Exam 70-511: *TS: Microsoft Windows Applications Development with Microsoft .NET Framework 4*

OBJECTIVE	CHAPTER	LESSON
1. BUILDING A USER INTERFACE BY USING BASIC TECHNIQUES (23%)		
1.1 Choose the most appropriate control class	1 4	1 1, 2, 3, 4
1.2 Implement screen layout by using nested control hierarchies.	1	1
1.3 Create and apply styles and theming.	1 5	3 3
1.4 Manage reusable resources.	1	2
1.5 Implement an animation in WPF.	2	3
2. ENHANCING A USER INTERFACE BY USING ADVANCED TECHNIQUES (21%)		
2.1 Manage routed events in WPF.	2	1
2.2 Configure WPF commanding.	2	2
2.3 Modify the visual interface at run time.	3	1, 2
2.4 Implement user-defined controls.	5	1, 3
2.5 Create and display graphics.	3	1
2.6 Add multimedia content to an application in WPF.	3	2
2.7 Create and apply control templates in WPF.	5	2
2.8 Create data, event, and property triggers in WPF.	1	3
3. MANAGING DATA AT THE USER INTERFACE LAYER (23%)		
3.1 Implement data binding.	6 7	1 1
3.2 Implement value converters in WPF.	6	2
3.3 Implement data validation.	6 8	3 2
3.4 Implement and consume change notification interfaces.	6	3
3.5 Prepare collections of data for display.	7	2
3.6 Bind to hierarchical data.	7	1
3.7 Implement data-bound controls.	8	1
3.8 Create a data template in WPF.	7	2
4. ENHANCING THE FUNCTIONALITY AND USABILITY OF A SOLUTION (17%)		
4.1 Integrate WinForms and WPF within an application.	9	3
4.2 Implement asynchronous processes and threading.	9	1
4.3 Incorporate globalization and localization features.	9	2
4.4 Implement drag and drop operations within and across applications.	10	3
4.5 Implement security features of an application.	10	1
4.6 Manage user and application settings.	10	2
4.7 Implement dependency properties.	5	3
5. STABILIZING AND RELEASING A SOLUTION (17%)		
5.1 Implement a WPF test strategy.	11	1, 2
5.2 Debug XAML by using the WPF Visualizer.	11	1
5.3 Debug WPF issues by using PresentationTraceSources.	11	2
5.4 Configure a ClickOnce deployment.	12	2
5.5 Create and configure a Windows Installer project.	12	1
5.6 Configure deployment security settings.	12	2

Exam Objectives The exam objectives listed here are current as of this book's publication date. Exam objectives are subject to change at any time without prior notice and at Microsoft's sole discretion. Please visit the Microsoft Learning Web site for the most current listing of exam objectives: http://www.microsoft.com/learning/en/us/exams /70-237.mspx.

MCTS Self-Paced Training Kit (Exam 70-511): Windows® Applications Development with Microsoft® .NET Framework 4

Matthew A. Stoecker

PUBLISHED BY
Microsoft Press
A Division of Microsoft Corporation
One Microsoft Way
Redmond, Washington 98052-6399

Library of Congress Control Number: 2010942625
ISBN: 978-0-7356-2742-0

Printed and bound in the United States of America.

2 3 4 5 6 7 8 9 10 11 QGT 6 5 4 3 2 1

Microsoft Press books are available through booksellers and distributors worldwide. For further information about international editions, contact your local Microsoft Corporation office or contact Microsoft Press International directly at fax (425) 936-7329. Visit our Web site at www.microsoft.com/mspress. Send comments to tkinput @microsoft.com.

Acquisitions Editor: Martin DelRe
Developmental Editor: Karen Szall
Project Editor: Iram Nawaz
Editorial Production: nSight, Inc.
Technical Reviewer: Kurt Meyer
Cover: Tom Draper Design

Body Part No. X17-40175

Contents at a Glance

Contents

What do you think of this book? We want to hear from you!

Microsoft is interested in hearing your feedback so we can continually improve our
books and learning resources for you. To participate in a brief online survey, please visit:

www.microsoft.com/learning/booksurvey/

Introduction

This training kit is designed for developers who plan to take Microsoft Certified Technology Specialist (MCTS) exam 70-511 as well as for developers who need to know how to develop applications by using Microsoft .NET Framework 4. Before you begin using this kit, you must have a working knowledge of Windows and Microsoft Visual Basic or Microsoft Visual C#. The topics in this training kit cover what you need to know for the exam as described on the Skills Measured tab for the exam, which is available at *http://www.microsoft.com/learning/en/us/exam.aspx?ID=70-511&locale=en-us#tab2*.

By using this training kit, you'll learn how to do the following:

- Choose the most appropriate control class
- Implement screen layout using nested control hierarchies
- Create and apply styles and theming
- Manage reusable resources
- Implement an animation in Windows Presentation Foundation (WPF)
- Manage routed events in WPF
- Configure WPF commanding
- Modify the visual interface at run time
- Implement user-defined controls
- Create and display graphics
- Add multimedia content to an application in WPF
- Create and apply control templates in WPF
- Create data, event, and property triggers in WPF
- Implement data binding
- Implement value converters in WPF
- Implement data validation
- Implement and consume change notification interfaces
- Prepare collections of data for display
- Bind to hierarchical data
- Implement data-bound controls
- Create a data template in WPF
- Integrate WinForms and WPF within an application
- Implement asynchronous processes and threading

- Incorporate globalization and localization features
- Implement drag and drop operations across applications
- Implement security features of an application
- Manage user and application settings
- Implement dependency properties
- Implement a WPF test strategy
- Debug XAML by using WPF Visualizer
- Debug WPF issues by using *PresentationTraceSources*
- Configure a ClickOnce deployment
- Create and configure a Windows Installer project
- Configure deployment security settings

Refer to the objective mapping page in the front of this book to see where in the book each exam objective is covered.

Hardware Requirements

You should use a computer that is not your primary workstation to do the practice exercises in this book because you will make changes to the operating system and application configuration.

To use the companion CD, you need a computer running Microsoft Windows XP with Service Pack 3 (SP3), Windows Vista with SP2, Windows 7, Windows Server 2003 with SP2, Windows Server 2003 R2, Windows Server 2008 with SP2, or Windows Server 2008 R2. The computer must meet the following minimum requirements:

- Personal computer with at least a 1-GHz 32-bit (x86) or 64-bit (x64) processor
- At least 1 GB of RAM (x86 systems) or 2 GB of RAM (x64 systems)
- At least a 40-GB hard disk
- DVD-ROM drive
- Super VGA (800 x 600) or higher resolution video adapter and monitor
- Keyboard and Microsoft mouse or compatible pointing device

For chapter 10 you will need a computer running Windows 7 Professional, Ultimate, or Enterprise Edition.

Software Requirements

The computer used with the companion CD-ROM should also have the following software:

- A Web browser such as Windows Internet Explorer
- An application that can display PDF files such as Adobe Acrobat Reader, which can be downloaded at *www.adobe.com/reader*
- Microsoft Visual Studio 2010 Professional, a trial version of which can be downloaded at *http://www.microsoft.com/visualstudio/en-us/products/2010-editions/professional*

These requirements will support use of the companion CD-ROM.

Using the Companion Media

The companion media (CD) included with this training kit contains the following:

- **Practice tests**   You can reinforce your understanding of programming with Microsoft .NET Framework 4 by using electronic practice tests that you customize to meet your needs from the pool of lesson review questions in this book, or you can practice for the 70-511 certification exam by using tests created from a pool of 200 realistic exam questions, which give you many practice exams to ensure that you are prepared.
- **An eBook**   An electronic version (eBook) of this book is included for when you do not want to carry the printed book with you.

> **NOTE**   **DIGITAL CONTENT FOR DIGITAL BOOK READERS**
>
> If you bought a digital-only edition of this book, you can enjoy select content from the print edition's companion media. Go to *http://go.microsoft.com/fwlink/?LinkId=207838* to get your downloadable content. This content is always up to date and available to all readers.

How to Install the Practice Tests

To install the practice test software from the companion CD to your hard disk, perform the following steps:

1. Insert the companion CD into your CD drive and accept the license agreement. A CD menu appears.

2.   Click Practice Tests and follow the instructions on the screen.

How to Use the Practice Tests

To start the practice test software, follow these steps:

1.   Click Start, click All Programs, and then select Microsoft Press Training Kit Exam Prep.
A window appears that shows all the Microsoft Press training kit exam prep suites
installed on your computer.

2.   Double-click the lesson review or practice test you want to use.

Lesson Review Options

When you start a lesson review, the Custom Mode dialog box appears so that you can configure your test. You can click OK to accept the defaults, or you can customize the number of
questions you want, how the practice-test software works, the exam objectives to which you
want the questions to relate, and whether you want your lesson review to be timed. If you
are retaking a test, you can select whether you want to see all the questions again or only the
questions you missed or did not answer.

After you click OK, your lesson review starts.

■ **Article I**   To take the test, answer the questions and use the Next and Previous buttons to move from question to question.

■ **Article II**   After you answer an individual question, if you want to see which answers
are correct—along with an explanation of each correct answer—click Explanation.

- **Article III**   If you prefer to wait until the end of the test to see how you did, answer all the questions and then click Score Test. You will see a summary of the exam objectives you chose and the percentage of questions you got right, both overall and per objective. You can print a copy of your test, review your answers, or retake the test.

Practice Test Options

When you start a practice test, you choose whether to take the test in Certification Mode, Study Mode, or Custom Mode.

- **Certification Mode**   Closely resembles the experience of taking a certification exam. The test has a set number of questions. It is timed, and you cannot pause and restart the timer.
- **Study Mode**   Creates an untimed test during which you can review the correct answers and the explanations after you answer each question.
- **Custom Mode**   Gives you full control over the test options so that you can customize them as you like. In all modes, the test user interface is basically the same but with different options enabled or disabled, depending on the mode. The main options are discussed in the previous section, "Lesson Review Options."

When you review your answer to an individual practice test question, you see a "References" section that lists where in the training kit you can find the information that relates to that question and provides links to other sources of information. After you click Test Results to score your entire practice test, you can click the Learning Plan tab to see a list of references for every objective.

How to Uninstall the Practice Tests

To uninstall the practice test software for a training kit, use the Uninstall A Program option in Windows Control Panel.

Microsoft Certified Professional Program

Microsoft certifications provide the best method for proving your command of current Microsoft products and technologies. The exams and corresponding certifications are developed to validate your mastery of critical competencies as you design and develop, or implement and support, solutions with Microsoft products and technologies. Computer professionals who become Microsoft certified are recognized as experts and are sought after industry-wide. Certification brings a variety of benefits to the individual and to employers and organizations.

> **MORE INFO** **ALL THE MICROSOFT CERTIFICATIONS**
>
> For a full list of Microsoft certifications, go to *www.microsoft.com/learning/mcp/default.asp*.

Errata and Book Support

We've made every effort to ensure the accuracy of this book and its companion content. If you do find an error, please report it on our Microsoft Press site at Oreilly.com:

1. Go to *http://microsoftpress.oreilly.com*.

2. In the Search box, enter the book's ISBN or title.

3. Select your book from the search results.

4. On your book's catalog page, under the cover image, you'll see a list of links. Click View/Submit Errata.

You'll find additional information and services for your book on its catalog page. If you need additional support, please email Microsoft Press Book Support at *tkinput@microsoft.com*.

Please note that product support for Microsoft software is not offered through the addresses above.

We Want to Hear from You

At Microsoft Press, your satisfaction is our top priority, and your feedback our most valuable asset. Please tell us what you think of this book at:

http://www.microsoft.com/learning/booksurvey

The survey is short, and we read every one of your comments and ideas. Thanks in advance for your input!

Stay in Touch

Let's keep the conversation going! We're on Twitter: *http://twitter.com/MicrosoftPress*

Preparing for the Exam

Microsoft certification exams are a great way to build your résumé and let the world know about your level of expertise. Certification exams validate your on-the-job experience and product knowledge. Although there is no substitution for on-the-job experience, preparation through study and hands-on practice can help you prepare for the exam. We recommend that you round out your exam preparation plan by using a combination of available study materials and courses. For example, you might use this Training Kit and another study guide for your at-home preparation and take a Microsoft Official Curriculum course for the classroom experience. Choose the combination you think works best for you.

CHAPTER 1

Building a User Interface

The user interface is the visual representation of your application. Users of your application use the user interface to interact with the application through the manipulation of controls, which are hosted in windows. Currently, you can use two Microsoft technologies in Visual Studio to build Microsoft Windows applications: Windows Forms and Windows Presentation Foundation (WPF).

> **IMPORTANT**
>
> **Have you read page xxi?**
>
> It contains valuable information regarding the skills you need to pass the exam.

Windows Forms historically has been the basis for most Microsoft Windows applications and can be configured to provide a variety of user interface (UI) options. The developer can create forms of various sizes and shapes and customize them to the user's needs. Forms are hosts for controls, which provide the main functionality of the UI.

WPF is the successor to Windows Forms for desktop application development. WPF applications differ from traditional Windows Forms applications in several ways, the most notable of which is that the code for the user interface is separate from the code for application functionality. Although the code for the functionality of a project can be defined using familiar languages such as Microsoft Visual Basic .NET or Microsoft Visual C#, the user interface of a WPF project is typically defined using a relatively new declarative syntax called Extensible Application Markup Language (XAML).

Although this training kit does cover some elements of Windows Forms programming, the primary focus for this training kit and the exam for which it prepares you is WPF technology.

This chapter introduces you to the fundamentals of creating a Windows application. Lesson 1 describes the kinds of WPF controls and how to use them. Lesson 2 explains using resources, and Lesson 3 describes how to incorporate styles into your WPF application.

Exam objectives in this chapter:

- Choose the most appropriate control class.
- Implement screen layout by using nested control hierarchies.
- Manage reusable resources.
- Create and apply styles and theming.
- Create data, event, and property triggers in WPF.

Lessons in this chapter:

Before You Begin

To complete the lessons in this chapter, you must have:

- A computer that meets or exceeds the minimum hardware requirements listed in the "Introduction" section at the beginning of the book.
- Microsoft Visual Studio 2010 Professional edition installed on your computer.
- An understanding of Visual Basic or C# syntax and familiarity with Microsoft .NET Framework 4.
- An understanding of XAML.

 REAL WORLD

Matt Stoecker

When I develop a Windows application, I pay special attention to the design of the UI. A well thought out UI that flows logically can help provide a consistent user experience from application to application and make learning new applications easy for users. Familiarity and common themes translate into increased productivity. With both Windows Forms and WPF available to create applications, an unprecedented number of options are now available for your programming tasks.

Lesson 1: Using WPF Controls

In this lesson, you learn to use WPF controls for WPF application development and how to use individual controls, item controls, and layout controls, each of which is necessary for creating WPF applications.

After this lesson, you will be able to:

- Explain what a content control is.
- Describe and use several common WPF controls.
- Use a dependency property.
- Create and use an item control in your user interface.
- Create a menu.
- Create a toolbar.
- Create a status bar.
- Explain the properties of a control that manage layout.
- Explain how to use the *Grid* control.
- Explain how to use the *UniformGrid* control.
- Explain how to use the *StackPanel* control.
- Explain how to use the *WrapPanel* control.
- Explain how to use the *DockPanel* control.
- Explain how to use the *Canvas* control.
- Configure control sizing.
- Align content at design time.
- Use the *GridSplitter* control.

Estimated lesson time: 2 hours

WPF Controls Overview

There are three basic types of controls in WPF. First, there are *individual controls*, which correspond with many of the familiar controls from Windows Forms programming. Controls such as *Button*, *Label*, and *TextBox* are familiar to developers and users alike. These controls generally have a single purpose in an application; for example, buttons are clicked, text boxes receive and display text, and so on. A subset of these controls comprises *content controls*, which are designed to display a variety of kinds of content. Content controls, discussed later in this lesson, typically contain a single nested element.

A second kind of WPF control is the *item control*, which is designed to contain groups of related items. Examples of these include *ListBox* controls, *Menu* controls, and *TreeView* controls. These controls typically enable the user to select an item from a list and perform an action with that item. Item controls can contain multiple nested elements. These controls are discussed later in this lesson.

Finally, *layout controls*, which contain multiple nested controls of any type, provide built-in logic for the visual layout of those controls. Examples include *Grid*, *StackPanel*, and *Canvas*. These controls are also discussed later in this lesson.

Content Controls

Many of the controls you use to build your WPF application are content controls. Simply, a content control derives from the *ContentControl* class and can contain a single nested element. This nested element can be of any type and can be set or retrieved in code through the *Content* property. The following XAML example demonstrates setting the content of a *Button* control to a string value (shown in bold):

```
<Button Height="23" Margin="36,0,84,15" Name="button2"
   VerticalAlignment="Bottom">This is the content string</Button>
```

You also can set the content in code, as shown in the following example:

Sample of Visual Basic Code

```
Button2.Content = "This is the content string"
```

Sample of C# Code

```
button2.Content = "This is the content string";
```

The type of the *Content* property is *Object*, so it can accept any object as content. How content is rendered, however, depends on the type of the object in the *Content* property. For items that do not derive from *UIElement*, the *ToString* method is called, and the resulting string is rendered as the control content. Items that derive from *UIElement,* however, are displayed as contained within the content control. The following example code demonstrates how to render a button that has an image as its content:

```
<Button Margin="20,20,29,74" Name="button1">
   <Image Source="C:\Pictures\HumpbackWhale.jpg"/>
</Button>
```

Assuming that the path to the image is valid, this code will render a button that displays a picture file of a humpback whale named HumpbackWhale.jpg.

Note that even though content controls can contain only a single nested element, there is no inherent limit on the number of nested elements that the content can contain. For example, it is possible for a content control to host a layout control that itself contains several additional UI elements. The following code shows a simple example of *Button* with a nested *StackPanel* control that itself has nested elements:

```
<Button Margin="20,20,-12,20" Name="button1">
   <StackPanel>
         <Image Source="C:\Pictures\HumpbackWhale.jpg"></Image>
         <TextBlock>This is a Humpback Whale</TextBlock>
```

```
    </StackPanel>
</Button>
```

At run time, this will be rendered as an image of a humpback whale with text beneath it.

Label Control and Mnemonic Keys

The *Label* control is one of the simplest WPF controls. It is mostly just a container for content. Typical usage for a *Label* control is as follows:

```
<Label Name="label1">This is a Label</Label>
```

Labels contain built-in support for mnemonic keys, which move the focus to a designated control when the Alt key is pressed with the mnemonic key. For example, if R were the mnemonic key for a particular control, the focus would shift to that control when Alt+R is pressed.

Typical usage for mnemonic keys in labels occurs when the label designates a control that can receive the focus, such as *TextBox*. The mnemonic key is specified by preceding the desired key with the underscore (_) symbol and appears underlined at run time when the Alt key is pressed. For example, the following code appears as Press Alt+A at run time when you press the Alt key:

```
<Label>Press Alt+_A</Label>
```

Although this code designates the mnemonic key for the label, it has no effect unless you designate a target control as well. You can designate a target control by setting the *Target* property of the *Label* control. The following example demonstrates how to create a mnemonic key with a target control named *TextBox1:*

```
<Label Target="{Binding ElementName=TextBox1}" Height="27"
   HorizontalAlignment="Left" VerticalAlignment="Top" Width="51">_Name
</Label>
<TextBox Name="TextBox1" Margin="53,1,94,0" Height="26"
   VerticalAlignment="Top">
</TextBox>
```

The syntax exemplified by {Binding ElementName=TextBox1} will be discussed further in Chapter 6, "Working with Data Binding."

Button Control

The *Button* control should be familiar to most developers. This control is designed to be clicked to enable the user to make a choice, to close a dialog box, or to perform another action. You can execute code by clicking the button to handle the *Click* event. (For information about handling events, see Chapter 2, "Working with Events and Commands.")

The *Button* control exposes two important properties useful when building user interfaces: the *IsDefault* property and the *IsCancel* property.

The *IsDefault* property determines whether a particular button is considered the default button for the user interface. When *IsDefault* is set to *True*, the button's *Click* event is raised when you press Enter. Similarly, the *IsCancel* property determines whether the button should be considered a *Cancel* button. When *IsCancel* is set to *True*, the button's *Click* event is raised when Esc is pressed.

ACCESS KEYS

Buttons provide support for access keys, which are similar to the mnemonic keys supported by labels. When a letter in a button's content is preceded by an underscore symbol (_), that letter will appear underlined when the Alt key is pressed, and the button will be clicked when the user presses Alt and that key together. For example, assume you have a button defined as follows:

```
<Button>_Click Me!</Button>
```

The text in the button appears as "Click Me" when Alt is pressed, and the button is clicked when Alt+C is pressed. If more than one button defines the same access key, neither is activated when the access key combination is pressed, but focus alternates between the buttons that define that key.

CHECKBOX CONTROL

The *Checkbox* control actually inherits from the *ButtonBase* class and typically enables the user to select whether an option is on or off. You can determine whether a check box is selected by accessing the *IsChecked* property. The *IsChecked* property is a Boolean? (bool? in C#) data type similar to the *Boolean* type but allows an indeterminate state as well. A check box will be in the indeterminate state when a window first opens.

Because *Checkbox* inherits from *ButtonBase,* it raises a *Click* event whenever the user selects or clears the check box. The best way to react to the user selecting or clearing a check box is to handle the *Click* event.

RADIOBUTTON CONTROL

Like *Checkbox*, *RadioButton* inherits from the *ButtonBase* class. *RadioButton* controls are typically used in groups to enable the user to select one option from a group. Clicking a radio button causes the *Click* event to be raised to react to user choices.

A fundamental feature of *RadioButton* controls is that they can be grouped. In a group of *RadioButton* controls, selecting one automatically clears all the others. Thus, it is not possible for more than one radio button in a group to be selected at one time.

Usually, all *RadioButton* controls in a single container are automatically in the same group. If you want to have a single group of three *RadioButton* controls in a window, all you need to do is add them to your window; they are automatically grouped. You can have multiple groups in a single container by setting the *GroupName* property. The following example demonstrates two groups of two radio buttons each.

```
<RadioButton GroupName="Group1" Name="RadioButton1" Height="22"
  VerticalAlignment="Top" Margin="15,10,0,0"
  HorizontalAlignment="Left" Width="76">Button 1</RadioButton>
<RadioButton GroupName="Group1" Name="RadioButton2"
  Margin="15,34,0,0" Height="22" VerticalAlignment="Top"
```

```
   HorizontalAlignment="Left" Width="76">Button 2</RadioButton>
<RadioButton GroupName="Group2" Name="RadioButton3"
   Margin="15,58,0,0" Height="21" HorizontalAlignment="Left"
   VerticalAlignment="Top" Width="76">Button 3</RadioButton>
<RadioButton GroupName="Group2" Name="RadioButton4"
   Margin="15,85,0,0" Height="22" HorizontalAlignment="Left"
   VerticalAlignment="Top" Width="76">Button 4</RadioButton>
```

You also can create groups of radio buttons by wrapping them in containers, such as in the code shown here:

```
<StackPanel Height="29" VerticalAlignment="Top">
   <RadioButton Name="RadioButton1">Button 1</RadioButton>
   <RadioButton Name="RadioButton2">Button 2</RadioButton>
</StackPanel>
<StackPanel Height="34" Margin="0,34,0,0" VerticalAlignment="Top">
   <RadioButton Name="RadioButton3">Button 3</RadioButton>
   <RadioButton Name="RadioButton4">Button 4</RadioButton>
</StackPanel>
```

EXAM TIP

It is important to realize that even though a content control can host only a single element, the element that it hosts can itself host child elements. Thus, a content control might host a grid, which in turn might host a number of objects.

Other Controls

There are other controls in the WPF suite that are not content controls. They do not have a *Content* property and typically are more limited in how they display or more specialized in terms of the content they display. For example, the *TextBlock* control displays text, and the *Image* control represents an image.

TextBlock Control

TextBlock is one of the simplest WPF elements. It just represents an area of text that appears in a window. The following example demonstrates a *TextBlock* control:

```
<TextBlock>Here is some text</TextBlock>
```

If you want to change the text in a *TextBlock* control in code, you must set the *Name* property of the *TextBlock* control so that you can refer to it in code, as shown here:

```
<TextBlock Name="TextBlock1">Here is some text</TextBlock>
```

Then you can change the text or any other property by referring to it in the code, as shown here:

Sample of Visual Basic Code

```
TextBlock1.Text = "Here is the changed text"
```

```csharp
TextBlock1.Text = "Here is the changed text";
```

By default, the font of the text in the *TextBlock* element will be the same as the font of the window. If you want different font settings for the *TextBlock*, you can set font-related properties, as shown here:

```xaml
<TextBlock FontFamily="Batang" FontSize="12"
  FontStyle="Italic" FontWeight="Bold"
  FontStretch="Normal">Here is some text</TextBlock>
```

Image Control

The *Image* control represents an image. The chief property of the *Image* control is the *Source* property, which takes a *System.Windows.Media.ImageSource* class in code, but, when set in XAML, it can be set as the Uniform Resource Identifier (URI) from which the image is loaded. For example, look at the following code.

```xaml
<Image Source="C:\Pictures\Humpbackwhale.jpg"/>
```

The URI can be either a local disk resource or a Web resource.

The *Image.Stretch* property determines how an image is displayed, whether it is shown at actual size and cropped (if necessary) to fit the image bounds, or whether it is shrunk or stretched to fit the bounds of the *Image* control. Table 1-1 describes the possible values for the *Stretch* property.

TABLE 1-1 Values for the *Stretch* Property

VALUE	DESCRIPTION
None	The image content is presented at its original size. If necessary, it is cropped to fit the available space.
Fill	The image content is resized (stretched or shrunk as needed) to fit the *Image* control size.
Uniform	The image content is resized to fit the destination dimensions while preserving its native aspect ratio. No cropping will occur, but unfilled space on the *Image* control edges might result.
UniformToFill	The image content is resized to fit the destination dimensions while preserving its native aspect ratio. If the aspect ratio of the *Image* control differs from the image content, the content is cropped to fit the *Image* control.

TextBox Control

The *TextBox* control is designed for the editing and display of text. The *Textbox* control enables the user to type text into the user interface. That text is accessible later by the application in the *TextBox.Text* property. You can use a *TextBox* control solely for text display by setting the *IsReadOnly* property to True, as shown in bold here:

```
<TextBox IsReadOnly="True" Height="93" Margin="16,14,97,0"
    Name="TextBox1" VerticalAlignment="Top"/>
```

The preceding code disables user input for the *TextBox1* control.

Although the *TextBox* control can be created as a rectangle of any size, it is single-line by default. To enable text wrapping in a *TextBox*, set the *TextWrapping* property to *Wrap*, as shown in bold here:

```
<TextBox TextWrapping="Wrap" Height="93" Margin="16,14,97,0"
    Name="TextBox1" VerticalAlignment="Top"/>
```

You can also set the *TextWrapping* property to *WrapWithOverflow*, which allows some words to overflow the edges of the text box if the wrapping algorithm is unable to break the text in an appropriate location.

The *TextBox* control includes automatic support for scroll bars. You can enable vertical scroll bars by setting the *VerticalScrollBarVisibility* property to *Auto* or *Visible*, as shown in bold here:

```
<TextBox VerticalScrollBarVisibility="Visible" Height="93"
    Margin="16,14,97,0" Name="TextBox1" VerticalAlignment="Top"/>
```

Setting *VerticalScrollBarVisibility* to *Visible* makes the vertical scroll bar visible at all times, whereas setting it to *Auto* makes the vertical scroll bar appear only when scrollable content is present. You also can enable a horizontal scroll bar by setting the *HorizontalScrollBar* property, but this setting is less useful.

ProgressBar Control

The *ProgressBar* control is designed to allow the application to provide visual feedback to the user regarding the progress of a time-consuming task. For example, you might use a progress bar to display progress for a file download. The progress bar appears as an empty box that gradually fills in to display progress. Table 1-2 shows important properties of the *ProgressBar* control.

TABLE 1-2 Properties of the *ProgressBar* Control

PROPERTY	DESCRIPTION
IsEnabled	Determines whether the *ProgressBar* control is enabled.
IsIndeterminate	Determines whether the progress bar is showing the actual value or generic progress. When IsIndeterminate is *False*, the progress bar will show the actual value represented by the *Value* property. When *True*, it will show generic progress.
LargeChange	Represents the amount added to or subtracted from the *Value* property when a large change is required.
Maximum	The *Maximum* value for the *ProgressBar* control. When the *Value* property equals the *Maximum* property, the *ProgressBar* control is filled.
Minimum	The *Minimum* value for the *ProgressBar* control. When the *Value* property equals the *Minimum* property, the *ProgressBar* control is empty.
Orientation	Determines whether the progress bar is shown horizontally or vertically.
SmallChange	Represents the amount added to or subtracted from the *Value* property when a small change is required.
Value	The Value displayed in the *ProgressBar* control. The Value will always be between the values of the *Minimum* and *Maximum* properties.

In code, you can change the *ProgressBar* display by adding to or subtracting from the *Value* property, as shown here:

Sample of Visual Basic Code

```
' Adds 1 to the Value
ProgressBar1.Value += 1
```

Sample of C# Code

```
// Adds 1 to the Value
ProgressBar1.Value += 1;
```

Slider Control

The *Slider* control enables the user to set a value by grabbing a graphic handle, or *thumb*, with the mouse and moving it along a track. This is often used to control volume, color intensity, or other application properties that can vary along a continuum. Table 1-3 shows important *Slider* properties.

TABLE 1-3 Properties of the *Slider* Control

PROPERTY	DESCRIPTION
IsDirectionReversed	Determines whether the direction is reversed. When set to *False* (the default), the minimum value is on the left and the maximum value is on the right. When set to *True*, the minimum is on the right and the maximum is on the left.
IsEnabled	Determines whether the slider is enabled.
LargeChange	Represents the amount added to or subtracted from the *Value* property when a large change is required. This amount is added or subtracted from the slider when the user clicks it on either side of the thumb or uses the PageUp or PageDown key.
Maximum	The maximum value for the *Slider* control. When the *Value* property equals the *Maximum* value, the thumb is completely on the right side of the slider (assuming the default direction and orientation of the control).
Minimum	The minimum value for the *Slider* control. When the *Value* property equals the *Minimum* value, the thumb is completely on the left side of the slider (assuming the default direction and orientation of the control).
Orientation	Determines whether the slider is shown horizontally or vertically.
SmallChange	Represents the amount added to or subtracted from the *Value* property when a small change is required. This amount is added to or subtracted from the slider when you use the arrow keys.
TickFrequency	Sets the interval between ticks that are displayed in the *Slider* control.
TickPlacement	Determines the location of ticks in the *Slider* control. The default setting is *None*, meaning that no tick marks appear.
Ticks	Used in advanced applications. You can determine the exact number and placement of tick marks by setting the *Ticks* collection directly.
Value	The value displayed in the *Slider* control. The *Value* property always is between the *Minimum* and *Maximum* values.

The *Slider* control raises the *ValueChanged* event whenever its *Value* property changes. You can handle this event to hook up the slider with whatever aspect of the application the slider controls.

Setting the Tab Order for Controls

A common mode of user interaction with the user interface is to cycle the focus through the controls by pressing the Tab key. By default, controls in the user interface will receive the focus from Tab key presses in the order in which they are defined in the XAML. You can set the tab order manually by setting the attached *TabIndex* property to an integer, as shown here:

```
<Button TabIndex="2" Name="button1"/>
```

See "Using Attached Properties" later in this chapter for more information about attached properties.

When the user presses the Tab key, the focus cycles through the controls in the order determined by the *TabIndex* value. Lower values receive focus first, followed by higher values. Controls whose *TabIndex* property is not explicitly set receive the focus after controls for which the property has been set, in the order that they are defined in the XAML. If two controls have the same *TabIndex* value, they receive the focus in the order the controls are defined in the XAML.

You can keep a control from receiving focus when the user presses the Tab key by setting the *KeyboardNavigation.IsTabStop* attached property to *False*, as shown in bold here:

```
<Button KeyboardNavigation.IsTabStop="False" Name="button1"/>
```

Item Controls

Item controls, also known as list-based controls, are designed to contain multiple child elements. Item controls are a familiar part of any user interface. Data is displayed frequently in item controls, and lists are used to allow the user to choose from a series of options. Item controls in WPF take the idea of lists one step further. Like content controls, item controls do not have restrictions on the kind of content they can present. Thus, an item control could present a list of strings or something more complex, such as a list of check box controls, or even a list that included various kinds of controls.

ListBox Control

The simplest form of item control is *ListBox*. As the name implies, *ListBox* is a simple control designed to display a list of items. A *ListBox* control typically displays a list of *ListBoxItem* controls, which are content controls, each of which hosts a single nested element. The simplest way to populate a *ListBox* control is by adding items directly in XAML, as shown here:

```
<ListBox Margin="19,0,0,36" Name="listBox1">
   <ListBoxItem>This</ListBoxItem>
   <ListBoxItem>Is</ListBoxItem>
   <ListBoxItem>A</ListBoxItem>
   <ListBoxItem>List</ListBoxItem>
</ListBox>
```

The *ListBox* control automatically lays out its content in a stack and adds a vertical scroll bar if the list is longer than the available space in the control.

By default, the *ListBox* control enables you to select a single item. You can retrieve the index of the selected item from the *ListBox.SelectedIndex* property, or you can retrieve the selected item itself through the *ListBox.SelectedItem* property. The *ListBoxItem* control also exposes an *IsSelected* property that is positive when the item is selected.

You can set the *SelectionMode* property to enable the user to select multiple items. Table 1-4 shows the possible values for the *SelectionMode* property.

TABLE 1-4 Values for the *SelectionMode* Property

VALUE	DESCRIPTION
Single	The user can select only one item at a time.
Multiple	The user can select multiple items without holding down a modifier key. Modifier keys have no effect.
Extended	The user can select multiple consecutive items while holding down the Shift key or nonconsecutive items by holding down the Ctrl key and clicking the items.

You can set the *SelectionMode* property in XAML as shown here:

```
<ListBox SelectionMode="Extended">
</ListBox>
```

When multiple items are selected, you can retrieve the selected items through the *ListBox.SelectedItems* property.

Although the *ListBox* control is used most commonly with *ListBoxItem* controls, it can display a list of any item types. For example, you might want to create a list of *CheckBox* controls. You can accomplish this by simply adding *CheckBox* controls to the *ListBox* control, as shown here:

```
<ListBox Name="listbox1" VerticalAlignment="Top">
   <CheckBox Name="Chk1">Option 1</CheckBox>
   <CheckBox Name="Chk2">Option 2</CheckBox>
   <CheckBox Name="Chk3">Option 3</CheckBox>
   <CheckBox Name="Chk4">Option 4</CheckBox>
</ListBox>
```

ComboBox Control

The *ComboBox* control works very similarly to the *ListBox* control. It can contain a list of items, each of which can be an object of any type, as in the *ListBox* control. Thus, the *ComboBox* control can host a list of strings, a list of controls such as for check boxes, or any other kind of list. The difference between the *ComboBox* control and the *ListBox* control is how the control is presented. The *ComboBox* control appears as a drop-down list. Like the *ListBox* control, you can get a reference to the selected item through the *SelectedItem* property, and you can retrieve the index of the selected item through the *SelectedIndex* property.

When an item is selected, the string representation of the content of that item is displayed in the *ComboBox* control. Thus, if the *ComboBox* control hosts a list of strings, the selected string is displayed. If the *ComboBox* control hosts a list of *CheckBox* controls, the string representation of the *ComboBox.Content* property is displayed. Then the selected value is available through the *ComboBox.Text* property.

Users also can edit the text displayed in the *ComboBox* control. They can even type in their own text, like in a text box. To make the *ComboBox* control editable, you must set the *IsReadOnly* property to *False* and set the *IsEditable* property to *True*.

You can open and close the *ComboBox* control programmatically by setting the *IsDropDownOpen* property to *True* (to open it) and *False* (to close it).

TreeView Control and *TreeViewItem* Control

TreeView is a simple item control that is very similar to *ListBox* in its implementation, but in practice, it is quite different. The primary purpose of the *TreeView* control is to host *TreeViewItem* controls, which enable the construction of trees of content.

The *TreeViewItem* control is the primary control used to construct trees. It exposes a *Header* property that enables you to set the text displayed in the tree. The *TreeViewItem* control itself also hosts a list of items. The list of items hosted in a *TreeViewItem* can be expanded or collapsed by clicking the icon to the left of the header. The following XAML demonstrates a *TreeView* control populated by a tree of items.

```
<TreeView>
   <TreeViewItem Header="Boy's Names">
          <TreeViewItem Header="Jack"/>
          <TreeViewItem Header="Jim"/>
          <TreeViewItem Header="Mark"/>
          <TreeViewItem Header="Ray"/>
   </TreeViewItem>
   <TreeViewItem Header="Girl's Names">
          <TreeViewItem Header="Betty"/>
          <TreeViewItem Header="Libby"/>
          <TreeViewItem Header="Janet"/>
          <TreeViewItem Header="Sandra"/>
   </TreeViewItem>
</TreeView>
```

You can create *TreeView* controls that have controls as the terminal nodes just as easily, as shown in this example:

```
<TreeView>
   <TreeViewItem Header="Pizza Toppings">
          <CheckBox Content="Pepperoni"/>
          <CheckBox Content="Sausage"/>
          <CheckBox Content="Mushroom"/>
          <CheckBox Content="Tomato"/>
```

```
    </TreeViewItem>
    <TreeViewItem Header="Sandwich Items">
            <CheckBox Content="Lettuce"/>
            <CheckBox Content="Tomato"/>
            <CheckBox Content="Mustard"/>
            <CheckBox Content="Hot Peppers"/>
    </TreeViewItem>
</TreeView>
```

You can obtain a reference to the selected item in the *TreeView* control with the *TreeView.SelectedItem* property.

Menus

Menus enable you to present the user with a list of controls that are typically associated with commands. Menus are displayed in hierarchical lists of items, usually grouped into related areas. WPF provides two types of menu controls: *Menu*, which is designed to be visible in the user interface, and *ContextMenu*, which is designed to function as a pop-up menu in certain situations.

Whereas the *Menu* control can be put anywhere in the user interface, it typically is docked to the top of the window. Menus expose an *IsMainMenu* property. When this property is *True*, pressing Alt or F10 causes the menu to receive focus, thereby enabling common Windows application behavior.

Although a *Menu* control can contain controls of any kind, the *Toolbar* control is better suited for presenting controls to the user. The *Menu* control is designed for presenting lists of *MenuItem* controls.

MenuItem Control

The *MenuItem* control is the main unit used to build menus. A *MenuItem* control represents a clickable section of the menu and has associated text. *MenuItem* controls are themselves item controls and can contain their own list of controls, which typically are also *MenuItem* controls. The following XAML example demonstrates a simple menu:

```
<Menu Height="22" Name="menu1" VerticalAlignment="Top"
   HorizontalAlignment="Left" Width="278">
   <MenuItem Header="_File">
            <MenuItem Header="Open"/>
            <MenuItem Header="Close"/>
            <MenuItem Header="Save" Command="ApplicationCommands.Save"/>
   </MenuItem>
</Menu>
```

The *Command* property indicates the command associated with that menu item. When the user clicks the menu item, the command specified by the *Command* property is invoked. If a shortcut key is associated with the command, it is displayed to the right of the *MenuItem* header. Commands are discussed in detail in Chapter 2 of this text.

Table 1-5 describes the important properties of the *MenuItem* control.

TABLE 1-5 Properties of the *MenuItem* Control

PROPERTY	DESCRIPTION
Command	The command associated with the menu item. This command is invoked when the menu item is clicked. If a keyboard shortcut is associated with the command, it is displayed to the right of the menu item.
Header	The text displayed in the menu.
Icon	The icon displayed to the left of the menu item. If *IsChecked* is set to *True*, the icon is not displayed even if it is set.
IsChecked	When this property is set to *True*, a check is displayed to the left of the menu item. If the *Icon* property is set, the icon is not displayed while *IsChecked* is set to *True*.
IsEnabled	Determines whether the menu item is enabled. When set to *False*, the item appears dimmed and does not invoke the command when clicked.
Items	The list of items contained by the *MenuItem* control. The list typically contains more *MenuItem* controls.

As with many other WPF controls, you can create an access key for a menu item by preceding the letter in the *Header* property with an underscore symbol (_), as shown here:

```
<MenuItem Header="_File">
```

The underscore symbol will not appear at run time, but when the Alt key is held down, it appears under the key it precedes. Pressing that key with the Alt key held down has the same effect as clicking the menu item.

Each MenuItem control can contain its own set of items, which are also typically *MenuItem* controls. These can be created in XAML by nesting *MenuItem* elements inside the parent *MenuItem* control. When a menu item that has sub-items is clicked, those items are shown in a new menu.

> **BEST PRACTICES** *MENUITEM* **CONTROLS WITH SUB-ITEMS**
>
> It is best practice not to assign a command to *MenuItem* controls that contain sub-items. Otherwise, the command is executed every time the user wants to view the list of sub-items.

You can add a separator bar between menu items by using the *Separator* control, as shown here:

```
<MenuItem Header="Close"/>
<Separator/>
<MenuItem Header="Save" Command="ApplicationCommands.Save"/>
```

The separator bar appears as a horizontal line between menu items.

ContextMenu Control

Unlike *Menu* controls, the *ContextMenu* control does not have a fixed location in the user interface. Rather, it is associated with other controls. To create a *ContextMenu* control for a control, define it in the XAML code for the *Control.ContextMenu* property, as shown in the following example with a *ListBox* control:

```
<ListBox Margin="77,123,81,39" Name="listBox1">
   <ListBox.ContextMenu>
         <ContextMenu>
            <MenuItem Header="Cut" Command="ApplicationCommands.Cut"/>
            <MenuItem Header="Copy" Command="ApplicationCommands.Copy"/>
            <MenuItem Header="Paste" Command="ApplicationCommands.Paste"/>
         </ContextMenu>
   </ListBox.ContextMenu>
</ListBox>
```

After a *ContextMenu* control has been set for a control, it is displayed whenever the user right-clicks the control or presses Shift+F10 while the control has the focus.

Another common scenario for adding *ContextMenu* controls to a control is to add them as a resource in the *Window.Resources* collection. Resources are discussed in Lesson 2 of this chapter, "Using Resources."

ToolBar Control

Like menus, the *ToolBar* control is designed to present controls to the user. The *ToolBar* control is ideally suited to host controls such as *Button*, *ComboBox*, *TextBox*, *CheckBox*, and *RadioButton*. The *ToolBar* control also can use the *Separator* control described in the previous section.

Toolbars automatically override the style of some of the controls they host. Buttons, for example, appear flat when shown in a toolbar and are highlighted in blue when the mouse is over the control. This gives controls in a toolbar a consistent appearance by default.

You add items to the *ToolBar* control in the same manner as any other item control. An example is shown here:

```
<ToolBar Height="26" Margin="43,23,35,0" Name="toolBar1"
   VerticalAlignment="Top">
   <Button>Back</Button>
   <Button>Forward</Button>
   <TextBox Name="textbox1" Width="100"/>
</ToolBar>
```

ToolBar.OverflowMode Property

When more controls are added to a *ToolBar* control than can fit, controls are removed until the controls fit in the space. Controls removed from the *ToolBar* control are placed automatically in the Overflow menu. The Overflow menu appears as a drop-down list on the right side of the toolbar when the toolbar is in the horizontal configuration. You can manage how controls are placed in the Overflow menu by setting the attached *ToolBar.OverflowMode* property. (See "Using Attached Properties" later in this chapter for more information.) Table 1-6 shows the possible values for this property.

Table 1-6 Values for the *ToolBar.OverflowMode* Property

VALUE	DESCRIPTION
OverflowMode.Always	The control always appears in the Overflow menu, even if there is space available in the toolbar.
OverflowMode.AsNeeded	The control is moved to the Overflow menu as needed. This is the default setting for this property.
OverflowMode.Never	Controls with this value are never placed in the Overflow menu. If there are more controls with the *Toolbar.OverflowMode* property set to *Never* than can be displayed in the space allotted to the toolbar, some controls will be cut off and unavailable to the user.

The following example demonstrates how to set the Toolbar.OverflowMode property:

```
<ToolBar Height="26" Margin="43,23,35,0" Name="toolBar1"
   VerticalAlignment="Top">
   <Button ToolBar.OverflowMode="Always">Back</Button>
</ToolBar>
```

ToolBarTray Class

WPF provides a special container class for *ToolBar* controls, called *ToolBarTray*. *ToolBarTray* enables the user to resize or move *ToolBar* controls that are contained in the tray at run time. When *ToolBar* controls are hosted in a *ToolBarTray* control, the user can move the *ToolBar* controls by grabbing the handle on the left side of the toolbar. The following example demonstrates the *ToolBarTray* control.

```
<ToolBarTray Name="toolBarTray1" Height="65" VerticalAlignment="Top">
  <ToolBar Name="toolBar1" Height="26" VerticalAlignment="Top">
     <Button>Back</Button>
     <Button>Forward</Button>
     <Button>Stop</Button>
  </ToolBar>
  <ToolBar>
     <TextBox Width="100"/>
     <Button>Go</Button>
  </ToolBar>
</ToolBarTray>
```

StatusBar Control

The *StatusBar* control is quite similar to the *ToolBar* control. The primary difference is in usage. *StatusBar* is used most commonly to host controls that convey information, such as *Label* and *ProgressBar* controls. Like the toolbar, the status bar overrides the visual style of many of the controls it hosts, but it provides a different appearance and behavior than the toolbar. The following example demonstrates a simple *StatusBar* control with hosted controls.

```
<StatusBar Height="32" Name="statusBar1" VerticalAlignment="Bottom">
  <Label>Application is Loading</Label>
  <Separator/>
  <ProgressBar Height="20" Width="100" IsIndeterminate="True"/>
</StatusBar>
```

 Quick Check

  ■ Describe the difference between a *Menu* control and a *ContextMenu* control.

Quick Check Answer

  ■ Both *Menu* elements and *ContextMenu* elements are list controls that host *MenuItem* elements. The primary difference between them is that *Menu* elements are visible elements that are part of the visual tree and can be hosted by content controls. *ContextMenu* elements, however, have no direct visual representation and are added to another individual control by setting the other control's *ContextMenu* property.

Layout Controls

WPF offers unprecedented support for a variety of layout styles. The addition of several specialized controls enables you to create a variety of layout models, and panels can be nested inside each other to create user interfaces that exhibit complex layout behavior. In this lesson, you learn how to use these specialized controls.

Control Layout Properties

Controls in WPF manage a great deal of their own layout and positioning and further interact with their container to determine their final positioning. Table 1-7 describes common control properties that influence layout and positioning.

TABLE 1-7 Properties That Control Layout

PROPERTY	DESCRIPTION
FlowDirection	Gets or sets the direction in which text and other UI elements flow within any parent element that controls their layout.
Height	Gets or sets the height of the control. When set to *Auto*, other layout properties determine the height.
HorizontalAlignment	Gets or sets the horizontal alignment characteristics applied to this element when it is composed within a parent element such as a panel or item control.
HorizonalContentAlignment	Gets or sets the horizontal alignment of the control's content.
Margin	Gets or sets the distance between each of the control's edges and the edge of the container or the adjacent controls, depending on the layout control hosting the child control.
MaxHeight	Gets or sets the maximum height for a control.
MaxWidth	Gets or sets the maximum width for a control.
MinHeight	Gets or sets the minimum height for a control.
MinWidth	Gets or sets the minimum width for a control.
Padding	Gets or sets the amount of space between a control and its child element.
VerticalAlignment	Gets or sets the vertical alignment characteristics applied to this element when it is composed within a parent element such as a layout or item control.
VerticalContentAlignment	Gets or sets the vertical alignment of the control's content.
Width	Gets or sets the width of the control. When set to *Auto*, other layout properties determine the width.

A few of these properties are worth a closer look.

Margin Property

The *Margin* property returns an instance of the *Thickness* structure that describes the space between the edges of the control and other elements that are adjacent. Depending on which layout panel is used, the adjacent element might be the edge of the container, such as a panel or Grid cell, or it might be a peer control, as would be the case in the vertical margins in a *StackPanel* control.

The *Margin* property can be set asymmetrically to allow different amounts of margin on each side. Consider the following example:

```
<Button Margin="0,48,96,1" Name="button1">Button</Button>
```

In this example, a different margin distance is set for each control edge. The order of edges in the *Margin* property is *Left*, *Top*, *Right*, *Bottom*, so in this example, the left margin is 0, the top margin is 48, the right margin is 96, and the bottom margin is 1.

Margins are additive. For example, if you have two adjacent controls in a *StackPanel* control and the topmost one has a bottom margin of 20 and the bottommost one has a top margin of 10, the total distance between the two control edges will be 30.

HorizontalAlignment and *VerticalAlignment* Properties

The *HorizontalAlignment* and *VerticalAlignment* properties determine how a control is aligned inside its parent when there is extra horizontal or vertical space. The values for these properties are mostly self-explanatory. The *HorizontalAlignment* property has possible values of *Left*, *Right*, *Center*, and *Stretch*. The *VerticalAlignment* property has possible values of *Top*, *Bottom*, *Center*, and *Stretch*. As you might expect, setting the *HorizontalAlignment* property to *Left*, *Right*, or *Center* aligns the control in its container to the left, right, or center, respectively. Similar results are seen with the *VerticalAlignment* property. The setting that is worth noting is the *Stretch* value. When set to *Stretch*, the control will stretch in the horizontal or vertical directions (depending on the property) until the control is the size of the available space after taking the value of the Margin property into account.

> **NOTE** **WHEN THERE IS NO EFFECT**
>
> In some containers, setting these properties might have no effect. For example, in *StackPanel*, the vertical layout is handled by the container, so setting the *VerticalAlignment* property has no effect, although setting the *HorizontalAlignment* property still does.

Using Attached Properties

WPF introduces a new concept in properties: *attached properties*. Because WPF controls contain the information required for their own layout and orientation in the user interface, it is sometimes necessary for controls to define information about the control that contains them. For example, a *Button* control contained by a *Grid* control will define in which grid column and row it appears. This is accomplished through attached properties. The *Grid* control attaches a number of properties to every control it contains, such as properties that determine the row and column in which the control exists. In XAML, you set an attached property with code like the following:

```
<Button Grid.Row="1" Grid.Column="1"></Button>
```

Refer to the class name (that is, *Grid*) rather than to the instance name (for example, grid1) when setting an attached property because attached properties are attached by the class and not by the instance of the class. In some cases, such as with the *TabIndex* property (shown in the next section), the class name is assumed and can be omitted in XAML.

Here's a full example of a *Grid* control that defines two rows and two columns and contains a single button that uses attached properties to orient itself in the grid:

```
<Grid>
  <Grid.ColumnDefinitions>
    <ColumnDefinition Width="139*"/>
    <ColumnDefinition Width="139*"/>
  </Grid.ColumnDefinitions>
  <Grid.RowDefinitions>
    <RowDefinition Height="126*"/>
    <RowDefinition Height="126*"/>
  </Grid.RowDefinitions>
  <Button Grid.Row="1" Grid.Column="1"></Button>
</Grid>
```

Layout Panels

WPF includes a variety of layout panels with which to design your user interface. This section explores these panels and explains when to use them.

Grid Panel

Grid is the most commonly used panel for creating user interfaces in WPF. The *Grid* panel enables you to create layouts that depend on the *Margin*, *HorizontalAlignment*, and *VerticalAlignment* properties of the child controls it contains. Controls hosted in a *Grid* control are drawn in the order in which they appear in markup or code, thereby enabling you to create layered user interfaces. In the case of overlapping controls, the last control to be drawn will be on top.

With the *Grid* control, you can define columns and rows in the grid. Then you can assign child controls to designated rows and columns to create a more structured layout. When assigned to a column or row, a control's *Margin*, *HorizontalAlignment*, and *VerticalAlignment* properties operate with respect to the edge of the row or column, not to the edge of the *Grid* container itself. Columns and rows are defined by creating *ColumnDefinition* and *RowDefinition* properties, as seen here:

```
<Grid>
  <Grid.RowDefinitions>
    <RowDefinition Height="125*"/>
    <RowDefinition Height="125*"/>
  </Grid.RowDefinitions>
  <Grid.ColumnDefinitions>
    <ColumnDefinition Width="80*"/>
    <ColumnDefinition Width="120*"/>
  </Grid.ColumnDefinitions>
</Grid>
```

Rows and columns can be either fixed or variable in their width and height. To designate a fixed width or height, simply set the *Width* or *Height* property to the size you would like, as shown here:

```
<RowDefinition Height="125"/>
```

In contrast, you can make a variable-sized row or column by appending an asterisk (*) to the end of the *Width* or *Height* setting, as shown here:

```
<RowDefinition Height="125*"/>
```

When the asterisk is added, the row or column grows or shrinks proportionally to fit the available space. Look at the following example:

```
<RowDefinition Height="10*"/>
<RowDefinition Height="20*"/>
```

Both the rows created by this code grow and shrink to fit the available space, but one row is always twice the height of the other. These numbers are proportional only among themselves. Thus, using 1* and 2* will have the same effect as using 100* and 200*.

You can have a *Grid* control that contains both fixed and variable rows or columns, as seen here:

```
<RowDefinition Height="125"/>
<RowDefinition Height="125*"/>
```

In this example, the first row always maintains a height of 125, and the second grows or shrinks as the window is resized.

GRID ATTACHED PROPERTIES

The *Grid* control provides attached properties to its child controls. You can position controls into specific *Grid* rows or columns by setting the attached properties *Grid.Column* and *Grid. Row*, as shown in bold here:

```
<Grid>
    <Grid.RowDefinitions>
      <RowDefinition Height="10*"/>
      <RowDefinition Height="5*"/>
    </Grid.RowDefinitions>
    <Grid.ColumnDefinitions>
      <ColumnDefinition Width="117"/>
      <ColumnDefinition Width="161"/>
    </Grid.ColumnDefinitions>
    <Button Name="button2" Grid.Row="0" Grid.Column="1">Button</Button>
</Grid>
```

Occasionally, you might have a control that spans more than one column or row. To indicate this, you can set the *Grid.ColumnSpan* or *Grid.RowSpan* property as shown here:

```
<Button Name="button2" Grid.ColumnSpan="2">Button</Button>
```

USING THE *GRIDSPLITTER* CONTROL

The *GridSplitter* control enables the user to resize grid rows or columns at run time and appears at run time as a vertical or horizontal bar between two rows or columns that the user can grab with the mouse and move to adjust the size of those columns or rows. Table 1-8 shows the important properties of the *GridSplitter* control.

TABLE 1-8 Properties of the *GridSplitter* Control

PROPERTY	DESCRIPTION
Grid.Column	This attached property from the *Grid* control determines the column in which the grid splitter exists.
Grid.ColumnSpan	This attached property from the *Grid* control determines the number of columns the grid splitter spans. For horizontal grid splitters, this property should equal the number of columns in the grid.
Grid.Row	This attached property from the *Grid* control determines the row in which the grid splitter exists.
Grid.RowSpan	This attached property from the *Grid* control determines the number of rows the grid splitter spans. For vertical grid splitters, this property should equal the number of rows in the grid.
Height	Determines the height of the grid splitter. For vertical grid splitters, this property should be set to *Auto*.
HorizontalAlignment	Determines the horizontal alignment of the grid splitter. For horizontal grid splitters, this property should be set to *Stretch*. For vertical grid splitters, this property should be set to *Top* or *Bottom*.
Margin	Determines the margin around the grid splitter. Typically, your margin will be set to 0 to make the grid splitter flush with grid columns and rows.
ResizeBehavior	Gets or sets which columns or rows are resized relative to the column or row for which the *GridSplitter* control is defined. The default value is *BasedOnAlignment*, which sets the resize behavior based on the alignment of the *GridSplitter* control relative to the row(s) or column(s) to which the grid splitter is adjacent.
ResizeDirection	Gets or sets a value that indicates whether the *GridSplitter* control resizes rows or columns. The default value is *Auto*, which automatically sets the resize direction based on the positioning of the *GridSplitter* control.
ShowsPreview	Gets or sets a value that indicates whether the *GridSplitter* control updates the column or row size as the user drags the control.

VerticalAlignment	Determines the vertical alignment of the grid splitter. For vertical grid splitters, this property should be set to *Stretch*. For horizontal grid splitters, this property should be set to *Left* or *Right*.
Width	Determines the width of the grid splitter. For horizontal grid splitters, this property should be set to *Auto*.

Although the *GridSplitter* control is easy for the user to use, it is not the most intuitive control for developers to use. Although you can drag and drop the grid splitter onto your window from the toolbox, you must do a fair amount of configuration to make the grid splitter useful. The *GridSplitter* control must be placed within a grid cell, even though it always resizes entire rows or columns, and it should be positioned either adjacent to the edge of the row or column that you want to resize or put into a dedicated row or column that is between the rows or columns you want to resize. You can position the grid splitter manually in the designer by grabbing the handle that appears at the upper left corner of the grid splitter. Figure 1-1 shows the grid splitter in the designer.

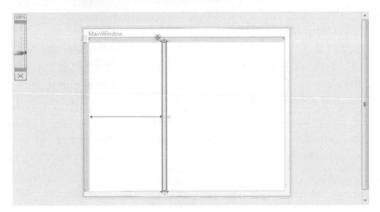

FIGURE 1 1 The grid splitter in the designer.

When the *ResizeBehavior* property is set to *Auto*, WPF automatically sets the correct resize behavior based on the alignment of the grid splitter.

The typical UI experience for the grid splitter is to have a visual element that spans all the rows or columns in a grid. Thus, you must manually set the *Grid.ColumnSpan* property for horizontal grid splitters or the *Grid.RowSpan* property for vertical grid splitters to span all the rows or columns the grid contains.

The following procedure describes how to add a grid splitter to your window at design time. To add a grid splitter to your window:

1. From the toolbox, drag a grid splitter onto your window and drop it in a cell that is adjacent to the row or column for which you want to set resizing. You might want to create a dedicated row or column to hold the grid splitter alone so there is no interference with other UI elements.

2. Set the Margin property of the grid splitter to **0**.

3. For vertical grid splitters, set the *VerticalAlignment* property to Stretch. For horizontal grid splitters, set the *HorizontalAlignment* property to Stretch. Set the remaining alignment property to the appropriate setting to position the GridSplitter control adjacent to the column(s) or row(s) for which you want to enable resizing.

4. For horizontal grid splitters, set the *Width* property to Auto and set the Height property to the appropriate height. For vertical grid splitters, set the Height property to Auto and set the *Width* property to the appropriate width.

5. For vertical grid splitters, set the *Grid.RowSpan* property to the number of rows in the grid. For horizontal grid splitters, set the *Grid.ColumnSpan* property to the number of columns in the grid.

Note that you can perform this configuration in the Properties window, in XAML, or (in most but not all cases) by manipulating the *GridSplitter* control in the designer with the mouse.

UniformGrid Control

Although similar in name, the *UniformGrid* control has very different behavior from the *Grid* control. In fact, the *UniformGrid* control is very limited. It automatically lays out controls in a grid of uniform size, adjusting the size and number of rows and columns as more controls are added. Grid cells are always the same size. The *UniformGrid* control typically is not used for designing entire user interfaces, but it can be useful for quickly creating layouts that require a grid of uniform size, such as a checkerboard or the buttons on a calculator.

You can set the number of rows and columns in the *UniformGrid* control by setting the *Rows* and *Columns* properties, as shown here:

```
<UniformGrid Rows="2" Columns="2">
</UniformGrid>
```

If you set the number of rows and columns in this manner, you fix the number of cells (and thus the controls that can be displayed) in a single uniform grid. If you add more controls than a uniform grid has cells, the controls will not be displayed. Cells defined first in XAML are the cells displayed in such a case.

If you set only the number of rows, additional columns will be added to accommodate new controls. Likewise, if you set only the number of columns, additional rows will be added.

StackPanel Control

The *StackPanel* control provides a simple layout model. It stacks the controls it contains one on top of the other in the order that they are defined. Typically, *StackPanel* containers stack controls vertically. You can also create a horizontal stack by setting the *Orientation* property to Horizontal, as shown here:

```
<StackPanel Orientation="Horizontal">
</StackPanel>
```

This creates a stack of controls from left to right. If you want to create a right-to-left stack of controls, you can set the *FlowDirection* property to *RightToLeft*, as shown here:

```
<StackPanel Orientation="Horizontal" FlowDirection="RightToLeft">
</StackPanel>
```

No combination of property settings in the stack panel creates a bottom-to-top stack.

Note that the layout properties of the controls contained in the *StackPanel* control also influence how the stack appears. For example, controls appear in the center of the *StackPanel* by default, but if the *HorizontalAlignment* property of a specific control is set at *Left*, that control appears on the left side of the *StackPanel*.

WrapPanel Control

The *WrapPanel* control provides another simple layout experience that typically is not used for creating entire user interfaces. Simply, the *WrapPanel* control lays out controls in a horizontal row side by side until the horizontal space available in the *WrapPanel* is used up. Then it creates additional rows until all its contained controls are positioned. Thus, controls are wrapped in the user interface like text is wrapped in a text editor like Notepad. A typical use for this layout panel is to provide automatic layout for a related set of controls that might be resized frequently, such as those in a toolbar.

You can wrap controls from right to left by setting the *FlowDirection* property to *RightToLeft*, as shown here:

```
<WrapPanel FlowDirection="RightToLeft">
</WrapPanel>
```

DockPanel Control

The *DockPanel* control provides a container that enables you to dock contained controls to the edges of the dock panel. In Windows Forms development, docking was accomplished by setting the Dock property on each individual dockable control. In WPF development, however, you use the *DockPanel* control to create interfaces with docked controls. Docking typically is useful for attaching controls such as toolbars or menus to edges of the user interface. The position of docked controls remains constant regardless of how the user resizes the user interface.

The *DockPanel* control provides docking for contained controls by providing an attached property called *Dock*. The following example demonstrates how to set the *DockPanel.Dock* property in a contained control:

```
<Button DockPanel.Dock="Top">Button</Button>
```

The *DockPanel.Dock* property has four possible values: *Top*, *Bottom*, *Left*, and *Right*, which indicate docking to the top, bottom, left, and right edges of the *DockPanel* control, respectively.

The *DockPanel* control exposes a property called *LastChildFill*, which can be set to *True* or *False*. When set to *True* (the default setting), the last control added to the layout will fill all remaining space.

The order in which controls are added to the *DockPanel* control is crucial in determining the layout. When controls are laid out in a *DockPanel* control, the first control to be laid out is allocated all the space on the edge it is assigned. For example, Figure 1-2 shows a *DockPanel* control with a single *Button* control docked to the top of the container.

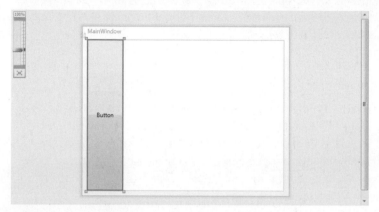

FIGURE 1-2 A *DockPanel* control with a single docked control.

As subsequent controls are added to other edges, they occupy the remaining space on those edges, as demonstrated by Figures 1-3, 1-4, and 1-5.

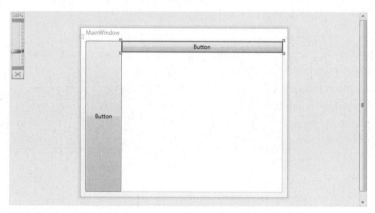

FIGURE 1-3 A *DockPanel* control with two docked controls.

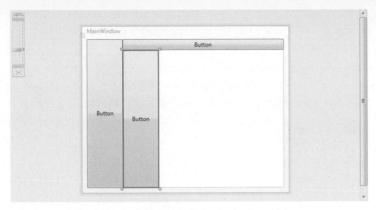

FIGURE 1-4 A *DockPanel* control with three docked controls.

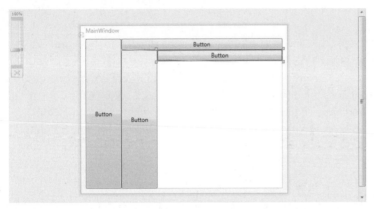

FIGURE 1-5 A *DockPanel* control with four docked controls.

In this sequence of figures, the second control is docked to the left edge. It occupies all the edge that is not occupied by the first control. The next control is docked again to the top edge, where it is docked adjacent to the first control that already is docked to the top, and it occupies the remaining space on the top edge that was not taken by the button docked on the left edge. The fourth figure shows a similar progression, with another control docked to the left edge.

DockPanel controls are typically not used as the sole basis for user interfaces, but rather are used to dock key components to invariant positions. Usually, the *LastChildFill* property in a *DockPanel* control is set to *True*, and the last child added is a *Grid* or other container control that can be used for the layout of the rest of the user interface. Figure 1-6 shows a sample user interface that has a menu docked to the top edge, a list box docked to the left edge, and a grid that fills the remaining space.

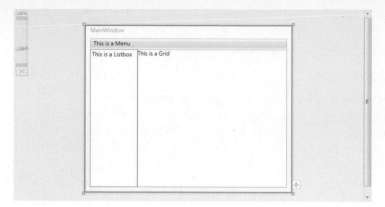

FIGURE 1-6 A *DockPanel* control that contains a menu, a list box, and a grid.

Canvas Control

The *Canvas* control is a container that allows absolute positioning of contained controls. It has no layout logic of its own, and all contained controls are positioned on the basis of four attached properties: *Canvas.Top*, *Canvas.Bottom*, *Canvas.Right*, and *Canvas.Left*. The value of each of these properties defines the distance between the indicated edge of the *Canvas* control and the corresponding edge of the child control. For example, the following XAML defines a button that is 20 units away from the top edge of the *Canvas* control and 30 units away from the left edge.

```
<Canvas>
    <Button Canvas.Top="20" Canvas.Left="30">Button</Button>
</Canvas>
```

You can define only one horizontal and one vertical attached property for each contained control. Thus, you can neither set the value of both *Canvas.Left* and *Canvas.Right* for a single control, nor both *Canvas.Top* and *Canvas.Bottom*.

When the *Canvas* container is resized, contained controls retain their fixed distance from the *Canvas* edges but can move relative to one another if different edges have been fixed for different controls.

Because the *Canvas* control allows for a freeform layout and does not incorporate any complex layout functionality of its own, contained controls can overlap in a *Canvas* control. By default, controls declared later in the XAML are shown on top of controls declared earlier in the XAML. However, you can set the Z-order (that is, which control appears on top) manually by setting the *Canvas.ZIndex* attached property. *Canvas.ZIndex* takes an arbitrary integer value. Controls with a higher *Canvas.ZIndex* value always appear on top of controls with a lower Canvas.ZIndex value. An example is shown here:

```
<Button Canvas.ZIndex="12">This one is on top</Button>
<Button Canvas.ZIndex="5">This one is on the bottom</Button>
```

Quick Check

- Describe what attached properties are and how they work.

Quick Check Answer

- Attached properties are properties that a containing element, such as a layout control, attaches to a contained element such as a content control. Properties are set by the contained element but typically affect how that element is rendered or laid out in the containing element. An example is the *Grid.Row* attached property, which is attached to all elements contained by a *Grid* element. By setting the *Grid.Row* property on a contained element, you set what row of the grid that element is rendered in.

Accessing Child Elements Programmatically

Layout controls expose a *Children* collection that enables you to access the child controls programmatically. You can obtain a reference to a child element by the index, as shown here:

Sample of Visual Basic Code

```
Dim aButton As Button
aButton = CType(grid1.Children(3), Button)
```

Sample of C# Code

```
Button aButton;
aButton = (Button)grid1.Children[3];
```

You can add a control programmatically by using the *Children.Add* method, as shown here:

Sample of Visual Basic Code

```
Dim aButton As New Button()
grid1.Children.Add(aButton)
```

Sample of C# Code

```
Button aButton = new Button();
grid1.Children.Add(aButton);
```

Similarly, you can remove a control programmatically with the *Children.Remove* method:

Sample of Visual Basic Code'

```
grid1.Children.Remove(aButton)
```

Sample of C# Code

```
grid1.Children.Remove(aButton);
```

And you can remove a control at a specified index by using the *RemoveAt* method, as shown here:

Sample of Visual Basic Code

```
grid1.Children.RemoveAt(3)
```

```
grid1.Children.RemoveAt(3);
```

Aligning Content

Frequently, you want to align the content contained in different controls as well as the edges of the controls themselves. You can align control edges and content at design time by using snaplines.

Snaplines are visual aids in the Visual Studio Integrated Development Environment (IDE) that provide feedback to the developer when control edges are aligned or when control content is aligned. When you position controls manually with the mouse in the designer, snaplines appear when the horizontal or vertical edges of the control are in alignment, as shown in Figures 1-7 and 1-8.

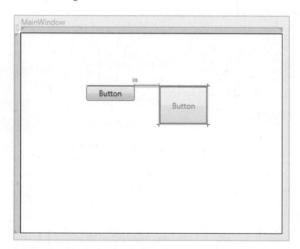

FIGURE 1-7 Horizontal snaplines.

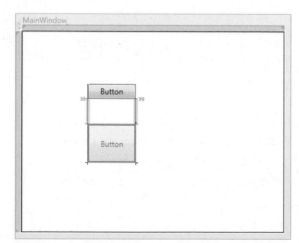

FIGURE 1-8 Vertical snaplines.

Snaplines also indicate when content is aligned, enabling you to align content across multiple controls. Figure 1-9 shows an example of content snaplines.

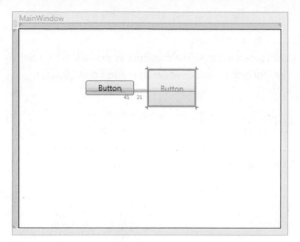

FIGURE 1-9 Content snaplines.

PRACTICE **Creating a Simple Application**

In this practice, you create a simple application to change the font of text in a *RichTextBox* control by using controls in a toolbar.

EXERCISE Using Layout Controls

1. In Visual Studio, create a new WPF application.

2. In XAML view, change the *Grid* opening and closing tags to be *DockPanel* tags, as shown here:

```
<DockPanel>
</DockPanel>
```

3. From the toolbox, drag a *ToolBar* control onto the window. Add a full-length closing tag and set the *DockPanel.Dock* property to *Top*, as shown here:

```
<ToolBar DockPanel.Dock="Top" Height="26" Name="toolBar1" Width="276">
</ToolBar>
```

Even though you have set the *DockPanel.Dock* property to *Top*, the toolbar remains in the center of the window because the *DockPanel.LastChildFill* property is set to *True* by default, and this setting overrides the *DockPanel.Dock* property.

4. In XAML view, use the following XAML to add a *Grid* container to the *DockPanel* control:

```
<Grid Name="grid1">
</Grid>
```

The toolbar now is at the top of the *DockPanel* control.

5. In XAML view, add the following *ColumnDefinition* elements to the *Grid* control:

```
<Grid.ColumnDefinitions>
  <ColumnDefinition Width="100"/>
  <ColumnDefinition Width="5"/>
  <ColumnDefinition Width="*"/>
</Grid.ColumnDefinitions>
```

6. In XAML view, use the following XAML to add a *ListBox* control to the first column:

```
<ListBox Grid.Column="0" Name="listBox1"></ListBox>
```

7. In XAML view, use the following XAML to add a *GridSplitter* control to the second column:

```
<GridSplitter Name="gridSplitter1" Margin="0" Width="5"
Grid.Column="1" HorizontalAlignment="Left"/>
```

In this practice, the *GridSplitter* control is given a dedicated column.

8. In XAML view, use the following XAML to add a *RichTextBox* control to the third column:

```
<RichTextBox Grid.Column="2" Name="richTextBox1"/>
```

9. In the XAML for the *ToolBar* control, use the following XAML to add three controls to the *ToolBar* control:

```
<Button>Bold</Button>
<Button>Italic</Button>
<Slider Name="Slider1" Minimum="2" Maximum="72" Width="100"/>
```

10. Double-click the button labeled Bold to open the *Click* event handler. Add the following code:

Sample of Visual Basic Code

```
richTextBox1.Selection.ApplyPropertyValue(FontWeightProperty, _
    FontWeights.Bold)
```

Sample of C# Code

```
richTextBox1.Selection.ApplyPropertyValue(FontWeightProperty,
    FontWeights.Bold);
```

11. In the designer, double-click the button labeled Italic to open the *Click* event handler. Add the following code:

Sample of Visual Basic Code

```
richTextBox1.Selection.ApplyPropertyValue(FontStyleProperty, _
    FontStyles.Italic)
```

Sample of C# Code

```
richTextBox1.Selection.ApplyPropertyValue(FontStyleProperty,
    FontStyles.Italic);
```

12. In the designer, double-click the slider to open the *ValueChanged* event handler. Add the following code:

Sample of Visual Basic Code

```
Try
    richTextBox1.Selection.ApplyPropertyValue(FontSizeProperty, _
      Slider1.Value.ToString())
Catch
End Try
```

Sample of C# Code

```
try
{
    richTextBox1.Selection.ApplyPropertyValue(FontSizeProperty,
      Slider1.Value.ToString());
}
catch { }
```

13. In the *Window1* constructor, add the following code after *InitializeComponent*. (In Visual Basic, you will have to add the entire constructor.)

Sample of Visual Basic Code

```
Public Sub New()
    InitializeComponent()
    For Each F As FontFamily In Fonts.SystemFontFamilies
      Dim l As ListBoxItem = New ListBoxItem()
      l.Content = F.ToString()
      l.FontFamily = F
      listBox1.Items.Add(l)
    Next
End Sub
```

Sample of C# Code

```
foreach (FontFamily F in Fonts.SystemFontFamilies)
{
    ListBoxItem l = new ListBoxItem();
    l.Content = F.ToString();
    l.FontFamily = F;
    listBox1.Items.Add(l);
}
```

14. In the designer, double-click the ListBox control to open the SelectionChanged event handler. Add the following code:

Sample of Visual Basic Code

```
richTextBox1.Selection.ApplyPropertyValue(FontFamilyProperty, _
    CType(listBox1.SelectedItem, ListBoxItem).FontFamily)
```

Sample of C# Code

```
richTextBox1.Selection.ApplyPropertyValue(FontFamilyProperty,
    ((ListBoxItem)listBox1.SelectedItem).FontFamily);
```

15. Press F5 to build and run your application. Note that you can resize the columns containing the *RichTextBox* and the *ListBox* by manipulating the grid splitter with the mouse.

Lesson Summary

- Controls in WPF are primarily divided into three types: content controls, which can contain a single nested element; item controls, which can contain a list of nested elements; and layout controls, which are designed to host multiple controls and provide layout logic for those controls. Certain specialized controls, such as the *TextBox*, *Image*, and *ProgressBar* controls, are individual controls and can be considered part of the content control category. Virtually any type of object can be assigned to the *Content* property of a content control. If the object inherits from *UIElement,* the control is rendered in the containing control. Other types are rendered as a string: the string returned by their content's *ToString* method.

- Item controls are designed to present multiple child items. Examples of item controls include *ListBox*, *ComboBox*, and *TreeView* as well as *Menu*, *ToolBar*, and *StatusBar* controls.

- *Menu* controls are designed to display hierarchical lists of *MenuItem* controls in the familiar menu format. Each *MenuItem* control can contain its own list of *MenuItem* controls and can have a command associated with it that is invoked when the *MenuItem* control is clicked, although typically not both at once.

- The *ContextMenu* control appears near an associated control when the user right-clicks the associated control. You can define a *ContextMenu* control in XAML for the associated control's *Control.ContextMenu* property.

- *ToolBar* controls are designed for displaying groups of associated controls, usually with related functionality. Controls displayed in a toolbar by default conform to the appearance and behavior of the toolbar itself. *StatusBar* controls are similar to *ToolBar* controls but typically are used more often for presenting information than for presenting controls that are an active part of the user interface.

- Layout controls are containers that provide layout logic for contained controls. A layout control is typically the child element in a window. How controls are arranged in a layout panel depends largely on the layout properties of the contained controls. The *HorizontalAlignment* and *VerticalAlignment* properties of child controls determine how a control is aligned in the horizontal and vertical directions, and the *Margin* property defines an area of space that surrounds the control. The impact of a control's layout properties can differ, depending on the control in which they are hosted.

- Attached properties are properties provided to a control by its container or by another class. Controls have these properties only when they are in the correct context to express them. Examples of attached properties include the *Grid.Row*, *Grid.Column*, and *KeyboardNavigation.TabIndex* properties.

- The *Grid* control is the most commonly used layout panel for the development of user interfaces. The *Grid* control enables you to define grid rows and columns and to host multiple elements in each cell. The *Grid* control provides attached properties to child controls that determine the grid column and row in which they are hosted.

- The *GridSplitter* control enables the user to resize grid columns and rows at run time.

- Layout panels such as *UniformGrid*, *StackPanel*, *WrapPanel*, *DockPanel*, and *Canvas* controls are commonly used to create specialized parts of the user interface and are usually not the highest-level panel in the user interface.

Lesson Review

You can use the following questions to test your knowledge of the information in Lesson 1, "Using WPF Controls." The questions are also available on the companion CD if you prefer to review them in electronic form.

NOTE **ANSWERS**

Answers to these questions and explanations of why each answer choice is correct or incorrect are located in the "Answers" section at the end of the book.

---

1. How many child controls can a content control contain?

    A. 0

    B. 1

    C. No limit

    D. Depends on the control

2. Which of the following XAML samples correctly shows a button in a cell created by the intersection of the second column and the second row of a grid with four cells?

    A.

```
<Grid>
  <Grid.ColumnDefinitions>
    <ColumnDefinition/>
    <ColumnDefinition/>
  </Grid.ColumnDefinitions>
  <Grid.RowDefinitions>
    <RowDefinition/>
    <RowDefinition/>
  </Grid.RowDefinitions>
  <Button Grid.Cell="1,1"></Button>
</Grid>
```

    B.

```
<Grid>
  <Grid.ColumnDefinitions>
    <ColumnDefinition/>
```

```
        <ColumnDefinition/>
    </Grid.ColumnDefinitions>
    <Grid.RowDefinitions>
        <RowDefinition/>
        <RowDefinition/>
    </Grid.RowDefinitions>
    <Button Grid.Column="1" Grid.Row="1"></Button>
</Grid>
```

C.

```
<Grid>
    <Grid.ColumnDefinitions>
        <ColumnDefinition/>
        <ColumnDefinition/>
    </Grid.ColumnDefinitions>
    <Grid.RowDefinitions>
        <RowDefinition/>
        <RowDefinition/>
    </Grid.RowDefinitions>
    <Button></Button>
</Grid>
```

D.

```
<Grid>
    <Grid.ColumnDefinitions>
        <ColumnDefinition/>
        <ColumnDefinition/>
    </Grid.ColumnDefinitions>
    <Grid.RowDefinitions>
        <RowDefinition/>
        <RowDefinition/>
    </Grid.RowDefinitions>
    <Button Grid.Cell="2,2"></Button>
</Grid>
```

3. Which XAML sample correctly defines a context menu for Button1?

    A.

```
<Grid>
    <ContextMenu name="mymenu">
        <MenuItem>MenuItem</MenuItem>
    </ContextMenu>
    <Button ContextMenu="mymenu" Height="23" HorizontalAlignment="Left"
        Margin="54,57,0,0" Name="button1" VerticalAlignment="Top"
        Width="75">Button</Button>
</Grid>
```

    B.

```
<ContextMenu Name="mymenu">
    <MenuItem>MenuItem</MenuItem>
</ContextMenu>
<Grid>
    <Button ContextMenu="mymenu" Height="23" HorizontalAlignment="Left"
```

```
        Margin="54,57,0,0" Name="button1" VerticalAlignment="Top"
        Width="75">Button</Button>
</Grid>
```

C.

```
<Menu Name="mymenu" ContextMenu="True">
    <MenuItem>MenuItem</MenuItem>
</Menu>
<Grid>
    <Button ContextMenu="mymenu" Height="23" HorizontalAlignment="Left"
        Margin="54,57,0,0" Name="button1" VerticalAlignment="Top"
        Width="75">Button</Button>
</Grid>
```

D.

```
<Grid>
    <Button Height="23" HorizontalAlignment="Left" Margin="54,57,0,0"
        Name="button1" VerticalAlignment="Top" Width="75">
        <Button.ContextMenu>
            <ContextMenu>
                <MenuItem>MenuItem</MenuItem>
            </ContextMenu>
        </Button.ContextMenu>
        Button
    </Button>
</Grid>
```

4. What is the maximum number of child elements that an item control can contain?

   A. 0

   B. 1

   C. No limit

   D. Depends on the control

5. Which layout panel would be the best choice for a user interface that requires evenly spaced controls laid out in a regular pattern?

   A. *Grid*

   B. *Canvas*

   C. *UniformGrid*

   D. *WrapPanel*

6. You are working with a *Button* control contained in a *Canvas* control. Which XAML sample will position the button edges 20 units from the bottom edge of the canvas and 20 units from the right edge of the canvas as well as maintain that positioning when the canvas is resized? (Each correct answer presents a complete solution. Choose all that apply.)

A.

```
<Button Margin="20" Canvas.Bottom="0" Canvas.Right="0"></Button>
```

B.

```
<Button Margin="20"></Button>
```

C.

```
<Button Canvas.Bottom="20" Canvas.Right="20"></Button>
```

D.

```
<Button Margin="20" Canvas.Bottom="20" Canvas.Right="20"></Button>
```

Lesson 2: Using Resources

Resources are files or objects an application uses but are not created in the actual executable code. Windows Forms uses binary resources to allow programs access to large files such as images or large text files. Although WPF technology uses binary resources, it also introduces the idea of logical resources, which define objects for use in your application and allow you to share objects among elements. In this lesson, you learn how to access encoded and binary resources in both Windows Forms and WPF applications. You learn how to create resource-only dynamic-link libraries (DLLs) and load resource-only assemblies. You also learn how to create logical resources and resource dictionaries and to access resources in code for your WPF applications. Last, you learn the difference between static and dynamic resources and when to use each.

> **After this lesson, you will be able to:**
> - Embed a binary resource in an application.
> - Retrieve a binary resource by using code.
> - Retrieve a binary resource by using pack URI syntax.
> - Access a resource in another assembly by using pack URI syntax.
> - Add a content file to an application.
> - Create a resource-only DLL.
> - Load and access a resource-only DLL.
> - Create a logical resource.
> - Create an application resource.
> - Access a resource in XAML.
> - Explain the difference between a static resource and a dynamic resource.
> - Create a resource dictionary.
> - Merge resource dictionaries.
> - Decide where to store a resource.
> - Access a resource object in code.
>
> **Estimated lesson time: 1 hour**

Using Binary Resources

Binary resources enable you to compile large binary files in your application assemblies and retrieve them for use in your application. Binary resources are different from logical resources, which can be defined and accessed in XAML files. Logical resources are discussed later in this lesson.

Embedding Resources

Embedding resources in your application is fairly easy. All you need to do is add the file to your project and set the file's *Build Action* property to *Resource*. When the application is compiled, the resource is compiled automatically as a resource and embedded in your application. You can use this procedure to embed resources in both Windows Forms and WPF applications.

To embed a resource in your application,

1. From the Project menu, choose Add Existing Item. The Add Existing Item dialog box opens.

2. Browse to the file you want to add. Click Add to add it to your project.

3. In the Properties window, set the *Build Action* property for this file to *Resource*.

> **NOTE** **THE *BUILD ACTION* PROPERTY**
>
> Do not set the *Build Action* property to Embedded Resource, which embeds the resource using a different resource management scheme that is less accessible from WPF applications.

You can update a resource that has been previously added to an application by following the previous procedure and recompiling your application.

Loading Resources

The WPF *Image* class is capable of interacting directly with embedded resources. To specify an image resource, all you have to do is refer to the embedded file path, as shown in bold here:

```
<Image Source="myPic.bmp" Margin="17,90,61,22"
  Name="Image1" Stretch="Fill"/>
```

This example refers to a resource that has been added directly to your project. In most cases, you want to organize your resources in folders in your application. Naturally, you must include the folder name in your path, as shown in bold here:

```
<Image Source="myFolder/myPic.bmp" Margin="17,90,61,22"
  Name="Image1" Stretch="Fill"/>
```

When accessing embedded resources, the forward slash (/) is used in the URI by convention, but either the forward slash or the back slash (\) will work.

Pack URIs

The syntax previously shown to access embedded resources is actually a shorthand syntax that represents the longer syntax for pack URIs, which is a way WPF accesses embedded resources directly by specifying a URI to that resource. The full syntax for using pack URIs to locate an embedded resource is as follows:

```
pack://<Authority>/<Folder>/<FileName>
```

The *<Authority>* specified in the pack URI syntax is one of two possible values. It can be either *application:,,,* which designates that the URI should look to the assembly the current application is in for resource or content files, or *siteOfOrigin:,,,* which indicates that the application should look to the site of the application's origin for the indicated resource files. The *siteOfOrigin* syntax is discussed further in the "Retrieving Loose Files with *siteOfOrigin* Pack URIs" section later in this chapter. If a relative URI is used, *application:,,,* is assumed to be the *<Authority>*.

Thus, the previous example of an *Image* element could be rewritten to use the full pack URI syntax, as shown in bold here:

```
<Image Source="pack://application:,,,/myFolder/myPic.bmp"
  Margin="17,90,61,22" Name="Image1" Stretch="Fill"/>
```

The full pack URI syntax comes in handy when you need to retrieve an embedded resource in code, as shown here:

Sample of Visual Basic Code

```
Dim myImage As Image
myImage.Source = New BitmapImage(New _
  Uri("pack://application:,,,/myFolder/myPic.bmp"))
```

Sample of C# Code

```
Image myImage;
myImage.Source = new BitmapImage(new
  Uri("pack://application:,,,/myFolder/myPic.bmp"));
```

Using Resources in Other Assemblies

You can also use the pack URI syntax to access resources embedded in other assemblies. The following example demonstrates the basic pack URI syntax for accessing embedded resources in other assemblies:

```
pack://application:,,,/<AssemblyName>;component/<Folder>/<FileName>
```

Thus, if you wanted to locate a file named myPic.bmp in the folder myFolder in another assembly named myAssembly, you would use the following pack URI:

```
Pack://application:,,,/myAssembly;component/myFolder/myPic.bmp
```

As with other pack URIs, if the embedded file does not exist within a folder, the folder is omitted in the URI.

Content Files

You do not want to embed all the files your application uses as resources. For example, files that need to be updated frequently should not be embedded, because embedding such files would require the application to be recompiled whenever a file is updated. Other examples of files that you do not want to embed are sound and media files. Because *MediaPlayer* and

MediaElement controls do not support the pack URI syntax, the only way to provide sound files is as content files. Fortunately, it is easy to add content files as unembedded resources.

To add a content file,

1. From the Project menu, choose Add Existing Item. The Add Existing Item dialog box opens.

2. Browse to the file you want to add. Click Add to add it to your project.

3. In the Properties window, set the *Build Action* property for this file to *Content*.

4. In the Properties window, set the *Copy To Output Directory* property to *Copy Always*. This ensures that this file is copied to your application directory when your application is built.

After a file has been added as a content file, you can refer to it using the relative URI, as shown in bold here:

```
<MediaElement Margin="52,107,66,35" Source="crash.mp3"
    Name="mediaElement1"/>
```

Retrieving Loose Files with *siteOfOrigin* Pack URIs

In some cases, you want to deploy an application that requires regular updating of resources. Because compiled XAML cannot reference a binary resource in its current directory unless that file has been added to the project, this requires any files referenced in XAML to be included as part of the application. That, in turn, requires users to install updated versions of a desktop application every time content files have changed.

You can solve this problem by using *siteOfOrigin* pack URIs to refer to the site from which the application was deployed.

The *siteOfOrigin:,,,* syntax means different things depending on the location from which the application was originally installed. If the application is a full-trust desktop application that was installed using Windows Installer, the *siteOfOrigin:,,,* syntax in a pack URI refers to the root directory of the application.

If the application is a full-trust application that was installed using ClickOnce, the *siteOfOrigin:,,,* syntax refers to the Uniform Resource Locator (URL) or the Universal Naming Convention (UNC) path from which the application was originally deployed.

For a partial-trust application deployed with ClickOnce or an XAML Browser Application (XBAP), *siteOfOrigin:,,,* refers to the URL or UNC path that hosts the application.

Pack URIs that use the *siteOfOrigin:,,,* syntax always point to loose files (that is, files that are copied to the output directory but are not compiled); they never point to embedded resources. Thus, the files they reference should always exist in the directory specified by the *siteOfOrigin:,,,* syntax in a loose, uncompiled state.

The following example demonstrates use of the *siteOfOrigin:,,,* syntax:

```
<Image Source="pack://siteOfOrigin:,,,/OfficeFrontDoor.jpg"/>
```

Retrieving Resources Manually

You might need to use resource files with objects that do not support the pack URI syntax. In these cases, you must retrieve the resources manually using the *Application* *.GetResourceStream* method. This method returns a *System.Windows.Resources* *.StreamResourceInfo* object that exposes two properties: the *ContentType* property, which describes the type of content contained in the resource, and the *Stream* property, which contains an *UnmanagedMemoryStream* object that exposes the raw data of the resource. Then you can manipulate that data programmatically. The following example demonstrates how to retrieve the text contained in an embedded resource text file:

Sample of Visual Basic Code

```
Dim myInfo As System.Windows.Resources.StreamResourceInfo
Dim myString As String
myInfo = Application.GetResourceStream( _
   New Uri("myTextFile.txt", UriKind.Relative))
Dim myReader As New System.IO.StreamReader(myInfo.Stream)
   ' myString is set to the text contained in myTextFile.txt
myString = myReader.ReadToEnd()
```

Sample of C# Code

```
System.Windows.Resources.StreamResourceInfo myInfo;
string myString;
myInfo = Application.GetResourceStream(
   new Uri("myTextFile.txt", UriKind.Relative));
System.IO.StreamReader myReader =
   new System.IO.StreamReader(myInfo.Stream);
// myString is set to the text contained in myTextFile.txt
myString = myReader.ReadToEnd();
```

Creating Resource-Only DLLs

You can create DLLs that contain only compiled resources. This can be useful in situations when resource files need to change frequently but recompiling the application is not an option. You can update and recompile the resources and then swap the old resource DLL for the new one.

Creating a resource-only DLL is fairly straightforward. To create a resource-only DLL, simply create an empty project in Visual Studio and add resource files to it. You can access resources in a resource-only DLL through the assembly resource stream.

To create a resource-only DLL:

1. In Visual Studio, create a new project with the Empty Project template.

2. In Solution Explorer, right-click the project name and choose Properties to open the Project Properties page. In the Application tab, set the Application Type to Class Library.

3. From the Project menu, choose Add Existing Item to add resource files to your project.

4. In Solution Explorer, select a resource file. In the Properties window, set the *Build Action* property to *Embedded Resource.* Repeat this step for each resource file.

5. From the Build menu, choose Build <application>, where <application> is the name of your application, to compile your resource-only DLL.

To access resources programmatically using the assembly resource stream:

1. Get the *AssemblyName* object that represents the resource-only assembly, as shown here:

Sample of Visual Basic Code

```
Dim aName As System.Reflection.AssemblyName
aName = System.Reflection.AssemblyName.GetAssemblyName("C:\myAssembly.dll"))
```

Sample of C# Code

```
System.Reflection.AssemblyName aName;
aName = System.Reflection.AssemblyName.GetAssemblyName("C:\\myAssembly.dll"));
```

2. Use the *AssemblyName* object to load the assembly, as shown here:

Sample of Visual Basic Code

```
Dim asm As System.Reflection.Assembly
asm = System.Reflection.Assembly.Load(aName)
```

Sample of C# Code

```
System.Reflection.Assembly asm;
asm = System.Reflection.Assembly.Load(aName);
```

3. After the assembly has been loaded, you can access the names of the resources through the *Assembly.GetManifestResourceNames* method and the resource streams through the *Assembly.GetManifestResourceStream* method. The following example demonstrates how to retrieve the names of the resources in an assembly and then load an image from the resource stream into a Windows Forms PictureBox control:

Sample of Visual Basic Code

```
Dim res() As String = asm.GetManifestResourceNames
PictureBox1.Image = New _
    System.Drawing.Bitmap(asm.GetManifestResourceStream(res(0)))
```

Sample of C# Code

```
String res[] = asm.GetManifestResourceNames();
pictureBox1.Image = new
    System.Drawing.Bitmap(asm.GetManifestResourceStream(res[0]));
```

Using Logical Resources

Logical resources enable you to define objects in XAML that are not part of the visual tree but are available for use by WPF elements in your user interface. Elements in your user interface can access the resource as needed. An example of an object that you might define as a resource is *Brush*, used to provide a common color scheme for the application.

By defining objects that several elements use in a *Resources* section, you gain a few advantages over defining an object each time you use it. First, you gain reusability because you define your object only once rather than multiple times. You also gain flexibility: By separating the objects used by your user interface from the user interface itself, you can refactor parts of the user interface without having to redesign it completely. For example, you might use different collections of resources for different cultures in localization or for different application conditions.

Any type of object can be defined as a resource. Every WPF element defines a *Resources* collection, which you can use to define objects available to that element and the elements in its visual tree. Although it is most common to define resources in the *Resources* collection of the window, you can define a resource in any element's *Resources* collection and access it so long as the accessing element is part of the defining element's visual tree.

Declaring a Logical Resource

You declare a logical resource by adding it to a *Resources* collection, as shown here:

```
<Window.Resources>
   <RadialGradientBrush x:Key="myBrush">
      <GradientStop Color="CornflowerBlue" Offset="0" />
      <GradientStop Color="Crimson" Offset="1" />
   </RadialGradientBrush>
</Window.Resources>
```

If you don't intend a resource to be available to the entire window, you can define it in the *Resources* collection of an element in the window, as shown in this example:

```
<Grid>
   <Grid.Resources>
      <RadialGradientBrush x:Key="myBrush">
         <GradientStop Color="CornflowerBlue" Offset="0" />
         <GradientStop Color="Crimson" Offset="1" />
      </RadialGradientBrush>
   </Grid.Resources>
</Grid>
```

The usefulness of this is somewhat limited, and the most common scenario is to define resources in the *Window.Resources* collection. One point to remember is that when using static resources, you must define the resource in the XAML code before you refer to it. Static and dynamic resources are explained later in this lesson.

Every object declared as a *Resource* must set the *x:Key* property. This is the name other WPF elements will use to access the resource. There is one exception to this rule: *Style* objects that set the *TargetType* property do not need to set the *x:Key* property explicitly because it is set implicitly behind the scenes. In the previous two examples, the key is set to *myBrush*.

The *x:Key* property does not have to be unique in the application, but it must be unique in the *Resources* collection in which it is defined. Thus, you could define one resource in the *Grid.Resources* collection with a key of *myBrush* and another in the *Window.Resources* collection with the same key. Objects within the visual tree of the grid that reference a resource with the key *myBrush* reference the object defined in the *Grid.Resources* collection, and objects that are not in the visual tree of the grid but are within the visual tree of the Window reference the object defined in the *Window.Resources* collection.

Application Resources

In addition to defining resources at the level of the element or Window, you can define resources that are accessible by all objects in a particular application. You can create an application resource by opening the App.xaml file (for C# projects) or the Application.xaml file (for Visual Basic projects) and adding the resource to the *Application.Resources* collection, as shown in bold here:

```
<Application x:Class="WpfApplication2.App"
    xmlns="http://schemas.microsoft.com/winfx/2006/xaml/presentation"
    xmlns:x="http://schemas.microsoft.com/winfx/2006/xaml"
    StartupUri="Window1.xaml">
    <Application.Resources>
        <SolidColorBrush x:Key="appBrush" Color="PapayaWhip" />
    </Application.Resources>
</Application>
```

Accessing a Resource in XAML

You can access a resource in XAML by using the following syntax:

```
{StaticResource myBrush}
```

In this example, the markup declares that a static resource with the *myBrush* key is accessed. Because this resource is a *Brush* object, you can plug that markup into any place that expects a *Brush* object. This example demonstrates how to use a resource in the context of a WPF element:

```
<Grid Background="{StaticResource myBrush}">
</Grid>
```

When a resource is referenced in XAML, the *Resources* collection of the declaring object is first searched for a resource with a matching key. If one is not found, the *Resources* collection of that element's parent is searched, and so on, up to the window that hosts the element and to the application *Resources* collection.

Static and Dynamic Resources

In addition to the syntax described previously, you can reference a resource with the following syntax:

```
{DynamicResource myBrush}
```

The difference between the DynamicResource and StaticResource syntax lies in how the referencing elements retrieve the resources. Resources referenced by the StaticResource syntax are retrieved once by the referencing element and used for the lifetime of the resource.

Resources referenced with the DynamicResource syntax are acquired every time the referenced object is used.

It might seem intuitive to think that, if you use StaticResource syntax, the referencing object does not reflect changes to the underlying resource, but this is not necessarily the case. WPF objects that implement dependency properties automatically incorporate change notification, and changes made to the properties of the resource are picked up by any objects using that resource. Take the following example:

```
<Window x:Class="WpfApplication2.Window1"
    xmlns="http://schemas.microsoft.com/winfx/2006/xaml/presentation"
    xmlns:x="http://schemas.microsoft.com/winfx/2006/xaml"
    Title="Window1" Height="300" Width="300">
    <Window.Resources>
        <SolidColorBrush x:Key="BlueBrush" Color="Blue" />
    </Window.Resources>
    <Grid Background="{StaticResource BlueBrush}">
    </Grid>
</Window>
```

This example renders the grid in the window with a blue background. If the *Color* property of the *SolidColorBrush* defined in the *Window.Resources* collection was changed in code to red, for instance, the background of the grid would render as red because change notification would notify all objects using that resource that the property had changed.

The difference between static and dynamic resources comes when the underlying object changes. If *Brush* defined in the *Windows.Resources* collection were accessed in code and set to a different object instance, the grid in the previous example would not detect this change. However, if the grid used the following markup, the change of the object would be detected, and the grid would render the background with the new brush:

```
<Grid Background="{DynamicResource BlueBrush}">
</Grid>
```

Accessing resources in code is discussed in the "Retrieving Resources in Code" section later in this chapter.

The downside of using dynamic resources is that they tend to decrease application performance because they are retrieved every time they are used, thus reducing the efficiency of an application. The best practice is to use static resources unless there is a specific reason for using a dynamic resource. Examples of instances in which you would want to use a dynamic resource include when you use the *SystemBrushes*, *SystemFonts*, and *SystemParameters* classes as resources (see Chapter 5, "Working With User Defined Controls," Lesson 3, for more information about these classes) or any other time when you expect the underlying object of the resource to change.

Creating a Resource Dictionary

A *resource dictionary* is a collection of resources that reside in a separate XAML file and can be imported into your application. They can be useful for organizing your resources in a single place or for sharing resources between multiple projects in a single solution. The following procedure describes how to create a new resource dictionary in your application.

To create a resource dictionary:

1. From the Project menu, choose Add Resource Dictionary. The Add New Item dialog box opens. Choose the name for the resource dictionary and click Add. The new resource dictionary is opened in XAML view.

2. Add resources to the new resource dictionary in XAML view. You can add resources to the file in XAML view, as shown in bold here:

```
<ResourceDictionary
    xmlns="http://schemas.microsoft.com/winfx/2006/xaml/presentation"
    xmlns:x="http://schemas.microsoft.com/winfx/2006/xaml">
    <SolidColorBrush x:Key="appBrush" Color="DarkSalmon" />
</ResourceDictionary>
```

Merging Resource Dictionaries

For objects in your application to access resources in a resource dictionary, you must merge the resource dictionary file with a *Resources* collection that is accessible in your application, such as the *Window.Resources* or *Application.Resources* collection. You merge resource dictionaries by adding a reference to your resource dictionary file in the *ResourceDictionary* *.MergedDictionaries* collection. The following example demonstrates how to merge the resources in a *Window.Resources* collection with the resources in resource dictionary files named Dictionary1.xaml and Dictionary2.xaml:

```
<Window.Resources>
    <ResourceDictionary>
        <ResourceDictionary.MergedDictionaries>
            <ResourceDictionary Source="Dictionary1.xaml" />
            <ResourceDictionary Source="Dictionary2.xaml" />
        </ResourceDictionary.MergedDictionaries>
        <SolidColorBrush x:Key="BlueBrush" Color="Blue" />
    </ResourceDictionary>
</Window.Resources>
```

If you define additional resources in your *Resources* collection, they must be defined within the bounds of the *ResourceDictionary* tags.

Choosing Where to Store a Resource

You have seen several options regarding where resources should be stored. The factors that should be weighed when deciding where to store a resource include ease of accessibility by referencing elements, readability and maintainability of the code, and reusability.

For resources to be accessed by all elements in an application, store resources in the *Application.Resources* collection. The *Window.Resources* collection makes resources available only to elements in that window, but that is typically sufficient for most purposes. If you need to share individual resources over multiple projects in a solution, your best choice is to store your resources in a resource dictionary that can be shared among different projects.

Readability is important for enabling maintenance of your code by other developers. The best choice for readability is to store resources in the *Window.Resources* collection because developers can then read your code in a single file rather than having to refer to other code files.

If making your resources reusable is important the ideal method for storing them is to use a resource dictionary. This allows you to reuse resources among different projects and extract those resources easily for use in other solutions as well.

Retrieving Resources in Code

You can access resources in code. The *FindResource* method enables you to obtain a reference to a resource by using the *Key* value. To use the *FindResource* method, you must call it from an element reference that has access to that resource. The following code example demonstrates how to obtain a reference to a resource with a *Key* value of *myBrush* through a *Button* element that has access to that resource:

Sample of Visual Basic Code

```
Dim aBrush As SolidColorBrush
aBrush = CType(Button1.FindResource("myBrush"), SolidColorBrush)
```

Sample of C# Code

```
SolidColorBrush aBrush;
aBrush = (SolidColorBrush)Button1.FindResource("myBrush");
```

The *FindResource* method throws an exception if the named resource cannot be found. To avoid possible exceptions, you can use the *TryFindResource* method instead.

You also can access resources directly through the *Resources* collection on the element that contains it. The caveat here is that you must know in which collection the resource is defined and use the correct *Resources* collection. The following example demonstrates how to access a resource with the *Key* value of *myBrush* through the *Resources* collection of the window:

Sample of Visual Basic Code

```
Dim aBrush As SolidColorBrush
aBrush = CType(Me.Resources("myBrush"), SolidColorBrush)
```

Sample of C# Code

```
SolidColorBrush aBrush;
aBrush = (SolidColorBrush)this.Resources["myBrush"];
```

When used in code, resources are read-write. Thus, you actually can change the object to which a resource refers. This example demonstrates how you can create a new object in code and set an existing resource to it:

Sample of Visual Basic Code

```vb
Dim aBrush As New SolidColorBrush(Colors.Red)
Me.Resources("myBrush") = aBrush
```

Sample of C# Code

```csharp
SolidColorBrush aBrush = new SolidColorBrush(Colors.Red);
this.Resources["myBrush"] = aBrush;
```

If the object a resource refers to is changed in code, objects that use that resource behave differently, depending on how the resource is referenced. Resources referenced with the *DynamicResource* markup use the new object when the resource is changed in code. Objects that reference resources with the *StaticResource* markup continue to use the object they initially retrieved from the *Resources* collection and are unaware of the change.

PRACTICE Practice with Logical Resources

In this practice, you create two resource dictionaries and merge them with the resources in your window.

EXERCISE Creating Resource Dictionaries

1. Open the partial solution for this practice.

2. From the Project menu, choose Add Resource Dictionary. Name the file **GridResources.xaml** and click Add.

3. Add another resource dictionary and name it **ButtonResources.xaml**.

4. In Solution Explorer, double-click GridResources.xaml to open the *GridResources* resource dictionary. Add the following *LinearGradientBrush* object to the GridResources.xaml file:

   ```xml
   <LinearGradientBrush x:Key="GridBackgroundBrush">
      <GradientStop Color="AliceBlue" Offset="0" />
      <GradientStop Color="Blue" Offset=".5" />
      <GradientStop Color="Black" Offset="1" />
   </LinearGradientBrush>
   ```

5. Double-click ButtonResources.xaml to open the *ButtonResources* resource dictionary. Add the following resources to this file:

   ```xml
   <LinearGradientBrush x:Key="ButtonBackgroundBrush">
      <GradientStop Color="Yellow" Offset="0" />
      <GradientStop Color="Red" Offset="1" />
   </LinearGradientBrush>
   <SolidColorBrush Color="Purple" x:Key="ButtonForegroundBrush" />
   <SolidColorBrush Color="LimeGreen" x:Key="ButtonBorderBrush" />
   <Style TargetType="Button">
   ```

```
<Setter Property="Background" Value="{StaticResource
    ButtonBackgroundBrush}" />
<Setter Property="Foreground" Value="{StaticResource
    ButtonForegroundBrush}" />
<Setter Property="BorderBrush" Value="{StaticResource
    ButtonBorderBrush}" />
</Style>
```

These resources include brushes for the background, foreground, and border as well as a style that automatically applies these brushes to *Button* elements.

6. Double-click Window1 to open the designer for the window. Above the definition for the *Grid* element, add the following *Resources* section to the XAML code for the window:

```
<Window.Resources>
    <ResourceDictionary>
        <ResourceDictionary.MergedDictionaries>
            <ResourceDictionary Source="ButtonResources.xaml" />
            <ResourceDictionary Source="GridResources.xaml" />
        </ResourceDictionary.MergedDictionaries>
    </ResourceDictionary>
</Window.Resources>
```

7. Modify the *Grid* definition to reference the resource that defines the brush to be used for the background of the grid, as shown here:

```
<Grid Background="{StaticResource GridBackgroundBrush}">
```

8. Press F5 to build and run your application. The *Brush* objects defined in the resource dictionaries are applied to your window.

Lesson Summary

- You can add binary resources to an application by using the Add Existing Item menu in Visual Studio and setting the *Build Action* property of the added file to *Resource*.

- For resource-aware classes such as the *Image* element, you can retrieve embedded resources by using pack URI syntax. The pack URI syntax also provides for accessing resources in other assemblies.

- If you are working with classes that are not resource-aware, you must retrieve resources manually by using the *Application.GetResourceStream* method to retrieve the *UnmanagedMemoryStream* that encodes the resource. Then you can use the File IO classes to read the stream.

- Content files can be added as loose files, which are files that are copied to the output directory but are not compiled. You must use content files to add sound or media files to an application because MediaPlayer and MediaElement are incapable of reading embedded resources.

- You can create resource-only DLLs and retrieve the resources stored within by using the *Assembly.GetManifestResourceStream* method.
- Logical resources are objects defined in XAML and can be used by elements in your application.
- You can define a resource in several locations: in the *Resources* collection for *Element*, in the *Resources* collection for the window, in the *Resources* collection for *Application*, or in a resource dictionary. Where you define a resource depends largely on reusability, maintainability of code, and how available the resource object needs to be to the rest of the application.
- Static resources retrieve an object from a *Resources* collection once, whereas dynamic resources retrieve the object each time it is accessed. Although changes made to an object are detected by static resources, a change within the actual underlying object is not.
- Resource dictionaries are separate XAML files that define resources. Resource dictionaries can be merged with an existing *Resources* collection for an element.
- Resources can be retrieved in code, either by accessing the *Resources* collection directly or by using the *FindResource* or *TryFindResource* method.

Lesson Review

You can use the following questions to test your knowledge of the information in Lesson 2, "Using Resources." The questions are also available on the companion CD if you prefer to review them in electronic form.

> **NOTE** **ANSWERS**
>
> Answers to these questions and explanations of why each answer choice is correct or incorrect are located in the "Answers" section at the end of the book.

1. Which of the following examples of the pack URI syntax accesses a file named myImage.jpg in a folder named MyFolder in another assembly named myAssembly?

   A.

   ```
   Pack://application:,,,/myAssembly;component/MyFolder/myImage.jpg
   ```

   B.

   ```
   Pack://application:,,,/myAssembly;MyFolder/component/myImage.jpg
   ```

   C.

   ```
   Pack://application:,,,;component/myAssemby/MyFolder/myImage.jpg
   ```

   D.

   ```
   Pack://application:,,,/myAssembly;component/myImage.jpg
   ```

2. You are adding an image to your application for use in an *Image* element. What is the best setting for the *Build Action* property in Visual Studio?

   A. *Embedded Resource*

   B. *Resource*

   C. *None*

   D. *Content*

3. You are adding a media file to your application for use in a *MediaElement* element. What is the best setting for the *Build Action* property in Visual Studio?

   A. *Embedded Resource*

   B. *Resource*

   C. *None*

   D. *Content*

4. You have created a series of customized *Brush* objects to create a common color scheme for every window in each of several applications in your company. The *Brush* objects have been implemented as resources. What is the best place to define these resources?

   A. In the *Resources* collection of each control that needs them

   B. In the *Resources* collection of each window that needs them

   C. In the *Application.Resources* collection

   D. In a separate resource dictionary

5. Look at the following XAML:

```
<Window x:Class="Window1"
    xmlns="http://schemas.microsoft.com/winfx/2006/xaml/presentation"
    xmlns:x="http://schemas.microsoft.com/winfx/2006/xaml"
    Title="Window1" Height="300" Width="300">
    <Window.Resources>
        <SolidColorBrush Color="Red" x:Key="ForegroundBrush" />
        <SolidColorBrush Color="Blue" x:Key="BackgroundBrush" />
    </Window.Resources>
    <Grid>
        <Button Background="{StaticResource BackgroundBrush}"
            Foreground="{DynamicResource ForegroundBrush}" Height="23"
            Margin="111,104,92,0" Name="Button1"
            VerticalAlignment="Top">Button</Button>
    </Grid>
</Window>
```

   What happens to the colors of the button when the following code is executed?

   Sample of Visual Basic Code

```
Dim aBrush As New SolidColorBrush(Colors.Green)
Me.Resources("ForegroundBrush") = aBrush
Dim bBrush As SolidColorBrush
bBrush = CType(Me.Resources("BackgroundBrush"), SolidColorBrush)
bBrush.Color = Colors.Black
```

Sample of C# Code

```
SolidColorBrush aBrush = new SolidColorBrush(Colors.Green);
this.Resources["ForegroundBrush"] = aBrush;
SolidColorBrush bBrush;
bBrush = (SolidColorBrush)this.Resources["BackgroundBrush"];
bBrush.Color = Colors.Black;
```

A. Nothing happens.

B. The background turns black.

C. The foreground turns green.

D. Both B and C.

Lesson 3: Using Styles and Triggers

Styles enable you to create a cohesive appearance and behavior for your application. You can use styles to define a standard color and sizing scheme for your application and use triggers to provide dynamic interaction with your UI elements. In this lesson, you learn to create and implement styles, apply a style to all instances of a single type, and to implement style inheritance. You learn to use setters to set properties and event handlers and triggers to change property values dynamically. Finally, you learn about the order of property precedence.

After this lesson, you will be able to:

- Create and implement a style.
- Apply a style to all instances of a type.
- Implement style inheritance.
- Use property and event setters.
- Explain the order of property value precedence.
- Use and implement triggers, including property triggers, data triggers, event triggers, and multiple triggers.

Estimated lesson time: 30 minutes

Using Styles

Styles can be thought of as analogous to cascading style sheets as used in Hypertext Markup Language (HTML) pages. Styles basically tell the presentation layer to substitute a new visual appearance for the standard one. They enable you to make changes to the user interface as a whole easily and to provide a consistent appearance and behavior for your application in a variety of situations. Styles enable you to set properties and hook up events on UI elements through the application of those styles. Further, you can create visual elements that respond dynamically to property changes through the application of triggers, which listen for a property change and then apply style changes in response.

Properties of Styles

The primary class in the application of styles is, unsurprisingly, the *Style* class, which contains information about styling a group of properties. A style can be created to apply to a single instance of an element, to all instances of an element type, or across multiple types. Table 1-9 shows the important properties of the *Style* class.

TABLE 1-9 Important Properties of the *Style* Class

PROPERTY	DESCRIPTION
BasedOn	Indicates another style that this style is based on. This property is useful for creating inherited styles.
Resources	Contains a collection of local resources the style uses. The *Resources* property is discussed in detail in Lesson 2 of this chapter.
Setters	Contains a collection of Setter or *EventSetter* objects. These are used to set properties or events on an element as part of a style.
TargetType	Identifies the intended element type for the style.
Triggers	Contains a collection of *Trigger* objects and related objects that enable you to designate a change in the user interface in response to changes in properties.

The basic skeleton of a <Style> element in XAML markup looks like the following:

```
<Style>
   <!-- A collection of setters is enumerated here -->
   <Style.Triggers>
   <!-- A collection of Trigger and related objects is enumerated here -->
   </Style.Triggers>
   <Style.Resources>
      <!-- A collection of local resources for use in the style -->
   </Style.Resources>
</Style>
```

Setters

The most common class you will use in the construction of styles is the *Setter*. As their name implies, setters are responsible for setting some aspect of an element. Setters come in two types: property setters (or just setters, as they are called in markup), which set values for properties, and event setters, which set handlers for events.

PROPERTY SETTERS

Property setters, represented by the <*Setter*> tag in XAML, enable you to set properties of elements to specific values. A property setter has two important properties: *Property*, which designates the property to be set by the setter, and *Value*, which indicates the value to which the property is to be set. The following example demonstrates a setter that sets the *Background* property of a *Button* element to red:

```
<Setter Property="Button.Background" Value="Red" />
```

The value for the *Property* property must take the following form:

```
Element.PropertyName
```

If you want to create a style that sets a property on multiple types of elements, you can set the style on a common class that the elements inherit, as shown here:

```
<Style>
    <Setter Property="Control.Background" Value="Red" />
</Style>
```

This style sets the *Background* property of all elements that inherit from the control to which it is applied.

EVENT SETTERS

Event setters (represented by the *<EventSetter>* tag) are similar to property setters, but they set event handlers rather than property values. The two important properties for *EventSetter* are the *Event* property, which specifies the event for which the handler is being set, and the *Handler* property, which specifies the event handler to attach to that event. An example is shown here:

```
<EventSetter Event="Button.MouseEnter" Handler="Button_MouseEnter" />
```

The value of the *Handler* property must specify an extant event handler with the correct signature for the type of event with which it is connected. Similar to property setters, the format for the *Event* property is

```
Element.EventName
```

where the element type is specified, followed by the event name.

Creating a Style

You've seen the simplest possible implementation of a style—a single setter between two *Style* tags—but you haven't yet seen how to apply a style to an element. There are several ways to do this. This section examines the various ways to apply a style to elements in your user interface.

SETTING THE *STYLE* PROPERTY DIRECTLY

The most straightforward way to apply a style to an element is to set the *Style* property directly in XAML. The following example demonstrates directly setting the *Style* property of a *Button* element:

```
<Button Height="25" Name="Button1" Width="100">
    <Button.Style>
        <Style>
            <Setter Property="Button.Content" Value="Style set directly" />
            <Setter Property="Button.Background" Value="Red" />
        </Style>
    </Button.Style>
</Button>
```

Although setting the style directly in an element might be the most straightforward, it is seldom the best method. When setting the style directly, you must set it for each element you want to be affected. In most cases, it is simpler to set the properties of the element directly at design time.

One scenario in which you might want to set the style directly in an element is to provide a set of triggers for that element. Because triggers must be set in a style (except for *EventTrigger*, as you will see in the next section), you could conceivably set the style directly to set triggers for an element.

SETTING A STYLE IN A *RESOURCES* COLLECTION

The most common method for setting styles is to create the style as a member of a *Resources* collection and then apply the style to elements in your user interface by referencing the resource. The following example demonstrates creating a style as part of the *Windows .Resources* collection:

```
<Window.Resources>
    <Style x:Key="StyleOne">
        <Setter Property="Button.Content" Value="Style defined in resources" />
        <Setter Property="Button.Background" Value="Red" />
    </Style>
</Window.Resources>
```

Under most circumstances, you must supply a key value for a style that you define in the *Resources* collection. Then you can apply that style to an element by referencing the resource, as shown in bold here:

```
<Button Name="Button1" Style="{StaticResource StyleOne}" Height="30"
    Width="200" />
```

The advantage of defining a style in the resources section is that you can then apply that style to multiple elements by simply referencing the resource.

APPLYING STYLES TO ALL CONTROLS OF A SPECIFIC TYPE

You can use the *TargetType* property to specify a type of element to be associated with the style. When you set the *TargetType* property on a style, that style is applied to all elements of that type automatically. Furthermore, you do not need to specify the qualifying type name in the *Property* property of any setters you use; you can just refer to the property name. When you specify *TargetType* for a style you have defined in a *Resources* collection, you do not need to provide a key value for that style. The following example demonstrates the use of the *TargetType* property:

```
<Window.Resources>
    <Style TargetType="Button">
        <Setter Property=" Content" Value="Style set for all buttons" />
        <Setter Property="Background" Value="Red" />
    </Style>
</Window.Resources>
```

When you apply the *TargetType* property, you do not need to add any additional markup to the elements of that type to apply the style.

If you want an individual element to opt out of the style, you can set the style on that element explicitly, as seen here:

```
<Button Style="{x:Null}" Margin="10">No Style</Button>
```

This example explicitly sets the style to *Null*, which causes the button to revert to its default look. You also can set the style to another style directly, as seen earlier in this lesson.

SETTING A STYLE PROGRAMMATICALLY

You can create and define a style programmatically. Although defining styles in XAML is usually the best choice, creating a style programmatically might be useful when you want to create and apply a new style dynamically, possibly based on user preferences. The typical method for creating a style programmatically is to create the *Style* object in code; create setters (and triggers if appropriate); add them to the appropriate collection on the *Style* object; and then, when finished, set the *Style* property on the target elements. The following example demonstrates creating and applying a simple style in code:

Sample of Visual Basic Code

```
Dim aStyle As New Style
Dim aSetter As New Setter
aSetter.Property = Button.BackgroundProperty
aSetter.Value = Brushes.Red
aStyle.Setters.Add(aSetter)
Dim bSetter As New Setter
bSetter.Property = Button.ContentProperty
bSetter.Value - "Style set programmatically"
aStyle.Setters.Add(bSetter)
Button1.Style = aStyle
```

Sample of C# Code

```
Style aStyle = new Style();
Setter aSetter = new Setter();
aSetter.Property = Button.BackgroundProperty;
aSetter.Value = Brushes.Red;
aStyle.Setters.Add(aSetter);
Setter bSetter = new Setter();
bSetter.Property = Button.ContentProperty;
bSetter.Value = "Style set programmatically";
aStyle.Setters.Add(bSetter);
Button1.Style = aStyle;
```

You can also define a style in a *Resources* collection and apply that style in code, as shown here:

Sample of XAML Code

```
<!-- XAML -->
<Window.Resources>
   <Style x:Key="StyleOne">
      <Setter Property="Button.Content" Value="Style applied in code" />
      <Setter Property="Button.Background" Value="Red" />
   </Style>
</Window.Resources>
```

```
Dim aStyle As Style
aStyle = CType(Me.Resources("StyleOne"), Style)
Button1.Style = aStyle
```

Sample of C# Code

```
Style aStyle;
aStyle = (Style)this.Resources["StyleOne"];
Button1.Style = aStyle;
```

Implementing Style Inheritance

You can use inheritance to create styles that conform to the basic appearance and behavior of the original style but provide differences that offset some controls from others. For example, you might create one style for all the *Button* elements in your user interface and create an inherited style to provide emphasis for one of the buttons. You can use the *BasedOn* property to create *Style* objects that inherit from other *Style* objects. The *BasedOn* property references another style, automatically inherits all the members of that style, and then enables you to build on that style by adding additional members. The following example demonstrates two *Style* objects: an original style and a style that inherits it:

```
<Window.Resources>
    <Style x:Key="StyleOne">
        <Setter Property="Button.Content" Value="Style set in original Style" />
        <Setter Property="Button.Background" Value="Red" />
        <Setter Property="Button.FontSize" Value="15" />
        <Setter Property="Button.FontFamily" Value="Arial" />
    </Style>
    <Style x:Key="StyleTwo" BasedOn="{StaticResource StyleOne}">
        <Setter Property="Button.Content" Value="Style set by inherited style" />
        <Setter Property="Button.Background" Value="AliceBlue" />
        <Setter Property="Button.FontStyle" Value="Italic" />
    </Style>
</Window.Resources>
```

Figure 1-10 displays the result of applying these two styles.

FIGURE 1-10 Two buttons: the original style and an inherited style.

When a property is set in both the original style and the inherited style, the property value set by the inherited style always takes precedence. But when a property is set by the original style and not set by the inherited style, the original property setting is retained.

 Quick Check

- Under what circumstances is a style automatically applied to an element? How else can a style be applied to an element?

Quick Check Answer

- A style is applied to an element automatically when it is declared as a resource in the page and the *TargetType* property of the style is set. If the *TargetType* property is not set, you can apply a style to an element by setting that element's *Style* property, either in XAML or in code.

Triggers

Along with setters, triggers make up the bulk of objects you use in creating styles. Triggers enable you to implement property changes declaratively in response to other property changes that would have required event-handling code in Windows Forms programming. There are five kinds of *Trigger* objects, as listed in Table 1-10.

TABLE 1-10 Types of *Trigger* Objects

TYPE	CLASS NAME	DESCRIPTION
Property trigger	*Trigger*	Monitors a property and activates when the value of that property matches the *Value* property
Multi-trigger	*MultiTrigger*	Monitors multiple properties and activates only when all the monitored property values match their corresponding *Value* properties
Data trigger	*DataTrigger*	Monitors a bound property and activates when the value of the bound property matches the *Value* property
Multi-data trigger	*MultDataTrigger*	Monitors multiple bound properties and activates only when all the monitored bound properties match their corresponding *Value* properties
Event trigger	*EventTrigger*	Initiates a series of actions when a specified event is raised

A trigger is active only when it is part of a Style.Triggers collection, with one exception. EventTrigger objects can be created within a Control.Triggers collection outside a style. The

Control.Triggers collection can accommodate only EventTrigger, and any other trigger placed in this collection causes an error. EventTrigger is used primarily with animation and is discussed further in Chapter 2, Lesson 3.

Property Triggers

The most commonly used type of trigger is the property trigger, which monitors the value of a property specified by the *Property* property. When the value of the specified property equals the *Value* property, the trigger is activated. Table 1-11 shows the important properties of property triggers.

TABLE 1-11 Important Properties of Property Triggers

PROPERTY	DESCRIPTION
EnterActions	Contains a collection of *Action* objects that are applied when the trigger becomes active. Actions are discussed in greater detail in Lesson 2 of this chapter.
ExitActions	Contains a collection of *Action* objects that are applied when the trigger becomes inactive. Actions are discussed in greater detail in Lesson 2 of this chapter.
Property	Indicates the property that is monitored for changes.
Setters	Contains a collection of *Setter* objects that are applied when the trigger becomes active.
Value	Indicates the value that is compared to the property referenced by the *Property* property.

Triggers listen to the property indicated by the *Property* property and compare that property to the *Value* property. When the referenced property and the *Value* property are equal, the trigger is activated. Any *Setter* objects in the *Setters* collection of the trigger are applied to the style, and any actions in the *EnterActions* collections are initiated. When the referenced property no longer matches the *Value* property, the trigger is inactivated. All *Setter* objects in the *Setters* collection of the trigger are inactivated, and any actions in the *ExitActions* collection are initiated.

> **NOTE ACTIONS IN ANIMATIONS**
>
> Actions are used primarily in animations, and they are discussed in greater detail in Lesson 2 of this chapter.

The following example demonstrates a simple *Trigger* object that changes the *FontWeight* value of a *Button* element to *Bold* when the mouse enters the button:

```
<Style.Triggers>
    <Trigger Property="Button.IsMouseOver" Value="True">
```

```
        <Setter Property="Button.FontWeight" Value="Bold" />
    </Trigger>
</Style.Triggers>
```

In this example, the trigger defines one setter in its *Setters* collection. When the trigger is activated, that setter is applied.

Multi-triggers

Multi-triggers are similar to property triggers in that they monitor the value of properties and activate when those properties meet a specified value. The difference is that multi-triggers are capable of monitoring several properties at a time, and they activate only when all monitored properties equal their corresponding *Value* properties. The properties that are monitored, and their corresponding *Value* properties, are defined by a collection of *Condition* objects. The following example demonstrates a *MultiTrigger* property that sets the *Button.FontWeight* property to *Bold* only when the button is focused and the mouse has entered the control:

```
<Style.Triggers>
    <MultiTrigger>
        <MultiTrigger.Conditions>
            <Condition Property="Button.IsMouseOver" Value="True" />
            <Condition Property="Button.IsFocused" Value="True" />
        </MultiTrigger.Conditions>
        <MultiTrigger.Setters>
            <Setter Property="Button.FontWeight" Value="Bold" />
        </MultiTrigger.Setters>
    </MultiTrigger>
</Style.Triggers>
```

Data Triggers and Multi-data Triggers

Data triggers are similar to property triggers in that they monitor a property and activate when the property meets a specified value, but they differ in that the property they monitor is a bound property. Instead of a *Property* property, data triggers expose a *Binding* property that indicates the bound property to listen to. The following shows a data trigger that changes the *Background* property of a label to red when the bound property *CustomerName* equals "Fabrikam":

```
<Style.Triggers>
    <DataTrigger Binding="{Binding Path=CustomerName}" Value="Fabrikam">
        <Setter Property="Label.Background" Value="Red" />
    </DataTrigger>
</Style.Triggers>
```

Multi-data triggers are to data triggers as multi-triggers are to property triggers. They contain a collection of *Condition* objects, each of which specifies a bound property through its *Binding* property, and a value to compare to that bound property. When all the conditions are satisfied, the multi-data trigger activates. The following example demonstrates a multi-data trigger that sets the *Label.Background* property to red when *CustomerName* equals "Fabrikam" and *OrderSize* equals 500:

```
<Style.Triggers>
   <MultiDataTrigger>
      <MultiDataTrigger.Conditions>
         <Condition Binding="{Binding Path=CustomerName}" Value="Fabrikam" />
         <Condition Binding="{Binding Path=OrderSize}" Value="500" />
      </MultiDataTrigger.Conditions>
      <MultiDataTrigger.Setters>
         <Setter Property="Label.Background" Value="Red" />
      </MultiDataTrigger.Setters>
   </MultiDataTrigger>
</Style.Triggers>
```

Event Triggers

Event triggers are different from the other trigger types. Whereas other trigger types monitor the value of a property and compare it to an indicated value, event triggers specify an event and activate when that event is raised. In addition, event triggers do not have a *Setters* collection; rather, they have an *Actions* collection. Most actions deal with animations, which are discussed in detail in Lesson 3 of Chapter 2. The following two examples demonstrate the *EventTrigger* class. The first example uses *SoundPlayerAction* to play a sound when a button is clicked:

```
<EventTrigger RoutedEvent="Button.Click">
   <SoundPlayerAction Source="C:\myFile.wav" />
</EventTrigger>
```

The second example demonstrates a simple animation that causes the button to grow in height by 200 units when clicked:

```
<EventTrigger RoutedEvent="Button.Click">
   <EventTrigger.Actions>
      <BeginStoryboard>
         <Storyboard>
            <DoubleAnimation Duration="0:0:5"
               Storyboard.TargetProperty="Height" To="200" />
         </Storyboard>
      </BeginStoryboard>
   </EventTrigger.Actions>
</EventTrigger>
```

Understanding Property Value Precedence

By now, you have probably noticed that properties can be set in many ways. They can be set in code, they can be set by styles, they can have default values, and so on. It might seem logical at first to believe that a property will have the value to which it was last set, but this is actually incorrect. A defined and strict order of precedence determines a property's value based on *how* it was set, not when. The precedence order is summarized here, with highest precedence listed first:

1. Set by coercion by the property system.
2. Set by active animations or held animations. (See Chapter 2 for a detailed discussion of animations.)
3. Set locally by code, by direct setting in XAML, or through data binding.
4. Set by *TemplatedParent*. Within this category is a sub-order of precedence, again listed in descending order:
   a. Set by triggers from the templated parent
   b. Set by the templated parent through property sets
5. Implicit style; this applies only to the *Style* property.
6. Set by *Style* triggers.
7. Set by *Template* triggers.
8. Set by *Style* setters.
9. Set by the default Style. There is a sub-order within this category, again listed in descending order:
   a. Set by triggers in the default style
   b. Set by setters in the default style
10. Set by inheritance.
11. Set by metadata.

EXAM TIP

The order of property precedence seems complicated, but actually it is fairly logical. Be sure you understand the concept behind the property order in addition to knowing the order itself.

This may seem like a complicated and arbitrary order of precedence, but upon closer examination it is actually very logical and based upon the needs of the application and the user. The highest precedence is property coercion. This takes place in some elements if an attempt is made to set a property beyond its allowed values. For example, if an attempt is made to set the *Value* property of a *Slider* control to a value higher than the *Maximum* property, *Value* is coerced to equal the *Maximum* property. Next in precedence come animations. For animations to have any meaningful use, they must be able to override preset property values. The next highest level of precedence is properties that have been set explicitly through developer or user action.

Properties set by *TemplatedParent* are next in the order of precedence. These are properties set on objects that come into being through a template, discussed further in Chapter 4. Next in the order is a special precedence item that applies only to the *Style* property of an element. Provided the *Style* property has not been set by any item with a higher-level precedence, it is set to a style whose *TargetType* property matches the type of element in question. Then come properties set by triggers, first those set by *Style,* then those set by *Template.* This is logical because for triggers to have any meaningful effect, they must override properties set by styles.

Properties set by styles come next, first properties set by user-defined styles and then properties set by the default style (also called the theme, which typically is set by the operating system). Finally come properties that are set through inheritance and the application of metadata.

For developers, there are a few important implications that are not intuitively obvious. The most important is that if you set a property explicitly—whether in XAML or in code—the explicitly set property blocks any changes dictated by a style or trigger. WPF assumes that you want that property value to be there for a reason and does not allow it to be set by a style or trigger, although it still can be overridden by an active animation.

A second, less obvious, implication is that when using the Visual Studio designer to drag and drop items onto the design surface from the toolbox, the designer explicitly sets several properties, especially layout properties. These property settings have the same precedence as they would if you had set them yourself. So if you are designing a style-oriented user interface, you should either enter XAML code directly in XAML view to create controls and set as few properties explicitly as possible, or you should review the XAML Visual Studio generates and delete settings as appropriate.

You can clear a property value that has been set in XAML or code manually by calling the *DependencyObject.ClearValue* method. The following code example demonstrates how to clear the value of the *Width* property on a button named *Button1*:

Sample of Visual Basic Code

```
Button1.ClearValue(WidthProperty)
```

Sample of C# Code

```
Button1.ClearValue(WidthProperty);
```

After the value has been cleared, it can be reset automatically by the property system.

PRACTICE Creating High-Contrast Styles

In this practice, you create a rudimentary, high-contrast style for *Button*, *TextBox*, and *Label* elements.

EXERCISE 1   Using Styles to Create High-Contrast Elements

1. Create a new WPF application in Visual Studio.

2. In XAML view, just above the *<Grid>* declaration, create a *Window.Resources* section, as shown here:

```
<Window.Resources>

</Window.Resources>
```

3. In the *Window.Resources* section, create a high-contrast style for *TextBox* controls that sets the background color to *Black* and the foreground to *White*. The *TextBox* controls also should be slightly larger by default. An example is shown here:

```
<Style TargetType="TextBox">
   <Setter Property="Background" Value="Black" />
   <Setter Property="Foreground" Value="White" />
   <Setter Property="BorderBrush" Value="White" />
   <Setter Property="Width" Value="135" />
   <Setter Property="Height" Value="30" />
</Style>
```

4. Create similar styles for *Button* and *Label,* as shown here:

```
<Style TargetType="Label">
   <Setter Property="Background" Value="Black" />
   <Setter Property="Foreground" Value="White" />
   <Setter Property="Width" Value="135" />
   <Setter Property="Height" Value="33" />
</Style>
<Style TargetType="Button">
   <Setter Property="Background" Value="Black" />
   <Setter Property="Foreground" Value="White" />
   <Setter Property="Width" Value="135" />
   <Setter Property="Height" Value="30" />
</Style>
```

5. Type the following in XAML view. Note that you should not add controls from the toolbox because that automatically sets some properties in the designer at a higher property precedence than styles:

```
<Label Margin="26,62,126,0" VerticalAlignment="Top">
   High-Contrast Label</Label>
<TextBox Margin="26,117,126,115">High-Contrast TextBox
   </TextBox>
<Button Margin="26,0,126,62" VerticalAlignment="Bottom">
   High-Contrast Button</Button>
```

6. Press F5 to build and run your application. Note that while the behavior of these controls is unaltered, their appearance has changed.

EXERCISE 2   Using Triggers to Enhance Visibility

1. In XAML view for the solution you completed in Exercise 1, add a Style.Triggers section to the *TextBox* style, as shown here:

```
<Style.Triggers>

</Style.Triggers>
```

2. In the Style.Triggers section, add triggers that detect when the mouse is over the control and enlarge *FontSize* in the control, as shown here:

```
<Trigger Property="IsMouseOver" Value="True">
   <Setter Property="FontSize" Value="20" />
</Trigger>
```

3. Add similar *Style.Triggers* collections to your other two styles.

4. Press F5 to build and run your application. The font size of a control now increases when you move the mouse over it.

Lesson Summary

- Styles enable you to define consistent visual styles for your application. Styles use a collection of setters to apply style changes. The most commonly used setter type is the property setter, which enables you to set a property. Event setters enable you to hook up event handlers as part of an applied style.

- Styles can be set inline, but more frequently, they are defined in a *Resources* collection and are set by referring to the resource. You can apply a style to all instances of a control by setting the *TargetType* property to the appropriate type.

- Styles are most commonly applied declaratively, but they can be applied in code by creating a new style dynamically or by obtaining a reference to a preexisting style resource.

- You can create styles that inherit from other styles by using the *BasedOn* property.

- Property triggers monitor the value of a dependency property and can apply setters from their *Setters* collection when the monitored property equals a predetermined value. Multi-triggers monitor multiple properties and apply their setters when all monitored properties match corresponding specified values. Data triggers and multi-data triggers are analogous but monitor bound values instead of dependency properties.

- Event triggers perform a set of actions when a particular event is raised. They are used most commonly to control animations.

- Property values follow a strict order of precedence, depending on how they are set.

Lesson Review

You can use the following questions to test your knowledge of the information in Lesson 3, "Using Styles and Triggers." The questions are also available on the companion CD if you prefer to review them in electronic form.

> **NOTE ANSWERS**
>
> Answers to these questions and explanations of why each answer choice is correct or incorrect are located in the "Answers" section at the end of the book.

1. Look at the following XAML sample:

```xaml
<Window.Resources>
    <Style x:Key="Style1">
        <Setter Property="Label.Background" Value="Blue" />
        <Setter Property="Button.Foreground" Value="Red" />
        <Setter Property="Button.Background" Value="LimeGreen" />
```

```
            </Style>
    </Window.Resources>
    <Grid>
        <Button Height="23" Margin="81,0,122,58" Name="Button1"
            VerticalAlignment="Bottom">Button</Button>
    </Grid>
```

Assuming that the developer hasn't set any properties any other way, what is the background color of *Button1?*

A. *Blue*

B. *Red*

C. *LimeGreen*

D. *System Default*

2. Look at the following XAML sample:

```
<Window.Resources>
    <Style x:Key="Style1">
        <Style.Triggers>
            <MultiTrigger>
                <MultiTrigger.Conditions>
                    <Condition Property="TextBox.IsMouseOver"
                        Value="True" />
                    <Condition Property="TextBox.IsFocused"
                        Value="True" />
                </MultiTrigger.Conditions>
                <Setter Property="TextBox.Background"
                    Value="Red" />
            </MultiTrigger>
        </Style.Triggers>
    </Style>
</Window.Resources>
<Grid>
    <TextBox Style="{StaticResource Style1}" Height="21"
        Margin="75,0,83,108" Name="TextBox1"
        VerticalAlignment="Bottom" />
</Grid>
```

When will *TextBox1* appear with a red background?

A. When the mouse is over *TextBox1*

B. When *TextBox1* is focused

C. When *TextBox1* is focused and the mouse is over *TextBox1*

D. All of the above

E. Never

3. Look at the following XAML sample:

```
<Window.Resources>
    <Style TargetType="Button">
        <Setter Property="Content" Value="Hello" />
        <Style.Triggers>
```

```
        <Trigger Property="IsMouseOver" Value="True">
            <Setter Property="Content" Value="World" />
        </Trigger>
        <Trigger Property="IsMouseOver" Value="False">
            <Setter Property="Content" Value="How are you?" />
        </Trigger>
      </Style.Triggers>
    </Style>
</Window.Resources>
<Grid>
    <Button Height="23" Margin="81,0,122,58" Name="Button1"
        VerticalAlignment="Bottom">Button</Button>
</Grid>
```

What does *Button1* display when the mouse is NOT over the button?

A. *Hello*

B. *World*

C. *Button*

D. *How are you?*

Case Scenarios

In the following case scenario, you apply what you've learned about how to use controls to design user interfaces. You can find answers to these questions in the "Answers" section at the end of this book.

Case Scenario 1: Streaming Stock Quotes

You're creating an application for a client that he can use to view streaming stock quotes. The geniuses in the Control Development department already have created a control that connects to the stock quote server and displays real-time streaming stock quotes, as well as a *Chart* control that displays live information about stocks in chart form. Your job is to create a simple application that hosts these controls along with a few controls (a text box and a pair of buttons) that the client can use to select the stock or stocks in which he is interested.

The technical requirements are:

- Users always must be able to access the controls that enable them to select the stock quote.
- The *Chart* control requires a fair amount of two-dimensional room and cannot be hosted in a toolbar.
- The *Stock Quote* control behaves like a stock ticker and requires linear space but minimal height.

Answer the following questions for your manager:

1. What kinds of item controls can be used to organize the controls that need to go into this application?
2. What kind of layout controls enable the design of an easy-to-use user interface?

Case Scenario 2: Cup Fever

You've had a little free time around the office, and you've decided to write a simple but snazzy application to organize and display results from World Cup soccer matches. The technical details are all complete: You've located a Web service that feeds up-to-date scores, and you've created a database that automatically applies updates from this service for match results and keeps track of upcoming matches. The database is exposed through a custom data object built on ObservableCollection lists. All that remains are the finishing touches. Specifically, when users choose an upcoming match from a drop-down list at the top of the window, you want the window's color scheme to match the colors of the teams in the selected matchup.

You've also identified the technical requirements. The user interface is divided into two sections, each of which is built on a *Grid* container. Each section represents a team in the current or upcoming match. The user interface for each section must apply the appropriate team colors automatically when the user chooses a new match.

Answer the following question for all your office mates, who are eagerly awaiting the application's completion.

- How can you implement these color changes to the user interface?

Suggested Practices

To help you successfully master the exam objectives presented in this chapter, complete the following tasks.

On Your Own

Complete these suggested practices on your own to reinforce the topics presented in this chapter.

- **Practice 1**   Build a calculator program that uses the *UniformGrid* control for the number button layout and a toolbar for the function key layout. Host both in a single *Grid* control. Then modify your solution to create a version that hosts both in a *DockPanel* control.

- **Practice 2**   Practice creating resources by creating resource dictionaries that contain a variety of *Brush* and *Style* objects. Incorporate these resource dictionaries into existing applications or build new applications around them.

Take a Practice Test

The practice tests on this book's companion CD offer many options. For example, you can test yourself on just one exam objective, or you can test yourself on all the 70-511 certification exam content. You can set up the test so that it closely simulates the experience of taking a certification exam, or you can set it up in study mode so that you can look at the correct answers and explanations after you answer each question.

> **MORE INFO**   **PRACTICE TESTS**
>
> For details about all the practice test options available, see the "How to Use the Practice Tests" section in this book's Introduction.

CHAPTER 2

Working with Events and Commands

Events and commands form the basis of the architecture for intra-application communication in Windows Presentation Foundation (WPF) applications. Routed events can be raised by multiple controls and enable a fine level of control over user input. Commands are a welcome addition to the Microsoft .NET Framework and provide a central architecture for enabling and disabling high-level tasks. Animation takes the concept of events a step further and enables you to design interactivity into your application by taking advantage of the WPF event infrastructure.

Exam objectives in this chapter:

- Manage routed events in WPF.
- Configure WPF commanding.
- Implement an animation in WPF.

Lessons in this chapter:

Before You Begin

To complete the lessons in this chapter, you must have:

- A computer that meets or exceeds the minimum hardware requirements listed in the "About This Book" section at the beginning of the book.
- Microsoft Visual Studio 2010 Professional Edition installed on your computer.
- An understanding of Microsoft Visual Basic or C# syntax and familiarity with the .NET Framework.

REAL WORLD

Matthew Stoecker

By using WPF routed events and commands, I find I have much finer control over how my user interfaces respond compared to how they behave in a Windows Forms application. The routed event architecture enables me to implement complex event handling strategies, and the command architecture provides a way to approach programming common tasks in my user interfaces.

Lesson 1: Configuring Events and Event Handling

Events in WPF programming are considerably different from those in traditional Windows Forms programming. WPF introduces routed events, which can be raised by multiple controls and handled by multiple handlers. *Routed events* enable you to add multiple levels of complexity and sophistication to your user interface and the way it responds to user input. In this lesson, you learn about routed events, including how to handle a routed event, define and register a new routed event, handle an application lifetime event, and use the *EventManager* class.

After this lesson, you will be able to:

- Explain the difference between a direct event, a bubbling event, and a tunneling event.
- Define and register a new routed event.
- Define static class event handlers.
- Handle an event in a WPF application.
- Handle an attached event in a WPF application.
- Handle application lifetime events.
- Use the *EventManager* class.

Estimated lesson time: 30 minutes

Events have been a familiar part of Microsoft Windows programming for years. An *event* is a message sent by an object, such as a control or another part of the user interface, that the program responds to (or handles) by executing code. Although the traditional .NET event architecture is still present in WPF programming, WPF builds upon the event concept by introducing routed events.

A key concept to remember in event routing is the control containment hierarchy. In WPF user interfaces, controls frequently contain other controls. For example, a typical user interface might consist of a top-level *Window* object, which contains a *Grid* object, which itself might contain several controls, one of which could be a *ToolBar* control, which in turn contains several *Button* controls. The routed event architecture allows for an event that originates in one control to be raised by another control in the containment hierarchy. Thus, if the user clicks one of the *Button* controls on the toolbar, that event can be raised by the button, the toolbar, the grid, or the window.

Why is it useful to route events? Suppose, for example, that you are designing a user interface for a calculator program. As part of this application, you might have several *Button* controls enclosed within a *Grid* control. Suppose you wanted all button clicks in this grid to be handled by a single event handler. WPF raises the click event from *Button, Grid,* and any other control in the control containment hierarchy. As the developer, you can decide where and how the event is handled. Thus, you can provide a single event handler for all *Button Click* events originating from *Button* controls in the grid, thereby simplifying code-writing tasks and ensuring consistency in event handling.

Types of Routed Events

There are three types of routed events: direct, bubbling, and tunneling.

Direct Events

Direct events are most similar to standard .NET events. Like a standard .NET event, a direct event is raised only by the control in which it originates. Because other controls in the control containment hierarchy do not raise these events, there is no opportunity for any other control to provide handlers for these events. An example of a direct event is the *MouseLeave* event.

Bubbling Events

Bubbling events are raised first in the control where they originate and then by each control in that control's control containment hierarchy, also known as a visual tree. The *MouseDown* event is an example of a bubbling event. Suppose you have a *Label* control contained inside a *FlowPanel* control contained inside a window. When the mouse button is pressed over the label, the first control to raise the *MouseDown* event would be *Label*. Then *FlowPanel* would raise the *MouseDown* event and then, finally, the window itself. You could provide an event handler at any or all stages of the event process.

Tunneling Events

Tunneling events are the opposite of bubbling events. A *tunneling event* is raised first by the topmost container in the visual tree and then down through each successive container until it is finally raised by the element in which it originates. An example of a tunneling event is the *PreviewMouseDown* event. In the previous example, although the event originates with the *Label* control, the first control to raise the *PreviewMouseDown* event is *Window*, then *FlowPanel*, and then, finally, *Label*. Tunneling events enable you to intercept and handle events in the window or container before the event is raised by the specific control so you can filter input, such as keystrokes, at varying levels.

In the .NET Framework, all tunneling events begin with the word *Preview*, such as *PreviewKeyDown*, *PreviewMouseDown*, and so on, and are typically defined in pairs with a complementary bubbling event. For example, the tunneling event *PreviewKeyDown* is paired with the *KeyDown* bubbling event. The tunneling event always is raised before its corresponding bubbling event, thus allowing higher-level controls in the visual tree to handle the event. Each tunneling event shares its instance of event arguments with its paired bubbling event. This fact is important to remember when handling events, and it will be discussed in greater detail later in this chapter.

RoutedEventArgs

All routed events include an instance of *RoutedEventArgs* (or a class that inherits *RoutedEventArgs*) in their signatures. The *RoutedEventArgs* class contains a wealth of information about the event and its source control. Table 2-1 describes the properties of the *RoutedEventArgs* class.

TABLE 2-1 *RoutedEventArgs* Properties

PROPERTY	DESCRIPTION
Handled	Indicates whether this event has been handled. By setting this property to *True*, you can halt further event bubbling or tunneling.
OriginalSource	Gets the object that originally raised the event. For most WPF controls, this will be the same as the object returned by the *Source* property. However, for some controls, such as composite controls, this property will return a different object.
RoutedEvent	Returns the *RoutedEvent* object for the event that was raised. When handling more than one event with the same event handler, you might need to refer to this property to identify which event has been raised.
Source	Returns the object that raised the event.

All *EventArgs* for routed events inherit the *RoutedEventArgs* class, but many of them provide additional information. For example, *KeyboardEventArgs* is used in keyboard events and provides information about keystrokes. Likewise, *MouseEventArgs,* used in mouse events, provides information about the state of the mouse when the event took place.

 Quick Check

- What are the three kinds of routed events in WPF and how do they differ?

Quick Check Answer

- Routed events in WPF come in three types: direct, tunneling, and bubbling. A direct event can be raised only by the element in which it originated. A bubbling event is raised first by the element in which it originated and then by each successive container in the visual tree. A tunneling event is raised first by the topmost container in the visual tree and then down through each successive container until it is finally raised by the element in which it originated. Tunneling and bubbling events enable elements of the user interface to respond to events raised by their contained elements.

Attaching an Event Handler

The preferred way to attach an event handler is directly in the Extensible Application Markup Language (XAML) code. You set the event to the name of a method with the appropriate signature for that event. The following example demonstrates setting the event handler for a *Button* control's *Click* event, as shown in bold:

```
<Button Height="23" Margin="132,80,70,0" Name="button1"
   VerticalAlignment="Top" Click="button1_Click">Button</Button>
```

Just like setting a property, you must supply a string value that indicates the name of the method.

Attached Events

It is possible for a control to define a handler for an event that the control cannot itself raise. These incidents are called *attached events*. For example, consider *Button* controls in a grid. The *Button* class defines a *Click* event, but the *Grid* class does not. However, you can still define a handler for buttons in the grid by attaching the *Click* event of the *Button* control in the XAML code. The following example demonstrates attaching an event handler for a button contained in a grid:

```
<Grid Button.Click="button_Click">
   <Button Height="23" Margin="132,80,70,0" Name="button1"
   VerticalAlignment="Top" >Button</Button>
</Grid>
```

Now every time a button contained in the grid shown here is clicked, the *button_Click* event handler will handle that event.

Handling a Tunneling or Bubbling Event

At times, you might want to halt the further handling of tunneling or bubbling events. For example, you might want to suppress keystroke handling at a particular level in the control hierarchy. You can handle an event and halt any further tunneling or bubbling by setting the *Handled* property of the *RoutedEventArgs* instance to *True*, as shown here:

Sample of Visual Basic Code

```
Private Sub TextBox1_KeyDown(ByVal sender As System.Object, _
   ByVal e As System.Windows.Input.KeyEventArgs)
   e.Handled = True
End Sub
```

Sample of C# Code

```
private void textBox1_KeyDown(object sender, KeyEventArgs e)
{
   e.Handled = true;
}
```

Note that tunneling events and their paired bubbling events (such as *PreviewKeyDown* and *KeyDown*) share the same instance of *RoutedEventArgs*. Thus, if you set the *Handled* property to *True* on a tunneling event, its corresponding bubbling event also is considered handled and is suppressed.

The *EventManager* Class

EventManager is a static class that manages the registration of all WPF routed events. Table 2-2 describes the methods of the *EventManager* class.

TABLE 2-2 *EventManager* Methods

METHOD	DESCRIPTION
GetRoutedEvents	Returns an array that contains all the routed events that have been registered in this application
GetRoutedEventsForOwner	Returns an array of all the routed events that have been registered for a specified element in this application
RegisterClassHandler	Registers a class-level event handler, as discussed in the "Creating a Class-Level Event Handler" section later in this chapter
RegisterRoutedEvent	Registers an instance-level event handler, as discussed in the next section

Defining a New Routed Event

You can use the *EventManager* class to define a new routed event for your WPF controls. The following procedure describes how to define a new routed event.

To define a new routed event:

1. Create a static, read-only definition for the event, as shown in this example:

   Sample of Visual Basic Code

   ```
   Public Shared ReadOnly SuperClickEvent As RoutedEvent
   ```

   Sample of C# Code

   ```
   public static readonly RoutedEvent SuperClickEvent;
   ```

2. Create a wrapper for the routed event that exposes it as a traditional .NET Framework event, as shown in this example:

   Sample of Visual Basic Code

   ```
   Public Custom Event SuperClick As RoutedEventHandler
     AddHandler(ByVal value As RoutedEventHandler)
       Me.AddHandler(SuperClickEvent, value)
     End AddHandler
   ```

```
RemoveHandler(ByVal value As RoutedEventHandler)
  Me.RemoveHandler(SuperClickEvent, value)
End RemoveHandler

RaiseEvent(ByVal sender As Object, _
  ByVal e As System.Windows.RoutedEventArgs)
  Me.RaiseEvent(e)
End RaiseEvent
End Event
```

Sample of C# Code

```
public event RoutedEventHandler SuperClick
{
  add
  {
    this.AddHandler(SuperClickEvent, value);
  }
  remove
  {
    this.RemoveHandler(SuperClickEvent, value);
  }
}
```

Use a different *EventArgs* class from *RoutedEventArgs*. You must derive a new class from *RoutedEventArgs* and create a new delegate that uses those event arguments.

3. Use *EventManager* to register the new event in the constructor of the class that owns this event. You must provide the name of the event, the routing strategy (direct, tunneling, or bubbling), the type of delegate that handles the event, and the type of the class that owns it. An example is shown here:

Sample of Visual Basic Code

```
EventManager.RegisterRoutedEvent("SuperClick", _
  RoutingStrategy.Bubble, GetType(RoutedEventArgs), GetType(Window1))
```

Sample of C# Code

```
EventManager.RegisterRoutedEvent("SuperClick",
  RoutingStrategy.Bubble, typeof(RoutedEventHandler), typeof(Window1));
```

Raising an Event

After an event is defined, you can raise it in code by creating a new instance of *RoutedEventArgs* and using the *RaiseEvent* method, as shown here:

Sample of Visual Basic Code

```
Dim myEventArgs As New RoutedEventArgs(myControl.myNewEvent)
MyBase.RaiseEvent(myEventArgs)
```

Sample of C# Code

```
RoutedEventArgs myEventArgs = new RoutedEventArgs(myControl.myNewEvent);
RaiseEvent(myEventArgs);
```

Creating a Class-Level Event Handler

You can use the *EventManager* class to register a class-level event handler. A class-level event handler handles a particular event for all instances of a class and is always invoked before instance handlers. Thus, you can screen and suppress events before they reach instance handlers. The following procedure describes how to implement a class-level event handler.

To create a class-level event handler:

1. Create a static method to handle the event. This method must have the same signature as the event. An example is shown here:

   Sample of Visual Basic Code

   ```
   Private Shared Sub SuperClickHandlerMethod(ByVal sender As Object, _
     ByVal e As RoutedEventArgs)
     ' Handle the event here
   End Sub
   ```

   Sample of C# Code

   ```
   private static void SuperClickHandlerMethod(object sender, RoutedEventArgs e)
   {
     // Handle the event here
   }
   ```

2. In the static constructor for the class for which you are creating the class-level event handler, create a delegate to this method, as shown here:

   Sample of Visual Basic Code

   ```
   Dim SuperClickHandler As New RoutedEventHandler( _
     AddressOf SuperClickHandlerMethod)
   ```

   Sample of C# Code

   ```
   RoutedEventHandler SuperClickHandler = new
     RoutedEventHandler(SuperClickHandlerMethod);
   ```

3. Also in the static constructor, call *EventManager.RegisterClassHandler* to register the class-level event handler, as shown here:

   Sample of Visual Basic Code

   ```
   EventManager.RegisterClassHandler(GetType(Window1), _
     SuperClickEvent, SuperClickHandler)
   ```

   Sample of C# Code

   ```
   EventManager.RegisterClassHandler(typeof(Window1),
     SuperClickEvent,SuperClickHandler);
   ```

Application-Level Events

Every WPF application is wrapped by an *Application* object, which provides a set of events that relate to the application's lifetime. You can handle these events to execute code in response to application startup or closure. The *Application* object also provides a set of events related to navigation in page-based applications. These events were discussed in Chapter 1, "Building a User Interface." Table 2-3 describes the available application-level events, excluding the navigation events.

TABLE 2-3 Selected Application-Level Events

EVENT	DESCRIPTION
Activated	Occurs when you switch from another application to your program. It also is raised the first time you show a window.
Deactivated	Occurs when you switch to another program
DispatcherUnhandledException	Raised when an unhandled exception occurs in your application. You can handle an unhandled exception in the event handler for this event by setting the *DispatcherUnhandledExceptionEventArgs.Handled* property to *True*.
Exit	Occurs when the application is shut down for any reason
SessionEnding	Occurs when the Windows session is ending, such as when the user shuts down the computer or logs off
Startup	Occurs as the application is started.

Application events are standard .NET events (rather than routed events), and you can create handlers for these events in the standard .NET way. The following procedure explains how to create an event handler for an application-level event.

To create an application-level event handler:

1. In Visual Studio, in Solution Explorer, right-click Application.xaml (in Visual Basic) or App.xaml (in C#) and choose View Code to open the code file for the *Application* object.

2. Create a method to handle the event, as shown here:

Sample of Visual Basic Code

```
Private Sub App_Startup(ByVal sender As Object, _
  ByVal e As StartupEventArgs)
  ' Handle event here
End Sub
```

Sample of C# Code

```
void App_Startup(object sender, StartupEventArgs e)
{
  // Handle the event here
}
```

3. In XAML view for the *Application* object, add the event handler to the Application declaration, as shown in bold here:

```
<Application x:Class="Application"
  xmlns="http://schemas.microsoft.com/winfx/2006/xaml/presentation"
  xmlns:x="http://schemas.microsoft.com/winfx/2006/xaml"
  StartupUri="Window1.xaml" Startup="App_Startup">
```

PRACTICE **Working with Routed Events**

In this practice, you use routed events. You create event handlers for the *TextBox.TextChanged* event in three controls in the visual tree and observe how the event is raised and handled by each one.

EXERCISE Creating an Event Handler

1. In Visual Studio, create a new WPF application.

2. From the toolbox, drag a *TextBox* and three *RadioButton* controls onto the design surface. Note that at this point, these controls are contained by a *Grid* control that is in itself contained in the top-level *Window* control. Thus, any bubbling events raised by the *TextBox* control will bubble up first to the *Grid* control and then to the *Window* control.

3. In XAML view, set the display contents of the *RadioButton* controls as follows:

RADIOBUTTON	CONTENT
RadioButton1	Handle Textbox.TextChanged in TextBox
RadioButton2	Handle Textbox.TextChanged in Grid
RadioButton3	Handle Textbox.TextChanged in Window

4. In the XAML for the *TextBox* control, just before the />, type **TextChanged** and then press the Tab key twice. An entry for an event handler is created and a corresponding method is created in the code. The event-handler entry should look like the following:

```
TextChanged="TextBox1_TextChanged"
```

5. In the XAML for the *Grid* control, type **TextBoxBase.TextChanged** and then press the Tab key twice to generate an event handler. The added XAML should look like this:

```
TextBoxBase.TextChanged="Grid_TextChanged"
```

6. In the XAML for the *Window* control, type **TextBoxBase.TextChanged** and then press the Tab key twice to generate an event handler. The added XAML should look like this:

```
TextBoxBase.TextChanged="Window_TextChanged"
```

7. In Code view, add the following code to the *Textbox1_TextChanged* method:

Sample of Visual Basic Code

```
MessageBox.Show("Event raised by Textbox")
e.Handled = RadioButton1.IsChecked
```

Sample of C# Code

```
MessageBox.Show("Event raised by Textbox");
e.Handled = (bool)radioButton1.IsChecked;
```

8. Add the following code to the *Grid_TextChanged* method:

Sample of Visual Basic Code

```
MessageBox.Show("Event raised by Grid")
e.Handled = RadioButton2.IsChecked
```

Sample of C# Code

```
MessageBox.Show("Event raised by Grid");
e.Handled = (bool)radioButton2.IsChecked;
```

9. Add the following code to the *Window_TextChanged* method:

Sample of Visual Basic Code

```
MessageBox.Show("Event raised by Window")
e.Handled = RadioButton3.IsChecked
```

Sample of C# Code

```
MessageBox.Show("Event raised by Window");
e.Handled = (bool)radioButton3.IsChecked;
```

10. Press F5 to build and run your application. Without first selecting any of the options, type a letter in the text box. Three message boxes are displayed, each one indicating the control that raised the event. You can handle the event by choosing one of the button options to halt event bubbling in the event handlers.

Lesson Summary

- WPF applications introduce a new kind of event called routed events, which are raised by WPF controls.

- There are three kinds of routed events: direct, bubbling, and tunneling. Direct events are raised only by the control in which they originate. Bubbling and tunneling events are raised by the control in which they originate and all controls that are higher in the visual tree.

- A tunneling event is raised first by the top-level control in the visual tree and tunnels down through the tree until it is finally raised by the control in which it originates. A bubbling event is raised first by the control in which the event originates and then bubbles up through the visual tree until it is finally raised by the top-level control in the visual tree.

- You can attach events that exist in contained controls to controls that are higher in the visual tree.

- The *EventManager* class exposes methods so you can manage events in your application. You can register a new routed event by using the *EventManager.RegisterRoutedEvent* class. You can create a class-level event handler by using *EventManager.RegisterClassHandler*.

- The *Application* object raises several events that can be handled to execute code at various points in the application's lifetime. You can handle application-level events in the code for the *Application* object.

Lesson Review

You can use the following questions to test your knowledge of the information in Lesson 1, "Configuring Events and Event Handling." The questions are also available on the companion CD of this book if you prefer to review them in electronic form.

> **NOTE ANSWERS**
>
> Answers to these questions and explanations of why each answer choice is correct or incorrect are located in the "Answers" section at the end of the book.

1. Suppose you have the following XAML code:

```
<Window x:Class="WpfApplication1.Window1"
  xmlns="http://schemas.microsoft.com/winfx/2006/xaml/presentation"
  xmlns:x="http://schemas.microsoft.com/winfx/2006/xaml"
  Title="Window1" Height="300" Width="300"
  ButtonBase.Click="Window_Click">
  <Grid ButtonBase.Click="Grid_Click">
    <StackPanel Margin="47,54,31,108" Name="stackPanel1"
     ButtonBase.Click="stackPanel1_Click">
    <Button Height="23" Name="button1" Width="75">Button</Button>
   </StackPanel>
  </Grid>
</Window>
```

Which method is executed first when *button1* is clicked?

A. *Button1_Click*

B. *StackPanel1_Click*

C. *Grid_Click*

D. *Window_Click*

2. Suppose you have the following XAML code:

```
<Window x:Class="WpfApplication1.Window1"
  xmlns="http://schemas.microsoft.com/winfx/2006/xaml/presentation"
  xmlns:x="http://schemas.microsoft.com/winfx/2006/xaml"
  Title="Window1" Height="300" Width="300" MouseDown="Window_MouseDown">
```

```
<Grid PreviewMouseDown="Grid_PreviewMouseDown">
    <StackPanel Margin="47,54,31,108" Name="stackPanel1"
      PreviewMouseDown="stackPanel1_PreviewMouseDown">
    <Button Click="button1_Click" Height="23" Name="button1"
        Width="75">Button</Button>
  </StackPanel>
  </Grid>
</Window>
```

Which method will be executed first when *button1* is clicked?

A. *Window_MouseDown*

B. *Grid_PreviewMouseDown*

C. *stackPanel1_PreviewMouseDown*

D. *button1_Click*

3. You are writing an application that consists of a single WPF window. You have code you want to execute when the window first appears and every time the window is activated. Which application event or events should you handle to accomplish this goal?

A. *Activated*

B. *Startup*

C. *Activated* and *Startup*

D. *Deactivated* and *Startup*

Lesson 2: Configuring Commands

WPF introduces new objects called *commands*. Commands represent high-level tasks that are performed in the application. *Paste* is an example of a command; it represents the task of copying an object from the clipboard into a container. WPF provides a cohesive architecture for creating commands, associating them with application tasks, and hooking those commands up to user interface (UI) elements. In this lesson, you will learn to use the built-in command library, associate these commands with UI elements, define command handlers, add a gesture to a command, and define custom commands.

After this lesson, you will be able to:

- Explain the different parts of a command.
- Associate a command with a UI element.
- Add a gesture to a command.
- Execute a command.
- Associate a command with a command handler.
- Disable a command.
- Create a custom command.

Estimated lesson time: 30 minutes

Commands, such as *Cut*, *Copy*, and *Paste*, represent tasks. In past versions of the .NET Framework, there was no complete architecture for associating code with tasks. For example, suppose you wanted to implement a *Paste* task in your application. You would create the code to execute the task and then associate your UI element with that code via events. You might have a *MenuItem* element that triggers the code when selected. You also might have context menu items and perhaps even a *Button* control. In past versions of the .NET Framework, you would have had to create event handlers for each control with which you wanted to associate the task. In addition, you would have had to implement code to inactivate each of these controls if the task was unavailable. Although not an impossible task, doing this requires tedious coding that can be fraught with errors.

Commands enable you to use a centralized architecture for tasks. You can associate any number of UI controls or input gestures with a command and bind that command to a handler that is executed when controls are activated or gestures are performed. Commands also keep track of whether they are available. If a command is disabled, UI elements associated with that command are disabled, too.

Command architecture consists of four principal parts. The *Command* object represents the task. There are also command sources. A *command source* is a control or gesture that triggers the command when invoked. The *command handler* is a method executed when the command is invoked, and *CommandBinding* is an object the .NET Framework uses to track which commands are associated with which sources and handlers.

The .NET Framework provides several predefined commands developers can use. These built-in commands are static objects that are properties of five static classes, which are the following:

- *ApplicationCommands*
- *ComponentCommands*
- *EditingCommands*
- *MediaCommands*
- *NavigationCommands*

Each of these classes exposes a variety of static command objects that you can use in your applications. Although some of these commands have default input bindings (for example, the *ApplicationCommands.Open* command has a default binding to the Ctrl+O key combination), none of these commands has any inherent functionality; you must create bindings and handlers for these commands to use them in your application.

A High-Level Procedure for Implementing a Command

The following section describes a high-level procedure for implementing command functionality. The steps of this procedure are discussed in greater detail in the subsequent sections.

To implement a command:

1. Decide on the command to use, whether it is one of the static commands exposed by the .NET Framework or a custom command.
2. Associate the command with any controls in the user interface and add any desired input gestures to the command.
3. Create a method to handle the command.
4. Create a *CommandBinding* control that binds the *Command* object to the command handler and, optionally, to a method that handles *Command.CanExecute*.
5. Add the command binding to the *Commands* collection of the control or *Window* control where the command is invoked.

Invoking Commands

After a command has been implemented, you can invoke it by associating it with a control, using a gesture, or invoking it directly from code.

Associating Commands with Controls

Many WPF controls implement the *ICommandSource* interface, which enables them to be associated with a command that is fired automatically when that control is invoked. For example, *Button* and *MenuItem* controls implement *ICommandSource* and thus expose a *Command* property. When this property is set to a command, that command is executed automatically when the control is clicked. You can set a command for a control in XAML, as shown here:

```
<Button Command="ApplicationCommands.Find" Height="23"
HorizontalAlignment="Right" Margin="0,0,38,80" Name="Button3"
VerticalAlignment="Bottom" Width="75">Button</Button>
```

Invoking Commands with Gestures

You also can register mouse and keyboard gestures with *Command* objects that invoke the command when those gestures occur. The following example code shows how to add a mouse gesture and a keyboard gesture to the *InputGestures* collection of the *Application.Find* command:

Sample of Visual Basic Code

```
ApplicationCommands.Find.InputGestures.Add(New _
  MouseGesture(MouseAction.LeftClick, ModifierKeys.Control))
ApplicationCommands.Find.InputGestures.Add(New _
  KeyGesture(Key.Q, ModifierKeys.Control))
```

Sample of C# Code

```
ApplicationCommands.Find.InputGestures.Add(new
  MouseGesture(MouseAction.LeftClick, ModifierKeys.Control));
ApplicationCommands.Find.InputGestures.Add(new
  KeyGesture(Key.Q, ModifierKeys.Control));
```

After the code in the previous example is executed, the *Find* command executes either when the Ctrl key is held down and the left mouse button is clicked or when the Ctrl key and the Q key are held down at the same time (Ctrl+Q).

Invoking Commands from Code

You might want to invoke a command directly from code, such as in response to an event in a control that does not expose a *Command* property. To invoke a command directly, simply call the *Command.Execute* method, as shown here:

Sample of Visual Basic Code

```
ApplicationCommands.Find.Execute(aParameter, TargetControl)
```

Sample of C# Code

```
ApplicationCommands.Find.Execute(aParameter, TargetControl);
```

In this example, *aParameter* represents an object that contains any required parameter data for the command. If no parameter is needed, you can use *null* (*Nothing* in Visual Basic). *TargetControl* is a control where the command originates. The run time will start looking for *CommandBindings* in this control and then bubble up through the visual tree until it finds an appropriate *CommandBinding*.

Command Handlers and Command Bindings

As stated previously, just invoking a command doesn't actually do anything. Commands represent tasks, but they do not contain any of the code for the tasks they represent. To execute code when a command is invoked, you must create a *CommandBinding* that binds the command to a command handler.

Command Handlers

Any method with the correct signature can be a command handler. Command handlers have the following signature:

Sample of Visual Basic Code

```
Private Sub myCommandHandler(ByVal sender As Object, _
  ByVal e As ExecutedRoutedEventArgs)
  ' Handle the command here
End Sub
```

Sample of C# Code

```
private void myCommandHandler(object sender, ExecutedRoutedEventArgs e)
{
  // Handle the command here
}
```

ExecutedRoutedEventArgs is derived from *RoutedEventArgs* and thus exposes all the members *RoutedEventArgs* does. In addition, it exposes a *Command* property that returns the *Command* object being handled.

Command Bindings

The *CommandBinding* object provides the glue that holds the whole command architecture together. A *CommandBinding* object associates a command with a command handler. Adding a *CommandBinding* object to the *CommandBindings* collection of the window or a control registers the *CommandBinding* object and enables the command handler to be called when the command is invoked. The following code demonstrates how to create and register a *CommandBinding* object:

Sample of Visual Basic Code

```
Dim abinding As New CommandBinding()
abinding.Command = ApplicationCommands.Find
AddHandler abinding.Executed, AddressOf myCommandHandler
Me.CommandBindings.Add(abinding)
```

Sample of C# Code

```
CommandBinding abinding = new CommandBinding();
abinding.Command = ApplicationCommands.Find;
abinding.Executed += new ExecutedRoutedEventHandler(myCommandHandler);
this.CommandBindings.Add(abinding);
```

In the preceding example, you first create a new *CommandBinding* object. You then associate that *CommandBinding* object with a *Command* object. Next, you specify the command handler to be executed when the command is invoked, and finally, you add the *CommandBinding* object to the *CommandBindings* collection of the window. Thus, if an object in the window invokes the command, the corresponding command handler will be executed.

You also can define command bindings directly in the XAML. You can create a new binding and declaratively set the command with which it is associated along with the associated handlers. The following example demonstrates a new *CommandBinding* object in the *CommandBindings* collection of the window that associates the *Application.Find* command with a handler:

```
<Window.CommandBindings>
  <CommandBinding Command="ApplicationCommands.Find"
   Executed="myCommandHandler" />
</Window.CommandBindings>
```

Command Bubbling

All controls have their own *CommandBindings* collection in addition to the window's *CommandBindings* collection. This is because commands, like routed events, bubble up through the visual tree when they are invoked. Commands look for a binding first in the *CommandBindings* collection of the control in which they originate and then in the *CommandBindings* collections of controls higher on the visual tree. Like *RoutedEvent*, you can stop further processing of the command by setting the *Handled* property of the *ExecutedRoutedEventArgs* parameter to *True*, as shown here:

Sample of Visual Basic Code

```
Private Sub myCommandHandler(ByVal sender As Object, _
  ByVal e As ExecutedRoutedEventArgs)
  ' Stops further Command bubbling
  e.Handled = True
End Sub
```

Sample of C# Code

```
private void myCommandHandler(object sender, ExecutedRoutedEventArgs e)
{
  // Handle the command here
  e.Handled = true;
}
```

EXAM TIP

Bubbling and tunneling are new concepts to WPF and play important roles both in commands and how WPF handles routed events. Be certain that you understand the concepts of bubbling and tunneling events and bubbling commands for the exam. Remember that a command or event doesn't need to be handled by the same element in which it originates.

Disabling Commands

Any command that is not associated with a command binding is automatically disabled. No action is taken when that command is invoked, and any control whose *Command* property is set to that command appears as disabled. However, there might be times when you want to disable a command that is in place and associated with controls and command bindings. For example, you might want the *Print* command to be disabled until the focus is on a document. The command architecture enables you to designate a method to handle the *Command. CanExecute* event. The *CanExecute* event is raised at various points in the course of application execution to determine whether a command is in a state that will allow execution.

Methods that handle the *CanExecute* event include an instance of *CanExecuteRoutedEventArgs* as a parameter. This class exposes a property called *CanExecute* that is a Boolean value. If *CanExecute* is true, the command can be invoked. If it is false, the command is disabled. You can create a method that handles the *CanExecute* event, determines whether the application is in an appropriate state to allow command execution, and sets *e.CanExecute* to the appropriate value.

To handle the *CanExecute* event:

1. Create a method to handle the *CanExecute* event. This method should query the application to determine whether the application's state is appropriate to enable the command. An example is shown here:

   Sample of Visual Basic Code

   ```
   Private canExecute As Boolean
   Private Sub abinding_CanExecute(ByVal sender As Object, _
     ByVal e As CanExecuteRoutedEventArgs)
     e.CanExecute = canExecute
   End Sub
   ```

   Sample of C# Code

   ```
   bool canExecute;
   void abinding_CanExecute(object sender, CanExecuteRoutedEventArgs e)
   {
     e.CanExecute = canExecute;
   }
   ```

   In this example, the method returns the value represented by a private variable called *canExecute*. Presumably, the application sets this to *False* whenever it requires the command to be disabled.

2. Set the *CanExecute* handler on *CommandBinding* to point to this method, as shown here:

   Sample of Visual Basic Code

   ```
   ' Assumes that you have already created a CommandBinding called abinding
   AddHandler abinding.CanExecute, AddressOf abinding_CanExecute
   ```

   Sample of C# Code

   ```
   // Assumes that you have already created a CommandBinding called abinding
   abinding.CanExecute += new CanExecuteRoutedEventHandler(abinding_CanExecute);
   ```

Alternatively, create a new binding in XAML and specify the handler there, as shown here in bold:

```xml
<Window.CommandBindings>
  <CommandBinding Command="ApplicationCommands.Find"
    Executed="CommandBinding_Executed"
    CanExecute="abinding_CanExecute" />
</Window.CommandBindings>
```

Creating Custom Commands

Although a wide variety of preexisting commands is at your disposal, you might want to create your own custom commands. The best practice for custom commands is to follow the example set in the .NET Framework and create static classes (in C#) or modules (in Visual Basic) that expose static instances of the custom command. This prevents the creations of multiple instances of the command. You also can provide any custom configuration for the command in the static constructor of the class—for example, if you want to map any input gestures to the command. The following example shows how to create a static class that exposes a custom command called *Launch*:

Sample of Visual Basic Code

```vb
Public Module MyCommands
  Private launch_command As RoutedUICommand
  Sub New()
    Dim myInputGestures As New InputGestureCollection
    myInputGestures.Add(New KeyGesture(Key.L, ModifierKeys.Control))
    launch_command = New RoutedUICommand("Launch", "Launch", _
    GetType(MyCommands), myInputGestures)
  End Sub
  Public ReadOnly Property Launch() As RoutedUICommand
    Get
      Return launch_command
    End Get
  End Property
End Module
```

Sample of C# Code

```csharp
public class MyCommands
{
  private static RoutedUICommand launch_command;
  static MyCommands()
  {
    InputGestureCollection myInputGestures = new
      InputGestureCollection();
    myInputGestures.Add(new KeyGesture(Key.L, ModifierKeys.Control));
    launch_command = new RoutedUICommand("Launch", "Launch",
      typeof(MyCommands), myInputGestures);
  }
  public RoutedUICommand Launch
  {
    get
    {
```

```
        return launch_command;
    }
  }
}
```

In this example, a static class or module is created to contain the custom command, which is exposed through a read-only property. In the static constructor, a new
InputGestureCollection collection is created and a key gesture is added to the collection.
This collection is then used to initialize the instance of *RoutedUICommand* that is returned
through the read-only property.

Using Custom Commands in XAML

After you have created a custom command, you are ready to use it in code. If you want to use
it in XAML, however, you also must map the namespace that contains the custom command
to an XAML namespace. The following procedure describes how to use a custom command
in XAML.

To use a custom command in XAML:

1. Create your custom command as described previously.

2. Add a namespace mapping to your *Window* XAML. The following example demonstrates how to map a namespace called *WpfApplication13.CustomCommands*. Note
   that, in this example, that would mean your custom commands are kept in a separate
   namespace:

   ```
   <Window x:Class="Window1"
     xmlns="http://schemas.microsoft.com/winfx/2006/xaml/presentation"
     xmlns:x="http://schemas.microsoft.com/winfx/2006/xaml"
     xmlns:CustomCommands="clr-namespace:WpfApplication13.CustomCommands"
     Title="Window1" Height="300" Width="300">


     <!-The rest of the XAML is omitted-->
   </Window>
   ```

3. Use the newly mapped XAML namespace in your XAML code, as shown here:

   ```
   <Button Command="CustomCommands:MyCommands.Launch" Height="23"
   HorizontalAlignment="Left" Margin="60,91,0,0" Name="Button1"
   VerticalAlignment="Top" Width="75">Button</Button>
   ```

> **PRACTICE** **Creating a Custom Command**

In this practice, you create a custom command and then connect your command to UI elements by using a command binding.

EXERCISE 1 Creating a Custom Command

1. From the CD, open the partial solution for this exercise.

2. From the Project menu, choose Add Class (in C#) or Add Module (in Visual Basic). Name the new item **CustomCommands** and click OK. Set the access modifier of this class or module to public.

3. If you are working in C#, add the following *using* statement to your class:

```
using System.Windows.Input;
```

   Otherwise, go on to Step 4.

4. Add a read-only property named **Launch** and a corresponding member variable that returns an instance of a *RoutedUICommand*, as shown here. (Note that these should be static members in C#.)

   Sample of Visual Basic Code

```
Private launch_command As RoutedUICommand
Public ReadOnly Property Launch() As RoutedUICommand
  Get
    Return launch_command
  End Get
End Property
```

   Sample of C# Code

```
private static RoutedUICommand launch_command;
public static RoutedUICommand Launch
{
  get
  {
    return launch_command;
  }
}
```

5. Add a constructor to your module (in Visual Basic) or a static constructor to your class (in C#) that creates a new *InputGestureCollection* collection, adds an appropriate input gesture to be associated with this new command, and then initializes the member variable that returns the custom command, as shown here:

   Sample of Visual Basic Code

```
Sub New()
  Dim myInputGestures As New InputGestureCollection
  myInputGestures.Add(New KeyGesture(Key.L, ModifierKeys.Control))
  launch_command = New RoutedUICommand("Launch", "Launch", _
    GetType(CustomCommands), myInputGestures)
End Sub
```

   Sample of C# Code

```
static CustomCommands()
{
  InputGestureCollection myInputGestures = new
    InputGestureCollection();
  myInputGestures.Add(new KeyGesture(Key.L, ModifierKeys.Control));
  launch_command = new RoutedUICommand("Launch", "Launch",
    typeof(CustomCommands), myInputGestures);
}
```

6. From the Build menu, choose Build Solution to build your solution.

EXERCISE 2 Using Your Custom Command

1. In XAML view, add the following code to your Window markup to create a reference to the class that contains your custom command:

```
xmlns:Local="clr-namespace:YourProjectNamespaceGoesHere"
```

The previous code in bold should be replaced with the namespace name of your project.

2. In XAML view, add the following attribute to both your *Button* control and your *Launch* MenuItem:

```
Command="Local:CustomCommands.Launch"
```

3. In the *Window1* code view, add the following method:

Sample of Visual Basic Code

```
Private Sub Launch_Handler(ByVal sender As Object, _
  ByVal e As ExecutedRoutedEventArgs)
  MessageBox.Show("Launch invoked")
End Sub
```

Sample of C# Code

```
private void Launch_Handler(object sender, ExecutedRoutedEventArgs e)
{
  MessageBox.Show("Launch invoked");
}
```

4. From the toolbox, drag a *CheckBox* control onto the form. Set the content of the control to **Enable Launch Command**.

5. In the code view for *Window1*, add the following method:

Sample of Visual Basic Code

```
Private Sub LaunchEnabled_Handler(ByVal sender As Object, _
  ByVal e As CanExecuteRoutedEventArgs)
  e.CanExecute = CheckBox1.IsChecked
End Sub
```

Sample of C# Code

```
private void LaunchEnabled_Handler(object sender,
  CanExecuteRoutedEventArgs e)
{
  e.CanExecute = (bool)checkBox1.IsChecked;
}
```

6. Create or replace the constructor for *Window1* that creates and registers a command binding for the *Launch* command. This command binding should bind the *Launch.Executed* event to the *Launch_Handler* method and bind the *Launch.CanExecute* event to the *LaunchEnabled_Handler* method. An example is shown here:

Sample of Visual Basic Code

```vb
Public Sub New()
  InitializeComponent()
  Dim abinding As New CommandBinding()
  abinding.Command = CustomCommands.Launch
  AddHandler abinding.Executed, AddressOf Launch_Handler
  AddHandler abinding.CanExecute, AddressOf LaunchEnabled_Handler
  Me.CommandBindings.Add(abinding)
End Sub
```

Sample of C# Code

```csharp
public Window1()
{
  InitializeComponent();
  CommandBinding abinding = new CommandBinding();
  abinding.Command = CustomCommands.Launch;
  abinding.Executed += new ExecutedRoutedEventHandler(Launch_Handler);
  abinding.CanExecute += new
    CanExecuteRoutedEventHandler(LaunchEnabled_Handler);
  this.CommandBindings.Add(abinding);
}
```

7. Press F5 to build and run your application. When the application starts, the Button and Launch menu items are disabled. Select the check box to enable the command. Now you can invoke the command from the button, from the menu, or by using the Ctrl+L input gesture.

Lesson Summary

- Commands provide a central architecture for managing high-level tasks. The .NET Framework provides a library of built-in commands that map to common tasks that can be used in your applications.

- Commands can be invoked directly, by an input gesture such as *MouseGesture* or *KeyGesture*, or by activating a custom control. A single command can be associated with any number of gestures or controls.

- Command bindings associate commands with command handlers. You can specify a method to handle the *Executed* event of a command and another method to handle the *CanExecute* event of a command.

- Methods handling the *CanExecute* event of a command should set the *CanExecute* property of *CanExecuteRoutedEventArgs* to *False* when the command should be disabled.

- Commands can be bound by any number of command bindings. Commands exhibit bubbling behavior. When invoked, commands first look for a binding in the collection of the element in which the command was invoked and then look in each higher element in the visual tree.

- You can create custom commands. When you have created a custom command, you must map the namespace in which it exists to an XAML namespace in your XAML view.

Lesson Review

You can use the following questions to test your knowledge of the information in Lesson 2, "Configuring Commands." The questions are also available on the companion CD if you prefer to review them in electronic form.

> **NOTE ANSWERS**
>
> Answers to these questions and explanations of why each answer choice is correct or incorrect are located in the "Answers" section at the end of the book.

1. Which of the following is required to bind a command to a command handler? (Choose all that apply.)

   A. Instantiate a new instance of *CommandBinding*.

   B. Set the *CommandBinding.Command* property to a command.

   C. Add one or more input gestures to your command.

   D. Add a handler for the *CommandBinding.Executed* event.

   E. Add a handler for the *CommandBinding.CanExecute* event.

   F. Add *CommandBinding* to the *CommandBindings* collection of the *Window* or other control associated with the command.

2. You are working with an application that exposes a command named *Launch*. This command is registered in the *CommandBindings* collection of a control called *Window11* and requires a −*String* parameter. Which of the following code samples invokes the command from code correctly?

   A.

   Sample of Visual Basic Code

   ```
   Launch.CanExecute = True
   Launch.Execute("Boom", Window11)
   ```

   Sample of C# Code

   ```
   Launch.CanExecute = true;
   Launch.Execute("Boom", Window11);
   ```

   B.

   Sample of Visual Basic Code

   ```
   Launch.Execute("Boom")
   ```

   Sample of C# Code

   ```
   Launch.Execute("Boom");
   ```

C.

Sample of Visual Basic Code

```
Launch.Execute("Boom", Window11)
```

Sample of C# Code

```
Launch.Execute("Boom", Window11);
```

D.

Sample of Visual Basic Code

```
Window11.CanExecute(Launch, True)
Launch.Execute("Boom", Window11)
```

Sample of C# Code

```
Window11.CanExecute(Launch, true);
Launch.Execute("Boom", Window11);
```

Lesson 3: Implementing Animation

Animations are another feature of WPF. They enable you to change the value of a property over the course of a set period of time. Using this technique, you can create a variety of visual effects, including causing controls to grow or move about the user interface, to change color gradually, or to change other properties over time. In this lesson, you learn how to create animations that animate a variety of property types and use *Storyboard* objects to control the playback of those animations.

After this lesson, you will be able to:

- Create and use animations.
- Control animations with the *Storyboard* class.
- Control timelines and playback of animations.
- Implement simultaneous animations.
- Use *Action* controls to control animation playback.
- Implement animations that use key frames.
- Create and start animations in code.

Estimated lesson time: 30 minutes

Using Animations

The term *animation* brings to mind hand-drawn anthropomorphic animals performing amusing antics in video media, but in WPF, animation has a far simpler meaning. Generally speaking, an animation in WPF refers to an automated property change over a set period of time. You can animate an element's size, location, color, or virtually any other property associated with an element. You can use the *Animation* classes to implement these changes.

The *Animation* classes are a large group of classes designed to implement these automated property changes. There are 42 *Animation* classes in the *System.Windows.Media.Animation* namespace, and each one has a specific data type it is designed to animate. *Animation* classes fall into three basic groups: Linear animations, key frame–based animations, and path-based animations.

Linear animations, which automate a property change in a linear way, are named in the *<TypeName>Animation* format, in which *<TypeName>* is the name of the type being animated. *DoubleAnimation* is an example of a linear animation class, and is the animation class you are likely to use the most.

Key frame–based animations perform their animation on the basis of several waypoints called key frames. The flow of a key-frame animation starts at the beginning and progresses to each of the key frames before ending. The progression is usually linear.

Key-frame animations are named in the *<TypeName>AnimationUsingKeyFrames* format, in which *<TypeName>* is the name of the type being animated. An example is *StringAnimationUsingKeyFrames*.

Path-based animations use a *Path* object to guide the animation. They are used most often to animate properties that relate to the movement of visual objects along a complex course. Path-based animations are named in the *<TypeName>AnimationUsingPath* format, in which *<TypeName>* is the name of the type being animated. There are currently only three path-based *Animation* classes: *PointAnimationUsingPath*, *DoubleAnimationUsingPath*, and *MatrixAnimationUsingPath*.

Important Properties of Animations

Although there are many *Animation* classes, they all work in the same fundamental way: They change the value of a designated property over a period of time. As such, they share common properties. Many of these properties are also shared with the *Storyboard* class, which organizes *Animation* objects, as you will see later in this lesson. Table 2-4 shows important common properties of the *Animation* and *Storyboard* classes.

TABLE 2-4 Important Properties of the *Animation* and *Storyboard* Classes

PROPERTY	DESCRIPTION
AccelerationRatio	Gets or sets a value specifying the percentage of the *Duration* property of the animation that is spent accelerating the passage of time from zero to its maximum rate
AutoReverse	Gets or sets a value that indicates whether the animation plays in reverse after it completes a forward iteration
BeginTime	Gets or sets the time at which the animation should begin, relative to the time it is executed. For example, an animation with *BeginTime* set to 0:0:5 exhibits a 5-second delay before beginning.
DecelerationRatio	Gets or sets a value specifying the percentage of the duration of the animation spent decelerating the passage of time from its maximum rate to zero
Duration	Gets or sets the length of time for which the animation plays
FillBehavior	Gets or sets a value that indicates how the animation behaves after it has completed
RepeatBehavior	Gets or sets a value that indicates how the animation repeats
SpeedRatio	Gets or sets the rate at which the animation progresses relative to its parent

In addition, the linear animation classes typically implement a few more important properties, which Table 2-5 describes.

TABLE 2-5 Important Properties of Linear Animation Classes

PROPERTY	DESCRIPTION
From	Gets or sets the starting value of the animation. If omitted, the animation uses the current property value.
To	Gets or sets the ending value of the animation
By	Gets or sets the amount by which to increase the value of the target property over the course of the animation. If both the *To* and *By* properties are set, the value of the *By* property is ignored.

The following example demonstrates a very simple animation that changes the value of a property that has a Double data type representation from 1 to 200 over the course of 10 seconds:

```
<DoubleAnimation Duration="0:0:10" From="1" To="200" />
```

In this example, the *Duration* property specifies a duration of 10 seconds for the animation, and the *From* and *To* properties indicate a starting value of 1 and an ending value of 200.

You might notice that something seems to be missing from this example. What property is this animation animating? The answer is that it is not animating any property; the *Animation* object carries no intrinsic information about the property being animated, but rather is applied to a property by means of *Storyboard*.

Storyboard Objects

Storyboard is the object that controls and organizes animations in your user interface. The *Storyboard* class contains a *Children* collection, which organizes a collection of *Timeline* objects, which include *Animation* objects. When created declaratively in XAML, all *Animation* objects must be enclosed within a *Storyboard* object, as shown here:

```
<Storyboard>
    <DoubleAnimation Duration="0:0:10" From="1" To="200" />
</Storyboard>
```

USING A STORYBOARD TO CONTROL ANIMATIONS

In XAML, *Storyboard* objects organize your *Animation* objects. The most important feature of the *Storyboard* object is that it contains properties for specifying the target element and target property of the child *Animation* objects, as shown in bold in this example:

```
<Storyboard TargetName="Button1" TargetProperty="Height">
    <DoubleAnimation Duration="0:0:10" From="1" To="200" />
</Storyboard>
```

This example is now usable. It defines a timeline during which, over the course of 10 seconds, the *Height* property of *Button1* goes from a value of *1* to a value of *200*.

The *TargetName* and *TargetProperty* properties are attached properties, so instead of defining them in the storyboard itself, you can define them in the child *Animation* objects, as shown in bold here:

```
<Storyboard>
    <DoubleAnimation Duration="0:0:10" From="1" To="200"
        Storyboard.TargetName="Button1"
        Storyboard.TargetProperty="Height" />
</Storyboard>
```

Because a storyboard can hold more than one animation at a time, this configuration enables you to set separate target elements and properties for each animation. Thus, it is more common to use the attached properties.

SIMULTANEOUS ANIMATIONS

The storyboard can contain multiple child *Animation* objects. When the storyboard is activated, all child animations are started at the same time and run simultaneously. The following example demonstrates two simultaneous animations that cause both the height and width of a *Button* element to grow over 10 seconds:

```
<Storyboard>
    <DoubleAnimation Duration="0:0:10" From="1" To="200"
        Storyboard.TargetName="Button1"
        Storyboard.TargetProperty="Height" />
    <DoubleAnimation Duration="0:0:10" From="1" To="100"
        Storyboard.TargetName="Button1"
        Storyboard.TargetProperty="Widtht" />
</Storyboard>
```

Using Animations with Triggers

You now have learned most of the story about using *Animation* objects. The *Animation* object defines a property change over time, and the *Storyboard* object contains *Animation* objects and determines which element and property the *Animation* objects affect. But one piece is still missing: How do you start and stop an animation?

All declaratively created *Animation* objects must be housed within a *Trigger* object. This can be either as part of a style or in the *Triggers* collection of an element, which accepts only *EventTrigger* objects.

Trigger objects define collections of *Action* objects, which control when an animation is started and stopped. The following example demonstrates an *EventTrigger* object with an inline animation:

```
<EventTrigger RoutedEvent="Button.Click">
    <EventTrigger.Actions>
        <BeginStoryboard>
            <Storyboard>
                <DoubleAnimation Duration="0:0:5"
                    Storyboard.TargetProperty="Height" To="200" />
            </Storyboard>
```

```
        </BeginStoryboard>
    </EventTrigger.Actions>
</EventTrigger>
```

As you can see in the preceding example, the *Storyboard* object is enclosed in a *BeginStoryboard* tag, which itself is enclosed in the *EventTrigger.Actions* tag. *BeginStoryboard* is an action; it indicates that the contained storyboard should be started. The *EventTrigger* class defines a collection of actions that should be initiated when the trigger is activated, and in this example, *BeginStoryboard* is the action that is initiated. Thus, when the button indicated in this trigger is clicked, the described animation runs.

USING ACTIONS TO CONTROL PLAYBACK

There are several *Action* classes you can use to manage animation playback. Table 2-6 summarizes these classes.

TABLE 2-6 Animation-Related *Action* Classes

ACTION	DESCRIPTION
BeginStoryboard	Begins the child *Storyboard* object
PauseStoryboard	Pauses the playback of an indicated storyboard at the current playback position
ResumeStoryboard	Resumes playback of an indicated storyboard
SeekStoryboard	Fast-forwards to a specified position in a target storyboard
SetStoryboardSpeedRatio	Sets the speed ratio of the specified storyboard
SkipStoryboardToFill	Moves the specified storyboard to the end of its timeline
StopStoryboard	Stops playback of the specified storyboard and returns the animation to the starting position

PauseStoryboard, *ResumeStoryboard*, *SkipStoryboardToFill*, and *StopStoryboard* are all fairly self-explanatory. They cause the indicated storyboard to pause, resume, stop, or skip to the end, as indicated by the action name. The one property that all these *Action* classes have in common is the *BeginStoryboardName* property. This property indicates the name of the *BeginStoryboard* object the action is to affect. The following example demonstrates a *StopStoryboard* action that stops the *BeginStoryBoard* object named *stb1:*

```
<Style.Triggers>
    <EventTrigger RoutedEvent="Button.MouseEnter">
        <EventTrigger.Actions>
            <BeginStoryboard Name="stb1">
                <Storyboard>
                    <DoubleAnimation Duration="0:0:5"
                        Storyboard.TargetProperty="Height" To="200" />
                </Storyboard>
            </BeginStoryboard>
        </EventTrigger.Actions>
```

```
        </EventTrigger>
        <EventTrigger RoutedEvent="Button.MouseLeave">
            <EventTrigger.Actions>
                <StopStoryboard BeginStoryboardName="stb1" />
            </EventTrigger.Actions>
        </EventTrigger>
    </Style.Triggers>
```

All actions that affect a particular *Storyboard* object must be defined in the same *Triggers* collection. The previous example shows both of these triggers being defined in the *Button. Triggers* collection. If you were to define these triggers in separate *Triggers* collections, storyboard actions would not function.

The *SetStoryboardSpeedRatio* action sets the speed ratio for the entire storyboard and all *Animation* objects in that storyboard. In addition to *BeginStoryboardName*, you must set the *SpeedRatio* property of this action as well. The following example demonstrates a *SetStoryboardSpeedRatio* action that speeds the referenced storyboard by a factor of 2:

```
<Style.Triggers>
    <EventTrigger RoutedEvent="Button.MouseEnter">
        <EventTrigger.Actions>
            <BeginStoryboard Name="stb1">
                <Storyboard>
                    <DoubleAnimation Duration="0:0:5"
                        Storyboard.TargetProperty="Height" To="200" />
                </Storyboard>
            </BeginStoryboard>
        </EventTrigger.Actions>
    </EventTrigger>
    <EventTrigger RoutedEvent="Button.MouseLeave">
        <EventTrigger.Actions>
            <SetStoryboardSpeedRatio BeginStoryboardName="stb1" SpeedRatio="2" />
        </EventTrigger.Actions>
    </EventTrigger>
</Style.Triggers>
```

The *SeekStoryboard* action requires that two additional properties be set. The *Origin* property can be a value of either *BeginTime* or *Duration* and specifies how the *Offset* property is applied. An *Origin* value of *BeginTime* specifies that the *Offset* is relative to the beginning of the storyboard. An *Origin* value of *Duration* specifies that the offset is relative to the *Duration* property of the storyboard. The *Offset* property determines the amount of the offset to jump to in the animation. The following example shows a *SeekStoryboard* action that skips the referenced timeline to 5 seconds ahead from its current point in the timeline.

```
<Style.Triggers>
    <EventTrigger RoutedEvent="Button.MouseEnter">
        <EventTrigger.Actions>
            <BeginStoryboard Name="stb1">
                <Storyboard>
                    <DoubleAnimation Duration="0:0:10"
                        Storyboard.TargetProperty="Height" To="200" />
                </Storyboard>
            </BeginStoryboard>
```

```
            </EventTrigger.Actions>
        </EventTrigger>
        <EventTrigger RoutedEvent="Button.MouseLeave">
            <EventTrigger.Actions>
                <SeekStoryboard BeginStoryboardName="stb1" Origin="BeginTime"
                    Offset="0:0:5" />
            </EventTrigger.Actions>
        </EventTrigger>
</Style.Triggers>
```

USING PROPERTY TRIGGERS WITH ANIMATIONS

In the examples shown in this section, you have seen actions being hosted primarily in *EventTrigger* objects. You can also host *Action* objects in other kinds of triggers. *Trigger*, *MultiTrigger*, *DataTrigger*, and *MultiDataTrigger* objects host two *Action* collections: *EnterActions* and *ExitActions* collections.

The *EnterActions* collection hosts a set of actions that are executed when the trigger is activated. Conversely, the *ExitActions* collection hosts a set of actions that are executed when the trigger is deactivated. The following demonstrates a trigger that begins a storyboard when activated and stops that storyboard when deactivated:

```
<Trigger Property="IsMouseOver" Value="True">
    <Trigger.EnterActions>
        <BeginStoryboard Name="stb1">
            <Storyboard>
                <DoubleAnimation Storyboard.TargetProperty="FontSize"
                    To="20" Duration="0:0:.5" />
            </Storyboard>
        </BeginStoryboard>
    </Trigger.EnterActions>
    <Trigger.ExitActions>
        <StopStoryboard BeginStoryboardName="stb1" />
    </Trigger.ExitActions>
</Trigger>
```

Managing the Playback Time Line

Both the *Animation* class and the *Storyboard* class contain several properties by which to manage the playback timeline with a fine level of control. Each of these properties is discussed in this section. When a property is set on an animation, the setting affects only that animation. Setting a property on a storyboard, however, affects all the *Animation* objects it contains.

ACCELERATIONRATIO AND DECELERATIONRATIO

The *AccelerationRatio* and *DecelerationRatio* properties enable you to designate part of the timeline for acceleration and deceleration of the animation speed rather than starting and playing at a constant speed. This is sometimes used to give an animation a more natural appearance. These properties are expressed in fractions of 1 and represent a percentage value of the total timeline. Thus, an acceleration ratio value of .2 indicates that 20 percent of the time line should be spent accelerating to the top speed. Therefore, the *AccelerationRatio* and *DecelerationRatio* properties should be equal to or less than 1 when added together. This example shows an animation with an acceleration ratio of .2:

```
<DoubleAnimation Duration="0:0:5" AccelerationRatio="0.2"
    Storyboard.TargetProperty="Height" To="200" />
```

AUTOREVERSE

As the name implies, the *AutoReverse* property determines whether the animation automatically plays out in reverse after the end is reached. A value of *True* indicates that the animation will play in reverse after it reaches the end of forward play. *False* is the default value. The following example demonstrates this property:

```
<DoubleAnimation Duration="0:0:5" AutoReverse="True"
    Storyboard.TargetProperty="Height" To="200" />
```

FILLBEHAVIOR

The *FillBehavior* property determines how the animation behaves after it has completed. A value of *HoldEnd* indicates that the animation holds the final value after it has completed, whereas a value of *Stop* indicates that the animation stops and returns to the beginning of the timeline when completed. An example follows here:

```
<DoubleAnimation Duration="0:0:5" FillBehavior="Stop"
    Storyboard.TargetProperty="Height" To="200" />
```

The default value for *FillBehavior* is *HoldEnd*.

REPEATBEHAVIOR

The *RepeatBehavior* property determines whether and how an animation repeats. The *RepeatBehavior* property can be set in three ways. First, it can be set to *Forever*, which indicates that an animation repeats for the duration of the application. Second, it can be set to a number followed by the letter *x* (for example, *2x*), which indicates the number of times to repeat the animation. Third, it can be set to a *Duration*, which indicates the amount of time an animation plays, irrespective of the number of iterations. The following three examples demonstrate these settings. The first demonstrates an animation that repeats forever, the second an animation that repeats three times, and the third an animation that repeats for 1 minute:

```
<DoubleAnimation Duration="0:0:5" RepeatBehavior="Forever"
    Storyboard.TargetProperty="Height" To="200" />
<DoubleAnimation Duration="0:0:5" RepeatBehavior="3x"
    Storyboard.TargetProperty="Height" To="200" />
<DoubleAnimation Duration="0:0:5" RepeatBehavior="0:1:0"
    Storyboard.TargetProperty="Height" To="200" />
```

The *SpeedRatio* property enables you to speed up or slow down the base timeline. The *SpeedRatio* value represents the coefficient for the speed of the animation. Thus, an animation with a *SpeedRatio* value of *0.5* takes twice the standard time to complete, whereas a value of *2* causes the animation to complete twice as fast. An example is shown here:

```
<DoubleAnimation Duration="0:0:5" SpeedRatio="0.5"
   Storyboard.TargetProperty="Height" To="200" />
```

Animating Non-Double Types

Most of the examples you have seen in this lesson have dealt with the *DoubleAnimation* class, but in fact, a class exists for every data type that can be animated. For example, the *ColorAnimation* class enables you to animate a color change, as shown here:

```
<Button Height="23" Width="100" Name="Button1">
   <Button.Background>
      <SolidColorBrush x:Name="myBrush" />
   </Button.Background>
   <Button.Triggers>
      <EventTrigger RoutedEvent="Button.Click">
         <BeginStoryboard>
            <Storyboard>
               <ColorAnimation Storyboard.TargetName="myBrush"
                  Storyboard.TargetProperty="Color" From="Red" To="LimeGreen"
                  Duration="0:0:5" />
            </Storyboard>
         </BeginStoryboard>
      </EventTrigger>
   </Button.Triggers>
</Button>
```

In this example, when the button is clicked, the background color of the button gradually changes from red to lime green over the course of 5 seconds.

> **NOTE   ANIMATIONS AND THE DEFAULT TEMPLATE**
>
> In the standard Windows theme, this animation can conflict with other animations in the button's default template, so you might need to move the mouse out of the button and defocus it to see the full effect.

ANIMATION WITH KEY FRAMES

Until now, all the animations you have seen have used linear interpolation; that is, the animated property changes take place over a linear time line at a linear rate. You can create nonlinear animations also, by using key frames.

Key frames are waypoints in an animation. Instead of allowing the animation to progress linearly from beginning to end, key frames divide the animation into short segments. The animation progresses from the beginning to the first key frame, then to the next, and through the *KeyFrames* collection until the end of the animation is reached. Each key frame defines its own *Value* and *KeyTime* properties, which indicate the value the animation will represent when it reaches the key frame and the time in the animation at which that key frame will be reached.

Every data type that supports a linear animation type also supports a key-frame animation type, and some types that do not have linear animation types have key-frame animation types. The key-frame animation types are named *<TargetType>AnimationUsingKeyFrames*, in which *<TargetType>* represents the name of the type animated by the animation. Key-frame animation types do not support the *From*, *To*, and *By* properties; rather, the course of the animation is defined by the collection of key frames.

There are three kinds of key frames. The first is linear key frames, which are named *Linear<TargetType>KeyFrame*. These key frames provide points in an animation that are interpolated between in a linear fashion. The following example demonstrates the use of linear key frames:

```
<DoubleAnimationUsingKeyFrames Storyboard.TargetProperty="Height">
    <LinearDoubleKeyFrame Value="10" KeyTime="0:0:1" />
    <LinearDoubleKeyFrame Value="100" KeyTime="0:0:2" />
    <LinearDoubleKeyFrame Value="30" KeyTime="0:0:4"/>
</DoubleAnimationUsingKeyFrames>
```

In the preceding example, the *Height* property goes from its starting value to a value of 10 in the first second, then to a value of 100 in the next second, and finally returns to a value of 30 in the last two seconds. The progression between each segment is interpolated linearly. In this example, it is similar to having several successive linear *Animation* objects.

DISCRETE KEY FRAMES

Some animatable data types do not support gradual transitions under any circumstances. For example, the String type can accept only discrete changes. You can use discrete key frame objects to make discrete changes in the value of an animated property. Discrete key frame classes are named *Discrete<TargetType>KeyFrame*, in which *<TargetType>* is the type being animated. Like linear key frames, discrete key frames use a *Value* and a *KeyTime* property to set the parameters of the key frame. The following example demonstrates an animation of a string by using discrete key frames:

```
<StringAnimationUsingKeyFrames Storyboard.TargetProperty="Content">
    <DiscreteStringKeyFrame Value="Soup" KeyTime="0:0:0" />
    <DiscreteStringKeyFrame Value="Sous" KeyTime="0:0:1" />
    <DiscreteStringKeyFrame Value="Sots" KeyTime="0:0:2" />
    <DiscreteStringKeyFrame Value="Nots" KeyTime="0:0:3" />
    <DiscreteStringKeyFrame Value="Nuts" KeyTime="0:0:4" />
</StringAnimationUsingKeyFrames>
```

SPLINE KEY FRAMES

Spline key frames enable you to define a Bézier curve that expresses the relationship between animation speed and animation time so you can create animations that accelerate and decelerate in complex ways. Although the mathematics of Bézier curves is beyond the scope of this lesson, a Bézier curve is simply a curve between two points, the shape of which is influenced by two control points. Using spline key frames, the start and end points of the curve are always (0,0) and (1,1), respectively, so you must define the two control points. The *KeySpline* property accepts two points to define the Bézier curve, as seen here:

```
<SplineDoubleKeyFrame Value="300" KeyTime="0:0:6" KeySpline="0.1,0.8 0.6,0.6" />
```

Spline key frames are difficult to create with the intended effect without complex design tools and are most commonly used when specialized animation design tools are available.

USING MULTIPLE TYPES OF KEY FRAMES IN AN ANIMATION

You can use multiple types of key frames in a single animation; you can freely mix *LinearKeyFrame*, *DiscreteKeyFrame*, and *SplineKeyFrame* objects in the *KeyFrames* collection. The only restriction is that all key frames you use must be appropriate to the type being animated. String animations, for example, can use only *DiscreteStringKeyFrame* objects.

 Quick Check

- What are the types of key frame objects? When would you use each one?

Quick Check Answer

- There are *LinearKeyFrame*, *DiscreteKeyFrame*, and *SplineKeyFrame* objects. *LinearKeyFrame* objects indicate a linear transition from the preceding property value to the value represented in the key frame. *DiscreteKeyFrame* objects represent a sudden transition from the preceding property value to the value represented in the key frame. *SplineKeyFrame* objects represent a transition whose rate is defined by the sum of an associated Bézier curve. You would use each of these types when the kind of transition represented was the kind you wanted to incorporate into your user interface. In addition, some animation types can use only *DiscreteKeyFrame* objects.

CREATING AND STARTING ANIMATIONS IN CODE

All the *Animation* objects you have seen so far in this lesson were created declaratively in XAML. However, you can also create and execute *Animation* objects just as easily in code.

The process of creating an animation should seem familiar to you; as with other .NET objects, you create a new instance of your animation and set the relevant properties, as seen in this example:

Sample of Visual Basic Code

```
Dim aAnimation As New System.Windows.Media.Animation.DoubleAnimation()
aAnimation.From = 20
```

```
aAnimation.To = 300
aAnimation.Duration = New Duration(New TimeSpan(0, 0, 5))
aAnimation.FillBehavior = Animation.FillBehavior.Stop
```

Sample of C# Code

```
System.Windows.Media.Animation.DoubleAnimation aAnimation = new
    System.Windows.Media.Animation.DoubleAnimation();
aAnimation.From = 20;
aAnimation.To = 300;
aAnimation.Duration = new Duration(new TimeSpan(0, 0, 5));
aAnimation.FillBehavior = Animation.FillBehavior.Stop;
```

After the animation has been created, however, the obvious question is: How do you start it? When creating *Animation* objects declaratively, you must use a storyboard to organize your animation and an action to start it. In code, however, you can use a simple method call. All WPF controls expose a method called *BeginAnimation* by which you can specify a dependency property on that control and an *Animation* object to act on that dependency property. The following code shows an example:

Sample of Visual Basic Code

```
Button1.BeginAnimation(Button.HeightProperty, aAnimation)
```

Sample of C# Code

```
button1.BeginAnimation(Button.HeightProperty, aAnimation);
```

PRACTICE Improving Readability with Animations

In this practice, you improve upon your solution to the practice in Lesson 1 of this chapter. You remove the triggers that cause the font size to expand and instead use an animation to make it look more natural. In addition, you create *Animation* objects to increase the size of the control when the mouse is over it.

EXERCISE Animating High-Contrast Styles

1. Open the completed solution from the practice in Lesson 3 of Chapter 1.

2. In each of the styles, remove the font size setter that is defined in the trigger and replace it with *Trigger.EnterActions* and *Trigger.ExitActions* sections, as shown here:

   ```
   <Trigger.EnterActions>

   </Trigger.EnterActions>
   <Trigger.ExitActions>

   </Trigger.ExitActions>
   ```

3. In each *Trigger.EnterActions* section, add a *BeginStoryboard* action, as shown here:

   ```
   <BeginStoryboard Name="Storyboard1">

   </BeginStoryboard>
   ```

4. Add the following *Storyboard* and *Animation* objects to the *BeginStoryboard* object in the style for the text box. Note that the values for the *ThicknessAnimation* object are crafted specifically for the completed version of the Lesson 1 practice on the CD. If you created your own solution, you must recalculate these values:

```
<Storyboard Duration="0:0:1">
    <DoubleAnimation Storyboard.TargetProperty="FontSize"
        To="20" />
    <ThicknessAnimation Storyboard.TargetProperty="Margin"
        To="26,118,45,104" />
    <DoubleAnimation Storyboard.TargetProperty="Width" To="210"/>
    <DoubleAnimation Storyboard.TargetProperty="Height" To="40"/>
</Storyboard>
```

5. Add a similar storyboard to the style for the label, as shown here:

```
<Storyboard Duration="0:0:1">
    <DoubleAnimation Storyboard.TargetProperty="FontSize" To="20" />
    <ThicknessAnimation Storyboard.TargetProperty="Margin"
        To="26,62,46,-10" />
    <DoubleAnimation Storyboard.TargetProperty="Width" To="210"/>
    <DoubleAnimation Storyboard.TargetProperty="Height" To="40"/>
</Storyboard>
```

6. Add a similar storyboard to the style for the button, as shown here:

```
<Storyboard Duration="0:0:1">
    <DoubleAnimation Storyboard.TargetProperty="FontSize" To="20" />
    <ThicknessAnimation Storyboard.TargetProperty="Margin"
        To="26,0,46,52" />
    <DoubleAnimation Storyboard.TargetProperty="Width" To="210"/>
    <DoubleAnimation Storyboard.TargetProperty="Height" To="40"/>
</Storyboard>
```

7. Add the following line to the *Trigger.ExitActions* section of each style:

```
<StopStoryboard BeginStoryboardName="Storyboard1" />
```

8. Press F5 to build and run your application. Now the font size expansion is animated and the control expands as well.

Lesson Summary

- *Animation* objects drive automated property changes over time. There are three types of *Animation* objects: linear animations, key frame-based animations, and path-based animations. Every animatable type has at least one animation type associated with it, and some types have more than one type of animation that can be applied.

- *Storyboard* objects organize one or more *Animation* objects. *Storyboard* objects determine which objects and properties their contained *Animation* objects are applied to.

- Both *Animation* and *Storyboard* objects contain a variety of properties that control animation playback behavior.

- *Storyboard* objects created declaratively are activated by a *BeginStoryboard* action in the *Actions* collection of a trigger. Triggers also can define actions that pause, stop, and resume *Storyboard* objects, as well as performing other storyboard-related functions.

- Key frame animations define a series of waypoints through which the animation passes. There are three kinds of key frames: linear key frames, discrete key frames, and spline key frames. Some animatable types, such as String, support only discrete key frames.

- You can create and apply *Animation* objects in code. When doing this, you do not need to define a *Storyboard* object; rather, you call the *BeginAnimation* method on the element with which you want to associate the animation.

Lesson Review

You can use the following questions to test your knowledge of the information in Lesson 3, "Implementing Animation." The questions are also available on the companion CD if you prefer to review them in electronic form.

> **NOTE ANSWERS**
>
> Answers to these questions and explanations of why each answer choice is correct or incorrect are located in the "Answers" section at the end of the book.

1. How many times does the animation shown here repeat (not counting the first iteration)?

   ```
   <DoubleAnimation Duration="0:0:15" RepeatBehavior="0:1:0"
       Storyboard.TargetProperty="Height" To="200" />
   ```

   A. 0

   B. 1

   C. 2

   D. 3

2. Look at this animation:

   ```
   <DoubleAnimation Duration="0:0:5" From="30" By="80" To="200" Storyboard.
   TargetProperty="Height" />
   ```

   Assuming that the element whose *Height* property it animates begins with a height of 50, what is the value of the element after the animation has completed?

   A. 50

   B. 110

   C. 130

   D. 200

Case Scenarios

In the following case scenarios, you will apply what you've learned about how to use commands, events, and settings to design user interfaces. You can find answers to these questions in the "Answers" section at the end of this book.

Case Scenario 1: Validating User Input

You're creating a form that Humongous Insurance data entry personnel will use to input data. The form consists of several *TextBox* controls that receive input. Data entry is expected to proceed quickly and without errors, but to help ensure this, you will be designing validation for this form. This validation is somewhat complex; there is a set of characters that is not allowed in any text box on the form, and each text box has additional limitations that differ from control to control. You would like to implement this validation scheme with a minimum of code to make troubleshooting and maintenance simple.

Answer the following question for your manager:

- What strategies can we use to implement these requirements?

Case Scenario 2: Humongous Insurance User Interface

The front end for this database is just as complex as the validation requirements. You are faced with a front end that exposes many menu options. Furthermore, for expert users, some of the more commonly used menu items can be triggered by holding down the Ctrl key while performing various gestures with the mouse. Functionality invoked by the menu items will sometimes be unavailable. Finally, you must enable the operator to edit data in this window quickly and easily.

The technical requirements are that:

- All main menu items must have access keys, and some must have mouse shortcuts.
- Availability of menu items must be communicated to the user in a way that is easy to understand but does not disrupt program flow.
- You must ensure that when a menu item is unavailable, corresponding shortcut keys and mouse gestures are also inactivated.
- Certain *TextBox* controls on the form must fill in automatically when appropriate keystrokes are entered.

The question is:

- How can this functionality be implemented?

Suggested Practices

To help you successfully master the exam objectives presented in this chapter, complete the following tasks.

- **Practice 1** Create a rudimentary text editor with buttons that implement the *Cut*, *Copy*, and *Paste* commands.

- **Practice 2** Build an application that consists of a window with a single button the user can chase around the window with the mouse but can never actually click.

- **Practice 3** Create an animation that moves elements across the user interface. Alternatively, use linear animations and key-frame animations to explore a variety of animation styles. Animate other properties of UI elements as well, such as their color, size, and content.

- **Practice 4** Use animations to create a slideshow application that reads all the image files in a given directory and displays each image for 10 seconds before automatically switching to the next one. Note that you have to create and apply the animation in code.

Take a Practice Test

The practice tests on this book's companion CD offer many options. For example, you can test yourself on just the content covered in this chapter, or you can test yourself on all the 70-511 certification exam content. You can set up the test so that it closely simulates the experience of taking a certification exam, or you can set it up in study mode so that you can look at the correct answers and explanations after you answer each question.

> *MORE INFO* **PRACTICE TESTS**
>
> For details about all the practice test options available, see the "How to Use the Practice Tests" section in this book's Introduction.

CHAPTER 3

Adding and Managing Content

Windows Presentation Foundation (WPF) provides unprecedented support for the construction and display of graphics, images, and media files. In this chapter, you learn to use WPF technology to create and display graphics, modify the visual interface, and add sound and video content.

Exam objectives in this chapter:

- Modify the visual interface at run time.
- Add multimedia content to an application in WPF.
- Create and display graphics.

Lessons in this chapter:

Before You Begin

To complete the lessons in this chapter, you must have

- A computer that meets or exceeds the minimum hardware requirements listed in the "About This Book" section at the beginning of the book.

- Microsoft Visual Studio 2010 Professional edition installed on your computer.

- An understanding of Microsoft Visual Basic or C# syntax and familiarity with the Microsoft .NET Framework.

 REAL WORLD

Matthew Stoecker

WPF makes it downright easy to add sound and video to my applications. Combined with the improved support for graphics, I find it easier than ever before to create content-rich applications.

Lesson 1: Managing the Visual Interface

WPF provides a previously unseen level of support for creating and displaying graphics. In this lesson, you learn to take advantage of this new support by creating your own graphics effects. You learn about using different brushes to create effects, creating a variety of shapes and transforming those shapes, and determining when the mouse is interacting with those shapes.

After this lesson, you will be able to:

- Create brushes that cause different effects and describe how brushes differ from each other.
- Apply a brush to various properties that affect the visual appearance of controls.
- Create different lines and shapes.
- Apply transformations to different lines and shapes.
- Determine when the mouse is over a shape.

Estimated lesson time: 30 minutes

Brushes

Brushes are the primary object WPF uses to paint the user interface, and every control has properties that accept a *Brush* object. You can affect the appearance of a control by assigning a different brush to each property. These properties represent several controls, but no control includes all the properties. Table 3-1 describes some of the properties.

TABLE 3-1 Element Properties That Accept a *Brush* Object

PROPERTY	DESCRIPTION
Background	The brush assigned to this property paints the background of the control.
BorderBrush	The brush assigned to this property paints the border of the control.
Fill	The brush assigned to this property paints the interior of a shape.
Foreground	The brush assigned to this property paints the foreground of the control, including the content of the control if the content is a string.
OpacityMask	This property accepts a *Brush* object, but only the opacity component is considered, which is determined by the opacity of the brush assigned. For example, if you assign a transparent brush to this property, the entire control appears transparent. You can use exotic brushes to create unusual transparency effects with this property.
Stroke	The brush assigned to this property paints the edge of a shape.

Brushes are freezable objects. Thus, you can make changes to *Brush* objects so long as the *Freeze* method has not been called. After the *Brush.Freeze* method is called, the brush becomes read-only and no further changes can be made.

SolidColorBrush

SolidColorBrush is the simplest of the *Brush* classes. As the name implies, it paints a single solid color without any patterns or gradients. Several solid-color brushes are available, and they are named by color in the *Brushes* class. You can access these brushes as shown here:

Sample of Visual Basic Code

```
Dim aBrush As Brush
aBrush = Brushes.AliceBlue
```

Sample of C# Code

```
Brush aBrush;
aBrush = Brushes.AliceBlue;
```

In Extensible Application Markup Language (XAML), you can assign a named brush to a property simply by referring to the name, as shown here:

```
<Button Background="Tomato"></Button>
```

You also can use hexadecimal notation to set the brush in XAML and specify an eight-digit number that defines the color. The first pair of digits denotes the value (from 00 to FF) of the opacity, the second pair of digits indicates the strength of the red channel, the third set indicates the strength of the green channel, and the final pair indicates the strength of the blue channel. The hexadecimal number is preceded by a number sign (#). The following example sets the background of a button to a pure red *SolidColorBrush* object:

```
<Button Background="#FFFF0000"></Button>
```

You also can create a new *SolidColorBrush* object by setting the value of each channel directly, as shown here:

```
<Button>
   <Button.Background>
      <SolidColorBrush>
         <SolidColorBrush.Color>
            <Color A="255" R="0" G="0" B="255"/>
         </SolidColorBrush.Color>
      </SolidColorBrush>
   </Button.Background>
</Button>
```

In code, you can use the *Color.FromArgb* method to define the individual channels, as shown here:

Sample of Visual Basic Code

```
Dim aBrush As SolidColorBrush
aBrush = New SolidColorBrush(Color.FromArgb(255, 0, 255, 0))
```

Sample of C# Code

```
SolidColorBrush aBrush;
aBrush = new SolidColorBrush(Color.FromArgb(255, 0, 255, 0));
```

LinearGradientBrush

LinearGradientBrush enables you to create a brush that blends two or more colors along a gradient, allowing a variety of effects. Figure 3-1 shows the effect of a *LinearGradientBrush* object painting the background of a window.

FIGURE 3-1 A window background painted by a *LinearGradientBrush*.

The code that creates this effect is shown here:

```
<Grid>
    <Grid.Background>
        <LinearGradientBrush>
            <GradientStop Color="Black" Offset="0"/>
            <GradientStop Color="White" Offset="1"/>
        </LinearGradientBrush>
    </Grid.Background>
</Grid>
```

The *LinearGradientBrush* object uses a system of coordinates to determine how the gradient is composed. The coordinate system is based on a rectangle that encloses the area to be painted. The upper left corner of this rectangle is coordinate (0,0), and the lower right corner is coordinate (1,1). Thus, coordinates are relative to the size of the drawn area and are not related to actual pixels.

Each *LinearGradientBrush* object contains a collection of *GradientStop* objects, each of which exposes two important properties: *Color* and *Offset*. The *Color* property determines the color to be blended, and the *Offset* is a number that specifies the point in the coordinate system where the indicated color is pure and not blended with other colors. In Figure 3-1, the upper left corner is completely black and the lower right corner is completely white, and the two colors are blended along the gradient.

The gradient along which colors are blended occurs in a line traveling from the start point to the end point. By default, the start point is (0,0) and the end point is (1,1), which creates a diagonal gradient that blends from the upper left corner to the lower right corner. You can specify other start and end points for *LinearGradientBrush* by using the *LinearGradientBrush.StartPoint* and *LinearGradientBrush.EndPoint* properties. For example, the following code creates a *LinearGradientPoint* object that paints a horizontal gradient instead of a diagonal one (shown in Figure 3-2):

```
<Grid>
   <Grid.Background>
      <LinearGradientBrush StartPoint="0,1" EndPoint="1,1">
         <GradientStop Color="Black" Offset="0"/>
         <GradientStop Color="White" Offset="1"/>
      </LinearGradientBrush>
   </Grid.Background>
</Grid>
```

FIGURE 3-2 A horizontal *LinearGradientBrush* object.

You can have more than two *GradientStop* objects in *LinearGradientBrush*. The following example demonstrates a *LinearGradientBrush* object that blends several colors along the gradient. Figure 3-3 shows the result of this code.

```
<Grid>
   <Grid.Background>
      <LinearGradientBrush StartPoint="0,0" EndPoint="1,1">
         <GradientStop Color="Black" Offset="0"/>
         <GradientStop Color="Red" Offset=".25"/>
         <GradientStop Color="Blue" Offset=".5"/>
         <GradientStop Color="Green" Offset=".75"/>
         <GradientStop Color="White" Offset="1"/>
      </LinearGradientBrush>
```

```
    </Grid.Background>
</Grid>
```

FIGURE 3-3 A multicolored *LinearGradientBrush* object.

The line defining the gradient need not start at a corner of the coordinate system. You could, for example, create a *LinearGradientBrush* object with *StartPoint* of (.3,.3) and *EndPoint* of (.7,.7) or any other pair of coordinates with values between 0 and 1. When the line defining the gradient does not stretch from one end of the coordinate system to the other, the value of the *LinearGradientBrush.Spread* property determines how the rest of the area is painted. Table 3-2 describes the possible values and effects of this property.

TABLE 3-2 Values of the *LinearGradientBrush.Spread* Property

VALUE	DESCRIPTION
Pad	This is the default value for the *Spread* property. It uses solid color on either side of the starting point of the gradient.
Reflect	When *SpreadMethod* is set to *Reflect,* the gradient is extended in the opposite orientation, like a mirror image.
Repeat	When *SpreadMethod* is set to *Repeat,* the gradient is repeated in the same orientation.

RadialGradientBrush

The *RadialGradientBrush* object is very similar to the *LinearGradientBrush* object; it blends a series of colors along a gradient and contains a collection of *GradientStop* objects that determine how the gradient is constructed. The key difference is that the gradient radiates out in concentric circles from a point in the coordinate system. The center of the gradient is defined by the *RadialGradientBrush.GradientOrigin* property (.5,.5 by default). The outermost circles of the *RadialGradientBrush* are defined by the *RadiusX* and *RadiusY* properties. *RadiusX* determines the distance of the outermost circle in the vertical dimension and *RadiusY* determines it in the horizontal dimension. The *GradientStop* objects function like they do in the *LinearGradientBrush,* indicating points where the colors are blended. Here's an example of code that defines *RadialGradientBrush*:

```
<Grid>
  <Grid.Background>
    <RadialGradientBrush Center=".5, .5" RadiusX=".5" RadiusY=".25">
      <GradientStop Color="Black" Offset="0"/>
      <GradientStop Color="White" Offset="1"/>
    </RadialGradientBrush>
  </Grid.Background>
</Grid>
```

Figure 3-4 displays the result of that code.

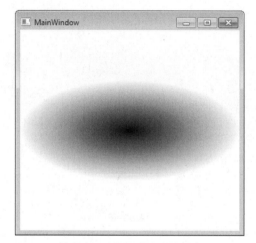

FIGURE 3-4 The *RadialGradientBrush*.

 Quick Check

- How is the gradient of *RadialGradientBrush* or *LinearGradientBrush* determined?

Quick Check Answer

- The gradient in these brushes is formed by a collection of *GradientStop* objects. Each *GradientStop* object defines a *Color* property and an *Offset* property, which indicate what color is to be blended and at what point in the gradient the color reaches maximum saturation.

ImageBrush

The *ImageBrush* object enables you to paint objects by using an image as the source for the brush. You can specify the source image for *ImageBrush* by setting the *ImageSource* property, as shown here:

```
<Grid.Background>
   <ImageBrush
      ImageSource="C:\Users\Public\Pictures\Sample Pictures\Forest.jpg">
   </ImageBrush>
</Grid.Background>
```

ImageBrush uses the designated image to paint the visual objects that are associated with it. If the designated image is smaller than the visual object to which the brush is assigned, the *Stretch* property controls how the brush paints the object. Table 3-3 shows the possible values of the *Stretch* property.

TABLE 3-3 Values of the *Stretch* Property

VALUE	DESCRIPTION
Fill	The image is stretched in both dimensions to fill available space. The aspect ratio of the image is not preserved.
None	The image is painted at original size. Any area outside the original image size is not painted.
Uniform	The image is stretched to fill the dimensions of the available space, but the aspect ratio of the image is preserved. Any area outside the stretched size is not painted.
UniformToFill	The image is expanded to fill all the available painting space. The aspect ratio is preserved, but content can be clipped if the aspect ratio of the image is different from the aspect ratio of the container.

You can select a portion of the source image to be used for painting by setting the *ViewBox* property, which defines a rectangle (usually relative to the imaginary box that surrounds the image) that is clipped to use for painting. The following example demonstrates cropping the upper left quarter of an image and using it for the *ImageBrush* object:

```
<Grid.Background>
   <ImageBrush Viewbox="0,0,.5,.5"
      ImageSource="C:\Users\Public\Pictures\Sample Pictures\Forest.jpg">
   </ImageBrush>
</Grid.Background>
```

If the *Stretch* property is set to *None,* you can also change the behavior of *ImageBrush* by setting the *TileMode* property. Table 3-4 displays the possible values for the *TileMode* property.

You can set the *Viewport* property to select a portion of the original source image to use as the tile source. An example is shown here:

```
<Grid.Background>
  <ImageBrush TileMode="FlipXY" Viewport="0,0,.5,.5"
    ImageSource="C:\Users\Public\Pictures\Sample Pictures\Forest.jpg">
  </ImageBrush>
</Grid.Background>
```

TABLE 3-4 Values of the *TileMode* Property

VALUE	DESCRIPTION
FlipX	The image is tiled in the original orientation in the vertical dimension and alternates original orientation and mirror-image orientation in the horizontal dimension.
FlipXY	The image is tiled in alternating original and mirror-image orientations in both the horizontal and vertical dimensions. Note that tiles to the lower right of an original orientation tile appear as though they have been rotated 180 degrees relative to the original orientation.
FlipY	The image is tiled in the original orientation in the horizontal dimension and alternates original orientation and mirror-image orientation in the vertical dimension.
None	No tiling takes place.
Tile	The image is tiled in the original orientation.

VisualBrush

The *VisualBrush* object is very similar to the *ImageBrush* object, but instead of using an image as the source for painting, it uses a *Visual* element, such as a WPF control or any other element that inherits the *Visual* class. The following demonstrates a *VisualBrush* object that uses a *Button* control as the source for the visual:

```
<VisualBrush Visual="{Binding ElementName=Button1}">
</VisualBrush>
```

You can use *VisualBrush* just as you would use *ImageBrush*, applying *Stretch* or *TileMode* properties.

Shapes

Shapes are drawing primitives. They represent individual drawn elements such as rectangles, ellipses, polygons, and lines. Although shapes appear as simple drawn elements, they support all the user interaction events that other WPF elements support and thus are used easily in the creation of new controls.

All shapes in WPF derive from the abstract *Shape* class, which itself ultimately derives from the *Visual* class. This class provides several properties to all the WPF shapes. Table 3-5 describes some of these properties.

TABLE 3-5 Properties of the *Shape* Class

PROPERTY	DESCRIPTION
Fill	The *Brush* object that paints the interior of the shape
Stroke	The *Brush* object that paints the edge of the shape
StrokeThickness	Sets the thickness of the border in device-independent units
Stretch	Determines how a shape fills the space it occupies

Like other controls, the *Shape* class provides *Width*, *Height*, *Margin*, and other properties that control the sizing and spacing of the visual element. If the *Width* and *Height* values are not explicitly set, the *Stretch* property describes how a shape will be stretched to fill the available space. Table 3-6 describes the possible values for the *Stretch* property.

TABLE 3-6 Values for the *Stretch* Property

VALUE	DESCRIPTION
None	The shape is rendered at full size.
Uniform	The shape is stretched to fill the dimensions of the available space, but the aspect ratio of the shape is preserved.
Fill	The shape is stretched in both dimensions to fill the available space. The aspect ratio of the shape is not preserved.
UniformToFill	The shape is expanded to fill all the available painting space. The aspect ratio is preserved. The shape can be clipped to fit the space.

Rectangle and *Ellipse* Classes

The *Rectangle* class represents a rendered rectangle and the *Ellipse* class represents a rendered ellipse. Both shapes are very simple. The visual depiction is defined primarily by the *Height* and *Width* properties. The following examples represent a rectangle and an ellipse that are each 100 units high and 200 units wide:

```
<Rectangle Height="100" Width="200" Fill="Blue"/>
<Ellipse Height="100" Width="200" Fill="Blue"/>
```

If the *Height* and *Width* properties are not explicitly set, you can use the *Stretch* property to describe how the shape in question fills the available space.

You can create a rectangle with rounded edges by setting the *RadiusX* and *RadiusY* properties. These properties represent the *x* and *y* radii of an ellipse, which are used to round the corners of the rectangle. The following XAML demonstrates drawing a rectangle with rounded edges:

```
<Rectangle RadiusX="20" RadiusY="10" Fill="blue" Height="50" Width="100"/>
```

Line and Polyline Classes

The *Line* class represents a line that connects two coordinate points. The coordinate system used for drawing *Line* objects is relative to the upper left corner of whatever contains the line. For example, if the line is contained in a grid cell, the (0,0) point represents the upper left corner of the grid cell. You create a *Line* object by setting the *X1*, *Y1*, *X2*, and *Y2* properties, as shown here:

```
<Line Stroke="Red" X1="0" Y1="50" X2="100" Y2="440"/>
```

The *Polyline* class is a somewhat more complex shape, essentially a set of collected points. The *Polyline* class exposes a *Points* collection that defines the points in the shape. The shape begins at the first point in the collection and then connects straight lines among the rest of the points in the collection before finishing with the last point. The following example demonstrates a *Polyline* class with a sawtooth shape:

```
<Polyline Stroke="Green"
    Points="300, 300 400, 400 400, 300 500, 400 500, 300"/>
```

The commas between the *x* and *y* coordinates of each point are not required but are allowed and facilitate readability of your code.

Polygon Class

The *Polygon* class is quite similar to the *Polyline* class. Like the *Polyline* class, it exposes a *Points* collection that defines the points of the shape and connects those points. The chief difference, however, is that the *Polygon* class also connects the first point with the last point and paints the interior of the shape with the *Brush* object defined in the *Fill* property. The following example demonstrates a *Polygon* class similar to the previous *Polyline* example:

```
<Polygon Fill="Green"
    Points="300, 300 400, 400 400, 300 500, 400 500, 300"/>
```

When lines in a *Polyline* or *Polygon* class cross one another, they create closed areas that can be filled by the shape's *Fill* brush. How enclosed areas are filled is determined by the value of the *FillRule* property. Table 3-7 shows the possible values for the *FillRule* property.

TABLE 3-7 Values for the *FillRule* Property

VALUE	DESCRIPTION
EvenOdd	WPF counts the number of lines it must cross to get to the bounded region. If a closed region can be reached by crossing an odd number of lines, it is filled. If it can be reached by crossing an even number of lines, it is not filled.
NonZero	WPF counts the number of lines that must be crossed to reach a bounded area and takes into account the direction in which they are drawn. If the number of lines that must be crossed that travel in one direction equals the number of lines that must be crossed that travel in the opposite direction, the area is filled. Otherwise, the area is not filled.

Path

Path is the most complex shape in WPF. A *Path* object describes a complex shape that can be built from one or more *Geometry* objects. A *Geometry* object can be thought of as a blueprint for a shape. It contains all the data regarding the physical appearance of a shape, such as coordinates and size, but it incorporates none of the event-handling or control-based functionality of a *Shape* class.

Table 3-8 describes the types of *Geometry* objects that can be used to create a *Path* object.

TABLE 3-8 *Geometry* Objects That Can Create a *Path* Object

VALUE	DESCRIPTION
CombinedGeometry	Combines two *Geometry* objects into a single object and enables you to apply different effects by setting the *CombineMode* property
EllipseGeometry	Contains data that represent the shape of an ellipse
GeometryGroup	Represents a group of *Geometry* objects that is added to the *Path* object
LineGeometry	Represents a straight line
PathGeometry	Represents a complex shape or figure that is composed of lines, arcs, and curves
RectangleGeometry	Represents a rectangle
StreamGeometry	A lightweight equivalent of *PathGeometry*; *StreamGeometry* differs from *PathGeometry* in that it is read-only after being created.

The simplest way to create a *Path* object is to add a single *Geometry* object to the *Path.Data* property, as shown here:

```
<Path Fill="Aqua">
  <Path.Data>
    <EllipseGeometry RadiusX="40" RadiusY="50"/>
  </Path.Data>
</Path>
```

You can create paths that consist of multiple shapes by using the *GeometryGroup* class. The following example adds a rectangle and an ellipse:

```
<Path Fill="Aqua" Margin="100">
  <Path.Data>
    <GeometryGroup FillRule="Nonzero">
      <EllipseGeometry RadiusX="40" RadiusY="50"/>
      <RectangleGeometry Rect="0,0,10,100"/>
    </GeometryGroup>
  </Path.Data>
</Path>
```

When a *GeometryGroup* contains overlapping *Geometry* objects, the *FillRule* property determines how the overlapping areas are filled, like with *Polygon* and *Polyline* shapes (see Table 3-7, cited previously).

The *CombinedGeometry* class enables you to create *Geometry* objects that represent combinations of two *Geometry* objects. The type of combination is determined by the *GeometryCombineMode* property. Table 3-9 shows values for the *GeometryCombineMode* property.

TABLE 3-9 Values of the *GeometryCombineMode* Property

VALUE	DESCRIPTION
Exclude	The resulting *Geometry* object represents the area that results when the second *Geometry* object is subtracted from the first *Geometry* object.
Intersect	The resulting *Geometry* object represents the intersection of the two input *Geometry* objects.
Xor	The resulting *Geometry* object represents the area that is not shared between the two input *Geometry* objects. This is the reverse of the *Intersect* value.
Union	The resulting *Geometry* object represents the union of the two input *Geometry* objects.

The following example demonstrates a *Path* object created by using a *CombinedGeometry* object:

```
<Path Fill="Aqua" Margin="100">
  <Path.Data>
```

```
    <CombinedGeometry GeometryCombineMode="Exclude">
        <CombinedGeometry.Geometry1>
            <EllipseGeometry RadiusX="40" RadiusY="50"/>
        </CombinedGeometry.Geometry1>
        <CombinedGeometry.Geometry2>
            <RectangleGeometry Rect="0,0,10,100"/>
        </CombinedGeometry.Geometry2>
    </CombinedGeometry>
    </Path.Data>
</Path>
```

Making extremely complex shapes is possible using the *PathGeometry* class. A full exploration of the capabilities of the *PathGeometry* class is beyond the scope of this lesson, but further reading is recommended for those interested in creating complicated graphical shapes.

Transformations

Transformations (also referred to as *transforms*) are objects that enable you to alter the shape of an element by altering the coordinate system used to draw it. You can use transforms to apply a variety of effects to shapes and elements, such as rotation, displacement, skewing, and more complicated effects.

Types of Transforms

Table 3-10 shows the kinds of *Transform* objects you can use to alter the appearance of a shape or element.

You can apply a *Transform* object to a shape by setting the *RenderTransform* property, as shown in this example that transforms a rectangle into a parallelogram:

```
<Rectangle Height="20" Width="50" Fill="blue">
   <Rectangle.RenderTransform>
      <SkewTransform AngleX="-30"></SkewTransform>
   </Rectangle.RenderTransform>
</Rectangle>
```

TABLE 3-10 Kinds of *Transform* Objects

CLASS	DESCRIPTION
MatrixTransform	Modifies the coordinate system of the object to which it is applied by applying a 3 x 3 affine transformation matrix to the underlying coordinate system. The matrix is defined by the *Matrix* property.
RotateTransform	Rotates the coordinate system around the point represented by the *CenterX* and *CenterY* properties. The *Angle* property determines the angle of rotation.

ScaleTransform	Transforms the coordinate system by increasing or reducing the scale of the transformation. The *ScaleX* property determines horizontal scaling, and the *ScaleY* property determines vertical scaling. The *CenterX* and *CenterY* properties determine the center point of the transformation.
SkewTransform	Skews the coordinate system of your object. The *AngleX* and *AngleY* properties determine the angle of skewing in the horizontal and vertical directions, respectively, and the *CenterX* and *CenterY* properties determine the center of the transformation.
TranslateTransform	Shifts the coordinate system of your object by the horizontal and vertical amounts indicated by the *X* and *Y* properties, respectively.
TransformGroup	Groups a series of *Transform* objects and applies each to the underlying coordinate system.

Typically, a transformation initiates at the upper left corner of the transformed element. You can specify a different origin for the transformation by setting the *RenderTransformOrigin* property. The coordinate system used by transformations sets (0,0) as the upper left corner of the rectangle bounding the element and (1,1) as the lower right corner. The code shown in bold in the following example sets the origin of the *Transform* to the center of the element:

```
<Rectangle Height="20" Width="50" Fill="blue"
   RenderTransformOrigin=".5, .5">
   <Rectangle.RenderTransform>
      <SkewTransform AngleX="-30"></SkewTransform>
   </Rectangle.RenderTransform>
</Rectangle>
```

Transforming Elements

In the same way you can transform shapes, you can apply *Transform* objects to elements to alter their appearance. Because all WPF elements are drawn by WPF, you can apply a *Transform* to any WPF element. A *Transform* object affects only the appearance of a control. A control's functionality remains unaffected, although applying dramatic *Transform* objects to user interface (UI) elements might affect how well a user can comprehend and use the UI.

You can apply *Transform* to an element in the same way as you would to a shape: by setting the *RenderTransform* property. The following example demonstrates a *Button* object with *SkewTransform* applied:

```
<Button Height="20" Width="50">
   <Button.RenderTransform>
      <SkewTransform AngleX="-30"></SkewTransform>
   </Button.RenderTransform>
</Button>
```

Flipping

A common requirement for visual transformations is to flip an element, either horizontally across the *y*-axis or vertically across the *x*-axis. You can flip an element by using *ScaleTransform*. To flip an element horizontally but maintain its size and shape, you use *ScaleTransform* with a *ScaleX* property of –1. To flip vertically, you use *ScaleTransform* with a *ScaleY* property of –1. Setting both *ScaleX* and *ScaleY* to –1 results in an element that is flipped across both axes. The following example demonstrates flipping a button horizontally:

```
<Button Height="50" Width="100" VerticalAlignment="Bottom">
   <Button.RenderTransform>
      <ScaleTransform ScaleX="-1"></ScaleTransform>
   </Button.RenderTransform>Flipped Button
</Button>
```

Using this transform displaces your element across the axis as though it were a mirror image. To flip an element but maintain its original position, set the element's *RenderTransformOrigin* property to .5,.5, as shown here in bold:

```
<Button RenderTransformOrigin=".5, .5" Height="50" Width="100"
   VerticalAlignment="Bottom">
   <Button.RenderTransform>
      <ScaleTransform ScaleX="-1"></ScaleTransform>
   </Button.RenderTransform>Flipped Button
</Button>
```

EXAM TIP

Be sure you understand the difference between each of the kinds of geometric transforms and know when each one is used. In particular, note that you use ScaleTransform rather than RotateTransform to flip an element,, which might not seem intuitive at first.

Clipping

In the "Path" section earlier in this chapter, you saw how you can use *Geometry* objects to create complex shapes. You can also use *Geometry* objects to clip the shape of elements by setting the *Clip* property, which is exposed by all WPF elements. Setting the *Clip* property constrains the visual appearance of the affected control to the shape described by the *Geometry* object to which the *Clip* property is set. This does not transform the element in any way; it merely clips the visible bounds of the control to conform to the *Geometry* object. Figure 3-5 shows two identically sized *Button* elements. The *Button* element on the left does not have the *Clip* property set, whereas the *Button* element on the right has the *Clip* property set to an *EllipseGeometry* object.

FIGURE 3-5 Two *Button* elements, one clipped, one not.

The following example demonstrates how to apply clipping to an element:

```
<Button Height="100" Width="100" Name="Button1">
  <Button.Clip>
     <!--Since the Button is 100 by 100 pixels, an EllipseGeometry
         with a Center of 50,50 and a RadiusX and RadiusY of 50 will
         clip the button so that it appears circular-->
     <EllipseGeometry Center="50,50" RadiusX="50" RadiusY="50"/>
  </Button.Clip>Button
</Button>
```

The Visual Tree

In WPF programming, the visual interface is defined by the visual tree, a hierarchical organization of the visual elements in your application. All WPF elements with an inherent visual representation inherit the *Visual* class. This includes controls and shapes as well as more specialized decorator classes that enhance the appearance of controls, but it does not include elements that do not have an inherent visual representation. An example of an element that does not have an inherent visual representation would be the *ListBoxItem* control, which can contain content but has no actual appearance itself.

The *Visual* class provides much of the background support for the visual elements of the user interface. The *Visual* class provides functionality for transformations, clipping, hit testing, and bounding box calculations for visual elements as well as persisting the serialized drawing information for the element. It is through the persistence of this drawing data that WPF is able to optimize graphics display by using *retained mode graphics*.

Retained mode graphics is one of the primary differences between rendering the user interfaces in WPF applications and rendering the user interfaces in Windows Forms applications. In Windows Forms, the application is responsible for invalidating regions of the user interface and sending commands to the system to redraw those regions. This is referred to as *immediate mode graphics*. When the application gets busy, this can cause repainting to be delayed or the user interface to become unresponsive.

In contrast, WPF retained mode graphics transmit the serialized drawing data to the system when a visual element is created, and the system is thereafter responsible for repainting the element. Thus, even if the application is busy, the system can still respond to paint requests and maintain a responsive user interface.

VisualTreeHelper

For navigating the tree of *Visual* elements in a WPF application, WPF provides a static helper class called *VisualTreeHelper*, which provides static methods that enable navigation among and interaction with elements in the visual tree. Table 3-11 describes the methods of *VisualTreeHelper*.

TABLE 3-11 Methods of the *VisualTreeHelper* Class

METHOD	DESCRIPTION
GetBitmapEffect	Returns the BitmapEffect value for the specified *Visual* object
GetBitmapEffectInput	Returns the BitmapEffectInput value for the specified *Visual* object
GetCacheMode	Retrieves the cached representation of the specified *Visual* object
GetChild	Returns the child visual object from the specified collection index within a specified parent
GetChildrenCount	Returns the number of children the specified *Visual* object contains
GetClip	Returns the clip region of the specified *Visual* object as a *Geometry* value
GetContentBounds(Visual)	Returns the cached bounding box rectangle for the specified *Visual* object
GetContentBounds(Visual3D)	Returns the cached bounding box rectangle for the specified *Visual3D* object
GetDescendantBounds(Visual)	Returns the union of all the content bounding boxes for all the descendants of the *Visual* object, which includes the content bounding box of the *Visual* object
GetDescendantBounds(Visual3D)	Returns the union of all the content bounding boxes for all the descendants of the specified *Visual3D* object, which includes the content bounding box of the *Visual3D* object

GetDrawing	Returns the drawing content of the specified *Visual* object
GetEdgeMode	Returns the edge mode of the specified *Visual* object as an *EdgeMode* value
GetEffect	Gets the bitmap effect for the specified *Visual* object
GetOffset	Returns the offset of the *Visual* object
GetOpacity	Returns the opacity of the *Visual* object
GetOpacityMask	Returns a *Brush* value that represents the opacity mask of the *Visual* object
GetParent	Returns a *DependencyObject* value that represents the parent of the *Visual* object
GetTransform	Returns a *Transform* value for the *Visual* object
GetXSnappingGuidelines	Returns an *x*-coordinate (vertical) guideline collection
GetYSnappingGuidelines	Returns a *y*-coordinate (horizontal) guideline collection
HitTest(Visual, Point)	Returns the topmost *Visual* object of a hit test by specifying a *Point*
HitTest(Visual, HitTestFilterCallback, HitTestResultCallback, HitTestParameters)	Initiates a hit test on the specified *Visual* object, with caller-defined *HitTestFilterCallback* and *HitTestResultCallback* methods
HitTest(Visual3D, HitTestFilterCallback, HitTestResultCallback, HitTestParameters3D)	Initiates a hit test on the specified *Visual3D* object, with caller-defined *HitTestFilterCallback* and *HitTestResultCallback* methods

The following example demonstrates the use of *VisualTreeHelper*. This example demonstrates how to use the *VisualTreeHelper* class to loop through all objects in the visual tree.

Sample of Visual Basic Code

```
Public Sub LoopVisuals(ByVal aVisual As Visual)
   For i As Integer = 0 To VisualTreeHelper.GetChildrenCount(aVisual) - 1
   ' Gets the child visual at specified index value.
      Dim bVisual As Visual = CType(VisualTreeHelper.GetChild(aVisual, i), Visual)
      ' Do whatever needs to be done to the Visual object.
      ' Call this method recursively to loop though all of the visuals of the child
      ' visual
      LoopVisuals(bVisual)
   Next i
End Sub
```

```
public void LoopVisuals(Visual aVisual)
{
    for (int i = 0; i < VisualTreeHelper.GetChildrenCount(aVisual); i++)
    {
        // Gets the child visual at specified index value.
        Visual bVisual = (Visual)VisualTreeHelper.GetChild(aVisual, i);
        // Do whatever needs to be done to the Visual object.
        // Call this method recursively to loop though all of the visuals of the child
        // visual
           LoopVisuals(bVisual);
    }
}
```

Adding to and Removing Controls from the Visual Interface at Run Time

Both Windows Forms and WPF applications enable you to add and remove controls at run time. In Windows Forms, you add a control to a form or other container control by accessing that control's *Controls* collection. The following example demonstrates how to add a button to the current form at run time:

Sample of Visual Basic Code

```
Dim aButton As New Button()
Me.Controls.Add(aButton)
```

Sample of C# Code

```
Button aButton = new Button();
this.Controls.Add(aButton);
```

Removing a control at run time is also accomplished through the *Controls* collection. You can either remove a control directly, based on a reference to that control, or, if you do not have a reference, you can remove a control based on its index in the collection. Both examples are shown here:

Sample of Visual Basic Code

```
' Removes the control referred to by the variable aButton.
Me.Controls.Remove(aButton)
' Removes the control at index 0 of the controls collection
Me.Controls.RemoveAt(0)
```

Sample of C# Code

```
// Removes the control referred to by the variable aButton.
this.Controls.Remove(aButton);
// Removes the control at index 0 of the controls collection
this.Controls.RemoveAt(0);
```

In WPF applications, the procedure is similar but somewhat complicated because controls can be hosted in any WPF container, list, or content control. For container controls, you can access child controls through the *Children* property. For list controls, such as *ListBox*, you can access list items through the *Items* property. Both the *Children* property of container controls and the *Items* property of list controls have *Add*, *Remove*, and *RemoveAt* methods that function similarly to their Windows Forms counterparts, as shown here:

Sample of Visual Basic Code

```vb
Dim aButton As New Button()
Dim bButton As New Button()
Grid1.Children.Add(aButton)
ListBox1.Items.Add(bButton)
' Removes the control referred to by the variables aButton and bButton.
Grid1.Children.Remove(aButton)
ListBox1.Items.Remove(bButton)
' Removes the control at index 0 of the controls collection
Grid1.Children.RemoveAt(0)
ListBox1.Items.RemoveAt(0)
```

Sample of C# Code

```csharp
Button aButton = new Button();
Button bButton = new Button();
Grid1.Children.Add(aButton);
ListBox1.Items.Add(bButton);
// Removes the control referred to by the variables aButton and bButton.
Grid1.Children.Remove(aButton);
ListBox1.Items.Remove(bButton);
// Removes the control at index 0 of the controls collection
Grid1.Children.RemoveAt(0);
ListBox1.Items.RemoveAt(0);
```

For content items, however, adding or removing a control is as simple as setting the *Content* property, as shown here:

Sample of Visual Basic Code

```vb
' Creates and adds a Button control to another Button control named Button1
Dim aButton As New Button()
Button1.Content = aButton
' Removes aButton from Button1
Button1.Content = Nothing
```

Sample of C# Code

```csharp
// Creates and adds a Button control to another Button control named Button1
Button aButton = new Button();
Button1.Content = aButton;
// Removes aButton from Button1
Button1.Content = null;
```

When a control is removed from its host collection, it will be garbage collected if no other active references to that control exist.

In this practice, you add a variety of effects to a previously created application. Although the result might not be useful in a business setting, it demonstrates some of the techniques you have learned in this lesson. Please note that this exercise, which creates a file in the root of your C: drive, requires appropriate file system access.

EXERCISE Practice with Graphics

1. From the CD, load the partial solution for Chapter 3, Lesson 1.

2. In XAML view, modify the XAML for *Button1* so that it defines a new *SolidColorBrush* for the *Background* property, as shown in bold here (note that the XAML for the C# practice files differs slightly):

```
<Button Height="23" Margin="30,76,0,0" Name="Button1"
    VerticalAlignment="Top" HorizontalAlignment="Left" Width="74">
    <Button.Background>
        <SolidColorBrush Color="Red"></SolidColorBrush>
    </Button.Background>Set Name
</Button>
```

3. Do the same with *Button2,* setting the background to a *SolidColorBrush* of a different color.

4. Modify the XAML for *TextBox* to add a *ScaleTransform* section, which flips the text box across the *y*-axis but maintains the same position, as shown in bold here:

```
<TextBox RenderTransformOrigin=".5,.5" Height="21" Margin="30,29,81,0"
    Name="textBox1" VerticalAlignment="Top">
    <TextBox.RenderTransform>
        <ScaleTransform ScaleX="-1"/>
    </TextBox.RenderTransform>
</TextBox>
```

5. Add a *SkewTransform* section to *Label1* to skew the rendering of the control, as shown in bold here:

```
<Label Margin="30,124,81,115" Name="label1">
    <Label.RenderTransform>
        <SkewTransform AngleX="30" AngleY="20"></SkewTransform>
    </Label.RenderTransform>
</Label>
```

6. Just before the *<Grid>* declaration, add the following code to set the window background to a *LinearGradientBrush* object:

```
<Window.Background>
    <LinearGradientBrush>
        <GradientStop Color="Red" Offset="0"/>
        <GradientStop Color="Yellow" Offset=".5"/>
        <GradientStop Color="Lime" Offset="1"/>
    </LinearGradientBrush>
</Window.Background>
```

7. Press F5 to build and run your application. Note that although the functionality remains the same, the user interface has a completely different appearance.

Lesson Summary

- *Brush* is the primary object that WPF uses to paint the user interface, and all *Brush* objects inherit the *Brush* abstract class. *SolidColorBrush* objects paint with a solid color, and *LinearGradientBrush* and *RadialGradientBrush* objects paint color gradients. *ImageBrush* and *VisualBrush* objects can be used to paint with images or other visual elements.

- WPF has built-in support for the creation of drawing primitive shapes. Shapes support all the user interaction events common to UI elements. Shapes range from the simple, such as *Rectangle* and *Ellipse,* to the complex, such as *Polygon* and *Path*.

- Transforms enable you to apply mathematical transformations to shapes and elements. You can apply *Transform* to a shape or element by setting the *RenderTransform* property of the object you want to transform.

- You can set the *Clip* property of an element to a specified *Geometry* object to clip the visual representation of that object. An element with the *Clip* property set will be painted only in the area represented by the intersection of the element's natural shape and the specified *Geometry* object.

- You can use the *VisualTreeHelper.HitTest* method to retrieve the object hit by a specified point. The point specified is relative to the upper left corner of the specified visual element.

Lesson Review

You can use the following questions to test your knowledge of the information in Lesson 1, "Managing the Visual Interface." The questions are also available on the companion CD of this book if you prefer to review them in electronic form.

> **NOTE ANSWERS**
>
> Answers to these questions and explanations of why each answer choice is correct or incorrect are located in the "Answers" section at the end of the book.

1. Which of the following XAML snippets renders the *Button* control flipped across the *y*-axis but renders it in the original coordinates?

A.

```
<Button Height="23" Margin="75,64,128,0" Name="Button1"
   VerticalAlignment="Top">
   <Button.RenderTransform>
      <ScaleTransform ScaleY="-1"/>
   </Button.RenderTransform>Button
</Button>
```

B.

```
<Button Height="23" Margin="75,64,128,0" Name="Button1"
   VerticalAlignment="Top" RenderTransformOrigin=".5,.5">
   <Button.RenderTransform>
      <ScaleTransform ScaleY="-1"/>
   </Button.RenderTransform>Button
</Button>
```

C.

```
<Button Height="23" Margin="75,64,128,0" Name="Button1"
   VerticalAlignment="Top">
   <Button.RenderTransform>
      <ScaleTransform ScaleX="-1"/>
   </Button.RenderTransform>Button
</Button>
```

D.

```
<Button Height="23" Margin="75,64,128,0" Name="Button1"
   VerticalAlignment="Top" RenderTransformOrigin=".5,.5">
   <Button.RenderTransform>
      <ScaleTransform ScaleX="-1"/>
   </Button.RenderTransform>Button
</Button>
```

2. Which of the following XAML samples correctly demonstrates how to create a
   LinearGradient brush by which the color is blended from red to yellow vertically?

   A.

```
<LinearGradientBrush>
   <GradientStop Color="Red" Offset="0"/>
   <GradientStop Color="Yellow" Offset="1"/>
</LinearGradientBrush>
```

   B.

```
<LinearGradientBrush StartPoint="0,1" EndPoint="1,1">
   <GradientStop Color="Red" Offset="0"/>
   <GradientStop Color="Yellow" Offset="1"/>
</LinearGradientBrush>
```

   C.

```
<LinearGradientBrush StartPoint="0,1" EndPoint="1,1">
   <GradientStop Color="Yellow" Offset="0"/>
   <GradientStop Color="Red" Offset="1"/>
</LinearGradientBrush>
```

   D.

```
<LinearGradientBrush StartPoint="1,0" EndPoint="1,1">
   <GradientStop Color="Red" Offset="0"/>
   <GradientStop Color="Yellow" Offset="1"/>
</LinearGradientBrush>
```

Lesson 2: Adding Multimedia Content

WPF enables you to integrate multimedia content into your applications. *SoundPlayer*, *MediaPlayer*, and *MediaElement* classes enable the seamless integration of sound and video into multiple facets of your application. In this lesson, you learn to use these three classes to incorporate sound and video content into your user interface.

After this lesson, you will be able to:

- Use the *SoundPlayer* class to play uncompressed .wav files.
- Describe the *SoundPlayerAction* class and explain how to use it in a trigger.
- Use the *MediaPlayer* class to play sound in a WPF application.
- Use the *MediaElement* to display video in a WPF application.
- Control aspects of media playback with *MediaPlayer* and *MediaElement*.
- Handle media-specific events.

Estimated lesson time: 20 minutes

Using *SoundPlayer*

The *SoundPlayer* class was introduced in .NET Framework 2.0 as a managed class to enable audio in Microsoft Windows applications. It is lightweight and easy to use, but it has significant limitations.

The *SoundPlayer* class can play only uncompressed .wav files. It cannot read compressed .wav files or files in other audio formats. Furthermore, the developer has no control over volume, balance, speed, or any other aspects of sound playback.

In spite of its limitations, *SoundPlayer* can be a useful and lightweight way to incorporate sound into your applications. It provides a basic set of members to load and play uncompressed .wav files easily. Table 3-12 shows important members of the *SoundPlayer* class.

TABLE 3-12 Important Members of the *SoundPlayer* Class

MEMBER	TYPE	DESCRIPTION
IsLoadCompleted	Property	Returns a Boolean value indicating whether the .wav file for the *SoundPlayer* class has completed loading.
Load	Method	Loads the .wav file from the indicated *Stream* or *SoundLocation* property synchronously.
LoadAsync	Method	Loads the .wav file from the indicated *Stream* or *SoundLocation* property asynchronously.

LoadComplete	Event	Is raised when the .wav file has completed loading.
LoadTimeout	Property	Gets or sets the time in milliseconds in which the .wav file must load.
Play	Method	Plays the indicated .wav file asynchronously.
PlayLooping	Method	Plays the indicated .wav file asynchronously. When the end of the file is reached, the file is started again at the beginning until it is stopped.
PlaySync	Method	Plays the indicated .wav file synchronously.
SoundLocation	Property	Gets or sets the file location of the .wav file.
SoundLocationChanged	Event	Is raised when the SoundLocation property changes.
Stop	Method	Stops playback by the SoundPlayer class.
Stream	Property	Gets or sets the Stream object that contains the .wav file.
StreamChanged	Event	Is raised when the Stream property changes.

To play a .wav file with the *SoundPlayer* class:

1. Declare a new instance of the *SoundPlayer* class, as shown here:

   Sample of Visual Basic Code

   ```
   Dim aPlayer As System.Media.SoundPlayer = New System.Media.SoundPlayer()
   ```

   Sample of C# Code

   ```
   System.Media.SoundPlayer aPlayer = new System.Media.SoundPlayer();
   ```

2. Specify the location of the .wav file either by setting the *SoundLocation* property to the file address for the .wav file or by setting the *Stream* property to a *Stream* object that contains the .wav file. See the following examples:

   Sample of Visual Basic Code

   ```
   aPlayer.SoundLocation = "C:\myFile.wav"
   ' OR
   aPlayer.Stream = myStream
   ```

   Sample of C# Code

   ```
   aPlayer.SoundLocation = "C:\\myFile.wav";
   // OR
   aPlayer.Stream = myStream;
   ```

3. Preload the .wav file. Although doing this is optional, it conserves system resources when the file is played more than once. If you do not preload the file, it is loaded automatically each time you play the file.

Sample of Visual Basic Code

```
aPlayer.Load()
' OR
aPlayer.LoadAsync()
```

Sample of C# Code

```
aPlayer.Load();
// OR
aPlayer.LoadAsync();
```

4. Use the *Play* or *PlaySync* method to play the .wav file, as shown here:

Sample of Visual Basic Code

```
aPlayer.Play()
' OR
aPlayer.PlaySync()
```

Sample of C# Code

```
aPlayer.Play();
// OR
aPlayer.PlaySync();
```

SoundPlayerAction

WPF provides a class named *SoundPlayerAction* for use in XAML that wraps a standard *SoundPlayer* object. The *SoundPlayerAction* class enables you to create a *SoundPlayer* object declaratively and play a .wav file in response to a trigger.

The only important property of the *SoundPlayerAction* class is the *Source* property, which should provide a path to the .wav file to be played. The line of code shown in bold in the following example demonstrates how to use the *SoundPlayerAction* class to play a sound when the mouse passes over a button:

```
<Button Height="23" Margin="93,57,110,0" Name="button1"
   VerticalAlignment="Top">
   <Button.Content>Button</Button.Content>
   <Button.Style>
      <Style>
         <Style.Triggers>
            <EventTrigger RoutedEvent="Button.MouseEnter">
               <SoundPlayerAction Source="C:\myFile.wav"/>
            </EventTrigger>
         </Style.Triggers>
      </Style>
   </Button.Style>
</Button>
```

MediaPlayer and MediaElement

The *MediaPlayer* and *MediaElement* classes provide deep support for playing audio and video media files in a variety of formats. Both of these classes use the functionality of Windows Media Player 10, so although they are guaranteed to be usable in applications running on Windows Vista, which comes with Media Player 11 as a standard feature, these classes will not function on Windows XP installations that do not have at least Windows Media Player 10 installed.

The *MediaPlayer* and *MediaElement* classes are very similar and expose many of the same members. The primary difference between the two classes is that although *MediaPlayer* loads and plays both audio and video, it has no visual interface and thus cannot display video in the user interface. However, *MediaElement* is a full-fledged WPF element that can be used to display video in your applications. *MediaElement* wraps a *MediaPlayer* object and provides a visual interface to play video files. Another important difference is that *MediaPlayer* cannot be used easily in XAML, whereas *MediaElement* is designed for XAML use.

Table 3-13 shows important properties of *MediaPlayer* and *MediaElement*, and Table 3-14 shows important methods of *MediaPlayer* and *MediaElement*.

TABLE 3-13 Important Properties of *MediaPlayer* and *MediaElement*

PROPERTY	DESCRIPTION
Balance	Gets or sets the balance between the left and right speakers. Possible values range between –1 (left speaker only) and 1 (right speaker only). A value of 0 represents equal balance between the speakers.
BufferingProgress	Returns a number between 0 and 1 that represents the percentage of the file that has been buffered if the file is in a streaming format that enables buffering.
DownloadProgress	Returns a number between 0 and 1 that represents the percentage of the file that has been downloaded.
HasAudio	Indicates whether the current media file has audio.
HasVideo	Indicates whether the current media file has video.
LoadedBehavior	Indicates whether the file should be played automatically when loaded. When set to *Play*, the file is played automatically when loaded. When set to *Manual*, the file is not played until the *Play* method is called. This property exists only in *MediaElement*.
NaturalDuration	Returns a *Duration* object that represents the duration of the current media file when played at natural speed.
NaturalVideoHeight	Indicates the unaltered video height of the current media file.
NaturalVideoWidth	Indicates the unaltered video width of the current media file.
Position	Returns a *TimeSpan* object that represents the current position in the media file.

Source	Returns the Uniform Resource Identifier (URI) from which the media file was loaded. For *MediaPlayer*, this is a read-only property and is set when the *Open* method is called. For *MediaElement*, however, you can set the *Source* property declaratively in XAML.
SpeedRatio	Gets or sets a positive *Double* value that represents the speed at which the media is played back. A value of 1 indicates normal speed. Values greater than or less than 1 represent the ratio of playback speed. For example, a value of 2 indicates double speed, and a value of .5 indicates half speed.

TABLE 3-14 Important Methods of *MediaPlayer* and *MediaElement*

METHOD	DESCRIPTION
Open	Opens the indicated media file. Takes a URI that points to the media file as an argument. This method is available only in *MediaPlayer*.
Pause	Pauses playback of the current file but does not change the *Position* property.
Play	Begins playback of the file or resumes playback of the file if the *Pause* method has been called.
Stop	Stops playback and sets the *Position* property to the beginning of the file.

To play audio with *MediaPlayer*:

1. Declare a new instance of *MediaPlayer*, as shown here:

   Sample of Visual Basic Code

   ```
   Dim aPlayer As New System.Windows.Media.MediaPlayer()
   ```

   Sample of C# Code

   ```
   System.Windows.Media.MediaPlayer aPlayer = new MediaPlayer();
   ```

2. Load the media file with the *Load* method, as shown here:

   Sample of Visual Basic Code

   ```
   aPlayer.Open(new Uri("crash.mp3"))
   ```

   Sample of C# Code

   ```
   aPlayer.Open(new Uri("crash.mp3"));
   ```

3. Use the *Play* method to play the file, as shown here:

   Sample of Visual Basic Code

   ```
   aPlayer.Play()
   ```

Sample of C# Code
```
aPlayer.Play();
```

To play audio or video automatically with *MediaElement*:

1. In XAML, declare a new *MediaElement*, as shown here:

   ```
   <MediaElement Margin="52,107,66,35" Name="mediaElement1"/>
   ```

2. Set the *Source* property declaratively, as shown in bold here:

   ```
   <MediaElement Margin="52,107,66,35" Source="crash.mp3"
     Name="mediaElement1"/>
   ```

3. The media will be played as soon as it is loaded, which will be soon after the window loads. To have manual control over when the media plays, see the next procedure.

To play audio or video manually with *MediaElement*:

1. In XAML, declare a new *MediaElement*, as shown here:

   ```
   <MediaElement Margin="52,107,66,35" Name="mediaElement1"/>
   ```

2. Set the *Source* property declaratively, as shown in bold here:

   ```
   <MediaElement Margin="52,107,66,35" Source="crash.mp3"
     Name="mediaElement1"/>
   ```

3. Set the *LoadedBehavior* property to *Manual*, as shown in bold here:

   ```
   <MediaElement Margin="52,107,66,35" Source="crash.mp3"
     LoadedBehavior="Manual" Name="mediaElement1"/>
   ```

4. In code, call the *Play* method to play the media, as shown here:

   Sample of Visual Basic Code
   ```
   mediaElement1.Play()
   ```

   Sample of C# Code
   ```
   mediaElement1.Play();
   ```

 Quick Check

- What is the difference between MediaPlayer and MediaElement?

Quick Check Answer

- Although both MediaPlayer and MediaElement encapsulate the same functionality, MediaElement has a visual representation, whereas MediaPlayer is a component without a visual interface. Thus, MediaElement should be used to play video in your applications.

Handling Media-Specific Events

MediaPlayer and *MediaElement* raise three media-specific events, detailed in Table 3-15.

TABLE 3-15 Media-Specific Events in *MediaPlayer* and *MediaElement*

EVENT	DESCRIPTION
MediaEnded	Raised when the media file has finished playing
MediaFailed	Raised when there is a problem finding or loading a file
MediaOpened	Raised when the media file has completed loading

The *MediaEnded* and *MediaOpened* events are standard WPF-routed events, and each provides an instance of *RoutedEventArgs* as a parameter to its handler. You can handle these events to run code when the file has loaded or ended in the same manner that you would any other event.

The *MediaFailed* event is somewhat different. Instead of raising an exception when media cannot be located or played, the *MediaElement* and *MediaPlayer* classes raise the *MediaFailed* event, thus allowing application execution to continue even if there is a problem with the media. Although an exception is raised by the initial media failure, this exception is wrapped in an instance of *ExceptionRoutedEventArgs*, which then is provided as a parameter to the handler for this event. You can retrieve an instance of the exception that was raised in the *ErrorException* property of the *ExceptionRoutedEventArgs* instance. By examining the properties of the wrapped exception, you can determine how you want your application to proceed. The following example demonstrates a simple method to handle the *MediaFailed* event and show a message box with the wrapped exception's message:

Sample of Visual Basic Code

```
Private Sub mediaElement1_MediaFailed(ByVal sender As System.Object, _
   ByVal e As System.Windows.ExceptionRoutedEventArgs)
   MessageBox.Show(e.ErrorException.Message)
End Sub
```

Sample of C# Code

```
private void mediaElement1_MediaFailed(object sender,
   ExceptionRoutedEventArgs e)
{
   MessageBox.Show(e.ErrorException.Message);
}
```

PRACTICE **Creating a Basic Media Player**

In this practice, you create a rudimentary media player with the capability to load and play audio and video files and to start, stop, and pause the playback.

EXERCISE Creating a Basic Media Player

1. From the CD, open the partial solution for Chapter 3, Lesson 2. The partial solution includes a reference to the *System.Windows.Forms* namespace. You use the *OpenFileDialog* class from this namespace to browse the file system.

2. In the XAML, add a *MediaElement* to the top row of the *Grid* control and set the *LoadedBehavior* property to *Manual*, as shown here:

```
<MediaElement LoadedBehavior="Manual" Margin="0" Name="MediaElement1"/>
```

3. In XAML, add four buttons to the toolbar with the *Open*, *Play*, *Pause*, and *Stop* display text and define *Click* event handlers for each, as shown here:

```
<ToolBar Grid.Row="1" Margin="0" Name="ToolBar1">
    <Button Click="Button_Click">Open</Button>
    <Button Click="Button_Click_1">Play</Button>
    <Button Click="Button_Click_2">Pause</Button>
    <Button Click="Button_Click_3">Stop</Button>
</ToolBar>
```

4. In the designer, double-click the *Open* button to open the *Click* event hander. Add the following code:

Sample of Visual Basic Code

```
aDialog.ShowDialog()
MediaElement1.Source = New Uri(aDialog.FileName)
MediaElement1.Play()
```

Sample of C# Code

```
aDialog.ShowDialog();
MediaElement1.Source = new Uri(aDialog.FileName);
MediaElement1.Play();
```

5. In the designer, double-click the *Play* button to open the *Click* event handler. Add the following code:

Sample of Visual Basic Code

```
MediaElement1.Play()
```

Sample of C# Code

```
MediaElement1.Play();
```

6. In the designer, double-click the *Pause* button to open the *Click* event handler. Add the following code:

Sample of Visual Basic Code

```
MediaElement1.Pause()
```

Sample of C# Code

```
MediaElement1.Pause();
```

7. In the designer, double-click the *Stop* button to open the *Click* event handler. Add the following code:

Sample of Visual Basic Code

```
MediaElement1.Stop()
```

Sample of C# Code

```
MediaElement1.Stop();
```

8. In the designer, add a definition for the *MediaElement1.MediaFailed* event, as shown in bold here:

```
<MediaElement MediaFailed="MediaElement1_MediaFailed"
   LoadedBehavior="Manual" Margin="0" Name="MediaElement1"/>
```

9. In the code editor, add the following code to the *MediaElement1_MediaFailed* method:

Sample of Visual Basic Code

```
MessageBox.Show("Media loading unsuccessful. " & e.ErrorException.Message)
```

Sample of C# Code

```
MessageBox.Show("Media loading unsuccessful. " + e.ErrorException.Message);
```

10. Press F5 to build and run your application. Click the *Open* button, browse to a media file, then test the functionality of each button. Now click *Open* and browse to a non-media file to ensure that the error-handling code works correctly.

Lesson Summary

- The *SoundPlayer* object provides lightweight support for playing uncompressed .wav files. It cannot play compressed .wav files or any other type of sound file. You can create a *SoundPlayer* object declaratively by creating a *SoundPlayerAction* object.

- *MediaPlayer* provides sophisticated support for playing media files. *MediaPlayer* can play a variety of audio and video file types, although it lacks a visual interface. *MediaElement* wraps a media player and provides a visual interface for playing video. Both elements provide support for influencing volume, balance, and playback of media.

- *MediaPlayer* and *MediaElement* do not throw exceptions when there is a problem with a media file. Instead, you must handle the *MediaFailed* event, which contains a wrapped exception that indicates the problem and enables you to take appropriate action.

Lesson Review

You can use the following questions to test your knowledge of the information in Lesson 2, "Adding Multimedia Content." The questions are also available on the companion CD of this book if you prefer to review them in electronic form.

1. Which is the correct strategy for handling errors caused by media failing to load in a *MediaElement*?

   A. Trap the error in a *Try...Catch* block and provide code to enable the application to recover from the failure.

   B. Ignore media errors because they do not cause the application to crash.

   C. Handle the *MediaElement.MediaFailed* event.

   D. Verify that the correct type of file has been opened in the *MediaElement .MediaOpened* event.

2. Which is the best choice for playing uncompressed .wav files in an application?

   A. *SoundPlayer*

   B. *MediaPlayer*

   C. *MediaElement*

   D. Either A or B, depending on the application requirements

Case Scenario

In the following case scenario, you apply what you've learned about how to add and manage content. You can find answers to these questions in the "Answers" section at the end of this book.

Case Scenario: The Company with Questionable Taste

You're creating an application for a company that has a strange sense of style; it seems to have been influenced by concerts that the founders attended in the early 1970s. They would like the main application to be stark black and white, but they want all user input to show up in tie-dyed colors. In addition, in the upper left corner of the application, they would like a media file containing concert video to run continuously—and the video must be in the shape of a dancing bear. The art department has supplied you with a *Path* object in the shape of a dancing bear, but the rest is up to you.

Answer the following questions for your manager:

1. How can you create tie-dyed user input?

2. How will you ever make video in the shape of a dancing bear?

Suggested Practices

To help you successfully master the exam objectives presented in this chapter, complete the following tasks.

On Your Own

Complete these suggested practices on your own to reinforce the topics presented in this chapter.

- **Practice 1**   Improve the media player application from Lesson 2 to allow the user to control volume, balance, and playback speed.

- **Practice 2**   Explore the *VisualBrush* and *ImageBrush* classes and create an application that uses these brushes to paint the background with a variety of effects.

- **Practice 3**   Create a media player application that can access media files embedded as binary resources. (Hint: You will need to use the File IO system more than once.)

Take a Practice Test

The practice tests on this book's companion CD offer many options. For example, you can test yourself on just the content covered in this chapter, or you can test yourself on all the 70-511 certification exam content. You can set up the test so that it closely simulates the experience of taking a certification exam, or you can set it up in study mode so that you can look at the correct answers and explanations after you answer each question.

> **MORE INFO PRACTICE TESTS**
>
> For details about all the practice test options available, see the "How to Use the Practice Tests" section in this book's Introduction.

CHAPTER 4

Windows Forms and Windows Forms Controls

Windows Forms is the basis for most Microsoft Windows applications, and you can configure it to provide a variety of user interface (UI) options. The developer can create forms of various sizes and shapes and customize them to the user's needs. Forms are hosts for *controls*, which provide the main functionality of the UI. You can use special controls called *container controls* to control the layout of the UI and individual controls to implement application-specific functionality. Menus and toolbars allow your users quick access to standard applicaton functionality. In this chapter, you learn about the building blocks of Windows Forms applications.

Exam objectives in this chapter:

- Choose the most appropriate control class.

Lessons in this chapter:

Before You Begin

To complete the lessons in this chapter, you must be familiar with Microsoft Visual Basic or Microsoft Visual C# and comfortable with the following tasks:

- Opening Visual Studio and creating a Windows Forms project
- Dragging controls from the Toolbox to the designer
- Setting properties in the Properties window

 REAL WORLD

Matt Stoecker

Although Windows Presentation Foundation (WPF) is definitely the future of Windows application development, Windows Forms represents its rich and colorful past. With many years of successful adoption behind it, many companies are still fully entrenched in Windows Forms development and are likely to remain that way for some time. It is essential for a Windows developer in today's world to have a grasp of both WPF and Windows Forms technology.

Lesson 1: Working with Windows Forms and Container Controls

This lesson describes how to create and configure Windows Forms and container controls. You learn how to create forms and refer to them in code, alter the visual properties of the forms, and control the behavior of the forms at run time. You learn how to add controls to a form or to a container control, and to configure various kinds of container controls to create dynamic and varied layouts for controls in your form.

> **After this lesson, you will be able to:**
> - Add a Windows form to a project at design time.
> - Add a new Windows form at run time.
> - Resize a window at design time or run time.
> - Identify and set the properties that determine a form's appearance and behavior at run time.
> - Refer to the default instance of a form in code.
> - Add a control to a form or container control at design time.
> - Add a control to a form or container at run time.
> - Group and arrange controls with the *Panel* control.
> - Group and arrange controls with the *GroupBox* control.
> - Group and arrange controls with the *TabControl* control.
> - Group and arrange controls with the *FlowLayoutPanel* control.
> - Group and arrange controls with the *TableLayoutPanel* control.
> - Create dynamic container areas with the *SplitContainer* control.
>
> **Estimated lesson time: 1 hour**

Overview of Windows Forms

Windows Forms is the basic building block of the UI. It provides a container that hosts controls and menus and enables you to present an application in a familiar and consistent fashion. Forms can receive user input in the form of keystrokes or mouse interactions and can display data to the user through hosted controls. Although it is possible to create applications that do not contain forms, such as console applications or services, most applications that require sustained user interaction will include at least one Windows form, and complex applications frequently require several forms to enable the program to execute in a consistent and logical fashion.

When you create a new Windows Forms project, a form named Form1 is added to your project by default. You can edit your form by adding controls and other visual elements in the designer, which is a graphic representation of a designable, visual element (such as a form) that appears in the Visual Studio Integrated Development Environment (IDE). Figure 4-1 shows the Visual Studio IDE.

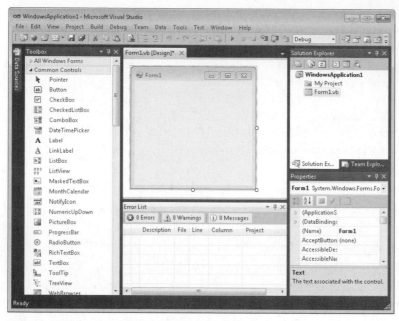

FIGURE 4-1 A Windows form in the Visual Studio IDE.

Adding Forms to Your Project

Most projects will require more than one form. You can add and configure additional forms at design time, or you can create instances of predesigned forms in code at run time.

To add a new form to your project at design time, first, from the Project menu, select Add Windows Form. The Add New Item dialog box opens. Then, select Windows Form and type a name for the new form in the Name box. Click Add to add the form to the development environment.

You can add and configure as many forms as your application needs at design time. You can also create new instances of forms in your code. This method is most often employed when you want to display a form that has already been designed. In Visual Basic, you can access default instances of a form by referring to that form by name. For example, if you have a form named *Form1* in your application, you can refer to it directly by its name, *Form1*. To access the default instance of a form at run time (Visual Basic only), refer to the form by its class name. You can call methods or access properties from this default instance. For example:

Sample of Visual Basic Code

```
Form1.Text = "This is my form"
Form1.Show()
```

Note that if you are referring to a form from within that form's code, you cannot use the default instance. To access a form's methods and properties from inside its code, use the keyword *Me* (Visual Basic) or *this* (C#). For example:

Sample of Visual Basic Code

```
Me.Text = "Coho Winery - Main Page"
```

Sample of C# Code

```
this.Text = "Coho Winery - Main Page";
```

You can also create new instances of forms at run time by declaring a variable that represents a type of form and creating an instance of that form. To add a form to your application at run time, declare and instantiate a variable that represents your form. This example assumes that you have already designed a form named *Form1* in your project:

Sample of Visual Basic Code

```
Dim myForm As Form1
myForm = New Form1()
' Displays the new form
myForm.Show()
```

Sample of C# Code

```
Form1 myForm;
myForm = new Form1();
// Displays the new form
myForm.Show();
```

Properties of Windows Forms

The visual appearance of your UI is an important part of your application. A UI that is poorly designed is difficult to learn and will increase training time and expense. You can modify the appearance of your UI by using Windows Forms properties.

Windows Forms contains a variety of properties to customize the appearance and behavior of the form. You can view and change these properties in the Properties window of the designer, as shown in Figure 4-2.

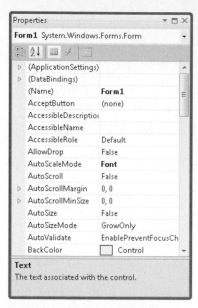

FIGURE 4-2 The Properties window.

Table 4-1 summarizes some of the Windows Forms properties that are important in the appearance and behavior of the application. This is not an exhaustive list of all Windows Forms properties, but rather a selected subset.

TABLE 4-1 Some Properties of the *Form* Class

PROPERTY	DESCRIPTION
(Name)	Sets the name of the *Form* class shown in the designer. This property can be set only at design time.
Backcolor	Indicates the background color of the form.
BackgroundImage	Indicates the background image of the form.
BackgroundImageLayout	Determines how the image indicated by the *BackgroundImage* property will be laid out on the form. If no background image is selected, this property has no effect.
ControlBox	Determines whether the form has a Control/System menu box.
Cursor	Indicates the cursor that appears when the cursor is moved over the form.
Enabled	Determines whether the form is able to receive user input. If *Enabled* is set to *False*, all controls contained by the form are likewise disabled.

Font	Sets the default font for the form. All controls contained by the form will also adopt this font unless their *Font* property is set separately.
ForeColor	Indicates the forecolor of the form, which is the color used to display text. All controls contained by the form will also adopt this forecolor unless their *ForeColor* property is set separately.
FormBorderStyle	Indicates the appearance and behavior of the form border and title bar.
HelpButton	Indicates whether the form has a Help button.
Icon	Indicates the icon used to represent this form.
Location	When the *StartPosition* property is set to Manual, this property indicates the starting location of the form relative to the upper left corner of the screen.
MaximizeBox	Indicates whether the form has a maximize box.
MaximumSize	Determines the maximum size for the form. If this property is set to a size of (0,0), the form has no upper size limit.
MinimizeBox	Indicates whether the form has a minimize box.
MinimumSize	Determines the minimum size to which the user can resize the form.
Opacity	Represents the opacity or, conversely, the transparency of the form from 0% to 100%. A form with 100% opacity is completely opaque, and a form with 0% opacity is completely transparent.
Size	Gets and sets the initial size of the form.
StartPosition	Indicates the position of the form when the form is first displayed.
Text	Determines the text caption of the form.
TopMost	Indicates whether the form always appears above all other forms that do not have this property set to *True*.
Visible	Determines whether the form is visible when running.
Windowstate	Determines whether the form is minimized, maximized, or set to the size indicated by the *Size* property when first shown.

Modifying the Appearance and Behavior of the Form

You can use the property grid to set properties of the form at design time. Properties set in this manner will retain their values until the application starts, at which time they can be set in code.

You can set most properties of a form at run time. The generalized scheme for setting a simple property is to use the assignment operator (=) to assign a value to a property. The following example demonstrates how to set the *Text* property of a form:

Sample of Visual Basic Code

```
Form1.Text = "This is Form 1"
```

Sample of C# Code

```
Form1.Text = "This is Form 1";
```

Some properties, such as the *Font* or *Size* properties, are more complex. Their value is represented by an instance of a class or structure. For these properties, you can either set the property to an existing instance of the class or create a new instance that specifies any subvalues of the property and assign it to the property, as shown in the following pseudocode example:

Sample of Visual Basic Code

```
PropertyY = New Class(value,value)
```

Sample of C# Code

```
PropertyY = new Class(value,value);
```

The (*Name*) property, which represents the name of the *Form* class, is an exception. This property is used within the namespace to identify the class of which the *Form* is a unique instance and, in the case of Visual Basic, accesses the default instance of the form.

Setting the Title of the Form

The name of the form is the name that refers to the *Form* class or the default instance of a form (Visual Basic only) in code, but it is also useful for the form to have a title that is visible to users. This title might be the same as the name of the form, but is more often a description of the form itself, such as Data Entry. The title can also convey information to the user, such as "Processing Entries—My Application" or "Customer Entry—My Application." The title appears in the title bar and on the taskbar.

You can change the title of a form by changing the *Text* property. To change the title of a form at design time, set the *Text* property of the form in the Property grid. To change the title of a form at run time, set the *Text* property of the form in code, as shown in the following code:

Sample of Visual Basic Code

```
Form1.Text = "Please enter your address"
```

Sample of C# Code

```
Form1.Text = "Please enter your address";
```

Setting the Border Style of the Form

The border style of a form determines how the border of the form looks and, to a certain extent, how a form behaves at run time. Depending on the setting, the *FormBorderStyle* property can control how the border appears, whether a form is resizable by the user at run time, and whether various control boxes appear (although these are also determined by other form properties). The *FormBorderStyle* property has seven possible values, explained in Table 4-2.

TABLE 4-2 Values for the *FormBorderStyle* Property

VALUE	DESCRIPTION
None	The form has no border and has no minimize, maximize, help, or control boxes.
FixedSingle	The form has a single border and the user cannot resize it. It can have a minimize, maximize, help, or control box as determined by other properties.
Fixed3D	The form's border has a three-dimensional appearance and the user cannot resize it. It can have a minimize, maximize, help, or control box as determined by other properties.
FixedDialog	The form has a single border and the user cannot resize it. Additionally, it has no control box. It can have a minimize, maximize, or help box as determined by other properties.
Sizable	This is the default setting for a form. The user can resize it, and it can contain a minimize, maximize, or help box as determined by other properties.
FixedToolWindow	The form has a single border and the user cannot resize it. The window contains no boxes except the close box.
SizableToolWindow	The form has a single border and the user can resize it. The window contains no boxes except the close box.

You can set the *FormBorderStyle* property at either design time or run time. To change the border style of a form at design time, set the *FormBorderStyle* property in the Property grid. To change the border style of a form at run time, set the *FormBorderStyle* property in code, as shown in the following example:

Sample of Visual Basic Code

```
aForm.FormBorderStyle = FormBorderStyle.Fixed3D
```

Sample of C# Code

```
aForm.FormBorderStyle = FormBorderStyle.Fixed3D;
```

Setting the Startup State of the Form

The *Windowstate* property determines what state the form is in when it first opens. This property has three possible values: *Normal*, *Minimized*, and *Maximized*. The default setting is *Normal*. When *Windowstate* is set to *Normal*, the form will start at the size determined by the *Size* property. When it is set to *Minimized*, the form will start up minimized in the taskbar. When it is set to *Maximized*, the form will start up maximized. Although you can set this property at run time, doing so will have no effect on the state of the form. Thus, it is useful to set this property in the Property grid at design time only.

Resizing the Form

When the *Windowstate* property is set to *Normal*, it will start at the size determined by the *Size* property—actually an instance of the *Size* structure, which has two members, *Width* and *Height*. You can resize the form by setting the *Size* property in the Property grid, or you can set *Width* and *Height* separately by expanding the *Size* property and setting the values for the individual fields.

You can also resize the form by grabbing and dragging the lower right corner, the lower edge, or the right-side edge of the form in the designer. As the form is visibly resized in the designer, the *Size* property is automatically set to the new size.

You can resize the form at run time by setting the *Size* property in code. The *Width* and *Height* fields of the *Size* property are also exposed as properties of the form itself. You can set either the individual *Width* and *Height* properties or the *Size* property to a new instance of the *Size* structure, as shown in the following example:

Sample of Visual Basic Code

```
' Set the Width and Height separately
aForm.Width = 300
aForm.Height = 200
' Set the Size property to a new instance of the Size structure
aForm.Size = New Size(300,200)
```

Sample of C# Code

```
// Set the Width and Height separately
aForm.Width = 300;
aForm.Height = 200;
// Set the Size property to a new instance of the Size structure
aForm.Size = new Size(300,200);
```

Note that if the form's *StartPosition* property is set to *WindowsDefaultBounds*, the size will be set to the window's default rather than to the size indicated by the *Size* property.

Specifying the Startup Location of the Form

The startup location of the form is determined by a combination of two properties. The first property is the *StartPosition* property, which determines where in the screen the form will be when first started. The *StartPosition* property can be set to any of the values contained within the *FormStartPosition* enumeration. Table 4-3 lists the *FormStartPosition* enumeration values.

TABLE 4-3 *StartPosition* Property Settings

VALUE	DESCRIPTION
Manual	The starting location of the form is set by the form's *Location* property. (See the following options.)
CenterScreen	The form starts up in the center of the screen.
WindowsDefaultLocation	The form is positioned at the Windows default location and is set to the size determined by the *Size* property.
WindowsDefaultBounds	The form is positioned at the Windows default location and the size is determined by the Windows default size.
CenterParent	The form's starting position is set to the center of the parent form.

If the *StartPosition* property is set to *Manual*, the form's starting position is set to the location specified by the form's *Location* property, which is dictated by the location of the form's upper left corner. For example, to start the form in the upper left corner of the screen, set the *StartLocation* property to *Manual* and the *Location* property to *(0,0)*. To start the form 400 pixels to the right and 200 pixels below the upper left corner of the screen, set the *Location* property to *(400,200)*.

Keeping a Form on Top of the User Interface

At times, you might want to designate a form to stay on top of other forms in the UI. For example, you might design a form that presents important information about the program's execution that you always want the user to be able to see. You can set a form to always be on top of the UI by setting the *TopMost* property to *True*. When the *TopMost* property is *True*, the form will always appear in front of any forms that have the *TopMost* property set to *False*, which is the default setting. Note that if you have more than one form with the *TopMost* property set to *True*, they can cover each other.

Opacity and Transparency in Forms

You can use the *Opacity* property to create striking visual effects in your form. The *Opacity* property sets the transparency of the form. When set in the Property grid, the opacity value can range from 0 percent to 100 percent, indicating the degree of opacity. An opacity of 100 percent indicates a form that is completely opaque (solid and visible), and a value of 0 percent indicates a form that is completely transparent. Values between 0 percent and 100 percent result in a partially transparent form.

You can also set the *Opacity* property in code. When the *Opacity* property is set in code, it is set to a value between 0 and 1, with 0 representing complete transparency and 1 representing complete opacity. The following example demonstrates how to set a form's opacity to 50 percent:

Sample of Visual Basic Code

```
aForm.Opacity = 0.5
```

Sample of C# Code

```
aForm.Opacity = 0.5;
```

The *Opacity* property can be useful when it is necessary to keep one form in the foreground but monitor action in a background form or to create interesting visual effects. A control usually inherits the opacity of the form that hosts it.

Setting the Startup Form

If your Windows Forms application contains multiple forms, you must designate one as the startup form; it is the first form to be loaded on execution of your application. The method for setting the startup form depends on whether you are programming in Visual Basic or C#.

In Visual Basic, you can designate a form as the startup form by setting the Startup Form project property, which is done in the project Properties window, as shown in Figure 4-3:

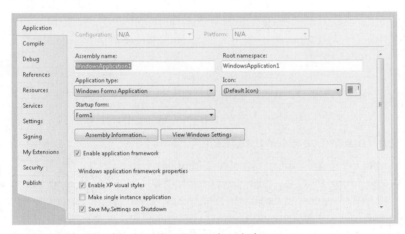

FIGURE 4-3 The Visual Basic project Properties window.

To set the startup form in Visual Basic:

1. In Solution Explorer, click the name of your project. The project name is highlighted.

2. In the Project menu, choose *<applicationName>* Properties, where *<applicationName>* represents the name of your project.

3. On the Application tab, under Startup Form, choose the appropriate form from the drop-down menu.

Setting the startup form in C# is slightly more complicated. The startup object is specified in the *Main* method. By default, this method is located in the *Program* class in a file called Program.cs, which Visual Studio automatically creates. The *Program* class contains, by default, a *Main* method, as follows:

```
static void Main()
{
    Application.EnableVisualStyles();
```

```
Application.SetCompatibleTextRenderingDefault(false);
Application.Run(new Form1());
}
```

The startup object is indicated by the line

```
Application.Run(new Form1());
```

You can set the startup form for the project by changing this line in the *Program* class to the form that you want to start the application. For example, if you wanted a form called *myForm* to be the startup form, you would change this line to read as follows:

```
Application.Run(new myForm());
```

To set the startup form in C#:

1. In Solution Explorer, double-click Program.cs to view the code. The code window opens.

2. Locate the *Main* method and then locate the line that reads:

    ```
    Application.Run(new Form());
    ```

    where *Form* represents the name of the form that is currently the startup form.

3. Change *Form* to the name of the form you want to set as the startup form.

Making the Startup Form Invisible

At times, you might want the startup form to be invisible at run time. For example, you might want a form to execute a time-consuming process when starting and not appear until that process is complete. The *Visible* property determines whether a form is visible at run time. You can set the *Visible* property either in the Property grid or in code. If you set *Visible* to *False* in the property window, the form will be invisible at startup.

To make a form invisible during execution, set the *Visible* property to *False* in code, as shown in the following example:

Sample of Visual Basic Code

```
aForm.Visible = False
```

Sample of C# Code

```
aForm.Visible = false;
```

 Quick Check

1. **How can you specify the startup location of a form?**

2. **How do you set the startup form?**

Overview of Container Controls

Container controls are specialized controls that serve as customizable containers for other controls. Examples of container controls include the *Panel*, *FlowLayoutPanel*, and *SplitContainer* controls. Container controls give the form logical and physical subdivisions that can group other controls into consistent UI subunits. For example, you might contain a set of related *RadioButton* controls in a *GroupBox* control. The use of container controls helps create a sense of style or information flow in your UI and enables you to manipulate contained controls in a consistent fashion.

When a container control holds other controls, changes to the properties of the container control can affect the contained controls. For example, if the *Enabled* property of a panel is set to *False*, all the controls contained in the panel are disabled. Likewise, changes to properties related to the UI, such as *BackColor*, *Visible*, or *Font*, are also applied to the contained controls. Note that you can still manually change any property inside a contained control, but if the container is disabled, all controls inside that container will be inaccessible, regardless of their individual property settings.

The *Controls* Collection

Each form and container control has a property called *Controls*, which represents the collection of controls contained by that form or control. When a control is added to a form or container control at design time, the designer automatically adds it to the controls collection of that form or container control and sets the location property as appropriate. You can also add a new control at run time dynamically by manually creating a new control and adding the control to the controls collection.

Adding a Control to a Form or Container Control in the Designer

There are four ways to add a control to a form or container control in the designer:

- Drag the control from the Toolbox to the surface of the form or container control.
- Select a control in the Toolbox and then draw it on the form with the mouse.
- Select a control in the Toolbox and double-click the form.
- Double-click the control in the Toolbox.

Adding a Control to a Form or Container Control at Run Time

To add a control to a form or container control at run time, manually instantiate a new control and add it to the *Controls* collection of the form, as shown in the following example. You must set any properties of the control, such as the *Location* or *Text* properties, before adding it to the *Controls* collection. The following sample code assumes that you have added a *Panel* container named *Panel1* (panels are discussed later in this chapter in the section "The *Panel* Control"):

Sample of Visual Basic Code

```
Dim aButton As New Button()
' Sets the relative location in the containing control or form
aButton.Location = New Point(20,20)
aButton.Text = "Test Button"
' Adds the button to a panel called Panel1
Panel1.Controls.Add(aButton)
' Adds the button to the current form
Me.Controls.Add(aButton)
```

Sample of C# Code

```
Button aButton = new Button();
// Sets the relative location in the containing control or form
aButton.Location = new Point(20,20);
aButton.Text = "Test Button";
// Adds the button to a panel called Panel1
Panel1.Controls.Add(aButton);
// Adds the button to the current form
this.Controls.Add(aButton);
```

The *Anchor* Property

The *Anchor* and *Dock* properties of a control dictate how it behaves inside its form or parent control. The *Anchor* property enables you to define a constant distance between one or more edges of a control and one or more edges of a form or other container. Thus, if a user resizes a form at run time, the control edges will always maintain a specific distance from the edges. The default setting for the *Anchor* property is *Top*, *Left*, meaning that the top and left edges of the control always maintain a constant distance from the top and left edges of the form. If the *Anchor* property was set to *Bottom*, *Right*, for example, the control would "float" when the form was resized to maintain the constant distance between the bottom and right edges of the form. If opposite properties are set for the *Anchor* property, such as *Top* and *Bottom*, the control will stretch to maintain the constant distance of the control edges to the form edges.

You can set the *Anchor* property to any combination of *Top*, *Bottom*, *Left*, *Right*, or none of these. The Properties window presents a visual interface, shown in Figure 4-4, that aids in choosing the value for the *Anchor* property.

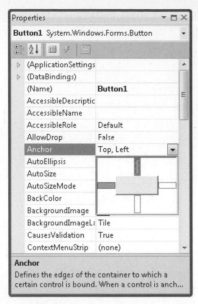

FIGURE 4-4 Choosing the *Anchor* property.

The *Dock* Property

The *Dock* property enables you to attach your control to the edge of a parent control, which can be a form or a container control, such as a *Panel* control or a *TabControl* control.

Like the *Anchor* property, the *Dock* property provides a special visual interface that enables you to choose the property value graphically. Figure 4-5 shows this interface.

FIGURE 4-5 Choosing the *Dock* property.

To set the *Dock* property, click the section of the interface that corresponds to where you want your control to dock. For example, to dock your control to the right side of the form, click the bar on the right of the interface. To release docking, choose None. Clicking the center of the *Dock* property interface sets the *Dock* property to a value of *Fill*, which means the control will dock to all four sides of the form and fill the control in which it resides.

The *GroupBox* Control

The *GroupBox* control is a container control that appears as a subdivision of the form surrounded by a border. It does not provide scrollbars, like the *Panel* control, nor does it provide any kind of specialized layout capabilities. *GroupBox* can have a caption, which is set by the *Text* property, or it can appear without a caption when the *Text* property is set to an empty string.

The most common use for *GroupBox* controls is for grouping *RadioButton* controls. *RadioButton* controls placed within a single *GroupBox* are mutually exclusive, but are not exclusive of *RadioButtons* elsewhere in the form or in other *GroupBox* controls. *RadioButton* controls are discussed in greater detail later in this chapter. Table 4-4 describes *Text*, the most important unique property of the *GroupBox* control.

TABLE 4-4 The *Text* Property of the *GroupBox* Control

PROPERTY	DESCRIPTION
Text	Represents the caption of the *GroupBox* enclosure. If no caption is desired, this property should be set to an empty string.

The *Panel* Control

The *Panel* control creates a subsection of a form that can host other controls. *Panel* can be indistinguishable from the rest of the surrounding form, or it can be surrounded by a border as determined by the *BorderStyle* property. *Panel* can have a *BorderStyle* property of *None*, which indicates no border; *FixedSingle*, which indicates a single edge around the *Panel*; or *Fixed3D*, which represents a border with a three-dimensional appearance.

The *Panel* control is a scrollable control, which means that it supports horizontal and vertical scroll bars. Controls can be hosted in *Panel* outside its visible bounds. When the *AutoScroll* property is set to *True*, scroll bars will automatically be available if any controls are placed outside the visible bounds of the control. If the *AutoScroll* property is set to *False*, controls outside the visible bounds of the *Panel* control are inaccessible. Table 4-5 shows the important properties of the *Panel* control.

TABLE 4-5 Important Properties of the *Panel* Control

PROPERTY	DESCRIPTION
AutoScroll	Determines whether *Panel* will display scroll bars when controls are hosted outside the visible bounds of the *Panel*. Scroll bars are displayed when this property is set to *True* and are not displayed when it is set to *False*.
BorderStyle	Represents the visual appearance of the *Panel* border. This property can be set to *None*, which indicates no border; *FixedSingle*, which creates a single-line border; or *Fixed3D*, which creates a border with a three-dimensional appearance.

The *FlowLayoutPanel* Control

The *FlowLayoutPanel* control is a subclass of the *Panel* control. Like the *Panel* control, it is most commonly used to create a distinct subsection of the form that hosts related controls. Unlike the *Panel* control, however, the *FlowLayoutPanel* dynamically repositions the controls it hosts when it is resized at either design time or run time. This provides a great aid to UI design, because control positions are automatically adjusted as the size and dimensions of the *FlowLayoutPanel* are adjusted, and it provides dynamic realignment of the UI (much like an HTML page) if the *FlowLayoutPanel* is resized at run time.

Like the *Panel* control, the *FlowLayoutPanel* control is scrollable. Scroll bars are enabled when *AutoScroll* is set to *True* and are disabled when *AutoScroll* is set to *False*.

The default flow direction of the *FlowLayoutPanel* is from left to right, meaning that controls placed in the *FlowLayoutPanel* will locate in the upper left corner and then flow to the right until they reach the edge of the panel. The *FlowDirection* property controls this behavior. You can set the *FlowDirection* property to four possible values: *LeftToRight*, which is the default; *RightToLeft*, which provides flow from right to left; *TopDown*, in which the controls flow from the top of the control to the bottom; and *BottomUp*, in which controls flow from the bottom of the *FlowLayoutPanel* to the top.

After the end of a row (in the case of *LeftToRight* and *RightToLeft FlowDirection* settings) or column (in the case of *TopDown* and *BottomUp FlowDirection* settings) is reached, the flow will wrap or not wrap to the next row or column as determined by the value of the *WrapContents* property. If *WrapContents* is set to *True* (which is the default), controls will automatically wrap to the next column or row. If it is set to *False*, controls will not automatically form new rows or columns.

You can manually create breaks in the flow of the controls that are analogous to line breaks in text. When the *WrapContents* property of a *FlowLayoutPanel* control is set to *False*, you must manually set flow breaks to manage the flow, but you can also set flow breaks when *WrapContents* is set to *True* if you desire individual breaks. You can set a flow break on a control by calling the *SetFlowBreak* method of the *FlowLayoutPanel*.

To set a flow break on a control hosted in *FlowLayoutPanel*, set the flow break by using the *SetFlowBreak* method as shown in the following example (which assumes that a *FlowLayoutPanel* control named *Flp* and a *Button* control named *aButton* have already been created):

Sample of Visual Basic Code

```
Flp.SetFlowBreak(aButton, True)
```

Sample of C# Code

```
Flp.SetFlowBreak(aButton, true);
```

Regardless of whether there is room in the *FlowLayoutPanel* control to continue the flow of controls, a control that has had a flow break set by this method will start a new row (or column, depending on the value of the *FlowDirection* property) in *FlowLayoutPanel*.

You can query a particular control to determine whether it has had a flow break set for it by calling the *GetFlowBreak* method, as shown in the following example:

Sample of Visual Basic Code

```
If Flp.GetFlowBreak(aButton) Then
    ' Continue processing
End If
```

Sample of C# Code

```
if (Flp.GetFlowBreak(aButton))
{
// Continue processing
}
```

Table 4-6 lists important properties and methods of the *FlowLayoutPanel* control.

TABLE 4-6 Important Members of the *FlowLayoutPanel* Control

PROPERTY/METHOD	DESCRIPTION
AutoScroll	Property. Determines whether the *FlowLayoutPanel* will display scroll bars when controls are hosted outside the visible bounds of the *Panel*. Scroll bars are displayed when set to *True* and are not displayed when set to *False*.
BorderStyle	Property. Represents the visual appearance of the *Panel* border. It can be set to *None*, which indicates no border; *FixedSingle*, which creates a single-line border; or *Fixed3D,* which creates a border with a three-dimensional appearance.
FlowDirection	Property. Determines the direction of flow in *FlowLayoutPanel*. Can be set to *LeftToRight*, *RightToLeft*, *TopDown*, or *BottomUp*.
WrapContents	Property. Determines whether controls will automatically wrap to the next column or row when the *FlowLayoutPanel* is resized.

GetFlowBreak	Method. Returns a Boolean value that indicates whether a particular control has had a flow break set.
SetFlowBreak	Method. Sets a flow break on a control contained in *FlowLayoutPanel*.

The *TableLayoutPanel* Control

Like the *FlowLayoutPanel* control, the *TableLayoutPanel* control is a specialized panel that aids in the design and layout of the UI. *TableLayoutPanel* is essentially a table that provides cells for the individual hosting of controls. Like other panels, it is a scrollable container that provides scroll bars when the *AutoScroll* property is set to *True*.

At design time, *TableLayoutPanel* appears on the form as a table of individual cells. You can drag controls from the Toolbox into each of the cells. Generally, only one control can be hosted in a single cell. However, for complicated UI designs, you can nest other container controls inside *TableLayoutPanel* cells, each of which can host multiple controls.

At run time, the *CellBorderStyle* property determines the appearance of the cells. You can set this property to *None*, which displays no cell lines, or to *Single*, *Inset*, *InsetDouble*, *Outset*, *OutsetDouble*, or *OutsetPartial*, each of which gives a distinctive behavior and appearance to the table cells.

The *ColumnStyle* and *RowStyle* collections manage the columns and rows of the *TableLayoutPanel* control. At design time, you can set the styles of the rows and columns by choosing the *ColumnStyles* or *RowStyles* collection in the Property grid and launching the Columns And Rows Styles editor, shown in Figure 4-6.

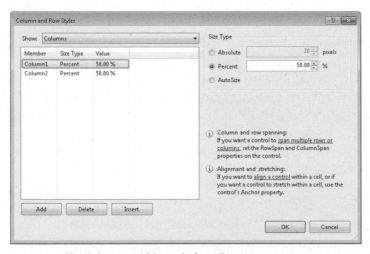

FIGURE 4-6 The Columns And Rows Styles editor.

You can alter column and row size styles with this editor. Column and row size styles can be set to *Absolute*, which indicates a fixed size in pixels, or they can be set to *Relative*, which indicates a percentage of the size of all columns or rows whose style is set to *Relative*. Columns and rows can also be set to *AutoSize*. When set to this value, the columns and rows will automatically adjust to the correct size.

Column and row styles can also be set manually in code by accessing the *ColumnStyles* and *RowStyles* collections in code. You can access the style for a particular column or row by the index of that column or row. Styles can be set as shown in the following example:

Sample of Visual Basic Code

```
TableLayoutPanel1.ColumnStyles(0).SizeType = SizeType.Absolute
TableLayoutPanel1.ColumnStyles(0).Width = 20
TableLayoutPanel1.RowStyles(0).SizeType = SizeType.Percent
TableLayoutPanel1.RowStyles(0).Height = 50
```

Sample of C# Code

```
TableLayoutPanel1.ColumnStyles[0].SizeType = SizeType.Absolute;
TableLayoutPanel1.ColumnStyles[0].Width = 20;
TableLayoutPanel1.RowStyles[0].SizeType = SizeType.Percent;
TableLayoutPanel1.RowStyles[0].Height = 50;
```

If you set a row or column style to a size type of anything other than *SizeType.Absolute*, you can also set *Width* (for columns) or *Height* (for rows). These values are set in either pixels or percentages, whichever is appropriate for the *SizeType* setting of *ColumnStyle*.

When adding new controls to *TableLayoutPanel* at run time, you can use either of two overloads of the *TableLayoutPanel.Controls.Add* method. The first is the standard *Add* method, as follows:

Sample of Visual Basic Code

```
TableLayoutPanel1.Controls.Add(aButton)
```

Sample of C# Code

```
TableLayoutPanel1.Controls.Add(aButton);
```

This method simply adds the control to the controls collection of *TableLayoutPanel*, and the control is inserted into the next open cell in the table. If there are no more open cells, the behavior of *TableLayoutPanel* is determined by the value of the *GrowStyle* property. If the *GrowStyle* property is set to *AddRows*, additional rows will be added to accommodate new controls. If the *GrowStyle* property is set to *AddColumns*, new columns will be added when needed. If the *GrowStyle* property is set to *FixedSize*, no new cells may be added. If you attempt to add a control to *TableLayoutPanel* with a *GrowStyle* value of *FixedSize*, an exception will be thrown.

You can also add a control to a specific cell by using the *Controls.Add* method, as follows:

Sample of Visual Basic Code

```
TableLayoutPanel1.Controls.Add(aButton,3,3)
```

Sample of C# Code

```
TableLayoutPanel1.Controls.Add(aButton,3,3);
```

Columns in *TableLayoutPanel* are numbers starting at 1, whereas rows are numbers starting at 0. Thus, the preceding example adds *aButton* to the cell in column 3 at row 3, which is actually the third column and the fourth row that the user sees. Note, however, that if a cell is already occupied by a control, your control might not be added to that cell. Controls added to cells at design time generally have precedence over controls added at run time. In these cases, the control is simply added to the next available cell. If you add the control to a cell that contains another control that has been added at run time, the cell already in that position will usually be moved down to the next available cell in favor of the control that was just added. As always, careful testing is important.

To add a control to a *TableLayoutPanel* control at run time:

1. Declare and instantiate a new control in code.

2. Use the *TableLayoutPanel.Controls.Add* method to add the control. An example follows:

Sample of Visual Basic Code

```
Dim aButton As New Button()
' Adds the Button to the next available cell
TableLayoutPanel1.Controls.Add(aButton)
' Adds the Button to a cell at (2,2)
TableLayoutPanel1.Controls.Add(aButton, 2, 2)
```

Sample of C# Code

```
Button aButton = new Button();
// Adds the Button to the next available cell
TableLayoutPanel1.Controls.Add(aButton);
// Adds the Button to a cell at (2,2)
TableLayoutPanel1.Controls.Add(aButton, 2, 2);
```

Table 4-7 lists important properties and methods of the *TableLayoutPanel* control.

TABLE 4-7 Important Members of the *TableLayoutPanel* Control

PROPERTY/METHOD	DESCRIPTION
AutoScroll	Property. Determines whether *TableLayoutPanel* will display scroll bars when controls are hosted outside the visible bounds of *Panel*. Scroll bars are displayed when this property is set to *True* and are not displayed when it is set to *False*.
CellBorderStyle	Property. Determines the style of the cell borders. This property can be set to *None*, which indicates no cell borders, or to a variety of different visual styles.
ColumnCount	Property. Indicates the number of columns. You can add or remove columns by incrementing or decrementing the *ColumnCount* property.

Columns	Property. Represents the collection of columns. Available only at design time; accessing this property launches the Columns And Rows Styles editor.
ColumnStyles	Property. Represents the collection of column styles. Available only at run time.
GrowStyle	Property. Represents how *TableLayoutPanel* grows when new controls are added to it. This property can be set to *AddColumns*, *AddRows*, or *FixedSize*.
RowCount	Property. Indicates the number of rows. You can add or remove rows by incrementing or decrementing the *RowCount* property.
Rows	Property. Represents the collection of rows. Available only at design time; accessing this property launches the Columns And Rows Styles editor.
RowStyles	Property. Represents the collection of row styles. Available only at run time.
Controls.Add	Method of the *Controls* collection. Can be used to add a control either to the next available cell or to a specific cell identified by its column and row coordinates.

The *TabControl* Control

The *TabControl* control enables you to group sets of controls in tabs, rather like files in a filing cabinet or dividers in a notebook. For example, you might create property pages for an application in which each page represents the properties of a specific component. *TabControl* serves as a host for one or more *TabPage* controls, which themselves contain controls. The user can switch between tab pages (and the controls contained therein) by clicking the tabs on *TabControl*.

The most important property of *TabControl* is the *TabPages* property. *TabPage* controls are specialized container controls that are hosted only inside *TabControl* controls. Each *TabPage* has its own set of properties, and you can access these properties by editing the *TabPages* property at design time. This launches the TabPage Collection Editor, as shown in Figure 4-7.

Individual *TabPage* controls are a lot like *Panel* controls. They are scrollable controls and will generate scroll bars as needed if the *AutoScroll* property is set to *True*. Individual *TabPage* controls also have a *Text* property, which represents the text shown in the tab that represents this page in the *TabControl*. Also, like *Panel* controls, *TabPage* controls have a *BorderStyle* property that can be set to *None*, *FixedSingle*, or *Fixed3D*, with results similar to those in the *Panel* control.

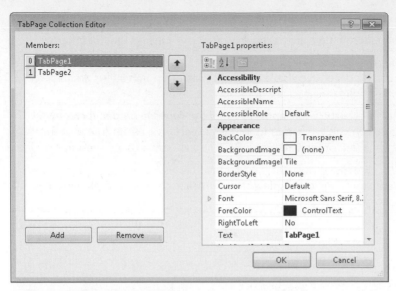

FIGURE 4-7 TabPage Collection Editor.

TabControl has several properties you can use to customize the behavior and appearance of the control. The *Appearance* property controls how the tabs look. This property can be set to *Normal*, *Buttons*, or *FlatButtons*, each of which generates a different visual style. The *Alignment* property determines whether the tabs appear on the top, bottom, left, or right of the tab control. *TabControl* also has a property called *Multiline*, which indicates whether more than one row of tabs is allowed. When it is set to *True*, multiple rows of tabs are supported. When it is set to *False*, only a single row of tabs is allowed. Important properties of the *TabControl* control and *TabPage* control are shown in Table 4-8 and Table 4-9, respectively.

TABLE 4-8 Important Properties of the *TabControl* Control

PROPERTY	DESCRIPTION
Appearance	Determines the visual style of *TabControl*
Alignment	Determines whether the tabs appear on the top, bottom, left, or right of the tab control
Multiline	Determines whether more than one row of tabs is allowed on the tab control
TabPages	Represents the collection of *TabPage* controls hosted by *TabControl*

TABLE 4-9 Important Properties of the *TabPage* Control

PROPERTY	DESCRIPTION
AutoScroll	Determines whether *TabPage* will display scroll bars when controls are hosted outside the visible bounds of the panel. Scroll bars are displayed when set to *True* and are not displayed when set to *False*.
BorderStyle	Represents the visual appearance of the *TabPage* border. It can be set to *None*, which indicates no border; *FixedSingle*, which creates a single-line border; or *Fixed3D*, which creates a border with a three-dimensional appearance.
Text	Represents the text displayed on the tab in the tab control that represents this *TabPage*.

The *SplitContainer* Control

The *SplitContainer* control creates a subsection of the form where *Splitter* divides *SplitContainer* into two *SplitterPanel* controls that function similarly to *Panel* controls. The user can grab *Splitter* with the mouse and move its location, thus changing the relative size of each *SplitterPanel* control. The *SplitContainer.Dock* property is set to *Fill* by default, because the most common use for *SplitContainer* controls is to create divided Windows forms.

SplitContainer exposes its two child *SplitterPanel* controls through its *Panel1* and *Panel2* properties. These properties enable you to access the properties of the contained *SplitterPanel* controls.

Each *SplitterPanel* control contained by the *SplitContainer* control functions in basically the same way as a *Panel* control. It can host controls and is distinct from the rest of the form. It can display scroll bars when the *AutoScroll* property is set to *True*. The individual *SplitterPanel* controls of a *SplitContainer* do not have individual borders, so they expose no *BorderStyle* property like stand-alone *Panel* controls do, but the *SplitContainer* control itself does have a *BorderStyle* property. Like the *BorderStyle* property of the *Panel* control, this property can be set to *None*, *FixedSingle*, or *Fixed3D*. When the *BorderStyle* property is set, it also affects the appearance of *Splitter*.

The orientation of *Splitter* is determined by the *Orientation* property. When it is set to *Vertical*, *Splitter* stretches from the top to the bottom of *SplitContainer*. When it is set to *Horizontal*, *Splitter* stretches from left to right.

The *FixedPanel* property enables you to designate a panel in *SplitContainer* that will remain constant in size if the control is resized. This property can be set to *Panel1* so that only *Panel2* will be resized, to *Panel2* so that only *Panel1* will be resized, or to *None* so that both panels will be resized proportionally when the control is resized. Note that a panel is fixed by the *FixedPanel* property only when the *SplitContainter* control is resized. The user is still able to resize the panels by grabbing and moving *Splitter* with the mouse.

You can disable the ability of the user to move *Splitter* by setting the *IsSplitterFixed* property. When it is set to *True*, *Splitter* is fixed in its location and the user cannot move it. You can manually move *Splitter* in code by changing the *SplitterDistance* property in code. This property represents the distance, in pixels, of *Splitter* from the left edge (when *Orientation* is *Horizontal*) or the top edge (when *Orientation* is *Vertical*). You can change the thickness of *Splitter* by setting the *SplitterWidth* property, which is also represented in pixels.

You can hide one of the panels in *SplitContainer* by setting either the *Panel1Collapsed* or *Panel2Collapsed* property to *True*. When one of these properties is set to *True*, the corresponding panel is collapsed, and the other panel expands to fill *SplitContainer*. Note that you cannot set both of these properties to *True*. For example, if you set *Panel1Collapsed* to *True* when *Panel2Collapsed* is already set to *True*, *Panel2Collapsed* will be set to *False*.

You can set a minimum size for individual panels by setting the *Panel1MinSize* and *Panel2MinSize* properties. These properties represent the minimum number of pixels to which a panel can be sized. Table 4-10 shows the important properties of the *SplitContainer* control.

TABLE 4-10 Important Properties of the *SplitContainer* Control

PROPERTY	DESCRIPTION
BorderStyle	Represents the visual appearance of the *TabPage* border. It can be set to *None*, which indicates no border; *FixedSingle*, which creates a single-line border; or *Fixed3D*, which creates a border with a three-dimensional appearance.
FixedPanel	Represents the panel of *SplitContainer* that is fixed in size. This property can be set to *Panel1*, *Panel2*, or *None* (in which case no panel has a fixed size).
IsSplitterFixed	Determines whether the location of *Splitter* is fixed and cannot be moved by the user.
Orientation	Determines whether *Splitter* is oriented horizontally or vertically in *SplitContainer*. It can be set to *Horizontal* or *Vertical*.
Panel1	Exposes the properties of the *SplitContainer* control's *Panel1*.
Panel1Collapsed	Determines whether *Panel1* is collapsed or regular size. The panel is collapsed when this property is set to *True*.
Panel1MinSize	Gets or sets the minimum size for *Panel1*.
Panel2	Exposes the properties of the *SplitContainer* control's *Panel2*.
Panel2Collapsed	Determines whether *Panel2* is collapsed or regular size. The panel is collapsed when this property is set to *True*.
Panel2MinSize	Gets or sets the minimum size for *Panel2*.
SplitterDistance	Represents the distance of *Splitter* from either the top or left edge of the form, depending on the value of the *Orientation* property.
SplitterWidth	Gets or sets the width of *Splitter* in pixels.

Quick Check

1. What is the purpose of the *Dock* property?

2. What are containers, and what are they used for?

Quick Check Answers

1. The *Dock* property enables you to attach a control to one of the sides of the form or to fill all available space in the form.

2. Containers are specialized controls that can host other controls. They can provide a variety of control-display layouts.

PRACTICE **Using Container Controls**

In this practice, you practice using container controls by creating a Windows form with a variety of container controls.

EXERCISE Practice with Container Controls

1. Open Visual Studio and create a new Windows Forms project.

2. From the Toolbox, drag a tab control to the surface of the form. In the Property grid, set the *Dock* property to *Fill*.

3. In the Property grid, choose the *TabPages* property to open the TabPages Collection Editor. Add tab pages until there is a total of four pages. Set the *Text* properties of these four *TabPage* controls to **GroupBox**, **FlowLayoutPanel**, **TableLayoutPanel**, and **SplitContainer**, respectively. Click OK.

4. In the form, select the tab labeled GroupBox. From the Toolbox, drag a *GroupBox* control onto the surface of the *TabPage* control.

5. Drag two *RadioButton* controls into the *GroupBox* control.

6. In the form, select the tab labeled FlowLayoutPanel. From the Toolbox, drag a *FlowLayoutPanel* control onto the surface of the *TabPage* control. Set the *Dock* property of the *FlowLayoutPanel* to *Fill*.

7. From the Toolbox, add four *Button* controls to *FlowLayoutPanel*.

8. Double-click Button1 and add the following code to the *Click* event handler:

   Sample of Visual Basic Code

   ```
   FlowLayoutPanel1.SetFlowBreak(Button3, True)
   ```

   Sample of C# Code

   ```
   flowLayoutPanel1.SetFlowBreak(button3, true);
   ```

9. Select the designer for the form. In the form, select the tab labeled TableLayoutPanel. From the toolbox, add a *TableLayoutPanel* control to the *TabPage* control. Set the *CellBorderStyle* property to *Inset* and *AutoScroll* to *True*.

10. From the Toolbox, add a *Button* control to the upper left cell of *TableLayoutPanel*.

11. Double-click the button and add the following code to the *Click* event handler:

Sample of Visual Basic Code

```
Dim aButton As New Button
TableLayoutPanel1.Controls.Add(aButton, 1, 1)
```

Sample of C# Code

```
Button aButton = new Button();
tableLayoutPanel1.Controls.Add(aButton, 1, 1);
```

12. In the designer, choose the SplitContainer tab. From the Toolbox, add a *SplitContainer* control to this tab page. Set the *BorderStyle* property to *Fixed3D*.

13. From the Toolbox, add two *Button* controls to *Panel1* of the *SplitContainer*. Set the *Text* properties of these buttons to **Fix/Unfix Panel1** and **Fix/Unfix Splitter**. Resize the form, *Panel1*, and the buttons as necessary to display the text.

14. Add a *Button* to *Panel2* and set the *Text* property to **Collapse/Uncollapse Panel1**. Resize the button as necessary to display the text.

15. Double-click the button labeled Fix/Unfix Panel1 and add the following code to the *Click* event handler:

Sample of Visual Basic Code

```
If SplitContainer1.FixedPanel = FixedPanel.Panel1 Then
      SplitContainer1.FixedPanel = FixedPanel.None
Else
      SplitContainer1.FixedPanel = FixedPanel.Panel1
End If
```

Sample of C# Code

```
if (splitContainer1.FixedPanel == FixedPanel.Panel1)
{
    splitContainer1.FixedPanel = FixedPanel.None;
}
else
{
    splitContainer1.FixedPanel = FixedPanel.Panel1;
}
```

16. Double-click the button labeled Fix/Unfix Splitter and add the following code to the *Click* event handler:

Sample of Visual Basic Code

```
SplitContainer1.IsSplitterFixed = Not SplitContainer1.IsSplitterFixed
```

Sample of C# Code

```
splitContainer1.IsSplitterFixed = !(splitContainer1.IsSplitterFixed);
```

17. Double-click the button labeled Collapse/Uncollapse Panel1 and add the following code to the *Click* event handler:

Sample of Visual Basic Code
```
SplitContainer1.Panel1Collapsed = Not SplitContainer1.Panel1Collapsed
```

Sample of C# Code
```
splitContainer1.Panel1Collapsed = !(splitContainer1.Panel1Collapsed);
```

18. Press F5 to run the application.

19. On the GroupBox tab, alternately select the option buttons and note that they are automatically mutually exclusive.

20. On the FlowLayoutPanel tab, resize the form with the mouse. Note the automatic change in layout that occurs. With the form resized to fit all the buttons on one row, click Button1 and note the effect of setting a flow break on Button3.

21. On the TableLayoutPanel tab, click Button5 several times to observe how new controls are added to *TableLayoutPanel*.

22. On the SplitContainer tab, resize the form and resize each panel by moving the splitter. Click each button in turn and observe the effect on the ability of the *SplitContainer* control to resize.

Lesson Summary

- You can alter the appearance and behavior of a form by changing the form's properties. Properties such as *Text*, *FormBorderStyle*, *Windowstate*, *Size*, *StartPosition*, *TopMost*, *Visible*, and *Opacity* enable you to create a variety of visual styles and effects.

- You can designate the startup form in the project properties window for Visual Basic or by changing the startup form in the *Main* method for C#. The *Main* method is usually found in the *Program* class, which is autogenerated.

- You can create nonrectangular forms by creating a new instance of the *Region* class and then setting the form's *Region* property to that new instance.

- You can use container controls to group and arrange controls on a form. Container controls include *Panel*, *GroupBox*, *FlowLayoutPanel*, *TableLayoutPanel*, and *SplitContainer* controls.

- *GroupBox* controls are usually used to group *RadioButton* controls.

- *Panel* controls create distinct subsections of a form. *FlowLayoutPanel* controls and *TableLayoutPanel* controls are derivatives of the *Panel* control that provide added layout capabilities.

- *SplitContainer* encapsulates two *SplitterPanel* controls and a *Splitter* control. The user can resize the panels by grabbing and moving the splitter.

- The *TabControl* control maintains a collection of *TabPage* controls that each function similarly to individual panels. The user can select each tab page at run time by choosing the corresponding tab displayed on the edge of the tab control.

Lesson Review

You can use the following questions to test your knowledge of the information in Lesson 1, "Working with Windows Forms and Container Controls." The questions are also available on the companion CD if you prefer to review them in electronic form.

> **NOTE ANSWERS**
>
> Answers to these questions and explanations of why each answer choice is correct or incorrect are located in the "Answers" section at the end of the book.

1. Which of the following code samples demonstrates how to add a new instance of a Windows form named *Form1* at run time?

   A.

   Sample of Visual Basic Code

   ```
   Dim myForm As Form1
   myForm = Form1.CreateForm()
   ```

   Sample of C# Code

   ```
   Form1 myForm;
   myForm = Form1.CreateForm();
   ```

   B.

   Sample of Visual Basic Code

   ```
   Dim myForm As Form1
   myForm.Show()
   ```

   Sample of C# Code

   ```
   Form1 myForm;
   myForm.Show();
   ```

   C.

   Sample of Visual Basic Code

   ```
   myForm = Form1
   myForm.Show()
   ```

   Sample of C# Code

   ```
   myForm = Form1;
   myForm.Show();
   ```

   D.

   Sample of Visual Basic Code

   ```
   Dim myForm As Form1
   myForm = New Form1()
   ```

Sample of C# Code

```
Form1 myForm;
myForm = new Form1();
```

2. Which of the following code samples correctly sets the title, border style, size, and opacity of a form?

A.

Sample of Visual Basic Code

```
Me.Text = "My Form"
Me.FormBorderStyle = FormBorderStyle.Fixed3D
Me.Size = New Size(300, 300)
Me.Opacity = 0.5
```

Sample of C# Code

```
this.Text = "My Form";
this.FormBorderStyle = FormBorderStyle.Fixed3D;
this.Size = new Size(300, 300);
this.Opacity = 0.5;
```

B.

Sample of Visual Basic Code

```
Me.Text = "My Form"
Me.BorderStyle = "Fixed3D"
Me.Size = New Size(300, 300)
Me.Opacity = 0.5
```

Sample of C# Code

```
this.Text = "My Form";
this.BorderStyle = "Fixed3D";
this.Size = new Size(300, 300);
this.Opacity = 0.5;
```

C.

Sample of Visual Basic Code

```
Me.Text = "My Form"
Me.FormBorderStyle = FormBorderStyle.Fixed3D
Me.Size = (300,300)
Me.Opacity = "100%"
```

Sample of C# Code

```
this.Text = "My Form";
this.FormBorderStyle = FormBorderStyle.Fixed3D;
this.Size = (300,300);
this.Opacity = "100%";
```

D.

Sample of Visual Basic Code

```
Me.Title = "My Form"
Me.FormBorderStyle = FormBorderStyle.Fixed3D
```

```
Me.Size = New Size(300,300)
Me.Opacity = "100%"
```

Sample of C# Code

```
this.Title = "My Form";
this.FormBorderStyle = FormBorderStyle.Fixed3D;
this.Size = new Size(300,300);
this.Opacity = "100%";
```

3. Which of the following code samples demonstrates how to set a flow break on a control named *aButton* in a *FlowLayoutPanel* control named *FLPanel1*?

A.

Sample of Visual Basic Code

```
aButton.SetFlowBreak()
```

Sample of C# Code

```
aButton.SetFlowBreak();
```

B.

Sample of Visual Basic Code

```
aButton.SetFlowBreak(FLPanel1)
```

Sample of C# Code

```
aButton.SetFlowBreak(FLPanel1);
```

C.

Sample of Visual Basic Code

```
FLPanel1.SetFlowBreak(aButton, True)
```

Sample of C# Code

```
FLPanel1.SetFlowBreak(aButton, true);
```

D.

Sample of Visual Basic Code

```
FLPanel1.aButton.SetFlowBreak
```

Sample of C# Code

```
FLPanel1.aButton.SetFlowBreak();
```

4. You are designing an application that includes a property page that enables the user to set properties of the application. These properties are divided into three categories: Appearance, Execution, and Memory Management. Which container control represents the best starting point for the user interface?

A. *TableLayoutPanel*

B. *FlowLayoutPanel*

C. *GroupBox*

D. *TabControl*

5. Which of the following is the correct way to add a control to a form at design time? (Choose all that apply.)

   A. Select a control in the Toolbox and double-click the form.

   B. Select a control in the Toolbox and draw on the form with the mouse.

   C. Double-click the control in the Toolbox.

   D. Select the control in the Toolbox and drag it to the form.

6. Which of the following code samples demonstrates the correct way to add a *Button* control to a form named *Form1* at run time?

   A.

   Sample of Visual Basic Code

   ```
   Form1.Controls.Add(Button)
   ```

   Sample of C# Code

   ```
   Form1.Controls.Add(Button);
   ```

   B.

   Sample of Visual Basic Code

   ```
   Dim aButton As New Button
   Form1.Controls.Add(aButton)
   ```

   Sample of C# Code

   ```
   Button aButton = new Button();
   Form1.Controls.Add(aButton);
   ```

   C.

   Sample of Visual Basic Code

   ```
   Dim aButton As New Button
   Form1.Add(aButton)
   ```

   Sample of C# Code

   ```
   Button aButton = new Button();
   Form1.Add(aButton);
   ```

   D.

   Sample of Visual Basic Code

   ```
   Form1.Add(New Button)
   ```

   Sample of C# Code

   ```
   Form1.Add(new Button);
   ```

7. Which code sample correctly demonstrates how to add a new panel to a *SplitContainer* control named *SpC1*?

A.

Sample of Visual Basic Code

```
SpC1.Controls.Add(New Panel)
```

Sample of C# Code

```
SpC1.Controls.Add(new Panel());
```

B.

Sample of Visual Basic Code

```
SpC1.Controls.Add(New SplitterPanel)
```

Sample of C# Code

```
SpC1.Controls.Add(new SplitterPanel());
```

C.

Sample of Visual Basic Code

```
SpC1.Add(New SplitterPanel)
```

Sample of C# Code

```
SpC1.Add(new SplitterPanel());
```

D.

Sample of Visual Basic Code

```
None of the above
```

Sample of C# Code

```
None of the above
```

Lesson 2: Configuring Controls in Windows Forms

This lesson describes general principles of creating and configuring controls and explores how to configure controls and create the UI in depth. Controls are graphical components that provide reproducible functionality you can use to create a consistent user interface experience over several applications. Microsoft Visual Studio provides controls for information display, data input, user interaction, and other specialized tasks.

After this lesson, you will be able to:

- Describe common properties of controls.
- Change the properties of controls at design time or at run time.
- Control the layout of your controls.
- Use the various mechanisms the IDE exposes to modify controls quickly.
- Design your UI in accordance with best practices.

Estimated lesson time: 1 hour

Overview of Controls

Controls are components that combine a graphical interface with predesigned functionality—reusable units of code designed to fulfill particular tasks. For example, the *TextBox* control is designed to display text and receive textual input from the user, and it provides properties, methods, and events that facilitate these tasks.

All controls inherit from the base class *Control* and, as such, share a variety of properties relating to size, location, and other general aspects of controls. Table 4-11 describes some of the common properties of controls.

TABLE 4-11 Common Properties of Controls

PROPERTY	DESCRIPTION
Anchor	Determines how the control is anchored in its parent form or container control.
BackColor	Gets or sets the *BackColor* of the control.
BackgroundImage	Represents the image painted as the background image of the control.
CausesValidation	Represents whether a control causes validation; validation enables you to verify that user input meets specific formatting and value requirements.
ContainsFocus	Indicates whether this control or one of its child controls has the focus.

Controls	Gets the collection of controls contained within this control. Used only for containers.
Cursor	Represents the cursor used when the mouse pointer is over this control.
Dock	Determines how the control is docked in its parent form or container control.
Enabled	Gets or sets whether the control is enabled. If a control is not enabled, it appears dimmed and cannot be selected or edited.
Font	Gets or sets the font used by this control to display text.
ForeColor	Represents the color used in the foreground of this control, primarily for displaying text.
HasChildren	Gets a value that indicates whether this control has any child controls.
Height	Represents the height of the control in pixels.
Location	Indicates the location of the upper left corner of this control relative to the upper left corner of its parent form or container control.
MaximumSize	Gets or sets the maximum size for the control.
MinimumSize	Gets or sets the minimum size for the control.
Name	Represents the name used to refer to the control in code. This property can be altered only at design time and cannot be modified at run time.
Parent	Gets or sets the parent form or container control for this control. Setting this property adds the control to the new parent's controls collection.
Region	Gets or sets the window region associated with the control.
Size	Represents the size of the control in pixels.
TabIndex	Indicates in what order the control is selected when the *Tab* key is used to navigate from control to control.
Tag	Enables the programmer to store a value or object associated with the control.
Text	Gets or sets the text associated with the control. The text might or might not be displayed, depending on the type of control and other property settings.
Visible	Indicates whether the control is visible.
Width	Represents the width of the control in pixels.

Configuring Controls at Design Time

You can add a control to a form or container control at design time by dragging it from the Toolbox, selecting it in the Toolbox and clicking the form, or double-clicking the control in the Toolbox. Using any of these methods, you can add the control to the design surface. When the control is in the designer, you can modify its properties. You can adjust many of the properties of a control graphically in the designer by using the mouse. For other properties, you can modify control properties in the Properties window.

Control Size and Location

The method of modifying a control with the mouse is intuitive and enables you to adjust the control to exactly the desired size. You adjust the size of a control with the mouse by first selecting the control, usually by clicking it in the designer. This causes the control to be outlined by white squares and a dotted line, as shown in Figure 4-8.

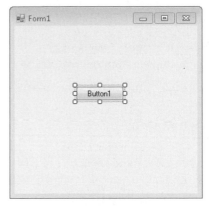

FIGURE 4-8 A selected *Button* control in the designer.

After the control has been selected, you can resize it in the designer by grabbing an edge or a corner and dragging it with the mouse.

You can also resize a control in the Properties window by modifying the *Size* property, which has two components—*Width* and *Height*—that represent the width and height of the control in pixels. You can modify these individual components by expanding the *Size* property and typing a new value for one of the components in the Properties window, or you can modify the *Size* property directly. The control is resized accordingly.

You can choose one of two ways to resize a control.

To resize a control at design time:

1. Select the control and then drag a corner or an edge to the appropriate size.
2. Modify the *Size* property in the Properties window by either changing the *Size* property directly or expanding the *Size* property and changing *Height* or *Width*.

The designer also provides an easy way to set the location of a control on a form or container control. You can change the location of a control graphically by grabbing the middle of the control with the mouse and dragging it to the new location.

You can also set the location of a control by modifying the *Location* property in the Properties window. The *Location* property represents the coordinates of the upper left corner of the control relative to the upper left corner of the parent form or container control. The *Location* property has two components, *X* and *Y*. You can modify the *Location* property directly in the Properties window, or you can expand the *Location* property and individually set the *X* and *Y* values. The property will relocate to the new location.

You can choose one of two ways to change the location of a control.

To change the location of a control at design time:

1. Grab the middle of the control with the mouse and drag it to the appropriate location.

2. Set the *Location* property of the control in the Properties window, either by setting the *Location* property directly or by expanding the *Location* property and modifying the values of *X* and *Y* as appropriate.

You can also reposition a group of controls graphically with the mouse. You must first select all the controls you want to move, either by outlining the appropriate controls with the mouse or by holding down the Ctrl key and clicking each control in turn. Figure 4-9 depicts a group of selected controls.

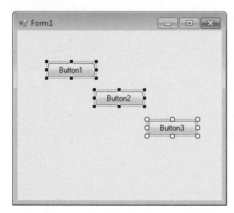

FIGURE 4-9 A group of selected controls in the designer.

After the group of controls is selected, you can move the group by grabbing the middle of one of the controls and moving it with the mouse. You can also set property values for multiple controls simultaneously by selecting multiple controls and setting a property in the Properties window.

Snaplines

Snaplines give you visual aid and feedback when locating controls on a form or within a container control. When you drag a control onto a form or container control, snaplines appear, providing cues relating to control alignment.

When you drag a control near the edge of a form, a container control, or another control, a snapline appears, indicating the distance represented by the *Margin* property. Also, snaplines indicating vertical and horizontal alignment of control edges appear when a control that is being dragged comes into alignment with an adjacent control. When a snapline appears, you can drop the control to create an aligned UI. Figure 4-10 displays horizontal, vertical, and margin snaplines.

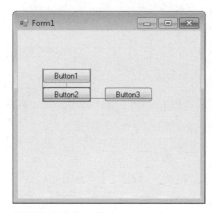

FIGURE 4-10 Snaplines.

If snaplines are disabled, you can enable them in the Options dialog box, as described in the following steps.

To enable snaplines:

1. From the Tools menu, select Options to open the Options dialog box.
2. In the left pane, expand Windows Forms Designer and select General.
3. In the right pane, set *LayoutMode* to *SnapLines*.
4. Click OK.

 Quick Check

- What is the purpose of snaplines?

Quick Check Answers

- Snaplines appear at design time and help you align controls to the form or to each other.

Modifying Control Properties at Design Time

Although you can modify properties of controls such as location and size by manipulating the control in the designer, other mechanisms enable you to set control properties in the designer, including those of the Properties window, smart tags, and Document Outline window.

The Properties Window

The primary interface for setting control properties is the Properties window, which exposes the properties of a form, component, or control that can be set at design time. You can set property values for most properties by selecting the property and typing a new value for the property into the Properties window. For some properties, such as the *Dock* and *Anchor* properties, the Properties window provides specialized graphical interfaces that assist in setting the property value. Figure 4-11 shows the Properties window.

FIGURE 4-11 The Properties window.

If the Properties window is not visible, you can open it with the following procedure.

To open the Properties window:

From the View menu, choose Properties Window or press F4.

To set a property in the Properties window:

1. Click the property you want to set.

2. Type the new value for the property or use the specialized interface if this property provides one.

The *Button* Control

One of the most familiar controls in the toolbox is the *Button* control, the primary control that enables command interaction between the user and the UI. The button can display a short string on its face and can respond to user clicks. The *Button* control gives a visual cue when clicked and exposes an *event handler* that enables the developer to write code that executes when the button is clicked.

The *Button* control exposes several properties that enable you to customize its appearance and behavior. Table 4-12 shows important properties of the *Button* control.

TABLE 4-12 Important Properties of the *Button* Control

PROPERTY	DESCRIPTION
AutoEllipsis	Enables the automatic handling of text that extends beyond the width of the button
DialogResult	Sets a *DialogResult* value that you can associate with the button, such as *DialogResult.OK* or *DialogResult.Cancel*
FlatAppearance	Defines styles that govern how the button appears and behaves when the *FlatStyle* property is set to *Flat*
FlatStyle	Sets the visual style of the button when a user moves the mouse over the button and clicks
Text	Sets the text that appears on the button
TextAlign	Indicates how the text displayed on the button is aligned

Responding to Clicks

The primary function of a *Button* control in the UI is to respond to user mouse clicks. When a user clicks a button, it typically causes code to be executed. For example, you might have an OK button that causes the application execution to continue after the user has provided necessary information, or you might have a Cancel button that returns execution to a previous step.

You can write code to be executed when the button is clicked by using the *Button.Click* event handler, a method activated when the button is clicked that then executes appropriate code.

To write code for the *Button.Click* event handler:

1. In the designer, double-click the button for which you want to write code.

   Visual Studio automatically generates a method declaration named *Button_Click* and adds code behind the scenes to configure the method to handle the *Button.Click* event. Visual Studio displays the new *Button_Click* method that runs when the user clicks the button.

2. Write the appropriate code in this method.

At run time, this code is executed when the button is clicked. The following code shows an example of a complete *Button_Click* method:

Sample of Visual Basic Code

```
Private Sub Button1_Click(ByVal sender As System.Object, ByVal e As _
    System.EventArgs)_
    Handles Button1.Click
    MsgBox("The Button has been clicked!")
End Sub
```

Sample of C# Code

```
private void button1_Click(object sender, EventArgs e)
{
    MessageBox.Show("The Button has been clicked!");
}
```

Responding to Other Clicks

Although the *Button.Click* event handler is useful for responding to simple clicks, you can also configure a button or other control to respond to other mouse clicks as well, such as right-clicks. You can respond to these clicks by using the *MouseDown* event.

One of the arguments for the *Button.MouseDown* event handler is an instance of *MouseEventArgs*. This argument contains detailed information about the location and click-state of the mouse and can be used to differentiate between left-clicks, right-clicks, double-clicks, and other mouse interactions. Table 4-13 describes the properties of the *MouseEventArgs* class.

TABLE 4-13 Properties of *MouseEventArgs*

PROPERTY	DESCRIPTION
Button	Indicates the mouse button that was pressed. Possible values are *Left*, *Right*, *Middle*, *None*, *XButton1*, or *XButton2*.
Clicks	Gets the number of times the button was pressed and released.
Delta	Gets a count of how many notches the mouse wheel has rotated.
Location	Gets the current location of the mouse pointer.
X	Gets the *X* coordinate of the mouse pointer.
Y	Gets the *Y* coordinate of the mouse pointer.

Using the values exposed by the *MouseEventArgs* instance, you can determine the button that was clicked and the position of the mouse wheel. Note that if any button other than the left button clicks a control, the control will not give the visual feedback (the "click" in the UI) that is customary for a button.

To respond to various mouse clicks:

1. In the designer, select the *Button* control for which you want to write code.

2. In the Properties window, click the lightning bolt toolbar button (shown in Figure 4-12) to view the *Button* control's events.

FIGURE 4-12 The lightning bolt toolbar button.

3. In the Properties window, double-click the cell next to *MouseDown* to have Visual Studio generate and display an event handler for *Button.MouseDown*.

4. Write code in this event handler that responds to the desired mouse click combination. The following example demonstrates how to differentiate between the left and right buttons:

Sample of Visual Basic Code

```
Private Sub Button1_MouseDown(ByVal sender As System.Object, ByVal e As _
  System.Windows.Forms.MouseEventArgs) Handles Button1.MouseDown
    Select Case e.Button
        Case Windows.Forms.MouseButtons.Left
            MsgBox("The left button was clicked")
        Case Windows.Forms.MouseButtons.Right
            MsgBox("The right button was clicked")
        Case Else
            MsgBox("Some other button was clicked")
    End Select
End Sub
```

Sample of C# Code

```
private void button1_MouseDown(object sender, MouseEventArgs e)
{
    switch (e.Button)
    {
        case MouseButtons.Left:
            MessageBox.Show("The left button was clicked");
            break;
        case MouseButtons.Right:
            MessageBox.Show("The right button was clicked");
            break;
        default:
            MessageBox.Show("Some other button was clicked");
            break;
    }
}
```

FlatStyle and FlatAppearance

The *FlatStyle* property determines whether the button has a three-dimensional, raised appearance or a flat appearance. You can give a button a flat appearance by setting the *FlatStyle* property to *Flat*.

When the *FlatStyle* property is set to *Flat*, the *FlatAppearance* property determines how the button looks and behaves in the UI. The *FlatAppearance* property is an instance of a structure that contains properties described in Table 4-14.

TABLE 4-14 Properties of *FlatAppearance*

PROPERTY	DESCRIPTION
BorderColor	Sets the color of the button border
BorderSize	Sets the size of the button border
MouseDownBackColor	Sets the color of the button when the left mouse button clicks this button
MouseOverBackColor	Sets the color of the button when the mouse pointer is over the button

When the *FlatStyle* is set to *Flat*, there are fewer built-in visual cues that allow the user to interact with the button. You can provide additional cues by setting appropriate values in the *FlatAppearance* property. The following procedure describes how to set the back color of the button when it is under the mouse.

To change the back color of a button when it is under the mouse:

1. In the Properties window, set the *FlatStyle* property to *Flat*.

2. Expand the *FlatAppearance* property.

3. In the *FlatAppearance* property, set the *MouseOverBackColor* property to the color you want the button to have when it is under the mouse.

Accept and Cancel Buttons

A common scenario when creating dialog forms is to create an Accept or Cancel button on the form that provides an appropriate *DialogResult* value to the form when clicked. You can use the *DialogResult* property of *Button* to create Accept or Cancel buttons.

To create an Accept or Cancel button:

1. From the Toolbox, drag a button onto the form and set the *Text* property to an appropriate value (for example, *Accept* for an Accept button).

2. In the Properties window, set the *DialogResult* property to *OK* for an Accept button or *Cancel* for a Cancel button.

3. In the designer, double-click the button to open the code window.

4. In the *Button_Click* event handler, close the form as shown here:

Sample of Visual Basic Code
```
Me.Close()
```

Sample of C# Code
```
this.Close();
```

When a form is shown with the *ShowDialog* method, it automatically returns the dialog result associated with the button that was clicked. The following example demonstrates how this form might be used. The hypothetical form is named *DialogForm*.

Sample of Visual Basic Code

```
Dim aForm As New DialogForm
Dim aResult As System.Windows.Forms.DialogResult
aResult = aForm.ShowDialog
If aResult = DialogResult.Ok Then
    ' Do something
    Else
    ' Do something else
End If
```

Sample of C# Code

```
Dialog aForm = new DialogForm();
System.Window.Forms.DialogResult aResult;
aResult = aForm.ShowDialog();
if (aResult == DialogResult.Ok)
{
    // Do something
}
else
{
    // Do something else
}
```

The *Label* Control

The *Label* control is primarily used to display read-only textual information to the user. For example, labels are frequently used to display an informative string beside a control, such as "First Name" beside a *TextBox* control meant to collect the user's first name. Labels can also be used to define shortcut keys for other controls.

The text displayed in a label is set in the label's *Text* property. You can set the label to resize itself automatically to the size of the text by setting the label's *AutoSize* property to *True*. If the *AutoSize* property is set to *False*, you can set the size of the label by grabbing and dragging the control edges in the designer.

You can use *Label* controls to define access keys for other controls. *Access keys* are keys that, when pressed in combination with the Alt key, move the focus to the desired control. The following procedure describes how to use a *Label* control to define an access key for another control.

To define an access key:

1. From the Toolbox, drag a *Label* control onto the form, near the control for which you want to define the access key (for example, a *TextBox* control).

2. In the Properties window, set the *Text* property to a descriptive name for the control. Precede the letter that you want to use for the access key with an ampersand

(&) character. For example, to use F as the access key, set the label's *Text* property to **&First Name**.

3. In the Properties window, set the *UseMnemonic* property to *True* (the default).

4. In the Properties window, set the *TabIndex* property to one less than the *TabIndex* property of the control for which you are defining an access key. Verify that no two controls have the same *TabIndex* value.

Creating Access Keys for Controls without Using Label Controls

Access keys enable the user to move the focus to a particular control by pressing the Alt key and the access key you have defined for a particular control. The following procedure describes how to create access keys for individual controls.

> **NOTE CREATING AN ACCESS KEY FOR A CONTROL**
>
> To create an access key for a control with this procedure, the control must be capable of receiving the focus, it must have a *Text* property, and it must have a *UseMnemonic* property. If the control for which you want to create an access key can receive the focus but does not have a *UseMnemonic* property, use the first procedure that uses a *Label* control to make the access key. If the control cannot receive the focus, you cannot create an access key for it by any procedure.

To create an access key for a control:

1. Set the *Text* property to the text you want the control to display.

2. In the *Text* property, prepend the letter you want to make the access key with the ampersand (&) symbol.

3. In the Properties window, set the *UseMnemonic* property to *True*. The letter preceded by the ampersand symbol appears underlined, and at run time the user is able to shift the focus to the control by pressing the Alt key along with the underlined key.

 Quick Check

1. What events of the *Button* control can be used to respond to mouse clicks?

2. What is the purpose of access keys?

Quick Check Answers

1. The *Click* event responds to the left-button click, and the *MouseDown* event can be used to respond to other button clicks.

2. Access keys enable you to provide keyboard shortcuts that move the focus to the control with which the access key is associated.

The *TextBox* Control

The *TextBox* control is the primary control used to receive textual input from the user; it enables you to receive text from and display text to the user. You can create text boxes that can display multiline text, and you can create text boxes that display a password character instead of the actual text.

The *TextBox* control exposes several properties that enable you to configure its behavior. Table 4-15 shows the important properties of the *TextBox* control.

TABLE 4-15 Important Properties of the *TextBox* Control

PROPERTY	DESCRIPTION
AutoCompleteCustomSource	Holds a string collection that contains autocomplete data when the *AutoCompleteMode* is set to a value other than *None* and the *AutoCompleteSource* is set to *Custom*.
AutoCompleteMode	Sets the *AutoComplete* mode of the control. Possible values are *None*, *Append*, *Suggest*, and *SuggestAppend*.
AutoCompleteSource	Sets the source for autocomplete data. Can be set to any of a variety of system sources or to a custom source provided by the *AutoCompleteCustomSource* property.
CharacterCasing	Indicates the casing of the characters in the *TextBox* control. Possible values are *Normal*, *Upper*, and *Lower*.
Lines	Returns a string array representing the individual lines of the text box. This property is most useful when *MultiLine* is set to *True*. Note that a line is defined as a string that is terminated by a carriage return character and does not refer to visible lines in the UI (as might be seen when the *WordWrap* property is set to *True*).
MaxLength	Specifies the maximum number of characters that can be entered into the text box.
MultiLine	Indicates whether the text box can contain only a single line of text or multiple lines.
PasswordChar	Sets the password character to be displayed in the text box instead of the actual text.
ReadOnly	Indicates whether the text in the text box can be edited.
ScrollBars	Indicates whether scroll bars are displayed in the text box when the *MultiLine* property is set to *True*.
Text	Gets or sets the text contained in the text box.

UseSystemPasswordChar	Indicates whether to display the system password instead of the actual text in the text box.
WordWrap	Indicates whether words automatically wrap from one line to the next when the *MultiLine* property is set to *True*.

The main purpose of the *TextBox* control is to provide a container for editable text. Users can input text into text boxes or edit textual data that the application displays. The text held by the *TextBox* property is accessible through the *Text* property. The text in *TextBox* is editable if the *ReadOnly* property is set to *False*, which is the default. If the *ReadOnly* property is set to *True*, the user cannot edit the text displayed.

Creating a Multiline *TextBox* Control

TextBox controls are single-line by default, but you can create a multiline *TextBox* control by setting the *MultiLine* property to *True*. This enables you to resize *TextBox* vertically as well as horizontally.

When the *MultiLine* property is set to *True*, several other properties become important. The *Lines* property exposes a string array that contains the individual lines of *TextBox*. The *ScrollBars* property indicates whether scroll bars are displayed for the text box and, if so, whether *Horizontal*, *Vertical*, or both are displayed. The *WordWrap* property indicates whether words automatically wrap from one line to the next. Note that if the *WordWrap* property is set to *True*, horizontal scroll bars never appear, even if the *ScrollBars* property is set to *Horizontal*.

Creating a Password *TextBox* Control

You can use the *PasswordChar* or *UseSystemPasswordChar* properties to create a text box that can receive text input but displays a masking character instead of the actual text, rendering the user input unreadable to observers. This is most commonly used to create a text box for entering a password. If the *PasswordChar* property is set to a character (for example, an asterisk ["*"]), that character is displayed whenever the user types a character into the text box. Note that the actual characters the user types are stored in the *Text* property; only the rendering of these characters in the UI changes. You can also set the *UseSystemPasswordChar* property to *True*, which will display the password character defined by the system for each character typed in the text box. If *UseSystemPasswordChar* is set to *True* and *PasswordChar* is set to a character, the system password character is used.

The *MaskedTextBox* Control

The *MaskedTextBox* control is a modified *TextBox* control that enables you to define a preset pattern for accepting or rejecting user input. The *Mask* property enables you to specify required or optional characters, specify whether input characters are letters or numbers, and apply formatting for the display of strings. Table 4-16 shows important properties of the *MaskedTextBox* control.

TABLE 4-16 Important Properties of the *MaskedTextBox* Control

PROPERTY	DESCRIPTION
AllowPromptAsInput	Indicates whether the prompt character is valid as input.
AsciiOnly	Indicates whether only ASCII characters are valid as input. When set to *True*, only A–Z and a–z are accepted as input.
BeepOnError	Indicates whether *MaskedTextBox* sends a system beep for every input character it rejects.
CutCopyMaskFormat	Determines whether literals and prompt characters are included when the text is cut or copied.
HidePromptOnLeave	Indicates whether prompt characters are hidden when *MaskedTextBox* loses the focus.
InsertKeyMode	Gets or sets the text insertion mode for *MaskedTextBox*.
Mask	Defines the input mask for *MaskedTextBox* (explained in detail in the following text).
PromptChar	Gets or sets the character used for the prompt.
RejectInputOnFirstFailure	Gets or sets a value indicating whether parsing of user input stops after the first invalid character is reached.
ResetOnPrompt	Indicates how an input character that matches the prompt character should be handled.
ResetOnSpace	Determines how a space input character should be handled.
SkipLiterals	Indicates whether literals in the mask should be reentered or skipped.
TextMaskFormat	Indicates whether prompt characters and literal characters are included in the text returned by the *Text* property.

The *Mask* Property

The most important property of the *MaskedTextBox* control is the *Mask* property, which enables you to define a string that represents the required format of an input string in *MaskedTextBox*. The *MaskedTextProvider* control associated with *MaskedTextBox* provides the parsing engine that parses the *Mask* format. Table 4-17 shows the code characters the default *MaskedTextProvider* uses.

TABLE 4-17 Elements of the Default *MaskedTextProvider* Control

MASKING ELEMENT	DESCRIPTION
0	Represents a required digit between 0 and 9.
9	Represents an optional digit between 0 and 9.
#	Represents an optional digit between 0 and 9 or a space. Plus (+) and minus (–) signs are also accepted.
L	Represents a required letter, either uppercase or lowercase (A–Z, a–z).
?	Represents an optional letter, either uppercase or lowercase (A–Z, a–z).
&	Represents a required character. If *AsciiOnly* is set to *True*, this element behaves like the *L* element.
C	Represents an optional character. If *AsciiOnly* is set to *True*, this element behaves like the [?] element.
A, a	Represents an optional alphanumeric character. If *AsciiOnly* is set to *True*, it accepts only A–Z and a–z.
.	Decimal placeholder. Represents a decimal character. The actual character used will be the decimal character set by the control's *FormatProvider*.
,	Thousands placeholder. Represents a thousands separator. The actual character used will be the thousands separator set by the control's *FormatProvider*.
:	Time separator. Represents a time separator. The actual character used will be the time separator character set by the control's *FormatProvider*.
/	Date separator. Represents a date separator. The actual character used will be the date separator set by the control's *FormatProvider*.
$	Currency symbol. Represents a currency symbol. The actual character used will be the currency symbol set by the control's *FormatProvider*.
<	Shift down. Converts all following characters to lowercase.
>	Shift up. Converts all following characters to uppercase.
|	Disables a previous shift up or shift down.
\	Escapes a mask character, turning it into a literal character. The double slash (\\) is the escape sequence for a backslash.
All other characters	All other characters appear as themselves in *MaskedTextBox*, and the user cannot move or delete them.

You can design a mask for the masked text box by creating a string made of characters described in Table 4-17. Setting the *Mask* property of *MaskedEditBox* restricts the input allowed to the format determined by the mask string. Table 4-18 shows some examples of mask strings, together with input strings and the output string displayed in the control.

TABLE 4-18 Examples of Mask Strings

MASK STRING	INPUT TEXT	DISPLAYED TEXT
(999)-000-0000	1234567890	(123)-456-7890
00/00/0000	07141969	07/14/1969 – Note that the actual date separator displayed is determined by the control's *FormatProvider*.
$99,999.00	1234567	$12,345.67 – Note that the actual currency symbol, thousands separator, and decimal separator are determined by the control's *FormatProvider*.
LL>L|LLL<LL	abcdABCD	abCdABcd

Configuring the *MaskedTextBox* Control for User Input

In addition to the *Mask* property, the *MaskedTextBox* control has several properties that affect how the control behaves when receiving user input. The *AsciiOnly* property determines whether only ASCII characters are allowed as input; when set to *True*, it restricts input to A–Z and a–z. Other inputs are rejected. You can set the control to notify users when an error has been committed by setting the *BeepOnError* property to *True*. The *SkipLiterals* property determines whether literal characters should be reentered by the user (if set to *False*) or skipped over in the masked text box (when set to *True*).

The *RejectInputOnFirstFailure* property governs how text pasted into *MaskedTextBox* is handled. If a string that does not match the *Mask* format is pasted into *MaskedTextBox*, *MaskedTextBox* rejects the entire string if the *RejectInputOnFirstFailure* is set to *True*. If set to *False*, *MaskedTextBox* accepts all the characters that match the *Mask* format.

The *Prompt* property sets the character displayed in *MaskedTextBox* when there is no input for a given position. The default value for the *Prompt* character is the underscore character (_). The *AllowPromptAsInput* and *ResetOnPrompt* properties govern how the prompt character is treated when entered as input. If the *ResetOnPrompt* property is set to *True*, prompt characters are accepted, *Mask* is reset for that character position, and the cursor advances to the next position. If the *ResetOnPrompt* property is set to *False* and the *AllowPromptAsInput* property is set to *True*, the prompt character is processed as regular input. If both properties are set to *False*, the prompt character is rejected. The *ResetOnSpace* property governs the treatment of spaces in the same way that *ResetOnPrompt* governs the treatment of prompt characters.

Manipulating Text in *MaskedTextBox*

The text shown in *MaskedTextBox* is not necessarily the text that is available to the user when cutting and pasting or to the application when text is manipulated programmatically. *CutCopyMaskFormat* determines how the text in *MaskedTextBox* is treated when the user cuts or copies it. The default value for this property is *IncludeLiterals*, in which case literals from the *Mask* are included when text is cut or copied, but prompt characters are not. You can also set this property to *ExcludePromptAndLiterals*, which excludes both literals and prompts; *IncludePrompt*, which includes prompt characters but excludes literals; and *IncludePromptAndLiterals*, which includes both prompts and literals. The *TextMaskFormat* property has the same possible values, and functions in the same way with respect to the text returned by the *Text* property.

 Quick Check

1. How can you create a *TextBox* control with more than one line?

2. What is the purpose of the *MaskedTextBox* control?

Quick Check Answers

1. You can create a multiline *TextBox* control by setting the *MultiLine* property to *True*.

2. The *MaskedTextBox* control is used to display a format to the user for data entry or display and to validate that data is input in the correct format.

PRACTICE **Using Text Display Controls**

In this lab, you add controls to a partial project. You add a multiline text box to prompt the user for an address, and you add a *MaskedTextBox* control to collect a phone number.

EXERCISE Adding Text Display Controls

1. In Visual Studio, load the partial solution for this lesson.

2. In Solution Explorer, double-click Form2 to open the designer for Form2.

3. From the Toolbox, drag a *TextBox* control onto the form. Drag a *Label* control onto the form next to the *TextBox* control.

4. Set the *Text* property of *Label* to **Address**.

5. Set the *Multiline* property of *TextBox* to *True* and set the *WordWrap* property to *False*. Set the *ScrollBars* property to *Both*. Resize *TextBox* to make it large enough to hold an address.

6. From the Toolbox, drag a *MaskedTextBox* control and a *Label* control onto the form.

7. Set the *Text* property of *Label* to **Phone Number**.

8. Set the *Mask* property of *MaskedTextBox* to **(999)-000-0000**.

9. *C# only*: Set the *Modifiers* property of *TextBox* and *MaskedTextBox* to **Internal**.

10. In Solution Explorer, right-click Form1 and choose View Code.

11. In the *LinkLabel1_LinkClicked* event handler, add the following code at the end of the *If* block:

Sample of Visual Basic Code

```
MsgBox("Your address is " & Form2.TextBox3.Text)
MsgBox("Your phone number is " & Form2.MaskedTextBox1.Text)
```

Sample of C# Code

```
MessageBox.Show("Your address is " + aForm.textBox3.Text);
MessageBox.Show("Your phone number is " + aForm.maskedTextBox1.Text);
```

12. Press F5 to run and test your application.

Lesson Summary

- You can modify individual properties of controls in the Properties window. Some properties provide specialized graphical interfaces to help you set the property value.

- The *Anchor* and *Dock* properties enable you to set specialized behaviors for controls on your form.

- The *Button* control is the primary command control for the UI. The *Button_Click* event handler is the method executed when the button is clicked. The button can respond to other mouse button clicks by means of the *MouseDown* event.

- The *FlatAppearance* property governs how a button looks and behaves when the *FlatStyle* property is set to *Flat*.

- By setting the *DialogResult* value of a *Button* control, you can create a Cancel or Accept button. You can then examine the result of the form as you would a standard dialog box.

- The *Label* control conveys read-only information to the user. You can use *Label* to define an access key by setting the *Text*, *TabOrder*, and *UseMnemonic* properties.

- The *TextBox* control enables the user to enter text. The text that is entered can be accessed through the *Text* property.

- *TextBox* controls can be single-line or multiline, depending on the value of the *MultiLine* property.

- The *MaskedTextBox* control can be configured for formatted text display and entry.

- The *Mask* property determines the formatting for text in *MaskedTextBox* controls.

Lesson Review

The following questions are intended to reinforce key information presented in Lesson 2, "Configuring Controls in Windows Forms." The questions are also available on the companion CD if you prefer to review them in electronic form.

> **NOTE ANSWERS**
>
> Answers to these questions and explanations of why each answer choice is correct or incorrect are located in the "Answers" section at the end of the book.

1. Which of the following can be used to modify the size of a control in a form at design time? (Choose all that apply.)

    A. Grabbing and dragging the edges of the control

    B. Setting the control size in the View menu

    C. Clicking the smart tag and entering a new size for the control

    D. Editing the *Size* property in the Properties window

2. Which of the following methods can be used to modify the location of controls in a form at design time? (Choose all that apply.)

    A. Changing the *Location* property in the Properties window

    B. Grabbing the control and moving it with the mouse

    C. Using the Layout toolbar to adjust control spacing

    D. Using the Location window to position controls graphically

3. Which setting of the *Anchor* property allows controls to float freely when the form is resized?

    A. *Top*

    B. *Top, Bottom*

    C. *None*

    D. *Right, Left*

4. Which setting of the *Dock* property causes the control to fill its form or container control?

    A. *Top*

    B. *Fill*

    C. *Top, Left, Right, Bottom*

    D. None; use the *Anchor* property

5. Which *Button* events can be used to respond to mouse clicks? (Choose all that apply.)

    A. *Button.Click*

    B. *Button.LinkClicked*

    C. *Button.MouseDown*

    D. *Button.MouseOver*

6. Which property does NOT control how a button looks or behaves when the *FlatStyle* property is set to *Flat*?

    A. *FlatAppearance.MouseOverBackColor*

    B. *FlatAppearance.MouseDownBackColor*

    C. *FlatAppearance.BorderSize*

    D. *FlatAppearance.Text*

7. Which is necessary to define an access key using a *Label* control? (Choose all that apply.)

    A. Set the *TabOrder* property so that the control for the access key is immediately after the *Label* control.

    B. Set the *UseMnemonic* property to *True*.

    C. Set the *Text* property with an ampersand to indicate the access key.

    D. Set the *CausesValidation* property to *True*.

8. Which of the following properties of the *TextBox* control should be set to the value indicated to ensure that the text box can accommodate a string 10,000 characters long?

    A. *MultiLine = True*

    B. *WordWrap = True*

    C. *ScrollBars = True*

    D. *MaxLength = 10000*

9. Which of the following *Mask* property settings will configure *MaskedTextBox* for the entry of a social security number, which is displayed as three digits followed by a hyphen, then two digits followed by another hyphen, and then finally four digits?

    A. *999-99-9999*

    B. *999/00/0000*

    C. *000-00-0000*

    D. *000/00/0000*

10. You have a *MaskedTextBox* control with the *Mask* property set to *000-0000* to indicate a seven-digit phone number. You want users to be able to cut and paste the entire string, including the "-" character, but when the program accesses *MaskedTextBox*, you want to exclude the "-" character. Which of the following will configure *MaskedTextBox* to provide this functionality?

    A. Set the *CutCopyMaskFormat* property to *ExcludePromptAndLiterals* and *TextMaskFormat* to *IncludeLiterals*.

    B. Set the *CutCopyMaskFormat* property to *IncludeLiterals* and *TextMaskFormat* to *ExcludePromptAndLiterals*.

    C. Set the *CutCopyMaskFormat* property to *ExcludePromptAndLiterals* and *TextMaskFormat* to *IncludePrompt*.

    D. Set the *CutCopyMaskFormat* property to *IncludeLiterals* and *TextMaskFormat* to *IncludeLiterals*.

Lesson 3: Using List-Display and Specialized Controls

This lesson continues where the previous lesson left off, with an in-depth examination of Windows Forms controls. In this lesson, you learn how to create and configure controls for displaying lists, setting values and dates, and displaying images.

After this lesson, you will be able to:

- Programmatically determine which item in a list appears in a given position.
- Add or remove items from a list of items in a list-based control.
- Bind a list-based control to a data source.
- Sort list data.
- Display data in a drop-down combo box.
- Select one or more items from a predefined list.
- Use the *ListView* control to display a list of items with icons.
- Use the *TreeView* control to display a list of items in a hierarchical view.
- Configure the *DomainUpDown* control to display a list of strings.
- Configure the *NumericUpDown* control to display a list of numbers.
- Set two or more mutually exclusive options in the user interface using a *RadioButton*.
- Use the *CheckBox* control to indicate whether a condition is on or off.
- Allow navigation through a large amount of information or visually adjust a numeric setting using a *TrackBar*.
- Enable the user to select a single item from a list of dates or times by using the *DateTimePicker* control.
- Present an intuitive graphical interface for users to view and set date information using the *MonthCalendar*.
- Add images to or remove images from the *ImageList* component.
- Display graphics by using the *PictureBox* control.

Estimated lesson time: 60 minutes

Overview of List-Based Controls

The basic list-based controls are *ListBox*, *ComboBox*, and *CheckedListBox*. Although differing somewhat in appearance and functionality, each of these controls organizes and presents lists of data in the same way, and each contains an *Items* collection that organizes the items contained in one of these controls.

The *Items* collection is basically a collection of objects. Although these objects are often strings, they do not have to be. If a collection does contain a string, however, the string representation of the object is displayed in the control.

ListBox Control

The *ListBox* control is the simplest of the list-based controls and serves primarily to display a simple list of items in an easy-to-navigate user interface from which users can select one or more items. Table 4-19 describes the important properties of the *ListBox* control.

TABLE 4-19 Important Properties of the *ListBox* Control

PROPERTY	DESCRIPTION
DataSource	Sets the source for data binding in this control.
DisplayMember	Represents the data member displayed in this control.
FormatString	Specifies a formatting string that will be used to format the entries in the control if *FormattingEnabled* is set to *True*.
FormattingEnabled	Determines whether the entries in the control are formatted using *FormatString*.
Items	Returns the collection of items contained in this control.
MultiColumn	Indicates whether this item shows multiple columns of items or only a single item.
SelectedIndex	Gets the index of the selected item or, if the *SelectionMode* property is set to *MultiSimple* or *MutilExtended*, returns the index to any selected item.
SelectedIndices	Returns a collection of all selected indexes.
SelectedItem	Returns the selected item or, if the *SelectionMode* property is set to *MultiSimple* or *MultiExtended*, returns the index to any selected item.
SelectedItems	Returns a collection of all selected items.
SelectedValue	In a data-bound control, returns the value associated with the selected item. If the control is not data-bound, or if *ValueMember* is not set, this property returns the *ToString* value of the selected item.
SelectionMode	Determines how many items can be selected in a list box. Can be set to *None*, *One*, *MultiSimple*, or *MultiExtended*. *MultiSimple* allows the selection of multiple objects, and *MultiExtended* allows the use of the Shift and Ctrl keys when making multiple selections.
ValueMember	Indicates the data member that will provide the values for the list box.

ComboBox Control

The *ComboBox* control is similar to the *ListBox* control, but, in addition to allowing the user to select items from a list, it provides a space for a user to type an entry. Additionally, you can configure the *ComboBox* to either display a list of options or to provide a drop-down list of options. Table 4-20 describes the important properties of the *ComboBox* control.

TABLE 4-20 Important Properties of the *ComboBox* Control

PROPERTY	DESCRIPTION
DataSource	Sets the source for data binding in this control.
DisplayMember	Represents the data member displayed in this control.
DropDownHeight	Sets the maximum height for the drop-down box.
DropDownStyle	Determines the style of the combo box. Can be set to *Simple*, which is similar to a *ListBox*; *DropDown*, which is the default; or *DropDownList*, which is similar to *DropDown* but does not allow the user to type a new value.
DropDownWidth	Sets the width of the drop-down section of the combo box.
FormatString	Specifies a formatting string that will be used to format the entries in the control if *FormattingEnabled* is set to *True*.
FormattingEnabled	Determines whether the entries in the control are formatted using *FormatString*.
Items	Returns the collection of items contained in this control.
SelectedIndex	Gets the index of the selected item.
SelectedItem	Returns the selected item.
SelectedValue	In a data-bound control, returns the value associated with the selected item. If the control is not data-bound, or if the *ValueMember* is not set, this property returns the *ToString* value of the selected item.
ValueMember	Indicates the data member that will provide the values for the *ComboBox*.

CheckedListBox Control

CheckedListBox displays a list of items to users and allows them to select multiple items by checking boxes that are displayed next to the items. Any number of items can be checked, but only one item can be selected at a time. You can retrieve a collection that represents the checked items by accessing the *CheckedItems* collection, and you can get a collection of the checked indexes by accessing the *CheckedIndices* collection. Table 4-21 describes the important properties of the *CheckedListBox* control.

TABLE 4-21 Important Properties of the *CheckedListBox* Control

PROPERTY	DESCRIPTION
CheckedIndices	Returns a collection that represents all the checked indexes
CheckedItems	Returns a collection that exposes all the checked items in the control
FormatString	Specifies a formatting string that will be used to format the entries in the control if *FormattingEnabled* is set to *True*
FormattingEnabled	Determines whether the entries in the control are formatted using *FormatString*
Items	Returns the collection of items contained in this control
MultiColumn	Indicates whether this control shows multiple columns of items or only a single item
SelectedIndex	Gets the index of the selected item, or, if the *SelectionMode* property is set to *MultiSimple* or *MultiExtended*, it can return any selected index
SelectedItem	Returns the selected item, or, if the *SelectionMode* property is set to *MultiSimple* or *MultiExtended*, it can return any selected item

You can set an item to be checked or unchecked by calling the *SetItemChecked* method, as shown here:

Sample of Visual Basic Code

```
CheckedListBox.SetItemChecked(0, True)
```

Sample of C# Code

```
checkedListBox.SetItemChecked(0, true);
```

Likewise, you can use the *SetItemCheckState* method to set the *CheckState* of an item:

Sample of Visual Basic Code

```
CheckedListBox.SetItemCheckState(0, CheckState.Indeterminate)
```

Sample of C# Code

```
checkedListBox.SetItemCheckState(0, CheckState.Indeterminate);
```

Adding Items to and Removing Items from a List-Based Control

You can add items to or remove items from a list-based control through either the designer at design time or the code at run time.

To add items to a list-based control at design time, you select the control in the designer and then, in the Properties window, select the *Items* property. The String Collection Editor (shown in Figure 4-13) opens. All the items currently contained in the control are shown. Items can then be added to or removed from this list.

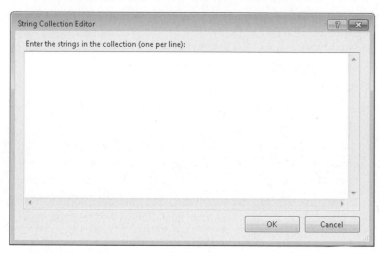

FIGURE 4-13 The String Collection Editor.

You can also use code to add and remove items programmatically from the control at run time. To add an item, you use the *Items.Add* method, as shown in the following code example:

Sample of Visual Basic Code

```
ListBox1.Items.Add("This string will be added to the list")
```

Sample of C# Code

```
listBox1.Items.Add("This string will be added to the list");
```

If you have several items to add at once, you can use the *AddRange* method to add an array of items to the control, as shown here:

Sample of Visual Basic Code

```
ListBox1.Items.AddRange(New String() {"Item1", "Item2", "Item3"})
```

Sample of C# Code

```
listBox1.Items.AddRange(new String[] {"Item1", "Item2", "Item3"});
```

You can use the *Items.Insert* method to add an item to a specific index in the list. The index of items is a zero-based index, so the first item in the control is at index 0. When you add an item to an index already occupied by an item, that item and any items beneath it are shifted down one index. The following code shows how to insert an item to be third in the displayed list, assuming that the *ListBox1* control is already populated with several items:

Sample of Visual Basic Code

```
ListBox1.Items.Insert(2, "This item will be third")
```

Sample of C# Code

```
listBox1.Items.Insert(2, "This item will be third");
```

You can use the *Items.Remove* method to remove an item from the list. This method requires a reference to the object you want to remove from the items collection. Note that if your control contains a collection of objects that are not strings, you will need to pass a reference to the object itself—not just to the string representation that appears in the control—to remove it. The following example demonstrates the *Items.Remove* method:

Sample of Visual Basic Code

```
ListBox1.Items.Remove("This string will be removed")
```

Sample of C# Code

```
listbox1.Items.Remove("This string will be removed");
```

If you do not know the actual item you want to remove at run time but have the index of the item you want to remove, you can use the *Items.RemoveAt* method to remove the item at a given index and adjust the indexes of the other items accordingly. The *Items.RemoveAt* method is demonstrated in the following code example:

Sample of Visual Basic Code

```
' Removes the third item in the list
ListBox1.Items.RemoveAt(2)
```

Sample of C# Code

```
// Removes the third item in the list
listbox1.Items.RemoveAt(2);
```

To remove all items from a list-based control, you can use the *Items.Clear* method, as shown here:

Sample of Visual Basic Code

```
ListBox1.Items.Clear()
```

Sample of C# Code

```
listBox1.Items.Clear();
```

Determining Where an Item Appears in a List

If you want to determine where an item appears in a list programmatically, you can do so by using the *Items.IndexOf* method. This method takes the item you want to find as an argument and returns an integer that represents the index of that item. If the item is not found in the *Items* collection, the *IndexOf* method returns -1. An example of the *IndexOf* method is shown here:

Sample of Visual Basic Code

```vb
Dim anIndex As Integer
anIndex = ListBox1.Items.IndexOf("A String")
```

Sample of C# Code

```csharp
int anIndex;
anIndex = listBox1.Items.IndexOf("A String");
```

You can also programmatically determine the index of an item that has been selected by the user by using the *SelectedIndex* property. The *SelectedIndex* property returns the item that has been selected in the user interface at run time. If more than one item has been selected, the *SelectedIndex* property can return any of the selected items. The *SelectedIndex* property is demonstrated here:

Sample of Visual Basic Code

```vb
Dim anIndex As Integer
anIndex = ListBox1.SelectedIndex
```

Sample of C# Code

```csharp
int anIndex;
anIndex = listBox1.SelectedIndex;
```

In controls in which the *SelectionMode* property is set to *MultiSimple* or *MultiExtended*, you can return all the selected indexes by using the *SelectedIndices* property, as shown in the following example:

Sample of Visual Basic Code

```vb
For Each i As Integer In ListBox1.SelectedIndices
    Console.WriteLine(ListBox1.Items(i).ToString)
Next
```

Sample of C# Code

```csharp
foreach (int i in listBox1.SelectedIndices)
{
    Console.WriteLine(listBox1.Items[i].ToString());
}
```

Binding List-Based Controls to Data Sources

You will frequently want to expose data to the user in list-based controls. You can bind *ListBox* controls and *ComboBox* controls (but not *CheckedListBox* controls) to a data source by using the *DataSource*, *DisplayMember*, and *ValueMember* properties to bind a list-based control to a column of data in a data table.

To bind a list-based control to a data source:

1. In the designer, select the list-based control you want to bind to a data source.

2. In the Properties window, click the *DataSource* property to open the data source configuration interface, as shown in Figure 4-14. Set the *DataSource* property to a table contained in one of the data sources in your project.

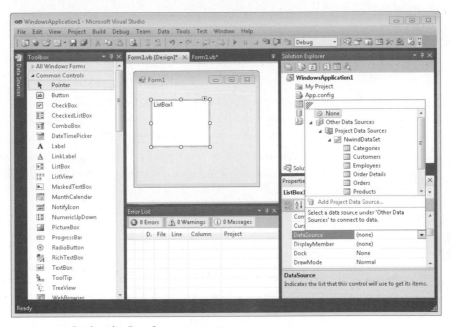

FIGURE 4-14 Setting the *DataSource* property.

3. In the Properties window, click the *DisplayMember* property. Visual Studio displays the columns in the selected table. This is the column whose rows will be displayed in the control.

4. In the Properties window, click the *ValueMember* property. Choose a column name in the interface to which to bind the control. This is the column whose members will provide the value that is returned from the selected index in the control.

The *DataSource* property indicates the data source (usually a data table) from which the data in the control is drawn. The *DisplayMember* property represents the column of data in the data source that is displayed to the user in the control. The *ValueMember* property enables you to designate an additional column of values to be represented in the control. For example, you might set the *DisplayMember* property to the Products column to display a list of products to the user, but set the *ValueMember* to a *ProductsCode* column that returns a numeric code for each product. In this instance, whenever an item is selected, the *SelectedItem* property returns the item displayed in the *ListBox*, and the *SelectedValue* property returns the corresponding item from the *ProductsCode* column.

Sorting in List-Based Controls

You can sort the objects displayed in a list-based control by setting the *Sorted* property to *True*, as shown here:

Sample of Visual Basic Code

```
ListBox1.Sorted = True
```

Sample of C# Code

```
listBox1.Sorted = true;
```

Setting a Format for Items Displayed in a List-Based Control

You can format the items you display in a list-based control. For example, if you are displaying a list of monetary values, you can format them all as currency, and they will be displayed in the currency format appropriate to the culture under which the application is running.

You can set a format for a list-based control by setting the *FormatString* property at design time. Selecting and clicking the *FormatString* property in the Properties window launches the Format String Dialog dialog box, shown in Figure 4-15.

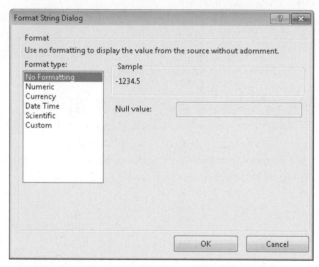

FIGURE 4-15 The Format String Dialog dialog box.

The *FormattingEnabled* property determines whether to use the formatting indicated by *FormatString*. When the *FormattingEnabled* property is set to *True*, the entries in the control are displayed in the format indicated by the *FormatString* property.

If the preset format strings do not provide the correct format for an item, you can create a custom format string. Table 4-22 describes the characters you can use to create a custom format string.

TABLE 4-22 Custom Format String Characters

CHARACTER	DESCRIPTION
0	Zero placeholder. If the value being formatted has a digit in the position where the "0" appears in the format string, that digit is copied to the result string. The position of the left-most "0" before the decimal point and the right-most "0" after the decimal point determine the range of digits that are always present in the result string. Note that the "00" specifier causes the value to be rounded to the nearest digit preceding the decimal, where rounding away from zero is always used. For example, formatting 34.5 with "00" would result in the value 35.
#	Digit placeholder. If the value being formatted has a digit in the position where the "#" appears in the format string, that digit is copied to the result string. Otherwise, nothing is stored in that position in the result string. Note that this specifier never displays the "0" character if it is not a significant digit, even if "0" is the only digit in the string. It will display the "0" character if it is a significant digit in the number being displayed. The "##" format string causes the value to be rounded to the nearest digit preceding the decimal, where rounding away from zero is always used. For example, formatting 34.5 with "##" would result in the value 35.
.	Decimal separator. The first "." character determines the location of the first decimal separator in the formatted value. Additional "." characters are ignored. Note that the actual character used will be the decimal separator determined by the current locale.
,	Thousands separator and scaling. First, if the format string contains a "," character between two digit placeholders (0 or #) and to the left of the decimal point (if one is present), the output will have thousand separators inserted between each group of three digits to the left of the decimal separator. The actual character used as the decimal separator in the result string is determined by the *NumberGroupSeparator* property of the current *NumberFormatInfo* property that controls formatting.
	If the format string contains one or more "," characters immediately to the left of the decimal point, the number will be divided by the number of "," characters multiplied by 1000 before it is formatted. For example, the format string "0," will represent 100 million simply as 100.
%	Percentage placeholder. The presence of the % symbol causes the number represented to be multiplied by 100 before formatting. The % symbol appears in the place in which it occurs in the format string.

E0, E+0, E-0, e0, e+0, e-0	Scientific notation. If any of the strings "E", "E+", "E-", "e", "e+", or "e-" are present in the format string and are followed immediately by at least one "0" character, the number is formatted using scientific notation with an "E" or "e" inserted between the number and the exponent. The number of "0" characters following the scientific notation indicator determines the minimum number of digits to output for the exponent. The "E+" and "e+" formats indicate that a sign character (plus or minus) should always precede the exponent. The "E", "E-", "e", or "e-" formats indicate that a sign character should precede only negative exponents.
\	Escape character. In C#, this character indicates that the character immediately following the "\" is to be interpreted as an escape sequence. In Visual Basic, this character has no effect.
"ABC", 'ABC'	Literal strings. Characters enclosed in "" or '' are displayed as literal strings in the formatted string.
;	Section separator. The ";" character separates sections for positive, negative, and zero numbers in the format string. You can provide up to three sections in a format string, each containing its own format. These sections should be separated by ";" characters and will be applied to positive, negative, and zero numbers, respectively.
Other Characters	Other characters in the format string are represented as literal strings.

Selecting Items in a List-Based Control

You can select items programmatically in a list-based control by using the *SelectedItem* or *SelectedIndex* property, as shown in the following example:

Sample of Visual Basic Code

```
ListBox1.SelectedItem = "This item will be selected"
```

Sample of C# Code

```
listBox1.SelectedItem = "This item will be selected";
```

If the *SelectedItem* property is set to an item that is not contained in the control, there is no effect, and no item is selected.

If the control allows multiple selections, you can select multiple items by setting the *SelectedItem* property multiple times if the *SelectionMode* property is set to *MultiSimple* or *MultiExtended* (which is supported by only the *ListBox* control). When selected, an item remains selected until cleared by the user. An example is shown here:

Sample of Visual Basic Code

```
ListBox1.SelectedItem = "This item will be selected"
ListBox1.SelectedItem = "This item will be selected too"
```

Sample of C# Code

```
listBox1.SelectedItem = "This item will be selected";
listBox1.SelectedItem = "This item will be selected too";
```

The *SelectedIndex* property functions in a way similar to the *SelectedItem* property except that it is an *Integer* type that corresponds to the sequential item in the list. You can select an item in the control by setting the *SelectedIndex* property to the corresponding index, and you can select multiple items by setting the property multiple times in succession. The main difference between the behavior of the *SelectedItem* property and the *SelectedIndex* property is that the *SelectedIndex* property throws an exception if an attempt is made to set it to a nonexistent index.

The *ListView* Control

The *ListView* control enables you to view lists of items with optional associated icons in the manner of Windows Explorer. Using the *ListView* control, you can display items with large associated icons, small associated icons, or additional details about the item. Table 4-23 shows important properties of the *ListView* control.

TABLE 4-23 Important Properties of the *ListView* Control

PROPERTY	DESCRIPTION
Columns	Contains the collection of columns to be displayed when the *View* property is set to *Details*.
Groups	Contains an optional collection of groups that can be used to categorize the items contained in the *Items* collection.
Items	A collection of *ListViewItems* displayed in the *ListView* control.
LargeImageList	The *ImageList* component from which images for *ListViewItems* are drawn when the *View* property is set to *LargeIcon*.
ShowGroups	Determines whether the groups contained in the *Groups* collection are shown.
SmallImageList	The *ImageList* component from which images for *ListViewItems* are drawn when the *View* property is set to *SmallIcon*.
View	Indicates the manner in which *ListView* items are displayed.

The most important property in the *ListView* control is the *Items* property. This property contains a collection of *ListViewItem* objects. Unlike the list-based controls examined earlier, *ListView* items are specific objects that contain additional information about the item being displayed, such as icons that are shown in the control. Table 4-24 shows important properties of the *ListViewItem* class.

TABLE 4-24 Important Properties of the *ListViewItem* Class

PROPERTY	DESCRIPTION
Group	The group, if any, in the *ListView* control's *Groups* collection to which this *ListViewItem* belongs.
ImageIndex	The index, if any, of the image to be used for this item when the *View* property is set to *LargeIcon* or *SmallIcon*. If the *ImageIndex* property is set, the *ImageKey* property is set to "."
ImageKey	The key of the image, if any, to be used for this item when the *View* property is set to *LargeIcon* or *SmallIcon*. If the *ImageKey* property is set, the *ImageIndex* property is set to -1.
SubItems	Contains the subitems that will be shown when the *View* property is set to *Details*. These items should correspond to the columns in the *ListView* control's *Columns* collection.
Text	The text that is shown in the *ListView* property.

You can add *ListView* items to *ListView* and edit the properties of individual items by clicking the *Items* property of the *ListView* control to open the ListViewItem Collection Editor, shown in Figure 4-16.

The *ListView* control organizes the images associated with the *ListView* items in *ImageList* objects that are exposed in the *SmallImageList* and *LargeImageList* properties. The *ImageList* class will be discussed in greater detail later in this lesson. You can set the images associated with a particular *ListView* item by setting either the *ImageIndex* or *ImageKey* property of each item. The *View* property determines whether the *ListView* items are shown with large images, with small images, or in a view that exposes the subitems of the *ListView* items.

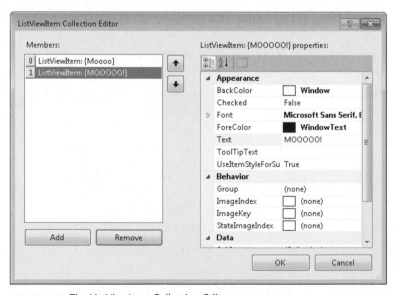

FIGURE 4-16 The ListViewItem Collection Editor.

To display a list of items with icons in a *ListView* control:

1. In the designer, drag an *ImageList* control from the Toolbox to a design surface that already contains a *ListView* control.

2. In the Properties window, click the *Images* property of *ImageList* to add images to the *Images* collection.

3. In the designer, select the *ListView* control. In the Properties window, set the *SmallImageList*, *LargeImageList*, or both to the *ImageList* object.

4. In the Properties window, click Items to add *ListView* items to *ListView*. In the ListViewItem Collection Editor, set either the *ImageIndex* or the *ImageKey* property for each *ListView* item to the appropriate image in *ImageList*. Also, set any other properties, such as *Text*, at this point.

5. In the designer, select the *ListView* control. In the Properties window, set the *View* property to either *LargeIcon* or *SmallIcon*.

TreeView Control

The *TreeView* control enables you to display a list of objects in a hierarchical manner. Each object in the *TreeView* control represents an instance of the *TreeNode* class, which contains information about the location of the node within the *TreeView* control. Nodes containing child nodes in the *TreeView* control can be collapsed and expanded. Figure 4-17 shows a *TreeView* control in a form.

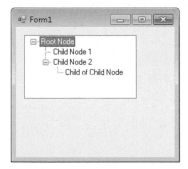

FIGURE 4-17 The *TreeView* control.

The primary property of the *TreeView* control is the *Nodes* property. This property contains the collection of tree nodes that comprise the root objects in *TreeView*. Each *TreeNode* object contains its own collection of tree nodes that represent child nodes of that node. Table 4-25 describes some of the important properties of the *TreeNode* class.

TABLE 4-25 Important Properties of the *TreeNode* Class

PROPERTY	DESCRIPTION
FirstNode	Returns the first node in the current group of child nodes.
LastNode	Returns the last node in the current group of child nodes.
NextNode	Returns the next sibling tree node.
NextVisibleNode	Returns the next visible node.
Nodes	Returns the collection of child nodes belonging to this node.
Parent	Returns the parent node of the current node. If the current node is a root node in *TreeView*, accessing this property will return null.
PrevNode	Returns the previous sibling tree node.
PrevVisibleNode	Returns the previous visible node.
TreeView	Returns a reference to the *TreeView* control in which the *TreeNode* is contained.

Adding and Removing Nodes from the *TreeView* Controls

At design time, you can add nodes to a *TreeView* control by clicking the *Nodes* property in the Properties window to display the TreeNode Editor (shown in Figure 4-18). You can add new root nodes or new child nodes and set the properties of each tree node.

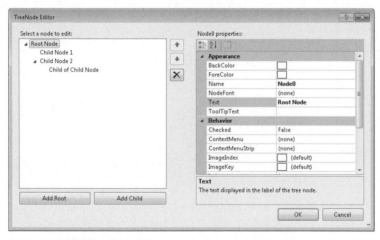

FIGURE 4-18 The TreeNode Editor.

At run time, you can create new *TreeNode* objects and add them to the *TreeView* control as root nodes, or add them to another *TreeNode* object as child nodes. For both of these procedures, you use the *Nodes.Add* method, as shown here:

```
Dim aNode As New TreeNode("New Node")
' Add a child node to the new node
aNode.Nodes.Add(New TreeNode("New Child"))
' Adds aNode and its child As a new root node in a TreeView control named TreeView1
TreeView1.Nodes.Add(aNode)
' Adds a second child node to the first node in TreeView1
TreeView1.Nodes(0).Nodes.Add(New TreeNode("Second Child"))
```

Sample of C# Code

```
TreeNode aNode = new TreeNode("New Node");
// Add a child node to the new node
aNode.Nodes.Add(new TreeNode("New Child"));
// Adds aNode and its child as a new root node in a TreeView control named TreeView1
treeView1.Nodes.Add(aNode);
// Adds a second child node to the first node in TreeView1
treeView1.Nodes[0].Nodes.Add(new TreeNode("Second Child"));
```

You can remove nodes from the *Nodes* collection by using the *Remove* and *RemoveAt* methods. The *Remove* method takes a reference to a particular node as a parameter and removes it from the collection if it exists in the collection. If the specified node does not exist in the collection, this method call is ignored. The *RemoveAt* method removes the node at a specified index. If the specified index is not present in the nodes collection, an *ArgumentOutOfRange* exception is thrown. The following example demonstrates the *Remove* and *RemoveAt* methods:

Sample of Visual Basic Code

```
' Removes the node named aNode from the collection
TreeView1.Nodes.Remove(aNode)
' Removes the node at index 3 from the collection.
TreeView1.Nodes.RemoveAt(3)
```

Sample of C# Code

```
// Removes the node named aNode from the collection
treeView1.Nodes.Remove(aNode);
// Removes the node at index 3 from the collection.
treeView1.Nodes.RemoveAt(3);
```

Expanding and Collapsing Nodes

The *TreeView* control presents a hierarchical view of nodes that can be expanded or collapsed to reveal or hide the child nodes as appropriate. You can expand or collapse child nodes programmatically at run time by using the *Expand* and *Collapse* methods, as shown in the following example:

Sample of Visual Basic Code

```
' Expands the child nodes of a TreeNode named aNode
aNode.Expand()
' Collapses the child nodes of a TreeNode named aNode
aNode.Collapse()
```

Sample of C# Code

```csharp
// Expands the child nodes of a TreeNode named aNode
aNode.Expand();
// Collapses the child nodes of a TreeNode named aNode
aNode.Collapse();
```

NumericUpDown Control

The *NumericUpDown* control enables you to set a range of numbers a user can browse and select. A range of numbers is presented in the control, and the user can click the up and down arrows to increase or decrease the number. Table 4-26 shows important properties of the *NumericUpDown* control.

TABLE 4-26 Important Properties of the *NumericUpDown* Control

PROPERTY	DESCRIPTION
Hexadecimal	Indicates whether the numeric value will be shown in hexadecimal.
Increment	Gets or sets the amount to increment or decrement with each button click.
Maximum	Indicates the maximum value for the control.
Minimum	Indicates the minimum value for the control.
ThousandsSeparator	Indicates whether the culture-appropriate thousands separator will be used when displaying values greater than 1000.
Value	Gets or sets the current value of the control.

To configure the *NumericUpDown* control:

1. Set the *Minimum* property to the minimum numeric value for the control.

2. Set the *Maximum* property to the maximum numeric value for the control.

3. Set the *Increment* property to the amount you want to increment and decrement with each arrow button click.

4. If desired, set the *Value* property to a default value.

DomainUpDown Control

The *DomainUpDown* control is similar to the *NumericUpDown* control in that it enables users to browse a specified series of data and set a value for the control. Instead of browsing numeric values, however, the *DomainUpDown* control enables the user to browse a collection of preset strings. Table 4-27 describes the important properties of the *DomainUpDown* control.

TABLE 4-27 Important Properties of the *DomainUpDown* Control

PROPERTY	DESCRIPTION
Items	Contains the collection of strings displayed in the *DomainUpDown* control.
ReadOnly	Indicates whether the user can alter the *Text* property of the control.
Text	Gets or sets the text of the control.

The *Items* collection contains the strings displayed in the *DomainUpDown* control. You can add strings by clicking the *Items* property in the Properties window to display the String Collection Editor. When *ReadOnly* is set to *False*, the user can choose to type a string in the *DomainUpDown* control instead of choosing one of the strings. Note that strings typed by the user are not added to the *Items* collection. Also note that the *Text* property defines the default value for the control, not for the *Items* collection.

 Quick Check

1. What is the purpose of the *TreeView* control?

2. What is the purpose of a *ListView* control, and when would you use one?

Quick Check Answers

1. The *TreeView* control enables you to display a list of data in a hierarchically re-lated manner.

2. The *ListView* control provides a highly configurable control that enables you to display lists of data in a variety of ways. You can use a *ListView* control when you want to provide different options to the user for the display of list data, such as providing icons or details about the data.

Value-Setting Controls

Value-setting controls enable the user to set values or pick options from a preset list in the user interface. The *CheckBox* control enables a user to select or clear particular options in a nonexclusive manner, and the *RadioButton* control enables you to present a range of options to the user, only one of which can be selected. The *TrackBar* control enables the user to set a value rapidly in a graphical interface.

The *CheckBox* Control

The *CheckBox* control is a very familiar control to users. It enables the user to mark a check box next to a label to indicate acceptance or rejection of the option presented. *CheckBox* controls function in a nonexclusive manner; you can have multiple *CheckBox* controls on a single form, and any combination of them can be selected or cleared at a single time. Table 4-28 shows important properties of the *CheckBox* control.

TABLE 4-28 Important Properties of the *CheckBox* Control

PROPERTY	DESCRIPTION
AutoCheck	Determines whether the *CheckBox* is automatically checked when the text is clicked.
Checked	Gets or sets whether the *CheckBox* is checked.
CheckState	Returns the *CheckState* of the control. Possible values for this property are *Checked*, *Unchecked*, and *Indeterminate*.
Text	The text displayed next to the check box.
ThreeState	Determines whether the *CheckBox* control allows two or three check states.

The most common use for the *CheckBox* control is to enable the user to make a binary decision about an option by either selecting the box or not selecting it. Typically, the check box is used for nonexclusive options; that is, selecting a particular check box usually does not affect the state of other text boxes. Figure 4-19 shows an example of a hypothetical pizza order form. Option buttons are used to choose between the exclusive options of Pizza or Calzone, and *CheckBox* controls are used to select toppings for the pizza or calzone selected.

FIGURE 4-19 Example of *CheckBox* and *RadioButton* controls.

You can determine programmatically whether a *CheckBox* control is selected by accessing the *Checked* property. This property returns *True* if the control is selected and *False* if the control is cleared or indeterminate.

A less common use for *CheckBox* is to enable the user to choose among three settings: *Checked*, *Unchecked*, or *Indeterminate*. This can be useful to indicate to the user that a conscious decision must be made for each option rather than simply setting a default option. You enable three-state *CheckBox* controls by setting the *ThreeState* property to *True* to enable the user to cycle through the three states, rather than just the two, for the check box. You can determine the state of the check box by accessing the *CheckState* property.

Note that you can set the *CheckState* property to *Indeterminate* at design time even if you set the *ThreeState* property to *False*. This causes the *CheckBox* controls to start in the indeterminate state, but after the user makes a selection, *CheckBox* must be either selected or cleared. In this case, the user is not allowed to reset the check box to *Indeterminate*.

The *RadioButton* Control

The *RadioButton* control is used to present exclusive options to the user. The hypothetical pizza order form in Figure 4-19 demonstrates the use of *RadioButton* controls, enabling the user to choose either a pizza or a calzone, but not both. Table 4-29 shows important properties of the *RadioButton* control.

TABLE 4-29 Important Properties of the *RadioButton* Control

PROPERTY	DESCRIPTION
Checked	Indicates whether the *RadioButton* is selected.
Text	The text displayed next to the option button.

You can determine whether a particular *RadioButton* is selected by accessing the *Checked* property, which returns *True* if selected.

All *RadioButton* controls in a given container control are exclusive of one another. That means that if one *RadioButton* control is selected, all the others will be cleared. This has the net effect of allowing the user to choose only one of a group of options.

If you want to have several exclusive groups of *RadioButton* controls, the most common method is to group them in a *GroupBox* control. Each group of *RadioButton* controls in a particular group box will be exclusive of one another, but unaffected by other *RadioButton* controls in other *GroupBox* containers. Figure 4-20 displays an example of *RadioButton* controls in *GroupBox* containers.

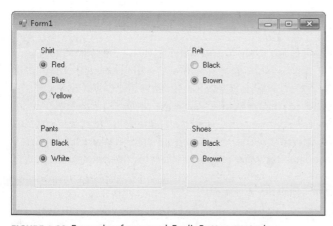

FIGURE 4-20 Example of grouped *RadioButton* controls.

The *TrackBar* Control

The *TrackBar* control provides a simple interface that enables the user to set a value from a predetermined range of values by graphically manipulating a slider with the mouse or keyboard commands. This enables the user to rapidly set a value from a potentially very large range. Table 4-30 shows important properties of the *TrackBar* control.

TABLE 4-30 Important Properties of the *TrackBar* Control

PROPERTY	DESCRIPTION
LargeChange	The number of positions the slider moves in response to mouse clicks or the Page Up and Page Down keys.
Maximum	The maximum value for *TrackBar*.
Minimum	The minimum value for *TrackBar*.
SmallChange	The number of positions the slider moves in response to arrow key keystrokes.
TickFrequency	The number of positions between tick marks on *TrackBar*.
TickStyle	Indicates where ticks appear on *TrackBar*.
Value	The value returned by *TrackBar*.

Figure 4.21 shows the *TrackBar* control.

FIGURE 4-21 The *TrackBar* control.

The *TrackBar* control can return an integer value in any range between the values of the *Minimum* and *Maximum* properties. The user can set this value by manipulating the graphical slider on the track bar. Clicking the control or using the Page Up and Page Down keys while the control is selected causes the value to change by the increment set in the *LargeChange* property. Using the arrow keys while the control is selected causes the value to change by the increment set in the *SmallChange* property. The user can also grab the slider with the mouse and adjust it to whatever value is needed. The *Value* property indicates the current value of the track bar.

Choosing Dates and Times

User interfaces frequently require the user to be allowed to set a date or time. For example, an application that enables a user to make a reservation would require a date for the reservation to be entered. Visual Studio provides two controls that enable date and time choosing: *DateTimePicker* and *MonthCalendar*.

DateTimePicker Control

The *DateTimePicker* control enables the user to set a date, a time, or both in an easy-to-understand graphical interface similar to a *ComboBox* control. The user can click the drop-down box to display a calendar interface to choose a day from a calendar or type a time into the text area in *DateTimePicker*. The chosen day or time is then displayed in the text area of *DateTimePicker*, and the *Value* property is set to the chosen date and time. Table 4-31 shows important properties of the *DateTimePicker* control.

TABLE 4-31 Important Properties of the *DateTimePicker* Control

PROPERTY	DESCRIPTION
CustomFormat	The custom *DateTime* format to be used when the *Format* property is set to *Custom*.
Format	Sets the format for the *DateTime* format displayed in *DateTimePicker*. Can be set to *Long*, which displays the value in long date format; *Short*, which displays the value in short date format; *Time*, which displays the time only; or *Custom*, which uses the custom *DateTime* format indicated by the *CustomFormat* property.
MaxDate	The maximum *DateTime* value the *DateTimePicker* will accept.
MinDate	The minimum *DateTime* value the *DateTimePicker* will accept.
Value	The *DateTime* value to which *DateTimePicker* is currently set.

When the *Format* property is set to *Long* or *Short*, only the date is displayed, and the date can only be set through the graphical interface. When the *Format* property is set to *Time*, the user can type a new time value into the text area of *DateTimePicker*. The user can still choose a day through the drop-down interface. Although this day is reflected in the *Value* property, it is not displayed when the *Format* property is set to *Time*.

MonthCalendar Control

The *MonthCalendar* control is a highly configurable control that enables the user to select a range of dates in a highly intuitive interface. Table 4-32 shows the important properties of the *MonthCalendar* control.

TABLE 4-32 Important Properties of the *MonthCalendar* Control

PROPERTY	DESCRIPTION
AnnuallyBoldedDates	Contains an array of dates and times that will appear bold every year.
BoldedDates	Contains an array of dates and times that will appear bold.
FirstDayOfWeek	Determines which day of the week is set as the first day of the week in the *MonthCalendar* control.
MaxDate	Sets the maximum date that can be chosen in *MonthCalendar*.
MinDate	Sets the minimum date that can be chosen in *MonthCalendar*.
MaxSelectionCount	Sets the maximum number of days that can be selected in *MonthCalendar*.
MonthlyBoldedDates	Contains an array of dates and times that will appear bold every month in *MonthCalendar*.
SelectionEnd	Indicates the ending date and time of the *SelectionRange* property.
SelectionRange	Contains the range of dates selected by the user.
SelectionStart	Indicates the starting date and time of the *SelectionRange* property.

The user can select a single date by clicking a date in *MonthCalendar* or a continuous range of dates by holding down the Shift key while clicking the starting date and the ending date. The range of dates selected cannot be a greater number of days than the *MaxSelectionCount* property indicates.

At run time, you can retrieve the selected dates by accessing the *SelectionStart* and *SelectionEnd* properties, which expose the *Start* and *End* properties of the *SelectionRange* property. The following example demonstrates how to access the *SelectionStart* and *SelectionEnd* properties:

Sample of Visual Basic Code

```
MsgBox("Your vacation starts on " & _
    MonthCalendar1.SelectionStart.ToLongDateString & _
    " and ends on " & MonthCalendar1.SelectionEnd.ToLongDateString)
```

Sample of C# Code

```
MessageBox.Show("Your vacation starts on " +
    monthCalendar1.SelectionStart.ToLongDateString() + " and ends on " +
    monthCalendar1.SelectionEnd.ToLongDateString());
```

Working with Images

Images enable you to liven up your user interface as well as provide important information to the user. Visual Studio contains several components and controls that facilitate the display of images. The *PictureBox* control is an all-around control that displays pictures in different formats. The *ImageList* component manages and organizes a collection of images and can be used to display images in *ListView* or to organize images for other controls.

PictureBox Control

The *PictureBox* control is the basic control used for displaying images in the user interface, and it can display pictures in a variety of formats, including .bmp, .jpg, .gif, metafiles, and icons. You can display images that are present in application resource files or compiled into the application, or you can load images from a Web or disk address. Table 4-33 describes important properties of the *PictureBox* control.

TABLE 4-33 Important Properties of the *PictureBox* Control

PROPERTY	DESCRIPTION
ErrorImage	The image that will be displayed if the selected image fails to load.
Image	The image to be loaded in *PictureBox*.
ImageLocation	A Web or disk address from which to load the image.
InitialImage	The image to be displayed in *PictureBox* while the image is loading.
SizeMode	Determines how the control handles image placement and sizing.

You can set the *Image* property at design time by clicking it in the Properties window, which opens the Select Resource dialog box, shown in Figure 4-22.

You can select an image resource already present in a project resource file by selecting the Project Resource File option button and selecting the .resx file that contains the image. You can also import a new image into a resource file by clicking the Import button and navigating to the image you want to import. The selected image is added to the selected .resx file. You can also import the image as a local resource by selecting the Local Resource option button and clicking the Import button to browse to the image you want to import. Importing an image as a local resource only makes it available to the *PictureBox* control and unavailable to the rest of the application.

Instead of loading an image from a resource, you can specify a URL from which to load an image by setting the *ImageLocation* property. When the *ImageLocation* property is set, the image is loaded from the specified address, and the *Image* property is set to that image.

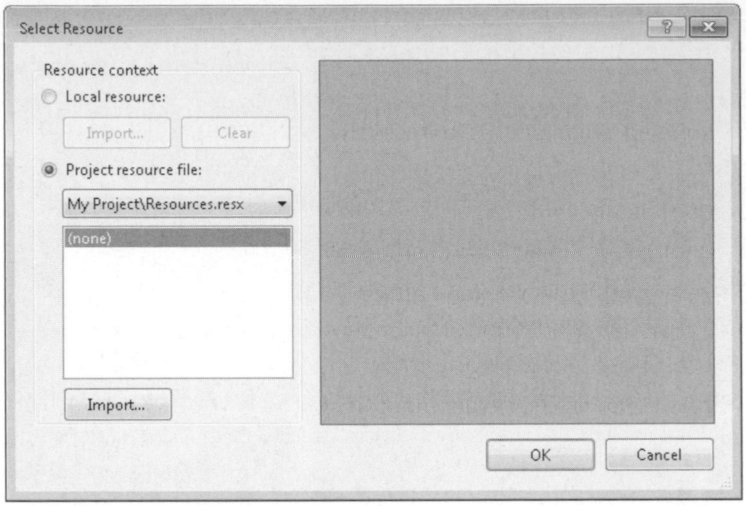

FIGURE 4-22 The Select Resource dialog box.

At run time, you can set the *Image* property to an instance of an image, as shown in the following example:

Sample of Visual Basic Code

```
Dim anImage As New System.Drawing.Bitmap("C:\anImage.bmp")
PictureBox1.Image = anImage
```

Sample of C# Code

```
System.Drawing.Bitmap anImage = new
    System.Drawing.Bitmap(@"C:\anImage.bmp");
pictureBox1.Image = anImage;
```

ImageList Component

The *ImageList* component is not a control as such, but it enables you to organize groups of images. Although it has no visual representation itself, it can supply images to other controls, such as *ListView*, or serve as a repository for images to be loaded into a picture box. You can set the size and color depth for the images and iterate through them as you would a collection. Table 4-34 shows important properties of the *ImageList* component.

TABLE 4-34 Important Properties of the *ImageList* Component

PROPERTY	DESCRIPTION
ColorDepth	Sets the color depth for the images contained in the *ImageList* component.
Images	The collection of images organized by the *ImageList* component.
ImageSize	Sets the size for the images contained in the *ImageList* component.

You can add new items to the *ImageList* component by clicking the *Images* property in the Properties window. This opens the Images Collection Editor, shown in Figure 4-23.

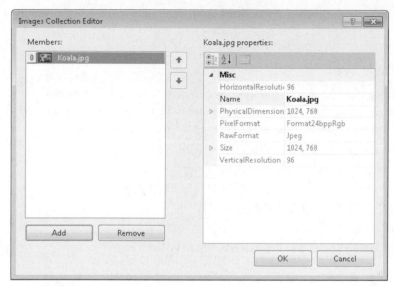

FIGURE 4-23 The Image Collection Editor.

You can use the Images Collection Editor to add or remove images. You can also use it to change their order. After you have added images to the *ImageList* component, you can set the color depth for each image by setting the *ColorDepth* property, and you can set all the images to a specified size by setting the *ImageSize* property.

At run time, you can access the images contained in the *ImageList* by means of the *Images* collection, as shown in the following example:

Sample of Visual Basic Code
```
PictureBox1.Image = ImageList1.Images(0)
```

Sample of C# Code
```
pictureBox1.Image = imageList1.Images[0];
```

You can use *ImageList* components to provide images to other controls in your user interface. Several controls, such as *Button*, *CheckBox*, *RadioButton*, and others host *ImageList*, *ImageKey*, and *ImageIndex* properties. You can provide images from an *ImageList* component to these controls by setting these properties.

To provide an image to a control from an *ImageList* component:

1. Set the *ImageList* property of the control to the *ImageList* component that hosts the image you want to provide.

2. Set either the *ImageIndex* property or the *ImageKey* property to the appropriate image in the *ImageList*.

1. What is the difference between how a *RadioButton* control and a *CheckBox* control are used?

2. What is the purpose of an *ImageList* control, and how is it used?

Quick Check Answers

1. Option buttons enable the user to choose a single option from a set of mutually exclusive options. *CheckBox* controls enable the user to select multiple options, usually regardless of whether any other options in the group are selected.

2. An *ImageList* control is used to organize a set of related images, generally to provide images to the controls on a form. You can set the *ImageList* property of the controls on a form to an instance of *ImageList* and then set either the *ImageIndex* or the *ImageKey* property to specify the image.

PRACTICE   **Adventure Works Ski Instructor Reservation Form**

In this lab, you use what you have learned in this lesson to add functionality to a simple application designed to reserve ski instructors. You add a *ComboBox* that enables the user to select the mountain on which he or she wants to ski, a *ListView* control to select a ski instructor, and a *NumericUpDown* control to select the length of the lesson. You add a group of *CheckBox* controls to enable the user to indicate required ski rental equipment, a group of *RadioButton* controls to enable the user to indicate his or her ski skill level, and an *ImageList* component to integrate with the *ListView* control so the user can see faces to go with the names.

EXERCISE   The Ski Instructor Reservation Form

1. In Visual Studio, load the partial solution for this lesson.

2. In Form1, beneath the Name text box, add a *Label* control and a *ComboBox* control. Set the *Text* property of the *Label* control to **Choose Ski Run**.

3. Set the *DropDownStyle* property of *ComboBox* to *DropDownList*.

4. Add the following items to the *ComboBox Items* property: **Camelback**, **Powder Point**, and **The Plunge**.

5. Add a *Label* control and a *NumericUpDown* control to the form. Set the *Text* property of *Label* to **Lesson Length**.

6. Set the *Minimum* property of the *NumericUpDown* control to **1** and the *Maximum* property to **3**.

7. Add a *Label* control and a *ListView* control to the form. Set the *Text* property of the *Label* control to **Choose Instructor**.

8. In the Properties window, set the *View* property of the *ListView* control to *SmallIcon*. Later in this practice, you will associate the items in this list with images.

9. In the Properties window, click the *Items* property to add four *ListView* items to *ListView*. In the ListViewItem Collection Editor, set their *Text* properties to **Sandy**, **Jack**, **Libby**, and **Christa**.

10. Add a *Button* control to the form and set the *Text* property to **Make Reservation**.

11. In the designer, double-click the button and add the following code to the *Button_Click* event handler:

Sample of Visual Basic Code

```
If  ListView1.SelectedItems.Count > 0 Then
    MsgBox("Your reservation with " &  listView1.SelectedItems(0).Text & _
        " is confirmed.")
End If
```

Sample of C# Code

```
if (listView1.SelectedItems.Count > 0)
{
    MessageBox.Show("Your reservation with " + listView1.SelectedItems[0].Text +
        " is confirmed.");
}
```

12. Drag a *GroupBox* container onto the form. Set the *Text* property of *GroupBox* to **Rental Equipment**.

13. Drag three *CheckBox* controls into *GroupBox*. Set the *Text* properties of the *CheckBox* controls to **Skis**, **Poles**, and **Boots**.

14. Drag a *GroupBox* container onto the form. Set the *Text* property of *GroupBox* to **Skill Level**.

15. Drag three *RadioButton* controls into *GroupBox*. Set the *Text* properties of the *RadioButton* controls to **Beginner**, **Intermediate**, and **Advanced**.

16. Drag a *Label* control and a *DateTimePicker* control onto the form. Set the *Text* property of *Label* to **Select Lesson Time**.

17. Set the *Format* property of *DateTimePicker* to **Time**.

18. Drag an *ImageList* component from the Toolbox onto the form.

19. In the Properties window, set the *ImageSize* property of the *ImageList* component to **32,32** and set the *ColorDepth* property to **Depth16Bit**.

20. In the Properties window, click Images to add four images to the *ImageList* component. You will find sample images on the Companion CD in the Images subfolder of the Code folder.

21. In the designer, select the *ListView* control. In the Properties window, set the *SmallImageList* property to **ImageList1**.

22. In the Properties window, click Items to open the ListViewItem Collection Editor. In the ListViewItem Collection Editor, set the *ImageIndex* property for *ListView* items 0, 1, 2, and 3 to **0**, **1**, **2**, and **3**, respectively. Images should now display next to the icons in the *ListView* control.

23. Press F5 to build and test your application.

Lesson Summary

- List-based controls are used to organize and present lists of information to the user. The *ListBox*, *ComboBox*, and *CheckedListBox* controls organize items through the *Items* property and share many common methods and properties.

- The *ListBox* control enables you to display a selection of items to the user and enables the user to select one or more items from that list.

- The *ComboBox* control can appear similar to a *ListBox* control or as a drop-down list. You can require users to select from a list or choose to enable them to type an entry that is not present in the list.

- The *CheckedListBox* control enables you to display a list of items with a check box beside each one, enabling the user to select as many items as desired. Although multiple items can be selected, only one item can be selected in the *CheckedListBox* at any time.

- The *ListView* control allows specialized displays of lists of items. Items can be displayed in association with icons provided by an *ImageList* component or with additional columns of subitems.

- The *TreeView* control enables you to display lists of items in a hierarchical format. Each node contains a collection of child nodes, which can themselves have child nodes. Nodes can be expanded or collapsed.

- The *NumericUpDown* control enables the user to click up or down arrows to select a numeric value. The *DomainUpDown* control enables the user to click up or down arrows to select from a preselected set of options.

- The *CheckBox* control enables users to select options nonexclusively. You can use groups of *CheckBox* controls to enable the user to select multiple options.

- The *RadioButton* control enables you to present a group of exclusive options to the user. You can use groups of *RadioButton* controls to present a list of options, only one of which can be chosen.

- The *TrackBar* control enables the user to set a numeric value rapidly and graphically by adjusting a slider with mouse or keyboard commands.

- The *DateTimePicker* control enables the user to set a date or time. When set to *Time* format, times can be typed into *DateTimePicker*. Days can be chosen from the drop-down calendar interface.

- The *MonthCalendar* control is a highly configurable control that enables the user to select a range of dates from an intuitive user interface. You can configure bold dates and set the maximum length of the date range to be selected by the user.

- The *PictureBox* control is an all-purpose control for displaying images in the user interface. It can display images in a variety of formats. The *ImageList* component organizes a collection of images and can set images to a common size and color depth.

Lesson Review

The following questions are intended to reinforce key information presented in Lesson 3, "Using List-Display and Specialized Controls." The questions are also available on the companion CD if you prefer to review them in electronic form.

> **NOTE ANSWERS**
>
> Answers to these questions and explanations of why each answer choice is correct or incorrect are located in the "Answers" section at the end of the book.

1. Which of the following properties and methods can be used to find the index of a selected item in a *ListBox* control? (Choose all that apply.)

    A. *ListBox.IndexOf*

    B. *ListBox.SelectedIndex*

    C. *ListBox.SelectedIndices*

    D. *ListBox.Select*

2. Which of the following methods CANNOT be used to add an item to the *Items* collection of a *ComboBox*, *ListBox*, or *CheckedListBox* control?

    A. *Items.Add*

    B. *Items.Insert*

    C. *Items.AddRange*

    D. *Items.Contains*

3. Which of the following is NOT a valid setting for the *View* property of the *ListView* control?

    A. *LargeIcon*

    B. *Details*

    C. *Tree*

    D. *SmallIcon*

4. Which of the following are possible values for the *Checked* property of a *CheckBox* control? (Choose all that apply.)

   A. *Checked*

   B. *False*

   C. *Indeterminate*

   D. *Unchecked*

   E. *True*

   F. *NotChecked*

5. You are designing an application that asks the user to select a period ranging from one day to seven days in a given month. Which of the following configurations for a *MonthCalendar* control are best choices to facilitate this functionality? (Choose all that apply.)

   A. Set the *MaxSelectionCount* property to 7.

   B. Set the *SelectionRange* property to the first and last days of the month in question.

   C. Set the *MaxDate* property to the last day of the month in question.

   D. Set the *MinDate* property to the first day of the month in question.

6. Which of the following code examples correctly associates an image from an *ImageList* component with a *Button* control? Assume an *ImageList* component named *ImageList1* and a *Button* control named *Button1*. (Choose all that apply.)

   A.

   Sample of Visual Basic Code

   ```
   Button1.Image = ImageList1
   ```

   Sample of C# Code

   ```
   button1.Image = imageList1;
   ```

   B.

   Sample of Visual Basic Code

   ```
   Button1.ImageList = ImageList1
   Button1.ImageKey = ImageList1.Images(0)
   ```

   Sample of C# Code

   ```
   button1.ImageList1 = imageList1;
   button1.ImageKey = imageList1.Images(0);
   ```

   C.

   Sample of Visual Basic Code

   ```
   Button1.ImageList = ImageList1
   Button1.ImageIndex = 0
   ```

Sample of C# Code

```csharp
button1.ImageList = imageList1;
button1.ImageIndex = 0;
```

D.

Sample of Visual Basic Code

```vb
Button1.ImageList = ImageList1
Button1.ImageKey = "myImage"
```

Sample of C# Code

```csharp
button1.ImageList = imageList1;
button1.ImageKey = "myImage";
```

Lesson 4: Using Tool Strips and Menus

The *ToolStrip* control is designed to facilitate the creation of custom toolbars that behave and look like Office and Microsoft Internet Explorer toolbars. Using the *ToolStrip* control, you can rapidly develop highly configurable, professional-looking toolbars that expose your custom functionality. Menus have always been part of Windows Forms applications. They give the user quick and easy access to important application commands in an easy-to-understand, easy-to-browse interface. The .NET Framework version 2.0 introduced MenuStrips, which enable the rapid creation of Forms menus as well as context menus (also known as shortcut menus, which appear when the user right-clicks an object).

> **After this lesson, you will be able to:**
> - Create toolstrips, menus, and context menus.
> - Configure them for use in your application.
>
> **Estimated lesson time: 60 minutes**

Overview of the *ToolStrip* Control

The *ToolStrip* control enables you to create toolbars that have professional and consistent behavior and appearance. *ToolStrip* controls are containers for *ToolStripItem* controls designed to be hosted inside a tool strip. You can use *ToolStripItem* controls to give the user a wide variety of options and functionality.

   ToolStrip controls encapsulate much of the functionality required for managing a toolbar. They manage the layout and positioning of their contained tool strip controls, enable the user to reorder the tool strip items, manage rendering, and create overflow buttons when a tool strip hosts more tool strip items than it can display. Table 4-35 shows some of the important properties of the *ToolStrip* control.

TABLE 4-35 Important Properties of the *ToolStrip* Control

PROPERTY	DESCRIPTION
AllowItemReorder	Indicates whether the user can reorder items. When set to *True*, contained tool strip items can be reordered when the user holds down the Alt key and grabs the item with the mouse.
AllowMerge	Indicates whether this tool strip can be merged with another tool strip.
CanOverflow	Indicates whether tool strip items can be automatically moved to the overflow button when needed.
Dock	Indicates how the tool strip is docked. Although *ToolStrip* controls can be free in the form, they are usually docked to one of the form edges.

LayoutStyle	Indicates how the controls on the tool strip are laid out. A value of *HorizontalStackWithOverFlow* indicates that items are stacked horizontally and overflow as needed. *VerticalStackWithOverFlow* stacks items vertically and overflows as needed. *StackWithOverflow* determines the stack model appropriate to the *Dock* property of the tool strip. *Flow* allows the items to stack horizontally or vertically as needed, and *Table* arranges all the items flush left.
RenderMode	Determines how the tool strip items are rendered. *System* uses system settings, *Professional* indicates an Office-style appearance, and *ManagerRenderMode* gets the setting automatically.
ShowItemToolTips	Indicates whether tool tips for individual tool strip items are displayed.
Stretch	When hosted in a *ToolStripContainer*, indicates whether the tool strip stretches to the full length of the *ToolStrip* panel.
TextDirection	Indicates the direction of the text in controls hosted in the tool strip.

The *StatusStrip* control is very similar to the *ToolStrip* control and can host the same controls a *ToolStrip* control can. The primary differences are in the default settings for the properties. *StatusStrip* controls are designed to dock at the bottom of the form and give the user status updates, and they have default properties set to values that facilitate this functionality. *ToolStrip* controls are designed for a variety of tool-based roles, and have default values for properties that indicate a more generalized role.

Adding Tool Strip Items to a Tool Strip

At design time, you can add tool strip items to a tool strip by choosing appropriate items from the drop-down menu in the designer, as shown in Figure 4-24.

The item you choose from the menu is added to the tool strip, and an instance of it is added to your application. You can set properties for the item in the Properties window and refer to the item in code.

FIGURE 4-24 Adding a tool strip item at design time.

At run time, you can add items dynamically to a tool strip by using the *ToolStrip.Items.Add* method. This method enables you to specify a reference to an existing tool strip item and add it to the toolbar, or it will create and add a new tool strip item when you specify text or an image. An example is shown here:

Sample of Visual Basic Code

```vb
Dim aToolStripItem As ToolStripItem
Dim bToolStripItem As ToolStripItem
aToolStripItem = myToolStrip.Items.Add("New Item")
bToolStripItem = myToolStrip.Items.Add(anImage)
```

Sample of C# Code

```csharp
ToolStripItem aToolStripItem;
ToolStripItem bToolStripItem;
aToolStripItem = myToolStrip.Items.Add("New Item");
bToolStripItem = myToolStrip.Items.Add(anImage);
```

In this example, a new tool strip item is added when text or an image is specified in the call to the *Add* method. When items are added in this way, the resulting item is always a *ToolStripButton* object. The *ToolStrip.Items.Add* method returns a reference to the new item so you can set properties and events for it at run time.

You can also create a new tool strip item and then add it directly, as shown here:

Sample of Visual Basic Code

```vb
Dim aComboBox As New ToolStripComboBox()
myToolStrip.Items.Add(aComboBox)
```

Sample of C# Code

```csharp
ToolStripComboBox aComboBox = new ToolStripComboBox();
myToolStrip.Items.Add(aComboBox);
```

By following this example, you can create a tool strip item of any kind and add it to a tool strip at run time.

Tool Strip Items

The .NET Framework provides several items designed to be hosted in tool strips. Items such as the *ToolStripLabel*, *ToolStripButton*, *ToolStripTextBox*, *ToolStripComboBox*, and *ToolStripProgressBar* controls are similar to the *Label*, *Button*, *TextBox*, *ComboBox*, and *ProgressBar* controls, but they are designed to be hosted in tool strips. *ToolStripSplitButton*, *ToolStripDropDownButton*, and *ToolStripSeparator* are designed to provide functionality specific to tool strips.

Common Properties of Tool Strip Items

Tool strip items have several common properties that govern their behavior in the tool strip. Table 4-36 describes the most important properties that all tool strip items share.

TABLE 4-36 Important Properties of Tool Strip Items

PROPERTY	DESCRIPTION
MergeAction	Determines how a tool strip item behaves with the tool strip that contains it when it is merged with another tool strip. Possible values are *Append, Insert, MatchOnly, Remove*, and *Replace*. Merging tool strips will be discussed later in this lesson.
MergeIndex	Indicates where a tool strip item appears in a merged tool strip if the *MergeAction* property is set to *Insert*.
ToolTipText	Gets or sets the text shown in a tool tip when the mouse hovers over the tool strip item if the *ToolStrip.ShowItemToolTips* property is set to *True*. Note that the *ToolStripSeparator* control does not have this property.

ToolStripLabel

The *ToolStripLabel* control combines the functionality of the *Label* control and the *LinkLabel* control. When the *IsLink* property is set to *False*, *ToolStripLabel* displays the text contained in its *Text* property in the tool strip and acts similarly to a basic *Label* control. When the *IsLink* property is set to *True*, the control behaves like a *LinkLabel* control. You can program actions to be taken when the label is clicked in the *ToolStripLabel.Click* event handler.

ToolStripButton

The *ToolStripButton* control is analogous to the familiar *Button* control. It appears on the tool strip as a button, usually displaying an icon that indicates its function. The user can click the button to execute an action. Clicking the button executes code in the *ToolStripButton.Click* event handler.

ToolStripSeparator

The *ToolStripSeparator* control is a visual cue that separates items in a tool strip from other items in a tool strip. Although it can respond to mouse clicks through the *ToolStripSeparator* *.Click* event handler, it primarily provides visual feedback.

ToolStripComboBox

The *ToolStripComboBox* control is similar to the *ComboBox* control but is hosted in a tool strip. Like the *ComboBox* control, it can be set to styles of *Simple, DropDown*, or *DropDownList*, and the items are found in the *Items* collection. When an item is selected or typed into *ToolStripComboBox*, that item is exposed through the *Text* property.

ToolStripTextBox

ToolStripTextBox is very similar to the basic *TextBox* control. The user can type a string into the text box, and this string will be accessible programmatically through the *ToolStripTextBox.Text* property. The main difference in functionality is that *ToolStripTextBox* does not have a *MultiLine* property and, thus, can have only one line.

ToolStripProgressBar

ToolStripProgressBar is a control designed to provide feedback to the user when progress is made on a time-consuming task, and it functions very similarly to the standard *ProgressBar* control. The *Minimum* and *Maximum* properties set the minimum and maximum values for *ToolStripProgressBar*, and the *Value* property determines the current setting. The visual appearance is set by the *Style* property, and when *Style* is set to *Blocks* or *Continuous*, the *Value* property is reflected in the visual interface as a percentage of the maximum that is filled in the progress bar. When it is set to *Marquee*, blocks continuously move across the progress bar at the rate specified by the *MarqueeAnimationSpeed* property. At run time, you can advance the value of *ToolStripProgressBar* either by setting the *Value* property directly or by using the *Increment* and *PerformStep* methods.

ToolStripDropDownButton

ToolStripDropDownButton enables you to create a drop-down menu that appears when the button is clicked. At design time, you can create the menu by typing text for menu items in the menu designer.

Each menu item has its own *ToolStripMenuItem.Click* event to which you can respond.

ToolStripSplitButton

The *ToolStripSplitButton* control combines the functionality of the *ToolStripButton* and *ToolStripDropDownButton* controls. It exposes a button a user can click to execute code, but it also exposes a drop-down menu in the style of the *ToolStripDropDownButton* control. You can handle the *ToolStripSplitButton.Click* event to write code for the button clicks, or you can write code that is executed for each *ToolStripMenuItem.Click* event.

Displaying Images on Tool Strip Items

The *ToolStripButton*, *ToolStripDropDownButton*, and *ToolStripSplitButton* controls can display text, images, or a combination of both. Table 4-37 shows how the properties of these controls govern how images are displayed.

TABLE 4-37 Image Display Properties of *ToolStripButton* Controls

PROPERTY	DESCRIPTION
DisplayStyle	Determines whether the control is displayed with text, image, or both.
Image	Gets or sets the image associated with this control.
ImageAlign	Indicates how the image is aligned in the control.
ImageScaling	Specifies whether the image will be resized to fit the control.
ImageTransparentColor	Indicates the color in the image that will appear as transparent when rendered in the UI.

To display an image on a tool strip:

1. Select the control. In the Properties window, ensure that the *DisplayStyle* property is set to *Image* or *ImageAndText*.

2. In the Properties window, select the image for the control by clicking the *Image* property and selecting or browsing to the appropriate image in the Select Resource dialog box.

The *ToolStripContainer* Class

The *ToolStripContainer* class is a specialized container control designed specifically for containing tool strips and enabling rafting, the process by which a user can grab a tool strip and move it from one edge of the container to another.

The *ToolStripContainer* contains five panels: four *ToolStrip* panels (one on each edge of the form) and one *Content* panel. The most common scenario for *ToolStripContainer* is to add it to a form and set the *Dock* property to *Fill*. This results in the *ToolStripContainer* filling the entire form and having tool strip panels available on all sides.

At design time, you can add a tool strip to a tool strip container by dragging it from the toolbox onto one of the tool strip panels. You can control which tool strip panels are available to the user by setting the *TopToolStripPanelVisible*, *BottomToolStripPanelVisible*, *LeftToolStripPanelVisible*, and *RightToolStripPanelVisible* properties. When these properties are set to *True*, the corresponding panel is available for tool strip rafting at run time. When they are set to *False*, the panel is not available.

Merging Tool Strips

You can merge *ToolStrip* controls at run time and incorporate their items into a single tool strip. You merge tool strips by invoking the *ToolStripManager.Merge* method, as shown here:

Sample of Visual Basic Code

```
ToolStripManager.Merge(sourceToolStrip, targetToolStrip)
```

Sample of C# Code

```
ToolStripManager.Merge(sourceToolStrip, targetToolStrip);
```

The *ToolStripManager* is a static class that manages the display and layout of the tool strips on a form. Because it is a static class, there is no need to instantiate it; you can invoke the methods directly.

The preceding example merges the first tool strip, *sourceToolStrip*, with the second tool strip, *targetToolStrip*. The tool strip items on *sourceToolStrip* are then merged with the items on *targetToolStrip*, as is determined by their *MergeAction* property value. Table 4-38 summarizes the merge action taken by the *MergeAction* property value.

TABLE 4-38 *ToolStripItem MergeAction* Property Values and Merge Actions

MERGEACTION VALUE	ACTION TAKEN
Append	Appends the item at the end of the list of items.
Insert	Inserts the item at the location specified by the *MergeIndex* property.
MatchOnly	Looks for a match but takes no action.
Remove	If a matching tool strip item is found, it is removed from the resulting tool strip.
Replace	If a matching tool strip item is found, it is replaced with this tool strip.

When tool strips are merged, each tool strip item in the source tool strip is compared to each tool strip item in the target tool strip. The comparison is based on the *Text* property of each tool strip item. Thus, if any two tool strip items have the same *Text* property, they are considered a match, even if they are different types. (For example, a *ToolStripLabel* item and a *ToolStripButton* item that both have a *Text* property set to *Execute* are considered a match.) If a match is found and the source tool strip item has the *MergeAction* property set to *MatchOnly*, *Remove*, or *Replace*, the appropriate action is taken. Otherwise, the tool strip item is appended or inserted, as determined by the *MergeAction* property.

For tool strips to be merged successfully, they must have their *AllowMerge* property set to *True*.

 Quick Check

1. What is the purpose of the *ToolStrip* control?

2. What kinds of *ToolStripItem* controls can be hosted in a *ToolStrip* control?

Overview of the *MenuStrip* Control

The *MenuStrip* control is essentially a *ToolStrip* control optimized for the display of *ToolStripMenu* items. The *MenuStrip* control derives from *ToolStrip* and can host all the tool strip items described in the previous lesson. Its primary function, however, is to host *ToolStripMenu* items.

ToolStripMenuItem controls are the controls that provide the visual representation for items on a menu. They can appear as text, an image, or both and can execute code found in their *ToolStripMenuItem.Click* event handlers when clicked. Each *ToolStripMenuItem* control can contain its own set of menu items, allowing for the creation of nested menus.

The menu strip exposes many properties that affect the behavior of its hosted *ToolStripMenu* items. Table 4-39 describes important properties of the *MenuStrip* control.

TABLE 4-39 Important Properties of the *MenuStrip* Control

PROPERTY	DESCRIPTION
AllowItemReorder	Indicates whether the user can reorder items. When set to *True*, contained items can be reordered when the user holds down the Alt key and grabs the item with the mouse.
AllowMerge	Indicates whether this menu strip can be merged with another tool strip.
Dock	Indicates how the menu strip is docked. Although *MenuStrip* controls can be free in the form, they are usually docked to one of the form edges.
LayoutStyle	Indicates how the controls on the tool strip are laid out. A value of *HorizontalStackWithOverflow* indicates that items are stacked horizontally and overflow as needed. *VerticalStackWithOverflow* stacks items vertically and overflows as needed. *StackWithOverflow* determines the stack model appropriate to the *Dock* property of the tool strip. *Flow* allows the items to stack horizontally or vertically as needed, and *Table* arranges all the items flush left.
RenderMode	Determines how the tool strip items are rendered. *System* uses system settings, *Professional* indicates an Office-style appearance, and *ManagerRenderMode* gets the setting automatically.

ShowItemToolTips	Indicates whether tool tips for individual tool strip items are displayed.
Stretch	When hosted in a *ToolStripContainer*, indicates whether the tool strip stretches to the full length of the *ToolStripPanel*.
TextDirection	Indicates the direction of the text in controls hosted in the tool strip.

Note that the properties of the *MenuStrip* control are very similar to the properties of the *ToolStrip* control. Because *MenuStrip* derives from *ToolStrip*, it exposes most of the same properties as the *ToolStrip* control and encapsulates most of the same functionality.

ToolStripMenuItem controls provide all the functionality expected of menus. Table 4-40 explains some of the important properties of the *ToolStripMenuItem* control.

TABLE 4-40 Important Properties of the *ToolStripMenuItem* Control

PROPERTY	DESCRIPTION
AutoSize	Determines whether the menu item is automatically sized to fit the text.
Checked	Determines whether the menu item appears as selected.
CheckOnClick	Determines whether the menu item is automatically selected when clicked.
CheckState	Returns the *CheckState* value of the menu item. *CheckState* can be *Checked*, *Unchecked*, or *Indeterminate*.
DisplayStyle	Determines how the tool strip menu item is displayed. This property can be set to *None*, which provides no visual representation; *Text*, which shows only text; *Image*, which displays the item with an image only; or *ImageAndText*, which displays the image next to the text.
DoubleClickEnabled	Determines whether the *DoubleClick* event fires.
DropDownItems	Contains a collection of tool strip items (usually, but not necessarily, tool strip menu items) that appear in the drop-down list when this item is chosen.
Enabled	Determines whether the tool strip menu item is enabled.
Image	Sets the image to be associated with this tool strip menu item.
MergeAction	Determines the action taken by this tool strip menu item when menus are merged.
MergeIndex	Determines the order of items in the resultant menu after menus are merged.

ShortcutKeyDisplayString	Sets a custom string for the shortcut key displayed next to the menu item. If shortcut keys are enabled and this property is left blank, the actual key combination is displayed.
ShortcutKeys	Defines the key combination that will act as a shortcut to execute the menu command.
ShowShortcutKeys	Indicates whether shortcut keys are displayed.
Text	Gets or sets the text displayed in the menu item.
TextImageRelation	Determines how the text and image are displayed together when the *DisplayStyle* property is set to *ImageAndText*.

Creating Menu Strips and Tool Strip Menu Items

You can create a *MenuStrip* control at design time in the same way you create any control: by dragging it from the Toolbox onto the design surface. After it has been added to the design surface, an interface for creating tool strip menu items appears. You can type a string into the box in the menu strip to create a new tool strip menu item. After a new item has been created, additional boxes appear to the right of and beneath the newly created tool strip menu item to enable you to create more items or subitems of the first item. This interface disappears if you move the focus elsewhere in the designer, but you can make it reappear by clicking the tool strip menu item. Figure 4-25 shows the *ToolStripMenuItem* control design interface.

Note that the default naming scheme for the *ToolStripMenuItem* control is different from the default naming scheme for other controls. Although controls such as *Button* are appended with a number when added to the form (such as *Button1*), tool strip menu items are prepended with the text of the menu item. For example, if you created a File menu item, the default name would be *fileToolStripMenuItem*. You can rename a menu item by changing the *Name* property in the Properties window.

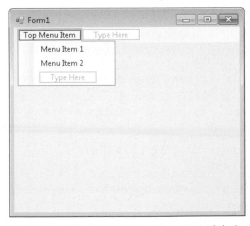

FIGURE 4-25 The *ToolStripMenuItem* control design interface.

Changing Properties for Multiple Tool Strip Menu Items at Once

At times, you might want to edit properties for several menu items (or any control) at the same time. You would usually do this to ensure that all controls have the same setting for a particular property. If you edit properties for a selection of types of controls, the Properties window displays only those properties and events that all controls have in common.

To change multiple menu item properties at once:

1. While holding down the Ctrl key, click each menu item you want to edit to select it.

2. Make the appropriate changes in the Properties window. Changes you make will apply to all selected menu items.

You can also add tool strip menu items to menu strips programmatically at run time. You can either add a preexisting menu item (for example, an item on another menu strip) or create a brand new menu item and add it to the menu strip. The following code example demonstrates each of these techniques:

Sample of Visual Basic Code

```
' Adds an existing ToolStripMenuItem to the MenuStrip
MenuStrip1.Items.Add(OpenToolStripMenuItem)
' Creates a new ToolStripMenuItem and adds it to the MenuStrip
Dim HelpToolStripMenuItem As New ToolStripMenuItem("Help")
MenuStrip1.Items.Add(HelpToolStripMenuItem)
```

Sample of C# Code

```
// Adds an existing ToolStripMenuItem to the MenuStrip
menuStrip1.Items.Add(OpenToolStripMenuItem);
// Creates a new ToolStripMenuItem and adds it to the MenuStrip
ToolStripMenuItem HelpToolStripMenuItem = new
    ToolStripMenuItem("Help");
menuStrip1.Items.Add(HelpToolStripMenuItem);
```

You can also use the *MenuStrip.Items.Add* method to add new tool strip menu items, even if you don't have a reference to an existing tool strip menu item. The following example shows how you can specify text or an image to create a tool strip menu item and get a reference to it:

Sample of Visual Basic Code

```
Dim newMenuItem1 As ToolStripMenuItem
Dim newMenuItem2 As ToolStripMenuItem
' Adds a new menu item by specifying text
newMenuItem1 = MenuStrip1.Items.Add("File")
' Adds a new menu item by specifying an image
newMenuItem2 = MenuStrip1.Items.Add(anImage)
```

Sample of C# Code

```
ToolStripMenuItem newMenuItem1;
ToolStripMenuItem newMenuItem2;
// Adds a new menu item by specifying text
newMenuItem1 = MenuStrip1.Items.Add("File");
```

```
// Adds a new menu item by specifying an image
newMenuItem2 = MenuStrip1.Items.Add(anImage);
```

You can use similar techniques to add new or existing tool strip menu items to the drop-down items of an existing tool strip menu item. This has the effect of creating new items in a submenu. The following example demonstrates programmatically adding a tool strip menu item to the *DropDownItems* collection of an existing tool strip menu item:

Sample of Visual Basic Code

```
Dim newMenuItem1 As ToolStripMenuItem
Dim newMenuItem2 As ToolStripMenuItem
' Adds an existing ToolStripMenuItem to another existing ToolStripMenuItem
FileToolStripMenuItem.DropDownItems.Add(OpenToolStripMenuItem)
' Creates a new ToolStripMenuItem and adds it to the MenuStrip
Dim HelpToolStripMenuItem As New ToolStripMenuItem("Help")
FileToolStripMenuItem.DropDownItems.Add(HelpToolStripMenuItem)
' Adds a new menu item by specifying text
newMenuItem1 = FileToolStripMenuItem.DropDownItems.Add("Open")
' Adds a new menu item by specifying an image
newMenuItem2 = FileToolStripMenuItem.DropDownItems.Add(anImage)
```

Sample of C# Code

```
ToolStripMenuItem newMenuItem1;
ToolStripMenuItem newMenuItem2;
// Adds an existing ToolStripMenuItem to another existing ToolStripMenuItem
FileToolStripMenuItem.DropDownItems.Add(OpenToolStripMenuItem);
// Creates a new ToolStripMenuItem and adds it to the MenuStrip
ToolStripMenuItem HelpToolStripMenuItem = new ToolStripMenuItem("Help");
FileToolStripMenuItem.DropDownItems.Add(HelpToolStripMenuItem);
// Adds a new menu item by specifying text
newMenuItem1 = (ToolStripMenuItem)FileToolStripMenuItem.DropDownItems.Add("Open");
// Adds a new menu item by specifying an image
newMenuItem2 = (ToolStripMenuItem)FileToolStripMenuItem.DropDownItems.Add(anImage);
```

Copying Menu Items at Design Time

At times, you might want to copy menu items from one location to another. For example, if you are creating different menus but you want to have a common set of options among them, you can easily copy menu items by copying and pasting in the designer.

To copy menu items at design time:

1. In the designer, right-click the menu item you want to copy and choose Copy from the context menu.

2. In the designer, right-click the menu item that is the intended location of the copied menu and choose Paste from the context menu. The menu item is copied into the new location.

Note that with this procedure, you can copy top-level items to sublevel items, sublevel items to top-level items, top-level items to top-level items, or sublevel items to sublevel items.

Adding Enhancements to Menus

Menus can display a variety of enhancements that streamline the user experience and enhance usability. This section covers how to create check marks, access keys, separator bars, and shortcut keys on menu items.

Adding Check Marks to Menu Items

You can display check marks next to any menu items except top-level menu items. This is useful when you want to indicate to the user that a menu option is selected or enabled. You can display a check mark beside a menu item by setting the *Checked* property to *True*, as shown here:

Sample of Visual Basic Code

```
OptionToolStripMenuItem.Checked = True
```

Sample of C# Code

```
optionToolStripMenuItem.Checked = true;
```

Alternatively, you can define whether the menu item is selected by setting the *CheckState* property to *Checked*, as shown here:

Sample of Visual Basic Code

```
OptionToolStripMenuItem.CheckState = CheckState.Checked
```

Sample of C# Code

```
optionToolStripMenuItem.CheckState = CheckState.Checked;
```

The *Checked* property is a Boolean property that returns whether an item is selected. If the item is selected, the *Checked* property returns *True*. If the item is in any other state, the *Checked* property returns *False*. The *CheckState*, however, indicates the actual state of the menu item and returns *CheckState.Checked*, *CheckState.Unchecked*, or *Checkstate.Indeterminate*.

If you want a menu item to appear selected when the user clicks the item, you can set the *CheckOnClick* property to *True*. This causes the check mark on the menu item to toggle between selected and cleared each time the user clicks the menu item. You can programmatically change the check state or determine whether the menu item is selected by using the *ToolStripMenuItem.CheckState* property or the *ToolStripMenuItem.Checked* property.

Adding Separator Bars to Menus

It can be useful to add separator bars to menus to set groups of menu options apart from one another. You can add a separator to any submenu at design time by choosing Separator from the drop-down box in the menu item design interface.

Note that if you want to add a separator to a top-level menu, you must do so programmatically by creating a new instance of the *ToolStripSeparator* control and inserting it into the correct location in the *MenuStrip.Items* collection, as shown here:

Sample of Visual Basic Code

```
Dim aSeparator As New ToolStripSeparator
MenuStrip1.Items.Insert(1, aSeparator)
```

Sample of C# Code

```
ToolStripSeparator aSeparator = new ToolStripSeparator();
menuStrip1.Items.Insert(1, aSeparator);
```

Creating Access Keys

Access keys enable you to access menu items by defining keys that, when pressed in combination with the Alt key, will execute the menu command. For example, if a File menu defines the F key as an access key, when Alt+F is pressed, the File menu opens. Menus that contain submenus open when the access key combination is pressed, and menus that invoke commands will invoke those commands. Note that the menu item must be visible for the access key to function. Thus, if you define an access key for an Open menu item that exists in the File submenu, the File menu must be opened first for the access key combination to function.

You can create an access key for a menu by preceding the letter for which you want to define the access key with an ampersand (&) symbol. For example, to create an Alt+F access key combination for the File menu, you would set the *Text* property of *FileToolStripMenuItem* to *&File*.

Creating Shortcut Keys

Unlike access keys, shortcut keys are a combination of keystrokes that enable direct invocation of a menu item, whether the menu item is visible or not. For example, you might define the Ctrl+E key combination to be a shortcut key for the Exit menu command in the File menu. Even if the File menu is not open, Ctrl+E causes the Exit menu command to be executed. Also, unlike access keys, you cannot create shortcut keys for top-level menus; you can create them only for items in submenus.

You can create a shortcut key at design time by setting the *ShortcutKeys* property in the Properties window. Clicking the *ShortcutKeys* property launches a visual interface that enables you to define a key combination. Figure 4-26 displays this interface.

FIGURE 4-26 The *ShortcutKeys* property user interface.

If you want to display the shortcut key combination next to the menu item, you can set the *ShowShortcutKeys* property of the *ToolStripMenuItem* control to *True*. You can also define custom text to be shown instead of the key combination. If you want to define custom text, you can set it in the *ShortcutKeyDisplayString* property.

Moving Items between Menus

You can move items from one menu to another at run time. This enables you to customize menus dynamically for special purposes. You can move a menu item to a new menu strip by using the *MenuStrip.Items.Add* method to add it to the new menu strip. It is removed from the previous menu strip automatically. If you want to add the menu item to a particular location in the new menu strip, you can use the *Insert* method to add it at a particular index. Examples are shown here:

Sample of Visual Basic Code

```vb
' Adds the FileToolStripMenuItem
MenuStrip2.Items.Add(FileToolStripMenuItem)
' Inserts FileToolStripMenuItem to the location corresponding to index 1
MenuStrip2.Items.Insert(1, FileToolStripMenuItem)
```

Sample of C# Code

```csharp
// Adds the FileToolStripMenuItem
menuStrip2.Items.Add(FileToolStripMenuItem);
// Inserts FileToolStripMenuItem to the location corresponding to index 1
menuStrip2.Items.Insert(1, FileToolStripMenuItem);
```

You can also use the analogous methods of the *ToolStripMenuItem.DropDownItems* property to move items from one menu to another. Examples are shown here:

Sample of Visual Basic Code

```
' Adds the FileToolStripMenuItem
AppToolStripMenuItem.DropDownItems.Add(FileToolStripMenuItem)
' Inserts FileToolStripMenuItem to the location corresponding to index 1
AppToolStripMenuItem.DropDownItems.Insert(1, FileToolStripMenuItem)
```

Sample of C# Code

```
// Adds the FileToolStripMenuItem
AppToolStripMenuItem.DropDownItems.Add(FileToolStripMenuItem);
// Inserts FileToolStripMenuItem to the location corresponding to index 1
AppToolStripMenuItem.DropDownItems.Insert(1, FileToolStripMenuItem);
```

Disabling, Hiding, and Deleting Menu Items

At times, it makes sense to remove certain options from a menu. You might want a menu item to be disabled when conditions aren't appropriate for it to be invoked, or you might want to hide a menu item that shouldn't be displayed. In some cases, you might want to delete a menu item completely.

You can disable a menu item by setting the *Enabled* property to *False*. This causes the menu item to appear dimmed. It is still visible to the user, but it cannot be invoked by mouse clicks or keystrokes.

You can hide a menu item by setting the *Visible* property to *False*. This keeps the menu item from appearing in the menu. Note, however, that it does not disable the menu item, and if the *Enabled* property is set to *True*, the menu item can still be invoked through shortcut keys if they have been defined for this menu item. Hide menu items sparingly; if a user is looking for a specific menu item, it is typically better for the user to see it dimmed because the *Enabled* property has been set to *False*. Otherwise, the user might continue looking for the hidden menu item on other menus.

If you need to delete a menu item from a menu entirely, you can do so by using the *MenuStrip.Items.Remove* and *MenuStrip.Items.RemoveAt* methods to remove an item from a top-level menu. Alternately, you can use the *ToolStripMenuItem.DropDownItems.Remove* and *ToolStripMenuItem.DropDownItems.RemoveAt* methods to remove an item from a submenu, as shown in the following examples:

Sample of Visual Basic Code

```
'Removes FileToolStripMenuItem from MenuStrip1
MenuStrip1.Items.Remove(FileToolStripMenuItem)
' Removes FileToolStripMenuItem from AppToolStripMenuItem
AppToolStripMenuItem.DropDownItems.Remove(FileToolStripMenuItem)
' Removes the ToolStripMenuItem at index 4 from MenuStrip1
MenuStrip1.Items.RemoveAt(4)
' Removes the ToolStripMenuItem at index 4 from AppToolStripMenuItem
AppToolStripMenuItem.DropDownItems.RemoveAt(4)
```

Sample of C# Code

```
// Removes FileToolStripMenuItem from menuStrip1
menuStrip1.Items.Remove(FileToolStripMenuItem);
// Removes FileToolStripMenuItem from AppToolStripMenuItem
AppToolStripMenuItem.DropDownItems.Remove(FileToolStripMenuItem);
// Removes the ToolStripMenuItem at index 4 from menuStrip1
menuStrip1.Items.RemoveAt(4);
// Removes the ToolStripMenuItem at index 4 from AppToolStripMenuItem
AppToolStripMenuItem.DropDownItems.RemoveAt(4);
```

Merging Menus

Menus can be merged and their items incorporated into a single menu at run time. You can merge *MenuStrip* or *ContextMenuStrip* controls (which are covered in greater detail later in this lesson), or both. In fact, you can even merge *MenuStrip* controls with *ToolStrip* controls. Like tool strips, you merge menu strips by invoking the *ToolStripManager.Merge* method on the static *ToolStripManager* class, as shown here:

Sample of Visual Basic Code

```
ToolStripManager.Merge(sourceMenuStrip, targetMenuStrip)
```

Sample of C# Code

```
ToolStripManager.Merge(sourceMenuStrip, targetMenuStrip);
```

The preceding example merges the first menu strip, *sourceMenuStrip*, with the second menu strip, *targetMenuStrip*. The tool strip menu items on *sourceMenuStrip* are then merged with the items on *targetMenuStrip* as determined by their *MergeAction* property value. Table 4-41 summarizes the merge action taken by the *MergeAction* property value.

TABLE 4-41 *ToolStripItem MergeAction* Property Values and Merge Actions

MERGEACTION VALUE	ACTION TAKEN
Append	Appends the item at the end of the list of items.
Insert	Inserts the item at the location specified by the *MergeIndex* property.
MatchOnly	Looks for a match but takes no action.
Remove	If a matching tool strip item is found, it is removed from the resulting tool strip.
Replace	If a matching tool strip item is found, it is replaced with this tool strip.

When menu strips are merged, each tool strip menu item in the source menu strip is compared to each menu item in the target menu strip. The comparison is based on the *Text* property of each menu item. Thus, if any two tool strip menu items have the same *Text* property, they are considered a match. If a match is found, and the source tool strip menu item has the *MergeAction* property set to *MatchOnly*, *Remove*, or *Replace*, the appropriate action will be taken. Otherwise, the tool strip menu item is appended or inserted, as determined by the *MergeAction* property.

For menu strips to be merged successfully, they must have their *AllowMerge* property set to *True*.

Switching between *MenuStrip* Controls Programmatically

As application conditions change, adding and removing menu items might not be sufficient to meet the needs of your application, and you might opt to completely replace a menu strip with another menu strip. You can remove a *MenuStrip* control from the form entirely by removing it from the form's *Controls* collection, and you can likewise add a new *MenuStrip* control by adding it to the form's *Controls* collection. The following example demonstrates how to remove *MenuStrip1* from the form and replace it with *MenuStrip2* at run time:

Sample of Visual Basic Code

```
Me.Controls.Remove(MenuStrip1)
Me.Controls.Add(MenuStrip2)
```

Sample of C# Code

```
this.Controls.Remove(MenuStrip1);
this.Controls.Add(MenuStrip2);
```

Note that the menu strip you add should not already be a member of the form's *Controls* collection.

Context Menus and the *ContextMenuStrip* Control

Context menus are familiar to all users of Windows Forms applications. These shortcut menus are displayed when the user right-clicks an object. The *ContextMenuStrip* control enables you to create context menus and associate them with a selected object.

The *ContextMenuStrip* control is similar to the *MenuStrip* control. Both controls have an intuitive design interface that enables you to create tool strip menu items quickly, and both expose a collection of tool strip menu items in the *Items* property. The main difference between the *ContextMenuStrip* and the *MenuStrip* controls is that the *ContextMenuStrip* control does not have a top-level menu and is not visible at run time unless invoked by right-clicking the control with which it is associated.

Adding and Removing Context Menu Items

You can easily add and remove items from a context menu strip by using the *ContextMenuStrip.Items.Add* and *ContextMenuStrip.Items.Remove* methods, as shown in the following example:

Sample of Visual Basic Code

```
' Adds an item to the ContextMenuStrip
ContextMenuStrip1.Items.Add(ExitToolStripMenuItem)
```

```
' Removes an item from the ContextMenuStrip
ContextMenuStrip1.Items.Remove(ExitToolStripMenuItem)
```

Sample of C# Code

```
// Adds an item to the ContextMenuStrip
contextMenuStrip1.Items.Add(ExitToolStripMenuItem);
// Removes an item from the ContextMenuStrip
contextMenuStrip1.Items.Remove(ExitToolStripMenuItem);
```

Associating a *ContextMenuStrip* Property with a Control

All controls that can display a context menu expose a *ContextMenuStrip* property that represents the context menu associated with that control. When this property is set to a valid *ContextMenuStrip* control, the context menu appears when the user right-clicks the control at run time. You can set this property at design time in the Properties window.

You can also set the *ContextMenuStrip* property for a control at run time. The following example demonstrates how to create a context menu dynamically from preexisting menu items and then associate it with a control:

Sample of Visual Basic Code

```
ContextMenuStrip1.Items.Add(ExitToolStripMenuItem)
ContextMenuStrip1.Items.Add(OpenToolStripMenuItem)
Button1.ContextMenuStrip = ContextMenuStrip1
```

Sample of C# Code

```
contextMenuStrip1.Items.Add(ExitToolStripMenuItem);
contextMenuStrip1.Items.Add(OpenToolStripMenuItem);
button1.ContextMenuStrip = contextMenuStrip1;
```

Copying Menu Items from Existing Menu Strips at Run Time

You will frequently want to create context menus that also expose the same menu items as items in regular menus. Although a single tool strip menu item can belong to only one menu strip at a time, it is easy to create an exact copy of a menu item at run time. The *ToolStripMenuItem* constructor has several overloads that enable you to specify the text, image, and click-event handler. The following example demonstrates how to make a copy of an existing tool strip menu item named *ExitToolStripMenuItem* and add it to a *ContextMenuStrip* control named *ContextMenuStrip1*. This example assumes the existence of a method named *ExitToolStripMenuItem_Click*, which is the event handler for the *ExitToolStripMenuItem.Click* event.

Sample of Visual Basic Code

```
Dim anItem As ToolStripMenuItem
anItem = New ToolStripMenuItem(ExitToolStripMenuItem.Text, _
    ExitToolStripMenuItem.Image, New EventHandler(addressof _
    ExitToolStripMenuItem_Click))
ContextMenuStrip1.Items.Add(anItem)
```

Sample of C# Code

```
ToolStripMenuItem anItem;
anItem = new ToolStripMenuItem(ExitToolStripMenuItem.Text,
   ExitToolStripMenuItem.Image, new
   EventHandler(ExitToolStripMenuItem_Click));
ContextMenuStrip1.Items.Add(anItem);
```

 Quick Check

1. What is the difference between a *MenuStrip* control and a *ContextMenuStrip* control?

2. How do you associate a *ContextMenuStrip* property with a control?

Quick Check Answers

1. A *ContextMenuStrip* control is designed to be shown when the user right-clicks a control. Thus, it contains no top-level elements and has no visual presence on the form until a control is right-clicked.

2. You can associate a *ContextMenuStrip* property with a control by setting that control's *ContextMenuStrip* property.

PRACTICE **Creating a *ToolStrip*–Based Web Browser**

In this practice, you explore the functionality of *ToolStrip* and *ToolStripItem* controls by creating a simple Web browser that uses *ToolStripItem* controls to enable its functionality. In the first exercise, you add a tool strip that implements basic Web browser functionality. In the second exercise, you add a tool strip that enables the user to search the Web. In the third exercise, you extend the capabilities of the Web browser by adding a menu with menu items that enable you to browse, print, or save a file.

EXERCISE 1   Creating a Web Browser

1. Start a new Windows Forms Project.

2. From the Toolbox, drag a *ToolStripContainer* control onto the form. Set the *Dock* property to *Fill*.

3. Enlarge the form to a comfortable size for a Web browser.

4. From the Toolbox, drag a *WebBrowser* control into the center panel of *ToolStripContainer*.

5. From the Toolbox, drag a *ToolStrip* control to the top panel of *ToolStripContainer*.

6. Using the drop-down menu in the tool strip, add the following controls to the tool strip in this order: two *ToolStripButton* controls, a *ToolStripComboBox* control, and two more *ToolStripButton* controls.

7. In the Properties window, set the *Name*, *Image*, and *ToolTipText* properties of the *ToolStripButton* controls, as shown in the following table. You can find the image files in the completed solutions installed from the CD.

DEFAULT NAME	NEW NAME	IMAGE	TOOLTIPTEXT
ToolStripButton1	*BackButton*	Back.bmp	Navigate Back
ToolStripButton2	*ForwardButton*	Forward.bmp	Navigate Forward
ToolStripButton3	*GoButton*	Go.bmp	Navigate
ToolStripButton4	*StopButton*	Stop.bmp	Stop Navigation

8. Double-click the *BackButton* button and add the following code to the *BackButton_Click* event handler:

Sample of Visual Basic Code

```
WebBrowser1.GoBack()
```

Sample of C# Code

```
webBrowser1.GoBack();
```

9. Double-click the *ForwardButton* button and add the following code to the *ForwardButton_Click* event handler:

Sample of Visual Basic Code

```
WebBrowser1.GoForward()
```

Sample of C# Code

```
webBrowser1.GoForward();
```

10. Double-click the *GoButton* button and add the following code to the *GoButton.Click* event handler:

Sample of Visual Basic Code

```
If Not ToolStripComboBox1.Text = "" Then
    WebBrowser1.Navigate(ToolStripComboBox1.Text)
    ToolStripComboBox1.Items.Add(ToolStripComboBox1.Text)
    If ToolStripComboBox1.Items.Count = 11 Then
        ToolStripComboBox1.Items.RemoveAt(0)
    End If
End If
```

Sample of C# Code

```
if (!(toolStripComboBox1.Text == ""))
{
    webBrowser1.Navigate(toolStripComboBox1.Text);
    toolStripComboBox1.Items.Add(toolStripComboBox1.Text);
    if (toolStripComboBox1.Items.Count == 11)
    {
        toolStripComboBox1.Items.RemoveAt(0);
    }
}
```

11. Double-click the *StopButton* button and add the following code to the *StopButton_Click* event handler:

Sample of Visual Basic Code
```
WebBrowser1.Stop()
```

Sample of C# Code
```
webBrowser1.Stop();
```

12. Press F5 to test your application.

EXERCISE 2   Adding a Search Tool Strip

1. From the Toolbox, drag a second *ToolStrip* control onto the *Top* panel of the *ToolStripContainer* control.

2. In the ToolStrip designer, add a *ToolStripTextBox* control and a *ToolStripButton* control to the new tool strip.

3. In the Properties window, set the *Text* property of *ToolStripButton* to **Search Bing** and the *DisplayStyle* property to *Text*.

4. Double-click the tool strip button and add the following code to its event handler:

Sample of Visual Basic Code
```
WebBrowser1.Navigate("http://search.msn.com/results.aspx?q=" & _
    ToolStripTextBox1.Text)
```

Sample of C# Code
```
webBrowser1.Navigate(@"http://search.msn.com/results.aspx?q=" +
    toolStripTextBox1.Text);
```

5. Press F5 to test your application. Note that the two tool strips can be individually positioned and moved to other panels in *ToolStripContainer*.

EXERCISE 3   Adding a Menu

1. Open the partial solution for this exercise on the companion CD.

2. Open Form1. In the designer, drag a *MenuStrip* control from the Toolbox to the top panel of *ToolStripContainer*.

3. Add a top-level tool strip menu item named **&File** to the menu strip.

4. Add the following submenu items to the File tool strip menu item: **&Open**, **&Print**, **P&rint Preview**, **&Save**, and **&Exit**.

5. From the Toolbox, drag an *OpenFileDialog* component onto the form.

6. In the designer, double-click *OpenToolStripMenuItem* to open the code window to the *OpenToolStripMenuItem_Click* event handler. Add the following code to this method:

Sample of Visual Basic Code
```
Dim result As DialogResult
result = OpenFileDialog1.ShowDialog()
```

```
If result = System.Windows.Forms.DialogResult.OK Then
    WebBrowser1.Navigate(OpenFileDialog1.FileName)
End If
```

Sample of C# Code

```
DialogResult result;
result = openFileDialog1.ShowDialog();
if (result == System.Windows.Forms.DialogResult.OK)
    webBrowser1.Navigate(openFileDialog1.FileName);
```

7. Double-click *PrintToolStripMenuItem* to open its *Click* event handler and add the following code:

   Sample of Visual Basic Code

   ```
   WebBrowser1.ShowPrintDialog()
   ```

   Sample of C# Code

   ```
   webBrowser1.ShowPrintDialog();
   ```

8. Double-click *PrintPreviewToolStripMenuItem* and add the following line to its *Click* event handler:

   Sample of Visual Basic Code

   ```
   WebBrowser1.ShowPrintPreviewDialog()
   ```

   Sample of C# Code

   ```
   webBrowser1.ShowPrintPreviewDialog();
   ```

9. Double-click *SaveToolStripMenuItem* and add the following line to its *Click* event handler:

   Sample of Visual Basic Code

   ```
   WebBrowser1.ShowSaveAsDialog()
   ```

   Sample of C# Code

   ```
   webBrowser1.ShowSaveAsDialog();
   ```

10. Double-click *ExitToolStripMenuItem* and add the following line to its *Click* event handler:

    Sample of Visual Basic Code

    ```
    Application.Exit()
    ```

    Sample of C# Code

    ```
    Application.Exit();
    ```

11. In the Properties window, set the *ShortCutKeys* property of *ExitToolStripMenuItem* to Ctrl+E.

12. Navigate to a page and test your application by pressing F5.

Lesson Summary

- The *ToolStrip* control is a host for *ToolStripMenuItem* controls you can use to create toolbar-style functionality for your forms. Toolbars provide support for item reordering, rafting, and overflow of items onto the overflow button.

- Many tool strip items duplicate functionality of full-size Windows Forms controls such as *ToolStripLabel*, *ToolStripButton*, *ToolStripTextBox*, *ToolStripComboBox*, and *ToolStripProgressBar*. Tool strip controls that do not have analogous Windows Forms controls include *ToolStripSeparator*, *ToolStripDropDownButton*, and *ToolStripSplitButton*.

- You can display images on the *ToolStripItems* control with the *Image* property.

- The *ToolStripContainer* control enables you to create forms that include support for rafting toolbars.

- The *ToolStripManager* class is a static class that exposes methods for tool strip management. You can use the *ToolStripManager.Merge* method to merge tool strips.

- The *MenuStrip* control is the host for *ToolStripMenuItem* properties, which represent individual menu items. The top-level menu items in a menu strip are contained in the *Items* collection.

- Individual tool strip menu items can host their own submenus, which are contained in the *DropDownItems* collection.

- Individual menu items can be displayed with check marks next to the menu items and can have access keys and shortcut keys to enable keyboard-based navigation.

- Menus can be merged by using the *ToolStripManager.Merge* method. The configuration of the menu resulting from a merge is determined by the individual *ToolStripMenuItem*, *MergeAction*, and *MergeIndex* properties.

- *ContextMenuStrip* enables you to create context menus for your application. Menus created with the *ContextMenuStrip* control are not visible at run time and do not host a top-level menu, but otherwise they behave like *MenuStrip* controls. You can associate *ContextMenuStrip* with a control by setting the control's *ContextMenuStrip* property.

Lesson Review

You can use the following questions to test your knowledge of the information in Lesson 4, "Using Tool Strips and Menus." The questions are also available on the companion CD if you prefer to review them in electronic form.

> **NOTE ANSWERS**
>
> Answers to these questions and explanations of why each answer choice is correct or incorrect are located in the "Answers" section at the end of the book.

1. Which of the following is required to create an access key for a menu item?

   A. The *UseMnemonic* property for the *ToolStripMenuItem* must be set to *True*.

   B. The *AccessKeys* property must be set to the correct key.

   C. The letter for the access key in the *Text* property must be preceded by an ampersand (&) symbol.

   D. The *ShortCutKeys* property must be set to Ctrl plus the letter for the access key.

2. Which of the following code samples will add a new menu named Menu1 to a form at run time?

   A.

   Sample of Visual Basic Code
   ```
   ToolStripManager.Menus.Add(Menu1)
   ```

   Sample of C# Code
   ```
   ToolStripManager.Menus.Add(Menu1);
   ```

   B.

   Sample of Visual Basic Code
   ```
   ToolStripManager.Merge(Form1, Menu1)
   ```

   Sample of C# Code
   ```
   ToolStripManager.Merge(Form1, Menu1);
   ```

   C.

   Sample of Visual Basic Code
   ```
   ToolStripManager.Controls.Add(Menu1)
   ```

   Sample of C# Code
   ```
   ToolStripManager.Controls.Add(Menu1);
   ```

   D.

   Sample of Visual Basic Code
   ```
   Me.Controls.Add(Menu1)
   ```

   Sample of C# Code
   ```
   this.Controls.Add(Menu1);
   ```

3. Which of the following is required to associate and enable a context menu strip named ContextMenu1 with a button named Button1?

   A. The *ContextMenuStrip* property for *Button1* must be set to *ContextMenu1*.

   B. The *ShowPopUp* property for *Button1* must be set to *True*.

   C. *Button1* must call the *ContextMenu1.ShowPopUp* method in its *RightClick* event handler.

   D. The *ContextMenu1.Control* property must be set to *Button1*.

4. Which of the following code samples will correctly merge two tool strips named aToolStrip and bToolStrip?

A.

Sample of Visual Basic Code

```
aToolStrip.Merge(bToolStrip)
```

Sample of C# Code

```
aToolStrip.Merge(bToolStrip);
```

B.

Sample of Visual Basic Code

```
ToolStripManager.Merge(aToolStrip, bToolStrip)
```

Sample of C# Code

```
ToolStripManager.Merge(aToolStrip, bToolStrip);
```

C.

Sample of Visual Basic Code

```
Dim aManager As New ToolStripManager()
aManager.Merge(aToolStrip, bToolStrip)
```

Sample of C# Code

```
ToolStripManager aManager = new ToolStripManager();
aManager.Merge(aToolStrip, bToolStrip);
```

D.

Sample of Visual Basic Code

```
ToolStrip.Merge(aToolStrip, bToolStrip)
```

Sample of C# Code

```
ToolStrip.Merge(aToolStrip, bToolStrip);
```

5. Which of the following code samples will add a new *ToolStripButton* property to a tool strip named aToolStrip?

A.

Sample of Visual Basic Code

```
aToolStrip.Items.Add(New ToolStripButton("Click me"))
```

Sample of C# Code

```
aToolStrip1.Items.Add(new ToolStripButton("Click me"));
```

B.

Sample of Visual Basic Code

```
ToolStripManager.Add(aToolStrip, New ToolStripButton("Click me"))
```

Sample of C# Code

```
ToolStripManager.Add(aToolStrip, new ToolStripButton("Click me"));
```

C.

Sample of Visual Basic Code

```
aToolStrip.Buttons.Add(New ToolStripButton("Click me"))
```

Sample of C# Code

```
aToolStrip.Buttons.Add(new ToolStripButton("Click me"));
```

D.

Sample of Visual Basic Code

```
aToolStrip.Items.NewItem(Items.ToolStripButton("Click me"))
```

Sample of C# Code

```
aToolStrip.Items.NewItem(Items.ToolStripButton("Click me"));
```

Case Scenarios

In the following case scenarios, you apply what you've learned about Windows Forms and Windows Forms Controls. You can find answers to these questions in the "Answers" section at the end of this book.

Case Scenario 1: Designing a Simple User Interface

Your organization, Humongous Insurance, is creating an application to help customers calculate the future value of bonds and other investments that will be held for a number of years. As a new employee, you are assigned a simple task: create the front-end interface and prepare the user input to be processed by the calculation engine that will be supplied by another development team. You begin by reviewing the following technical requirements.

Create a UI that accepts the following information from users in a simple, straightforward way:

- Current investment value
- Assumed interest rate
- Time span in years

Answer the following questions for your manager:

1. How can you provide an easy-to-understand interface that provides visual cues to the user, clearly indicates currency when appropriate, and accepts user input for all three of the aforementioned factors?

2. How can you provide a keyboard-based system of navigation as an alternative to mouse use?

Case Scenario 2: Designing a User Interface

Your company has been contracted to design and implement a reservation system for a ski resort and chalet. You have been handed the job of creating a page to enter and display client data. You begin by reviewing the following technical requirements.

Create a UI that accepts the following information from users in a simple, straightforward way:

- First and last name
- Address
- City, state, and postal code
- Credit card number
- A general area for comments about the client

At the bottom of the technical requirements section is a note from the head of security that reads, "We need to be extra careful about our customers' credit card information. Make sure it isn't displayed with the rest of the data."

Answer the following questions for your manager:

1. Which controls are most appropriate for the design of the UI?
2. How can you keep customer credit card data from being displayed but still enable its entry?

Suggested Practices

To help you successfully master the exam objective presented in this chapter, complete the following tasks.

- **Practice 1**   Build an application that duplicates the functionality of Windows Explorer. You should be able to display a directory tree in one pane and files in a particular directory in another pane.

- **Practice 2**   Build an application that acts like an appointment book. It should allow the user to choose a date and time, add information about the appointment, track and display details about the appointment, and visually display what days have appointments set to the user on a *MonthCalendar* control.

- **Practice 3**   Create toolbars with similar members and practice merging them together, changing the *MergeIndex* and *MergeAction* properties of each tool strip item.

Take a Practice Test

The practice tests on this book's companion CD offer many options. For example, you can test yourself on just one exam objective, or you can test yourself on all the 70-511 certification exam content. You can set up the test so that it closely simulates the experience of taking a certification exam, or you can set it up in study mode so that you can look at the correct answers and explanations after you answer each question.

> ***MORE INFO***   **PRACTICE TESTS**
>
> For details about all the practice test options available, see the "How to Use the Practice Tests" section in this book's introduction.

CHAPTER 5

Working with User-Defined Controls

Windows Presentation Foundation (WPF) and Windows Forms both provide support for creating your own controls when the pre-built controls do not provide the required functionality for your application. In this chapter, you learn how to create custom controls in both Windows Forms and WPF and user controls in Windows Forms and how to extend pre-existing controls through inheritance. You also learn to extend the appearance of standard WPF elements by providing new control templates that alter their appearance and behavior while retaining their inherent functionality. Finally, you learn how to create custom WPF controls completely from the beginning.

Exam objectives in this chapter:

- Implement user-defined controls.
- Create and apply control templates in WPF.
- Create and apply styles and theming (themes only in this chapter).
- Implement dependency properties.

Lessons in this chapter:

Before You Begin

To complete the lessons in this chapter, you must have:

- A computer that meets or exceeds the minimum hardware requirements listed in the "About This Book" section at the beginning of the book.

- Microsoft Visual Studio 2010 Professional installed on your computer.

- An understanding of Microsoft Visual Basic or C# syntax and familiarity with Microsoft .NET Framework 4.0.

- An understanding of Extensible Application Markup Language (XAML).

 REAL WORLD

Matthew Stoecker

> I find that WPF provides most of the controls I need to create my applications, but there are a few notable exceptions, particularly concerning the file dialog boxes and some of the more specialized Windows Forms controls. Fortunately, it is easy to integrate that functionality into my applications, so I don't have to spend hours reinventing Windows Forms controls or creating complex workarounds.

Lesson 1: Creating Controls in Windows Forms

Composite controls are the simplest form of user-created controls. The composite control designer includes a graphical interface similar to a Windows form that you can use to add preexisting controls and components, which you then bind together in a single functional unit. In this lesson, you learn some general methods for control development as well as how to create a composite control.

After this lesson, you will be able to:

- Develop a user (composite) Windows Forms control.
- Create properties, methods, and events for Windows Forms controls.
- Expose properties of constituent controls.
- Configure a control to be invisible at run time.
- Configure a control to have a transparent background.
- Provide a Toolbox bitmap for a control.
- Develop an extended control (inherited from an existing Windows Forms control).

Estimated lesson time: 45 minutes

Introduction to Composite Controls

Composite controls (also known as *user controls*) are just as they sound: controls that are made up of other controls. Composite controls inherit from the *UserControl* class, which provides a base level of functionality you can build on by adding other controls as well as additional properties, methods, and events. The *UserControl* class has its own designer that enables you to use the Visual Studio Integrated Development Environment (IDE) to drag additional controls from the Toolbox to the design surface and configure them. Figure 5-1 shows the *UserControl* designer.

FIGURE 5-1 The *UserControl* designer.

To add a composite control to a solution at design time:

1. From the Project menu, choose Add User Control. The Add New Item dialog box opens.

2. Name your control and click Add. The new control is added to the project and opened for editing in the designer.

You can create a composite control in code by inheriting from the *UserControl* class, as shown here:

Sample of Visual Basic Code

```
Public Class myControl
    Inherits UserControl
    ' Add implementation here
End Class
```

Sample of C# Code

```
public class myControl : UserControl
{
    // Add implementation here
}
```

The subordinate controls that make up the composite control are called constituent controls. You can add constituent controls to your composite control in the same way you would add a control to a form: by dragging it onto the design surface from the Toolbox. Then you can configure these constituent controls in the same way you would configure them in a form: by setting properties, altering the appearance, and creating methods that handle control events. When the composite control is built, the functionality you have coded will be built into it.

Adding Methods, Properties, and Events to Controls

In addition to adding constituent controls, you can also add functionality to your control in the form of methods, properties, and events.

> **NOTE CLASSES, CONTROLS, AND COMPOSITE CONTROLS**
>
> The information in this section can be applied to classes and controls of all types, not just to composite controls.

ADDING METHODS TO A CONTROL

You can add a method to a control in the same way that you would add a method to a form or to any other class. Within the bounds of the class declaration in the Code window, add the method declaration and the method body. For a method that does not return a value, create a *Sub* (Visual Basic) or a *void* (C#) method, as shown here:

Sample of Visual Basic Code

```
Public Sub DisplayString(ByVal aString As String)
    Msgbox(aString)
End Sub
```

```
public void DisplayString(string aString)
{
    MessageBox.Show(aString);
}
```

For methods that return a value, create a *Function* (Visual Basic) or specify a return type (C#), as shown in this example:

Sample of Visual Basic Code

```
Public Function DisplayString(ByVal aString As String, ByVal bString As String) As
    String
    Return aString & bString
End Function
```

Sample of C# Code

```
public string DisplayString(string aString, string bString)
{
    return aString + bString;
}
```

ADDING PROPERTIES TO A CONTROL

Adding a property is similar to adding a method. You create a property definition and then implement the functionality required to return and set the value represented by the property. Usually, the underlying value for the property is stored in a private member variable. In Visual Basic, you use the *Property* keyword to create a property. In C#, you simply implement the getter and setter for the property. The following example demonstrates how to implement a property, including a member variable to contain the value:

Sample of Visual Basic Code

```
Private mUnitsOnHand
Public Property UnitsOnHand() As Integer
    Get
        Return mUnitsOnHand
    End Get
    Set(ByVal value As Integer)
        mUnitsOnHand = value
    End Set
End Property
```

Sample of C# Code

```
private int mUnitsOnHand;
public int UnitsOnHand
{
    get { return mUnitsOnHand; }
    set { mUnitsOnHand = value; }
}
```

You can create a read-only property by using the *ReadOnly* keyword in Visual Basic or by omitting the setter in C#. An example is shown here:

Sample of Visual Basic Code

```
Private mUnitsOnHand
Public ReadOnly Property UnitsOnHand() As Integer
    Get
        Return mUnitsOnHand
    End Get
End Property
```

Sample of C# Code

```
private int mUnitsOnHand;
public int UnitsOnHand
{
    get { return mUnitsOnHand; }
}
```

If you are creating a read-only property, you must set the member variable that represents the property's value in code.

ADDING EVENTS TO A CONTROL

You can add to a control events that can be raised to notify the rest of the application that something interesting has happened. Once an event has been added to a class or control, it can be raised in code to send a notification to the rest of the application.

In Visual Basic, you can create an event by using the *Event* keyword and specifying the name and signature of the event, as shown here:

Sample of Visual Basic Code

```
Public Event Bang(ByVal decibels As Integer)
```

C#, however, requires an explicit delegate to be present to specify the signature before the *Event* keyword can be used to create a new event. The following example demonstrates how to create an event in C#:

Sample of C# Code

```
public delegate void Sound(int decibels);
public event Sound Bang;
```

Note that you specify the delegate itself, not an instance of the delegate.

You can raise an event in code by using the *RaiseEvent* keyword in Visual Basic or by calling the event like you would a method in C#. An example is shown here:

Sample of Visual Basic Code

```
RaiseEvent Bang(100)
```

Sample of C# Code

```
this.Bang(100);
```

Exposing the Properties of Constituent Controls

When constituent controls are added to a composite control, they are given an access level of *Friend* by default in Visual Basic and *private* by default in C#. In both cases, the constituent controls will be inaccessible to classes in other assemblies. If you want to enable other assemblies to configure parts of the constituent controls, you must expose the properties of the constituent controls by wrapping them in a property declaration and then writing code in the property of the composite control to get and set the value of the property of the constituent control. For example, suppose you wanted to expose the *BackColor* property of a constituent button. You might create a property in the composite control called *ButtonBackColor*, in which you return the *BackColor* property of the constituent button in the getter and set the constituent *BackColor* property of the button in the setter. An example of how you might implement this is shown here:

Sample of Visual Basic Code

```vb
Public Property ButtonBackColor() As System.Drawing.Color
    Get
        Return Button1.BackColor
    End Get
    Set(ByVal value As System.Drawing.Color)
        Button1.BackColor = value
    End Set
End Property
```

Sample of C# Code

```csharp
public System.Drawing.Color ButtonBackColor
{
    get { return Button1.BackColor; }
    set { Button1.BackColor = value; }
}
```

Configuring a Control to Be Invisible at Run Time

At times, you might want your control to be invisible at run time. You can create an invisible control by setting the *Visible* property to *False*. Controls that are invisible cannot interact with the user through the UI, but they can still interact with the application and other controls. The following example demonstrates how to set the *Visible* property to *False*:

Sample of Visual Basic Code

```vb
myUserControl.Visible = False
```

Sample of C# Code

```csharp
myUserControl.Visible = false;
```

Note that you can set the *Visible* property only at run time. To ensure that a control is invisible at startup, set the *Visible* property to *False* in the control's *Load* event handler.

Configuring a Control to Have a Transparent Background

When configuring your control to have a transparent background, you have two types of transparencies to consider. A control can be transparent so that the appearance of the form underneath the control is seen through the background of the control. A control can also appear as a transparent window through the form, displaying whatever is on the desktop beneath the form.

To create a control with a transparent background color, all you need to do is set the *BackColor* property to *Color.Transparent*. Whatever is displayed on the form beneath the control will show through the background of the control. You can set the *BackColor* to *Transparent* in the Properties window at design time, or you can set the *BackColor* to *Transparent* in code, as shown here:

Sample of Visual Basic Code

```
Me.BackColor = Color.Transparent
```

Sample of C# Code

```
this.BackColor = Color.Transparent;
```

Creating a transparent control that acts as a window through the form is a little more complex. Each form has a property called *TransparencyKey*, which represents a color that appears as transparent when represented on the form. By setting the *BackColor* property of the control to the same color as the form's *TransparencyKey* property, you can create a window of transparency through the form. You can set the form's *TransparencyKey* property and the control's *BackColor* property in the designer at design time or in code, as shown here:

Sample of Visual Basic Code

```
Form1.TransparencyKey = Color.Red
myUserControl.BackColor = Color.Red
```

Sample of C# Code

```
Form1.TransparencyKey = Color.Red;
myUserControl.BackColor = Color.Red;
```

Providing a Toolbox Bitmap for Your Control

After you have built a control, it automatically appears in the Toolbox if you are using it in the same solution that contains the control, or, if it was created in a different project, you can add it to the Toolbox. When you add the control to the Toolbox, it appears in the Toolbox as the name of the control next to an icon. If no icon is specified, a generic icon is supplied. You can specify the icon displayed next to the name of your control by using *ToolboxBitmapAttribute*. You can attach instances of the *ToolboxBitmapAttribute* class to your control declaration and use it to specify a 16-by-16 pixel bitmap that will represent your control in the Toolbox.

You can specify the Toolbox bitmap in three ways. The most straightforward way is to specify the path to the bitmap you want to use. Here is an example of how to do this:

Sample of Visual Basic Code

```
<ToolboxBitmap("C:\myToolboxBitmap.bmp")> Class myControl
    Inherits UserControl
    ' Implementation omitted
End Class
```

Sample of C# Code

```
[ToolboxBitmap(@"C:\myToolboxBitmap.bmp")]
class myControl : UserControl
{}
```

You can also use *ToolboxBitmap* from an existing type. For example, you could specify the same Toolbox bitmap that the *Button* control uses with the following code:

Sample of Visual Basic Code

```
<ToolBoxBitmap(GetType(System.Windows.Forms.Button))> Class myControl
    Inherits UserControl
    ' Implementation omitted
End Class
```

Sample of C# Code

```
[ToolBoxBitmap(GetType(System.Windows.Forms.Button))]
class myControl : UserControl
{}
```

Finally, you can specify an assembly by specifying a type defined in that assembly and then load an icon resource that is specified by a string name, as shown here:

Sample of Visual Basic Code

```
<ToolBoxBitmap(GetType(myControl), "myControl.bmp")> Class myControl
    Inherits UserControl
    ' Implementation omitted
End Class
```

Sample of C# Code

```
[ToolBoxBitmap(GetType(myControl), "myControl.bmp")]
class myControl : UserControl
{}
```

 Quick Check

1. Briefly define a composite control.

2. How can you expose properties of constituent controls to developers?

Creating Extended Controls

Extended controls are user-created controls that extend a preexisting .NET Framework control. By extending existing controls, you can retain all the functionality of the control while adding properties and methods and, in some cases, altering the rendered appearance of the control.

Extending a Control

You can create an extended control by creating a class that inherits the control in question. The following example demonstrates how to create a control that inherits the *Button* class:

Sample of Visual Basic Code

```
Public Class ExtendedButton
    Inherits System.Windows.Forms.Button
End Class
```

Sample of C# Code

```
public class ExtendedButton : System.Windows.Forms.Button
{}
```

The *ExtendedButton* class created in the previous example has the same appearance, behavior, and properties as the *Button* class, but you can now extend this functionality by adding custom properties or methods. For example, the following example demonstrates adding a property called *ButtonValue* that returns an integer:

Sample of Visual Basic Code

```
Public Class ExtendedButton
    Inherits System.Windows.Forms.Button
    Private mValue As Integer
    Public Property ButtonValue() As Integer
        Get
            Return mValue
        End Get
        Set(ByVal Value As Integer)
            mValue = Value
        End Set
    End Property
End Class
```

```csharp
public class ExtendedButton : System.Windows.Forms.Button
{
    int mValue;
    public int ButtonValue
    {
        get
        {
            return mValue;
        }
        set
        {
            mValue = value;
        }
    }
}
```

Overriding Methods

In addition to adding new methods and properties to your control, you can also provide a new implementation for existing methods by overriding them. Overriding enables you to substitute your own implementation for the base implementation of a method or to add to the functionality already there. The following demonstrates how to override the *OnClick* method in a class that inherits from *Button*. The new implementation increments a variable called *Clicks* and then calls the base implementation of *OnClick*.

Sample of Visual Basic Code

```vbnet
Protected Overrides Sub OnClick(ByVal e As System.EventArgs)
    Clicks += 1
    MyBase.OnClick(e)
End Sub
```

Sample of C# Code

```csharp
protected override void OnClick(System.EventArgs e)
{
    Clicks++;
    base.OnClick(e);
}
```

Altering the Appearance of an Inherited Control

You can change the visual appearance of some controls by overriding the *OnPaint* method. This enables you to either add to or replace the rendering logic of the control. To add to the default rendering of the control, call the *MyBase.OnPaint* (Visual Basic) or *base.OnPaint* (C#) method to call the base class's rendering code in addition to your own. To provide a completely custom appearance for the control, you can omit the call to the base class's *OnPaint* method. The following example demonstrates how to create a simple elliptical button. Note, however, that it changes only the shape of the control and does not address subtler rendering tasks such as outlining.

Sample of Visual Basic Code

```
Protected Overrides Sub OnPaint(ByVal pevent As System.Windows.Forms.PaintEventArgs)
    Dim x As New System.Drawing.Drawing2D.GraphicsPath
    x.AddEllipse(0, 0, Me.Width, Me.Height)
    Me.Region = New Region(x)
    MyBase.OnPaint(pevent)
End Sub
```

Sample of C# Code

```
protected override void OnPaint(System.Windows.Forms.PaintEventArgs pevent)
{
    System.Drawing.Drawing2D.GraphicsPath x = new System.Drawing.Drawing2D.
        GraphicsPath();
    x.AddEllipse(0, 0, this.Width, this.Height);
    this.Region = new Region(x);
    base.OnPaint(pevent);
}
```

PRACTICE Create a Composite Control

In this practice, you create a simple composite control that acts as a digital clock. You add a *Label* control to your composite control that displays the correct time and a *Timer* component that updates the *Label* every second. Finally, you expose the *Enabled* property of the *Timer* control through your composite control so users can enable and disable the clock.

EXERCISE Create a Digital Clock

1. Create a new Windows Forms application in Visual Studio.

2. From the Project menu, choose Add User Control and click Add in the Add New Item dialog box. A new user control is added to your project and opens in the designer.

3. From the Toolbox, drag a *Label* control onto the user control. Resize the user control so that it is approximately the size of the *Label* control.

4. From the Toolbox, drag a *Timer* component onto the user control.

5. In the Properties window, set the *Interval* property for the *Timer* component to **1000** and the *Enabled* property to *True*.

6. Double-click the *Timer* component to open the Code window to the default event handler for the *Timer.Tick* event and add the following line of code:

   Sample of Visual Basic Code

   ```
   Label1.Text = Now.ToLongTimeString
   ```

   Sample of C# Code

   ```
   label1.Text = DateTime.Now.ToLongTimeString();
   ```

7. In the Code window, add the following *Property* declaration:

Sample of Visual Basic Code

```
Public Property TimeEnabled() As Boolean
    Get
        Return Timer1.Enabled
    End Get
    Set(ByVal value As Boolean)
        Timer1.Enabled = value
    End Set
End Property
```

Sample of C# Code

```
public bool TimeEnabled
{
    get { return timer1.Enabled; }
    set { timer1.Enabled = value; }
}
```

8. From the File menu, choose Save All to save your solution.

9. From the Build menu, build your solution.

10. In Solution Explorer, open *Form1*. From the Toolbox in the designer, drag *UserControl1* onto the form. An instance of your user control is added to the form and begins to keep time every second. Note that you can pause it by setting the *TimeEnabled* property to *False* in the Properties window.

11. Press F5 to build and run your application. Note that the user control functions the same way at run time as it does in the designer.

Lesson Summary

- Composite controls, also called user controls, consist of preexisting Windows Forms controls and components bound together by common functionality in a common UI. Controls that are contained in a composite control are called constituent controls. You can add methods, properties, and events to a composite control to create custom functionality.

- Properties of constituent controls are not generally accessible to developers. You can expose properties of constituent controls by wrapping them in new properties of the composite control.

- You can configure a control to be invisible at run time by setting the *Visible* property to *False*. You can create a control with a transparent background by setting the *BackColor* property to *Color.Transparent*. You can create a window through the control and its owning form by setting the control's *BackColor* property to the same color as the form's *TransparencyKey* property.

- You can provide a Toolbox bitmap for a control by configuring the *ToolboxBitmap* attribute.

- Dialog boxes are special forms that are designed to collect information from the user. Dialog boxes can be displayed either modally or modelessly. Modal dialog boxes halt program execution until the dialog box is closed, whereas modeless dialog boxes allow program execution to continue while they are displayed.

- You can use the *ShowDialog* method to set the parent form of a dialog box. You can then retrieve information from the parent form by casting a reference to the parent form to the appropriate type.

- You can create an extended control by creating a class that inherits a preexisting control. Extended controls encapsulate all the functionality of the inherited control. In addition, you can create new properties, methods, and events for an inherited control or override existing methods to replace preexisting functionality.

- You can alter the appearance of an extended control by overriding the *OnPaint* method. You should call the base class's *OnPaint* method to provide rendering for the base class or omit the call to the base class's *OnPaint* method to provide completely different rendering for the control.

Lesson Review

The following questions are intended to reinforce key information presented in Lesson 1, "Creating Controls in Windows Forms." The questions are also available on the companion CD if you prefer to review them in electronic form.

> **NOTE ANSWERS**
>
> Answers to these questions and explanations of why each answer choice is correct or incorrect are located in the "Answers" section at the end of the book.

1. Which of the following are characteristics of a composite control? (Choose all that apply.)

   A. Composite controls are made up of preexisting Windows Forms controls.

   B. Composite controls can have custom functionality in the form of new methods, properties, or events.

   C. Composite controls must provide their own rendering code.

   D. Composite controls automatically expose the properties of their constituent controls as their own properties.

2. Which of the following are required to provide a Toolbox bitmap for a control? (Choose all that apply.)

   A. You must provide a 16-by-16 pixel bitmap to act as the Toolbox bitmap.

   B. You must provide a bitmap to act as the Toolbox bitmap, but size is unimportant because the .NET Framework will automatically resize it.

C. You must set the *Image* property of the control to the appropriate bitmap for the Toolbox bitmap.

D. You must configure the *ToolboxBitmap* attribute to specify a path, a type, or a type and a resource name.

3. Which of the following are required to create an extended control?

A. You must override the *OnPaint* method to provide custom rendering.

B. You must provide a Toolbox bitmap for the new control.

C. You must inherit from a preexisting control.

D. You must expose any necessary properties of the inherited control by wrapping them in new properties.

Lesson 2: Using Control Templates

WPF controls are designed to be lookless, which means that an element's functionality is completely separate from the element's appearance. Consequently, it is easy to provide a new UI appearance for a WPF element by creating a new control template. In this lesson, you learn how to create a new control template for a preexisting control.

After this lesson, you will be able to:

- Create and apply a new control template.
- Insert a *Trigger* object in a control template.
- Apply properties of the template parent in the template.
- Apply a template within a *Style*.
- View the source code for a preexisting template.
- Use predefined part names in a new control template.

Estimated lesson time: 30 minutes

Creating Control Templates

A *control template* is an XAML document that describes how a control will appear in the presentation layer. The template represents the visual tree of the control; it defines any of the parts that make up a control as well as the appearance and behavior of those parts.

Because WPF elements are designed to be lookless, the visual layer is distinct from the logical layer, and you can change the appearance of any WPF element radically by creating a new template for that element.

Control templates are defined within a *<ControlTemplate>* element (as you might expect). The following example shows a very simple control template:

```
<Button Height="23" Width="100" Name="Button3">
   <Button.Template>
      <ControlTemplate>
         <Rectangle Fill="RoyalBlue" />
      </ControlTemplate>
   </Button.Template>
</Button>
```

When this control template is applied, the regular appearance of the *Button* is replaced with a *RoyalBlue* rectangle. Although it is not particularly exciting, it maintains all the functionality of the *Button* control. You can click it to raise the *Button.Click* event, and it maintains all the positioning and layout functionality of any other WPF element.

More complex templates are made up of multiple parts. The following example includes a *Border* element that contains the ellipse and appears as a *Chocolate* border around the *RoyalBlue* rectangle:

```xml
<Button Height="24" Name="Button3" Margin="89,0,89,61"
    VerticalAlignment="Bottom">
    <Button.Template>
        <ControlTemplate>
            <Border BorderBrush="Chocolate" BorderThickness="3">
                <Rectangle Fill="RoyalBlue" />
            </Border>
        </ControlTemplate>
    </Button.Template>
</Button>
```

Border is a content control; thus, it can contain only a single child element. If you want to build multiple visual elements into your template, you must use a layout control, as shown in the following example, which overlays a red ellipse onto our *RoyalBlue* rectangle:

```xml
<Button Height="67" Name="Button3" Margin="89,0,35,18"
    VerticalAlignment="Bottom">
    <Button.Template>
        <ControlTemplate>
            <Border BorderBrush="Chocolate" BorderThickness="3">
                <Grid>
                    <Rectangle Fill="RoyalBlue" />
                    <Ellipse Fill="Red" />
                </Grid>
            </Border>
        </ControlTemplate>
    </Button.Template>
</Button>
```

One major component is still missing from this template. There is no way to display the value of the *Content* property. You can provide support for the *Content* property by using the *ContentPresenter* class, as shown in bold here:

```xml
<Button Height="67" Name="Button3" Margin="89,0,35,18"
    VerticalAlignment="Bottom">
    <Button.Template>
        <ControlTemplate TargetType="{x:Type Button}">
            <Border BorderBrush="Chocolate" BorderThickness="3">
                <Grid>
                    <Rectangle Fill="RoyalBlue" />
                    <Ellipse Fill="Red" />
                    <ContentPresenter HorizontalAlignment="Center"
                        VerticalAlignment="Center" />
                </Grid>
            </Border>
        </ControlTemplate>
    </Button.Template>
</Button>
```

The *ContentPresenter* is essentially a placeholder for the *Content* property of the element. Whatever the value of the *Content* property, it is inserted into the space occupied by the *ContentPresenter*. For *List* controls, a similar class—*ItemsPresenter*—presents the objects in the *Items* property.

Note also in the previous example the addition of the *TargetType={x:Type Button}* property in the *ControlTemplate* tag. This is required for *ContentPresenter* to work because the *ContentPresenter* control contains an implicit *TemplateBinding* markup that requires the target type to be defined. Template bindings will be discussed later in this lesson. Note that unlike with styles, setting the *TargetType* property does not automatically set the template on elements of that type. You must set the element's *Template* property, either in XAML or by using styles, as you will see later in this lesson.

The previous template takes a *Button* control and completely redefines its visual appearance while retaining all its inherent functionality. The final product still requires some work, however; there is no visual cue when the user moves the mouse over the *Button* control or clicks it, as you would see in a *Button* control with the standard appearance. Later in this lesson you will see how to implement that functionality as well.

Creating a Template as a Resource

In the previous section, you saw how to define a control template inline in a control. Although this is technically possible, it is really useful only for demonstration purposes. Templates are generally created to provide a common appearance for multiple controls, and, therefore, they are defined as resources to facilitate their reuse. To define a template as a resource, you must define it in a *Resource* section and apply a *Key* property, as shown in the following example:

```
<Window.Resources >
    <ControlTemplate TargetType="{x:Type Button}" x:Key="ButtonTemplate">
        <Border BorderBrush="Chocolate" BorderThickness="3">
            <Grid>
                <Rectangle Fill="RoyalBlue" />
                <Ellipse Fill="Red" />
                <ContentPresenter HorizontalAlignment="Center"
                    VerticalAlignment="Center" />
            </Grid>
        </Border>
    </ControlTemplate>
</Window.Resources>
```

Applying a Template to a Control

After you have defined a template as a resource, you can apply it to a control by setting the *Template* property to that resource, as shown here:

```
<Button Template="{StaticResource ButtonTemplate}" Margin="112,123,91,116"
    Name="Button1">Button</Button>
```

Inserting a *Trigger* Object in a Template

So far in this lesson, you have seen how to create a template that provides a different visual representation for a WPF element, but this is only part of creating new and exciting visual elements for your application. A large part of the interface of an element is interactivity with the user. For example, a button with the standard template is highlighted when the mouse rolls over it and gives a visual cue when it is clicked. You can replicate this functionality by incorporating triggers into your template.

The *ControlTemplate* object contains a collection of *Trigger* objects in the *ControlTemplate .Triggers* collection. You can add triggers here to provide visual interactivity just as you would in a style. The following example demonstrates a *Trigger* object in a *Button* template that highlights the button when the mouse moves over it. The relevant portions are shown in bold:

```xml
<ControlTemplate TargetType="{x:Type Button}" x:Key="ButtonTemplate">
    <Border Name="Bord1" BorderBrush="Chocolate" BorderThickness="3">
        <Grid>
            <Rectangle Name="Rect1" Fill="RoyalBlue" />
            <Ellipse Name="Elli1" Fill="Red" />
            <ContentPresenter HorizontalAlignment="Center"
                VerticalAlignment="Center" />
        </Grid>
    </Border>
    <ControlTemplate.Triggers>
        <Trigger Property="IsMouseOver" Value="True">
            <Setter TargetName="Rect1" Property="Fill" Value="AliceBlue" />
            <Setter TargetName="Bord1" Property="BorderBrush" Value="Red" />
            <Setter TargetName="Elli1" Property="Fill" Value="Yellow" />
        </Trigger>
    </ControlTemplate.Triggers>
</ControlTemplate>
```

There are a few important things to notice about this example. First, each element affected by the *Trigger* object has had the *Name* property set so that the *Setter* objects in the *Trigger* object can refer to the correct object. Second, the *Trigger* object is defined in the XAML *after* the constituent elements of the template. This is required by the template engine. It is, therefore, a good idea to define triggers at the end of your template.

You also can define animations in your template triggers. This example provides an *Animation* object, shown in bold, that is executed when the button is clicked:

```xml
<ControlTemplate TargetType="{x:Type Button}" x:Key="ButtonTemplate">
    <Border Name="Bord1" BorderBrush="Chocolate" BorderThickness="3">
        <Grid>
            <Rectangle Name="Rect1" Fill="RoyalBlue" />
            <Ellipse Name="Elli1" Fill="Red" />
            <ContentPresenter HorizontalAlignment="Center"
                VerticalAlignment="Center" />
        </Grid>
    </Border>
    <ControlTemplate.Triggers>
        <Trigger Property="IsMouseOver" Value="True">
            <Setter TargetName="Rect1" Property="Fill" Value="AliceBlue" />
```

```
                    <Setter TargetName="Bord1" Property="BorderBrush" Value="Red" />
                    <Setter TargetName="Elli1" Property="Fill" Value="Yellow" />
                </Trigger>
                <Trigger Property="IsPressed" Value="True">
                    <Trigger.EnterActions>
                        <BeginStoryboard Name="bst1">
                            <Storyboard AutoReverse="True">
                                <ThicknessAnimation
                                    Storyboard.TargetProperty="Margin"
                                    To="0,0,0,0" Duration="0:0:.3" />
                            </Storyboard>
                        </BeginStoryboard>
                    </Trigger.EnterActions>
                    <Trigger.ExitActions>
                        <StopStoryboard BeginStoryboardName="bst1" />
                    </Trigger.ExitActions>
                </Trigger>
        </ControlTemplate.Triggers>
</ControlTemplate>
```

Respecting the Templated Parent's Properties

Up to this point in this lesson, you have seen how to create a fully functional template with support for triggers that provides user interactivity. However, your template is not easy to configure. The *Border* color is always *Chocolate*, the *Rectangle* object is always *RoyalBlue*, and the *Ellipse* object is always *Red*, no matter how the developer sets the properties. Although you might intend for a template to be unalterable in some cases, there are other times when you want to provide user configurability. You can use *TemplateBinding* to respect the properties of the template parent.

Using *TemplateBinding*

The *TemplateBinding* markup is essentially a data-binding expression that binds a property within the template to a named property of the templated parent, which is a fancy way of saying the control for which you are designing the template. The *TemplateBinding* expression takes the following form:

```
{TemplateBinding <PropertyName>}
```

where *<PropertyName>* is the name of the property on the templated parent to which you want to bind. The following example shows the template from the previous example with the *Border.BorderThickness* property bound to the parent *BorderThickness* property:

```
<ControlTemplate TargetType="{x:Type Button}" x:Key="ButtonTemplate">
    <Border Name="Bord1" BorderBrush="Chocolate"
        BorderThickness="{TemplateBinding BorderThickness}">
        <Grid>
            <Rectangle Name="Rect1" Fill="RoyalBlue" />
            <Ellipse Name="Elli1" Fill="Red" />
            <ContentPresenter HorizontalAlignment="Center"
                VerticalAlignment="Center" />
```

```
        </Grid>
      </Border>
      <!--Triggers omitted-->
</ControlTemplate>
```

Using Template Data Binding

There is one significant problem with the *TemplateBinding* expression. *TemplateBinding* does not support *Freezable* types (which include *Brush* objects) when used in triggers. Fortunately, there is an easy way to deal with this issue: You can use a regular *Binding* expression. A regular *Binding* expression can refer to a property of the template parent by setting the *RelativeSource* property to *TemplatedParent* and by setting the *Path* property to the desired property for binding. The following example demonstrates the use of this binding technique (note the bold code):

```
<ControlTemplate TargetType="{x:Type Button}" x:Key="ButtonTemplate">
<!--Grid and buttons omitted for brevity-->
    <ControlTemplate.Triggers>
        <Trigger Property="IsMouseOver" Value="True">
            <Setter TargetName="Rect1" Property="Fill" Value="AliceBlue" />
            <Setter TargetName="Bord1" Property="BorderBrush" Value="Red" />
            <Setter TargetName="Elli1" Property="Fill" Value="{Binding
                RelativeSource={RelativeSource TemplatedParent},
                Path=Background}" />
        </Trigger>
<!--Trigger omitted for brevity-->
    </ControlTemplate.Triggers>
</ControlTemplate>
```

You can use any other type of data-binding expression in a template as well. For example, you could create a *Binding* object that sets *Path* in the XAML template (shown here in bold) and then sets *DataContext* for *Window* in code, as shown here:

```
<ControlTemplate TargetType="{x:Type Button}" x:Key="ButtonTemplate">
    <Border Name="Bord1" BorderBrush="Chocolate" BorderThickness="3">
        <Grid>
            <Rectangle Name="Rect1" Fill="{Binding Path=Background}" />
            <Ellipse Name="Elli1" Fill="Red" />
            <ContentPresenter HorizontalAlignment="Center"
                VerticalAlignment="Center" />
        </Grid>
    </Border>
        <!--Triggers omitted-->
    </ControlTemplate.Triggers>
</ControlTemplate>
```

Sample of Visual Basic Code

```
Window1.DataContext = Me
```

Sample of C# Code

```
Window1.DataContext = this;
```

When this code is applied, all the *Button* elements set to this template in *Window1* have the ellipse painted by the same brush as the background of the window.

Applying Templates with *Style*

You can use *Style* to apply templates automatically. By setting the *TargetType* property of *Style* and using *Setter* to set the *Template* property, the specified template is applied automatically to all elements of that type. The following example demonstrates an instance of *Style* that automatically applies a template to *Button* elements:

```
<Style TargetType="{x:Type Button}">
   <Setter Property="Template" Value="{StaticResource ButtonTemplate}" />
</Style>
```

It is important to remember that when you set a template with *Style*, it must be defined in XAML after the template is defined.

Viewing the Source Code for an Existing Template

Creating a template for a *Button* control is fairly easy; there isn't a lot of nuance to the layout, and there aren't too many visual states to monitor. However, when designing templates for other controls, you might want to use the default template as a reference. You can view the default template for a WPF element easily, as described in the following procedure:

To view the source code for an existing template:

1. Instantiate an example of the element whose template you want to view. The element must actually be created in the visual tree so you can add it to *Window* at design time or add it programmatically, as shown here:

    Sample of Visual Basic Code

    ```
    Dim aTextBox As New TextBox
    Grid1.Children.Add(aTextBox)
    ```

    Sample of C# Code

    ```
    TextBox aTextBox = new TextBox();
    Grid1.Children.Add(aTextBox);
    ```

2. Use the *System.Windows.Markup.XamlWriter* class to serialize the template. There are several ways to do this. The following example demonstrates how to save the template to an Extensible Markup Language (XML) file:

    Sample of Visual Basic Code

    ```
    Dim aStream As New System.IO.FileStream("C:\template.xml", _
        System.IO.FileMode.Append)
    System.Windows.Markup.XamlWriter.Save(aTextBox.Template, aStream)
    ```

    Sample of C# Code

    ```
    System.IO.FileStream  aStream = new
        System.IO.FileStream("C:\\template.xml",
    ```

```
System.IO.FileMode.Append);
System.Windows.Markup.XamlWriter.Save(aTextBox.Template, aStream);
```

Using Predefined Part Names in a Template

Although WPF elements are designed to be lookless, this is not always completely the case. When inspecting the template of the *TextBox* control in the previous section, you might have noticed the following line:

```
<ScrollViewer Name="PART_ContentHost" SnapsToDevicePixels="{TemplateBinding
    UIElement.SnapsToDevicePixels}" />
```

The part of this line that deserves particular notice is "Name="PART_ContentHost". Despite the goal of lookless controls, some WPF elements interact with their code through named elements in their templates. By convention, all these elements that interact with the element code are named *PART_<name>*, where *<name>* is a description of the role of that part. In the *TextBox* example, *Part_ContentHost* interacts with the element code to provide the editable surface of *TextBox*. If you are providing a new template for any control with named parts, you should give the corresponding elements the same name to keep the functionality of the control consistent.

PRACTICE Creating a Control Template

In this practice, you create a new template for the *Button* control. You provide a custom appearance for the button and implement the functionality to change that appearance when the button is disabled, when the mouse moves over the button, and when the button is clicked.

EXERCISE Creating a New Control Template

1. Create a new WPF application.

2. In XAML view, create a *Window.Resources* section just before the *Grid* section, as shown here:

   ```
   <Window.Resources>

   </Window.Resources>
   ```

3. Add the following *ControlTemplate* template to the *Window.Resources* section. This template defines an *Ellipse* object and a *ContentPresenter* object that make up the visual appearance of *Button*. *Ellipse* is filled by a custom *RadialGradientBrush* property that gives it a colorful appearance:

   ```
   <ControlTemplate x:Key="ButtonTemplate" TargetType="Button">
       <Grid>
           <Ellipse Name="Ellipse1" Stroke="{TemplateBinding BorderBrush}"
               StrokeThickness="{TemplateBinding BorderThickness}">
               <Ellipse.Fill>
   ```

```
        <RadialGradientBrush GradientOrigin=".5, .5">
            <GradientStop Color="Red" Offset="0" />
            <GradientStop Color="Orange" Offset=".25" />
            <GradientStop Color="Blue" Offset=".5" />
            <GradientStop Color="Yellow" Offset=".75" />
            <GradientStop Color="Green" Offset="1" />
        </RadialGradientBrush>
      </Ellipse.Fill>
    </Ellipse>
    <ContentPresenter HorizontalAlignment="Center"
        VerticalAlignment="Center"/>
  </Grid>
</ControlTemplate>
```

4. Add a *ControlTemplate.Triggers* section and add the following trigger to highlight the button when the mouse is over it:

```
<ControlTemplate.Triggers>
    <Trigger Property="IsMouseOver" Value="True">
      <Setter TargetName="Ellipse1" Property="Fill">
        <Setter.Value>
          <RadialGradientBrush GradientOrigin=".5, .5">
              <GradientStop Color="LightCoral" Offset="0" />
              <GradientStop Color="LightSalmon" Offset=".25" />
              <GradientStop Color="LightBlue" Offset=".5" />
              <GradientStop Color="LightYellow" Offset=".75" />
              <GradientStop Color="LightGreen" Offset="1" />
          </RadialGradientBrush>
        </Setter.Value>
      </Setter>
    </Trigger>
</ControlTemplate.Triggers>
```

5. Add another trigger to disable *Button* when the *IsEnabled* property is set to *False*, as shown here:

```
<Trigger Property="IsEnabled" Value="False">
    <Setter TargetName="Ellipse1" Property="Fill">
      <Setter.Value>
        <RadialGradientBrush GradientOrigin=".5,.5">
            <GradientStop Color="Gray" Offset="0" />
            <GradientStop Color="LightGray" Offset=".25" />
            <GradientStop Color="Black" Offset=".5" />
            <GradientStop Color="White" Offset=".75" />
            <GradientStop Color="DarkGray" Offset="1" />
        </RadialGradientBrush>
      </Setter.Value>
    </Setter>
</Trigger>
```

6. Add *EventTrigger* that plays an animation when the button is clicked to the *Triggers* section. The following example causes the button to shrink to a point and re-expand:

```
<EventTrigger RoutedEvent="Button.Click">
    <BeginStoryboard>
```

```
            <Storyboard AutoReverse="True">
                <DoubleAnimation To="0" Duration="0:0:0.1"
                    Storyboard.TargetProperty="Width" />
                <DoubleAnimation To="0" Duration="0:0:0.1"
                    Storyboard.TargetProperty="Height" />
            </Storyboard>
        </BeginStoryboard>
    </EventTrigger>
```

7. In the *Window.Resources* section, after the end of *ControlTemplate,* add the following *Style* element to set the template for *Button* elements in this application automatically:

```
<Style TargetType="{x:Type Button}">
    <Setter Property="Template" Value="{StaticResource ButtonTemplate}" />
</Style>
```

8. Add the following *Button* tags as children to the *Grid* control in the XAML for this window:

```
<Button Height="80" Width="90" Name="Button1">Button</Button>
<Button Height="60" HorizontalAlignment="Left" Name="Button2"
    VerticalAlignment="Top" Width="75">Button</Button>
```

Do not set the Margin property because this interferes with the *Animation* property you defined in Step 6.

9. Set the *IsEnabled* property of the second *Button* object to *False,* as shown here.

```
<Button IsEnabled="False" Height="60" HorizontalAlignment="Left"
    Name="Button2" VerticalAlignment="Top" Width="75">Button</Button>
```

10. Press F5 to run your application. Note that your *Button* object is highlighted when the mouse moves over it and that the animation runs when the button is clicked.

Lesson Summary

- Control templates define the visual interface for a control but do not affect the inherent functionality of a control directly. By setting the *Template* property of a WPF element, you can provide a new visual interface for that control while leaving its core functionality intact.

- Control templates are typically defined as resources and are set on a target element by setting the element's *Template* property to reference the appropriate resource. Alternatively, templates can be applied automatically to all elements of a given type by using a *Style* element that has the *TargetType* property set to the appropriate element type.

- Control templates can contain *Trigger* objects as part of the template. *Trigger* objects typically provide visual cues to the user when conditions change for the element.

- You can use the *TemplateBinding* markup to bind a property inside a template to a property of the templated parent. This markup does not function with *Freezable* objects in *Trigger* objects; in that case, you should use a regular *Binding* control with the *RelativeSource* property set to *TemplatedParent*.

- Some templates contain elements that are acted on directly by the source code of the element. These elements are named *PART_<partname>*. When you are creating a template for an element with named parts, you should keep the same name for corresponding parts of the template to avoid having to re-implement the functionality.

Lesson Review

You can use the following questions to test your knowledge of the information in Lesson 2, "Using Control Templates." The questions are also available on the companion CD if you prefer to review them in electronic form.

> **NOTE ANSWERS**
>
> Answers to these questions and explanations of why each answer choice is correct or incorrect are located in the "Answers" section at the end of the book.

1. Which of the following XAML samples correctly binds the *Background* property of the *Label* control in the template to the *Background* property of its templated parent? (Choose all that apply.)

   A.

   ```
   <ControlTemplate x:Key="TestTemplate">
     <Label Background="Background" />
   </ControlTemplate>
   ```

   B.

   ```
   <ControlTemplate x:Key="TestTemplate">
     <Label Background="{Binding Background}" />
   </ControlTemplate>
   ```

   C.

   ```
   <ControlTemplate x:Key="TestTemplate">
     <Label Background="{TemplateBinding Background}" />
   </ControlTemplate>
   ```

   D.

   ```
   <ControlTemplate x:Key="TestTemplate">
     <Label Background="{Binding RelativeSource={RelativeSource
       TemplatedParent}, Path=Background}" />
   </ControlTemplate>
   ```

2. Which of the following XAML samples correctly applies the control template to all instances of *Label* in *Window*?

A.

```xml
<Window.Resources>
   <ControlTemplate x:Key="TestTemplate" TargetType="Label">
      <Label Background="{Binding RelativeSource={RelativeSource
         TemplatedParent}, Path=Background}" />
   </ControlTemplate>
   <Style TargetType="Label">
      <Setter Property="Template" Value="{StaticResource
         TestTemplate}" />
   </Style>
</Window.Resources>
```

B.

```xml
<Window.Resources>
   <Style TargetType="Label">
      <Setter Property="Template" Value="{StaticResource
         TestTemplate}" />
   </Style>
   <ControlTemplate x:Key="TestTemplate" TargetType="Label">
      <Label Background="{Binding RelativeSource={RelativeSource
         TemplatedParent}, Path=Background}" />
   </ControlTemplate>
</Window.Resources>
```

C.

```xml
<Window.Resources>
   <Style TargetType="Label">
   </Style>
   <ControlTemplate x:Key="TestTemplate" TargetType="Label">
      <Label Background="{Binding RelativeSource={RelativeSource
         TemplatedParent}, Path=Background}" />
   </ControlTemplate>
</Window.Resources>
```

D.

```xml
<Window.Resources>
   <ControlTemplate x:Key="TestTemplate" TargetType="Label">
      <Label Background="{Binding RelativeSource={RelativeSource
         TemplatedParent}, Path=Background}" />
   </ControlTemplate>
</Window.Resources>
```

Lesson 3: Creating Custom Controls in WPF

Although the array of element possibilities that WPF exposes through control templates is vast, there are times when the functionality you want to create in your applications is not matched by any preexisting WPF or Windows Forms control. In these cases, you can create custom controls that incorporate the functionality you need. In this lesson, you learn how to create a dependency property and how to create user and custom controls.

After this lesson, you will be able to:

- Choose among using a control template, a user control, or a custom control.
- Implement a dependency property.
- Create a new user control.
- Create a new custom control.
- Consume a custom or user control.
- Render theme-based appearances for your custom controls.

Estimated lesson time: 30 minutes

Control Creation in WPF

With the enormous amount of customization available for WPF elements, the number of scenarios in which you have to build a control from the beginning is fairly small. Nonetheless, occasionally you might want to create your own custom controls. Custom controls in WPF fall into two categories: *user controls*, which inherit the *UserControl* class and are made up of constituent controls bound together by a common functionality in a shared user interface; and *custom controls*, which inherit the *Control* or *ContentControl* class and define their own visual appearance and functionality. Because of the template-based mechanism of creating user interfaces, the line between user controls and custom controls is somewhat blurred. The important distinction from a developer's standpoint is that user controls provide a designable surface at design time and custom controls do not.

Whether creating a user control or a custom control, you likely want to provide new properties for your control. To take advantage of built-in data binding and change notification features in WPF, you should implement dependency properties.

Choosing among User Controls, Custom Controls, and Templates

User controls, custom controls, and templates all enable you to create custom elements with custom appearances. Because each of these methods is so powerful, you might be confused about which technique to use when creating a custom element for your application. The key to making the right decision isn't based on the appearance you want to create but, rather, on the functionality you want to incorporate into your application.

The standard WPF controls provide a great deal of built-in functionality. If the functionality of one of the preset controls, such as a progress bar or a slider, matches the functionality that you want to incorporate, then you should create a new template for that preexisting control to achieve the appearance you want. Creating a new template is the simplest solution to creating a custom element, so you should consider that option first.

If the functionality you want to incorporate into your application can be achieved through a combination of preexisting controls and code, consider creating a user control. User controls enable you to bind together multiple preexisting controls in a single interface and add code that determines how they behave.

If no preexisting control or combination of controls can achieve the functionality you want, create a custom control. Custom controls enable you to create a completely new template that defines the visual representation of the control and to add custom code that determines the control's functionality.

Implementing and Registering Dependency Properties

Dependency properties are the standard form that properties in WPF take. They support change notification, animation, property value inheritance, and data binding, and they support multiple property value providers.

Dependency properties can be implemented only on objects that derive from the *DependencyObject* class. All WPF elements derive from *DependencyObject*. If you want to implement dependency properties on a custom class, the class must inherit from *DependencyObject*.

Dependency properties are implemented as normal .NET properties with some extra WPF infrastructure. The dependency property must be registered with the run time in a static constructor, and then it can be set using a standard .NET property wrapper.

To implement and register a dependency property:

1. In a class that inherits from *DependencyObject*, declare a public, static, read-only variable of the type *DependencyProperty*. By convention, the name of this variable should be your desired name for the property with the suffix "Property" added to it. Look at the following example:

Sample of Visual Basic Code
```
Public Shared ReadOnly FlavorProperty As DependencyProperty
```

Sample of C# Code
```
public static readonly DependencyProperty FlavorProperty;
```

2. Create a static constructor for the class that registers the dependency property. The *DependencyProperty.Register* method requires you to provide the name of the .NET property wrapper, the type of the property, the type that owns that property, and an instance of *FrameworkPropertyMetadata*, which can be used to add optional features to your dependency property. The following example shows a static constructor that registers the dependency property and assumes that your class is named *PieClass*:

Sample of Visual Basic Code

```
Shared Sub New()
    Dim md As New FrameworkPropertyMetadata()
    PieClass.FlavorProperty = DependencyProperty.Register("Flavor", _
        GetType(String), GetType(PieClass), md)
End Sub
```

Sample of C# Code

```
static PieClass()
{
    FrameworkPropertyMetadata md = new FrameworkPropertyMetadata();
    PieClass.FlavorProperty = DependencyProperty.Register("Flavor",
        typeof(string), typeof(PieClass), md);
}
```

3. Finally, create a .NET property wrapper to allow the dependency property to be accessed in code, as shown here:

Sample of Visual Basic Code

```
Public Property Flavor() As String
    Get
        Return CType(GetValue(PieClass.FlavorProperty), String)
    End Get
    Set
        SetValue(PieClass.FlavorProperty, value)
    End Set
End Property
```

Sample of C# Code

```
public string Flavor
{
    get
    {
        return (string)GetValue(PieClass.FlavorProperty);
    }
    set
    {
        SetValue(PieClass.FlavorProperty, value);
    }
}
```

It is important to note that when dependency properties are set by the run time, they are set directly through the *GetValue* and *SetValue* methods, not through the .NET property wrapper. Thus, you should not put any additional code in the wrapper because it does not run unless the property is set directly in code. You can provide a static callback method that executes when the property value is changed by specifying a delegate in *FrameworkPropertyMetadata*, as shown here:

Sample of Visual Basic Code

```vb
Shared Sub New()
   Dim md As New FrameworkPropertyMetadata(New _
      PropertyChangedCallback(AddressOf FlavorPropertyChanged))
   PieClass.FlavorProperty = DependencyProperty.Register("Flavor", _
      GetType(String), GetType(PieClass), md)
End Sub

Private Shared Sub FlavorPropertyChanged(ByVal o As DependencyObject, _
   ByVal e As DependencyPropertyChangedEventArgs)
   ' Implementation omitted
End Sub
```

Sample of C# Code

```csharp
static PieClass()
{
   FrameworkPropertyMetadata md = new FrameworkPropertyMetadata(new
      PropertyChangedCallback(FlavorPropertyChanged));
   PieClass.FlavorProperty = DependencyProperty.Register("Flavor",
      typeof(string), typeof(PieClass), md);
}

private static void FlavorPropertyChanged(DependencyObject o,
   DependencyPropertyChangedEventArgs e)
{
   // Implementation omitted
}
```

Creating User Controls

You can create a user control to combine the functionality of multiple preexisting controls with code that makes them work together in a specific way. When creating user controls, you are typically not attempting to create a lookless control but, rather, a reusable amalgam of preconfigured controls.

Creating a user control is easy. Visual Studio provides a designable surface for user control creation that enables drag-and-drop functionality from the Toolbox. Thus, you can design a user control in exactly the same way as you would design an application interface. After the interface of the control is created, you can implement the functionality your control requires.

To create a user control:

1. In Visual Studio, create a new WPF User Control Library project, using the template in the Windows project type. The designer opens to a new designable user control.

2. Create the user interface for your control. You can drag constituent controls from the Toolbox, or you can create them in XAML.

3. Add any functionality your control requires. If you need to implement any properties, implement dependency properties, as described earlier in this lesson. For events, implement routed events, as described in Chapter 2, "Working with Events and Commands."

4. Press F5 to build your control.

Consuming user controls is discussed in the "Consuming User Controls and Custom Controls" section later in this lesson.

Creating Custom Controls

Custom controls are different from user controls in that they are designed to be lookless. Visual Studio provides no designable surface for a custom control; rather, you must create the template for the custom control in the XAML designer. When you create a new custom control project in Visual Studio, it creates a Themes folder that contains a file named Generic.xaml. This file contains the default template for your custom control, which you can alter to create the template for your control.

To create a custom control:

1. In Visual Studio, create a new WPF Custom Control Library project using the template in the Windows project type. The designer opens to the Code window.

2. In Solution Explorer, open the Themes folder and double-click Generic.xaml to open the default template for your custom control.

3. In XAML view, create the template for your control.

4. Add any functionality your control requires. If you need to implement any properties, implement dependency properties as described earlier in this lesson. For events, implement routed events as described in Chapter 2, "Working with Events and Commands."

5. Press F5 to build your control.

In the practice for this lesson, you create a custom control from the beginning.

Custom controls typically inherit the *Control* class, which provides all the infrastructure a control needs but contains no control-specific implementation. In some cases, however, you want to inherit another class. For example, if you wanted to create a WPF implementation of *MaskedTextBox*, you might start by inheriting the *TextBox* class. If you want to inherit a class other than *Control,* you must manually change the class your control inherits in the code file.

Consuming User Controls and Custom Controls

To test or otherwise consume a user control or a custom control, you must add it to another project. This involves creating a reference to the assembly and then instantiating the control.

To consume a user control or a custom control:

1. In Solution Explorer, right-click the project and choose Add Reference. The Add Reference dialog box opens.

2. Click the Browse tab and browse to the .dll file that contains the control you want to use. Select it and click OK.

3. In XAML view, add an XAML reference to the newly added assembly, as shown in this example:

```
xmlns:cc="clr-namespace:WpfCustomControlLibrary1;
    assembly=WpfCustomControlLibrary1"
```

4. In XAML, add your custom control, as shown in this example:

```
<cc:CustomControl1 />
```

5. Press F5 to build your application.

If you are testing a control, be sure you reference the dynamic-link library (DLL) in the Debug folder. When you make changes to the control and rebuild it, your test application detects any changes and prompts you to rebuild the application.

 Quick Check

- What is the difference between a user control and a custom control?

Quick Check Answer

- A user control is a composite control composed of preexisting WPF controls bound together by a common functionality. A custom control is a user-defined control composed of a new control template and a new associated functionality.

Rendering a Theme-Based Appearance

The Windows Vista operating system enables the user to select themes for the desktop environment. When a theme is selected, applications that render a theme-based appearance automatically change to render an appearance and behavior consistent with that theme. Although in some cases you might want your custom controls to have a distinct appearance, rendering a theme-based appearance enables your controls to integrate seamlessly with other user interfaces.

The keys to rendering a theme-based appearance are the *SystemColors*, *SystemFonts*, and *SystemParameters* classes. These classes provide user-accessible instances of the brushes, fonts, and miscellaneous parameters that the current theme uses. When the user changes the theme, the *System* colors, fonts, and parameters are updated automatically to reflect the new theme.

You can access these settings as resources. Because they are system objects, they are already declared and don't need to be declared as resources in your *Resources* section. You can bind a property to one of these system objects, as shown in bold in this example:

```
<Label Background ="{DynamicResource {x:Static
    SystemColors.ControlBrushKey}}" Content="Hello World" />
```

Because *System* resources often are changed by the user, you should use the *DynamicResource* markup instead of the more familiar *StaticResource* markup. The difference between static and dynamic resources is explained in Lesson 2 of Chapter 1, "Building a User Interface."

Note that you refer to the resource key in this example. If you want to use this object in code, you would omit the key suffix, as shown here:

Sample of Visual Basic Code

```
Label1.Background = SystemColors.ControlBrush
```

Sample of C# Code

```
label1.Background = SystemColors.ControlBrush;
```

Providing Theme-Specific Templates for Custom Controls

In some cases, you might want to provide a completely different appearance for a control when it is rendered in one theme as opposed to another. You can create templates that are specific to individual themes and designate them for use with *ThemeInfoAttribute*.

The template defined in the Generic.xaml file is the template used for every theme that does not have a specific template defined for it. You create templates for specific themes by creating an XAML file named *<ThemeName>.<ThemeColor>*.xaml, except for the Windows Classic theme, which is named simply Classic.xaml. Table 5-1 shows several examples of Windows themes and their corresponding XAML filenames.

TABLE 5-1 Selected Windows Themes and Matching XAML Filenames

WINDOWS THEME	XAML FILENAME
Windows Vista theme	Aero.NormalColor.xaml
Default Windows XP theme	Luna.NormalColor.xaml
Silver Windows XP theme	Luna.Metallic.xaml
Windows Classic theme	Classic.xaml

No matter which themes you provide specific support for, you must create a fallback template in the Generic.xaml file.

In addition to creating alternate templates in theme-specific files, you must apply *ThemeInfoAttribute*. This is an *Assembly* attribute, and it is applied in the AssemblyInfo.vb or AssemblyInfo.cs file. *ThemeInfoAttribute* takes two arguments. The first argument designates where to look for theme-specific templates and resources, and the second argument indicates where to look for generic templates. Possible values for these arguments are as follows:

- *ResourceDictionaryLocation.None*: This value indicates not to look for theme-specific templates.

- *ResourceDictionaryLocation.SourceAssembly*: This value indicates to look in the source assembly.

- *ResourceDictionaryLocation.ExternalAssembly*: This value indicates to look in an external assembly, which must be named *<AssemblyName>.<ThemeName>*.dll, where *<AssemblyName>* is the current assembly name and *<ThemeName>* is the name of the appropriate theme.

The following example demonstrates *ThemeInfoAttribute*:

Sample of Visual Basic Code

```
<Assembly: _
    ThemeInfo(ResourceDictionaryLocation.SourceAssembly, _
    ResourceDictionaryLocation.SourceAssembly)>
```

Sample of C# Code

```
[assembly: ThemeInfo(ResourceDictionaryLocation.SourceAssembly,
    ResourceDictionaryLocation.SourceAssembly)]
```

You can use this technique to provide theme-specific resource dictionaries as well. (Resource dictionaries are discussed in Chapter 1, "Building a User Interface.") The only adjustment you have to make is to create a Themes folder if it does not exist. You must also create a Generic.xaml file that includes a resource set for any themes that are unsupported.

EXAM TIP

Although it is important to understand the differences between Windows Forms custom controls and WPF custom controls when taking the exam, the exam is more likely to focus on WPF control creation, so be sure you understand all aspects of this process, especially control templates and using themes.

PRACTICE Creating a Custom Control

In this practice, you create a custom control that takes the form of a digital clock that is updated every second. You create a dependency property that represents the current time and implement the functionality to update this property every second. You then create the default template for your control and bind *TextBlock* in that template to the *Time* property. Finally, you create a test project to test your new control.

EXERCISE Creating a Custom Control

1. Create a new WPF Custom Control Library project, using the template in the Windows project type.

2. In code view, create variables that represent a *System.Timers.Timer* class and a dependency property named *TimeProperty*. Also, declare a new delegate called *SetterDelegate* that takes no arguments, as shown here:

Sample of Visual Basic Code

```vb
Public Shared ReadOnly TimeProperty As DependencyProperty
Private myTimer As New System.Timers.Timer
Delegate Sub SetterDelegate()
```

Sample of C# Code

```csharp
public static readonly DependencyProperty TimeProperty;
System.Timers.Timer myTimer = new System.Timers.Timer();
delegate void SetterDelegate();
```

3. In the shared (static) constructor, add the following code to register a new dependency property. No arguments are necessary for the metadata for this property:

Sample of Visual Basic Code

```vb
Dim metadata As New FrameworkPropertyMetadata()
TimeProperty = DependencyProperty.Register("Time", GetType(String), _
    GetType(CustomControl1), metadata)
```

Sample of C# Code

```csharp
FrameworkPropertyMetadata metadata = new FrameworkPropertyMetadata();
TimeProperty = DependencyProperty.Register("Time", typeof(string),
    typeof(CustomControl1), metadata);
```

4. Create an instance constructor that initializes *Timer* and sets the *DataContext* property. In addition, add a handler for the *Timer.Elapsed* event. (You will create the method that handles this event in a subsequent step.)

Sample of Visual Basic Code

```vb
Public Sub New()
    AddHandler myTimer.Elapsed, AddressOf timer_elapsed
    myTimer.Interval = 1000
    myTimer.Start()
    Me.DataContext = Me
End Sub
```

Sample of C# Code

```csharp
public CustomControl1()
{
    myTimer.Elapsed += timer_elapsed;
    myTimer.Interval = 1000;
    myTimer.Start();
    this.DataContext = this;
}
```

5. Create a method that sets the *Time* property to a string that represents the current time in the long time format. This method is called by *Dispatcher* in the *Timer.Elapsed* event handler. Note that you are setting the *Time* property directly through the *SetValue* method in WPF. Because this property is not meant to be set by other controls, you do not need to provide a .NET property wrapper for this dependency property.

Sample of Visual Basic Code

```
Private Sub TimeSetter()
    SetValue(TimeProperty, Now.ToLongTimeString)
End Sub
```

Sample of C# Code

```
void TimeSetter()
{
    SetValue(TimeProperty, DateTime.Now.ToLongTimeString());
}
```

6. Create the *timer_elapsed* method to handle the *Timer.Elapsed* event. Because *Timer* code is executed on a different thread from the user interface, this method should use *Dispatcher* to invoke the *TimeSetter* method safely. An example is shown here:

Sample of Visual Basic Code

```
Private Sub timer_elapsed(ByVal sender As Object, ByVal e As _
    System.Timers.ElapsedEventArgs)
    Dispatcher.Invoke(Windows.Threading.DispatcherPriority.Normal, _
        New SetterDelegate(AddressOf TimeSetter))
End Sub
```

Sample of C# Code

```
void timer_elapsed(object sender, System.Timers.ElapsedEventArgs e)
{
    Dispatcher.Invoke(System.Windows.Threading.DispatcherPriority.Normal,
        new SetterDelegate(TimeSetter));
}
```

7. In Solution Explorer, expand the Themes folder and double-click Generic.xaml to open the Generic.xaml file in XAML view. Within the *Border* declaration, add the following XAML code to create the visual template for your control:

```
<TextBlock Foreground="{TemplateBinding Foreground}"
    VerticalAlignment="Center" HorizontalAlignment="Center" Text="{Binding
    Path=Time}" />
```

8. Press F6 to build your control.

9. Now you will add a project to test your control. From the File menu, choose Add and then choose New Project. The Add New Project dialog box opens. Choose WPF Application and click OK.

10. In Solution Explorer, right-click the new project and choose Add Reference to open the Add Reference dialog box. Choose the Projects tab and then select the custom control library you created in the previous steps. Click OK.

11. In the namespaces section of your XAML code for the test project, add the following line to import the custom control namespace into your project. Note that if your project and namespace are called something other than Lesson3, you have to modify this line accordingly:

```
xmlns:MyNamespace="clr-namespace:Lesson3;assembly=Lesson3"
```

12. Add the following XAML within the *Grid* declaration in the XAML code for your test project:

```
<MyNamespace:CustomControl1/>
```

An instance of your control is added to your test project.

13. In Solution Explorer, right-click your test project and select Set As Startup Project. Press F5 to build and run your project.

Lesson Summary

- The choice among templates, custom controls, and user controls should be based on functionality. If an existing WPF control contains the functionality you need, create a template to provide a new appearance for it. If multiple existing WPF controls can be bound together with code to create your needed functionality, create a user control. If you need completely new functionality, create a custom control.

- Dependency properties have built-in change notification and support animation, property value inheritance, and data binding. When creating new properties for user controls or custom controls, create dependency properties.

- User controls are created in a designer and consist of one or more WPF controls bound together in a single interface and incorporating custom code.

- Custom controls are WPF elements that incorporate custom functionality. The appearance of custom controls is defined by a new template. They typically inherit from the *Control* class.

- You can provide theme-based rendering for your custom controls by using the *SystemColors*, *SystemFonts*, and *SystemParameters* classes. To provide completely different appearances for your control based on theme, you can create multiple templates and use *ThemeInfoAttribute* to designate where to look for the alternate theme templates.

Lesson Review

You can use the following questions to test your knowledge of the information in Lesson 3, "Creating Custom Controls in WPF." The questions are also available on the companion CD if you prefer to review them in electronic form.

> **NOTE ANSWERS**
>
> Answers to these questions and explanations of why each answer choice is correct or incorrect are located in the "Answers" section at the end of the book.

1. You are designing a control that retrieves current stock prices and displays them in a *ListBox* object that is updated regularly. Which of the following is the best strategy for creating your custom element?

   A. Use a preexisting Windows Forms control.

   B. Use a preexisting WPF element with a custom template.

   C. Create a user control.

   D. Create a custom control.

2. You are designing a control that downloads stock market quotes and displays them in a rolling stock-ticker format that moves constantly across the top of the window. Which of the following is the best strategy for creating your custom element?

   A. Use a preexisting Windows Forms control.

   B. Use a preexisting WPF element with a custom template.

   C. Create a user control.

   D. Create a custom control.

3. Which of the following is required to implement theme-specific templates for a custom control? (Choose all that apply.)

   A. Create separate templates for each theme.

   B. Create separate folders for each theme.

   C. Set *ThemeInfoAttribute*.

   D. Provide a generic template for themes that are not supported.

Case Scenarios

In the following case scenarios, you apply what you've learned about user-defined controls. You can find answers to these questions in the "Answers" section at the end of this book.

Case Scenario 1: Full Support for Styles

You've just been hired to create an application for one of your most important clients. There is nothing too technically difficult about this application; it basically takes customer information as input and stores it in a database. The problem is that the design of the application requires the use of a *MaskedTextBox*-style control, but the client insists that the application must be fully visually extensible like other WPF applications, including support for *Style* elements and templates.

The technical requirements are that:

- The user interface must incorporate several text boxes that have full masking ability.
- Every control in the user interface must be visually extensible through *Style* and *Template*.

Answer the following question for all your office mates, who are eagerly awaiting the application's completion:

- What possible approaches can we use to solve these problems?

Case Scenario 2: The Pizza Progress Bar

You're designing an internal application for a well-known pizza company, and the stakeholders have requested a few fun details to personalize the application for their company. Specifically, they'd like a custom progress bar. Instead of showing a bar that gradually fills as the task nears completion, they'd like to show an image of a pizza that gradually disappears as the task nears completion.

Answer the following questions for your manager:

1. What approach should you use to implement this control?
2. How can you implement the disappearing-pizza visual effect?

Suggested Practices

To help you successfully master the exam objectives presented in this chapter, complete the following tasks.

- **Practice 1**   Implement the custom *ProgressBar* control described in Case Scenario 2.
- **Practice 2**   Re-create the custom control you created in the practice accompanying Lesson 3 as a user control.

- **Practice 3**   Create templates that create *Button* controls that appear as triangles, pentagons, or other complex geometric shapes.

- **Practice 4**   Practice creating *Mask* properties for the *MaskedTextBox* control that accept a variety of standard formats, such as Lastname-Firstname, ZIP codes, phone numbers, and other input formats.

- **Practice 5**   Create a custom controller that displays an image, automatically extracts the image name from the metadata, and displays the image name below the image.

Take a Practice Test

The practice tests on this book's companion CD offer many options. For example, you can test yourself on just the content covered in this chapter, or you can test yourself on all the 70-511 certification exam content. You can set up the test so that it closely simulates the experience of taking a certification exam, or you can set it up in study mode so that you can look at the correct answers and explanations after you answer each question.

MORE INFO   **PRACTICE TESTS**

For details about all the practice test options available, see the "How to Use the Practice Tests" section in this book's Introduction.

CHAPTER 6

Working with Data Binding

D*ata binding* is the mechanism by which information contained in an object is associated with elements in your user interface. The most common scenario is seen when binding a control in the user interface to a record in a database. When a field in the database is bound to a control, that field's value is displayed in the control. Changes made to the value in the control can then be reflected back to the original record in the database if the programmer so desires. This kind of data binding has been a staple of Windows Forms programming for years.

Data binding in Windows Presentation Foundation (WPF) takes this paradigm to a whole new level. Using WPF data-binding technology, any property can be bound to any other object or source. You can create richly data-bound interfaces that eliminate much of the back-end coding required by Windows Forms. In this chapter, you learn about the *Binding* class and how to configure it. In addition, you learn how to configure data binding for WPF, apply custom conversions to your data to format strings, return objects, or apply conditional formatting to your presentation layer. You also learn how to validate data and configure custom data objects for data change notification.

Exam objectives in this chapter:

- Implement data binding.
- Implement value converters in WPF.
- Implement data validation.
- Implement and consume change notification interfaces.

Lessons in this chapter:

Before You Begin

To complete the lessons in this chapter, you must have:

- A computer that meets or exceeds the minimum hardware requirements listed in the "About This Book" section at the beginning of the book.

- Microsoft Visual Studio 2010 Professional installed on your computer.

- An understanding of Microsoft Visual Basic or C# syntax and familiarity with Microsoft .NET Framework 4.0.

- An understanding of Extensible Application Markup Language (XAML).

 REAL WORLD

Matthew Stoecker

WPF takes data binding to a level that was unheard of in the Windows Forms world. Now I can create rich user interfaces that have properties bound to just about anything imaginable. Creating the user interface (UI) functionality by which manipulating one control changes the value of another is now simple; no more complicated event-handling code. Just set the binding and you're ready to go!

Lesson 1: Configuring Data Binding

WPF makes it easy to bind almost any property on any element to any other object, property, collection, or data source. In this lesson, you learn about *Binding*, the central class that defines data binding in WPF. You learn how to create a binding between two properties and how to configure the binding mode and the update mode.

> **After this lesson, you will be able to:**
> - Describe the important members of the *Binding* class.
> - Create a binding between an element property and an object or object property.
> - Configure the *BindingMode* property of the *Binding* object.
> - Configure the *UpdateMode* property of the *Binding* object.
> - Bind to a nullable value.
>
> **Estimated lesson time: 30 minutes**

The term *data binding* describes the process of creating a dependence for the value of one property, called the *target property*, on the value of another property, called the *source property*. The target property takes on the value of the source property. Many variations on the style of binding are possible. In some cases, changes to the source property are transmitted to the target immediately, but in other cases, they are not. In some cases, changes the user makes to the target property also are transmitted back to the value of the source property, although in other cases, they are not. The class that makes all this possible is the *Binding* class.

The *Binding* Class

The *Binding* class is the glue that makes data binding possible. Simply put, the *Binding* class establishes and describes a relationship between the target and source properties. You can use a *Binding* object to create a relationship between a target property and another object, a list, an ADO.NET data object, or any other object. Table 6-1 shows important properties of the *Binding* class discussed in this chapter.

TABLE 6-1 Important Properties of the *Binding* Class

PROPERTY	DESCRIPTION
ElementName	Gets or sets the name of the element to use as the binding source object. When binding to a WPF element, this property is used instead of the *Source* property.
FallbackValue	Gets or sets the value to use when the binding is unable to return a value.

Mode	Gets or sets a value that determines the direction of the data flow in the binding.
NotifyOnSourceUpdated	Gets or sets a value that indicates whether to raise the *SourceUpdated* event when a value is transferred from the target to the source.
NotifyOnTargetUpdated	Gets or sets a value that indicates whether to raise the *SourceUpdated* event when a value is transferred from the source to the target.
Path	Gets or sets the path to the source property of the binding source object.
RelativeSource	Gets or sets the binding source by specifying its location relative to the position of the binding target. When you want to specify an element at a relative position in the visual tree, this property is used instead of the *ElementName* property or the *Source* property to specify the source object.
Source	Gets or sets the object to use as the binding source. When not binding to a WPF element, this property is used instead of the *ElementName* property.
TargetNullValue	Gets or sets the value used in the target when the value of the source is null.
XPath	Gets or sets an *XPath* query that returns the value on the Extensible Markup Language (XML) binding source to use.

At the core of a data binding are two properties: the source property and the target property. The source property is defined by the combined setting of two properties on the *Binding* object: The *ElementName* property, the *Source* property, or the *RelativeSource* property specifies the source object to which the binding is bound; the *Path* property specifies to which property of that object the binding is bound. Each of these kinds of sources is discussed in this lesson.

You might notice that there is no property on the *Binding* class that specifies the target object or target property. This is because you set the target property *to* the binding; the binding automatically transmits the value retrieved from the source property to the target property.

Binding to a WPF Element

The simplest data-binding scenario involves binding a property on a WPF element to a property on another element. Consider, for example, a *Label* element and a *Slider* element. You might want to bind the *Content* property of the *Label* element to the *Value* property of the *Slider* element. You can accomplish this declaratively, as shown in bold here:

```
<Label Content="{Binding ElementName=Slider1, Path=Value}" Height="25" Width="100"></
Label>
```

In this example, the binding is created declaratively. The object to which the *Content* property is bound is specified by the *ElementName* property, and the property on that object that actually supplies the value is indicated by the *Path* property. When the *Slider.Value* property changes, that change is now reflected immediately in the *Label.Content* property.

In some cases, you might need to define more complex bindings declaratively, and you might find it more useful to use more formal syntax. The following example uses nested declarations instead of the curly braces shown previously. The binding created is the same as the previous one:

```xml
<Label Height="25" Width="100">
    <Label.Content>
        <Binding ElementName="Slider1" Path="Value" />
    </Label.Content>
</Label>
```

Although this syntax is more cumbersome, it is occasionally useful, as will be demonstrated later in this lesson.

Creating a Binding in Code

Although it is easiest to create bindings declaratively, you might find it useful to create a binding in code if you want to set or remove a binding dynamically. A binding can be created in code like any other object. To set the binding, however, you must use the *SetBinding* method on the WPF element and specify the dependency property to which the binding will be bound. The following code demonstrates how to create in code the binding shown in the previous two examples:

Sample of Visual Basic Code

```vb
Dim aBinding As New Binding()
aBinding.ElementName = "Slider1"
aBinding.Path = New System.Windows.PropertyPath("Value")
' In the previous two examples, the Name property of the Label was not set.
' In this example, a name is required so it is assumed to be Label1.
Label1.SetBinding(ContentProperty, aBinding)
```

Sample of C# Code

```csharp
Binding aBinding = new Binding();
aBinding.ElementName = "Slider1";
aBinding.Path = new System.Windows.PropertyPath("Value");
// In the previous two examples, the Name property of the Label was not set.
// In this example, a name is required so it is assumed to be Label1.
Label1.SetBinding(ContentProperty, aBinding);
```

To remove a binding dynamically, you call the *BindingOperations.ClearBinding* method, as shown here:

Sample of Visual Basic Code

```vb
BindingOperations.ClearBinding(Me.Label1, ContentProperty)
```

Sample of C# Code

```
BindingOperations.ClearBinding(this.Label1, ContentProperty);
```

Binding to an Object

When binding to an object that is not a WPF element, you use the *Source* property to specify the *Source* object. This can be any object you are able to access from the XAML view. When binding to a non-WPF object, a common scenario is to bind to static objects such as system colors and fonts. The following example demonstrates how to use the *Source* property to bind the *Background* property of a button to the *SystemColors.WindowColor* static object:

```
<Button Background="{Binding Source={x:Static SystemColors.WindowColor}}"
    Height="23" Width="75">Button</Button>
```

In this example, because the *Background* property is bound to the brush exposed by *SystemColors.WindowColor*, you can omit the *Path* property.

Another common scenario is to bind to a logical resource. (Logical resources are discussed in detail in Chapter 1, "Building a User Interface.") The following code (shown in bold) demonstrates binding to a logical resource. It shows importing a namespace from the application, creating an instance of a class from that namespace in the *Window.Resources* tag, and then binding to a property of that instance:

```
<Window x:Class="WpfApplication1.Window1"
    xmlns="http://schemas.microsoft.com/winfx/2006/xaml/presentation"
    xmlns:x="http://schemas.microsoft.com/winfx/2006/xaml"
    xmlns:local="clr-namespace:WpfApplication1"
    Title="Window1" Height="300" Width="300">
    <Window.Resources>
        <local:aClass x:Key="theObject" />
    </Window.Resources>
    <Grid>
        <Button Content="{Binding Source={StaticResource theObject},
            Path=myProperty}" />
    </Grid>
</Window>
```

Using the *DataContext* Property

It is not actually necessary to set the *Source* property at all to create a data binding. You can instead set the *DataContext* property for an element or a container in the visual tree. If the *Source*, *RelativeSource*, or *Element* property of a *Binding* class is not set, WPF looks for a *DataContext* setting, starting with the element that is bound by the binding and then moving up the visual tree until an element is found for which the *DataContext* property is not null. The object specified by the *DataContext* property then serves as the source object for all bindings in that element's visual tree that do not already have the *Source*, *Element*, or *RelativeSource* property set. This is useful for binding multiple elements in a single container to the same data source. The lines of code shown in bold in the following example demonstrate the *DataContext* property. The *DataContext* property of the grid is set to a resource object called *aDataObject*, and then the *Content* property of the contained *Label* element is bound to a member of *myDataObject* named *myTitle*.

```
<Window x:Class="WpfApplication1.Window1"
    xmlns="http://schemas.microsoft.com/winfx/2006/xaml/presentation"
    xmlns:x="http://schemas.microsoft.com/winfx/2006/xaml"
    xmlns:local="clr-namespace:WpfApplication1"
    Title="Window1" Height="300" Width="300">
    <Window.Resources>
        <local:myDataObject x:Key="aDataObject" />
    </Window.Resources>
    <Grid DataContext="{StaticResource aDataObject}">
        <Label Content="{Binding Path=myTitle}" />
    </Grid>
</Window>
```

A common scenario when using *DataContext* is to set it in code. For example, this is required frequently when using ADO.NET objects that must be initialized in code and cannot be filled declaratively. In this case, you still can create the bindings declaratively, omitting the *Source* property, as shown in bold here:

```
<Grid Name="Grid1">
    <Label Content="{Binding Path=myTitle}" />
</Grid>
```

Then set the *DataContext* property in code, as shown here:

Sample of Visual Basic Code

```
Dim aDataObject As New myDataObject()
Grid1.DataContext = aDataObject
```

Sample of C# Code

```
myDataObject aDataObject = new myDataObject();
Grid1.DataContext = aDataObject;
```

When the *DataContext* property is set in code, the bound controls affected by it will not display any bound data until the code setting the property is executed.

Binding to Ancestor Properties with the *RelativeSource* Property

The *RelativeSource* property enables you to create bindings that specify a source element in a position in the visual tree relative to the target element. The type of *RelativeSource* binding is determined by the *RelativeSource.Mode* property. Table 6-2 shows the possible values for the *RelativeSource.Mode* property.

TABLE 6-2 Possible Values for the *RelativeSource.Mode* Property

VALUE	DESCRIPTION
FindAncestor	Refers to the ancestor in the visual tree of the data-bound element, which is an element in the visual tree one or more levels above the current element. When using this mode, you must set the *AncestorType* and *AncestorLevel* properties.
PreviousData	Enables you to bind the previous data item (not the control that contains the data item) in the list of data items being displayed.
Self	Refers to the element on which you are setting the *Binding* object; generally used to bind one property of an element to another property of that same element.
TemplatedParent	Refers to the element to which the control template (in which the data-bound element exists) is applied. This is applicable only if the *Binding* object is within a template. Control templates are discussed in detail in Chapter 5, "Working with User-Defined Controls."

When binding to an ancestor source object, you must set both the *AncestorType* and the *AncestorLevel* properties. The *AncestorType* property specifies the type of source object to bind to, and the *AncestorLevel* property indicates how many levels up in *VisualTree* the ancestor is located. The following example demonstrates binding the *Content* property of a button to the *Tag* property of the grid that contains the button:

```
<Grid Tag="Button Text">
  <Button Content="{Binding Path=Tag, RelativeSource={RelativeSource
    Mode=FindAncestor, AncestorType=Grid, AncestorLevel=1}}"
    Height="23" Width="75">
  </Button>
</Grid>
```

Because setting so many properties inline can be cumbersome, you might find it more useful to use the more formal syntax, as shown here:

```
<Grid Tag="Button Text">
  <Button Height="23" Name="Button1" VerticalAlignment="Bottom">
    <Button.Content>
      <Binding Path="Tag">
        <Binding.RelativeSource>
          <RelativeSource Mode="FindAncestor" AncestorType="Grid"
            AncestorLevel="1" />
        </Binding.RelativeSource>
      </Binding>
    </Button.Content>
  </Button>
</Grid>
```

Setting the Binding Mode

The *Binding.Mode* property determines how bound controls behave in response to changes in either the source or the target value. Table 6-3 shows the possible values for the *Binding.Mode* property.

TABLE 6-3 Possible Values for the *Binding.Mode* Property

VALUE	DESCRIPTION
Default	Specifies that the *Binding* object should use the default mode for the target property.
OneTime	Specifies that the *Binding* object should update the target when the application starts or when the data context changes, but that the *Binding* object should not update the target upon subsequent source value changes.
OneWay	Specifies that the *Binding* object should update the target property when the source property changes. Changes in the target property value have no effect on the source property value.
OneWayToSource	Specifies that the *Binding* object should update the source property when the target property changes. Changes in the source property have no effect on the target property value.
TwoWay	Specifies that changes to either the source property or the target property update the other automatically.

The most commonly used values for the *Binding.Mode* property are *OneWay* and *TwoWay*. A value of *OneWay* is typically used in applications that display data but do not allow data to be edited. A value of *TwoWay* is more commonly used in data-editing applications, where the data in the source is displayed but the user has the option of editing that data and saving it to the source object.

Binding to a Nullable Value

At times you might want to bind to a value of a data type that can be null. To provide a default value, you can set *TargetNullValue* to a value if the target value is null. The following example demonstrates binding the *Text* property of a text box to the *IsChecked* property of a check box, which can be *True*, *False*, or *null*. If the value of the *CheckBox.IsChecked* value is null, the string "Value Not Selected" is displayed in the text box.

```
<Grid>

    <CheckBox Content="CheckBox" Name="CheckBox1" IsChecked="{x:Null}" />
```

```
<TextBox Text="{Binding ElementName=CheckBox1, Path=IsChecked,
    TargetNullValue='Value Not Selected'}" HorizontalAlignment="Left"
    Margin="0,29,0,0" Name="TextBox1" VerticalAlignment="Top" Width="120" />

</Grid>
```

Setting the *UpdateSourceTrigger* Property

The *UpdateSourceTrigger* property controls how the source property in a data-binding relationship is updated. Bindings with a *Binding.Mode* property setting of *TwoWay* or *OneWayToSource* listen for changes in the target property and transfer the changes back to the source. The *UpdateSourceTrigger* property controls how frequently these transfers are made. Table 6-4 describes the possible values for the *UpdateSourceTrigger* property.

TABLE 6-4 Possible Values for the *UpdateSourceTrigger* Property

VALUE	DESCRIPTION
Default	A setting of *Default* indicates that the source property is updated according to the default value for the target property. Most properties have a default value of *PropertyChanged*, which updates the source property whenever the property changes. However, properties that are likely to be edited by a user at run time, such as text properties, often have a default *UpdateSourceTrigger* value of *LostFocus*.
Explicit	The source property is updated only when *Binding.UpdateSource()* is called.
LostFocus	The source property is updated when the element containing the target property loses focus. This is usually used for properties that are likely to be edited by the user.
PropertyChanged	The source property is updated whenever the target property changes.

In most cases, you want to leave the *UpdateSourceTrigger* property on the default value. Most properties have a default value of *PropertyChanged*, so the source is updated whenever the property changes. Some properties, though, such as *Text*, have a default value of *LostFocus* because the *Text* property is found in elements that are designed to be user-editable, such as the *TextBox* element. For most scenarios involving a *TextBox* element, you will want to update the source only when *TextBox* loses focus (that is, when the user has finished entering data). If you want to have changes that are being made reflected somewhere else in the user interface immediately, for example, you would set the *UpdateSourceTrigger* property to *PropertyChanged*.

Quick Check

- When creating a *Binding* object, when would you use the *Source* property? When would you use the *ElementName* property? When would you use the *RelativeSource* property? When would you explicitly use none of these properties at all?

Quick Check Answer

- When creating a *Binding* object, you use the *ElementName* property to identify the source object when that object is another WPF element. You use the *Source* property to specify an object that is not a WPF element, such as a resource. The *RelativeSource* property specifies a source object that exists in the visual tree in a location relative to the target object. You do not need to specify any of these if the *DataContext* property has been set for the element or for a visual parent in code.

PRACTICE **Using Bindings**

In this practice, you bind properties of one element to properties of another element. You re-create the application you created earlier in this book, but you use data binding instead of code to implement the functionality.

EXERCISE Using Bindings

1. Load the partial solution for Chapter 6, Lesson 1 from the CD. This solution shows a user interface with a *RichTextBox* control in which you can type text and observe the effect of changing *FontFamily* and *FontSize*. *ListBox*, on the left of the user interface, is populated by *FontFamily* names automatically when the application opens. You implement the bindings that make the application work.

2. In XAML view, add to the *RichTextBox* declaration a *Binding* object that binds the *FontFamily* property to the *SelectedItem.Content* property of *ListBox1*. When finished, your code should resemble this, with the added binding shown in bold:

```
<RichTextBox FontFamily="{Binding ElementName=listBox1,
   Path=SelectedItem.Content}" Grid.Column="2" Name="richTextBox1" />
```

3. Add a binding to the longer of the two *TextBox* controls in the toolbar to bind *Text* to the selected item in *ListBox*. Your code should look like the following when finished:

```
<TextBox Text="{Binding ElementName=listBox1, Path=SelectedItem.Content}"
   BorderBrush="Black" Width="100"></TextBox>
```

4. Add a binding to bind the *Slider* value to the *FontSize* property of *RichTextBox*. Your code should resemble the following when finished:

```
<RichTextBox FontSize="{Binding ElementName=Slider1, Path=Value}"
   FontFamily="{Binding ElementName=listBox1, Path=SelectedItem.Content}"
   Grid.Column="2" Name="richTextBox1" />
```

5. Add a binding to bind the *Text* property of the smaller of the two *TextBox* controls in the toolbar. Make it a *TwoWay* binding so that changes in *TextBox* are propagated automatically back to *Slider*, and set the *UpdateSourceTrigger* property to *PropertyChanged* so that changes are propagated as soon as a new value is entered. The following example demonstrates the code:

```
<TextBox Text="{Binding ElementName=Slider1, Path=Value, Mode=TwoWay,
    UpdateSourceTrigger=PropertyChanged}" BorderBrush="Black"
    Width="25"></TextBox>
```

6. Press F5 to run and test your application.

Lesson Summary

- The *Binding* class defines a binding between a source and a target. The *ElementName* property indicates the source when the source is a WPF element. The *RelativeSource* property indicates the source when the source object is located in the visual tree at a location relative to the target, and the *Source* property identifies a source that is not a WPF element.

- The *DataContext* property of elements is useful for creating the general data environment for a control or container control. You frequently set *DataContext* in code when the binding source must be initialized in code. You can then create *Binding* objects in XAML that do not set the source and instead find the nearest set *DataContext* property in the visual tree.

- The *Mode* property enables you to set the binding mode of a *Binding* object. Modes are typically *OneWay*, which updates the target property whenever the source changes, or *TwoWay*, which updates either the target property or the source property whenever the other changes. Other possible binding modes include *OneTime*, which binds the target property only when the application starts, and *OneWayToSource*, which updates the source property when the target changes, but not vice versa.

- The *UpdateSourceTrigger* property enables you to set when the data transmitted to the source by a binding is updated. The most commonly used types of update triggers are *PropertyChanged*, which transmits a bound value whenever the property value changes, and *LostFocus*, which transmits the new value when the element loses focus.

Lesson Review

You can use the following questions to test your knowledge of the information in Lesson 1, "Configuring Data Binding." The questions are also available on the companion CD if you prefer to review them in electronic form.

> **NOTE ANSWERS**
>
> Answers to these questions and explanations of why each answer choice is correct or incorrect are located in the "Answers" section at the end of the book.

1. Which of the following is sufficient to establish a binding between a source and a target, assuming that a target property is already being set to the *Binding* object in question? (Choose all that apply.)

   A. Setting the *ElementName* property and the *Path* property

   B. Setting the *DataContext* property on the target element

   C. Setting the *Source* property

   D. Setting the *Path* property and the *RelativeSource* property

2. You are creating an application that enables the user to review data in a database and save local changes to a separate file, but not to save changes to the database. What is the appropriate value for the *Mode* property of your *Binding* objects?

   A. *OneTime*

   B. *OneWay*

   C. *TwoWay*

   D. *Default*

3. You are creating an application that enables the user to load a complex object in a data-bound state, make multiple changes that are interdependent, and then accept or reject those changes before updating the database. Assuming that the relationship between the user interface and the database is expressed through a binding, which is the best value for the *UpdateSourceTrigger* property?

   A. *Default*

   B. *PropertyChanged*

   C. *LostFocus*

   D. *Explicit*

Lesson 2: Converting Data

WPF incorporates rich functionality for converting data displayed in the presentation layer. Using value converters, you can format data for display, localize data, create objects based on underlying data, and even create objects and values that derive from multiple bound elements. In this lesson, you learn how to implement *IValueConverter* to create custom value converters for your data presentation layer.

After this lesson, you will be able to:

- Implement *IValueConverter*.
- Use a converter to format data.
- Use a converter to return an object.
- Format data conditionally using a converter.
- Localize data using a converter.
- Implement *IMultiValueConverter*.

Estimated lesson time: 30 minutes

Implementing *IValueConverter*

At the center of conversion is the *IValueConverter* interface, which has two member methods: *Convert*, which converts an input type to an output type; and *ConvertBack*, which reverses the conversion. By implementing *IValueConverter*, you can create specialized classes for a variety of conversion and formatting duties. An empty implementation of *IValueConverter* is shown here:

Sample of Visual Basic Code

```vb
Public Class myConverter
   Implements IValueConverter

   Public Function Convert(ByVal value As Object, ByVal targetType As _
      System.Type, ByVal parameter As Object, ByVal culture As _
      System.Globalization.CultureInfo) As Object Implements _
      System.Windows.Data.IValueConverter.Convert
         Throw New NotImplementedException()
   End Function

   Public Function ConvertBack(ByVal value As Object, ByVal targetType As _
      System.Type, ByVal parameter As Object, ByVal culture As _
      System.Globalization.CultureInfo) As Object Implements _
      System.Windows.Data.IValueConverter.ConvertBack
         Throw New NotImplementedException()
   End Function
End Class
```

```csharp
public class myConverter : IValueConverter
{
    public object Convert(object value, Type targetType, object parameter,
        System.Globalization.CultureInfo culture)
    {
        throw new NotImplementedException();
    }

    public object ConvertBack(object value, Type targetType, object
        parameter, System.Globalization.CultureInfo culture)
    {
        throw new NotImplementedException();
    }
}
```

The *Convert* method converts the object represented by the value parameter into the output object, and the *ConvertBack* method reverses the conversion performed by the *Convert* method. In some cases, a reverse conversion is not possible, and in other cases you never call the *ConvertBack* method, so it is common practice not to provide an explicit implementation for the *ConvertBack* method if it will never be called. Note, however, that for cases in which two-way binding will be implemented, you must implement both the *Convert* and *ConvertBack* methods. Unless you are certain that *ConvertBack* will never be called, provide an implementation.

In addition to implementing *IValueConverter*, you must decorate the class with the *ValueConversion* attribute, which specifies the source type and the target type for the converter. An example that specifies a source type of *Integer* and a target type of *String* is shown here:

Sample of Visual Basic Code

```vbnet
<ValueConversion(GetType(Integer), GetType(String))> _
```

Sample of C# Code

```csharp
[ValueConversion(typeof(int), typeof(string))]
```

The next example shows a simple converter that converts a numeric code representing a job title into a string containing that job title, and vice versa:

Sample of Visual Basic Code

```vbnet
<ValueConversion(GetType(Integer), GetType(String))> _
Public Class myConverter
    Implements IValueConverter

    Public Function Convert(ByVal value As Object, ByVal targetType As _
        System.Type, ByVal parameter As Object, ByVal culture As _
        System.Globalization.CultureInfo) As Object Implements _
        System.Windows.Data.IValueConverter.Convert
        Dim a As Integer = CInt(value)
        Select Case a
          Case 1
```

```vb
            Return "Group Manager"
        Case 2
            Return "Manager"
        Case 3
            Return "Programmer"
        Case Else
            Return "Title not defined"
    End Select
End Function

Public Function ConvertBack(ByVal value As Object, ByVal targetType As _
    System.Type, ByVal parameter As Object, ByVal culture As _
    System.Globalization.CultureInfo) As Object Implements _
    System.Windows.Data.IValueConverter.ConvertBack
    Dim aString As String = value.ToString()
    Select Case aString
        Case "Group Manager"
            Return 1
        Case "Manager"
            Return 2
        Case "Programmer"
            Return 3
        Case Else
            Return 4
    End Select
End Function
End Class
```

Sample of C# Code

```csharp
[ValueConversion(typeof(int), typeof(string))]
public class myConverter : IValueConverter
{
    public object Convert(object value, Type targetType, object parameter,
        System.Globalization.CultureInfo culture)
    {
        int a = int.Parse(value.ToString());
        switch (a)
        {
            case 1:
                return "Group Manager";
            case 2:
                return "Manager";
            case 3:
                return "Programmer";
            default:
                return "Title not defined";
        }
    }
    public object ConvertBack(object value, Type targetType, object
        parameter, System.Globalization.CultureInfo culture)
    {
        string a = value.ToString();
        switch (a)
        {
```

```
            case "Group Manager":
                return 1;
            case "Manager":
                return 2;
            case "Programmer":
                return 3;
            default:
                return 4;
        }
    }
}
```

To use a converter in your XAML code, you first must create a reference to the namespace that contains it in the XAML, as shown in bold here:

```
<Window x:Class="WpfApplication5.Window1"
    xmlns="http://schemas.microsoft.com/winfx/2006/xaml/presentation"
    xmlns:x="http://schemas.microsoft.com/winfx/2006/xaml"
    xmlns:local="clr-namespace:WpfApplication5"
    Title="Window1" Height="300" Width="300">
```

You then must create an object instance, typically by adding it to one of the element *Resource* collections, and assign a key value. Resources are discussed in depth in Chapter 1, "Building a User Interface." An example is shown here:

```
<Window.Resources>
    <local:myConverter x:Key="EmployeeConverter"></local:myConverter>
</Window.Resources>
```

After an object instance is created, you can set the *Converter* property of your binding to it by referring to the resource, as shown here:

```
<Label Content="{Binding Path=EmployeeCode, Converter={StaticResource
    EmployeeConverter}}" />
```

Most of the cases discussed in this chapter require only one-way conversion of data for display purposes. It is unnecessary to provide a real implementation for *ConvertBack* in these cases.

Using Converters to Format Strings

One of the most convenient uses for converters is to format strings. Because data is usually stored in a database without formatting, formatting is generally up to the data presentation layer to accomplish. Phone numbers, dates, currency, and Social Security numbers are all examples of data that might benefit from string formatting.

Formatting as Currency

Currency is a prime example of the need for string formatting. Monetary values are typically stored in numeric data types, but most data presentation designs would want to present this data as a currency-formatted string. The *ToString* method of numeric data types allows you to specify a string that indicates how the resulting string should be formatted. To format a resultant string as currency, you insert "C", as shown here:

Sample of Visual Basic Code

```vb
aString = aDouble.ToString("C")
```

Sample of C# Code

```csharp
aString = aDouble.ToString("C");
```

You can incorporate this functionality into a simple converter that takes a *Decimal* value and outputs a currency-formatted string. The *Convert* method of such a converter is shown here:

Sample of Visual Basic Code

```vb
Public Function Convert(ByVal value As Object, ByVal targetType As _
    System.Type, ByVal parameter As Object, ByVal culture As _
    System.Globalization.CultureInfo) As Object Implements _
    System.Windows.Data.IValueConverter.Convert
    Dim a As Decimal = CDec(value.ToString)
    Return a.ToString("C")
End Function
```

Sample of C# Code

```csharp
public object Convert(object value, Type targetType, object parameter,
    System.Globalization.CultureInfo culture)
{
    decimal a = decimal.Parse(value.ToString());
    return a.ToString("C");
}
```

The next example shows the *ConvertBack* method from this same converter:

Sample of Visual Basic Code

```vb
Public Function ConvertBack(ByVal value As Object, ByVal targetType As _
    System.Type, ByVal parameter As Object, ByVal culture As _
    System.Globalization.CultureInfo) As Object Implements _
    System.Windows.Data.IValueConverter.ConvertBack
    Dim result As Decimal
    Dim a As String = value.ToString()
    If Decimal.TryParse(a, System.Globalization.NumberStyles.Any, Nothing, _
        result) Then
        Return result
    Else
        ' Implement code to determine or return a default value here
        Return 0
    End If
End Function
```

Sample of C# Code

```csharp
public object ConvertBack(object value, Type targetType, object parameter,
    System.Globalization.CultureInfo culture)
{
```

```
decimal result;
string a = value.ToString();
if (decimal.TryParse(a, System.Globalization.NumberStyles.Any, null,
    out result))
    return result;
else
    // Implement code to determine or return a default value here
    return 0;
}
```

Currency formatting takes the current culture setting into account. The currency symbol shown in the formatted string varies depending on the culture setting.

Formatting Dates

You can use the same general scheme for formatting dates. The *DateTime.ToString* method accepts the format strings shown in Table 6-5.

TABLE 6-5 Format Strings for the *DateTime* Structure

FORMAT STRING	FORMAT NAME	EXAMPLE	USAGE EXAMPLE
d	*Short Date*	07/14/1969	ToString("d")
D	*Long Date*	Monday, July 14, 1969	ToString("D")
f	*Long Date and Short Time*	Monday, July 14, 1969 11:07 PM	ToString("f")
F	*Long Date and Long Time*	Monday, July 14, 1969 11:07:17 PM	ToString("F")
G	*General*	07/14/1969 11:07:17 PM	ToString("G")
M	*Month and Day*	July 14	ToString("M")
s	*ISO Sortable Standard*	1969-07-14 11:07:17	ToString("s")

The format returned by *General* formatting ("G") varies according to the local culture setting.

In addition to format strings, the *DateTime* structure contains several built-in methods for returning date and time strings in a variety of formats.

Other String Formatting

The *ToString* method of numeric data types provides a variety of additional format strings, a complete list of which can be found in the Visual Studio documentation. However, you might need to create a converter to convert to a custom string format. In that case, you have to write code to perform the conversion explicitly. The following example demonstrates a converter that accepts a nine-digit integer and returns a string representation of that integer formatted as a Social Security number:

Sample of Visual Basic Code

```vb
<ValueConversion(GetType(Integer), GetType(String))> _
Public Class SSConverter
    Implements IValueConverter

    Public Function Convert(ByVal value As Object, ByVal targetType As _
        System.Type, ByVal parameter As Object, ByVal culture As _
        System.Globalization.CultureInfo) As Object Implements _
        System.Windows.Data.IValueConverter.Convert
        Dim a As String = value.ToString()
        If Not a.Length = 9 Then
            Throw New ArgumentException("Number is in the wrong format")
        End If
        a = a.Insert(5, "-")
        a = a.Insert(3, "-")
        Return a
    End Function

    Public Function ConvertBack(ByVal value As Object, ByVal targetType As _
        System.Type, ByVal parameter As Object, ByVal culture As _
        System.Globalization.CultureInfo) As Object Implements _
        System.Windows.Data.IValueConverter.ConvertBack
        Dim a As String = value.ToString()
        a = a.Remove(6, 1)
        a = a.Remove(3, 1)
        Return CInt(a)
    End Function
End Class
```

Sample of C# Code

```csharp
[ValueConversion(typeof(int), typeof(string))]
public class SSConverter : IValueConverter
{
    public object Convert(object value, Type targetType, object parameter,
        System.Globalization.CultureInfo culture)
    {
        string a = value.ToString();
        if (!(a.Length==9))
            throw new ArgumentException("Number is in the wrong format");
        a = a.Insert(5, "-");
        a = a.Insert(3, "-");
        return a;
    }

    public object ConvertBack(object value, Type targetType, object
        parameter, System.Globalization.CultureInfo culture)
    {
        string a = value.ToString();
        a = a.Remove(6, 1);
        a = a.Remove(3, 1);
```

```
        return int.Parse(a);
    }
}
```

Using Converters to Return Objects

In addition to formatting, you can return objects using converters. For example, you might store references to images as string paths in your database but want to load and display the images when viewing data. Returning an object is as simple as creating the object in code and returning it as shown in previous examples. The following example takes a string formatted as a path and returns a *BitmapImage* object that represents the image stored at that path:

Sample of Visual Basic Code

```
<ValueConversion(GetType(String), GetType(BitmapImage))> _
Public Class ImageConverter
    Implements IValueConverter

    Public Function Convert(ByVal value As Object, ByVal targetType As  _
        System.Type, ByVal parameter As Object, ByVal culture As  _
        System.Globalization.CultureInfo) As Object Implements _
        System.Windows.Data.IValueConverter.Convert
        Try
            Dim myPath As String = CType(value, String)
            Dim myUri As New Uri(myPath)
            Dim anImage As New BitmapImage(myUri)
            Return anImage
        Catch ex As Exception
            Return New BitmapImage(New Uri("C:\ImageNotAvailable.jpg"))
        End Try
    End Function

    Public Function ConvertBack(ByVal value As Object, ByVal targetType _
        As System.Type, ByVal parameter As Object, ByVal culture As  _
        System.Globalization.CultureInfo) As Object Implements _
        System.Windows.Data.IValueConverter.ConvertBack
        Throw New NotImplementedException()
    End Function
End Class


Sample of C# Code

[ValueConversion(typeof(string), typeof(BitmapImage))]
public class ImageConverter : IValueConverter
{
    public object Convert(object value, Type targetType, object parameter,
        System.Globalization.CultureInfo culture)
    {
        try
        {
            string myPath = (string)value;
            Uri myUri = new Uri(myPath);
            BitmapImage anImage = new BitmapImage(myUri);
```

```
            return anImage;
        }
        catch
        {
            return new BitmapImage(new Uri("C:\\ImageNotAvailable.jpg"));
        }
    }

    public object ConvertBack(object value, Type targetType, object
        parameter, System.Globalization.CultureInfo culture)
    {
        throw new NotImplementedException();
    }
}
```

In this example, a string is converted to a Universal Resource Identifier (URI), and then that URI generates the *BitmapImage* that is returned. In the event of an error, a default image is returned. Note that because it would be problematic to convert an image back to a path, the *ConvertBack* method is not implemented. Nevertheless, it is a best practice to implement *ConvertBack* whenever possible.

Localizing Data with Converters

Converters can be useful for localizing data. Although some built-in conversions (such as the string currency conversion) take the current culture into account, there are several cases in which you need to provide your own localization code.

The parameters for the *Convert* and *ConvertBack* methods contain a reference to the *Culture* object to be used for the conversion. You can examine the value of this parameter and use that information to return localized data. The following example demonstrates a converter that reads the *Culture* object provided and invokes a method on a translation class that returns the appropriate string for the culture. This example assumes that this application might be run in the United States, France, or Germany and provides methods to convert English strings to German and French strings, and vice versa:

Sample of Visual Basic Code

```
<ValueConversion(GetType(String), GetType(String))> _
Public Class DateBrushConverter
    Implements IValueConverter
    ' Note: the Translator class is assumed to be a class that contains a
    ' dictionary used to translate the provided strings.
    Dim myTranslator As New Translator
    Public Function Convert(ByVal value As Object, ByVal targetType As _
        System.Type, ByVal parameter As Object, ByVal culture As _
        System.Globalization.CultureInfo) As Object Implements _
        System.Windows.Data.IValueConverter.Convert
        Dim astring As String = CType(value, String)
        Select Case culture.ToString
            Case "fr-FR"
                Return myTranslator.EnglishToFrench(astring)
            Case "de-DE"
```

```vb
                Return myTranslator.FrenchToEnglish(astring)
            Case Else
                Return astring
        End Select
    End Function

    Public Function ConvertBack(ByVal value As Object, ByVal targetType _
        As System.Type, ByVal parameter As Object, ByVal culture As _
        System.Globalization.CultureInfo) As Object Implements _
        System.Windows.Data.IValueConverter.ConvertBack
        Dim astring As String = CType(value, String)
        Select Case culture.ToString
            Case "fr-FR"
                Return myTranslator.FrenchToEnglish(astring)
            Case "de-DE"
                Return myTranslator.GermanToEnglish(astring)
            Case Else
                Return astring
        End Select
    End Function
End Class
```

Sample of C# Code

```csharp
[ValueConversion(typeof(string), typeof(string))]
public class LanguageConverter : IValueConverter
{
    // Note: the Translator class is assumed to be a class that contains a
    // dictionary used to translate the provided strings.
    Translator myTranslator = new Translator();
    public object Convert(object value, Type targetType, object parameter,
        System.Globalization.CultureInfo culture)
    {
        string aString = (string)value;
        switch(culture.ToString())
        {
            case "de-DE":
                return myTranslator.EnglishToGerman(aString);
            case "fr-FR":
                return myTranslator.EnglishToFrench(aString);
            default:
                return aString;
        }
    }
    public object ConvertBack(object value, Type targetType, object
        parameter, System.Globalization.CultureInfo culture)
    {
        string aString = (string)value;
        switch(culture.ToString())
        {
            case "de-DE":
                return myTranslator.GermanToEnglish(aString);
            case "fr-FR":
                return myTranslator.FrenchToEnglish(aString);
            default:
```

```
            return aString;
        }
    }
}
```

 Quick Check

- Describe the general process for using a converter to apply conditional formatting for bound data.

Quick Check Answer

- First, you must implement a converter that performs the appropriate conversion. For example, if you wanted to highlight records with a *Date* property value older than 30 days, you would implement a converter that changed a *DateTime* value into a *Color* value based on the value of the *DateTime* property. After the converter has been implemented, you should bind the appropriate value in the data template to the property that is converted and supply a reference to the converter in the *Binding* object. In this example, you would bind the *Background* property of the control in the data template, which is used to present the data, to the *Date* property and reference an instance of the converter in that binding.

Using Multi-value Converters

Multi-value converters enable you to return a converted value that results from multiple fields. For example, you might perform a calculation, such as multiplying a *UnitsPurchased* field by a *UnitPrice* field, to return a value representing total cost. You can also use a multi-value converter to provide complicated conditional formatting that takes multiple fields into account.

To create a multi-value converter, you must implement the *IMultiValueConverter* interface. This interface is very similar to the *IValueConverter* interface. The only differences are that the *Convert* method takes an *Object* array instead of a single *Object* as the first parameter, and the *ConvertBack* method returns an *Object* array and takes a *Type* array as one of the parameters. An unimplemented example is shown here:

Sample of Visual Basic Code

```
Public Class myMultiConverter
    Implements IMultiValueConverter

    Public Function Convert(ByVal values As Object(), ByVal targetType As _
        System.Type, ByVal parameter As Object, ByVal culture As _
        System.Globalization.CultureInfo) As Object Implements _
        System.Windows.Data.IMultiValueConverter.Convert
            Throw New NotImplementedException()
    End Function
```

```
    Public Function ConvertBack(ByVal value As Object, ByVal targetTypes() _
        As System.Type, ByVal parameter As Object, ByVal culture As _
        System.Globalization.CultureInfo) As Object() Implements _
        System.Windows.Data.IMultiValueConverter.ConvertBack
            Throw New NotImplementedException()
    End Function
End Class
```

Sample of C# Code

```
public class myMultiConverter : IMultiValueConverter
{
    public object Convert(object[] values, Type targetType, object
        parameter, System.Globalization.CultureInfo culture)
    {
        throw new NotImplementedException();
    }

    public object[] ConvertBack(object value, Type[] targetTypes, object
        parameter, System.Globalization.CultureInfo culture)
    {
        throw new NotImplementedException();
    }
}
```

The following example demonstrates how to implement *IMultiValueConverter*. This example takes an *Integer* object and a *Decimal* object that represent units ordered and unit price, respectively, and returns a currency-formatted string that represents the total price:

Sample of Visual Basic Code

```
Public Class TotalCostConverter
    Implements IMultiValueConverter

    Public Function Convert(ByVal values() As Object, ByVal targetType As _
        System.Type, ByVal parameter As Object, ByVal culture As _
        System.Globalization.CultureInfo) As Object Implements _
        System.Windows.Data.IMultiValueConverter.Convert
        Dim UnitsOrdered As Integer = CType(values(0), Integer)
        Dim UnitCost As Decimal = CType(values(1), Decimal)
        Dim TotalCost As Decimal = UnitsOrdered * UnitCost
        Return TotalCost.ToString("C")
    End Function

    Public Function ConvertBack(ByVal value As Object, ByVal targetTypes() _
        As System.Type, ByVal parameter As Object, ByVal culture As _
        System.Globalization.CultureInfo) As Object() Implements _
        System.Windows.Data.IMultiValueConverter.ConvertBack
        Throw New NotImplementedException()
    End Function
End Class
```

Sample of C# Code

```
public class TotalCostConverter : IMultiValueConverter
{
    public object Convert(object[] values, Type targetType, object
```

```
        parameter, System.Globalization.CultureInfo culture)
    {
        int UnitsOrdered = (int)values[0];
        decimal UnitCost = (decimal)values[1];
        decimal TotalCost = UnitsOrdered * UnitCost;
        return TotalCost.ToString("C");
    }

    public object[] ConvertBack(object value, Type[] targetTypes, object
        parameter, System.Globalization.CultureInfo culture)
    {
        throw new NotImplementedException();
    }
}
```

To bind a property to a value returned by a multi-value converter, you must create a reference to the assembly that contains the multi-value converter and then add an instance to an available resource collection, as you saw earlier in this lesson. To actually create the binding, however, you must use a class called *MultiBinding*. The *MultiBinding* class is essentially a collection of bindings that specifies a converter that takes the value of those bindings into account. You can set a property to a *MultiBinding* object in the same manner that you would set it to a *Binding* object. The following example demonstrates setting the *Content* property of a *Label* element to the value returned by an instance of the *TotalCostConverter* class used in the previous example. This example assumes that you have created an instance of this converter in the *Window.Resources* collection with a key value of *myTotalCostConverter* and that the *DataContext* property of *Window* has been set to an object with properties named *Units-Ordered* and *UnitCost*:

```
<Label>
   <Label.Content>
      <MultiBinding Converter="{StaticResource myTotalCostConverter}">
         <Binding Path=UnitsOrdered />
         <Binding Path=UnitCost />
      </MultiBinding>
   </Label.Content>
</Label>
```

PRACTICE Applying String Formatting and Conditional Formatting

In this practice, you use custom converters to provide string formatting and conditional formatting in your application.

EXERCISE 1   Using a Converter to Apply String Formatting

1. Open the partial solution for this lesson. Press F5 to compile and run the application.

   Note that customer records are displayed in the upper-left Contact Name list box, and when you click a customer record, dates indicating order dates are displayed in the upper-right list box. In this lesson, you will add color coding to these dates based on the year. In the next chapter, you will drill deeper into the functionality behind this application.

2. In the code window, beneath the *CountryGrouper* class, add the following class to convert a *Decimal* value to a currency-formatted string:

Sample of Visual Basic Code

```vb
<ValueConversion(GetType(Decimal), GetType(String))> _
Public Class CurrencyConverter
    Implements IValueConverter

    Public Function Convert(ByVal value As Object, ByVal targetType As _
        System.Type, ByVal parameter As Object, ByVal culture As _
        System.Globalization.CultureInfo) As Object Implements _
        System.Windows.Data.IValueConverter.Convert
        Dim aDec As Decimal
        aDec = CDec(value)
        Return aDec.ToString("C")
    End Function

    Public Function ConvertBack(ByVal value As Object, ByVal targetType As _
        System.Type, ByVal parameter As Object, ByVal culture As _
        System.Globalization.CultureInfo) As Object Implements _
        System.Windows.Data.IValueConverter.ConvertBack
      Throw (New NotImplementedException)
    End Function
End Class
```

Sample of C# Code

```csharp
[ValueConversion(typeof(Decimal), typeof(String))]
public class CurrencyConverter : IValueConverter
{
    public object Convert(object value, Type targetType, object parameter,
      System.Globalization.CultureInfo culture)
    {
        decimal aDec;
        aDec = (decimal)value;
        return aDec.ToString("C");
    }

    public object ConvertBack(object value, Type targetType, object
        parameter, System.Globalization.CultureInfo culture)
    {
        throw new NotImplementedException();
    }
}
```

3. In the *Namespaces* section of XAML view, add the following line to import the local namespace into XAML view, where *<local namespace name>* represents the namespace of your local project, for example, **Lesson_2**:

```
xmlns:local="clr-namespace:<local namespace name>"
```

4. Just before the *Grid* declaration in XAML view, add the following *Windows.Resources* section to create an instance of *CurrencyConverter*:

```
<Window.Resources>
    <local:CurrencyConverter x:Key="myCurrencyConverter" />
</Window.Resources>
```

5. From the Build menu, choose Build Solution.

6. In the XAML view, in *DataTemplate* for *listBox3,* change the last *Label* declaration to read as shown in bold here:

```
<Label Background="Red" Content="{Binding Path=ExtendedPrice,
    Converter={StaticResource myCurrencyConverter}}" Width="60" />
```

7. Press F5 to build and run your application. Note that the field representing total price for orders now is formatted as currency.

EXERCISE 2 Using a Converter to Apply Conditional Formatting

1. In code view, beneath the code for *CurrencyConverter*, add the following class:

Sample of Visual Basic Code

```
<ValueConversion(GetType(DateTime), GetType(Brush))> _
Public Class YearConverter
    Implements IValueConverter

    Public Function Convert(ByVal value As Object, ByVal targetType As _
        System.Type, ByVal parameter As Object, ByVal culture As _
        System.Globalization.CultureInfo) As Object Implements _
        System.Windows.Data.IValueConverter.Convert
        Dim aDate As DateTime
        aDate = CDate(value)
        Select Case aDate.Year.ToString
            Case "1994"
                Return New SolidColorBrush(Colors.Purple)
            Case "1995"
                Return New SolidColorBrush(Colors.Green)
            Case "1996"
                Return New SolidColorBrush(Colors.Red)
            Case Else
                Return New SolidColorBrush(Colors.Yellow)
        End Select
    End Function

    Public Function ConvertBack(ByVal value As Object, ByVal targetType As _
        System.Type, ByVal parameter As Object, ByVal culture As _
        System.Globalization.CultureInfo) As Object Implements _
        System.Windows.Data.IValueConverter.ConvertBack
        Throw New NotImplementedException
    End Function
End Class
```

Sample of C# Code

```
[ValueConversion(typeof(DateTime), typeof(Brush))]
```

```
public class YearConverter : IValueConverter
{
    public object Convert(object value, Type targetType, object parameter,
        System.Globalization.CultureInfo culture)
    {
        DateTime aDate;
        aDate = (DateTime)value;
        switch (aDate.Year.ToString())
        {
            case "1994":
                return new SolidColorBrush(Colors.Purple);
            case "1995":
                return new SolidColorBrush(Colors.Green);
            case "1996":
                return new SolidColorBrush(Colors.Red);
            default:
                return new SolidColorBrush(Colors.Yellow);
        }
    }

    public object ConvertBack(object value, Type targetType, object
        parameter, System.Globalization.CultureInfo culture)
    {
        throw new NotImplementedException();
    }
}
```

2. In XAML view, add the following line to the *Windows.Resources* section:

```
<local:YearConverter x:Key="myYearConverter" />
```

3. In the XAML declaration for *listBox2*, delete the following:

```
DisplayMemberPath="OrderDate"
```

Then add the following data template:

```
<ListBox.ItemTemplate>
    <DataTemplate>
        <Label Content="{Binding OrderDate}" Background="{Binding
            Path=OrderDate, Converter={StaticResource myYearConverter}}" />
    </DataTemplate>
</ListBox.ItemTemplate>
```

4. Press F5 to build and run your application. Note that the order dates now are color coded by year.

Lesson Summary

- *IValueConverter* is the interface you must implement in your converters. You can use custom converters to provide string formatting, apply conditional formatting in data templates, return objects, or localize data.

- *IValueConverter* contains two members you must implement: *Convert* and *ConvertBack*. The *Convert* method accepts a value and converts it to the return value. *ConvertBack* performs this operation in reverse. In many cases, the reverse operation will be impossible, in which case *ConvertBack* typically is not implemented.

- You can convert multiple values into a single value by implementing *IMultiValueConverter*. *IMultiValueConverter* is similar to *IValueConverter*, but it is designed to operate on an array of values and return a single value.

- To bind to a multi-value converter, you must use the *MultiBinding* class, which contains a collection of *Binding* objects and specifies a multi-value converter that returns a value based on those bindings.

Lesson Review

You can use the following questions to test your knowledge of the information in Lesson 2, "Converting Data." The questions are also available on the companion CD if you prefer to review them in electronic form.

> **NOTE ANSWERS**
>
> Answers to these questions and explanations of why each answer choice is correct or incorrect are located in the "Answers" section at the end of the book.

1. You have implemented a converter called *DateBrushConverter* that returns a different colored *Brush* object for each month of the year. Assuming that you have added an instance of this converter as a static resource in the *Windows.Resources* collection with the *myConverter* key, and that you are binding to a field called *Date*, which of the following XAML snippets shows the correct way to bind a *Label* control so that it displays the date with a background color returned by the converter?

   A.

   ```
   <Label Content="{Binding Path=Date}" Background="{Binding Path=Date,
      Converter={StaticResource myConverter}} />
   ```

   B.

   ```
   <Label Content="{Binding Path=Date}" Background="{Binding Path=Date}" />
   ```

   C.

   ```
   <Label Content="{Binding Path=Date}" Background="{Binding Path=Date}" >
      <Label.Resources>
         <local:DateBrushConverter x:Key="myConverter" />
      </Label.Resources>
   </Label>
   ```

   D.

   ```
   <Label Content="{Binding Path=Date}" Background="{Binding Path=Date,
      Converter=myConverter} />
   ```

2. You have implemented a multi-value converter named *ShapeConverter* that takes a string and an integer as arguments and outputs a *Shape* object. You have added an instance of *ShapeConverter* as a resource to the *Windows.Resources* collection with the *myConverter* key. Assuming that you are binding to properties called *ShapeName* and *ShapeSize* (string and integer data types, respectively), which of the following XAML samples renders the returned shape correctly as the content of a label control?

A.

```
<Label Content={Binding Source=ShapeName Path=ShapeSize,
    Converter={StaticResource myConverter}}">
```

B.

```
<Label Content={Binding Path=ShapeName/ShapeSize,
    Converter={StaticResource  myConverter}}">
```

C.

```
<Label>
    <Label.Content>
        <MultiBinding Converter="{StaticResource myConverter}">
            <Binding Path=ShapeName />
            <Binding Path=ShapeSize />
        </MultiBinding>
    </Label>
</Label>
```

D.

```
<Label>
    <Label.Content>
        <MultiBinding Converter="{StaticResource myConverter}">
            <Binding Path=ShapeSize />
            <Binding Path=ShapeName />
        </MultiBinding>
    </Label>
</Label>
```

Lesson 3: Validating Data and Configuring Change Notification

This lesson deals with validating data and configuring change notification for custom data objects. Although seemingly unrelated, both of these topics are essential for ensuring that the data presented by your applications is always accurate, current, and uncorrupted. In this lesson, you learn how to validate your data by using validation rules, to create custom validation rules, and to configure data change notification by implementing *INotifyPropertyChanged* and inheriting from *ObservableCollection*.

> **After this lesson, you will be able to:**
> - Apply *ExceptionValidationRule*.
> - Create custom validation rules.
> - Handle and respond to validation errors.
> - Implement *INotifyPropertyChanged*.
> - Use *ObservableCollection* to create bindable collections.
>
> **Estimated lesson time: 30 minutes**

Validating Data

To be useful, data must be valid. The act of validating data involves ensuring that data conforms to the standards of its type. For example, a data field that represents an item price never should contain a negative number. WPF enables you to create validation rules and apply them to your *Binding* objects so that data added is always valid.

Binding Validation Rules

WPF enables you to set validation rules that define how your application validates its data. Each *Binding* object exposes a *ValidationRules* collection. You can add new rules to *ValidationCollection*, as shown in bold in this example:

```
<TextBox>
   <TextBox.Text>
      <Binding Path="CandyBars">
         <Binding.ValidationRules>
            <local:CandyBarValidationRule />
            <local:SweetTreatsValidationRule />
         </Binding.ValidationRules>
      </Binding>
   </TextBox.Text>
</TextBox>
```

In this example, the *CandyBarValidationRule* and *SweetTreatsValidationRule* declarations represent two custom validation rules that have been defined in your application. When a new value is bound, each of the validation rules is evaluated in the order in which the rules are declared. In this example, *CandyBarValidationRule* is evaluated first, followed by *SweetTreatsValidationRule*. If there are no validation problems, the application proceeds normally. If a problem violates a validation rule, however, the following things happen:

- The element with the validation error is outlined in red.
- The attached property *Validation.HasError* is set to *True*.
- A new *ValidationError* object is created and added to the attached *Validation.Errors* collection.
- If the *Binding.NotifyOnValidationError* property is set to *True*, the *Validation.Error* attached event is raised.
- The data-binding source is not updated with the invalid value and instead remains unchanged.

Setting *ExceptionValidationRule*

You might have noticed when working with data that exceptions are not thrown from data binding. This is primarily to preserve application flow and prevent application crashes that result from data errors. However, you can report data errors by setting *ExceptionValidationRule*, which causes all exceptions thrown in the data-binding process to be reported as validation errors. Note that this still does not halt application execution as an unhandled exception would. Rather, it creates a validation error as described previously. The following example demonstrates how to set *ExceptionValidationRule*:

```
<Binding Path="CandyBars">
    <Binding.ValidationRules>
        <ExceptionValidationRule />
    </Binding.ValidationRules>
</Binding>
```

Implementing Custom Validation Rules

You can create specific validation rules by creating classes that inherit the abstract *ValidationRule* class, which has one virtual method that must be overridden: the *Validate* method. The *Validate* method receives an object parameter, which represents the value being evaluated, and returns a *ValidationResult* object, which contains an *IsValid* property and an *ErrorCondition* property. The *IsValid* property represents a Boolean value that indicates whether the value is valid, and the *ErrorCondition* property is text that can be set to provide a descriptive error condition. If a *ValidationResult* object with an *IsValid* value of *True* is returned, the value is considered to be valid and application execution proceeds normally. If a *ValidationResult* object with an *IsValid* result of *False* is returned, a *ValidationError* object is created as described previously.

The following example demonstrates a simple implementation of the abstract *ValidationRule* class:

Sample of Visual Basic Code

```vb
Public Class NoNullStringsValidator
    Inherits ValidationRule

    Public Overrides Function Validate(ByVal value As Object, ByVal _
        cultureInfo As System.Globalization.CultureInfo) As _
        System.Windows.Controls.ValidationResult
        Dim astring As String = value.ToString
        If astring = "" Then
            Return New ValidationResult(False, "String cannot be empty")
        Else
            Return New ValidationResult(True, Nothing)
        End If
    End Function
End Class
```

Sample of C# Code

```csharp
public class NoNullStringsValidator : ValidationRule
{
    public override ValidationResult Validate(object value,
        System.Globalization.CultureInfo cultureinfo)
    {
        string aString = value.ToString();
        if (aString == "")
            return new ValidationResult(false, "String cannot be empty");
        return new ValidationResult(true, null);
    }
}
```

In this example, the string contained in the *value* object is evaluated. If it is a zero-length string, the validation fails; otherwise, the validation succeeds.

Handling Validation Errors

When validation errors are raised, you must decide how to respond to them. In some cases, the visual cues provided by the validation error are enough; the user can see that the element is surrounded by a red outline and can detect and fix the problem. In other cases, however, you might need to provide feedback to the user regarding the nature of the validation problem.

When validation is enabled for a binding, the *Validation.Error* event is attached to the bound element. *Validation.Error* includes an instance of *ValidationErrorEventArgs*, which contains two important properties, as described in Table 6-6.

TABLE 6-6 Important Properties of *ValidationErrorEventArgs*

PROPERTY	DESCRIPTION
Action	Describes whether the error in question is a new error or an old error that is being cleared
Error	Contains information about the error that occurred, the details of which are described in further detail in Table 6-7

The *Error* object of *ValidationErrorEventArgs* contains a host of useful information regarding the error that occurred. Important properties of the *Error* object are described in Table 6-7.

TABLE 6-7 Important Properties of the *Error* Object

PROPERTY	DESCRIPTION
BindingInError	Contains a reference to the *Binding* object that caused the validation error
ErrorContent	Contains the string set by the *ValidationRule* object that returned the validation error
Exception	Contains a reference to the exception, if any, that caused the validation error
RuleInError	Contains a reference to the *ValidationRule* exception that caused the validation error

The *Validation.Error* event is not fired unless the *NotifyOnValidationError* property of the *Binding* object is specifically set to *True,* as shown in bold here:

```
<Binding NotifyOnValidationError="True" Mode="TwoWay"
    Source="{StaticResource StringCollection}" Path="name">
    <Binding.ValidationRules>
        <local:NoNullStringsValidator/>
    </Binding.ValidationRules>
</Binding>
```

When this property is set to *True,* the *Validation.Error* event is raised anytime any *ValidationRule* in the *ValidationRules* collection of the *Binding* object detects a validation error. The *Validation.Error* event is a bubbling event. It is raised first in the element where the validation error occurs and then in each higher-level element in the visual tree. Thus, you can create a local error-handling method that specifically handles validation errors from a single element, as shown in bold here:

```
<TextBox Validation.Error="TextBox1_Error" Height="21" Width="100"
    Name="TextBox1" >
```

Alternatively, you can create an error-handling routine that is executed higher in the visual tree to create a more generalized validation error handler, as shown in bold here:

```
<Grid Validation.Error="Grid_Error">
```

The *Validation.Error* event is fired both when a new validation error is detected and when an old validation error is cleared. Thus, it is important to check the *e.Action* property to determine whether the error is being cleared or is a new error. The following example demonstrates a sample validation error handler that displays the error message to the user when a new error occurs and writes information to *Trace* when a validation error is cleared:

Sample of Visual Basic Code

```
Private Sub Grid_Error(ByVal _
sender As System.Object, ByVal e As _
    System.Windows.Controls.ValidationErrorEventArgs)
    If e.Action = ValidationErrorEventAction.Added Then
        MessageBox.Show(e.Error.ErrorContent.ToString)
    Else
        Trace.WriteLine("Validation error cleared")
    End If
End Sub
```

Sample of C# Code

```
private void Grid_Error(object sender, ValidationErrorEventArgs e)
{
    if (e.Action == ValidationErrorEventAction.Added)
        MessageBox.Show(e.Error.ErrorContent.ToString());
    else
        System.Diagnostics.Trace.WriteLine("Validation error cleared");
}
```

EXAM TIP

Data validation is an important feature that is considerably different in WPF than it is in Windows Forms. It promises to figure prominently on the exam, so be certain you get lots of practice with validating data. In particular, note that the Validation.Error event is raised both when an error is detected and when an error is cleared. Code that handles this event should test to determine whether an error has been added or cleared.

Configuring Data Change Notification

You saw earlier in this chapter how data binding in WPF is virtually unlimited. Nearly any object can act as a data source, any collection can be bound as a list, and nearly any property can be bound. However, there are some limits. Your own custom data objects can be bound in the same manner as any other object, but if changes occur to properties of your data objects, or if more members are added to your data collections, these changes are not detected by WPF data binding unless you implement data change notification.

Fortunately, data change notification is fairly easy to implement in custom classes. For custom data objects, you can implement the *INotifyPropertyChanged* interface, which provides notification for changed properties in your data objects. For custom collections, you can derive from *ObservableCollection*, which has change notification built in.

Implementing *INotifyPropertyChanged*

The *INotifyPropertyChanged* interface has one member: the *PropertyChanged* event. This event contains an instance of *PropertyChangedEventArgs*, which indicates the property that is changing. When you implement *INotifyPropertyChanged*, raise the *PropertyChanged* event from every property for which you want to provide data change notification. On a practical level, this is essentially every public property that might change. The only properties for which you might not raise this event are properties that never change, such as unique identifiers. The following example shows a simple class with one property that implements *INotifyPropertyChanged*:

Sample of Visual Basic Code

```
Public Class LastName
    Implements System.ComponentModel.INotifyPropertyChanged
    Public Event PropertyChanged(ByVal sender As Object, ByVal e As _
        System.ComponentModel.PropertyChangedEventArgs) Implements _
        System.ComponentModel.INotifyPropertyChanged.PropertyChanged
    Dim mLastName As String
    Public Property Name()
        Get
            Return mLastName
        End Get
        Set (ByVal value)
            mLastName = value
            RaiseEvent PropertyChanged(Me, _
                New System.ComponentModel.PropertyChangedEventArgs("LastName"))
        End Set
    End Property
End Class
```

Sample of C# Code

```
public class LastName : System.ComponentModel.INotifyPropertyChanged
{
    public event System.ComponentModel.PropertyChangedEventHandler
        PropertyChanged;
    string mLastName;
    public string Name
    {
        get
        {
            return mLastName;
        }
        set
        {
            mLastName = value;
            PropertyChanged(this,
```

```
        new System.ComponentModel.PropertyChangedEventArgs("LastName"));
    }
  }
}
```

Using *ObservableCollection*

Just as properties must provide change notification in order for that change to be detected by WPF data binding, collections must provide notification whenever a member is added or removed. Just for this purpose, .NET Framework 3.5 provides the *ObservableCollection* class.

ObservableCollection is a generic collection with built-in collection change notification. Thus, when items are added to or removed from *ObservableCollection*, the changes are detected automatically by WPF data binding. As with other generic classes, you must specify the type with which the collection works. You can create a new instance of *ObservableCollection*, as shown here:

Sample of Visual Basic Code

```
Dim LastNames As New _
    System.Collections.ObjectModel.ObservableCollection(Of LastName)
```

Sample of C# Code

```
System.Collections.ObjectModel.ObservableCollection<LastName> LastNames =
    new System.Collections.ObjectModel.ObservableCollection<LastName>();
```

In most cases, however, this is insufficient for your purposes. You likely want to provide initialization code for your collection or add other code to facilitate your data object. *ObservableCollection* implements *INotifyCollectionChanged,* the collection-based version of *INotifyPropertyChanged*. Although it is possible to create your own observable collection class by implementing *INotifyCollectionChanged*, inheriting from *ObservableCollection* to build your own class is almost always the best choice. In this case, you should inherit from the appropriately typed *ObservableCollection* and add code as your business needs require. An example is shown here:

Sample of Visual Basic Code

```
Public Class LastNames
    Inherits System.Collections.ObjectModel.ObservableCollection(Of _
        LastName)
    Public Sub New()
      ' Initialization code omitted
    End Sub
End Class
```

Sample of C# Code

```
public class LastNames :
    System.Collections.ObjectModel.ObservableCollection<LastName>
{
    public LastNames()
    {
      // Initialization code omitted
```

```
    }
}
```

Configuring Change Notification and Data Validation

In this practice, you configure change notification and validating data. You build a simple data object, create a simple collection of objects of that type, create a simple user interface for viewing and adding data objects, and implement a simple validation scheme for your user interface.

EXERCISE 1 Creating Simple Data Objects

1. In Visual Studio, create a new WPF application.

2. In code view, add the following class, which implements *INotifyPropertyChanged*:

   Sample of Visual Basic Code

```
Public Class Name
    Implements System.ComponentModel.INotifyPropertyChanged
    Public Event PropertyChanged(ByVal sender As Object, ByVal e As _
        System.ComponentModel.PropertyChangedEventArgs) Implements _
        System.ComponentModel.INotifyPropertyChanged.PropertyChanged
    Public Sub New(ByVal fName As String, ByVal lName As String)
        mFirstName = fName
        mLastName = lName
    End Sub


    Private mFirstName As String
    Private mLastName As String
    Public Property FirstName()
        Get
            Return mFirstName
        End Get
        Set (ByVal value)
            mFirstName = value
            RaiseEvent PropertyChanged(Me, _
                New System.ComponentModel.PropertyChangedEventArgs("FirstName"))
        End Set
    End Property
    Public Property LastName()
        Get
            Return mLastName
        End Get
        Set (ByVal value)
            mLastName = value
            RaiseEvent PropertyChanged(Me, _
                New System.ComponentModel.PropertyChangedEventArgs("LastName"))
        End Set
    End Property
End Class
```

Sample of C# Code

```csharp
public class Name : System.ComponentModel.INotifyPropertyChanged
{
    public event System.ComponentModel.PropertyChangedEventHandler
    PropertyChanged;
    public Name(string fName, string lName)
    {
        mFirstName=fName;
        mLastName = lName;
    }
    string mFirstName;
    string mLastName;
    public string FirstName
    {
        get
        {
            return mFirstName;
        }
        set
        {
            mFirstName = value;
            PropertyChanged(this,
              new System.ComponentModel.PropertyChangedEventArgs("FirstName"));
        }
    }
    public string LastName
    {
        get
        {
            return mLastName;
        }
        set
        {
            mLastName = value;
            PropertyChanged(this,
                new System.ComponentModel.PropertyChangedEventArgs("LastName"));
        }
    }
}
```

3. Beneath this class, add the following class to create a collection of *Name* objects that inherits *ObservableCollection*:

Sample of Visual Basic Code

```vbnet
Public Class Names
    Inherits System.Collections.ObjectModel.ObservableCollection(Of Name)
    Public Sub New()
        Dim aName As New Name("FirstName " & (Me.Count+1).ToString(), _
            "LastName " & (Me.Count+1).ToString())
        Me.Add(aName)
    End Sub
End Class
```

```csharp
public class Names :
    System.Collections.ObjectModel.ObservableCollection<Name>
{
    public Names()
    {
        Name aName = new Name("FirstName " + (this.Count+1).ToString(),
            "LastName " + (this.Count+1).ToString());
        this.Add(aName);
    }
}
```

4. Add a line similar to the line shown here to import the local namespace into your XAML:

```
xmlns:local="clr-namespace:Lesson_3"
```

5. Add the following *Windows.Resources* section to your XAML to create an instance of the *Names* collection:

```xml
<Window.Resources>
    <local:Names x:Key="myNames"></local:Names>
</Window.Resources>
```

6. Replace the *Grid* declaration with the following:

```xml
<Grid>
    <TextBox Height="21" Margin="12,62,0,0" Name="TextBox1"
        VerticalAlignment="Top" HorizontalAlignment="Left" Width="120" >
        <TextBox.Text>
            <Binding Source="{StaticResource myNames}" Path="FirstName"
                NotifyOnValidationError="True">
                <Binding.ValidationRules>

                </Binding.ValidationRules>
            </Binding>
        </TextBox.Text>
    </TextBox>
    <TextBox Height="21" HorizontalAlignment="Right" Margin="0,62,12,0"
        Name="TextBox2" VerticalAlignment="Top" Width="120" >
        <TextBox.Text>
            <Binding Source="{StaticResource myNames}" Path="LastName"
                NotifyOnValidationError="True">
                <Binding.ValidationRules>

                </Binding.ValidationRules>
            </Binding>
        </TextBox.Text>
    </TextBox>
    <Button HorizontalAlignment="Left" Margin="35,122,0,116"
        Name="Button1" Width="75">Back</Button>
    <Button HorizontalAlignment="Right" Margin="0,122,34,117"
        Name="Button2" Width="75">Forward</Button>
```

```
    <Button Height="22" Margin="101,0,101,56" Name="Button3"
        VerticalAlignment="Bottom">Add</Button>
</Grid>
```

7. In code view, add the following code to create two class-level variables and to add (or replace) the constructor:

Sample of Visual Basic Code

```
Dim aView As System.ComponentModel.ICollectionView
Dim myNames As Names
Public Sub New()

    ' This call is required by the Windows Form Designer.
    InitializeComponent()

    ' Add any initialization after the InitializeComponent() call.
    myNames = CType(Me.Resources("myNames"), Names)
    aView = CollectionViewSource.GetDefaultView(myNames)
End Sub
```

Sample of C# Code

```
Names myNames;
System.ComponentModel.ICollectionView aView;
public MainWindow1()
{
    InitializeComponent();
    myNames=(Names)(this.Resources["myNames"]);
    aView = CollectionViewSource.GetDefaultView(myNames);
}
```

8. In the designer, double-click *Button1* to open the default *Click* event handler. Add the following code:

Sample of Visual Basic Code

```
If Not aView.CurrentPosition = 0 Then
    aView.MoveCurrentToPrevious()
End If
```

Sample of C# Code

```
if (!(aView.CurrentPosition == 0))
    aView.MoveCurrentToPrevious();
```

9. In the designer, double-click *Button2* to open the default *Click* event handler. Add the following code:

Sample of Visual Basic Code

```
If Not aView.CurrentPosition = myNames.Count - 1 Then
    aView.MoveCurrentToNext()
End If
```

Sample of C# Code

```
if (!(aView.CurrentPosition == myNames.Count - 1))
    aView.MoveCurrentToNext();
```

10. In the designer, double-click *Button3* to open the default *Click* event handler. Add the following code:

Sample of Visual Basic Code

```vb
Dim aName As New Name("", "")
myNames.Add(aName)
aView.MoveCurrentToNext()
```

Sample of C# Code

```csharp
Name aName = new Name("", "");
myNames.Add(aName);
aView.MoveCurrentToNext();
```

11. Press F5 to build and run your application. Click Add to add a new record to your collection. Navigate back to the first record and change the entries in the text boxes. Navigate forward and then back again. Note that changes are persisted to both the property values and the collection.

EXERCISE 2   Implementing Simple Validation

1. In code view, add the following class to perform validation:

Sample of Visual Basic Code

```vb
Public Class StringValidator
    Inherits ValidationRule

    Public Overrides Function Validate(ByVal value As Object, ByVal _
        cultureInfo As System.Globalization.CultureInfo) As _
        System.Windows.Controls.ValidationResult
        Dim astring As String = value.ToString
        If astring = "" Then
            Return New ValidationResult(False, "String cannot be empty")
        Else
            Return New ValidationResult(True, Nothing)
        End If
    End Function
End Class
```

Sample of C# Code

```csharp
public class StringValidator : ValidationRule
{
    public override ValidationResult Validate(object value,
        System.Globalization.CultureInfo cultureinfo)
    {
        string aString = value.ToString();
        if (aString == "")
            return new ValidationResult(false, "String cannot be empty");
        return new ValidationResult(true, null);
    }
}
```

2. In XAML view, add the following line to both of the *<Binding.ValidationRules>* tags to set *StringValidator* as the validation rule for these bindings:

```
<local:StringValidator />
```

3. Press F6 to build your application.

4. Modify the *Grid* declaration, as shown here in bold, to create an error handler for the grid.

```
<Grid Validation.Error="Grid_Error">
```

5. In code view, add the following code to the *Grid.Error* event handler:

Sample of Visual Basic Code

```
If e.Action = ValidationErrorEventAction.Added Then
   MessageBox.Show(e.Error.ErrorContent.ToString)
End If
```

Sample of C# Code

```
if (e.Action == ValidationErrorEventAction.Added)
   MessageBox.Show(e.Error.ErrorContent.ToString());
```

6. Press F5 to build and run your application. Delete all text in the first text box and then press Tab to move away from that box. Note that a message box informing you of a validation error appears and that the text box is outlined in red.

Lesson Summary

- Data binding does not surface exceptions; they all are handled internally. You can use validation rules to validate data in your application. Validation rules are placed in the *ValidationRules* collection of the binding and are evaluated in the order in which they are set.

- When a validation error occurs, the element causing the validation rule is outlined in red; the *Validation.HasError* property is set to *True*; a *ValidationError* object is created and added to the *Validation.Errors* collection; and, if the *Binding.NotifyOnValidationError* property is set to *True*, the *Validation.Error* event is raised.

- The *ExceptionValidationRule* causes a validation error to occur whenever an unhandled exception occurs in your data-binding code, but it does not surface the exception.

- You can create custom validation rules by implementing the *IValidationRule* class.

- To configure data change notification, you should implement the *INotifyPropertyChanged* interface and raise the *PropertyChanged* event in all properties that might be bound. For notification-enabled collections, you should inherit from *ObservableCollection*.

Lesson Review

You can use the following questions to test your knowledge of the information in Lesson 3, "Validating Data and Configuring Change Notification." The questions are also available on the companion CD if you prefer to review them in electronic form.

> **NOTE ANSWERS**
>
> Answers to these questions and explanations of why each answer choice is correct or incorrect are located in the "Answers" section at the end of the book.

1. Look at the following XAML sample:

```xaml
<TextBox>
    <TextBox.Text>
        <Binding Path="CandyBars">
            <Binding.ValidationRules>
                <local: CandyBarValidationRule />
                <local: SweetTreatsValidationRule />
            </Binding.ValidationRules>
        </Binding>
    </TextBox.Text>
</TextBox>
```

   Assuming that *SweetTreatsValidationRule* detects a validation error, which of the following does NOT occur? (Choose all that apply.)

   A. An exception is raised and surfaced to the user.

   B. The *Validation.HasError* property on the text box is set to *True*.

   C. A new *ValidationError* object is added to the *Validation.Errors* collection of *TextBox*.

   D. The *Validation.Error* event is raised.

2. You are implementing *INotifyPropertyChanged* in a custom data class. Which of the following code samples demonstrates a property with correct change notification? You can assume that the rest of the interface has been implemented correctly.

   A.

   Sample of Visual Basic Code

```vb
Dim maProp As String
Public Property aProp() As String
    Get
        Return maProp
    End Get
    Set (ByVal Value As String)
        maProp = Value
    End Set
End Property
```

   Sample of C# Code

```csharp
string maProp;
public string aProp
```

```
{
  get
  {
    return maProp;
  }
  set
  {
    maProp = value;
  }
}
```

B.

Sample of Visual Basic Code

```
Dim maProp As String
Public Property aProp() As String
    Get
        Return maProp
    End Get
    Set (ByVal Value As String)
        RaiseEvent PropertyChanged(Me, _
            New System.ComponentModel.PropertyChangedEventArgs("aProp"))
        maProp = Value
    End Set
End Property
```

Sample of C# Code

```
string maProp;
public string aProp
{
  get
  {
    return maProp;
  }
  set
  {
    PropertyChanged(this,
        new System.ComponentModel.PropertyChangedEventArgs("aProp"));
    maProp = value;
  }
}
```

C.

Sample of Visual Basic Code

```
Dim maProp As String
Public Property aProp() As String
    Get
        Return maProp
    End Get
    Set (ByVal Value As String)
        maProp = Value
        RaiseEvent PropertyChanged(Me, _
            New System.ComponentModel.PropertyChangedEventArgs("aProp"))
```

```
   End Set
End Property
```

Sample of C# Code

```csharp
string maProp;
public string aProp
{
    get
    {
        return maProp;
    }
    set
    {
        maProp = value;
        PropertyChanged(this,
            new System.ComponentModel.PropertyChangedEventArgs("aProp"));
    }
}
```

D.

Sample of Visual Basic Code

```vb
Dim maProp As String
Public Property aProp() As String
    Get
        Return maProp
        RaiseEvent PropertyChanged(Me, _
            New System.ComponentModel.PropertyChangedEventArgs("aProp"))
  End Get
   Set (ByVal Value As String)
       maProp = Value
       RaiseEvent PropertyChanged(Me, _
           New System.ComponentModel.PropertyChangedEventArgs("aProp"))
   End Set
End Property
```

Sample of C# Code

```csharp
string maProp;
public string aProp
{
    get
    {
        return maProp;
        PropertyChanged(this,
            new System.ComponentModel.PropertyChangedEventArgs("aProp"));
    }
    set
    {
        maProp = value;
        PropertyChanged(this,
            new System.ComponentModel.PropertyChangedEventArgs("aProp"));
    }
}
```

3. Which of the following samples demonstrates the best way to use *ObservableCollection* to create a collection of *Employee* objects?

A.

Sample of Visual Basic Code

```
Public Class Employees
    Inherits ObservableCollection(Of Object)
    ' Implementation omitted
End Class
```

Sample of C# Code

```
public class Employees : ObservableCollection<object>
{
    // Implementation omitted
}
```

B.

Sample of Visual Basic Code

```
Public Class Employees
    Inherits ObservableCollection(Of Employee)
    ' Implementation omitted
End Class
```

Sample of C# Code

```
public class Employees : ObservableCollection<Employee>
{
    // Implementation omitted
}
```

C.

Sample of Visual Basic Code

```
Public Class Employees
    Dim mEmployees As New ObservableCollection(Of Object)
    ' Implementation omitted
End Class
```

Sample of C# Code

```
public class Employees
{
    ObservableCollection<object> mEmployees = new
        ObservableCollection<object>();
    // Implementation omitted
}
```

D.

Sample of Visual Basic Code

```vb
Public Class Employees
    Dim mEmployees As New ObservableCollection(Of Employee)
    ' Implementation omitted
End Class
```

Sample of C# Code

```csharp
public class Employees
{
    ObservableCollection<object> mEmployees = new
        ObservableCollection<Employee>();
    // Implementation omitted
}
```

Case Scenarios

In the following case scenarios, you apply what you've learned about databinding. You can find answers to these questions in the "Answers" section at the end of this book.

Case Scenario 1: The Currency Trading Review Console

You have been commissioned to create a review console for currency trades transacted by Humongous Insurance Co. This application will enable managers to view currency transactions that traders have made over the past week. All the data is stored in the company's central currency exchange database. In addition to the values of the transactions in dollars and in the purchased currency, the managers want to view the value of each transaction in eight other standard currencies. A Web service is available to provide up-to-date exchange rates.

In addition, the managers want to be alerted to transactions that exceed the trading limit of individual traders.

The technical requirements are that:

- You must display transaction data in eight currencies that are not stored in the database, with correct values and correct currency formatting.

- You must enable the managers to easily spot transactions that exceed an individual trader's authority. Each trader has a different transaction limit, and this value is available in the database as well.

Answer the following questions for your manager:

1. What is the easiest way to provide the currency transaction data?

2. How can you alert the managers to transactions that exceed an individual trader's limits?

Case Scenario 2: Currency Trading Console

Based on the good results from the currency trading review console, you have been asked to implement updates in their currency trading console. Traders use this application to create orders they then submit to a central orders database. Because there were some problems with individual traders going over their trading limits, Humongous Insurance would like you to improve its console to prevent any trades that exceed an individual's trading limit from being submitted.

Answer the following question for your manager:

- What strategy can you use to implement this requirement?

Suggested Practices

To help you successfully master the exam objectives presented in this chapter, complete the following tasks.

- **Practice 1**   Implement *IMultiValveConverter* to create a converter that accepts integers signifying the day, month, and year, and that returns a *DateTime* object. Be sure to implement the *ConvertBack* method as well.

- **Practice 2**   Implement validation rules that validate the data used by the *IMultiValueConverter* object just described. Be sure to implement rules so that it is impossible to set dates that don't exist, such as April 31. For a particularly difficult challenge, implement a validation rule that validates February 29 only when the year is a leap year.

- **Practice 3**   Use *ObservableCollection* to create two custom data collections of *Employee* objects and *Division* objects, in which *Division* has a one-to-many relationship with *Employee*. Implement *INotifyPropertyChanged* in each object. Create a user interface that displays *Employee* objects grouped by the division they are in.

Take a Practice Test

The practice tests on this book's companion CD offer many options. For example, you can test yourself on just the content covered in this chapter, or you can test yourself on all the 70-511 certification exam content. You can set up the test so that it closely simulates the experience of taking a certification exam, or you can set it up in study mode so that you can look at the correct answers and explanations after you answer each question.

> **MORE INFO**   **PRACTICE TESTS**
>
> For details about all the practice test options available, see the "How to Use the Practice Tests" section in this book's Introduction.

CHAPTER 7

Configuring Data Binding

M ost applications that access data do not simply deal with individual fields, but rather deal with lists and tables of data. Today, the relevant data for an application can come in the form of a traditional database, or it can be in a list contained in memory, data from an XML file, or any number of other formats. Binding your application to a variety of data sources is a crucial skill in the development of applications for today's world.

Once you have bound your data, manipulation of that data allows you to present it in a variety of ways to your application users. In this chapter, you will learn to bind to a variety of data sources, and then in your second lesson use data templates to format the display of your data, as well as sorting grouping and filtering data.

Exam objectives in this chapter:
- Implement data binding.
- Prepare collections of data for display.
- Bind to hierarchical data.
- Create a data template in WPF.

Lessons in this chapter:

Before You Begin

To complete the lessons in this chapter, you must have:

- A computer that meets or exceeds the minimum hardware requirements listed in the "About This Book" section at the beginning of the book.

- Microsoft Visual Studio 2010 Professional Edition installed on your computer.

- An understanding of Microsoft Visual Basic or C# syntax and familiarity with Microsoft .NET Framework 3.5.

- An understanding of Extensible Application Markup Language (XAML).

 REAL WORLD

Matthew Stoecker

WPF takes data binding to a level that was unheard of in the Windows Forms world. Now I can create rich user interfaces that have properties bound to just about anything imaginable. Creating the user interface (UI) functionality by which manipulating one control changes the value of another is now simple—no more complicated event handling code. Just set the binding and you're ready to go!

Lesson 1: Binding to Data Sources

In the previous chapter, you saw how to bind a property to another property of an element or object. In this lesson, you learn how to bind properties to a variety of data sources: how to bind to and navigate a list, how to bind to ADO.NET data sources, and how to create a master-detail binding with hierarchical data. Then you learn how to use the *XMLDataSource* and *ObjectDataSource* classes to bind to XML and specialized data.

> **After this lesson, you will be able to:**
> - Bind an item control to a list of data.
> - Bind a property to a list.
> - Navigate a list.
> - Bind to an ADO.NET object.
> - Bind to hierarchical data.
> - Use the *ObjectDataProvider* class to bind to objects and methods.
> - Use the *XmlDataProvider* class to bind to XML.
>
> **Estimated lesson time: 30 minutes**

Binding to a List

Frequently, you want to bind an element to a list of objects rather than just to a single object. There are two scenarios in this case: binding a single element to a list and enabling navigation of that list, and binding a collection (such as the items in *ListBox*) to a list so that the list's elements are all displayed at one time.

Binding an Item Control to a List

One common scenario in binding to a list of data or a collection is to display all items in that collection in a list-based element such as *ListBox*. Item controls have built-in properties that enable data binding. These are described in Table 7-1.

TABLE 7-1 Data-Related Properties of Item Controls

PROPERTY	DESCRIPTION
DisplayMemberPath	Indicates the property of the bound collection that will be used to create the display text for each item.
IsSynchronizedWithCurrentItem	Determines whether the selected item is kept synchronized with the *CurrentItem* property in the *Items* collection. Not strictly a data-related property, but useful for building master-detail views.

ItemsSource	Represents the collection that contains the items that make up the source of the list. You set this property to a *Binding* object that is bound to the appropriate collection.
ItemTemplate	The data template used to create the visual appearance of each item. Data templates will be discussed in Lesson 2 of this chapter, "Manipulating and Displaying Data."

For simple displaying of bound members, you must set the *ItemsSource* property to the collection to which you are binding and set the *DisplayMemberPath* property to the collection member that is to be displayed. More complex displays using data templates are discussed in Lesson 2. The following example demonstrates how to bind a *ListBox* collection to a static resource named *myList* and a display member called *FirstName*:

```
<ListBox Width="200" ItemsSource="{Binding Source={StaticResource myList}}"
   DisplayMemberPath="FirstName" />
```

A more common scenario when working with bound lists, however, is to bind to an object that is defined and filled with data in code. In this case, the best way to bind to the list is to set *DisplayMemberPath* in XAML and then set the *DataContext* property of the element or its container in code. The following example demonstrates how to bind a *ListBox* control to an object called *myCustomers* that is created at run time. The *ListBox* control displays the entries from the *CustomerName* property:

Sample of Visual Basic Code

```
' Code to initialize and fill myCustomers has been omitted
grid1.DataContext = myCustomers;
```

Sample of C# Code

```
// Code to initialize and fill myCustomers has been omitted
grid1.DataContext = myCustomers;
```

Sample of XAML Code

```
<!-- XAML -->

<Grid Name="grid1">
   <ListBox ItemsSource="{Binding}" DisplayMemberPath="CustomerName"
      Margin="92,109,66,53" Name="ListBox1" />
</Grid>
```

Note that in the XAML for this example, the *ItemsSource* property is set to a *Binding* object that has no properties initialized. The *Binding* object binds the *ItemsSource* property of *ListBox*, but because the *Source* property of the *Binding* object is not set, WPF searches upward through the visual tree until it finds a *DataContext* object that has been set. Because *DataContext* for *grid1* has been set in code to *myCustomers*, this then becomes the source for the binding.

Binding a Single Property to a List

You can also bind a single property to a list or collection. The process is much the same as binding an item control to a list except that, initially, only the first item in the list is displayed. You can navigate through the list to display subsequent items in the list. Navigation of lists is discussed in the next section. The following example demonstrates creating the data source object in code and setting the data context for a grid and then, in XAML, binding a *Label* object to the *FirstName* property of the items contained in the data source object:

Sample of Visual Basic Code

```
' Code to initialize and fill myCustomers omitted
grid1.DataContext = myCustomers;
```

Sample of C# Code

```
Code to initialize and fill myCustomers omitted
grid1.DataContext = myCustomers;
```

Sample of XAML Code

```
<!-- XAML -->
<Grid Name="grid1">
    <Label Content="{Binding Path=FirstName}" Height="23"
        Width="100"></Label>
</Grid>
```

Navigating a Collection or List

When individual properties, such as the *Content* property of *Label*, are bound to a collection, they are capable of displaying only a single member of that collection at a time. This is a common pattern seen in data access applications: A window might be designed to display one record at a time and have individual controls display each data column. Because only one record is displayed at a time, it becomes necessary to have a mechanism that enables the user to navigate through the records.

WPF has a built-in navigation mechanism for data and collections. When a collection is bound to a WPF binding, an *ICollectionView* interface is created behind the scenes. The *ICollectionView* interface contains members that manage data currency as well as views, grouping, and sorting, all of which are discussed in Lesson 2 of this chapter. Table 7-2 describes members involved in navigation.

TABLE 7-2 *ICollectionView* Members Involved in Navigation

MEMBER	DESCRIPTION
CurrentItem	This property returns the current item.
CurrentPosition	This property returns the numeric position of the current item.
IsCurrentAfterLast	This property indicates whether the current item is after the last item in the collection.

IsCurrentBeforeFirst	This property indicates whether the current item is before the first item in the collection.
MoveCurrentTo	This method sets the current item to the indicated item.
MoveCurrentToFirst	This method sets the current item to the first item in the collection.
MoveCurrentToLast	This method sets the current item to the last item in the collection.
MoveCurrentToNext	This method sets the current item to the next item in the collection.
MoveCurrentToPosition	This method sets the current item to the item at the designated position.
MoveCurrentToPrevious	This method sets the current item to the previous item.

You can get a reference to *ICollectionView* by calling the *CollectionViewSource.GetDefaultView* method, as shown here:

Sample of Visual Basic Code

```
' This example assumes a collection named myCollection
Dim myView As System.ComponentModel.ICollectionView
myView = CollectionViewSource.GetDefaultView (myCollection)
```

Sample of C# Code

```
// This example assumes a collection named myCollection
System.ComponentModel.ICollectionView myView;
myView = CollectionViewSource.GetDefaultView (myCollection);
```

When calling this method, you must specify the collection or list for which to retrieve the view (which is *myCollection* in the previous example). *CollectionViewSource.Get-DefaultView* returns an *ICollectionView* object that is actually one of three classes, depending on the class of the source collection.

If the source collection implements *IBindingList*, the view returned is a *BindingList-CollectionView* object. If the source collection implements *IList* but not *IBindingList*, the view returned is a *ListCollectionView* object. If the source collection implements *IEnumerable* but not *IList* or *IBindingList*, the view returned is a *CollectionView* object.

For navigational purposes, working with the *ICollectionView* should be sufficient. If you need to access members of the other classes, you must cast the *ICollectionView* object to the correct class.

When an item control or content control is bound to a data source, the default collection view handles currency and navigation by default. The current item in the view is returned by the *CurrentItem* property. This is the item currently displayed in all content controls bound to this view. Navigation backward and forward through the list is accomplished using the *MoveCurrentToNext* and *MoveCurrentToPrevious* methods, as shown here:

Sample of Visual Basic Code

```
Dim myView As System.ComponentModel.ICollectionView
myView = CollectionViewSource.GetDefaultView (myCollection)
' Sets the CurrentItem to the next item in the list
myView.MoveCurrentToNext()
' Sets the CurrentItem to the previous item in the list
myView.MoveCurrentToPrevious()
```

Sample of C# Code

```
System.ComponentModel.ICollectionView myView;
myView = CollectionViewSource.GetDefaultView (myCollection);
// Sets the CurrentItem to the next item in the list
myView.MoveCurrentToNext();
// Sets the CurrentItem to the previous item in the list
myView.MoveCurrentToPrevious();
```

Because item controls typically are bound to all the items in a list, navigation through the list is not usually essential. However, you can use an item control to enable the user to navigate records by setting *IsSynchronizedWithCurrentItem* to *True*, as shown in bold here:

```
<ListBox ItemsSource="{Binding}" DisplayMemberPath="City"
    Margin="92,109,66,53" Name="ListBox1"
    IsSynchronizedWithCurrentItem="True" />
```

When the *IsSynchronizedWithCurrentItem* property is set to *True*, the *SelectedItem* property of the item control always is synchronized with the *CurrentItem* property of the view. Thus, if the user selects an item in an item control, the *CurrentItem* property of the view is set to that item. This change then is reflected in all other controls bound to the same data source. This concept is illustrated in the lab for this lesson.

Binding to ADO.NET Objects

Binding to ADO.NET objects is basically the same as binding to any other collection or list. Because ADO.NET objects usually are initialized in code, the general pattern is to initialize the ADO.NET objects in code and set the data context for the user interface. Bindings in XAML should point to the appropriate ADO.NET object.

Setting *DataContext* to an ADO.NET *DataTable* Object

When setting *DataContext* to an ADO.NET *DataTable* object that contains the data to which you want to bind, set the *ItemsSource* property of any item controls you are binding to that table to an empty *Binding* object and specify the column to be displayed in the *DisplayMemberPath* property. For content controls or other single properties, you should set the appropriate property to a *Binding* object that specifies the appropriate column in the *Path* property. The following example demonstrates the code to initialize an ADO.NET data set and set the *DataContext*, and the XAML to bind a *ListBox* control and a *Label* control to that dataset:

Sample of Visual Basic Code

```vb
Public Class Window1
    Dim aset As NwindDataSet = New NwindDataSet()
    Dim custAdap As _
        NwindDataSetTableAdapters.CustomersTableAdapter = _
        New NwindDataSetTableAdapters.CustomersTableAdapter()
    Dim ordAdap As NwindDataSetTableAdapters.OrdersTableAdapter _
        = New NwindDataSetTableAdapters.OrdersTableAdapter()
    Public Sub New()
        InitializeComponent()
        custAdap.Fill(aset.Customers)
        OrdAdap.Fill(aset.Orders)
        Grid1.DataContext = aset.Customers
End Sub
```

Sample of C# Code

```csharp
public partial class Window1 : Window
{
    NwindDataSet aset = new NwindDataSet();
    NwindDataSetTableAdapters.CustomersTableAdapter custAdap =
        new NwindDataSetTableAdapters.CustomersTableAdapter();
    NwindDataSetTableAdapters.OrdersTableAdapter ordAdap =
        new NwindDataSetTableAdapters.OrdersTableAdapter();
    public Window1()
    {
        InitializeComponent();
        custAdap.Fill(aset.Customers);
        ordAdap.Fill(aset.Orders);
        Grid1.DataContext = aset.Customers;
    }
}
```

Sample of XAML Code

```xml
<!-- XAML -->
<Grid Name="Grid1">
    <ListBox ItemsSource="{Binding}" DisplayMemberPath="ContactName"
        Name="listBox1" Width="100" Height="100" VerticalAlignment="Top" />

    <Label Content="{Binding Path=ContactTitle}" Height="23" Width="100"
        Name="label1" VerticalAlignment="Top"></Label>
</Grid>
```

Setting *DataContext* to an ADO.NET *DataSet* Object

You can also set *DataContext* to an ADO.NET *DataSet* object instead of to a *DataTable* object. Because a *DataSet* object is a collection of *DataTable* objects, you must provide the name of the *DataTable* object as part of the *Path* property. Examples are shown here:

Sample of Visual Basic Code

```vb
' The rest of the code is identical to the previous example
```

```
' and has been omitted.
Grid1.DataContext = aset
```

Sample of C# Code

```csharp
// The rest of the code is identical to the previous example
// and has been omitted.
Grid1.DataContext = aset;
```

```xml
<!--XAML-->
<Grid Name="Grid1">
    <ListBox ItemsSource="{Binding Path=Customers}"
        DisplayMemberPath="ContactName" Name="listBox1" Width="100"
        Height="100" VerticalAlignment="Top" />
    <Label Content="{Binding Path=Customers/ContactTitle}" Height="23"
        Width="100" Name="label1" VerticalAlignment="Top"></Label>
</Grid>
```

Using the Visual Studio Designer Tools for ADO.NET

In Visual Studio 2010, substantial design time support has been added for working with ADO. NET in WPF applications. After you have added an ADO.NET data source to your application, you can navigate the available data fields in that data source in the Data Sources window, shown here in Figure 7-1.

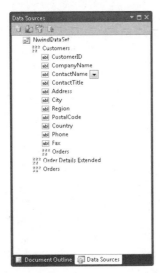

FIGURE 7-1 The Data Sources window.

The Data Sources window enables you to drag fields from your data source and drop them onto the design surface. When a data field is dropped onto the design surface, a bound control is automatically generated along with any required XAML code to create required data resources, such as *CollectionViewSource* objects. You can change the type of bound control that is created by clicking the field in the Data Sources window and selecting the control from the drop-down box. If the control you desire is not listed, you can add it to the default list by selecting Customize.

Binding to Hierarchical Data

When binding to lists of complex objects, you might want to create a master-detail view that enables the user to select one item from an upper-level list and view the details about the selected object. For lists of complex objects, this is as simple as setting the *Path* property of each detail binding to the correct property to display and making sure that the upper-level item controls in the user interface have the *IsSynchronizedWithCurrentItem* property set to *True* so that the selected item is set to the current item and the detail lists are updated automatically. The following example demonstrates a simple master-detail view. Each *Division* object contains a list of *Group* objects, each *Group* object contains a list of *Employee* objects, and all objects in this example have a *Name* property:

```
<Grid DataContext="{Binding Source={StaticResource Divisions}}">
    <StackPanel>
        <Label>Divisions</Label>
        <ListBox ItemsSource="{Binding}" DisplayMemberPath="Name"
            IsSynchronizedWithCurrentItem="True" />
    </StackPanel>

    <StackPanel>
        <Label Content="{Binding Path=Name}" />
        <ListBox ItemsSource="{Binding Path=Groups}" DisplayMemberPath="Name"
            IsSynchronizedWithCurrentItem="True" />
    </StackPanel>

    <StackPanel>
        <Label Content="{Binding Path=Groups/Name}" />
        <ListBox DisplayMemberPath="Name"
            ItemsSource="{Binding Path=Groups/Employees}" />
    </StackPanel>
</Grid>
```

For displaying hierarchical data, see Using Hierarchical Data Templates in Lesson 2.

Binding to Related ADO.NET Tables

When hierarchical data is retrieved from databases, it typically is presented in related tables. In ADO.NET, these relationships between tables are established by *DataRelation* objects, which link a column in one table to a column in another table. In WPF, you can retrieve related records by binding to the data relation. The pattern for creating a binding to a relation is as follows, where *ParentTable* represents a table, *Relation* represents a child relation of that table, and *relation2* represents a child relation of the data returned by *Relation*:

```
{Binding Path=ParentTable/Relation/Relation2}
```

You can bind through child relations only; you cannot bind up through parent relations.

The following example demonstrates initializing a data set with two related tables: *Customers* and *Orders*. The *Orders* table has a foreign key called *CustomerID* that relates to the primary key of the *Customers* table, also called *CustomerID*. The name of the relation in the database is *CustomersOrders*. The code shows the initializing of this data set and the setting of *DataContext* to the parent table. The XAML shows how to bind the related table to the data relation to view related records automatically:

Sample of Visual Basic Code

```vb
Public Class Window1
    Dim aset As NwindDataSet = New NwindDataSet()
    Dim custAdap As _
        NwindDataSetTableAdapters.CustomersTableAdapter = _
            New NwindDataSetTableAdapters.CustomersTableAdapter()
    Dim ordAdap As NwindDataSetTableAdapters.OrdersTableAdapter = _
        New NwindDataSetTableAdapters.OrdersTableAdapter()
    Public Sub New()
        InitializeComponent()
        custAdap.Fill(aset.Customers)
        OrdAdap.Fill(aset.Orders)
        Grid1.DataContext = aset.Customers
    End Sub
End Sub
```

Sample of C# Code

```csharp
public partial class Window1 : Window
{
    NwindDataSet aset = new NwindDataSet();
    NwindDataSetTableAdapters.CustomersTableAdapter custAdap =
        new NwindDataSetTableAdapters.CustomersTableAdapter();
    NwindDataSetTableAdapters.OrdersTableAdapter ordAdap =
        new NwindDataSetTableAdapters.OrdersTableAdapter();
    public Window1()
    {
        InitializeComponent();
        custAdap.Fill(aset.Customers);
        ordAdap.Fill(aset.Orders);
        Grid1.DataContext = aset.Customers;
    }
}
```

Sample of XAML Code

```xml
<!-- XAML -->
<Grid Name="Grid1">
    <ListBox ItemsSource="{Binding}" DisplayMemberPath="ContactName"
        Name="listBox1" Width="100" Height="100" VerticalAlignment="Top" />
    <ListBox ItemsSource="{Binding Path=CustomersOrders}"
        DisplayMemberPath="OrderID" Height="100" Width="100"
        Name="listBox2" VerticalAlignment="Bottom" />
</Grid>
```

Binding to an Object with *ObjectDataProvider*

The *ObjectDataProvider* class enables you to bind a WPF element or property to a method called on an object. You can specify an object type and a method on that type, then bind to the results of that method call. Table 7-3 lists the important properties of *ObjectDataProvider*.

TABLE 7-3 Important Properties of *ObjectDataProvider*

PROPERTY	DESCRIPTION
ConstructorParameters	Represents the list of parameters to pass to the constructor.
IsAsynchronous	Indicates whether object creation and method calls are performed on the foreground thread or on a background thread.
MethodName	Represents the name of the method of the source object to call.
MethodParameters	Represents the list of parameters to pass to the method specified by the *MethodName* property.
ObjectInstance	Gets or sets the object used as the binding source.
ObjectType	Gets or sets the type of object of which to create an instance.

The following example demonstrates how to create a simple *ObjectDataProvider* object for an object with a method that takes no parameters:

```
<Window.Resources>
  <ObjectDataProvider x:Key="myObjectProvider" ObjectType="{x:Type
      local:myObject}" MethodName="GetCollection" />
</Window.Resources>
```

You can also bind to this *ObjectDataProvider* object, using a *Binding* object, as shown here:

```
<ListBox Name="ListBox1" DisplayMemberPath="ItemID"
    ItemsSource="{Binding Source={StaticResource myObjectProvider}}" />
```

If the method requires parameters, you can provide them in the *MethodParameters* property. Likewise, if the constructor requires parameters, they are provided in the *ConstructorParameters* property. Examples are shown here:

```
<Window.Resources>
    <ObjectDataProvider x:Key="myObjectProvider"
        ObjectType="{x:Type local:myObject}" MethodName="GetCollection">
        <ObjectDataProvider.ConstructorParameters>
            <system:Double>12</system:Double>
        </ObjectDataProvider.ConstructorParameters>
        <ObjectDataProvider.MethodParameters>
            <system:String>Items</system:String>
        </ObjectDataProvider.MethodParameters>
    </ObjectDataProvider>
</Window.Resources>
```

Although you can bind to data presented by *ObjectDataProvider,* you cannot update data; that is, the binding is always going to be read-only.

Binding to XML Using *XmlDataProvider*

The *XmlDataProvider* class enables you to bind WPF elements to data in the XML format. Important properties of the *XmlDataProvider* class are shown in Table 7-4.

TABLE 7-4 Important Properties of *XmlDataProvider*

PROPERTY	DESCRIPTION
Document	Gets or sets the *XmlDocument* object to be used as the binding source.
Source	Gets or sets the Uniform Resource Indicator (URI) of the XML file to be used as the binding source.
XPath	Gets or sets the *XPath* query used to generate the XML data.

The following example demonstrates an *XmlDataProvider* object providing data from a source file called Items.xml:

```
<Window.Resources>
    <XmlDataProvider x:Key="Items" Source="Items.xml" />
</Window.Resources>
```

You can also provide the XML data inline as an XML data island. In this case, you wrap the XML data in *XData* tags, as shown here:

```
<Window.Resources>
    <XmlDataProvider x:Key="Items">
        <x:XData>
            <!--XML Data omitted-->
        </x:XData>
    </XmlDataProvider>
</Window.Resources>
```

You can bind elements to the data provided by *XmlDataProvider* in the same way you would bind to any other data source: namely, using a *Binding* object and specifying the *XmlDataProvider* object in the *Source* property, as shown here:

```
<ListBox ItemsSource="{Binding Source={StaticResource Items}}"
    DisplayMemberPath="ItemName" Name="listBox1" Width="100" Height="100"
    VerticalAlignment="Top" />
```

Using *XPath* with *XmlDataProvider*

You can use *XPath* expressions to filter the results exposed by *XmlDataProvider* or to filter the records displayed in the bound controls. By setting the *XPath* property of *XmlDataProvider* to an *XPath* expression, you can filter the data provided by the source. The following example filters the results exposed by an *XmlDataProvider* object to include only those nodes called *<ExpensiveItems>* in the *<Items>* top-level node:

```
<Window.Resources>
    <XmlDataProvider x:Key="Items" Source="Items.xml"
    XPath="Items/ExpensiveItems" />
</Window.Resources>
```

You can also apply *XPath* expressions in the bound controls. The following example sets the *XPath* property to *Diamond* (shown in bold), which indicates that only data contained in *<Diamond>* tags will be bound:

```
<ListBox ItemsSource="{Binding Source={StaticResource Items}
    XPath=Diamond}" DisplayMemberPath="ItemName" Name="listBox1" Width="100"
    Height="100" VerticalAlignment="Top" />
```

EXAM TIP

There are different methods for binding to different data sources. Be sure you understand how to bind not only to lists of data but also to ADO.NET objects, *ObjectDataProvider* objects, and *XmlDataProvider* objects because each one has its own individual subtleties.

PRACTICE **Accessing a Database**

In this lab, you create an application to view related data in a database. You use the Northwind sample database and create an application that enables you to choose a contact name, view a list of dates on which orders were placed, and see the details about shipping and which products were ordered. In Lesson 2, you will build on this application.

EXERCISE 1 Adding a Data Source

1. From the top-level folder of the companion CD, copy the Nwind database to a convenient location.

2. In Visual Studio, open a new WPF Application project.

3. In Visual Studio, from the Data menu choose Add New Data Source. The Data Source Configuration Wizard opens, with Database selected in the first page. Click Next to continue.

4. On the Choose A Database Model page, select Dataset and click Next.

5. On the Choose Your Data Connection page, click New Connection to open the Add Connection dialog box. Change Data Source to Microsoft Access Database File, click Continue, and then click Browse to browse to the location where you copied your Nwind database file. After selecting your database file, click Open. In the Add Connection dialog box, click Test Connection to test the connection. If the test is successful, click OK, click OK in the Add Connection dialog box, click Next in the Choose

Your Data Connection dialog box, and then click Yes in the pop-up window. Click Next again.

6. On the Choose Your DataBase Objects page, expand the Tables node and select the Customers table and the Orders table. Expand the Views node, select Order Details Extended, and click Finish. A new class called *NwindDataSet* is added to your solution, and table adapters are created.

7. In Solution Explorer, double-click NwindDataSet.xsd to open the Dataset Designer. Right-click the Dataset Designer; choose Add and then choose Relation to open the Relation window.

8. In the Relation window, set Parent Table to Orders and set Child Table to Order Details Extended. Verify that Key Columns and Foreign Key Columns are set to OrderID. Click OK to create the new data relation.

9. From the Build menu, choose Build Solution to build and save your solution.

EXERCISE 2 Binding to Relational Data

1. In the designer, add the namespace attribute (shown bolded in the following code) to the Window element to import your project. Please note that, depending on the name of your project, you will have to update the namespace of this project.

```
<Window x:Class="Window1"
        xmlns="http://schemas.microsoft.com/winfx/2006/xaml/presentation"
        xmlns:x="http://schemas.microsoft.com/winfx/2006/xaml"
        Title="Window1" Height="350" Width="523" xmlns:my="clr-namespace:Lesson_1">
</Window.Resources>
```

2. From the Data menu, choose Show Data Sources to open the Data Sources window. Expand the Customers node.

3. Click one of the fields—for example, CompanyName—under the Customers node. Open the drop-down box and select Customize. The Customize Control Binding window opens.

4. In the Customize Control Binding window, set the Data Type drop-down box to String and ensure that the box next to ListBox is selected. Repeat this procedure with the Data Type drop-down box set to DateTime. Click OK.

5. In the Data Sources window, under the Customers node, open the drop-down box for ContactName and then select ListBox.

6. From the Data Sources window, drag the ContactName node to the design surface. A bound list box with an appropriate label is created.

7. In the Data Sources window, within the Customers node, expand the Orders node and open the drop-down box for OrderDate and select ListBox.

8. From the Data Sources Window, drag the OrderDate node to the Design surface to create a bound list box.

9. In the Data Sources window, within the Customers node and within the Orders node, open the Order Details Extended node. Open the drop-down box for ProductName and select ListBox.

10. From the Data Sources window, drag the ProductName node to the design surface to create a bound list box.

11. In the Data Sources window, within the Customers node, under the Orders node, drag the ShipName, ShipAddress, ShipCity, and ShipCountry nodes to the design surface to create bound text boxes.

12. Press F5 to run your application. Note that when a Contact Name is selected in the first list box, the other bound controls automatically sync to the selected item. Similarly, if an order date is selected in the second list box, the items in the third list (for product name) box are synchronized with the selected item.

Lesson Summary

- When binding an item control to a list of data, you must set the *ItemsSource* property to a *Binding* class that specifies the source of the list. *DisplayMemberPath* indicates which property of the list should be displayed in the item control.

- Individual properties can be bound to lists of data. Initially, the first member of any such bound list is displayed, but the list can be navigated through the default *ICollectionView* property retrieved through the *CollectionViewSource* object.

- When binding to hierarchical data, set the *IsSynchronizedWithCurrentItem* property on each item control to *True* to enable automatic UI updates of hierarchical data. You can set a *Binding* class to detail lists by specifying the detail list through the *Path* property.

- You can bind to the value returned by a method through *ObjectDataProvider*.

- You can bind to XML with *XmlDataProvider*. *XmlDataProvider* requires XML as a file, an *XmlDocument* object, or a data island.

Lesson Review

You can use the following questions to test your knowledge of the information in Lesson 1, "Binding to Data Sources." The questions are also available on the companion CD if you prefer to review them in electronic form.

> **NOTE ANSWERS**
>
> Answers to these questions and explanations of why each answer choice is correct or incorrect are located in the "Answers" section at the end of the book.

1. Which of the following code samples shows a *ListBox* object correctly bound to the *CustomerAddress* field of a data table? The data table is named *Customers* in an ADO.

NET data set named *mySet*. Take both XAML and code into account in the possible answers.

A.

Sample of Visual Basic Code

```
Grid1.DataContext=mySet
```

Sample of C# Code

```
Grid1.DataContext=mySet;
```

Sample of XAML Code

```
<!-- XAML -->
<Grid Name="Grid1">
    <ListBox ItemsSource="{Binding}"
    DisplayMemberPath="CustomerAddress"
    Name="listBox1" Width="100" Height="100" VerticalAlignment="Top" />
</Grid>
```

B.

Sample of Visual Basic Code

```
Grid1.DataContext=mySet
```

Sample of C# Code

```
Grid1.DataContext=mySet;
```

Sample of XAML Code

```
<!-- XAML -->
<Grid Name="Grid1">
<ListBox ItemsSource="{Binding Path=mySet.Customers}"
    DisplayMemberPath="CustomerAddress"
    Name="listBox1" Width="100" Height="100" VerticalAlignment="Top" />
</Grid>
```

C.

Sample of Visual Basic Code

```
Grid1.DataContext=mySet.Customers
```

Sample of C# Code

```
Grid1.DataContext=mySet.Customers;
```

Sample of XAML Code

```
<!-- XAML -->
<Grid Name="Grid1">
<ListBox ItemsSource="{Binding}"
    DisplayMemberPath="CustomerAddress"
    Name="listBox1" Width="100" Height="100" VerticalAlignment="Top" />
</Grid>
```

D.

Sample of Visual Basic Code

```
Grid1.DataContext=mySet.Customers
```

Sample of C# Code

```
Grid1.DataContext=mySet.Customers;
```

Sample of XAML Code

```xaml
<!-- XAML -->
<Grid Name="Grid1">
<ListBox ItemsSource="{Binding}"
    DisplayMemberPath="Customers/CustomerAddress"
    Name="listBox1" Width="100" Height="100" VerticalAlignment="Top" />
</Grid>
```

2. You're binding a *ListBox* object to the Price field in an ADO.NET data table called Details. This table is related to the Orders table through a parent relation called OrdersDetails. The Orders table is related to a table called Customers through a parent relation called CustomersOrders. The *DataContext* property for your list box has been set to the Customers table, which is the parent table of the CustomersOrders relation. Which of the following correctly binds *ListBox* to the *Price* field?

A.

```xaml
<ListBox ItemsSource="{Binding}"
    DisplayMemberPath="Price" Name="listBox1"
    Width="100" Height="100" VerticalAlignment="Top" />
```

B.

```xaml
<ListBox ItemsSource="{Binding Path=OrdersDetails}"
    DisplayMemberPath="Price" Name="listBox1"
    Width="100" Height="100" VerticalAlignment="Top" />
```

C.

```xaml
<ListBox ItemsSource="{Binding Path=CustomersOrders/OrdersDetails}"
    DisplayMemberPath="Price" Name="listBox1"
    Width="100" Height="100" VerticalAlignment="Top" />
```

D.

```xaml
<ListBox ItemsSource="{Binding Path=Customers/CustomersOrders/OrdersDetails}"
    DisplayMemberPath="Price" Name="listBox1"
    Width="100" Height="100" VerticalAlignment="Top" />
```

Lesson 2: Manipulating and Displaying Data

WPF has built-in functionality for sorting, grouping, and filtering data. In addition, it provides unprecedented support for customizing data display through data template technology. In this lesson, you learn to apply sorting and grouping through the *ICollectionView* interface. You learn to create and implement custom filters for data displayed in WPF, and you learn to use data templates to customize the appearance of data in your user interface.

After this lesson, you will be able to:

- Create and implement a data template.
- Sort data through *ICollectionView*.
- Apply grouping to data with *ICollectionView*.
- Use an *IComparer* to create a custom sorting scheme.
- Apply a custom filter to bound data.
- Apply a filter to a bound ADO.NET object.
- Implement and use a *DataTemplateSelector* class.
- Create and use *HierarchicalDataTemplate*.

Estimated lesson time: 30 minutes

Data Templates

So far, you have seen how to bind content controls and item controls to data to display bound data in the user interface. The results, however, have been underwhelming. You have seen how to present data fields as simple text in content controls and lists of text in item controls. You can create a rich data presentation experience, however, by incorporating data templates into your UI design.

A *data template* is a bit of XAML that describes how bound data is displayed. A data template can contain elements that are each bound to a data property, along with additional markup that describes layout, color, and other aspects of appearance. The following example demonstrates a simple data template that describes a *Label* element bound to the *ContactName* property. The *Foreground*, *Background*, *BorderBrush*, and *BorderThickness* properties are also set:

```
<DataTemplate>
    <Label Content="{Binding Path=ContactName}" BorderBrush="Black"
        Background="Yellow" BorderThickness="3" Foreground="Blue" />
</DataTemplate>
```

Figure 7-2 shows a list box displaying a list of bound data. Figure 7-3 shows the same list box displaying the same bound data with the previously cited data template set to the *ListBox.ItemsTemplate* property.

FIGURE 7-2 A bound list box without a data template.

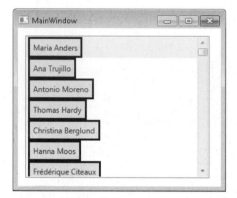

FIGURE 7-3 A bound list box with a data template applied.

When binding a property or list directly to a control, you are limited to binding a single property. With data templates, however, you can bind more than one property in each item, thereby displaying multiple bits of related data together. The following example demonstrates this concept. It is a modification of the template shown in the previous example, but a header is added to each *ContactName* item that consists of the text "Company Name:" and the *CompanyName* value associated with that contact name. Additional properties are set to provide style, and both labels are placed within a *StackPanel* class to facilitate layout:

```
<DataTemplate>
  <StackPanel>
    <Label Background="Purple" Foreground="White" BorderBrush="Red"
      BorderThickness="4">
      <Label.Content>
        <WrapPanel HorizontalAlignment="Stretch">
          <TextBlock>Company Name: </TextBlock>
          <TextBlock Text="{Binding CompanyName}" />
        </WrapPanel>
      </Label.Content>
    </Label>
    <Label Content="{Binding Path=ContactName}" BorderBrush="Black"
```

```
        HorizontalAlignment="Stretch" Background="Yellow"
        BorderThickness="3" Foreground="Blue" />
    </StackPanel>
</DataTemplate>
```

Figure 7-4 shows the results of applying this data template.

FIGURE 7-4 A bound list box with a data template that includes a header with related data.

You can apply data templates to content controls as well. Although a content control can display only a single record at a time, it can use all the formatting features of the data template technology.

Setting the Data Template

You set the data template on a control by setting one of two properties. For content controls, you set the *ContentTemplate* property, as shown in bold here:

```
<Label Height="23" HorizontalAlignment="Left" Margin="56,0,0,91"
    Name="label1" VerticalAlignment="Bottom" Width="120">
    <Label.ContentTemplate>
        <DataTemplate>
            <!  Actual data template omitted-->
        </DataTemplate>
    </Label.ContentTemplate>
</Label>
```

For item controls, you set the *ItemsTemplate* property, as shown in bold here:

```
<ListBox ItemsSource="{Binding}" IsSynchronizedWithCurrentItem="True"
    Margin="18,19,205,148" Name="listBox1">
    <ListBox.ItemTemplate>
        <DataTemplate>
            <!--Actual data template omitted-->
        </DataTemplate>
    </ListBox.ItemTemplate>
</ListBox>
```

Note that for item controls, the *DisplayMemberPath* and *ItemTemplate* properties are mutually exclusive; you can set one but not the other.

A frequent pattern with data templates is to define them in a resource collection and reference them in your element rather than defining them inline as shown in the previous examples. All that is required to reuse a data template in this manner is to define the template in a resource collection and set a *Key* property for the template, as shown here:

```
<Window.Resources>
   <DataTemplate x:Key="myTemplate">
      <Label Content="{Binding Path=ContactName}" BorderBrush="Black"
         Background="Yellow" BorderThickness="3" Foreground="Blue" />
   </DataTemplate>
</Window.Resources>
```

Then you can set the template by referring to the resource, as shown in bold here:

```
<ListBox ItemTemplate="{StaticResource myTemplate}"
   Name="ListBox1" />
```

EXAM TIP

Although data templates appear to be rather simple, be sure that you have lots of practice implementing and using them. Data templates are an extremely powerful feature of WPF and promise to figure prominently on the exam.

Using Converters to Apply Conditional Formatting in Data Templates

One of the most useful things you can do with converters is to apply conditional formatting to displayed data. For example, suppose you are writing an application that binds to a list of dates on which orders were placed. You might want orders that were placed in the current month to have a different foreground color than the other orders. You can accomplish this by binding the *Foreground* property of the control used to bind the date to the *Date* field and providing a converter that evaluates the date and returns a brush of the appropriate color. The following examples show such a converter, an instance of that converter added to the *Window.Resources* collection, and, finally, the *Foreground* property bound to the *Date* property using the converter to return a *Brush* object. First, here's the converter:

Sample of Visual Basic Code

```
<ValueConversion(GetType(DateTime), GetType(Brush))> _
Public Class DateBrushConverter
   Implements IValueConverter

   Public Function Convert(ByVal value As Object, ByVal targetType As _
      System.Type, ByVal parameter As Object, ByVal culture As _
      System.Globalization.CultureInfo) As Object Implements _
      System.Windows.Data.IValueConverter.Convert
      Dim aDate As DateTime
      aDate = CType(value, DateTime)
      If aDate.Month = Now.Month Then
         Return New SolidColorBrush(Colors.Red)
      Else
         Return New SolidColorBrush(Colors.Black)
      End If
```

```
      End Function

      Public Function ConvertBack(ByVal value As Object, ByVal targetType _
         As System.Type, ByVal parameter As Object, ByVal culture As  _
         System.Globalization.CultureInfo) As Object Implements _
           System.Windows.Data.IValueConverter.ConvertBack
         Throw New NotImplementedException()
      End Function
End Class
```

Sample of C# Code

```csharp
[ValueConversion(typeof(DateTime), typeof(Brush))]
public class DateBrushConverter : IValueConverter
{
   public object Convert(object value, Type targetType, object parameter,
      System.Globalization.CultureInfo culture)
   {
      DateTime aDate = (DateTime)value;
      if (aDate.Month == DateTime.Now.Month)
         return new SolidColorBrush(Colors.Red);
      else
         return new SolidColorBrush(Colors.Black);
   }

   public object ConvertBack(object value, Type targetType, object
      parameter, System.Globalization.CultureInfo culture)
   {
      throw new NotImplementedException();
   }
}
```

An instance is then added to the *Window.Resources* collection, as shown in bold here:

```xml
<Window x:Class="WpfApplication5.Window1"
   xmlns="http://schemas.microsoft.com/winfx/2006/xaml/presentation"
   xmlns:x="http://schemas.microsoft.com/winfx/2006/xaml"
   xmlns:local="clr-namespace:WpfApplication5"
   Title="Window1" Height="300" Width="300">
   <Window.Resources>
      <local:DateBrushConverter
          x:Key="myDateConverter"></local:DateBrushConverter>
   </Window.Resources>
   <!--- the rest of the window is omitted --!>
</Window>
```

Finally, you can bind the *Foreground* property to a date by using the converter, as shown in bold here:

```xml
<ListBox Margin="60,58,98,104" Name="ListBox1">
   <ListBox.ItemTemplate>
      <DataTemplate>
         <Label Content="{Binding Path=OrderDate}" Foreground="{Binding
            Path=OrderDate, Converter={StaticResource myDateConverter}}" />
      </DataTemplate>
   </ListBox.ItemTemplate>
</ListBox>
```

Using *DataTemplateSelector*

The *DataTemplateSelector* class enables you to assign data templates dynamically to collection objects based on the content of the data. For example, consider that you have two data templates, shown in XAML here:

```
<Window.Resources>
        <DataTemplate x:Key="BasicTemplate">
                <TextBlock Text="{Binding Path=RequiredDate}"/>
        </DataTemplate>
        <DataTemplate x:Key="PriorityTemplate">
                <TextBlock Text="{Binding Path=RequiredDate}" Background="Red"/>
        </DataTemplate>
</Window.Resources>
```

Both templates in this example are quite simple. They each define a text block that displays a field called RequiredDate—in this example, the date an order is required by the customer. However, in the template called PriorityTemplate, the background of the text block is red. Suppose you want your application to examine the value of the RequiredDate field and use PriorityTemplate for orders that are due this month and BasicTemplate for all others. You can implement this logic by using the *DataTemplateSelector* class.

DataTemplateSelector is an abstract class that exposes a single method (which can be overridden) called *SelectTemplate*. *SelectTemplate* returns a *DataTemplate* object and, when overridden, should incorporate the logic required to determine the correct template based on the data. The *SelectTemplate* method accepts two parameters: an *Object* parameter that represents the object bound by the data template, and a *DependencyObject* parameter that represents the container for the bound object. The following example shows a simple implementation of *DataTemplateSelector* that examines a field in a data row and returns a data template based on the value of that field.

Sample of Visual Basic Code

```
Public Class DateDataTemplateSelector
    Inherits DataTemplateSelector
    Public Overrides Function SelectTemplate(ByVal item As Object, ByVal container As
DependencyObject) _
        As DataTemplate
        Dim element As FrameworkElement
        element = TryCast(container, FrameworkElement)
        ' Tests to ensure that both the item and the container are not null, and that
        ' the item is of the expected data type.
        If element IsNot Nothing AndAlso item IsNot Nothing AndAlso TypeOf item Is
System.Data.DataRowView Then
            ' Casts the item as the expected type, in this case a System.Data.
DataRowView
            Dim dateitem As System.Data.DataRowView = CType(item, System.Data.
DataRowView)
            ' Compares the value of the expected field with the current month
            If CType(dateitem("RequiredDate"), Date).Month = DateTime.Now.Month Then
                ' Returns the PriorityTemplate in the case of a match
                Return TryCast(element.FindResource("PriorityTemplate"), DataTemplate)
```

```
            Else
                ' Returns the BasicTemplate for other cases
                Return TryCast(element.FindResource("BasicTemplate"), DataTemplate)
            End If
        End If
        Return Nothing
    End Function
End Class
```

Sample of C# Code

```
public class DateDataTemplateSelector : DataTemplateSelector
{
    public override DataTemplate SelectTemplate(object item, DependencyObject container)
    {
     FrameworkElement element;
     System.Data.DataRowView dateitem;
     element = container as FrameworkElement;
     // Tests to ensure that both the item and the container are not null, and that the
     // item is of the expected data type.
     if (element != null && item != null && item is System.Data.DataRowView)
        {
        // Casts the item as the expected type, in this case a System.Data.DataRowView
        dateitem = (System.Data.DataRowView)item;
        // Compares the value of the expected field with the current month
        if (((DateTime)dateitem["RequiredDate"]).Month == DateTime.Now.Month)
            // Returns the PriorityTemplate in the case of a match
            return element.FindResource("PriorityTemplate") as DataTemplate;
        else
            // Returns the BasicTemplate for other cases
            return element.FindResource("BasicTemplate") as DataTemplate;
        }
     return null;
    }
}
```

After you have created your inherited *DataTemplateSelector* class, you can create an instance of it in your Resources section, as shown here:

```
<Window x:Class="MainWindow"
    xmlns="http://schemas.microsoft.com/winfx/2006/xaml/presentation"
    xmlns:x="http://schemas.microsoft.com/winfx/2006/xaml"
    xmlns:my="clr-namespace:WpfApplication4"
    Title="MainWindow" Height="350" Width="525" >
    <Window.Resources>
        <my:DateDataTemplateSelector x:Key="myTemplateSelector" />
    </Window.Resources>
    <!--  Implementation omitted -->
</Window>
```

After you have defined a *DataTemplateSelector* resource, you can assign the resource to the *ItemTemplateSelector* property of an item control, as shown here:

```
<ListBox ItemTemplateSelector="{StaticResource myTemplateSelector}" />
```

When an item is added to the list box in this example, the *SelectTemplate* method of *DataTemplateSelector* is executed on that item, and the appropriate template is returned and applied to the display of that item.

Using Hierarchical Data Templates

When displaying hierarchical data, such as in a *TreeView* or a *Menu* control, you can use *HierarchicalDataTemplate* to provide formatting and layout for both items in a list and related sub-items. The *HierarchicalDataTemplate* class incorporates all the properties of the *DataTemplate* class and serves as the standard data template for list items. *HierarchicalDataTemplate* also incorporates a number of properties that apply to sub-items, which Table 7-5 summarizes.

TABLE 7-5 Item-Related Properties of *HierarchicalDataTemplate*

PROPERTY	DESCRIPTION
ItemBindingGroup	Gets or sets the *BindingGroup* property that is copied to each child item
ItemContainerStyle	Gets or sets the *Style* property that is applied to the item container for each child item
ItemContainerStyleSelector	Gets or sets custom style-selection logic for a style that can be applied to each item container
ItemsSource	Gets or sets the binding for this data template, which indicates where to find the collection that represents the next level in the data hierarchy
ItemStringFormat	Gets or sets a composite string that specifies how to format the items in the next level in the data hierarchy if they are displayed as strings
ItemTemplate	Gets or sets the data template to apply to the *ItemTemplate* property on a generated *HeaderedItemsControl* control (such as *MenuItem* or *TreeViewItem*) to indicate how to display items from the next level in the data hierarchy
ItemTemplateSelector	Gets or sets *DataTemplateSelector* to apply to the *ItemTemplateSelector* property on a generated *HeaderedItemsControl* control (such as *MenuItem* or *TreeViewItem*) to indicate how to select a template to display items from the next level in the data hierarchy

The *ItemsSource* property is a binding that points to the sub-items to be displayed in the hierarchical display. The *ItemTemplate* property represents the data template for the sub-items. Normally, this is a regular data template, but note that sub-items can have sub-items of their own, in which case you can set this property to another *HierarchicalDataTemplate* class.

If you want to examine the sub-items programmatically and provide different data templates based on the data values, you can set the *ItemTemplateSelector* property to an instance of a class deriving from *DataTemplateSelector*, as described in the previous section.

The following XAML code demonstrates an example of *HierarchicalDatatemplate*. In this example, a window defines two CollectionViewResource objects, which represent an ADO. NET *DataTable* object and a *DataRelation* object that defines the relationship between it and a related table. The user interface of the window contains a *TreeView* control that will display a list of items, each of which will have sub-items. *HierarchicalDataTemplate*, in this example, is applied to the items that are displayed in *ListView*, and the *ItemTemplate* property of *HierarchicalDataView* refers to the DataTemplate class applied to sub-items in *ListView*.

```xml
<Window x:Class="MainWindow"
    xmlns="http://schemas.microsoft.com/winfx/2006/xaml/presentation"
    xmlns:x="http://schemas.microsoft.com/winfx/2006/xaml"
    xmlns:my="clr-namespace:WpfApplication4"
    Title="MainWindow" Height="350" Width="525" >
    <Window.Resources>
        <!-- Creates a resource that refers to a DataSet defined in code -->
        <my:NwindDataSet x:Key="NwindDataSet" />
        <!-- Creates a resource that refers to the Customers table of the DataSet -->
        <CollectionViewSource x:Key="CustomersViewSource" Source="{Binding
Path=Customers,
            Source={StaticResource NwindDataSet}}" />
        <!-- Creates a resource that refers to a DataRelation defined by the Customers
table -->
        <CollectionViewSource x:Key="CustomersOrdersViewSource" Source="{Binding
Path=CustomersOrders,
            Source={StaticResource CustomersViewSource}}" />
        <!-- The DataTemplate that is applied to sub-items in the list view -->
        <DataTemplate x:Key="BasicTemplate">
            <TextBlock Text="{Binding Path=RequiredDate}"/>
        </DataTemplate>
        <!-- The HierarchicalDataTemplate that is applied to Listview items -->
        <HierarchicalDataTemplate x:Key="HierarchTemplate" ItemsSource="{Binding
Path=CustomersOrders}"
            ItemTemplate="BasicTemplate" >
            <TextBlock Foreground="Red" Text="{Binding Path=CompanyName}" />
        </HierarchicalDataTemplate>
    </Window.Resources>
    <Grid DataContext="{StaticResource CustomersViewSource}">
        <TreeView Height="248" HorizontalAlignment="Left" Margin="46,39,0,0"
Name="TreeView1"
            VerticalAlignment="Top" Width="394" ItemsSource="{Binding}"
            ItemTemplate="{StaticResource HierarchTemplate}" />
    </Grid>
</Window>
```

Sorting Data

When presenting data in the user interface, you want to sort it in various ways. Bound data can be sorted through the default *ICollectionView* element for the data list. You saw previously how to obtain a reference to the default collection view through the *CollectionViewSource* object, as shown again here:

Sample of Visual Basic Code

```
Dim myView As System.ComponentModel.ICollectionView
myView = CollectionViewSource.GetDefaultView(myCollection)
```

Sample of C# Code

```
System.ComponentModel.ICollectionView myView;
myView = CollectionViewSource.GetDefaultView(myCollection);
```

ICollectionView exposes a property called *SortDescriptions*, which contains a collection of *SortDescription* objects. *SortDescription* objects describe the column name to sort by and a direction that specifies either an ascending or a descending sort order. The following example demonstrates sorting by a column named LastName in ascending order:

Sample of Visual Basic Code

```
myView.SortDescriptions.Add(New _
    System.ComponentModel.SortDescription("LastName", _
    System.ComponentModel.ListSortDirection.Ascending)
```

Sample of C# Code

```
myView.SortDescriptions.Add(new
    System.ComponentModel.SortDescription("LastName",
    System.ComponentModel.ListSortDirection.Ascending);
```

SortDescription objects are applied to a collection in the order in which they are added to the collection view. Thus, if you wanted to sort first by the LastName column and then by the FirstName column, you first would add a *SortDescription* object that specified sorting by *LastName* and then add a *SortDescription* object that specified sorting by *FirstName*, as shown here:

Sample of Visual Basic Code

```
myView.SortDescriptions.Add(New _
    System.ComponentModel.SortDescription("LastName", _
    System.ComponentModel.ListSortDirection.Ascending)
myView.SortDescriptions.Add(New _
    System.ComponentModel.SortDescription("FirstName", _
    System.ComponentModel.ListSortDirection.Ascending)
```

Sample of C# Code

```
myView.SortDescriptions.Add(new
    System.ComponentModel.SortDescription("LastName",
    System.ComponentModel.ListSortDirection.Ascending);
myView.SortDescriptions.Add(new
    System.ComponentModel.SortDescription("FirstName",
    System.ComponentModel.ListSortDirection.Ascending);
```

Applying Custom Sorting

If you are binding to a class whose default view is *ListCollectionView* (that is, it implements *IList* but not *IBindingList*), such as *ObservableCollection*, you can implement custom sort orders by setting the *ListCollectionView.CustomSort* property. The *CustomSort* property takes an object that implements the *IComparer* interface. The *IComparer* interface requires a single method called *Compare* that takes two arguments and returns an integer that represents the result of the comparison of those two objects. The following example demonstrates an implementation of the *IComparer* interface that takes two *Employee* objects and sorts by the length of the *LastName* property:

Sample of Visual Basic Code

```
Public Class myComparer
    Implements IComparer

    Public Function Compare(ByVal x As Object, ByVal y As Object) As _
        Integer Implements System.Collections.IComparer.Compare
        Dim empX As Employee = CType(x, Employee)
        Dim empY As Employee = CType(y, Employee)
        Return empX.LastName.Length.CompareTo(empY.LastName.Length)
    End Function
End Class
```

Sample of C# Code

```
public class myComparer : System.Collections.IComparer
{
    public int Compare(object x, object y)
    {
        Employee empX = (Employee)x;
        Employee empY = (Employee)y;
        return empX.LastName.Length.CompareTo(empY.LastName.Length);
    }
}
```

Then you can create an instance of this class to set to the *CustomSort* property of your *ICollectionView* element, as shown here:

Sample of Visual Basic Code

```
Dim myView As ListCollectionView
myView = CType(CollectionViewSource.GetDefaultView(myCollection), _
    ListCollectionView)
myView.CustomSort = New myComparer()
```

Sample of C# Code

```
System.ComponentModel.ICollectionView myView;
myView =
    (ListCollectionView)CollectionViewSource.GetDefaultView(myCollection);
myView.CustomSort = new myComparer();
```

Grouping

ICollectionView also supports grouping data. Grouping data is similar to sorting but takes advantage of the built-in functionality of item controls to provide formatting for different groups, thus enabling the user to distinguish groups visually at run time. You can create a group by adding a *PropertyGroupDescription* object to the *ICollectionView.GroupDescriptions* collection. The following example demonstrates creating groups based on the value of the *EmployeeTitle* property:

Sample of Visual Basic Code

```
Dim myView As System.ComponentModel.ICollectionView
myView = CollectionViewSource.GetDefaultView(myCollection)
myView.GroupDescriptions.Add( _
    New PropertyGroupDescription("EmployeeTitle"))
```

Sample of C# Code

```
System.ComponentModel.ICollectionView myView;
myView = CollectionViewSource.GetDefaultView(myCollection);
myView.GroupDescriptions.Add(
    new PropertyGroupDescription("EmployeeTitle"));
```

At first glance, applying this grouping seems to have the same effect as sorting by *EmployeeTitle*. The difference becomes evident when this data is displayed in an item control with the *GroupStyle* property set. The *GroupStyle* property provides formatting information for grouped items and enables you to set how they are displayed. Table 7-6 explains the properties of the *GroupStyle* object.

TABLE 7-6 Properties of *GroupStyle*

PROPERTY	DESCRIPTION
ContainerStyle	Gets or sets the style applied to the GroupItem object generated for each item
ContainerStyleSelector	Represents an instance of StyleSelector that determines the appropriate style to use for the container
HeaderTemplate	Gets or sets the template used to display the group header
HeaderTemplateSelector	Represents an instance of StyleSelector that determines the appropriate style to use for the header
Panel	Gets or sets a template that creates the panel used to lay out the items

The following example demonstrates setting the *GroupHeader* and *Panel* properties. In this example, the *Panel* property is replaced by a *WrapPanel* element that causes the groups to wrap horizontally, and the *HeaderTemplate* is set to display the header in purple text on a red background:

```
<ListBox ItemsSource="{Binding}" IsSynchronizedWithCurrentItem="True"
    DisplayMemberPath="ContactName" Margin="18,19,25,0" Name="listBox1"
```

```
        Height="100" VerticalAlignment="Top">
    <ListBox.GroupStyle>
        <GroupStyle>
            <GroupStyle.HeaderTemplate>
                <DataTemplate>
                    <Label Content="{Binding Path=Name}" Foreground="Purple"
                        Background="Red" Padding="4" />
                </DataTemplate>
            </GroupStyle.HeaderTemplate>
            <GroupStyle.Panel>
                <ItemsPanelTemplate>
                    <WrapPanel/>
                </ItemsPanelTemplate>
            </GroupStyle.Panel>
        </GroupStyle>
    </ListBox.GroupStyle>
</ListBox>
```

Note that in the data template for the *GroupStyle.HeaderTemplate* property, the *Content* property is bound to the *Name* property. This is not the *Name* property of the objects bound in the *ListBox* control, but, actually, the *Name* property of the *PropertyGroupDescription* element. Thus, when you want the header to reflect the name of the category, you always bind to the *Name* property rather than to the name of the property you are using to group your data.

Creating Custom Grouping

In addition to creating groupings based on the values of object properties, you can create custom groups to arrange your items in an item control. To create a custom group, you must create a class that implements the *IValueConverter* interface, which exposes two methods: *Convert* and *ConvertBack*. For the purposes of creating custom grouping, you need to provide only a "real" implementation for the *Convert* method; the *ConvertBack* method will never be called. The *Convert* method takes an object as a parameter, which will be the object represented by the property named in *PropertyGroupDescription*. In the *Convert* method, examine the value of the object, determine which custom group it belongs to, and then return a value that represents that custom group. The following example is a simple demonstration of this concept. It is designed to examine a value from a *Region* property and determine whether that region is the Isle of Wight. If it is, it returns Isle Of Wight as the group header; otherwise, it returns Everyplace Else.

Sample of Visual Basic Code

```
Public Class RegionConverter
    Implements IValueConverter

    Public Function Convert(ByVal value As Object, ByVal targetType As _
        System.Type, ByVal parameter As Object, ByVal culture As _
        System.Globalization.CultureInfo) As Object Implements _
        System.Windows.Data.IValueConverter.Convert
        If Not value.ToString = "" Then
            Dim region As String = value.ToString
```

```
        If region = "Isle of Wight" Then
            Return "Isle of Wight"
        End If
    End If
    Return "Everyplace else"
End Function

Public Function ConvertBack(ByVal value As Object, ByVal targetType _
    As System.Type, ByVal parameter As Object, ByVal culture As _
    System.Globalization.CultureInfo) As Object Implements _
    System.Windows.Data.IValueConverter.ConvertBack
    Throw New NotImplementedException()
End Function
End Class
```

Sample of C# Code

```csharp
public class RegionGrouper : IValueConverter
{
    public object Convert(object value, Type targetType, object parameter,
        System.Globalization.CultureInfo culture)
    {
        if (!(value.ToString() == ""))
        {
            string Region = (string)value;
            if (Region == "Isle of Wight")
                return "Isle of Wight";
        }
        return "Everyplace else";
    }

    public object ConvertBack(object value, Type targetType, object
        parameter, System.Globalization.CultureInfo culture)
    {
        throw new NotImplementedException();
    }
}
```

Then you can add your custom *PropertyGroupDescription* parameter by specifying the *Region* property and a new instance of the *RegionGrouper* property, as shown here:

Sample of Visual Basic Code

```vbnet
Dim myView As System.ComponentModel.ICollectionView
myView = CollectionViewSource.GetDefaultView(myCollection)
myView.GroupDescriptions.Add(New PropertyGroupDescription("Region", _
    New RegionGrouper()))
```

Sample of C# Code

```csharp
System.ComponentModel.ICollectionView myView;
myView = CollectionViewSource.GetDefaultView(myCollection);
myView.GroupDescriptions.Add(new PropertyGroupDescription("Region",
    new RegionGrouper()));
```

Filtering Data

ICollectionView has built-in functionality that enables you to designate a method to filter the data in your collection view. The *ICollectionView* property accepts a *Predicate* delegate that specifies a Boolean method, which takes the object from the collection as an argument, examines it, and returns *True* if the object is included in the filtered view and *False* if the object is excluded. The following two examples demonstrate setting a simple filter. The first example demonstrates setting the filter on an *ICollectionView* object, and the second example demonstrates the method that implements that filter. These examples involve a collection of items named *myItems*:

Sample of Visual Basic Code

```
Dim myView As System.ComponentModel.ICollectionView
myView = CollectionViewSource.GetDefaultView(myItems)
myView.Filter = New Predicate(Of Object)(AddressOf myFilter)
```

Sample of C# Code

```
System.ComponentModel.ICollectionView myView;
myView = CollectionViewSource.GetDefaultView(myItems);
myView.Filter = new Predicate<object>(myFilter);
```

The next example shows *myFilter*, a simple method that excludes all objects whose *ToString* method returns a string length of eight characters or fewer:

Sample of Visual Basic Code

```
Public Function myFilter(ByVal param As Object) As Boolean
    Return (param.ToString.Length > 8)
End Function
```

Sample of C# Code

```
public bool myFilter(object param)
{
    return (param.ToString().Length > 8);
}
```

Note that the *Predicate* delegate to which the *Filter* property is set must be *Predicate<object>* [*Predicate(Of Object)* in Visual Basic] rather than a strongly typed *Predicate* delegate such as *Predicate<Item>*. You must perform any necessary casting in the method that implements the filter.

Filtering ADO.NET Objects

The filtering method described in the previous section does not work when binding to ADO.NET objects or anytime the underlying *ICollectionView* object is actually a *BindingListCollectionView* object. This is because the data collection bound to in this view actually is connected through an ADO.NET *DataView* layer, which implements its own filtering scheme. However, you can take advantage of the filtering capabilities of *DataView* by setting the *BindingListCollectionView.CustomFilter* property. This property applies a string-based expression directly to the underlying *DataView* layer. The filter expression is a string expression in the following format:

```
<ColumnName> <Operator> <Value>
```

For example, the following filter limits the rows returned to rows whose *Sandwich* property has a value of 'Muffaletta':

```
Sandwich = 'Muffaletta'
```

To set the filter, you would create the following code:

Sample of Visual Basic Code
```
Dim myView As BindingListCollectionView
myView = CType(CollectionViewSource.GetDefaultView(myItems), _
    BindingListCollectionView;
myView.CustomFilter = "Sandwich = 'Muffaletta'"
```

Sample of C# Code
```
BindingListCollectionView myView;
myView =
    (BindingListCollectionView)CollectionViewSource.GetDefaultView(myItems);
myView.CustomFilter = "Sandwich = 'Muffaletta'";
```

String literals for the filter expression must be enclosed in single quotes, as shown in the preceding code. Although the complete rules for filter expressions are beyond the scope of this lesson, they follow the same syntax as comparison expressions for the *DataColumn.Expression* property, and you can view a complete reference in the Microsoft reference topic of that name at *http://msdn2.microsoft.com/en-us/library/system.data .datacolumn.expression(VS.71).aspx*.

 Quick Check

- What is the difference between sorting by a particular property and creating a group based on that property?

Quick Check Answer

- When you create a group, you have access to the *GroupStyle* object created for that group. You can set individual templates for the header and container and supply a different layout panel.

PRACTICE **Practice with Data Templates**

In this lab, you expand on the application you completed in the previous lab. You add data templates to display greater detail and visual appeal to the *ContactNames* and *ProductNames* lists.

EXERCISE Adding Data Templates

1. Open the completed solution for Lesson 1 of this chapter from either the CD or your completed exercise. You might want to expand the user interface horizontally and increase the width of listbox1 (for contact name) and listbox3 (for product name).

2. In XAML view, delete the following code from the declaration for listBox1:

```
DisplayMemberPath="ContactName"
```

3. In XAML view, add the following data template and set it to the *ItemTemplate* property of listBox1:

```xml
<DataTemplate>
    <StackPanel Orientation="Horizontal">
        <Label Background="Purple" Foreground="White" BorderBrush="Red"
            BorderThickness="4" Width="300">
            <Label.Content>
                <StackPanel HorizontalAlignment="Stretch">
                    <TextBlock>Company Name: </TextBlock>
                    <TextBlock Text="{Binding CompanyName}" />
                </StackPanel>
            </Label.Content>
        </Label>
        <Label Content="{Binding Path=ContactName}" BorderBrush="Black"
            HorizontalAlignment="Stretch" Background="Yellow"
            BorderThickness="3" Foreground="Blue" Width="200" />
    </StackPanel>
</DataTemplate>
```

This data template does a lot of things. It creates *StackPanel*, in which is bound the *CompanyName* field, and then lays it out so that it appears to the left of the *ContactName* property for that company. It also adds some colorful UI effects.

4. Delete the following code from the declaration for listBox3:

```
DisplayMemberPath="ProductName"
```

5. In XAML view, set the following data template to the *ItemTemplate* property of listBox3:

```xml
<DataTemplate>
    <StackPanel Orientation="Horizontal">
        <Label Background="Yellow" Content="{Binding Path=Quantity}"
            Width="25" />
        <Label Background="AliceBlue" Content="{Binding Path=ProductName}"
            MinWidth="120" />
        <Label Background="Red" Content="{Binding Path=ExtendedPrice}"
            Width="50" />
    </StackPanel>
</DataTemplate>
```

This data template binds to the *Quantity* and *ExtendedPrice* fields, as well as to the *ProductName* fields, and sets the background color for each field.

6. Press F5 to build and run your application. Note that the display is now more color-ful and that additional fields are bound in the *ListBox* elements. Note that although a *Label* object in the data template for listBox3 is bound to the *ExtendedPrice* field, it appears as a regular number instead of being formatted as currency.

Lesson Summary

- Data templates are pieces of XAML markup that specify how bound data should be displayed. They enable you to set the appearance and behavior of bound data as well as specify related fields to be displayed. You can set a data template for an item control by setting the *ItemTemplate* property, and you can set the data template for a content control by setting the *ContentTemplate* property.

- You can apply sorting to data by accessing the default collection view and adding a new sort description to the *SortDescriptions* property. Standard sorting enables you to sort based on a data field value in either ascending or descending mode. You can create custom sorts by creating a class that implements *IComparer* and setting it to the *CustomSort* property.

- You can create groups of data by adding a new *PropertyGroupDescription* param-eter to the *GroupDescriptions* property of the default collection view. You can set the header and other formatting for groups by setting the *GroupStyle* property of the item control that binds the data.

- You can specify a delegate to perform filtering by creating a Boolean method that performs the filtering and specifying a *Predicate<object>* delegate that points to that method. This does not work with ADO.NET objects, however, and you must set the *CustomFilter* property to a filter expression to filter ADO.NET records.

Lesson Review

You can use the following questions to test your knowledge of the information in Lesson 2, "Manipulating and Displaying Data." The questions are also available on the companion CD if you prefer to review them in electronic form.

> **NOTE ANSWERS**
>
> Answers to these questions and explanations of why each answer choice is correct or incor-rect are located in the "Answers" section at the end of the book.

1. Which of the following code samples correctly demonstrates a data template that binds the *ContactName* field set in *ListBox*? Assume that *DataContext* is set correctly.

   A.

```
<ListBox ItemsSource="{Binding}" name="ListBox1">
   <DataTemplate>
      <Label Content="{Binding Path=ContactName}" BorderBrush="Black"
```

```
              Background="Yellow" BorderThickness="3" Foreground="Blue" />
      </DataTemplate>
   </ListBox>
```

B.

```
<ListBox name="ListBox1">
   <ListBox.ItemsSource>
      <DataTemplate>
         <Label Content="{Binding Path=ContactName}" BorderBrush="Black"
              Background="Yellow" BorderThickness="3" Foreground="Blue" />
      </DataTemplate>
   </ListBox.ItemsSource>
</ListBox>
```

C.

```
<ListBox ItemsSource="{Binding}" name="ListBox1">
   <ListBox.ItemTemplate>
      <Label Content="{Binding Path=ContactName}" BorderBrush="Black"
           Background="Yellow" BorderThickness="3" Foreground="Blue" />
   </ListBox.ItemTemplate>
</ListBox>
```

D.

```
<ListBox ItemsSource="{Binding}" name="ListBox1">
   <ListBox.ItemTemplate>
      <DataTemplate>
         <Label Content="{Binding Path=ContactName}" BorderBrush="Black"
              Background="Yellow" BorderThickness="3" Foreground="Blue" />
      </DataTemplate>
   </ListBox.ItemTemplate>
</ListBox>
```

2. Which of the following code samples correctly sets the filter on the *CollectionView* object *myView*?

   A.

   Sample of Visual Basic Code

```
myView.Filter = New Predicate(Of Object)(AddressOf myFilter)

Public Function myFilter(ByVal param As Object) As Boolean
   Return (param.ToString.Length > 8)
End Function
```

   Sample of C# Code

```
myView.Filter = new Predicate<object>(myFilter);

public bool myFilter(object param)
{
   return (param.ToString().Length > 8);
}
```

B.

Sample of Visual Basic Code

```
myView.Filter = New Predicate(Of Object)(AddressOf myFilter)
Public Function myFilter(ByVal param As Object) As Object
    Return (param.ToString.Length > 8)
End Function
```

Sample of C# Code

```
myView.Filter = new Predicate<object>(myFilter);

public object myFilter(object param)
{
    return (param.ToString().Length > 8);
}
```

C.

Sample of Visual Basic Code

```
myView.CustomFilter = New Predicate(Of Object)(AddressOf myFilter)

Public Function myFilter(ByVal param As Object) As Boolean
    Return (param.ToString.Length > 8)
End Function
```

Sample of C# Code

```
myView.CustomFilter = new Predicate<object>(myFilter);

public bool myFilter(object param)
{
    return (param.ToString().Length > 8);
}
```

D.

Sample of Visual Basic Code

```
myView.CustomFilter = New Predicate(Of Object)(AddressOf myFilter)
Public Function myFilter(ByVal param As Object) As Object
    Return (param.ToString.Length > 8)
End Function
```

Sample of C# Code

```
myView.CustomFilter = new Predicate<object>(myFilter);

public object myFilter(object param)
{
    return (param.ToString().Length > 8);
}
```

Case Scenarios

In the following case scenarios, you apply what you've learned about configuring data binding. You can find answers to these questions in the "Answers" section at the end of this book.

Case Scenario 1: Getting Information from the Field

Field agents are diligently scouring the world trying to locate new supplies of "stuff" for your company's ongoing research efforts. They need to relay regular reports to us in a specific format, which will be logged into our central database. Each of the agents is equipped with a laptop and a satellite Internet connection, but direct connections to the company database are impossible. They also have a report generator that outputs XML files and e-mails them to the mail-handling program, which stores them as raw XML in a queue where they can be vetted by support staff before being saved in the database. You are in charge of creating an application to help these support staff handle the data processing.

Technical Requirements

- XML files can be read, but they must not be altered in any way.
- The user must be able to edit the information before saving it into the central database.

Answer the following question for your manager:

- What is the ideal data access strategy for our application?

Case Scenario 2: Viewing Customer Data

One of your company's clients has contracted with you to create an application to help maximize his business potential. He wants to view customer records that meet any of several specific sets of criteria: customers who buy big-ticket items, customers who buy a lot of small items, customers who buy only in April, and so on. And he wants to view them all at once, but he wants them to be arranged in groups by these criteria. He does not want to see any records that do not match any of the criteria groups. All the information required by the application is available in the database he is supplying.

Technical Requirements

- The application should display only records that fall into one of the criteria groups.
- The records should be arranged by criteria group.

Answer the following question for your manager:

- How can you design the application to achieve the grouping the client wants, with minimal development time?

Suggested Practices

To help you successfully master the exam objectives presented in this chapter, complete the following tasks.

- **Practice 1** Create a Really Simple Syndication (RSS) reader that downloads and formats RSS data by using *XmlDataProvider*.

- **Practice 2** Create an application that accesses the Northwind database and enables the user to filter on the *CompanyName* element.

Take a Practice Test

The practice tests on this book's companion CD offer many options. For example, you can test yourself on just the content covered in this chapter, or you can test yourself on all the 70-511 certification exam content. You can set up the test so that it closely simulates the experience of taking a certification exam, or you can set it up in study mode so that you can look at the correct answers and explanations after you answer each question.

> **MORE INFO** **PRACTICE TESTS**
>
> For details about all the practice test options available, see the "How to Use the Practice Tests" section in this book's Introduction.

CHAPTER 8

Working with Data Grids and Validating User Input

The display of data in a grid form has been a constant meme in data display ever since the introduction of spreadsheets and, to this day, remains one of the most popular formats for presenting data to the user. In Lesson 1, "Implementing Data-bound Controls in Windows Forms," you learn to use the *DataGridView* control for viewing data in Windows Forms applications and the *DataGrid* control for viewing data in Windows Presentation Foundation (WPF) applications. In Lesson 2, "Validating User Input," you learn how to validate user input at the field level in both Windows Forms and WPF and implement *IDataErrorInfo* for WPF applications.

Exam objectives in this chapter:

- Implement data validation.
- Implement data-bound controls.

Lessons in this chapter:

Before You Begin

To complete the lessons in this chapter, you must have:

- A computer that meets or exceeds the minimum hardware requirements listed in the "About This Book" section at the beginning of the book.
- Microsoft Visual Studio 2010 Professional installed on your computer.
- An understanding of Microsoft Visual Basic or C# syntax and familiarity with Microsoft .NET Framework 4.0.
- An understanding of Extensible Application Markup Language (XAML).

 REAL WORLD

Matthew Stoecker

For simple display of data tables, nothing beats *DataGrid*. A glaring hole in previous versions of WPF development technology was the lack of a *DataGrid* control, but with the release of Visual Studio 2010, this highly flexible and useful control is now available for use in your applications.

Lesson 1: Implementing Data-bound Controls in Windows Forms

Binding data is one of the fundamental tasks in developing a user interface. In this lesson, you learn how to bind Windows Forms controls to data and navigate a bound data source. You can bind simple controls, such as *TextBox* or *Label*, to a single element of data, or you can bind complex controls, such as *DataGridView* and *ComboBox*, to multiple elements of data. You also learn how to use a *BindingSource* component and a *DataNavigator* component to navigate data in your user interface. Additionally, you learn to use the *DataGridView* control for viewing complex data in Windows Forms applications and the *DataGrid* control for WPF applications.

> **After this lesson, you will be able to:**
>
> - Use a simple data-bound control to display a single data element on a Windows Form.
> - Implement complex data binding to integrate data from multiple sources.
> - Navigate forward and backward through records in a data set in Windows Forms.
> - Enhance navigation through a data set by using the *DataNavigator* component.
> - Define a data source by using a *DataConnector* component.
>
> **Estimated lesson time: 45 minutes**

Binding Controls to Data

Binding controls to data is the process of displaying data in Windows Forms controls and creating a connection between the control and the underlying data source.

Simple *data binding* describes the process of displaying a single element of data in a control—for example, a *TextBox* control displaying the value from a single column in a table, such as a company name.

Complex data binding describes the process of binding a control to more than one source of data. For example, consider a combo box that displays a list of category names. What if the table you are displaying has only a category ID, such as the Products and Categories tables in the Northwind sample database? You can use complex data binding to display the value from a column in one *DataTable* source based on a foreign key value in another *DataTable* source.

Simple Data Binding

Simple data binding is the process of binding a single element of data to a single control property, such as a *TextBox* control displaying the *ProductName* column from a table (in its *Text* property).

The following code shows how to bind the *ProductName* column from a data table to a text box named *TextBox1*:

Sample of Visual Basic Code

```
TextBox1.DataBindings.Add("Text", productsBindingSource, "ProductName")
```

Sample of C# Code

```
TextBox1.DataBindings.Add("Text", productsBindingSource, "ProductName");
```

Complex Data Binding

Complex data binding is binding more than one element of data to more than one property of a control—for example, a *DataGridView* control that displays an entire table, or a *List* control that displays multiple columns of data.

Controls that enable complex data binding typically contain a *DataSource* property and a *DataMember* property. The *DataSource* property is usually a *BindingSource* or *DataSet* object. The *DataMember* property is typically the table or collection to actually display.

The following code shows how to bind *DataGridView* to the Northwind Customers table, using a *BindingSource* component:

Sample of Visual Basic Code

```
Dim customersBindingSource As New BindingSource(NorthwindDataSet1, "Customers")
DataGridView1.DataSource = customersBindingSource
```

Sample of C# Code

```
BindingSource customersBindingSource = new BindingSource(northwindDataSet1,
"Customers");
DataGridView1.DataSource = customersBindingSource;
```

The following code shows how to bind *DataGridView* to the Northwind Customers table, using a data set:

Sample of Visual Basic Code

```
DataGridView1.DataSource = NorthwindDataSet1
DataGridView1.DataMember = "Customers"
```

Sample of C# Code

```
DataGridView1.DataSource = northwindDataSet1;
DataGridView1.DataMember = "Customers";
```

Navigating Records in a Data Set

You can use a *BindingNavigator* component to navigate the records in a data source. Assign the *BindingNavigator.BindingSource* property a valid *BindingSource* component, and you can use *BindingNavigator* to move back and forth through the records in that data source.

BindingNavigator uses the navigational methods available on the *BindingSource* component to navigate records. For example, *MoveNext* and *MovePrevious* methods are available on the *BindingSource* component.

Defining a Data Source Using a *BindingSource* Component

The *BindingSource* component contains the information that a control needs to bind to a binding source by passing it a reference to a *DataTable* component in *DataSet*. By binding to *BindingSource* instead of to *DataSet*, you can easily redirect your application to another source of data without having to redirect all the data-binding code to point to the new data source.

The following code shows how to create a *BindingSource* component and assign it a reference to the Northwind Customers table:

Sample of Visual Basic Code

```
customersBindingSource = New BindingSource(NorthwindDataSet1, "Customers")
```

Sample of C# Code

```
customersBindingSource = new BindingSource(northwindDataSet1, "Customers");
```

 Quick Check

1. What is the difference between simple and complex binding?
2. How do you navigate back and forth through the records in a data table?

Quick Check Answers

1. Simple binding binds an individual bit of data (such as a field or column) to a single property of the control to bind to, whereas complex binding binds multiple bits of data to multiple properties of a control.
2. Navigate by calling the *Move* methods of a *BindingSource* component or by displaying a data set in the *DataGridView* control.

Displaying Data in *DataGridView*

To display a data set in a *DataGridView* control or, more specifically, to display a data table in *DataGridView*, set the *DataSource* property of *DataGridView* to *DataSet* and set the *DataMember* property of *DataGridView* to the name of the data table. For example, the following code displays the Northwind Customers table in *DataGridView*:

Sample of Visual Basic Code

```
DataGridView1.DataSource = NorthwindDataSet1
DataGridView1.DataMember = "Customers"
```

Sample of C# Code

```
DataGridView1.DataSource = northwindDataSet1;
DataGridView1.DataMember = "Customers";
```

You can also set a *DataGridView* control to display a data set by using the smart tag available on a *DataGridView* control: this is accomplished by selecting the data set in the Choose Data Source combo box available on the smart tag. The Choose Data Source command enables you to select a data set and data table to display from the *DataSet* list already defined in your project, or you can create a new data set to display by selecting Add Project Data Source on the smart tag, which starts the Data Source Configuration wizard.

Configuring *DataGridView* Columns

There are six built-in types of columns you can use in *DataGridView*, as outlined in Table 8-1. When adding columns to *DataGridView*, select the type of column based on the data you plan to display in it.

TABLE 8-1 *DataGridView* Column Types

COLUMN TYPE	DESCRIPTION
DataGridViewTextBoxColumn	Use this column type to display text and numeric values. A data-bound *DataGridView* control automatically generates this type of column when binding to strings and numeric values.
DataGridViewCheckBoxColumn	Use this column to display Boolean values. *DataGridView* automatically generates this type of column when binding to Boolean values.
DataGridViewImageColumn	Use this column to display images. *DataGridView* automatically generates this type of column when binding to *Image* and *Icon* objects. You can also bind a *DataGridViewImage* column to a byte array.
DataGridViewButtonColumn	Use this column to provide users with a button control.
DataGridViewComboBoxColumn	Use this column type to present lists of choices. This would typically be used for lookups to other tables.
DataGridViewLinkColumn	Use this column type to display links to other data.
Custom Column	If none of the preceding column types provides the specific functionality you require, you can always create a custom column type. To create a custom column, define your class to inherit from *DataGridViewColumn* or any class with a base class of *DataGridViewColumn*. (For example, inherit from *DataGridViewTextBoxColumn* to extend the functionality of that type.)

Adding Tables and Columns to *DataGridView*

To display a table in *DataGridView*, define the columns that make up the schema of the table and add them to *DataGridView*. You can add columns to *DataGridView* with designers using the Add Column dialog box or programmatically in code.

First, decide which type of column to use (refer to Table 8-1) and then use one of the following procedures to add the column to your *DataGridView* control.

Adding Columns to *DataGridView* Using the Designer

To add columns to *DataGridView* in the designer, follow these steps:

1. Select *DataGridView* on your form.
2. Open the smart tag of *DataGridView*.
3. Select Add Column.
4. In the Add Column dialog box, define the column by setting the appropriate values in the dialog box.

Adding Columns to *DataGridView* Programmatically

To add columns to *DataGridView* in code, create an instance of the appropriate type of column, define the column by setting the appropriate properties, and then add the column to the *DataGridView.Columns* collection.

For example, the following code sample creates a new text box column named ProductName:

Sample of Visual Basic Code

```
Dim ProductNameColumn As New DataGridViewTextBoxColumn
ProductNameColumn.Name = "ProductName"
ProductNameColumn.HeaderText = "Product Name"
ProductNameColumn.ValueType = System.Type.GetType("System.String")
DataGridView1.Columns.Add(ProductNameColumn)
```

Sample of C# Code

```
DataGridViewTextBoxColumn ProductNameColumn = new DataGridViewTextBoxColumn();
ProductNameColumn.Name = "ProductName";
ProductNameColumn.HeaderText = "Product Name";
ProductNameColumn.ValueType = System.Type.GetType("System.String");
DataGridView1.Columns.Add(ProductNameColumn); .
```

Deleting Columns in *DataGridView*

You can delete columns in *DataGridView* by using the designer in Visual Studio or programmatically in code.

Deleting Columns in *DataGridView* Using the Designer

To delete columns in a *DataGridView* using the designer, complete the following steps:

1. Select the *DataGridView* on your form.

2. Open the smart tag for the *DataGridView*.

3. Select Edit Columns.

4. In the Edit Columns dialog box, select the column you want to remove from the *DataGridView*.

5. Click the Remove button.

Deleting Columns in a *DataGridView* Programmatically

To delete columns in *DataGridView* in code, call the *Remove* method and provide the name of the column you want to delete. For example, the following code example deletes a column named ProductName from *DataGridView1*:

Sample of Visual Basic Code

```
DataGridView1.Columns.Remove("ProductName")
```

Sample of C# Code

```
DataGridView1.Columns.Remove["ProductName"];
```

Determining the Clicked Cell in *DataGridView*

To determine the clicked cell, use the *DataGridView.CurrentCell* property. *CurrentCell* provides a reference to the currently selected cell and provides properties to access the value of the data in the cell, as well as the row and column index of the cell's current location in *DataGridView*. For example:

Sample of Visual Basic Code

```
Dim CurrentCellValue As String
CurrentCellValue = CustomersDataGridView.CurrentCell.Value.ToString
```

Sample of C# Code

```
String CurrentCellValue;
CurrentCellValue = CustomersDataGridView.CurrentCell.Value.ToString();
```

Validating Input in the *DataGridView* Control

To validate input in an individual cell in a *DataGridView* control, handle the *DataGridView.CellValidating* event and cancel the edit if the value fails validation. The *CellValidating* event is raised when a cell loses focus. Add code to the event handler for the *CellValidating* event to verify that the values in specific columns conform to your business rules and application logic. The event arguments contain the proposed value in the cell, as well as the row and column index of the cell being edited.

For example, the following code validates that the ProductName column does not contain an empty string (use this sample for a *DataGridView* control that is not bound to data):

Sample of Visual Basic Code

```vb
If DataGridView1.Columns(e.ColumnIndex).Name = "ProductName" Then
    If e.FormattedValue.ToString = "" Then
        dataGridView1.Rows(e.RowIndex).ErrorText = "Product Name is a required field"
        e.Cancel = True
    Else
        dataGridView1.Rows(e.RowIndex).ErrorText = ""
    End If
End If
```

Sample of C# Code

```csharp
if (DataGridView1.Columns[e.ColumnIndex].Name == "ProductName")
{
    if (e.FormattedValue.ToString() == "")
    {
        DataGridView1.Rows[e.RowIndex].ErrorText = "Product Name is a required field";
        e.Cancel = true;
    }
    else
    {
        DataGridView1.Rows[e.RowIndex].ErrorText = "";
    }
}
```

The following code also validates that the ProductName column does not contain an empty string. Use this example for a *DataGridView* control that *is* bound to data. The difference from the preceding example is shown in bold.

Sample of Visual Basic Code

```vb
If DataGridView1.Columns(e.ColumnIndex).DataPropertyName = "ProductName" Then
    If e.FormattedValue.ToString = "" Then
        dataGridView1.Rows(e.RowIndex).ErrorText = "Product Name is a required field"
        e.Cancel = True
    Else
        dataGridView1.Rows(e.RowIndex).ErrorText = ""
    End If
End If
```

Sample of C# Code

```csharp
if (DataGridView1.Columns[e.ColumnIndex].DataPropertyName == "ProductName")
{
    if (e.FormattedValue.ToString() == "")
    {
        DataGridView1.Rows[e.RowIndex].ErrorText = "Product Name is a required field";
        e.Cancel = true;
    }
    else
    {
        DataGridView1.Rows[e.RowIndex].ErrorText = "";
    }
}
```

Format a *DataGridView* Control by Using Custom Painting

To format a *DataGridView* control by using custom painting, you can handle the *CellPainting* event and insert your own custom painting code. When you handle the *CellPainting* event, *DataGridViewCellPaintingEventArgs* provides access to many properties that simplify custom painting. When you handle the *CellPainting* event, be sure to set *e.Handled* to *True* so the grid does not call its own cell painting routine.

To paint all cells *LightSkyBlue*, place the following code in the *CellPainting* event handler:

Sample of Visual Basic Code

```
' Paint the cell background color LightSkyBlue
e.Graphics.FillRectangle(Brushes.LightSkyBlue, e.CellBounds)

' Draw the contents of the cell
If Not (e.Value Is Nothing) Then
    e.Graphics.DrawString(e.Value.ToString, e.CellStyle.Font, _
        Brushes.Black, e.CellBounds.X, e.CellBounds.Y)
End If
e.Handled = True
```

Sample of C# Code

```
// Paint the cell background color LightSkyBlue
e.Graphics.FillRectangle(Brushes.LightSkyBlue, e.CellBounds);
// Draw the contents of the cell
if (e.Value != null)
{
    e.Graphics.DrawString(e.Value.ToString(), e.CellStyle.Font,
        Brushes.Black, e.CellBounds.X, e.CellBounds.Y);
}
e.Handled = true;
```

> ✔ **Quick Check**
>
> 1. What properties do you set on a *DataGridView* control to display a specific data table?
>
> 2. How do you determine what cell is clicked in a *DataGridView* control?
>
> **Quick Check Answers**
>
> 1. Set the *DataSource* property to the *DataSet* and the *DataMember* properties to the name of the data table.
>
> 2. Inspect the *DataGridView.CurrentCell* property.

Using *DataGrid* in WPF Applications

The WPF *DataGrid* control is analogous to the Windows Forms *DataGridView* control in that it is designed to display tables of data in a cohesive format. You can add columns manually to your *DataGrid* control, or it will automatically create appropriate columns for your data based on the schema of the data source.

Binding Data Sources to a *DataGrid* Control

A *DataGrid* control can be bound to a data source that implements the *IEnumerable* interface. By default, it will automatically create columns for the properties of the bound object and will create rows that display the values of those properties for each object in the data source. You can set the data source for a *DataGrid* control by setting the *ItemsSource* property in code, as shown here:

Sample of Visual Basic Code

```
' Refers to a Binding already present in code
DataGrid1.ItemsSource = myCustomersBinding
```

Sample of C# Code

```
// Refers to a DataTableView already present in code
dataGrid1.ItemsSource = myCustomersBinding;
```

Or, more commonly, you will set the data source in XAML by setting the *ItemsSource* property, as shown here:

```
<Window.Resources>
        <my:NwindDataSet x:Key="NwindDataSet" />
        <CollectionViewSource x:Key="CustomersViewSource" Source="{Binding
Path=Customers,
            Source={StaticResource NwindDataSet}}" />
</Window.Resources>
    <Grid DataContext="{StaticResource CustomersViewSource}">
        <DataGrid ItemsSource="{Binding}"
            <!-- Additional implementation omitted -->
        </DataGrid>
    </Grid>
```

For changes in the collection to be updated automatically in the *DataGrid* control, the collection to which the *DataGrid* control is bound must implement *INotifyCollectionChanged*, such as *ObservableCollection*. For changes to property values to be reflected in real time, the bound properties must implement *INotifyPropertyChanged*.

Binding a *DataGrid* Control to a Data Source in Your Project

If you have already added a data source, such as an ADO.NET database, to your project, you can easily create a bound *DataGrid* control in your application through the Data Sources window.

To create a bound data grid through the Data Sources window:

1. If the Data Sources window is not already visible, choose Show Data Sources from the Data menu. The Data Sources window opens.

2. In the Data Sources window, each available data table should have a grid symbol next to it. If a grid symbol is not shown, highlight the data table, click the drop-down menu, and choose DataGrid.

3. With the grid symbol showing next to the data table, drag the data table from the Data Sources window to the design surface of the form. A *DataGrid* control representing the data table is added to your project.

Using *DataGrid* Columns

The columns displayed in the *DataGrid* control are very configurable and can be manipulated at design time through the Columns Collection editor in Visual Studio, shown in Figure 8-1. To make the Columns Collection editor appear, click the ellipses (...) to the right of the *Columns* property in the Property grid.

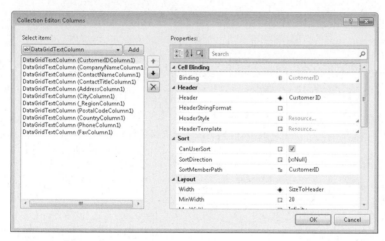

FIGURE 8-1 The Collection Editor.

Using the Collection editor, you can add and remove *DataGrid* columns, as well as change the properties of individual columns.

When a *DataGrid* control is bound to a data source, appropriate columns are automatically generated for the data set. Depending on the data type of the bound property, types of columns are generated as shown in Table 8-2.

TABLE 8-2 DataGrid Column Types

DATA TYPE	GENERATED COLUMN TYPE
Boolean	DataGridCheckBoxColumn
Enum	DataGridComboBoxColumn
String	DataGridTextBoxColumn
Uri	DataGridHyperlinkColumn

If you want to provide custom functionality during column auto-generation, handle the *DataGrid.AutoGeneratingColumn* property. To turn automatic column generation off and set all columns manually, set the *AutoGenerateColumns* property to *False*.

Using *DataGridTemplateColumn*

For other data types, or to create your own custom data columns, you can use a column of type *DataGridTemplateColumn*, which is a customizable column that enables you to define three *DataTemplate* objects that govern the appearance and behavior of the column. The *HeaderTemplate* property of *DataGridTemplateColumn* determines the data template that will be used for the column header. The *CellTemplate* property determines the data template that will be used for cells when data is being displayed, and the *CellEditingTemplate* property indicates the data template used when data in the cell is being edited. These templates should be defined in your Windows or Application resources as shown here:

```
<Window.Resources>
    <my:NwindDataSet x:Key="NwindDataSet" />
    <CollectionViewSource x:Key="CustomersViewSource"
        Source="{Binding Path=Customers, Source={StaticResource NwindDataSet}}" />
    <DataTemplate x:Key="myHeaderTemplate">
        <Label Background="Purple" Foreground="Yellow" Content="{Binding}"/>
    </DataTemplate>
    <DataTemplate x:Key="myCellTemplate">
        <Button Foreground="Red" Content="{Binding Path=CompanyName}"/>
    </DataTemplate>
    <DataTemplate x:Key="myCellEditingTemplate">
        <TextBox Background="Red" Text="{Binding Path=CompanyName}"/>
    </DataTemplate>
</Window.Resources>
```

In this example, *HeaderTemplate* defines a purple label with yellow text. This will be seen only in the *DataGrid* header, and the empty binding the *Content* property is set to ensure that the *Content* property will be bound to the *Header* property of the column.

CellTemplate in this example creates a *Button* control that displays the bound CompanyName in red as the content of the button. *CellEditingTemplate* displays a text box with the background in red, also bound to the same CompanyName. *CellEditingTemplate* is displayed whenever *BeginEditCommand* is processed for that cell—for example, when the cell is selected and the F2 button is pressed, and *CellTemplate* will be displayed when editing is committed or cancelled.

In addition to providing templates, you can instead set *TemplateSelector* controls to provide dynamic selection of the template to use for the header, cell, and cell editing. You can provide these through the *HeaderTemplateSelector*, *CellTemplateSelector*, and *CellEditingTemplateSelector* properties, respectively. See Chapter 7, "Configuring Data Binding," for further information about using *TemplateSelector* controls.

Using Row Details

In some cases, you might want to display some data about a row only when that row is selected. For example, if a data table has several columns, you might want to display only a subset in the grid itself, and then display other columns in a specialized format only when a row of data is being inspected. You can access this functionality through the *RowDetailsTemplate* property, which enables you to create a data template that will display additional data beneath a row in the data grid when that row is selected. Consider the following example:

```
<DataTemplate x:Key="myRowDetailsTemplate">
    <StackPanel DataContext="{StaticResource OrdersViewSource}"
        Orientation="Horizontal">
        <Label Content="Order Date" Background="Red" />
        <DatePicker Text="{Binding Path=OrderDate}" />
        <Label Content="Required Date" Background="Red" />
        <DatePicker Text="{Binding Path=RequiredDate}" />
    </StackPanel>
</DataTemplate>
```

This example demonstrates a data template to be used for a *RowDetailsTemplate* control. It defines a *StackPanel* control that contains four other controls: two labels and two *DatePicker* controls that are bound to the *OrderDate* and *RequiredDate* fields. At run time, the values of these bound fields will be displayed next to the labels underneath the selected row. By default, row details are visible only for the selected row. You can make them visible for all rows by setting the *RowDetailsVisibilityMode* property to *Visible*, or you can always hide them by setting the *RowDetailsVisibilityMode* to *Collapsed*.

You can also define a template selector to use for row details by setting the *RowDetailsTemplateSelector* property.

PRACTICE   **Working with *DataGridView***

In this practice, you work with data in a *DataGridView* control.

EXERCISE   Working with *DataGridView*

First, you create a Windows Forms application and see how to manipulate the definition as well as the columns and data in a *DataGridView* control.

1. Create a Windows Forms application and name it **DataGridViewExample**.

2. Open the Data Sources window (on the Data menu, select Show Data Sources).

3. Click Add New Data Source to start the Data Source Configuration Wizard.

4. Leave the default of Database and click Next twice.

5. Select (or create) a connection to the Northwind sample database by browsing to the database file and selecting it; click Next. When prompted, click Yes and then Next again.

6. Expand the Tables node. Select the Customers table and then click Finish.

7. Drag the Customers node from the Data Sources window onto the form.

   At this point, you can actually run the application, and the form appears with the Customers table loaded into a *DataGridView* control.

8. Drag two *Button* controls onto the form below *DataGridView* and set the following properties:

   - Button1:
     - *Name* = AddColumnButton
     - *Text* = Add Column
   - Button2:
     - *Name* = DeleteColumnButton
     - *Text* = Delete Column

9. Double-click the Add Column button to create the button-click event handler and to open the form in code view.

10. Add the following code to *Form1*. The additional code in the *Form1_Load* event creates a new column on the data table, and the code in the *AddColumnButton_Click* event handler adds a new column to *DataGridView*:

Sample of Visual Basic Code

```vb
Private Sub Form1_Load(ByVal sender As System.Object, _
    ByVal e As System.EventArgs) _
    Handles MyBase.Load
    'TODO: This line of code loads data into the
    'NwindDataSet.Customers table. You can move, or remove
    'it, As needed.
    Me.CustomersTableAdapter.Fill(Me.NwindDataSet.Customers)

    ' Add a new column to the Customers DataTable
    ' to be used to demonstrate adding and removing
    ' columns in a DataGridView in the methods below
    Dim Location As New DataColumn("Location")
    Location.Expression = "City + ', ' + Country"
    NwindDataSet.Customers.Columns.Add(Location)
End Sub

Private Sub AddColumnButton_Click(ByVal sender As System.Object, _
    ByVal e As System.EventArgs) _
    Handles AddColumnButton.Click
```

```vb
    Dim LocationColumn As New DataGridViewTextBoxColumn
    LocationColumn.Name = "LocationColumn"
    LocationColumn.HeaderText = "Location"
    LocationColumn.DataPropertyName = "Location"
    CustomersDataGridView.Columns.Add(LocationColumn)
End Sub
```

Sample of C# Code

```csharp
private void Form1_Load(object sender, EventArgs e)
{
    // TODO: This line of code loads data into the
    // nwindDataSet.Customers table. You can move, or
    // remove it, as needed.
    this.customersTableAdapter.Fill(this.nwindDataSet.Customers);
    // Add a new column to the Customers DataTable
    // to be used to demonstrate adding and removing
    // columns in a DataGridView in the methods below
    DataColumn Location = new DataColumn("Location");
    Location.Expression = "City + ', ' + Country";
    nwindDataSet.Customers.Columns.Add(Location);
}

private void AddColumnButton_Click(object sender, EventArgs e)
{
    DataGridViewTextBoxColumn LocationColumn = new
        DataGridViewTextBoxColumn();
    LocationColumn.Name = "LocationColumn";
    LocationColumn.HeaderText = "Location";
    LocationColumn.DataPropertyName = "Location";
    customersDataGridView.Columns.Add(LocationColumn);
}
```

11. In the designer, double-click the Delete Column button to create the
    DeleteColumnButton_Click event handler. Add the following code to the
    DeleteColumnButton_Click event handler:

    Sample of Visual Basic Code

    ```vb
    Try
        CustomersDataGridView.Columns.Remove("LocationColumn")
    Catch ex As Exception
        MessageBox.Show(ex.Message)
    End Try
    ```

    Sample of C# Code

    ```csharp
    try
    {
        customersDataGridView.Columns.Remove("LocationColumn");
    }
    catch (Exception ex)
    {
        MessageBox.Show(ex.Message);
    }
    ```

12. Drag another *Button* control onto the form and set the following properties:

- *Name* = GetClickedCellButton
- *Text* = Get Clicked Cell

13. Drag a *Label* control onto the form and place it next to the Get Clicked Cell button.

14. Double-click the Get Clicked Cell button and add the following code to the *GetClickedCellButton_Click* event handler:

Sample of Visual Basic Code

```
Dim CurrentCellInfo As String
CurrentCellInfo = _
    CustomersDataGridView.CurrentCell.Value.ToString & _
    Environment.NewLine
CurrentCellInfo += "Column: " & _
    CustomersDataGridView.CurrentCell.OwningColumn.DataPropertyName & _
    Environment.NewLine
CurrentCellInfo += "Column Index: " & CustomersDataGridView.CurrentCell.
ColumnIndex.ToString & _
    Environment.NewLine
CurrentCellInfo += "Row Index: " & _
    CustomersDataGridView.CurrentCell.RowIndex.ToString

Label1.Text = CurrentCellInfo
```

Sample of C# Code

```
string CurrentCellInfo;
CurrentCellInfo = customersDataGridView.CurrentCell.Value.ToString() +
    Environment.NewLine;
CurrentCellInfo += "Column: " +
    customersDataGridView.CurrentCell.OwningColumn.DataPropertyName +
    Environment.NewLine;
CurrentCellInfo += "Column Index: " + customersDataGridView.CurrentCell.
ColumnIndex.ToString() +
    Environment.NewLine;
CurrentCellInfo += "Row Index: " +
    customersDataGridView.CurrentCell.RowIndex.ToString();

label1.Text = CurrentCellInfo;
```

15. Create an event handler for the *CustomersDataGridView.CellValidating* event. (Select the *CustomersDataGridView* control on the form, click the Events icon in the Properties window, and double-click the *CellValidating* event.)

16. Add the following code to the *CellValidating* event handler:

Sample of Visual Basic Code

```
If CustomersDataGridView.Columns(e.ColumnIndex).DataPropertyName = _
    "ContactName" Then
    If e.FormattedValue.ToString = "" Then
        CustomersDataGridView.Rows(e.RowIndex).ErrorText = _
            "ContactName is a required field"
        e.Cancel = True
    Else
```

```
        CustomersDataGridView.Rows(e.RowIndex).ErrorText = ""
    End If
End If
```

Sample of C# Code

```csharp
if (customersDataGridView.Columns[e.ColumnIndex].DataPropertyName ==
    "ContactName")
{
    if (e.FormattedValue.ToString() == "")
    {
        customersDataGridView.Rows[e.RowIndex].ErrorText =
        "ContactName is a required field";
        e.Cancel = true;
    }
    else
    {
        customersDataGridView.Rows[e.RowIndex].ErrorText = "";
    }
}
```

17. Drag another *Button* control onto the form and set the following properties:

    ■ *Name* = ApplyStyleButton

    ■ *Text* = Apply Style

18. Double-click the Apply Style button and add the following code to the *ApplyStyleButton_Click* event handler:

    Sample of Visual Basic Code

    ```vb
    CustomersDataGridView.AlternatingRowsDefaultCellStyle.BackColor = _
        Color.LightGray
    ```

    Sample of C# Code

    ```csharp
    customersDataGridView.AlternatingRowsDefaultCellStyle.BackColor =
        Color.LightGray;
    ```

19. Run the application.

20. Click the Add Column button and then scroll to the end of the columns to verify that the new Location column is there.

21. Click the Delete Column button and verify that the Location column is deleted from *DataGridView*.

22. Select any cell in the grid and then click the Get Clicked Cell button. The *Label* control displays the contents of the cell, the name of the column the cell is in, and the column and row index of the cell.

23. Finally, click the Apply Style button. The *AlternatingRowsDefaultCellStyle* style is set up to display alternating rows with a light gray background.

Lesson Summary

- *DataGridView* is the preferred control for displaying tabular data such as a data table in a Windows Forms application. In a WPF application, the *DataGrid* control is used.

- You can add columns to and remove columns from a *DataGridView* control in the designer by using the Add Column and Edit Column dialog boxes available from the smart tag of *DataGridView*.

- The *DataGridView.CurrentCell* property provides access to the currently selected cell in a *DataGridView* control.

- *DataGridView* raises a *CellValidating* event through which you can add code that verifies that the value in a column conforms to your business rules and application logic.

- You can format the look of *DataGridView* by using styles and custom painting.

- You can create custom columns in a data grid by setting the *HeaderTemplate*, *CellTemplate*, and *CellEditingTemplate* properties of *DataGridTemplateColumn*.

- You can provide customized row details by setting the *RowDetailsTemplate* property of *DataGrid*.

Lesson Review

You can use the following questions to test your knowledge of the information in Lesson 1, "Implementing Data-bound Controls in Windows Forms." The questions are also available on the companion CD if you prefer to review them in electronic form.

> **NOTE ANSWERS**
>
> Answers to these questions and explanations of why each answer choice is correct or incorrect are located in the "Answers" section at the end of the book.

1. What is the best way to determine which cell a user clicks in *DataGridView*?

    A. Use the column and row index of the selected cell.

    B. Use the *DataGridView.CurrentCell* property.

    C. Use the cursor position's *x* and *y* coordinates.

    D. Use the currently selected column and row in the bound *DataTable* control to determine the clicked cell.

2. What is the preferred method of validating input in *DataGridView*?

    A. By adding validation code to the *CellPainting* event handler

    B By adding validation code to the *DataGridView.CellClick* event handler

    C. By adding validation code to the *DataGridView.CellValidating* event handler

    D. By adding code to the *DataGridView* partial class file

3. What is the best way to display a Boolean value in *DataGridView*?

   A. Configure *DataGridViewTextBoxColumn* and display *True* or *False*.

   B. Configure *DataGridViewCheckBoxColumn* to display a check box that is selected or cleared.

   C. Configure *DataGridViewButtonColumn* to display a button that indicates pressed or not pressed.

   D. Configure a custom column to display *Yes* or *No*.

Lesson 2: Validating User Input

In most applications, the user enters information for the application through the user inter-face. Data validation ensures that all data entered by a user falls within acceptable parameters before proceeding with program execution. For example, you might have a field in which a user enters a ZIP code as part of an address. Using validation, you could verify that the field contained five and only five characters, all of which were numeric, before proceeding. Validating user input reduces the chance of an input error and makes your application more robust.

In this lesson, you learn how to use events to validate user input and direct the focus on your forms. You learn how to use field-level validation, which validates entries as they are made, and form-level validation, which validates all the entries on a form at once. You learn how to use control properties to help restrict input and use the *ErrorProvider* component to provide informative error messages to your users.

After this lesson, you will be able to:

- Explain the difference between form-level and field-level validation.
- Direct the focus using control methods and events.
- Implement form-level validation for your form.
- Implement field-level validation for your form.

Estimated lesson time: 30 minutes

You can choose between two types of validation for user input: form-level validation and field-level validation. Form-level validation verifies data after the user has filled all the fields. For example, a user might be directed to fill in a name, address, and phone number on a form and then click OK. With form-level validation, all the fields on the form would be validated when the user clicked OK.

Field-level validation, alternatively, verifies the data in each field as the field is filled in. For example, if a user fills in a field that holds a phone number, field-level validation could verify that the number contains a valid area code before moving to the next field. As each digit is entered, you could also use control events to verify that only numbers are entered.

Field-Level Validation

You might want to validate data as it is entered into each field. Field-level validation gives the developer control over user input as it occurs. In this section, you learn how to use control events to validate user input and how to use some properties of the *TextBox* control to help restrict input to appropriate parameters.

Using *TextBox* Properties

The most commonly used control for user input is *TextBox*. Several properties of the *TextBox* control enable you to restrict the values of user input that those properties will accept. Some of these properties include:

- *MaxLength*
- *PasswordChar*
- *ReadOnly*
- *MultiLine*

Setting the *MaxLength* Property

The *MaxLength* property limits the number of characters that can be entered into a text box. If the user attempts to exceed the number returned by *MaxLength*, the text box will accept no further input, and the system beeps to alert the user. This property is useful for text boxes that always contain data of the same length, such as a ZIP code field.

Using the *PasswordChar* Property

The *PasswordChar* property enables you to hide user input at run time. For example, if you set the *PasswordChar* property to an asterisk (*), the text box will display an asterisk for each character, regardless of user input. This type of behavior is commonly seen in password logon boxes.

Although the password character is most commonly an asterisk, you can set it to any valid character. Thus, you could display all semicolons or ampersands, for example. The value of the *Text* property will always be set to the value the user enters, regardless of the password character.

Setting the *ReadOnly* Property

The *ReadOnly* property determines whether a user can edit the value displayed in a text box. If *ReadOnly* is set to *True*, the text cannot be changed by user input. If *ReadOnly* is set to *False*, the user can edit the value normally.

Using the *MultiLine* Property

The *MultiLine* property determines whether a text box can accept multiple lines. When set to *True*, the user can enter multiple lines in the text box, each separated by a carriage return. The individual lines are stored as an array of strings in the *TextBox.Lines* collection and can be accessed by their index.

Using Events in Field-Level Validation

Field-level keyboard events enable you to validate user input immediately. Controls that can receive keyboard input raise three keyboard events. They are:

- *KeyDown*
- *KeyPress*
- *KeyUp*

KeyDown and KeyUp

The *KeyDown* and *KeyUp* events are raised when a key is pressed and when a key is released, respectively. The control that has the focus raises the event. When these events are raised, they package information about which key or combination of keys has been pressed or released in an instance of *KeyEventArgs*, a class that describes the key combination pressed. A method that handles the *KeyDown* or *KeyUp* event must include a *KeyEventArgs* parameter in its signature.

The *KeyUp* and *KeyDown* events are most commonly used for determining whether the Alt, Ctrl, or Shift key has been pressed. This information is exposed through properties in the *KeyEventArgs* reference that is passed to the handler. The *KeyEventArgs* properties—Alt, Control, and Shift—are properties that return a Boolean value, which indicates whether those keys are down. A value of *True* is returned if the corresponding key is down, and *False* is returned if the key is up. The following example demonstrates a *KeyUp* event handler that checks whether the Alt key is pressed.

Sample of Visual Basic Code

```
Private Sub TextBox1_KeyUp(ByVal sender As Object, ByVal e As _
   System.Windows.Forms.KeyEventArgs) Handles TextBox1.KeyUp
   If e.Alt = True Then
      MessageBox.Show("The ALT key still is down")
   End If
End Sub
```

Sample of Visual C# Code

```
private void textBox1_KeyUp(object sender,
   System.Windows.Forms.KeyEventArgs e)
{
   if (e.Alt == true)
   MessageBox.Show("The ALT key is still down");
}
```

You can also use the *KeyEventArgs.KeyCode* property to examine the actual key that triggered the event. This property returns a *Key* value that represents the key that was pressed (in the case of a *KeyDown* event) or released (in the case of a *KeyUp* event). The following example shows a simple event handler that displays a message box containing a string representation of the key that was pressed.

```
Private Sub TextBox1_KeyDown(ByVal sender As Object, ByVal e As _
    System.Windows.Forms.KeyEventArgs) Handles TextBox1.KeyDown
    MessageBox.Show(e.KeyCode.ToString())
End Sub
```

Sample of Visual C# Code

```
private void textBox1_KeyDown(object sender,
    System.Windows.Forms.KeyEventArgs e)
{
    MessageBox.Show(e.KeyCode.ToString());
}
```

KeyPress

When a user presses a key that has a corresponding ASCII value, the *KeyPress* event is raised. These keys include any alphabetic and numeric characters (alphanumeric a–z, A–Z, and 0–9), as well as some special keyboard characters such as the Enter and Backspace keys. If a key or key combination does not produce an ASCII value, it will not raise the *KeyPress* event. Examples of keys that do not raise this event include Ctrl, Alt, and the function keys.

This event is most useful for intercepting keystrokes and evaluating them. When this event is raised, an instance of *KeyPressEventArgs* is passed as a parameter to the event handler. The *KeyPressEventArgs.KeyChar* property contains the ASCII character represented by the keystroke that raised the event. If you want to make sure the key pressed is a numeric key, for example, you can evaluate the *KeyChar* property in your *KeyPress* event handler.

Validating Characters

The *Char* data type contains several *Shared* (static) methods that are useful for validating characters trapped by the *KeyPress* event. These methods include:

- *Char.IsDigit*
- *Char.IsLetter*
- *Char.IsLetterOrDigit*
- *Char.IsPunctuation*
- *Char.IsLower*
- *Char.IsUpper*

Each of these methods evaluates a character and returns a Boolean value; they are fairly self-explanatory. The *Char.IsDigit* function returns *True* if a character is a numeric digit, *False* if it is not. The *Char.IsLower* function returns *True* if a character is a lowercase letter, otherwise it returns *False*. The other methods behave similarly. The following example uses the *Char.IsNumber* method to test whether the key pressed is a numeric key:

Sample of Visual Basic Code

```
Private Sub TextBox1_KeyPress (ByVal sender as Object, ByVal e As _
    System.Windows.Forms.KeyPressEventArgs) Handles TextBox1.KeyPress
```

```
    If Char.IsDigit(e.KeyChar) = True Then
        MessageBox.Show("You pressed a number key")
    End If
End Sub
```

Sample of Visual C# Code

```
private void textBox1_KeyPress (object sender,
    System.Windows.Forms.KeyPressEventArgs e)
{
    if (Char.IsDigit(e.KeyChar) == true)
        MessageBox.Show("You pressed a number key");
}
```

Handling the Focus

Focus is the ability of an object to receive user input through the mouse or keyboard. Although you can have several controls on your form, only one can have the focus at any given time. The control that has the focus is always on the active form of the application.

Every control implements the *Focus* method. This method sets the focus to the control that called it. The *Focus* method returns a Boolean value that indicates whether the control was successful in setting the focus. Controls that are disabled or invisible cannot receive the focus. You can determine whether a control can receive the focus by checking the *CanFocus* property, which returns *True* if the control can receive the focus and *False* if the control cannot.

Sample of Visual Basic Code

```
' This example checks to see if TextBox1 can receive the focus and
' sets the focus to it if it can.
If TextBox1.CanFocus = True Then
    TextBox1.Focus()
End If
```

Sample of Visual C# Code

```
// This example checks to see if textBox1 can receive the focus and
// sets the focus to it if it can.
if (textBox1.CanFocus == true)
    textBox1.Focus();
```

Focus events occur in the following order:

1. *Enter*
2. *GotFocus*
3. *Leave*
4. *Validating*
5. *Validated*
6. *LostFocus*

The *Enter* and *Leave* events are raised when the focus arrives at a control and when the focus leaves a control, respectively. *GotFocus* and *LostFocus* are raised when a control first obtains the focus and when the focus has been lost from the control, respectively. Although you can use these events for field-level validation, the *Validating* and *Validated* events are more suited to that task.

The *Validating* and *Validated* Events

The easiest way to validate data is to use the *Validating* event, which occurs before a control loses the focus. This event is raised only when the *CausesValidation* property of the control that is about to receive the focus is set to *True*. Thus, if you want to use the *Validating* event to validate data entered in your control, the *CausesValidation* of the next control in the tab order should be set to *True*. To use *Validating* events, the *CausesValidation* property of the control to be validated must also be set to *True*. By default, the *CausesValidation* property of all controls is set to *True* when controls are created at design time. Controls such as Help buttons are typically the only kind of controls that have *CausesValidation* set to *False*.

The *Validating* event enables you to perform sophisticated validation on your controls. You could, for example, implement an event handler that tests whether the value entered corresponds to a very specific format. Another possible use is an event handler that doesn't allow the focus to leave the control until a value has been entered.

The *Validating* event includes an instance of the *CancelEventArgs* class. This class contains a single property, *Cancel*. If the input in your control does not fall within required parameters, you can use the *Cancel* property within your event handler to cancel the *Validating* event and return the focus to the control.

The *Validated* event fires after a control has been validated successfully. You can use this event to perform any actions based upon the validated input.

The following example demonstrates a handler for the *Validating* event. This method requires an entry in TextBox1 before it will allow the focus to move to the next control.

Sample of Visual Basic Code

```vb
Private Sub TextBox1_Validating(ByVal sender As Object, ByVal e As _
    System.ComponentModel.CancelEventArgs) Handles TextBox1.Validating
    ' Checks the value of TextBox1
    If TextBox1.Text = "" Then
        ' Resets the focus if there is no entry in TextBox1
        e.Cancel = True
    End If
End Sub
```

Sample of Visual C# Code

```csharp
private void textBox1_Validating(object sender,
    System.ComponentModel.CancelEventArgs e)
{
    // Checks the value of textBox1
    if (textBox1.Text == "")
        // Resets the focus if there is no entry in TextBox1
        e.Cancel = true;
}
```

To use the *Validating* event of a text box:

1. Add a text box to a form.

2. Create an event handler to handle the *Validating* event of the text box. In the event handler, set the *e.Cancel* property to *True* to cancel validating and return the focus to the text box.

3. Set the *CausesValidation* property to *False* for any controls for which you do not want the *Validating* event to fire.

Form-Level Validation

Form-level validation is the process of validating all the fields on a form at once. A central procedure implements form-level validation and is usually called when the user is ready to proceed to another step. A more advanced method of form-level validation is implementing a form-level keyboard handler.

The following example demonstrates how to create a form-level validation method. The sample tests that all the text boxes on a form have received input when a button called *btnValidate* is pressed, and resets the focus to the first text box it encounters without input.

Sample of Visual Basic Code

```
Private Sub btnValidate_Click(ByVal sender As System.Object, ByVal e _
    As System.EventArgs) Handles btnValidate.Click
    Dim aControl As System.Windows.Forms.Control
    ' Loops through each control on the form
    For Each aControl In Me.Controls
        ' Checks to see if the control being considered is a Textbox and
        ' if it contains an empty string
        If TypeOf aControl Is TextBox AndAlso aControl.Text = "" Then
        ' If a textbox is found to contain an empty string, it is
            ' given the focus and the method is exited.
            aControl.Focus()
            Exit Sub
        End If
    Next
End Sub
```

Sample of Visual C# Code

```
private void btnValidate_Click(object sender, System.EventArgs e)
    {
    // Loops through each control on the form
    foreach (System.Windows.Forms.Control aControl in this.Controls)
    {
        // Checks to see if the control being considered is a Textbox and
        // if it contains an empty string
        if (aControl is System.Windows.Forms.TextBox & aControl.Text ==
            "")
        {
            // If a textbox is found to contain an empty string, it is
            // given the focus and the method is exited.
            aControl.Focus();
```

```
            return;
        }
    }
}
```

Form-Level Keyboard Handler

A keyboard handler is a somewhat more sophisticated technique for form-level validation. A centralized keyboard handler enables you to manage data input for all fields on a form. For example, you could create a method that enables command buttons only after appropriate input has been entered into each field and that performs specific actions with each keystroke.

The *KeyPress*, *KeyDown*, and *KeyUp* events implement a form-level keyboard handler. If a form has no visible and enabled controls, it will automatically raise keyboard events. If there are any controls on the form, however, the form will not automatically raise these events. For the form to raise these events, the *KeyPreview* property of the form must be set to *True*. When set to *True*, the form will raise keystroke events before the control that has the focus. For example, assume there is a *KeyPress* handler for the form and a *KeyPress* handler for a text box on that form, and that the *KeyPreview* property of the form is set to *True*. When a key is pressed, the form will raise the *KeyPress* event first, and the form's *KeyPress* event handler will execute first. When execution has completed, the text box's *KeyPress* event handler will execute.

Providing User Feedback

When invalid input is entered in a field, the user should be alerted and given an opportunity to correct the error. There are many ways to inform the user of an input error. If the error is obvious and self-explanatory, an audio cue can alert the user to the problem. You can use the *Beep* method to produce an attention-getting sound.

Sample of Visual Basic Code

```
' This line causes an audible beep
Beep()
```

Sample of C# Code

```
// This line causes an audible beep
System.Console.Beep();
```

Other ways to draw a user's attention to an error include changing the *BackColor* or *ForeColor* property of a control. For example, a text box with invalid input might have its *BackColor* changed to red.

If more detailed messages are required, you can use the *MessageBox.Show* method. This method displays a small, modal dialog box that contains an informative message. Because it is displayed modally, it halts program execution and is impossible for the user to ignore. The following shows how to call the *MessageBox.Show* method, which includes an informative message:

Sample of Visual Basic Code

```
MessageBox.Show("That value is not valid for this control")
```

Sample of Visual C# Code

```
MessageBox.Show("That value is not valid for this control");
```

The *ErrorProvider* Component

The *ErrorProvider* component provides an easy way to communicate validation errors to your users. It enables you to set an error message for each control on your form when the input is not valid. When an error message is set, an icon indicating the error will appear next to the control, and the error message text will be shown as a tool tip when the mouse hovers over the affected control. The *ErrorProvider* component can be found in the Windows Forms tab of the Toolbox.

Displaying an Error

To cause an error condition to be displayed next to a control, use the *SetError* method of the *ErrorProvider* component. The *SetError* method requires the name of the control to be set and the text to be provided. It is invoked as shown here:

Sample of Visual Basic Code

```
' This example assumes the existence of a control named nameTextBox and
' an ErrorProvider named myErrorProvider
myErrorProvider.SetError(nameTextBox, "Name cannot be left blank!")
```

Sample of Visual C# Code

```
// This example assumes the existence of a control named nameTextBox and
// an ErrorProvider named myErrorProvider
myErrorProvider.SetError(nameTextBox, "Name cannot be left blank!");
```

When this line of code is executed, an icon will be displayed next to the *nameTextBox* control, and the specified text will appear in a tool tip box when the mouse hovers over the control.

You can also set an error at design time. In the Properties window, you will find that when you add an *ErrorProvider* control to your form, each control has a new property called *Error on x* where *x* is the name of the *ErrorProvider* component. You can set this property to a value at design time in the Properties window. If a value is set for the error, the control will immediately show an error at run time.

Different properties of the *ErrorProvider* component affect how the information is displayed to the user. The *Icon* property controls which icon is displayed next to the control. You might want to have multiple error providers on a single form: one that reports errors and one that reports warnings. You could use different icons for each to provide visual cues to the user. Another property is the *BlinkStyle* property. This property determines whether the error icon blinks when displayed. The *BlinkRate* property determines how rapidly the icon blinks.

To create a validation handler that uses the *ErrorProvider* component:

1. Create your form and add an *ErrorProvider* component to it.

   The *ErrorProvider* component appears in the component tray.

2. Set the *CausesValidation* property of the control for which you want to provide errors to *True* if it is not already true.

3. In the event handler for that control's *Validating* event, test the value. If an error condition occurs, use the *SetError* method to set the error to be displayed. The following example demonstrates a validation handler for a text box named pswordTextBox and an error provider named myErrorProvider:

Sample of Visual Basic Code

```
Private Sub pswordTextBox_Validating(ByVal sender as Object, _
   ByVal e As System.ComponentModel.CancelEventArgs) Handles _
   pswordTextBox.Validating
   ' Validate the entry
   If pswordTextBox.Text = "" Then
      ' Set the error for an invalid entry
      myErrorProvider.SetError(pswordTextBox, _
         "Password cannot be blank!")
   Else
      ' Clear the error for a valid entry-no error will be displayed
      myErrorProvider.SetError(pswordTextBox, "")
   End If
End Sub
```

Sample of Visual C# Code

```
private void pswordTextBox_Validating(object sender,
   System.ComponentModel.CancelEventArgs e)
{
   // Validate the entry
   if (pswordTextBox.Text == "")
      // Set the error for an invalid entry
      myErrorProvider.SetError(pswordTextBox,
         "Password cannot be blank!");
   else
      // Clear the error for a valid entry-no error will be displayed
      myErrorProvider.SetError(pswordTextBox, "");
}
```

Implementing *IDataErrorInfo* in WPF Applications

Validation for WPF applications was covered extensively in Chapter 6, "Working with Data Binding." By adding *ValidationRule* objects to the *Binding.ValidationRules* collection, you can validate user input data. Implementing *IDataErrorInfo* in your custom classes, however, enables you to build validation into your data objects to provide an additional level of validation control.

IDataErrorInfo consists of two members: *Error*, which provides an error message that indicates the problem with the object, and *Item*, which provides an error message that indicates what the problem is with a property of the object. The value of the *Error* property can be accessed only by directly querying the property value and is frequently not implemented. However, the *Item* property provides information to the *Validation.Errors* collection in WPF and can be used by built-in validation mechanisms.

Implementing *IDataErrorInfo*

Typically, the bulk of implementation of *IDataErrorInfo* is found in the *Item* property. Implementation of the *Item* property requires you to provide validation for each property that requires validation. Consider the following example:

Sample of Visual Basic Code

```vb
Default Public ReadOnly Property Item(ByVal columnName As String) _
    As String Implements System.ComponentModel.IDataErrorInfo.Item
    Get
        Dim result As String = Nothing
        If columnName = "FirstName" Then
            If Not FirstName = "John" Then
                result = "First name must equal John"
            End If
        End If
        If columnName = "LastName" Then
            If Not LastName = "Smith" Then
                result = "Last name must equal Smith"
            End If
        End If
        Return result
    End Get
End Property
```

Sample of C# Code

```csharp
public string this[string columnName]
{
    get
    {
        string result = null;
        if (columnName == "FirstName")
        {
            if (!(FirstName == "John"))
                result = "First Name must be John";
        }
        if (columnName == "LastName")
        {
            if (!(LastName == "Smith"))
                result = "Last Name must be Smith";
        }
        return result;
    }
}
```

In this rather useless example, the *Item* property provides validation for two properties: *FirstName* and *LastName*, in which the *FirstName* property must be set to "John" and the *LastName* property must be set to "Smith". The name of the column being validated by the method is passed to the method in the *columnName* parameter, and you can test which column is being validated. You can then validate the value of the property in question. In this example, if the property being tested is not set to an appropriate value, an error string is returned. Otherwise, a null string is returned.

After *IDataErrorInfo* is implemented, the WPF Validation apparatus can be used to validate values for the object's properties. A control bound to an object implementing *IDataErrorInfo* should set *ValidatesonDataErrors* to *True*, as shown here:

```
<TextBox.Text>
    <Binding Source="{StaticResource TheCollection}"
        Path="LastName" UpdateSourceTrigger="LostFocus"
        ValidatesOnDataErrors="True"/>
</TextBox.Text>
```

Also note in this example that the *UpdateSourceTrigger* property is set to *LostFocus*. This also determines when the bound content in the control is validated. When the control loses focus, the *Item* method of *IDataErrorInfo* is executed. You can validate the bound content every time it changes by setting this property to *PropertyChanged*, but that tends to be processor-intensive.

If a validation error is found and an error string is returned by the *Item* method, it is added to the *Validation.Errors* collection and can be accessed at run time. You can use a *Style* element to set the tool tip on the error string at run time, as shown here:

```
<Style TargetType="{x:Type TextBox}">
    <Style.Triggers>
        <Trigger Property="Validation.HasError" Value="true">
            <Setter Property="ToolTip"
        Value="{Binding RelativeSource={RelativeSource Self},
                Path=(Validation.Errors)[0].ErrorContent}"/>
        </Trigger>
    </Style.Triggers>
</Style>
```

In this example, *Style* is applied to controls of type *TextBox*, and it invokes a trigger when the *Validation.HasError* property that sets the *ToolTip* property to the error string for this control is true. That string will be visible when the mouse hovers over the control and will remain until the error is cleared.

You can set the *Validation.ErrorTemplate* attached property to provide a different template for the control when a validation error is present. The *Validation.ErrorTemplate* attached property takes a *ControlTemplate* value. This lesson's practice demonstrates creating an *ErrorTemplate* attached property.

Implementing *IDataErrorInfo*

In this practice, you implement *IDataErrorInfo* in a simple class and then bind it to controls in the user interface. You create a style that automatically sets *ToolTip* to an error string and creates an *ErrorTemplate* attached property that alters the appearance of the control when an error is present.

EXERCISE Implementing *IDataErrorInfo*

1. In Visual Studio, create a new WPF application named **Lesson 2**.

2. In the Code editor for the *MainWindow* class, add the following class.

   Note that it contains an empty implementation for *IDataErrorInfo*; this is the implementation that is automatically generated by Visual Studio.

   Sample of Visual Basic Code

```
Public Class Customer
    Implements System.ComponentModel.IDataErrorInfo
    Private mFirstName As String = ""
    Public Property FirstName As String
        Get
            Return mFirstName
        End Get
        Set(ByVal value As String)
            mFirstName = value
        End Set
    End Property
    Private mLastName As String = ""
    Public Property LastName As String
        Get
            Return mLastName
        End Get
        Set(ByVal value As String)
            mLastName = value
        End Set
    End Property
    Public ReadOnly Property [Error] As String _
        Implements System.ComponentModel.IDataErrorInfo.Error
        Get

        End Get
    End Property

    Default Public ReadOnly Property Item(ByVal columnName As String) As String _
        Implements System.ComponentModel.IDataErrorInfo.Item
        Get

        End Get
    End Property
End Class
```

```csharp
public class Customer : System.ComponentModel.IDataErrorInfo
{
    string mFirstName = "";
    public string FirstName
    {
        get
        {
            return mFirstName;
        }
        set
        {
            mFirstName = value;
        }
    }
    string mLastName = "";
    public string LastName
    {
        get
        {
            return mLastName;
        }
        set
        {
            mLastName = value;
        }
    }

    public string Error
    {
        get { }
    }

    public string this[string columnName]
    {
        get { }
    }
}
```

3. In the *Error* property, add the following line to the getter.

   Sample of Visual Basic Code

   ```vb
   Throw New NotImplementedException
   ```

   Sample of C# Code

   ```csharp
   throw new NotImplementedException();
   ```

4. In the *Item* property, add the following implementation:

   ```vb
   Get
       Dim Result As String = Nothing
       Select Case columnName
           Case "FirstName"
               If Not FirstName.Length > 1 Then
                   Result = "First Name must be at least 2 characters long"
   ```

```
            ElseIf FirstName.Length > 10 Then
                Result = "First Name cannot be longer than 10 characters"
            End If
        Case "LastName"
            If Not LastName.Length > 1 Then
                Result = "Last Name must be at least 2 characters long"
            End If
    End Select
    Return Result
End Get
```

Sample of C# Code

```csharp
get
{
    string result = null;
    switch (columnName)
    {
        case "FirstName":
            if (!(FirstName.Length > 1))
                result = "First Name must be at least 2 characters long";
            else if (FirstName.Length > 10)
                result =
                    "First Name cannot be longer than 10 characters";
            break;
        case "LastName":
            if (!(LastName.Length > 1))
                result = "Last Name must be at least 2 characters long";
            break;
    }
    return result;
}
```

5. In the XAML designer, add the following line to the Window declaration to import the project namespace.

   Note that if your project is named anything other than Lesson 2, you will have to modify this line accordingly.

   ```
   xmlns:my="clr-namespace:Lesson_2"
   ```

6. In the XAML designer, add a Windows.Resources section as follows to create an instance of the *Customer* class as a resource for your application.

   ```xml
   <Window.Resources>
       <my:Customer x:Key="myCustomer" />
   </Window.Resources>
   ```

7. In the XAML designer, add the following XAML code to the Grid declaration.

   Note that the *Text* property of each text box is bound to a property of the myCustomer resource and that the *UpdateSourceTrigger* and the *ValidatesOnDataErrors* properties of the binding are set to *LostFocus* and *True*, respectively.

   ```xml
   <TextBox Height="23" HorizontalAlignment="Left"
       Margin="61,32,0,0" Name="TextBox1" VerticalAlignment="Top" Width="120"
   ```

```
>
    <TextBox.Text>
        <Binding Source="{StaticResource myCustomer}" Path="FirstName"
            UpdateSourceTrigger="LostFocus" ValidatesOnDataErrors="True"/>
    </TextBox.Text>
</TextBox>
<TextBox Height="23" HorizontalAlignment="Left" Margin="61,81,0,0"
    Name="TextBox2" VerticalAlignment="Top" Width="120" >
    <TextBox.Text>
        <Binding Source="{StaticResource myCustomer}" Path="LastName"
            UpdateSourceTrigger="LostFocus" ValidatesOnDataErrors="True"/>
    </TextBox.Text>
</TextBox>
```

8. In the XAML designer, add the following style to the Windows.Resources section.

This style has a target type of *Textbox*, so it is applied automatically to both *Textbox* controls in this application and includes a trigger that fires when the *Validaton.HasError* property for the bound control is *True*. When the trigger fires, it invokes a setter that sets the *ToolTip* property for *Textbox* to the *ErrorContent* component of the validation error, which will display the string returned by the *Item* method in the form of a tool tip whenever the mouse hovers over the control.

```
<Style TargetType="{x:Type TextBox}">
    <Style.Triggers>
        <Trigger Property="Validation.HasError" Value="true">
            <Setter Property="ToolTip"
        Value="{Binding RelativeSource={RelativeSource Self},
                Path=(Validation.Errors)[0].ErrorContent}"/>
        </Trigger>
    </Style.Triggers>
</Style>
```

9. Add the following setter to the trigger in the style described previously.

This setter sets the *ErrorTemplate* property for the control when the *Validation.HasError* property is true. The template described here outlines the text box with the error in purple and displays red exclamation points as well.

```
<Setter Property="Validation.ErrorTemplate">
    <Setter.Value>
        <ControlTemplate>
            <DockPanel LastChildFill="True">
                <TextBlock DockPanel.Dock="Right" Foreground="Red"
                    FontSize="16pt">!!!</TextBlock>
                <Border BorderBrush="Purple" BorderThickness="3">
                    <AdornedElementPlaceholder />
                </Border>
            </DockPanel>
        </ControlTemplate>
    </Setter.Value>
</Setter>
```

10. Press F5 to build and run your application.

Lesson Summary

- Form-level validation validates all fields on a form simultaneously. Field-level validation validates each field as data is entered and provides a finer level of control over validation.

- The *TextBox* control contains several design-time properties that restrict the values users can enter.

- Keyboard events enable you to validate keystrokes; they are raised by the control that has the focus and is receiving input. The form will also raise these events if the *KeyPreview* property is set to *True*.

- The *Char* structure contains several static methods that are useful for validating character input.

- The *Validating* event occurs before the control loses focus and should be used to validate user input. This event occurs only when the *CausesValidation* property of the control that is about to receive the focus is true. To keep the focus from moving away from the control in the *Validating* event handler, set the *CancelEventArgs.Cancel* property to *True* in the event handler.

- The *ErrorProvider* component enables you to set an error for a control at run time that displays a visual cue and an informative message to the user. To display an error at run time, use the *ErrorProvider.SetError* method.

- *IDataErrorInfo* is an interface in the *System.ComponentModel* namespace that can be implemented in classes to provide validation in WPF applications. Error strings returned by the *Item* property are automatically set to the *ErrorContent* property of the first *Validation.Errors* item for the binding in question.

- You can provide a different template for a control to be displayed when there is a validation error by setting the *ErrorTemplate* attached property of that control.

Lesson Review

You can use the following questions to test your knowledge of the information in Lesson 2, "Validating User Input." The questions are also available on the companion CD if you prefer to review them in electronic form.

> **NOTE ANSWERS**
>
> Answers to these questions and explanations of why each answer choice is correct or incorrect are located in the "Answers" section at the end of the book.

1. How can you set the *ErrorContent* string of a *Validation.Errors* object for a specific control from a class that implements *IDataErrorInfo*?

    A. Return the error string as the return value of the *Error* property. It will automatically be set to the *ErrorContent* string of the correct *Validation.Errors* object when an error occurs in a control bound to this object.

    B. Return the error string as the return value of the *Item* property. It will automatically be set to the *ErrorContent* string of the correct *Validation.Errors* object when an error occurs in a control bound to this object.

    C. Set the *ErrorContent* string directly in the *Error* property.

    D. Set the *ErrorContent* string directly in the *Item* property.

2. Which of the following represents the correct order in which focus events are raised?

    A. *Enter, GotFocus, Validating, Validated, Leave, LostFocus*

    B. *Enter, GotFocus, Validating, Validated, LostFocus, Leave*

    C. *Enter, GotFocus, Leave, Validating, Validated, LostFocus*

    D. *Enter, GotFocus, LostFocus, Leave, Validating, Validated*

Case Scenario

In the following case scenarios, you apply what you've learned about how to use datagrids and input validation. You can find answers to these questions in the "Answers" section at the end of this book.

Case Scenario: The Writer Completeness Chart

You have been contracted by a firm that manages a large group of technical writers, each one working on a different book. The firm has asked you to develop an application to help manage the status and schedule of its writers. You are building a database and associated application for this purpose. Your task is to build the user interface for an overview screen.

The technical requirements are as follows:

- The application should be built using WPF.

- The database will provide a data row about each writer with the following information: Name, Project Title, Projected Number of Chapters, Completed Number of Chapters.

- The application should display the percentage of the project done, expressed as the completed number of chapters divided by the projected number of chapters, and it should be displayed graphically as a pie chart.

- Information for all writers should be visible at once in the application so that it can be browsed easily.

Answer the following question for your manager:

- What is the best strategy for meeting these requirements?

Suggested Practices

To help you successfully master the exam objectives presented in this chapter, complete the following tasks.

- **Practice 1**   Implement the project described in the case scenario.

- **Practice 2**   Create a *DataGridTemplateColumn* property that accepts a date as data type and displays the date as a text box when not editing and as a date picker when editing.

- **Practice 3**   Create a Windows Forms application to enter data for the Northwind Customers table with appropriate field-level validation on each control.

Take a Practice Test

The practice tests on this book's companion CD offer many options. For example, you can test yourself on just the content covered in this chapter, or you can test yourself on all the 70-511 certification exam content. You can set up the test so that it closely simulates the experience of taking a certification exam, or you can set it up in study mode so that you can look at the correct answers and explanations after you answer each question.

> **MORE INFO** **PRACTICE TESTS**
>
> For details about all the practice test options available, see the "How to Use the Practice Tests" section in this book's Introduction.

CHAPTER 9

Enhancing Usability

Developers of both Windows Presentation Foundation (WPF) and Windows Forms applications can access the built-in functionality of the Microsoft .NET Framework to enhance the usability of the applications they develop. In this chapter, you learn to use this built-in functionality to create applications that are responsive, global, and interoperational. In Lesson 1, "Implementing Asynchronous Processing," you learn how to implement asynchronous processing and programming for your applications; in Lesson 2, "Incorporating Globalization and Localization," you learn how to globalize and localize your applications; and in Lesson 3, "Integrating Windows Forms and WPF," you learn how to use WPF controls in Windows Forms applications, and vice versa.

Exam objectives in this chapter:

- Implement asynchronous processes and threading.
- Incorporate globalization and localization features.
- Integrate WinForms and WPF within an application.

Lessons in this chapter:

Before You Begin

To complete the lessons in this chapter, you must have:

- A computer that meets or exceeds the minimum hardware requirements listed in the "About This Book" section at the beginning of the book.

- Microsoft Visual Studio 2010 Professional installed on your computer.

- An understanding of Microsoft Visual Basic or C# syntax and familiarity with .NET Framework 4.0.

- An understanding of Extensible Application Markup Language (XAML).

 REAL WORLD

Matthew Stoecker

Even with ever-increasing processor speeds, time-consuming tasks are still a central part of many of the applications I write. The *BackgroundWorker* component enables the creation of simple, asynchronous operations and is easily accessible to programmers of all levels. For more advanced operations, delegates and threads provide the needed level of functionality.

Lesson 1: Implementing Asynchronous Processing

You are frequently required to perform tasks that consume fairly large amounts of time, such as file downloads. The *BackgroundWorker* component provides an easy way to run time-consuming processes in the background, thereby leaving the user interface (UI) responsive and available for user input.

> **After this lesson, you will be able to:**
>
> - Run a background process by using the *BackgroundWorker* component.
> - Announce the completion of a background process by using the *BackgroundWorker* component.
> - Cancel a background process by using the *BackgroundWorker* component.
> - Report the progress of a background process by using the *BackgroundWorker* component.
> - Request the status of a background process by using the *BackgroundWorker* component.
>
> **Estimated lesson time: 45 minutes**

The *BackgroundWorker* component is designed to enable you to execute time-consuming operations on a separate, dedicated thread so you can run operations that take a lot of time, such as file downloads and database transactions, asynchronously while the UI remains responsive.

The key method of the *BackgroundWorker* component is the *RunWorkerAsync* method. When this method is called, the *BackgroundWorker* component raises the *DoWork* event. The code in the *DoWork* event handler is executed on a separate, dedicated thread so that the UI remains responsive. Table 9-1 shows the important members of the *BackgroundWorker* component.

TABLE 9-1 Important Members of the *BackgroundWorker* Component

MEMBER	DESCRIPTION
CancellationPending	Property. Indicates whether the application has requested cancellation of a background operation.
IsBusy	Property. Indicates whether the *BackgroundWorker* is currently running an asynchronous operation.
WorkerReportsProgress	Property. Indicates whether the *BackgroundWorker* component can report progress updates.
WorkerSupportsCancellation	Property. Indicates whether the *BackgroundWorker* component supports asynchronous cancellation.

CancelAsync	Method. Requests cancellation of a pending background operation.
ReportProgress	Method. Raises the *ProgressChanged* event.
RunWorkerAsync	Method. Starts the execution of a background operation by raising the *DoWork* event.
DoWork	Event. Occurs when the *RunWorkerAsync* method is called. Code in the *DoWork* event handler is run on a separate and dedicated thread.
ProgressChanged	Event. Occurs when *ReportProgress* is called.
RunWorkerCompleted	Event. Occurs when the background operation has been completed or cancelled or has raised an exception.

Running a Background Process

The *RunWorkerAsync* method of the *BackgroundWorker* component starts the execution of the background process by raising the *DoWork* event. The code in the *DoWork* event handler is executed on a separate thread. The following procedure explains how to create a background process.

To create a background process with the *BackgroundWorker* component:

1. From the Toolbox, drag a *BackgroundWorker* component onto the form.

2. In the component tray, double-click the *BackgroundWorker* component to create the default event handler for the *DoWork* event. Add the code that you want to run on the separate thread. An example is shown here.

    Sample of Visual Basic Code

    ```
    Private Sub BackgroundWorker1_DoWork(ByVal sender As System.Object, _
        ByVal e As System.ComponentModel.DoWorkEventArgs) _
        Handles BackgroundWorker1.DoWork
        ' Insert time-consuming operation here
    End Sub
    ```

    Sample of C# Code

    ```
    private void backgroundWorker1_DoWork(object sender, DoWorkEventArgs e)
    {
        // Insert time-consuming operation here
    }
    ```

3. Elsewhere in your code, start the time-consuming operation on a separate thread by calling the *RunWorkerAsync* method, as shown:

    Sample of Visual Basic Code

    ```
    BackgroundWorker1.RunWorkerAsync()
    ```

```
backgroundWorker1.RunWorkerAsync();
```

Providing Parameters to the Background Process

Sometimes you will want to run a background process that requires a parameter. For example, you might want to provide the address of a file for download. You can provide a parameter in the *RunWorkerAsync* method. This parameter will be available as the *Argument* property of the instance of *DoWorkEventArgs* in the *DoWork* event handler.

To provide a parameter to a background process:

1. Include the parameter in the *RunWorkerAsync* call, as shown here:

Sample of Visual Basic Code

```
BackgroundWorker1.RunWorkerAsync("C:\myfile.txt")
```

Sample of C# Code

```
backgroundWorker1.RunWorkerAsync("C:\\myfile.txt");
```

2. Retrieve the parameter from the *DoWorkEventArgs.Argument* property and cast it appropriately to use it in the background process. An example is shown here:

Sample of Visual Basic Code

```
Private Sub BackgroundWorker1_DoWork(ByVal sender As System.Object, _
    ByVal e As System.ComponentModel.DoWorkEventArgs) _
    Handles BackgroundWorker1.DoWork
    Dim myPath As String
    myPath = CType(e.Argument, String)
    ' Use the argument in the process
    RunTimeConsumingProcess()
End Sub
```

Sample of C# Code

```
private void backgroundWorker1_DoWork(object sender, DoWorkEventArgs e)
{
    string myPath;
    myPath = (string)e.Argument;
    // Use the argument in the process
    RunTimeConsumingProcess();
}
```

Announcing the Completion of a Background Process

When the background process terminates, whether because the process is completed or cancelled, the *RunWorkerCompleted* event is raised. You can alert the user to the completion of a background process by handling the *RunWorkerCompleted* event. Here is an example:

Sample of Visual Basic Code

```
Private Sub BackgroundWorker1_RunWorkerCompleted( _
    ByVal sender As System.Object, _
```

```
        ByVal e As System.ComponentModel.RunWorkerCompletedEventArgs) _
        Handles BackgroundWorker1.RunWorkerCompleted
        MsgBox("Background process completed!")
End Sub
```

Sample of C# Code

```
private void backgroundWorker1_RunWorkerCompleted(object sender,
    RunWorkerCompletedEventArgs e)
{
    System.Windows.Forms.MessageBox.Show("Background process completed");
}
```

You can ascertain whether the background process was cancelled by reading the *e.Cancelled* property, as shown here:

Sample of Visual Basic Code

```
Private Sub BackgroundWorker1_RunWorkerCompleted( _
    ByVal sender As System.Object, _
    ByVal e As System.ComponentModel.RunWorkerCompletedEventArgs) _
    Handles BackgroundWorker1.RunWorkerCompleted
    If e.Cancelled Then
        MsgBox("Process was cancelled!")
    Else
        MsgBox("Process completed")
    End If
End Sub
```

Sample of C# Code

```
private void backgroundWorker1_RunWorkerCompleted(object sender,
    RunWorkerCompletedEventArgs e)
{
    if (e.Cancelled)
    {
        System.Windows.Forms.MessageBox.Show ("Process was cancelled!");
    }
    else
    {
        System.Windows.Forms.MessageBox.Show("Process completed");
    }
}
```

Returning a Value from a Background Process

You might want to return a value from a background process. For example, if your process is a complex calculation, you would want to return the result. You can return a value by setting the *Result* property of *DoWorkEventArgs* in *DoWorkEventHandler*. This value will then be available in the *RunWorkerCompleted* event handler as the *Result* property of the *RunWorkerCompletedEventArgs* parameter, as shown in the following example:

Sample of Visual Basic Code

```
Private Sub BackgroundWorker1_DoWork(ByVal sender As System.Object, _
    ByVal e As System.ComponentModel.DoWorkEventArgs) _
```

```
      Handles BackgroundWorker1.DoWork
      ' Assigns the return value of a method named ComplexCalculation to
      ' e.Result
      e.Result = ComplexCalculation()
End Sub
Private Sub BackgroundWorker1_RunWorkerCompleted( _
   ByVal sender As System.Object, _
   ByVal e As System.ComponentModel.RunWorkerCompletedEventArgs) _
   Handles BackgroundWorker1.RunWorkerCompleted
   MsgBox("The result is " & e.Result.ToString)
End Sub
```

Sample of C# Code

```
private void backgroundWorker1_DoWork(object sender, DoWorkEventArgs e)
{
   // Assigns the return value of a method named ComplexCalculation to
   // e.Result
   e.Result = ComplexCalculation();
}
private void backgroundWorker1_RunWorkerCompleted(object sender,
   RunWorkerCompletedEventArgs e)
{
   System.Windows.Forms.MessageBox.Show("The result is " +
      e.Result.ToString());
}
```

Cancelling a Background Process

You might want to implement the ability to cancel a background process. *BackgroundWorker* supports this ability, but you must implement most of the cancellation code yourself. The *WorkerSupportsCancellation* property of the *BackgroundWorker* component indicates whether the component supports cancellation. You can call the *CancelAsync* method to attempt to cancel the operation; doing so sets the *CancellationPending* property of the *BackgroundWorker* component to *True*. By polling the *CancellationPending* property of the *BackgroundWorker* component, you can determine whether to cancel the operation.

To implement cancellation for a background process:

1. In the Properties window, set the *WorkerSupportsCancellation* property to *True* to enable the *BackgroundWorker* component to support cancellation.

2. Create a method that is called to cancel the background operation. The following example demonstrates how to cancel a background operation in a *Button.Click* event handler:

    Sample of Visual Basic Code

    ```
    Private Sub btnCancel_Click(ByVal sender As System.Object, _
        ByVal e As System.EventArgs) Handles btnCancel.Click
        BackgroundWorker1.CancelAsync()
    End Sub
    ```

```csharp
private void btnCancel_Click(object sender, EventArgs e)
{
    backgroundWorker1.CancelAsync();
}
```

3. In the *BackgroundWorker.DoWork* event handler, poll the *BackgroundWorker*
   .CancellationPending property and implement code to cancel the operation if it is *True*.
   You should also set the *e.Cancel* property to *True,* as shown in the following example:

   Sample of Visual Basic Code

```vb
Private Sub BackgroundWorker1_DoWork(ByVal sender As System.Object, _
    ByVal e As System.ComponentModel.DoWorkEventArgs) _
    Handles BackgroundWorker1.DoWork
    For i As Integer = 1 to 1000000
        TimeConsumingMethod()
        If BackgroundWorker1.CancellationPending Then
            e.Cancel = True
            Exit Sub
        End If
    Next
End Sub
```

   Sample of C# Code

```csharp
private void backgroundWorker1_DoWork(object sender, DoWorkEventArgs e)
{
    for (int i = 0; i < 1000000; i++)
    {
        TimeConsumingMethod();
        if (backgroundWorker1.CancellationPending)
        {
            e.Cancel = true;
            return;
        }
    }
}
```

Reporting Progress of a Background Process with *BackgroundWorker*

For particularly time-consuming operations, you might want to report progress back to
the primary thread. You can report progress of the background process by calling the
ReportProgress method. This method raises the *BackgroundWorker.ProgressChanged* event
and enables you to pass a parameter that indicates the percentage of progress that has been
completed to the methods that handle that event. The following example demonstrates how
to call the *ReportProgress* method from within the *BackgroundWorker.DoWork* event handler
and then how to update a *ProgressBar* control in the *BackgroundWorker.ProgressChanged*
event handler:

Sample of Visual Basic Code

```vb
Private Sub BackgroundWorker1_DoWork(ByVal sender As System.Object, _
    ByVal e As System.ComponentModel.DoWorkEventArgs) _
```

```
    Handles BackgroundWorker1.DoWork
    For i As Integer = 1 to 10
        RunTimeConsumingProcess()
        ' Calls the Report Progress method, indicating the percentage
        ' complete
        BackgroundWorker1.ReportProgress(i*10)
    Next
End Sub
Private Sub BackgroundWorker1_ProgressChanged( _
    ByVal sender As System.Object, _
    ByVal e As System.ComponentModel.ProgressChangedEventArgs) _
    Handles BackgroundWorker1.ProgressChanged
    ProgressBar1.Value = e.ProgressPercentage
End Sub
```

Sample of C# Code

```
private void backgroundWorker1_DoWork(object sender, DoWorkEventArgs e)
{
    for (int i = 1;i < 11; i++)
    {
        RunTimeConsumingProcess();
        // Calls the Report Progress method, indicating the percentage
        // complete
        backgroundWorker1.ReportProgress(i*10);
    }

}
private void backgroundWorker1_ProgressChanged(object sender,
    ProgressChangedEventArgs e)
{
    progressBar1.Value = e.ProgressPercentage;
}
```

Note that to report progress with the *BackgroundWorker* component, you must set the *WorkerReportsProgress* property to *True*.

Requesting the Status of a Background Process

You can determine whether a *BackgroundWorker* component is executing a background process by reading the *IsBusy* property, which returns a Boolean value. If *True*, the *BackgroundWorker* component is currently running a background process. If *False*, the *BackgroundWorker* component is idle. An example follows:

Sample of Visual Basic Code

```
If Not BackgroundWorker1.IsBusy
    BackgroundWorker1.RunWorkerAsync()
End If
```

Sample of C# Code

```
if (!(backgroundWorker1.IsBusy))
{
    backgroundWorker1.RunWorkerAsync();
}
```

Quick Check

1. What is the purpose of the *BackgroundWorker* component?

2. Briefly describe how to implement cancellation for a background process with *BackgroundWorker*.

Quick Check Answers

1. The *BackgroundWorker* component enables you to run operations on a separate thread while allowing the UI to remain responsive without complicated implementation or coding patterns.

2. First, you set the *WorkerSupportsCancellation* property of the *BackgroundWorker* component to *True*. Then you create a method that calls the *BackgroundWorker* *.CancelAsync* method to cancel the operation. Finally, in the background process, you poll the *BackgroundWorker.CancellationPending* property and set *e.Cancel* to *True* if *CancellationPending* is *True*, and take appropriate action to halt the process.

Using Delegates

Special classes called *delegates* enable you to call methods in a variety of ways. A delegate is essentially a type-safe function pointer that enables you to pass a reference to an entry point for a method and invoke that method in a variety of ways without making an explicit function call. You use the *Delegate* keyword (*delegate* in C#) to declare a delegate, and you must specify the same method signature as the method that you want to call with the delegate. The following example demonstrates a sample method and the declaration of a delegate that can be used to call that method:

Sample of Visual Basic Code

```
Public Function TestMethod(ByVal I As Integer) As String
    ' Insert method implementation here
End Function
Public Delegate Function myDelegate(ByVal I As Integer) As String
```

Sample of C# Code

```
public string TestMethod(int I)
{
    // Insert method implementation here
}
public delegate string myDelegate(int i);
```

After a delegate has been declared, you can create an instance of it that specifies a method that has the same signature. In C#, you can specify the method by simply naming the method. In Visual Basic, you must use the *AddressOf* operator to specify the method. The following example demonstrates how to create an instance of the delegate that specifies the method shown in the previous example.

Sample of Visual Basic Code
```
Dim del As New myDelegate(AddressOf TestMethod)
```

Sample of C# Code
```
myDelegate del - new myDelegate(TestMethod);
```

After an instance of a delegate has been created, you can invoke the method that refers to the delegate by simply calling the delegate with the appropriate parameters or by using the delegate's *Invoke* method. Both are shown in the following example:

Sample of Visual Basic Code
```
del(342)
del.Invoke(342)
```

Sample of C# Code
```
del(342);
del.Invoke(342);
```

Using Delegates Asynchronously

Delegates can be used to call any method asynchronously. In addition to the *Invoke* method, every delegate exposes two methods, *BeginInvoke* and *EndInvoke*, that call methods asynchronously. Calling the *BeginInvoke* method on a delegate starts the method that it refers to on a separate thread. Calling *EndInvoke* retrieves the results of that method and ends the separate thread.

The *BeginInvoke* method begins the asynchronous call to the method represented by the delegate. It requires the same parameters as the method the delegate represents, as well as two additional parameters: an *AsyncCallback* delegate that references the method to be called when the asynchronous method is completed, and a user-defined object that contains information about the asynchronous call. *BeginInvoke* returns an instance of *IAsyncResult*, which monitors the asynchronous call.

The *EndInvoke* method retrieves the results of the asynchronous call and can be called any time after *BeginInvoke* has been called. The *EndInvoke* method signature requires as a parameter the instance of *IAsyncResult* returned by *BeginInvoke* and returns the value that is returned by the method represented by the delegate. The method signature also contains any *Out* or *ByRef* parameters of the method it refers to in its signature.

You can use *BeginInvoke* and *EndInvoke* in several ways to implement asynchronous methods. Among them are the following:

- Calling *BeginInvoke*, doing work, and then calling *EndInvoke* on the same thread
- Calling *BeginInvoke*, polling *IAsyncResult* until the asynchronous operation is completed, and then calling *EndInvoke*
- Calling *BeginInvoke*, specifying a callback method to be executed when the asynchronous operation has completed, and calling *EndInvoke* on a separate thread

Waiting for an Asynchronous Call to Return with *EndInvoke*

The simplest way to implement an asynchronous method call is to call *BeginInvoke*, do some work, and then call *EndInvoke* on the same thread that *BeginInvoke* was called on. Although this approach is simplest, a potential disadvantage is that the *EndInvoke* call blocks execution of the thread until the asynchronous operation is completed if it has not completed yet. Thus, your main thread might still be unresponsive if the asynchronous operation is particularly time-consuming. The *–DelegateCallback* and *–AsyncState* parameters are not required for this operation, so *Nothing* (*null* in C#) can be supplied for these parameters. The following example demonstrates how to implement an asynchronous call in this way, using the *TestMethod* and *myDelegate* methods that were defined in the preceding examples:

Sample of Visual Basic Code

```
Dim del As New myDelegate(AddressOf TestMethod)
Dim result As IAsyncResult
result = del.BeginInvoke(342, Nothing, Nothing)
' Do some work while the asynchronous operation runs
Dim ResultString As String
ResultString = del.EndInvoke(result)
```

Sample of C# Code

```
myDelegate del = new myDelegate(TestMethod);
IAsyncResult result;
result = del.BeginInvoke(342, null, null);
// Do some work while the asynchronous operation runs
string ResultString;
ResultString = del.EndInvoke(result);
```

Polling *IAsyncResult* until Completion

Another way of executing an asynchronous operation is to call *BeginInvoke* and then poll the *IsCompleted* property of *IAsyncResult* to determine whether the operation has finished. When the operation has finished, you can then call *EndInvoke*. An advantage of this approach is that you do not need to call *EndInvoke* until the operation is complete. Thus, you do not lose any time by blocking your main thread. The following example demonstrates how to poll the *IsCompleted* property:

Sample of Visual Basic Code

```
Dim del As New myDelegate(AddressOf TestMethod)
Dim result As IAsyncResult
    result = del.BeginInvoke(342, Nothing, Nothing)
While Not result.IsCompleted
    ' Do some work
End While
Dim ResultString As String
ResultString = del.EndInvoke(result)
```

Sample of C# Code

```
myDelegate del = new myDelegate(TestMethod);
    IAsyncResult result;
```

```
result = del.BeginInvoke(342, null, null);
while (!(result.IsCompleted))
{
    // Do some work while the asynchronous operation runs
}
string ResultString;
ResultString = del.EndInvoke(result);
```

Executing a Callback Method When the Asynchronous Operation Returns

If you do not need to process the results of the asynchronous operation on the same thread that started the operation, you can specify a callback method to be executed when the operation is completed. This enables the operation to complete without interrupting the thread that initiated it. To execute a callback method, you must provide an instance of *AsyncCallback* that specifies the callback method. You can also supply a reference to the delegate itself so that *EndInvoke* can be called in the callback method to complete the operation. The following example demonstrates how to specify and run a callback method:

Sample of Visual Basic Code

```
Private Sub CallAsync()
    Dim del As New myDelegate(AddressOf TestMethod)
    Dim result As IAsyncResult
    Dim callback As New AsyncCallback(AddressOf CallbackMethod)
    result = del.BeginInvoke(342, callback, del)
End Sub

Private Sub CallbackMethod(ByVal result As IAsyncResult)
    Dim del As myDelegate
    Dim ResultString As String
    del = CType(result.AsyncState, myDelegate)
    ResultString = del.EndInvoke(result)
End Sub
```

Sample of C# Code

```
private void CallAsync()
{
    myDelegate del = new myDelegate(TestMethod);
    IAsyncResult result;
    AsyncCallback callback =  new AsyncCallback(CallbackMethod);
    result = del.BeginInvoke(342, callback, del);
}

private void CallbackMethod(IAsyncResult result)
{
    myDelegate del;
    string ResultString;
    del = (myDelegate)result.AsyncState;
    ResultString = del.EndInvoke(result);
}
```

Creating Process Threads

For applications that require more precise control over multiple threads, you can create new threads with the *Thread* object, which represents a separate thread of execution that runs concurrently with other threads. You can create as many *Thread* objects as you like, but the more threads there are, the greater the impact on performance and the greater the possibility of adverse threading conditions, such as deadlocks.

> **MORE INFO** **THREADING**
>
> Multithreading and use of the *Thread* object is an extremely complex and detailed subject. The information in this section should not be considered comprehensive. For more information, see Managed Threading at *http://msdn.Microsoft.com/en-us/library/3e8s7xdd.aspx*.

Creating and Starting a New Thread

The *Thread* object requires a delegate to the method that will serve as the starting point for the thread. This method must be a *Sub* (*void* in C#) method and must either have no parameters or take a single −*Object* parameter. In the latter case, the −*Object* parameter passes any required parameters to the method that starts the thread. After a thread is created, you can start it by calling the *Thread.Start* method. The following example demonstrates how to create and start a new thread:

Sample of Visual Basic Code

```
Dim aThread As New System.Threading.Thread(Addressof aMethod)
aThread.Start()
```

Sample of C# Code

```
System.Threading.Thread aThread = new
    System.Threading.Thread(aMethod);
aThread.Start();
```

For threads that accept a parameter, the procedure is similar except that the starting method can take a single *Object* as a parameter, and that object must be specified as the parameter in the *Thread.Start* method. Here is an example:

Sample of Visual Basic Code

```
Dim aThread As New System.Threading.Thread(Addressof aMethod)
aThread.Start(anObject)
```

Sample of C# Code

```
System.Threading.Thread aThread = new
    System.Threading.Thread(aMethod);
aThread.Start(anObject);
```

Destroying Threads

You can destroy a *Thread* object by calling the *Thread.Abort* method. This method causes the thread on which it is called to cease its current operation and to raise a *ThreadAbortException* exception. If a *Catch* block is capable of handling the exception, it will execute along with any *Finally* blocks. The thread is then destroyed and cannot be restarted.

Sample of Visual Basic Code
```
aThread.Abort()
```

Sample of C# Code
```
aThread.Abort();
```

Synchronizing Threads

Two of the most common difficulties involved in multithread programming are deadlocks and race conditions. A deadlock occurs when one thread has exclusive access to a particular variable and then attempts to gain exclusive access to a second variable at the same time that a second thread has exclusive access to the second variable and attempts to gain exclusive access to the variable locked by the first thread. The result is that both threads wait indefinitely for the other to release the variables, and they cease operating.

A race condition occurs when two threads attempt to access the same variable at the same time. For example, consider two threads that access the same collection. The first thread might add an *object* to the collection. The second thread might then remove an object from the collection based on the index of the object. The first thread might then attempt to access the object in the collection to find that it had been removed. Race conditions can lead to unpredictable effects that can destabilize your application.

The best way to avoid race conditions and deadlocks is by careful programming and judicious use of thread synchronization. You can use the *SyncLock* keyword in Visual Basic and the *lock* keyword in C# to obtain an exclusive lock on an object. This enables the thread that has the lock on the object to perform operations on that object without allowing any other threads to access it. Note that if any other threads attempt to access a locked object, those threads will pause until the lock is released. The following example demonstrates how to obtain a lock on an object:

Sample of Visual Basic Code
```
SyncLock anObject
    ' Perform some operation
End SyncLock
```

Sample of C# Code
```
lock (anObject)
{
    // Perform some operation
}
```

Some objects, such as collections, implement a synchronization object that should be used to synchronize access to the greater object. The following example demonstrates how to obtain a lock on the *SyncRoot* object of an *ArrayList* object:

Sample of Visual Basic Code

```vb
Dim anArrayList As New System.Collections.ArrayList
SyncLock anArrayList.SyncRoot
    ' Perform some operation on the ArrayList
End SyncLock
```

Sample of C# Code

```csharp
System.Collections.Arraylist anArrayList = new System.Collections.ArrayList();
lock (anArrayList.SyncRoot)
{
    // Perform some operation on the ArrayList
}
```

It is generally good practice when creating classes that will be accessed by multiple threads to include a synchronization object for synchronized access by threads. This enables the system to lock only the synchronization object, thus conserving resources by not having to lock every single object contained in the class. A synchronization object is simply an instance of *Object*, and does not need to have any functionality except to be available for locking. The following example demonstrates a class that exposes a synchronization object:

Sample of Visual Basic Code

```vb
Public Class aClass
    Public SynchronizationObject As New Object()
    ' Insert additional functionality here
End Class
```

Sample of C# Code

```csharp
public class aClass
{
    public object SynchronizationObject = new Object();
    // Insert additional functionality here
}
```

Special Considerations when Working with Controls

Because controls are always owned by the UI thread, it is generally unsafe to make calls to controls from a different thread. In WPF applications, you can use the *Dispatcher* object, discussed later in this lesson, to make safe function calls to the UI thread. In Windows Forms applications, you can use the *Control.InvokeRequired* property to determine whether it is safe to make a call to a control from another thread. If *InvokeRequired* returns *False*, it is safe to make the call to the control. If *InvokeRequired* returns *True*, however, you should use the *Control.Invoke* method on the owning form to supply a delegate to a method to access the control. Using *Control.Invoke* enables the control to be accessed in a thread-safe manner. The following example demonstrates setting the *Text* property of a *TextBox* control named *Text1*:

Sample of Visual Basic Code

```vbnet
Public Delegate Sub SetTextDelegate(ByVal t As String)
Public Sub SetText(ByVal t As String)
    If TextBox1.InvokeRequired = True Then
        Dim del As New SetTextDelegate(AddressOf SetText)
        Me.Invoke(del, New Object() {t})
    Else
        TextBox1.Text = t
    End If
End Sub
```

Sample of C# Code

```csharp
public delegate void SetTextDelegate(string t);
public void SetText(string t)
{
    if (textBox1.InvokeRequired)
    {
        SetTextDelegate del = new SetTextDelegate(SetText);
        this.Invoke(del, new object[]{t});
    }
    else
    {
        textBox1.Text = t;
    }
}
```

In the preceding example, the method tests *InvokeRequired* to determine whether it is dangerous to access the control directly. In general, this will return *True* if the control is being accessed from a separate thread. If *InvokeRequired* does return *True*, the method creates a new instance of a delegate that refers to itself and calls *Control.Invoke* to set the *Text* property in a thread-safe manner.

 Quick Check

1. What is a delegate? How is a delegate used?
2. What is thread synchronization, and why is it important?

Quick Check Answers

1. A delegate is a type-safe function pointer. It contains a reference to the entry point of a method and can be used to invoke that method. A delegate can be used to invoke a method synchronously on the same thread or asynchronously on a separate thread.

2. When you are working with multiple threads of execution, problems can occur if multiple threads attempt to access the same resources. Thread synchronization is the process of ensuring that threads do not attempt to access the same resource at the same time. One way to synchronize threads is to obtain exclusive locks on the objects you want to access, thereby prohibiting other threads from affecting them at the same time.

Using *Dispatcher* to Access Controls Safely on Another Thread in WPF

At times, you might want to change the user interface from a worker thread. For example, you might want to enable or disable buttons based on the status of the worker thread, or to provide more detailed progress reporting than is allowed by the *ReportProgess* method. The WPF threading model provides the *Dispatcher* class for cross-thread calls. Using *Dispatcher*, you can update your user interface safely from worker threads.

You can retrieve a reference to the *Dispatcher* object for a UI element from its *Dispatcher* property, as shown here:

Sample of Visual Basic Code

```
Dim aDisp As System.Windows.Threading.Dispatcher
aDisp = Button1.Dispatcher
```

Sample of C# Code

```
System.Windows.Threading.Dispatcher aDisp;
aDisp = button1.Dispatcher;
```

Dispatcher provides two principal methods you will use: *BeginInvoke* and *Invoke*. Both methods enable you to call a method safely on the UI thread. The *BeginInvoke* method enables you to call a method asynchronously, and the *Invoke* method enables you to call a method synchronously. Thus, a call to *Dispatcher.Invoke* will block execution on the thread on which it is called until the method returns, whereas a call to *Dispatcher.BeginInvoke* will not block execution.

Both the *BeginInvoke* and *Invoke* methods require you to specify a delegate that points to a method to be executed. You can also supply a single parameter or an array of parameters for the delegate, depending on the requirements of the delegate. You also are required to set the *DispatcherPriority* property, which determines the priority with which the delegate is executed. In addition, the *Dispatcher.Invoke* method enables you to set a period of time for the *Dispatcher* to wait before abandoning the invocation. The following example demonstrates how to invoke a delegate named *MyMethod*, using *BeginInvoke* and *Invoke*:

Sample of Visual Basic Code

```
Dim aDisp As System.Windows.Threading.Dispatcher = Button1.Dispatcher
' Invokes the delegate synchronously
aDisp.Invoke(System.Windows.Threading.DispatcherPriority.Normal, MyMethod)
' Invokes the delegate asynchronously
aDisp.BeginInvoke(System.Windows.Threading.DispatcherPriority.Normal, MyMethod)
```

Sample of C# Code

```
System.Windows.Threading.Dispatcher aDisp = button1.Dispatcher;
// Invokes the delegate synchronously
aDisp.Invoke(System.Windows.Threading.DispatcherPriority.Normal, MyMethod);
// Invokes the delegate asynchronously
aDisp.BeginInvoke(System.Windows.Threading.DispatcherPriority.Normal, MyMethod);
```

In this practice, you use the *BackgroundWorker* component. You write a time-consuming method to be executed on a separate thread. You implement cancellation functionality, and you use *Dispatcher* to update the user interface from the worker thread.

EXERCISE   Practice with *BackgroundWorker*

1. Open the partial solution for this exercise from its location on the companion CD. The partial solution already has a user interface built and has code for a *BackgroundWorker* component and stubs for methods. Note that the *WorkerSupportsCancellation* property of *BackgroundWorker* is set to *True* in the constructor in the partial solution.

2. In Code view, add the following code to the *Window1* class for a delegate to the *UpdateLabel* method:

Sample of Visual Basic Code

```
Private Delegate Sub UpdateDelegate(ByVal i As Integer)
Private Sub UpdateLabel(ByVal i As Integer)
    Label1.Content = "Cycles: " & i.ToString
End Sub
```

Sample of C# Code

```
private delegate void UpdateDelegate(int i);
private void UpdateLabel(int i)
{
    Label1.Content = "Cycles: " + i.ToString();
}
```

3. In the *DoWork* event handler, add the following code:

Sample of Visual Basic Code

```
For i As Integer = 0 To 500
    For j As Integer = 1 To 10000000
    Next
    If aWorker.CancellationPending Then
        e.Cancel = True
        Exit For
    End If
    Dim update As New UpdateDelegate(AddressOf UpdateLabel)
    Label1.Dispatcher.BeginInvoke(Windows.Threading. _
        DispatcherPriority.Normal, update, i)
Next
```

Sample of C# Code

```
for (int i = 0; i <= 500; i++)
{
    for (int j = 1; j <= 10000000; j++)
    {

    }
    if (aWorker.CancellationPending)
```

```
        {
            e.Cancel = true;
            return;
        }
        UpdateDelegate update = new UpdateDelegate(UpdateLabel);
        Label1.Dispatcher.BeginInvoke(
            System.Windows.Threading.DispatcherPriority.Normal, update, i);
    }
```

4. In Code view, add the following code to the *RunWorkerCompleted* event handler:

   Sample of Visual Basic Code

   ```
   If Not e.Cancelled Then
       Label2.Content = "Run Completed"
   Else
       Label2.Content = "Run Cancelled"
   End If
   ```

   Sample of C# Code

   ```
   if (!(e.Cancelled))
       Label2.Content = "Run Completed";
   else
       Label2.Content = "Run Cancelled";
   ```

5. In the designer, double-click the button marked Start to open the *Button1_Click* event handler and add the following code:

   Sample of Visual Basic Code

   ```
   Label2.Content = ""
   aWorker.RunWorkerAsync()
   ```

   Sample of C# Code

   ```
   label2.Content = "";
   aWorker.RunWorkerAsync();
   ```

6. In the designer, double-click the Cancel button to open the *Button2_Click* event handler and add the following code:

   Sample of Visual Basic Code

   ```
   aWorker.CancelAsync()
   ```

   Sample of C# Code

   ```
   aWorker.CancelAsync();
   ```

7. Press F5 to run your application and test the functionality.

Lesson Summary

- The *BackgroundWorker* component enables you to execute operations on a separate thread of execution. You call the *RunWorkerAsync* method of the *BackgroundWorker* component to begin the background process. The event handler for the *DoWork* method contains the code that will execute on a separate thread.

- The *BackgroundWorker.RunCompleted* event is fired when the background process is completed.

- You can enable cancellation of a background process by setting the *BackgroundWorker .WorkerSupportsCancellation* property to *True*. You then signal *BackgroundWorker* to cancel the process by calling the *CancelAsync* method, which sets the *CancellationPending* method to *True*. You must poll the *CancellationPending* property and implement cancellation code if the *CancellationPending* property registers as *True*.

- You can report progress from the background operation. First you must set the *WorkerReportsProgress* property to *True*. You can then call the *ReportProgress* method from within the background process to report progress. This raises the *ProgressChanged* event, which you can handle to take any action.

- A control's *Dispatcher* object can be used to execute code safely in the user interface from a worker thread. *Dispatcher.BeginInvoke* is used to execute code asynchronously, and *Dispatcher.Invoke* is used to execute code synchronously.

- Delegates are type-safe function pointers that enable you to call methods with the same signature. You can call methods synchronously by using the delegate's *Invoke* method, or asynchronously by using *BeginInvoke* and *EndInvoke*.

- When *BeginInvoke* is called, an operation specified by the delegate is started on a separate thread. You can retrieve the result of the operation by calling *EndInvoke*, which will block the calling thread until the background process is completed. You can also specify a callback method to complete the operation on the background thread if the main thread does not need the result.

- Thread objects represent separate threads of operation and provide a high degree of control of background processes. You can create a new thread by specifying a method that serves as an entry point for the thread.

- You can use the *SyncLock* (Visual Basic) and *lock* (C#) keywords to restrict access to a resource to a single thread of execution.

- You must not make calls to controls from background threads. Use the *Control. InvokeRequired* property to determine whether it is safe to make a direct call to a control. If it is not safe to make a direct call to the control, use the *Control.Invoke* method to make a safe call to the control.

Lesson Review

You can use the following questions to test your knowledge of the information in Lesson 1, "Implementing Asynchronous Processing." The questions are also available on the companion CD if you prefer to review them in electronic form.

> **NOTE** ANSWERS
>
> Answers to these questions and explanations of why each answer choice is correct or incorrect are located in the "Answers" section at the end of the book.

1. Which of the following are required to start a background process with the *BackgroundWorker* component? (Choose all that apply.)

   A. Calling the *RunWorkerAsync* method

   B. Handling the *DoWork* event

   C. Handling the *ProgressChanged* event

   D. Setting the *WorkerSupportsCancellation* property to *True*

2. Which of the following are good strategies for updating the user interface from the worker thread? (Choose all that apply.)

   A. Use *Dispatcher.BeginInvoke* to execute a delegate to a method that updates the user interface.

   B. Invoke a delegate to a method that updates the user interface.

   C. Set the *WorkerReportsProgress* property to *True*, call the *ReportProgress* method in the background thread, and handle the *ProgressChanged* event in the main thread.

   D. Call a method that updates the user interface from the background thread.

Lesson 2: Implementing Globalization and Localization

Applications that display data in formats appropriate to a particular culture and that display locale-appropriate strings in the user interface (UI) are considered globally ready applications. You can create globally ready applications with Visual Studio by taking advantage of the built-in support for globalization and localization. In this lesson, you learn how to implement localization and globalization in a Windows Forms application and a WPF application.

> **After this lesson, you will be able to:**
> - Implement globalization and localization within a Windows Form.
> - Implement globalization and localization within a WPF application.
>
> **Estimated lesson time: 30 minutes**

Globalization and Localization

Globalization and *localization* are different processes of internationalization. Globalization refers to formatting existing data in formats appropriate for the current culture setting. Localization, however, refers to retrieving appropriate data based on the culture. The following examples illustrate the difference between globalization and localization:

- **Globalization** In some countries, currency is formatted using a period (.) as a thousand separator and a comma (,) as a decimal separator, whereas other countries use the opposite convention. A globalized application formats currency data with the appropriate thousand separator and decimal separator based on the current culture settings.

- **Localization** The title of a form is displayed in a given language based on the locale in which it is deployed. A localized application retrieves the appropriate string and displays it based on the current culture settings.

Culture

Culture refers to cultural information about the country or region in which the application is deployed. In the .NET Framework, cultures are represented by a culture code that indicates the current language. For example, the following culture codes represent the following languages:

- **en** Specifies the English language
- **eu** Specifies the Basque language
- **tr** Specifies the Turkish language

Culture codes can specify only the language, like the ones shown here, or they can specify both the language and the region. Culture codes that specify only the language are called neutral culture codes, whereas culture codes that specify both the language and the region are called specific culture codes. Examples of specific culture codes are shown in the following list:

- **en-CA** Specifies the English language and Canada as the region
- **af-ZA** Specifies the Afrikaans language and South Africa as the region
- **kn-IN** Specifies the Kannada language and India as the region

You can find a complete list of culture codes in the *CultureInfo* class reference topic (*http://msdn.Microsoft.com/en-us/library/system.globalization.cultureinfo.aspx*) in the .NET Framework reference documentation.

Most culture codes follow the format just described, but some culture codes are exceptions. The following culture codes are examples that specify the character sets in addition to other information:

- **uz-UZ-Cyrl** Specifies the Uzbek language, the Uzbekistan region, and the Cyrillic alphabet
- **uz-UZ-Latn** Specifies the Uzbek language, the Uzbekistan region, and the Latin alphabet
- **zh-CHT** Specifies the traditional Chinese language, no region
- **zh-CHS** Specifies the simplified Chinese language, no region

Changing the Current Culture

Your application automatically reads the culture settings of the system and implements them. Thus, in most circumstances, you do not have to change the culture settings manually. You can, however, change the current culture of your application in code by setting the current culture to a new instance of the *CultureInfo* class. The *CultureInfo* class contains information about a particular culture and how it interacts with the application and system. For example, the *CultureInfo* class contains information about the type of calendar, date formatting, currency formatting, and so on for a specific culture. You set the current culture of an application programmatically by setting the *CurrentThread.CurrentCulture* property to a new instance of the *CultureInfo* class. The *CultureInfo* constructor requires a string that represents the appropriate culture code as a parameter. The following code example demonstrates how to set the current culture to French Canadian:

Sample of Visual Basic Code

```
System.Threading.Thread.CurrentThread.CurrentCulture = New _
    System.Globalization.CultureInfo("fr-CA")
```

Sample of C# Code

```
System.Threading.Thread.CurrentThread.CurrentCulture = new
    System.Globalization.CultureInfo("fr-CA");
```

Implementing Globalization

The *CurrentThread.CurrentCulture* property controls the culture used to format data. When *CurrentCulture* is set to a new instance of *CultureInfo*, any data formatted by the application is updated to the new format. Data that is not formatted by the application is not affected by a change in the current culture. Consider the following examples:

Sample of Visual Basic Code

```
Label1.Text = "$500.00"
Label2.Text = Format(500, "Currency")
```

Sample of C# Code

```
label1.Text = "$500.00";
label2.Text = (500).ToString("C");
```

When the culture is set to en-US, which represents the English language and the United States as the region (which is the default culture setting for computers in the United States), both labels display the same string—that is, "$500.00". When the current culture is set to fr-FR, which represents the French language and France as the region, the text in the two labels differs. The text in *Label1* always reads "$500.00" because it is not formatted by the application. The text in *Label2*, however, reads "500,00 €". Note that the currency symbol is changed to the appropriate symbol for the locale—in this case, the euro symbol—and the decimal separator is changed to the separator that is appropriate for the locale (in this case, the comma).

Implementing Localization

You can implement localization—that is, provide a user interface (UI) specific to the current locale—by using the built-in localization features of Visual Studio, which enable you to create alternative versions of forms that are culture-specific and automatically manages retrieval of resources appropriate for the culture.

Changing the Current User Interface Culture

The UI culture is represented by an instance of *CultureInfo* and is distinct from the *CultureInfo* .*CurrentCulture* property. The *CurrentCulture* setting determines the formatting that will be applied to system-formatted data, whereas the *CurrentUICulture* setting determines the resources that will be loaded into localized forms at run time. You can set the UI culture by setting the *CurrentThread.CurrentUICulture* property, as shown in the following example:

Sample of Visual Basic Code

```
' Sets the current UI culture to Thailand
System.Threading.Thread.CurrentThread.CurrentUICulture = New _
    System.Globalization.CultureInfo("th-TH")
```

Sample of C# Code

```
// Sets the current UI culture to Thailand
System.Threading.Thread.CurrentThread.CurrentUICulture = new
    System.Globalization.CultureInfo("th-TH");
```

When the current UI culture is set, the application loads resources specific to that culture if they are available. If culture-specific resources are unavailable, the UI displays resources for the default culture.

Note that the UI culture must be set before a form that displays any localized resources is loaded. If you want to set the UI culture programmatically, you must set it before the form has been created, either in the form's constructor or in the application's *Main* method.

Creating Localized Forms

Every form exposes a *Localizable* property that determines whether the form is localized. Setting this property to *True* enables localization for the form.

When the *Localizable* property of a form is set to *True*, Visual Studio .NET automatically handles the creation of appropriate resource files and manages their retrieval according to the *CurrentUICulture* setting.

At design time, you can create localized copies of a form by using the *Language* property. It is available only at design time and assists in the creation of localized forms. When the *Language* property is set to *(Default)*, you can edit any of the form's UI properties or controls to provide a representation for the default UI culture. To create a localized version of the form, you can set the *Language* property to any value other than *(Default)*. Visual Studio will create a resource file for the new language and store any values you set for the UI in that file.

To create localized forms:

1. Set the *Localizable* property of your form to *True*.
2. Design the UI of your form and translate any UI elements into the localized languages.
3. Add UI elements for the default culture. This is the culture that will be used if no other culture is specified.
4. Set the *Language* property of your form to the culture for which you want to create a localized form.
5. Add the localized UI content to your form.
6. Repeat steps 4 and 5 for each localized language.
7. Build your application.

When *CurrentUICulture* is set to a localized culture, your application loads the appropriate version of the form by reading the corresponding resource files. If no resource files exist for a specified culture, the default culture UI is displayed.

Localizing a WPF application

Localization in WPF is enabled through satellite assemblies. Localizable elements of your application are segregated into resource assemblies that are loaded automatically, depending on the current UI culture. When a localized application is started, the application first looks for resource assemblies targeted to the specific culture and region (*fr-CA* in the previous example). If those assemblies are not found, it looks for assemblies targeted to the language only (*fr* in the previous example). If neither is found, the application looks for a neutral resource set. If this is not found either, an exception is raised. You should localize your application for every language in which you expect it to be used.

You can avoid localization-based exceptions by setting the *NeutralResourcesLanguage* attribute. This attribute designates the resource set to be used if a specific set of resources cannot be found. The following example demonstrates how to use the *NeutralResourcesLanguage* attribute:

Sample of Visual Basic Code

```
<Assembly: NeutralResourcesLanguage("en-US", _
UltimateResourceFallbackLocation.Satellite)>
```

Sample of C# Code

```
[assembly: NeutralResourcesLanguage("en-US",
UltimateResourceFallbackLocation.Satellite)]
```

Localizing an Application

Localization in WPF is a multi-step process. The following procedure is a high-level protocol for localizing a WPF application. Each of the steps is discussed in greater detail later in this lesson.

To localize an application:

1. Add a *UICulture* attribute to the project file and build the application to generate culture-specific subdirectories.

2. Mark localizable properties with the *Uid* attribute to identify them uniquely. You must perform this step for each XAML file in your application.

> **NOTE LOCALIZABLE PROPERTIES**
>
> Localizable properties include more than just text strings; they might include colors, layout properties, or any other UI property that has cultural significance.

3. Extract the localizable content from your application using a specialized tool (as discussed later in this chapter).

4. Translate the localizable content.

5. Create subdirectories to hold satellite assemblies for the new cultures.

6. Generate satellite assemblies using a specialized tool.

Adding the *UICulture* Attribute to the Project File

By default, a WPF application is not culture-aware. You can make your application culture-aware by adding the *UICulture* attribute to the project file and building the application. The *UICulture* attribute indicates the default culture for the application (usually *en-US* for applications created and run in the United States). After adding this attribute, building the application generates a subdirectory for the culture in the application directory with localizable content in a satellite assembly.

To add the *UICulture* attribute to the project file:

1. Open the project file for your project (<ProjectName>.csproj for C# applications and <ProjectName>.vbproj for Visual Basic applications) with Notepad or a similar text editor.

2. Locate the first <PropertyGroup> tag. Within that tag, add the following set of XAML tags:

   ```
   <UICulture>en-US</UICulture>
   ```

   If you are creating your application in a location other than the United States, or are using a language other than English, adjust the culture code in this tag accordingly.

3. Save the project file and build your application.

Marking Localizable Elements

The first step in actually localizing your application is to mark elements that are localizable; this includes all strings displayed in the user interface, but many other properties are localizable as well. For example, languages that use different alphabets might require the *FontWidth* property of visual elements to be localized, and languages that are read from right to left (rather than from left to right, as English is) require localization of the *FlowDirection* property of visual elements. Images are typically localized; thus, *ImageSource* properties have to be adjusted to point to the appropriate images. Different languages require the localization of font or other UI element sizes to account for differences in string lengths. Even color combinations can be culturally sensitive and require you to localize the *Foreground* and *Background* brushes. Deciding what to localize in an application is often the most difficult part of the entire process, but it is also the most important and should be given a great deal of thought. The point to keep in mind is that localization involves much more than simple translation; it is a complex process that requires sufficient research and planning.

You can mark elements for localization by adding the *Uid* attribute to the element in XAML. This is an attribute that uniquely identifies an element for the purpose of localization. You can add the *Uid* attribute as shown here in bold:

```
<Button x:Uid="Button_1" Margin="112,116,91,122"
   Name="Button1">Button</Button>
```

Alternatively, you can use the Msbuild.exe tool to mark every element in your application with the *Uid* attribute by using the *updateuid* flag and pointing it to your project file, as shown here:

```
msbuild /t:updateuid myApplication.vbproj
```

This tool should be run from the command prompt in Visual Studio, which is available in the Visual Studio Tools subdirectory of your Visual Studio folder on the Start menu.

When localizable resources are extracted from your application, every localizable property of every element marked with the *Uid* attribute is extracted.

Note that you must mark every element in your application that is in an XAML file and that you want to localize. This includes resources and resources in resource dictionaries.

Extracting Localizable Content

Extraction of localizable content from your application requires a specialized tool. You can download a command-line tool named LocBaml that can extract localizable content, and third-party solutions are also available. To acquire LocBaml, navigate to *http://msdn.microsoft .com/en-us/library/ms771568.aspx* and download the source files from the link in the LocBaml Tool Sample topic.

The LocBaml tool is not a compiled application. You must compile it before you can use it, and then you must run it as a command-line application from the directory that contains your compiled application and use the */parse* switch to provide the path to the resources dynamic link library (DLL). An example is shown here:

```
locbaml /parse en-US\myApplication.resources.dll
```

LocBaml outputs a .csv file that contains all localizable properties from all the elements that have been marked with the *Uid* attribute.

Translating Localizable Content

Content typically is not translated by the developer. Rather, localization specialists are employed to provide translated strings and values for other translatable properties. The .csv file generated by LocBaml provides a row of data pertaining to each localizable property extracted from the application. Each row contains the following information:

- The name of the localizable resource
- The *Uid* of the element and the name of the localizable property
- The localization category, such as Title or Text
- Whether the property is readable (that is, whether it is visible as text in the user interface)
- Whether the property value can be modified by the translator (always true unless you indicate otherwise)
- Any additional comments you provide for the translator
- The value of the property

The final entry in each row, the value of the property, is the property that must be translated by the translator. When translation is complete, the .csv file is returned to you with the translated values in the final column.

Creating Subdirectories

Before satellite assemblies can be created, you must create a subdirectory named for the appropriate culture code to house them. This subdirectory should be created in the directory where your compiled application exists, and it should be named for the culture code for which you are creating satellite assemblies. For example, if you were creating satellite assemblies for French as spoken in Canada, you would name your directory fr-CA.

Generating Satellite Assemblies

After the resources have been translated and the subdirectories have been created, you are ready to generate your *satellite assemblies*, which hold culture-specific resources for a localized application. If you are using LocBaml, you can generate satellite assemblies by running LocBaml again from the directory in which your compiled application resides and using the */generate* switch to generate a satellite assembly. The following example demonstrates a command-line use of LocBaml to generate a satellite assembly:

```
locbaml /generate en-US\myApplication.resources.dll
/trans:myApplication.resources.FrenchCan.csv /cul:fr-CA /out:fr-CA
```

Let's break down what this command does. The */generate* switch tells LocBaml to generate a satellite assembly based on the indicated assembly, which, in this example, is en-US\myApplication.resources.dll. The */trans* switch specifies the .csv file used to generate the satellite assembly (myApplication.resources.FrenchCan.csv in this example). The */cul* switch associates the indicated culture with the satellite assembly, and the */out* switch specifies the name of the folder, which must match the specified culture exactly.

Loading Resources by Locale

After satellite assemblies have been created, your application automatically loads the appropriate resources for the culture. As described previously, you can change the current UI culture by setting the *CurrentThread.CurrentUICulture* property to a new instance of *System.Globalization.CultureInfo*, or you can change culture settings through the system. If the culture changes while an application is running, you must restart the application to load culture-specific resources. If you use code to change the UI culture, you must set *UICulture* to a new instance of *CultureInfo* before any of the user interface is rendered. Typically, the best place to do this is in the *Application.Startup* event handler.

EXAM TIP

Localization is a complex process that typically involves localization specialists in addition to the developer. Focus on learning the aspects of localization that involve the developer directly, such as preparing the application for localization and marking localizable elements. Processes that probably will be performed by a different person, such as extracting content and translation, are likely to be emphasized less on the exam.

Using Culture Settings in Validators and Converters

Although localizing UI elements is an invaluable part of localization, you must also format data appropriately for the current culture setting. In some cases, this happens automatically. For example, the *String.Format* method uses the correct decimal and time separators based on the current UI culture. But when you provide formatting for data presented in your user interface or provide validation, your code must take the current culture into account.

The *Convert* and *ConvertBack* methods of the *IValueConverter* interface and the *Validate* method of the *ValidationRule* class provide a parameter that indicates the culture. In the case of *IValueConverter*, the parameter is named *culture*, and in the *Validate* method, the parameter is called *cultureInfo*. In both cases, the parameter represents an instance of *System.Globalization.CultureInfo*. Whenever you create a validation rule or converter in a localized application, you always should test the culture value and provide culture-appropriate formatting for your data. The following shows an example:

Sample of Visual Basic Code

```
<ValueConversion(GetType(String), GetType(String))> _
Public Class DateBrushConverter
    Implements IValueConverter
    ' Note: the Translator class is assumed to be a class that contains a
    ' dictionary used to translate the provided strings.
    Dim myTranslator As New Translator
```

```vb
    Public Function Convert(ByVal value As Object, ByVal targetType As _
        System.Type, ByVal parameter As Object, ByVal culture As _
        System.Globalization.CultureInfo) As Object Implements _
        System.Windows.Data.IValueConverter.Convert
        Dim astring As String = CType(value, String)
        Select Case culture.ToString
            Case "fr-FR"
                Return myTranslator.EnglishToFrench(astring)
            Case "de-DE"
                Return myTranslator.EnglishToGerman(astring)
            Case Else
                Return astring
        End Select
    End Function

    Public Function ConvertBack(ByVal value As Object, ByVal targetType _
        As System.Type, ByVal parameter As Object, ByVal culture As _
        System.Globalization.CultureInfo) As Object Implements _
        System.Windows.Data.IValueConverter.ConvertBack
        Dim astring As String = CType(value, String)
        Select Case culture.ToString
            Case "fr-FR"
                Return myTranslator.FrenchToEnglish(astring)
            Case "de-DE"
                Return myTranslator.GermanToEnglish(astring)
            Case Else
                Return astring
        End Select
    End Function
End Class
```

Sample of C# Code

```csharp
[ValueConversion(typeof(string), typeof(string))]
public class LanguageConverter : IValueConverter
{
    // Note: the Translator class is assumed to be a class that contains a
    // dictionary used to translate the provided strings.
    Translator myTranslator = new Translator();
    public object Convert(object value, Type targetType, object parameter,
        System.Globalization.CultureInfo culture)
    {
        string aString = (string)value;
        switch(culture.ToString())
        {
            case "fr-FR":
                return myTranslator.EnglishToFrench(aString);
            case "de-DE":
                return myTranslator.EnglishToGerman(aString);
            default:
                return aString;
        }
    }

    public object ConvertBack(object value, Type targetType, object
```

```
         parameter, System.Globalization.CultureInfo culture)
    {
        string aString = (string)value;
        switch(culture.ToString())
        {
          case "fr-FR":
              return myTranslator.FrenchToEnglish(aString);
          case "de-DE":
              return myTranslator.GermanToEnglish(aString);
          default:
              return aString;
        }
    }
  }
}
```

 Quick Check

1. What is the difference between globalization and localization?
2. What is the difference between *CurrentCulture* and *CurrentUICulture*?

Quick Check Answers

1. Globalization refers to formatting data in formats appropriate for the current culture setting. Localization refers to retrieving and displaying appropriately localized data based on the culture.
2. The *CurrentCulture* determines how data is formatted as appropriate for the current culture setting. The *CurrentUICulture* determines what set of resource strings should be loaded for display in the UI.

PRACTICE **Create Localized Forms**

In this practice, you create localized forms. You create a form for the default culture that demonstrates date/time display and currency display as well as strings for the default culture. Then you create a localized version of this form that includes German strings. Finally, you create a form that enables you to choose the locale for which you would like to display your localized form and sets the culture appropriately. A completed solution to this practice can be found in the files installed from the companion CD.

EXERCISE Creating Localized Forms

1. In Visual Studio, create a new Windows Forms application.
2. From the Project menu, choose Add Windows Form to add a new Form to your project. Name the new form **Form2**.

3. In the designer, click the tab for *Form2*. From the Toolbox, add four *Label* controls. Set the *Text* properties as follows:

LABEL	TEXT PROPERTY VALUE
Label1	*Currency Format*
Label2	*(nothing)*
Label3	*Current Date and Time*
Label4	*(nothing)*

4. Double-click Form2 to open the *Form2_Load* event handler. Add the following code to the *Form2_Load* event handler:

Sample of Visual Basic Code

```
Label2.Text = Format(500, "Currency")
Label4.Text = Now.ToShortDateString
```

Sample of C# Code

```
label2.Text = (500).ToString("C");
label4.Text = System.DateTime.Now.ToShortDateString();
```

5. In the designer, set the *Form2.Localizable* property to *True* and set the *Language* property to *German (Germany)*.

6. Set the *Text* properties of *Label1* and *Label3* as follows:

LABEL	TEXT PROPERTY VALUE
Label1	*Währung-Format*
Label3	*Aktuelle Uhrzeit*

7. In the designer, click the tab for Form1.

8. From the Toolbox, add three *Button* controls to the form and set their *Text* properties as shown here:

BUTTON	BUTTON TEXT PROPERTY VALUE
Button1	*United States*
Button2	*United Kingdom*
Button3	*Germany*

9. In the designer, double-click the Button1 control to open the *Button1_Click* default event handler and add the following code:

Sample of Visual Basic Code

```
System.Threading.Thread.CurrentThread.CurrentCulture = New _
   System.Globalization.CultureInfo("en-US")
System.Threading.Thread.CurrentThread.CurrentUICulture = New _
   System.Globalization.CultureInfo("en-US")
```

```
Dim aform As New Form2()
aform.Show()
```

Sample of C# Code

```
System.Threading.Thread.CurrentThread.CurrentCulture = new
    System.Globalization.CultureInfo("en-US");
System.Threading.Thread.CurrentThread.CurrentUICulture = new
    System.Globalization.CultureInfo("en-US");
Form2 aform = new Form2();
aform.Show();
```

10. In the designer, double-click the *Button2* control to open the *Button2_Click* default event handler and add the following code:

Sample of Visual Basic Code

```
System.Threading.Thread.CurrentThread.CurrentCulture = New _
    System.Globalization.CultureInfo("en-GB")
System.Threading.Thread.CurrentThread.CurrentUICulture = New _
    System.Globalization.CultureInfo("en-GB")
Dim aform As New Form2()
aform.Show()
```

Sample of C# Code

```
System.Threading.Thread.CurrentThread.CurrentCulture = new
    System.Globalization.CultureInfo("en-GB");
System.Threading.Thread.CurrentThread.CurrentUICulture = new
    System.Globalization.CultureInfo("en-GB");
Form2 aform = new Form2();
aform.Show();
```

11. In the designer, double-click the *Button3* control to open the *Button3_Click* default event handler and add the following code:

Sample of Visual Basic Code

```
System.Threading.Thread.CurrentThread.CurrentCulture = New _
    System.Globalization.CultureInfo("de-DE")
System.Threading.Thread.CurrentThread.CurrentUICulture = New _
    System.Globalization.CultureInfo("de-DE")
Dim aform As New Form2()
aform.Show()
```

Sample of C# Code

```
System.Threading.Thread.CurrentThread.CurrentCulture = new
    System.Globalization.CultureInfo("de-DE");
System.Threading.Thread.CurrentThread.CurrentUICulture = new
    System.Globalization.CultureInfo("de-DE");
Form2 aform = new Form2();
aform.Show();
```

12. Press F5 to build and run your application. Click each button to see a localized form. Note that the appropriate format for currency and the date are displayed in the localized form and that the new strings are loaded for the German form.

Lesson Summary

- Culture refers to cultural information about the country or region in which the application is deployed and is represented by a culture code. Globalization refers to the process of formatting application data in formats appropriate for the locale. Localization refers to the process of loading and displaying localized strings in the UI.

- The *CurrentCulture* setting for the thread determines the culture used to format application data. The *CurrentUICulture* setting for the thread determines the culture used to load localized resources.

- You can create localized forms by setting the *Localizable* property of a form to *True* and then setting the *Language* property to a language other than *(Default)*. A new copy of the form is created for this culture, and localized resources can be added to this form.

- You can implement right-to-left display in a control by setting the *RightToLeft* property to *True*. You can reverse the control layout of an entire form by setting the *RightToLeftLayout* and *RightToLeft* properties of a form to *True*.

- Localization in WPF requires localizable elements to be marked with the *Uid* attribute, which uniquely identifies localizable elements in your application.

- LocBaml is a command-line application available from Microsoft as a downloadable, compilable sample. LocBaml can be used to extract localizable resources from your application and to build satellite assemblies with localized resources.

- Methods in *IValueConverter* and *ValidationRule* provide a reference to the *CultureInfo* object to be used in the operation. Whenever culture-specific formatting or validation is required, your code should check the culture to provide the appropriate functionality.

Lesson Review

The following questions are intended to reinforce key information presented in Lesson 2, "Implementing Globalization and Localization." The questions are also available on the companion CD if you prefer to review them in electronic form.

> **NOTE ANSWERS**
>
> Answers to these questions and explanations of why each answer choice is correct or incorrect are located in the "Answers" section at the end of the book.

1. Which of the following lines of code should be used to format data appropriately for Germany?

   A.

   Sample of Visual Basic Code

   ```
   System.Threading.Thread.CurrentThread.CurrentUICulture = New _
       System.Globalization.CultureInfo("de-DE")
   ```

Sample of C# Code

```
System.Threading.Thread.CurrentThread.CurrentUICulture = New
    System.Globalization.CultureInfo("de-DE");
```

B.

Sample of Visual Basic Code

```
Me.CurrentUICulture = New System.Globalization.CultureInfo("de-DE")
```

Sample of C# Code

```
this.CurrentUICulture = New System.Globalization.CultureInfo("de-DE");
```

C.

Sample of Visual Basic Code

```
System.Threading.Thread.CurrentThread.CurrentCulture = New _
    System.Globalization.CultureInfo("de-DE")
```

Sample of C# Code

```
System.Threading.Thread.CurrentThread.CurrentCulture = New
    System.Globalization.CultureInfo("de-DE");
```

D.

Sample of Visual Basic Code

```
Me.CurrentCulture = New System.Globalization.CultureInfo("de-DE")
```

Sample of C# Code

```
this.CurrentCulture = New System.Globalization.CultureInfo("de-DE");
```

2. Given a form that contains a *Label* control named *Label1* and a *Button* control named *Button1*, all with default settings, which of the following must you do to display the entire form and all controls in a right-to-left layout with right-to-left text display? (Choose all that apply.)

   A. Set the *Label1.RightToLeft* property to *True*.

   B. Set the *Button1.RightToLeft* property to *True*.

   C. Set the *Form1.RightToLeft* property to *True*.

   D. Set the *Form1.RightToLeftLayout* property to *True*.

Lesson 3: Integrating Windows Forms Controls and WPF Controls

The WPF suite of controls is very full, and, together with the WPF control customization abilities, you can create a very wide array of control functionality for your applications. Some types of functionality, however, are absent from the WPF elements and can be difficult to implement on your own. Fortunately, WPF provides a method for using Windows Forms controls in your application. Likewise, you can incorporate WPF controls into your Windows Forms applications. In this lesson, you learn how to use Windows Forms controls in WPF applications, and vice versa.

> **After this lesson, you will be able to:**
> - Describe how to use a Windows Forms control in a WPF application.
> - Integrate Windows Forms dialog boxes into WPF applications.
> - Integrate WPF controls into Windows Forms applications.
>
> **Estimated lesson time: 30 minutes**

Using Windows Forms Controls in WPF Applications

Although WPF provides a wide variety of useful controls and features, you might find that some familiar functionality you used in Windows Forms programming is not available. Notably absent are controls such as *MaskedTextBox* and *PropertyGrid*, as well as simple dialog boxes. Fortunately, you can still use many Windows Forms controls in your WPF applications.

Using Dialog Boxes in WPF Applications

Dialog boxes are one of the most notable things missing from the WPF menagerie of controls and elements. Because dialog boxes are separate user interfaces, however, they are relatively easy to incorporate into your WPF applications.

File Dialog Boxes

The file dialog boxes *OpenFileDialog* and *SaveFileDialog* are components that you want to use frequently in your applications. They enable you to browse the file system and return the path to the selected file. The *OpenFileDialog* and *SaveFileDialog* classes are very similar and share most important members. Table 9-2 shows important properties of the file dialog boxes, and Table 9-3 shows important methods.

TABLE 9-2 Important Properties of the File Dialog Boxes

PROPERTY	DESCRIPTION
AddExtension	Gets or sets a value indicating whether the dialog box automatically adds an extension to a file name if the user omits the extension.
CheckFileExists	Gets or sets a value indicating whether the dialog box displays a warning if the user specifies a file name that does not exist.
CheckPathExists	Gets or sets a value indicating whether the dialog box displays a warning if the user specifies a path that does not exist.
CreatePrompt	Gets or sets a value indicating whether the dialog box prompts the user for permission to create a file if the user specifies a file that does not exist. Available only in *SaveFileDialog*.
FileName	Gets or sets a string containing the file name selected in the file dialog box.
FileNames	Gets the file names of all selected files in the dialog box. Although this member exists for both the *SaveFileDialog* and the *OpenFileDialog* classes, it is relevant only to the *OpenFileDialog* class because it is only possible to select more than one file in *OpenFileDialog*.
Filter	Gets or sets the current file name filter string, which determines the choices that appear in the Save As File Type or Files Of Type box in the dialog box.
InitialDirectory	Gets or sets the initial directory displayed by the file dialog box.
Multiselect	Gets or sets a value indicating whether the dialog box allows multiple files to be selected. Available only in *OpenFileDialog*.
OverwritePrompt	Gets or sets a value indicating whether the Save As dialog box displays a warning if the user specifies a file name that already exists. Available only in *SaveFileDialog*.
ValidateNames	Gets or sets a value indicating whether the dialog box accepts only valid Win32 file names.

TABLE 9-3 Important Methods of the File Dialog Boxes

METHOD	DESCRIPTION
OpenFile	Opens the selected file as a *System.IO.Stream* object. For *OpenFileDialog* objects, it opens a read-only stream. For *SaveFileDialog* objects, it saves a new copy of the indicated file and then opens it as a read-write stream. You need to be careful when using the *SaveFileDialog.OpenFile* method to keep from overwriting preexisting files of the same name.
ShowDialog	Shows the dialog box modally, thereby halting application execution until the dialog box has been closed. Returns a *DialogResult* result.

To use a file dialog box in a WPF application:

1. In Solution Explorer, right-click the project name and choose Add Reference. The Add Reference dialog box opens.

2. On the .NET tab, select *System.Windows.Forms* and then click OK.

3. In code, create a new instance of the desired file dialog box, as shown here:

Sample of Visual Basic Code

```
Dim aDialog As New System.Windows.Forms.OpenFileDialog()
```

Sample of C# Code

```
System.Windows.Forms.OpenFileDialog aDialog =
    new System.Windows.Forms.OpenFileDialog();
```

4. Use the *ShowDialog* method to show the dialog box modally. After the dialog box is shown, you can retrieve the file name that was selected from the *FileNames* property. An example is shown here:

Sample of Visual Basic Code

```
Dim aResult As System.Windows.Forms.DialogResult
aResult = aDialog.ShowDialog()
If aResult = System.Windows.Forms.DialogResult.OK Then
    ' Shows the path to the selected file
    MessageBox.Show(aDialog.FileName)
End If
```

Sample of C# Code

```
System.Windows.Forms.DialogResult aResult;
aResult = aDialog.ShowDialog();
if (aResult == System.Windows.Forms.DialogResult.OK)
{
    // Shows the path to the selected file
    MessageBox.Show(aDialog.FileName);
}
```

> **NOTE AVOIDING NAMING CONFLICTS**
>
> It is not advisable to import the System.Windows.Forms namespace because this leads to naming conflicts with several WPF classes.

WindowsFormsHost

Although using dialog boxes in WPF applications is fairly straightforward, using controls is a bit more difficult. Fortunately, WPF provides an element, *WindowsFormsHost*, specifically designed to ease this task.

WindowsFormsHost is a WPF element capable of hosting a single child element that is a Windows Forms control. The hosted Windows Forms control automatically sizes itself to the size of *WindowsFormsHost*. You can use *WindowsFormsHost* to create instances of

Windows Forms controls declaratively, and you can set properties on hosted Windows Forms declaratively.

Adding a Windows Forms Control to a WPF Application

To use the *WindowsFormsHost* element in your WPF applications, first you must add a reference to the *System.Windows.Forms.Integration* namespace to the XAML view in the *WindowsFormsIntegration* assembly, as shown here. (This line has been formatted to fit on the printed page, but it should be on a single line in your XAML.)

```
xmlns:my="clr-namespace:System.Windows.Forms.Integration;
    assembly=WindowsFormsIntegration"
```

If you drag a *WindowsFormsHost* element from the Toolbox to the designer, this reference is added automatically. You must also add a reference to the *System.Windows.Forms* namespace, as shown here:

```
xmlns:wf="clr-namespace:System.Windows.Forms;assembly=System.Windows.Forms"
```

Then you can create an instance of the desired Windows Forms control as a child element of a *WindowsFormsHost* element, as shown here:

```
<my:WindowsFormsHost Margin="48,106,30,56" Name="windowsFormsHost1">
    <wf:Button Text="Windows Forms Button" />
</my:WindowsFormsHost>
```

Setting Properties of Windows Forms Controls in a WPF application

You can set properties on a hosted Windows Forms control declaratively in XAML like you would any WPF element, as shown in bold here:

```
<my:WindowsFormsHost Margin="48,106,30,56" Name="windowsFormsHost1">
    <wf:Button Text="Windows Forms Button" />
</my:WindowsFormsHost>
```

Although you can set properties declaratively on a hosted Windows Forms control, some of those properties will not have any meaning. For example, properties dealing with layout, such as *Anchor*, *Dock*, *Top*, and *Left*, have no effect on the position of the Windows Forms control. This is because its container is *WindowsFormsHost,* and the Windows Forms control occupies the entire interior of that element. To manage layout for a hosted Windows Forms control, set the layout properties of *WindowsFormsHost* as shown in bold here:

```
<my:WindowsFormsHost Margin="48,106,30,56" Name="windowsFormsHost1">
    <wf:Button Text="Windows Forms Button" />
</my:WindowsFormsHost>
```

Setting Event Handlers on Windows Forms Controls in a WPF Application

Similarly, you can set event handlers declaratively in XAML, as shown in bold in the following example:

```
<my:WindowsFormsHost Margin="48,106,30,56" Name="windowsFormsHost1">
    <wf:Button Click="Button_Click" Name="Button1" />
</my:WindowsFormsHost>
```

Note that events raised by Windows Forms controls are regular .NET events, not routed events, and therefore they must be handled at the source.

Obtaining a Reference to a Hosted Windows Forms Control in Code

In most cases, using simple declarative syntax with hosted Windows Forms controls is not sufficient; you have to use code to manipulate hosted Windows Forms controls. Although you can set the *Name* property of a hosted Windows Forms control, that name does not give you a code reference to the control. Instead, you must obtain a reference by using the *WindowsFormsHost.Child* property and casting it to the correct type. The following code example demonstrates how to obtain a reference to a hosted Windows Forms *Button* control:

Sample of Visual Basic Code

```
Dim aButton As System.Windows.Forms.Button
aButton = CType(windowsFormsHost1.Child , System.Windows.Forms.Button)
```

Sample of C# Code

```
System.Windows.Forms.Button aButton;
aButton = (System.Windows.Forms.Button)windowsFormsHost1.Child;
```

Adding a WPF User Control to Your Windows Form Project

You can add preexisting WPF user controls to your Windows Forms project by using the *ElementHost* control. As the name implies, the *ElementHost* control hosts a WPF element.

The most important property of *ElementHost* is the *Child* property, which indicates the type of WPF control to be hosted by the *ElementHost* control. If the WPF control to be hosted is in a project that is a member of the solution, you can set the *Child* property in the Property grid. Otherwise, the *Child* property must be set to an instance of the WPF control in code, as shown here:

Sample of Visual Basic Code

```
Dim aWPFcontrol As New WPFProject.UserControl1
ElementHost1.Child = aWPFcontrol
```

Sample of C# Code

```
WPFProject.UserControl1 aWPFcontrol = new WPFProject.UserControl1;
ElementHost1.Child = aWPFcontrol;
```

PRACTICE   **Practice with Windows Forms Elements**

In this practice, you practice using Windows Forms elements in a WPF application. You create a simple application that uses *MaskedTextBox* to collect phone numbers and then write a list of phone numbers to a file that you select using a *SaveFileDialogBox*.

EXERCISE Using Windows Forms Elements

1. Create a new WPF application.

2. From the Toolbox, drag a *WindowsFormsHost* element onto the design surface and size it to the approximate size of an average text box.

3. In XAML view, add the following line to the *Window* tag to import the *System.Windows.Forms* namespace:

   ```
   xmlns:wf="clr-namespace:System.Windows.Forms;assembly=System.Windows.Forms"
   ```

4. Modify *WindowsFormsHost* in XAML so that it encloses a child *MaskedTextBox*. When finished, your code should look like this:

   ```
   <indowsFormsHost Margin="26,30,125,0" Name="windowsFormsHost1"
       Height="27" VerticalAlignment="Top">
       <wf:MaskedTextBox />
   <WindowsFormsHost>
   ```

5. Set the name of *MaskedTextBox* to *MaskedTextBox1* and set the *Mask* property to *(000)-000-0000*, as shown here:

   ```
   <wf:MaskedTextBox Name="MaskedTextBox1" Mask="(000)-000-0000" />
   ```

6. In XAML, add the following two buttons as additional children of the *Grid:*

   ```
   <Button Height="23" Margin="21,76,125,0" Name="Button1"
       VerticalAlignment="Top">Add to collection</Button>
   <Button Margin="21,0,125,118" Name="Button2" Height="22"
       VerticalAlignment="Bottom">Save collection to file</Button>
   ```

7. In the code window, add variables that represent a generic *List* of string objects and a Windows Forms *SaveFileDialog* element, as shown here:

   Sample of Visual Basic Code

   ```
   Dim PhoneNumbers As New List(Of String)
   Dim aDialog As System.Windows.Forms.SaveFileDialog
   ```

   Sample of C# Code

   ```
   List<string> PhoneNumbers = new List<String>();
   System.Windows.Forms.SaveFileDialog aDialog;
   ```

8. In the designer, double-click the button labeled Add To Collection to open the default *Click* event handler. Add the following code:

   Sample of Visual Basic Code

   ```
   Dim aBox As System.Windows.Forms.MaskedTextBox
   aBox = CType(windowsFormsHost1.Child, System.Windows.Forms.MaskedTextBox)
   PhoneNumbers.Add(aBox.Text)
   aBox.Clear()
   ```

   Sample of C# Code

   ```
   System.Windows.Forms.MaskedTextBox aBox;
   aBox = (System.Windows.Forms.MaskedTextBox)windowsFormsHost1.Child;
   ```

```
PhoneNumbers.Add(aBox.Text);
aBox.Clear();
```

9. In the designer, double-click the button labeled Save Collection To File to open the
   default *Click* event handler. Add the following code:

   Sample of Visual Basic Code

   ```
   aDialog = New System.Windows.Forms.SaveFileDialog
   aDialog.Filter = "Text Files | *.txt"
   aDialog.ShowDialog()
   Dim myWriter As New System.IO.StreamWriter(aDialog.FileName, True)
   For Each s As String In PhoneNumbers
       myWriter.WriteLine(s)
   Next
   myWriter.Close()
   ```

   Sample of C# Code

   ```
   aDialog = new System.Windows.Forms.SaveFileDialog();
   aDialog.Filter = "Text Files | *.txt";
   aDialog.ShowDialog();
   System.IO.StreamWriter myWriter = new
       System.IO.StreamWriter(aDialog.FileName, true);
   foreach(string s in PhoneNumbers)
       myWriter.WriteLine(s);
   myWriter.Close();
   ```

10. Press F5 to build and run your application. Add a few phone numbers to the collection
    by filling in *MaskedTextBox* and pressing the Add To Collection button. Then press the
    Save Collection To File button to open *SaveFileDialogBox*, and then select a file and
    save the list.

Lesson Summary

- Windows Forms dialog boxes can be used in WPF applications as they are. Dialog
  boxes can be shown modally by calling the *ShowDialog* method. Although they can be
  used without problems in WPF applications, Windows Forms dialog boxes typically use
  Windows Forms types. Therefore, conversion might be necessary in some cases.

- WPF provides the *WindowsFormsHost* element to host Windows Forms controls in the
  user interface. You can obtain a reference to the hosted Windows Forms control in
  code by casting the *WindowsFormsHost.Child* property to the appropriate type.

- Windows Forms provides the *ElementHost* control to host a WPF element.

Lesson Review

You can use the following questions to test your knowledge of the information in Lesson 3,
"Integrating Windows Forms Controls and WPF." The questions are also available on the companion CD if you prefer to review them in electronic form.

1. Look at the following XAML sample:

```
<my:WindowsFormsHost Margin="31,51,118,0" Name="windowsFormsHost1"
    Height="39" VerticalAlignment="Top">
    <wf:MaskedTextBox Name="MaskedTextBox1" />
</my:WindowsFormsHost>
```

Assuming that the namespaces for both of these objects are referenced and imported properly, which of the following code samples set(s) the background of *MaskedTextBox* to black? (Choose all that apply.)

A.

```
<my:WindowsFormsHost Background="Black" Margin="31,51,118,0"
    Name="windowsFormsHost1" Height="39" VerticalAlignment="Top">
    <wf:MaskedTextBox Name="MaskedTextBox1" />
</my:WindowsFormsHost>
```

B.

```
<my:WindowsFormsHost Margin="31,51,118,0" Name="windowsFormsHost1"
    Height="39" VerticalAlignment="Top">
    <wf:MaskedTextBox Name="MaskedTextBox1" BackColor="Black" />
</my:WindowsFormsHost>
```

C.

Sample of Visual Basic Code

```
MaskedTextBox1.BackColor = System.Drawing.Color.Black
```

Sample of C# Code

```
MaskedTextBox1.BackColor = System.Drawing.Color.Black;
```

D.

Sample of Visual Basic Code

```
Dim aMask as System.Windows.Forms.MaskedTextBox
aMask = CType(windowsFormsHost1.Child, System.Windows.Forms.MaskedTextBox)
aMask.Backcolor = System.Drawing.Color.Black
```

Sample of C# Code

```
System.Windows.Forms.MaskedTextBox aMask;
aMask = (System.Windows.Forms.MaskedTextBox)windowsFormsHost1.Child;
aMask.BackColor = System.Drawing.Color.Black;
```

Case Scenarios

In the following case scenarios, you apply what you've learned about enhancing usability. You can find answers to these questions in the "Answers" section at the end of this book.

Case Scenario 1: The Publishing Application

Now that the great document management application for Fabrikam, Inc., is complete, you have been asked to help design an application for distribution to its clients. This application should enable clients to download large, book-length documents from an online library while enabling clients to continue browsing the library and selecting other documents for download. When download of a single document is complete, download of the next document should begin if more are selected. When download of a document is complete, the UI should be updated to reflect that.

- What strategies can you use to coordinate document download with the UI interaction and how can the UI be constantly updated without fear of deadlocks or other problems?

Case Scenario 2: Creating a Simple Game

You finally have a day off from your job, so you decide to spend some time writing a nice, relaxing solitaire program. You have the actual gameplay pretty well done, and you are now just adding the bells and whistles. You would like to implement functionality that plays sounds in the background based on user interactions. These sounds are in a specialized format, and you must use a proprietary player that does not intrinsically support asynchronous play. You have a list of five sound files you can play, and you would like to save time and make the coding easy on yourself.

- What is a strategy for implementing the required functionality with a minimum of complexity in your program?

Suggested Practices

To help you successfully master the exam objectives presented in this chapter, complete the following tasks.

- **Practice 1**   Create an application that computes the value of pi on a separate thread and continually updates the UI with the value in a thread-safe manner.

- **Practice 2**   Create a localized form using a language that reads right to left. The localized version of the form should include appropriate strings and the layout should be reversed.

Take a Practice Test

The practice tests on this book's companion CD offer many options. For example, you can test yourself on just the content covered in this chapter, or you can test yourself on all the 70-511 certification exam content. You can set up the test so that it closely simulates the experience of taking a certification exam, or you can set it up in study mode so that you can look at the correct answers and explanations after you answer each question.

> **MORE INFO** **PRACTICE TESTS**
>
> For details about all the practice test options available, see the "How to Use the Practice Tests" section in this book's Introduction.

CHAPTER 10

Advanced Topics

In this chapter, you learn about three topics that are important features for application development: how to configure your application to request permissions from code access security and user account controls, as well as how to configure software restriction policies; how to manage user and application settings for your application; and how to implement drag and drop operations in your application.

Exam objectives in this chapter:

- Implement security features of an application.
- Manage user and application settings.
- Implement drag and drop operations within and across applications.

Lessons in this chapter:

Before You Begin

To complete the lessons in this chapter, you must have:

- A computer that meets or exceeds the minimum hardware requirements listed in the "About This Book" section at the beginning of the book.
- Microsoft Visual Studio 2010 Professional installed on your computer.
- An understanding of Microsoft Visual Basic or C# syntax and familiarity with Microsoft .NET Framework 4.0.
- An understanding of Extensible Application Markup Language (XAML).
- Windows 7 Professional, Ultimate, or Enterprise (for Lesson 1).

 REAL WORLD

Matthew Stoecker

In the early days of computing, security wasn't given a second thought. But as soon as networks connected computers together, malicious users sought to disrupt work or steal valuable data. Windows 7 Professional provides great new tools for managing the security of your computer so that you can ensure that only applications from trusted sources are executed, thus safeguarding your data and the integrity of your system.

Lesson 1: Working with Security

Your applications will be run in a variety of computer environments. The target computer for your application might be secured by the most current software restriction policy technology, or it might rely on User Account Control or code access security technology. In this chapter, you learn to configure your application to request permissions for the target computer and to create a software restriction policy on a computer running Windows 7.

> **After this lesson, you will be able to:**
> - Configure code access security for your application.
> - Configure User Account Control requests for your application.
> - Create a software restriction policy.
>
> **Estimated lesson time: 30 minutes**

When deploying an application, security for that application and the host system is always a concern. Although applications deployed with setup projects are deployed under full-trust conditions, you can configure applications deployed with ClickOnce to request a variety of permission classes. This section demonstrates how to configure your application to request permissions under code access security policy and User Account Control. You also learn how to create a software restriction policy.

Table 10-1 lists general operations that are not safe in partial-trust environments.

TABLE 10-1 Features That Are Unsafe for Use in Partial-Trust Environments

FEATURE AREA	FEATURES
General	<ul><li>Window (application-defined windows and dialog boxes)</li><li>SaveFile dialog box</li><li>File system</li><li>RegistryAccess</li><li>Drag and drop</li><li>XAML serialization (through XamlWriter.Save)</li><li>UIAutomation clients</li><li>Source window access (HwndHost)</li><li>Full speech support</li><li>Windows Forms interoperability</li></ul>

Web Integration	■ Web Services (using Windows Communication Foundation)
	■ Scripting
	■ Document object model
Visuals	■ Bitmap effects
Editing	■ Rich text format clipboard
	■ Full XAML support

When writing applications that might be deployed in partial-trust environments, try to avoid using the features listed in Table 10-1 as much as possible. For applications that might be run in both partial trust and full trust, you can use code access security (CAS) to check at run time whether a specific operation is permitted and, if not, to recover gracefully from that attempt rather than cause the application to crash. The following example demonstrates creating a demand for *FileIOPermission* to determine whether it is safe to write to a file. If the application does not have permission to write to the specified file, an exception is thrown.

Sample of Visual Basic Code

```vb
Try
   Dim perm As New System.Security.Permissions.FileIOPermission( _
      System.Security.Permissions.FileIOPermissionAccess.AllAccess, _
      "C:\myFile")
   perm.Demand()
   ' proceed with writing the file
Catch ex As Exception
   ' recover from being unable to write the file
End Try
```

Sample of C# Code

```csharp
try
{
    System.Security.Permissions.FileIOPermission perm =
        new System.Security.Permissions.FileIOPermission(
        System.Security.Permissions.FileIOPermissionAccess.AllAccess,
        "C:\\myFile");
    perm.Demand();
    // proceed with writing the file
}
catch
{
    // recover from being unable to write the file
}
```

Working with Code Access Security Policies

You can configure code access security requirements on the Security properties page, which you can access by right-clicking your project in Solution Explorer, choosing Properties, and then choosing the Security tab. The Security properties page is shown in Figure 10-1.

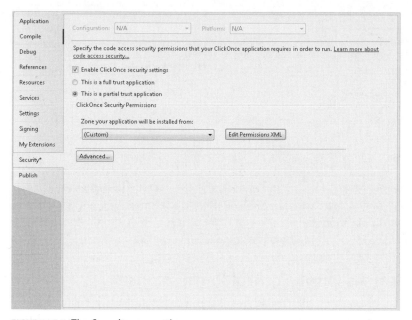

FIGURE 10-1 The Security properties page.

You can configure the permissions requested by your application on this page by first selecting the Enable ClickOnce Security Settings check box and then selecting the option button labeled This Is A Partial Trust Application. Use the ClickOnce Security Permissions group beneath this option button to configure the permissions requested by your application. You can set your requested permissions to the defaults allowed by the Internet or local intranet zones by selecting the zone in the drop-down box labeled Zone Your Application Will Be Installed From. You also can create custom security requests by selecting (Custom) and then clicking the Edit Permissions XML button, opening the app.manifest.xml file, which you can then edit directly. You can add XML representing custom permissions to the *ApplicationRequestMinimum* node to request custom permissions.

Generating XML for Custom Permission Sets

You can use the *ToXml* method of *Permission* classes to generate the required XML nodes to use to request additional permissions. The following example demonstrates how to generate XML for an unrestricted FileIO permission set and write it to a text file.

Sample of Visual Basic Code

```
Dim aPermission As New _
System.Security.Permissions.FileIOPermission(Security.Permissions.PermissionState _
```

```
.Unrestricted)
Dim anElement As System.Security.SecurityElement
anElement = aPermission.ToXml
Dim aWriter As New System.IO.StreamWriter("C:\myPermissionXml.txt")
aWriter.Write(anElement.ToString)
aWriter.Flush()
aWriter.Close()
```

Sample of C# Code

```
System.Security.Permissions.FileIOPermissionaPermission= new
    System.Security.Permissions.FileIOPermission(Security.Permissions.PermissionState
    .Unrestricted);
System.Security.SecurityElementanElement;
anElement = aPermission.ToXml;
System.IO.StreamWriteraWriter= new System.IO.StreamWriter("C:\\myPermissionXml.txt");
aWriter.Write(anElement.ToString);
aWriter.Flush();
aWriter.Close();
```

After you have created the text for a permission set, you can copy that text to the app.manifest.xml file in the *ApplicationRequestMinimum* node to request that permission set. Then set the Zone Your Application Will Be Installed From drop-down box to *Custom* and click the Edit Permissions XML button to open the app.manifest.xml file.

Requesting User Account Control Permissions

You can also request User Account Control (UAC) permissions through the app.manifest.xml file. To open the app.manifest.xml file, first select the Enable ClickOnce Security Settings check box and then select the option button labeled This Is A Partial Trust Application.

In the app.manifest.xml file, you can request UAC permissions by setting the *requestedExecutionLevel* node in the requestedPrivileges node. By default, your application is set to request UAC permissions as invoker, which means that it runs under the same permissions the user has. The *requestedExecutionLevel* node that requests these permissions is shown below:

```
<requestedExecutionLevel level="asInvoker" uiAccess="false" />
```

To request that your application require administrator access, replace this node with the following node:

```
<requestedExecutionLevel  level="requireAdministrator" uiAccess="false" />
```

The following node enables your application to ask for the highest available level of permissions:

```
<requestedExecutionLevel  level="highestAvailable" uiAccess="false" />
```

Software Restriction Policies

Windows 7 Ultimate enables you to create software restriction policies so you can fine-tune the software executed on your machine. Windows 7 Ultimate provides the gpedit.msc application that enables you to create and configure software restriction policies. You can start gpedit.msc by typing **gpedit.msc** in the Windows search box and pressing Enter. This opens the Local Group Policy Editor, shown in Figure 10-2.

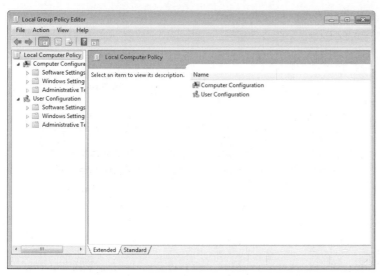

FIGURE 10-2 The gpedit application.

After you have opened the gpedit application, you can create a new software restriction policy by selecting Windows Settings, Security Settings, and then Software Restriction Policies. The gpedit application will then be in the state shown in Figure 10-3:

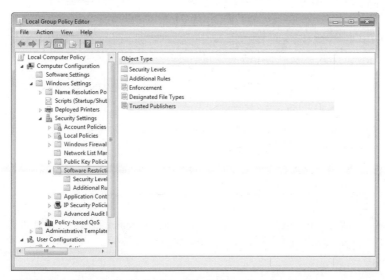

FIGURE 10-3 The gpedit application with nodes opened.

From this screen, you can select a base security level for your software restriction policy by clicking Security Levels. This displays three security levels, as shown in Table 10-2:

TABLE 10-2 Security Levels

SECURITY LEVEL	DESCRIPTION
Disallowed	Software will not run, regardless of the rights of the user.
Basic User	Allows programs to execute as a user who does not have Administrator access rights but can still access resources accessible by normal users.
Unrestricted	Software access rights are determined by the access rights of the user.

You can set one of these access levels as the default level for the SRP by clicking it and then clicking Set As Default.

You can create additional rules for your SRP by clicking the Additional Rules folder in the right-side pane. (Refer to Figure 10-3.) These rules enable you to create exceptions to your global software restriction policy. You can create a new rule by selecting a new rule from the Action menu and then configuring that rule in the resulting dialog box. Table 10-3 summarizes the types of rules:

TABLE 10-3 Additional Rule Types

ADDITIONAL RULE TYPE	DESCRIPTION
Certificate Rule	Enables you to override the default security setting for applications signed by the indicated certificate
Hash Rule	Enables you to override the default security setting for applications in a particular file
Network Zone Rule	Enables you to override the default security setting for an indicated network security zone
Path Rule	Enables you to override the default security setting for files in an indicated path

Each of these rules can be set to either Unrestricted or Disallowed, which indicates that the specified resource either has unrestricted access or is completely restricted.

You can also configure your software restriction policy for Enforcement, Designated File Types, and Trusted Publishers. Clicking each of these brings up a dialog box that enables you to configure each of these policies.

Clicking Enforcement enables you to designate whether this policy should apply to all software files or libraries such as .DLLs will be excluded, whether the policy applies to all users or all users except administrators, and whether to apply certificate rules or enforce them.

Clicking Designated File Types enables you to designate file types affected by the policy. You can add or remove file types in this dialog box.

Clicking Trusted Publishers enables you to designate which users can manage the Trusted Publishers files.

PRACTICE Creating a Software Restriction Policy

In this practice, you create a software restriction policy for your computer that restricts software execution to allow only software installed to the Users folder to execute and disallows all other software.

EXERCISE Creating a Software Restriction Policy

1. In Windows 7, type **gpedit.msc** into the Search box and press Enter to open the gpedit application. Note that this functionality is available only in Windows 7 Professional, Ultimate, or Enterprise.

2. In gpedit, expand Windows Settings and Security Settings and then select Software Restriction Policies.

3. From the Action menu, select New Software Restriction Policies to create a new default Software Restriction Policy.

4. In the right-side pane, double-click Enforcement to open the Enforcement Properties dialog box. Apply enforcement to all software files and apply enforcement to all users except local administrators. Click OK.

5. In the right-side pane, double-click Designated File Types to open the Designated File Types Properties dialog box. Under Designated File Types, select LNK, click Remove, and then click Yes to enable shortcuts to continue functioning.

6. Click Additional Rules and inspect both additional rules already in place.

   Note that these are path rules that exempt system files and files in the Program Files folder from this rule by default.

7. Double-click Security Levels, double click Set As Default, and click Yes.

   Your new software restriction policy is now in place.

8. Double-click Additional Rules. From the Action menu, choose New Path Rule to open the New Path Rule dialog box.

9. In the New Path Rule dialog box, click Browse and browse to your user folder. Under Security Level, select Unrestricted and click OK. Your rule now allows unrestricted access for applications installed to your user directory. If you do not want to retain this Software Restriction Policy on your computer, you can delete it by selecting Software Restriction Policies and selecting Delete Software Restriction Policies from the Action menu.

Lesson Summary

- You can configure options for requesting code access security and User Account controls by editing the app.manifest.xml file.
- You can create software restriction policies using gpedit.msc that enable you to fine-tune security policies on your local machine.

Lesson Review

You can use the following questions to test your knowledge of the information in Lesson 1, "Working with Security." The questions are also available on the companion CD if you prefer to review them in electronic form.

> **NOTE ANSWERS**
>
> **Answers to these questions and explanations of why each answer choice is correct or incorrect are located in the "Answers" section at the end of the book.**

1. Which of the following is required to request custom code access permissions for your application? (Choose all that apply.)

    A. Select (Custom) in the Security Properties page.

    B. Modify the *applicationRequestMinimum* node in the app.manifest.xml file.

    C. Modify the *requestedPrivileges* node in the app.manifest.xml file.

    D. Create a software restriction policy that grants unrestricted access to your application.

2. Which of the following are safe features to use when you are deploying your application to a partial-trust environment? (Choose all that apply.)

    A. File IO

    B. Isolated Storage

    C. Registry Access

    D. Using Images in content controls (WPF)

Lesson 2: Managing Settings

The .NET Framework enables you to create and access values called *settings* that persist from application session to application session. Settings can represent any kind of information an application might need from session to session, such as user preferences, the address of a Web server, or any other kind of necessary information. In this lesson, you learn how to create and access settings. You learn the difference between a user setting and an application setting and how to load and save settings at run time.

After this lesson, you will be able to:

- Explain the difference between a user setting and an application setting.
- Create a new setting at design time.
- Load settings at run time.
- Save user settings at run time.

Estimated lesson time: 15 minutes

Settings can store information that is valuable to the application but might change from time to time. For example, you can use settings to store user preferences such as the color scheme of an application or the address of a Web server the application uses.

Settings have four properties:

- *Name*, which indicates the name of the setting. This is used to access the setting at run time.
- *Type*, which represents the data type of the setting.
- *Value*, which is the value returned by the setting.
- *Scope*, which can be either *User* or *Application*.

The *Name*, *Type*, and *Value* properties should be fairly self-explanatory. The *Scope* property, however, bears a little closer examination. The *Scope* property can be set to either *Application* or *User*. A setting with *Application* scope represents a value that is used by the entire application regardless of the user, whereas an application with *User* scope is more likely to be user-specific and less crucial to the application.

An important distinction between user settings and application settings is that user settings are read/write. They can be read and written to at run time, and newly written values can be saved by the application. In contrast, *Application settings* are read-only and the values can be changed only at design time or by editing the Settings file between application sessions.

Creating Settings at Design Time

Visual Studio provides an editor, shown in Figure 10-4, to create settings for your application at design time.

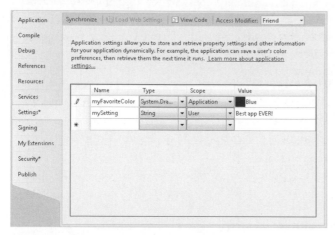

FIGURE 10-4 The Settings editor.

The Settings editor enables you to create new settings and set each of their four properties. The *Name* property—that is, the name you use to retrieve the setting value—must be unique in the application. The *Type* property represents the type of the setting. The *Scope* property is either *Application*, which represents a read-only property, or *User*, which represents a read-write setting. Finally, the *Value* property represents the value returned by the setting. The *Value* property must be of the type specified by the Type property.

To create a setting at design time:

1. If you are working in C#, in Solution Explorer, under Properties, locate and double-click Settings.settings to open the Settings editor. If you are working in Visual Basic, in Solution Explorer, double-click MyProject and select the Settings tab.

2. Set Name, Type, Scope, and Value for the new setting.

3. If your application has not yet been saved, choose Save All from the File menu to save your application.

Loading Settings at Run Time

At run time, you can access the values contained by the settings. In Visual Basic, settings are exposed through the *My* object, whereas in C#, you access settings through the *Properties.Settings.Default* object. At design time, individual settings appear in IntelliSense as properties of the *Settings* object and can be treated in code as such. Settings are strongly typed and are retrieved as the same type as specified when they were created. The following example code demonstrates how to copy the value from a setting to a variable:

Sample of Visual Basic Code

```
Dim aString As String
aString = My.Settings.MyStringSetting
```

Sample of C# Code

```
String aString;
aString = Properties.Settings.Default.MyStringSetting;
```

Saving User Settings at Run Time

You can save the value of user settings at run time. To change the value of a user setting, simply assign it a new value, just as you would any property or field. Then you must call the *Save* method to save the new value. An example is shown here:

Sample of Visual Basic Code

```
My.Settings.Headline = "This is tomorrow's headline"
My.Settings.Save
```

Sample of C# Code

```
Properties.Settings.Default.Headline = "This is tomorrow's headline";
Properties.Settings.Default.Save();
```

 Quick Check

- What is the difference between a user setting and an application setting?

Quick Check Answer

- A user setting is designed to be user-specific, such as a background color. User settings can be written at run time and can vary from user to user. An application setting is designed to be constant for all users of an application, such as a database connection string. Application settings are read-only at run time.

PRACTICE **Practice with Settings**

In this practice, you create an application that uses settings. You define settings while building the application, read the settings, apply them in your application, and enable the user to change one of the settings.

EXERCISE Using Settings

1. In Visual Studio, create a new WPF application.

2. In Solution Explorer, expand Properties and double-click Settings.settings (in C#) or double-click My Project and choose the Settings tab (in Visual Basic) to open the Settings editor.

3. Add two settings, as described in this table. For the second setting, you must browse to find and expand the *PresentationCore* node, then expand *the System.Windows.Media* type to find the *System.Windows.Media.Color* type:

NAME	TYPE	SCOPE	VALUE
ApplicationName	String	*Application*	*Settings App*
BackgroundColor	System.Windows.Media.Color	*User*	*#ff0000ff*

4. In XAML view, add the following XAML to the *Grid* element to add a *ListBox* control with four items and a *Button* control to your user interface:

```
<ListBox Margin="15,15,0,0" Name="listBox1" Height="78"
    HorizontalAlignment="Left" VerticalAlignment="Top" Width="107">
<ListBoxItem>Red</ListBoxItem>
    <ListBoxItem>Blue</ListBoxItem>
    <ListBoxItem>Green</ListBoxItem>
    <ListBoxItem>Tomato</ListBoxItem>
</ListBox>
<Button Margin="15,106,110,130" Name="button1">Change Background
    Color</Button>
```

5. In the designer, double-click *button1* to open the code view to the default handler for the *Click* event. Add the following code:

Sample of Visual Basic Code

```
If Not listBox1.SelectedItem Is Nothing Then
    Dim astring As String = CType(listBox1.SelectedItem, _
        ListBoxItem).Content.ToString
    Select Case astring
        Case "Red"
            My.Settings.BackgroundColor = Colors.Red
        Case "Blue"
            My.Settings.BackgroundColor = Colors.Blue
        Case "Green"
            My.Settings.BackgroundColor = Colors.Green
        Case "Tomato"
            My.Settings.BackgroundColor = Colors.Tomato
    End Select
    Me.Background = New _
        System.Windows.Media.SolidColorBrush(My.Settings.BackgroundColor)
    My.Settings.Save()
End If
```

Sample of C# Code

```
if (!(listBox1.SelectedItem == null))
{
    String astring =
        ((ListBoxItem)listBox1.SelectedItem).Content.ToString();
    switch (astring)
```

```
        {
            case "Red":
                Properties.Settings.Default.BackgroundColor = Colors.Red;
                break;
            case "Blue":
                Properties.Settings.Default.BackgroundColor = Colors.Blue;
                break;
            case "Green":
                Properties.Settings.Default.BackgroundColor = Colors.Green;
                break;
            case "Tomato":
                Properties.Settings.Default.BackgroundColor = Colors.Tomato;
                break;
        }
        this.Background = new
            System.Windows.Media.SolidColorBrush(
            Properties.Settings.Default.BackgroundColor);
            Properties.Settings.Default.Save();
    }
```

6. Create or replace the constructor for this class with the following code to read and apply the settings:

Sample of Visual Basic Code

```
Public Sub New()
    InitializeComponent()
    Me.Title = My.Settings.ApplicationName
    Me.Background = New _
        System.Windows.Media.SolidColorBrush(My.Settings.BackgroundColor)
End Sub
```

Sample of C# Code

```
public MainWindow ()
{
    InitializeComponent();
    this.Title = Properties.Settings.Default.ApplicationName;
    this.Background = new
        System.Windows.Media.SolidColorBrush(
            Properties.Settings.Default.BackgroundColor);
}
```

7. Press F5 to build and run your application. Note that the title of the window is the value of your *ApplicationName* setting and the background color of your window is the value indicated by the *BackgroundColor* setting. You can change the background color by selecting an item in *the list box* and clicking the button. After changing the background color, close the application and restart it. Note that the background color of the application at startup is the same as it was when the previous application session ended.

Lesson Summary

- Settings enable you to persist values between application sessions. You can add new settings at design time by using the Settings editor.

- Settings can be one of two scopes. Settings with Application scope are read-only at run time and can be changed only by altering the Settings file between application sessions. Settings with User scope are read-write at run time.

- You can access settings in code through *My.Settings* in Visual Basic or *Properties.Settings.Default* in C#.

Lesson Review

You can use the following questions to test your knowledge of the information in Lesson 2, "Managing Settings." The questions are also available on the companion CD if you prefer to review them in electronic form.

> **NOTE ANSWERS**
>
> Answers to these questions and explanations of why each answer choice is correct or incorrect are located in the "Answers" section at the end of the book.

1. Which of the following code samples correctly sets the value of a setting called *Title* and persists it?

   A.

   Sample of Visual Basic Code

   ```
   My.Settings("Title") = "New Title"
   My.Settings.Save
   ```

   Sample of C# Code

   ```
   Properties.Settings.Default["Title"] = "New Title";
   Properties.Settings.Default.Save();
   ```

   B.

   Sample of Visual Basic Code

   ```
   My.Settings("Title") = "New Title"
   ```

   Sample of C# Code

   ```
   Properties.Settings.Default["Title"] = "New Title";
   ```

   C.

   Sample of Visual Basic Code

   ```
   My.Settings.Title = "New Title"
   My.Settings.Save()
   ```

Sample of C# Code

```csharp
Properties.Settings.Default.Title = "New Title";
Properties.Settings.Default.Save();
```

D.

Sample of Visual Basic Code

```vbnet
My.Settings.Title = "New Title"
```

Sample of C# Code

```csharp
Properties.Settings.Default.Title = "New Title";
```

2. Which of the following code samples reads a setting of type *System.Windows.Media*
   .Color named *MyColor* correctly?

   A.

   Sample of Visual Basic Code

   ```vbnet
   Dim aColor As System.Windows.Media.Color
   aColor = CType(My.Settings.MyColor, System.Windows.Media.Color)
   ```

   Sample of C# Code

   ```csharp
   System.Windows.Media.ColoraColor;
   aColor = (System.Windows.Media.Color)Properties.Settings.Default.MyColor;
   ```

   B.

   Sample of Visual Basic Code

   ```vbnet
   Dim aColor As System.Windows.Media.Color
   aColor = My.Settings.MyColor.ToColor()
   ```

   Sample of C# Code

   ```csharp
   System.Windows.Media.ColoraColor;
   aColor = Properties.Settings.Default.MyColor.ToColor();
   ```

   C.

   Sample of Visual Basic Code

   ```vbnet
   Dim aColor As Object
   aColor = My.Settings.MyColor
   ```

   Sample of C# Code

   ```csharp
   Object aColor;
   aColor = Properties.Settings.Default.MyColor;
   ```

   D.

   Sample of Visual Basic Code

   ```vbnet
   Dim aColor As System.Windows.Media.Color
   aColor = My.Settings.MyColor
   ```

   Sample of C# Code

   ```csharp
   System.Windows.Media.ColoraColor;
   aColor = Properties.Settings.Default.MyColor;
   ```

Lesson 3: Implementing Drag and Drop

Drag and drop functionality refers to being able to grab data—such as a string or an object—by pressing and holding down the left mouse button, moving the mouse with the left button held down over another control that is able to accept the data, and then releasing the mouse button to transfer the data. Drag and drop functionality is implemented primarily by handling events. In this lesson, you learn how to implement basic drag and drop functionality and how to implement drag and drop functionality between applications.

> **After this lesson, you will be able to:**
> - Perform drag and drop operations within a Windows Forms application.
> - Perform drag and drop operations within a WPF application.
> - Perform drag and drop operations between applications.
>
> **Estimated lesson time: 45 minutes**

Implementing Drag and Drop Functionality

Drag and drop functionality is ubiquitous in Windows programming. It refers to enabling the user to grab data—such as text, an image, or another object—with the mouse and drag it to another control. When the mouse button is released over the other control, the data being dragged is dropped onto the control, and a variety of effects can then occur.

Dragging and dropping is similar to cutting and pasting. The mouse pointer is positioned over a control and the mouse button is pressed. Data is copied from a source control; when the mouse button is released, the drop action is completed. All code for copying the data from the source control and any actions taken on the target control must be explicitly coded.

Drag and drop operations are very similar in WPF and Windows Forms applications. The primary difference is that in Windows Forms, drag and drop methods and events are exposed on individual controls, and in WPF, the methods are exposed on a static class called *DragDrop*, which also provides attached events to WPF controls to facilitate drag and drop operations.

The drag and drop process is primarily an event-driven process. There are events that occur on the source control and events that occur on the target control. Table 10-4 describes the drag and drop events for the source control. The drag and drop events for the target control are described in Table 10-5.

TABLE 10-4 Source Control Events Involved in Implementing Drag and Drop

EVENT	DESCRIPTION
MouseDown	Occurs when the mouse button is pressed while the pointer is over the control. In general, the *DoDragDrop* method is called in the method that handles this event. In WPF applications, this is a bubbling event.
GiveFeedBack	Provides an opportunity for the user to set a custom mouse pointer. In WPF applications, this is a bubbling event.
QueryContinueDrag	Enables the drag source to determine whether a drag event should be cancelled. In WPF applications, this is a bubbling event.
PreviewMouseDown	WPF only; the tunneling version of the *MouseDown* event.
PreviewGiveFeedBack	WPF only; the tunneling version of the *GiveFeedback* event.
PreviewQueryContinueDrag	WPF only; the tunneling version of the *QueryContinueDrag* event.

TABLE 10-5 Target Control Events Involved in Implementing Drag and Drop

EVENT	DESCRIPTION
DragEnter	Occurs when an object is dragged within a control's bounds. The handler for this event receives a *DragEventArgs* object. In WPF, this is a bubbling event.
DragOver	Occurs when an object is dragged over a target control. The handler for this event receives a *DragEventArgs* object. In WPF, this is a bubbling event.
DragDrop	Occurs when the mouse button is released over a target control. The handler for this event receives a *DragEventArgs* object. In WPF, this is a bubbling event.
DragLeave	Occurs when an object is dragged out of the control's bounds. In WPF, this is a bubbling event.
PreviewDragEnter	WPF only; the tunneling version of *DragEnter*.
PreviewDragOver	WPF only; the tunneling version of *DragOver*.
PreviewDragDrop	WPF only; the tunneling version of *DragDrop*.
PreviewDragLeave	WPF only; the tunneling version of *DragLeave*.

In addition, the *DoDragDrop* method on the source control is required to initiate the drag and drop process in Windows Forms, or the *DoDragDrop* method of the *DragDrop* class is required for WPF. Furthermore, the target control must have the *AllowDrop* property set to *True*.

General Sequence of a Drag and Drop Operation

The general sequence of events that takes place in a drag and drop operation is as follows:

1. The drag and drop operation is initiated by calling the *DoDragDrop* method on the source control (for Windows Forms) or the *DragDrop.DoDragDrop* method for WPF applications. This is usually done in the *MouseDown* event handler. *DoDragDrop* copies the desired data from the source control to a new instance of *DataObject* and sets flags that specify which effects are allowed with this data.

2. The *GiveFeedBack* and *QueryContinueDrag* events are raised at this point. The GiveFeedback event handler can set the mouse pointer to a custom shape, and you can use the *QueryContinueDrag* event handler to determine whether the drag operation should be continued or aborted.

3. The mouse pointer is dragged over a target control. Any control that has the *AllowDrop* property set to *True* is a potential drop target. When the mouse pointer enters a control with the *AllowDrop* property set to *True*, the *DragEnter* event for that control is raised. The *DragEventArgs* object the event handler receives can be examined to determine whether data appropriate for the target control is present. If so, the *Effect* property of the *DragEventArgs* object can then be set to an appropriate value.

4. The user releases the mouse button over a valid target control, raising the *DragDrop* event. The code in the *DragDropevent* handler then obtains the dragged data and takes whatever action is appropriate in the target control.

The *DragDropEffects* Enumeration

To complete a drag and drop operation, the drag effect specified in the *DoDragDrop* method must match the value of the *Effect* parameter of the *DragEventArgs* object associated with the drag and drop event, which is generally set in the *DragEnter* handler. The *Effect* property is an instance of the *DragDropEffects* enumeration. Table 10-6 describes the members of the *DragDropEffects* enumeration.

TABLE 10-6 *DragDropEffects* Enumeration Members

MEMBER	EXPLANATION
All	Data is copied, removed from the drag source, and scrolled in the target.
Copy	The data is copied to the target.
Link	The data is linked to the target.
Move	The data is moved to the target.
None	The target does not accept the data.
Scroll	Scrolling is about to start or is currently occurring in the target.

Note that the main function of the *Effect* parameter is to change the mouse cursor when it is over the target control. The value of the *Effect* parameter has no actual effect on the action that is executed except that when the *Effect* parameter is set to *None*, no drop can take place on that control because the *DragDrop* event will not be raised.

Initiating the Drag and Drop Operation in Windows Forms Applications

The drag and drop operation is initiated by calling the *DoDragDrop* method on the source control. The *DoDragDrop* method takes two parameters: *Object*, which represents the data to be copied to *DataObject*, and an instance of *DragDropEffects*, which specifies which drag effects will be allowed with this data. The following example demonstrates how to copy the text from a text box and set the allowed effects to *Copy* or *Move*:

Sample of Visual Basic Code

```vb
Private Sub TextBox1_MouseDown(ByVal sender As System.Object, _
    ByVal e As System.Windows.Forms.MouseEventArgs) _
    Handles TextBox1.MouseDown
    TextBox1.DoDragDrop(TextBox1.Text, DragDropEffects.Copy Or DragDropEffects.Move)
End Sub
```

Sample of C# Code

```csharp
private void textBox1_MouseDown(object sender, MouseEventArgs e)
{
    textBox1.DoDragDrop(textBox1.Text, DragDropEffects.Copy | DragDropEffects.Move);
}
```

Note that you can use the *Or* operator (Visual Basic) or the | operator (C#) to combine members of the *DragDropEffects* enumeration to indicate multiple effects.

Initiating the Drag and Drop Operation in WPF Applications

In WPF applications, you initiate the drag and drop operation by calling *DragDrop.DoDragDrop*. This method takes three parameters: *DependencyObject*, which represents the source control for the drag operation; *Object*, which represents the data that will be copied to *DataObject*; and an instance of *DragDropEffects*, which specifies which drag effects will be allowed with this data. The following example demonstrates how to copy the text from a text box and set the allowed effects to *Copy* or *Move*:

Sample of Visual Basic Code

```vb
Private Sub TextBox1_MouseDown(ByVal sender As System.Object, _
    ByVal e As System.Windows.Input.MouseButtonEventArgs) _
    Handles TextBox1.MouseDown
DragDrop.DoDragDrop(TextBox1, TextBox1.Text, DragDropEffects.Copy Or DragDropEffects.
Move)
End Sub
```

Sample of C# Code

```csharp
private void textBox1_MouseDown(object sender, MouseButtonEventArgs e)
{
```

```
DragDrop.DoDragDrop(textBox1, textBox1.Text, DragDropEffects.Copy | DragDropEffects.
Move);
}
```

Handling the *DragEnter* Event

The *DragEnter* event should be handled for every target control. This event occurs when
a drag and drop operation is in progress and the mouse pointer enters the control. This
event passes a *DragEventArgs* object to the method that handles it, and you can use the
DragEventArgs object to query the *DataObject* object associated with the drag and drop operation. If the data is appropriate for the target control, you can set the *Effect* property to an
appropriate value for the control. The following example demonstrates how to examine the
data format of the *DataObject* and set the *Effect* property:

Sample of Visual Basic Code

```
' This is a Windows Forms example
Private Sub TextBox2_DragEnter(ByVal sender As System.Object, _
    ByVal e As System.Windows.Forms.DragEventArgs) _
    Handles TextBox2.DragEnter
    If e.Data.GetDataPresent(DataFormats.Text) = True Then
        e.Effect = DragDropEffects.Copy
    End If
End Sub


' This is a WPF example
Private Sub TextBox2_DragEnter(ByVal sender As System.Object, _
    ByVal e As System.Window.DragEventArgs) _
    Handles TextBox2.DragEnter
    If e.Data.GetDataPresent(DataFormats.Text) = True Then
        e.Effect = DragDropEffects.Copy
    End If
End Sub
```

Sample of C# Code

```
// The Windows Forms and WPF examples look the same in C#

private void textBox2_DragEnter (object sender, DragEventArgs e)
{
    if (e.Data.GetDataPresent(DataFormats.Text))
    {
        e.Effect = DragDropEffects.Copy;
    }
}
```

Note that in WPF applications, this is an attached event that is based off the *DragDrop*
class. You can attach this event in the Events pane of the Properties window in Visual Studio.

Handling the DragDrop Event

When the mouse button is released over a target control during a drag and drop operation, the *DragDrop* event is raised. In the method that handles the *DragDrop* event, you can use the *GetData* method of *DataObject* to retrieve the copied data from *DataObject* and take whatever action is appropriate for the control. The following example demonstrates how to drop a string into a text box:

Sample of Visual Basic Code

```
' This is a Windows Forms example

Private Sub TextBox2_DragDrop(ByVal sender As System.Object, ByVal e As _
    System.Windows.Forms.DragEventArgs) Handles TextBox2.DragDrop
    TextBox2.Text = TryCast(e.Data.GetData(DataFormats.Text), String)
End Sub

' This is a WPF example

Private Sub TextBox2_DragDrop(ByVal sender As System.Object, ByVal e As _
    System.Windows.DragEventArgs) Handles TextBox2.DragDrop
    TextBox2.Text = TryCast(e.Data.GetData(DataFormats.Text), String)
End Sub
```

Sample of C# Code

```
// The Windows Forms and WPF examples look the same in C#

private void textBox2_DragDrop(object sender, DragEventArgs e)
{
    textBox2.Text = (string)e.Data.GetData(DataFormats.Text);
}
```

Note that in WPF applications, this is an attached event that is based off the *DragDrop* class. You can attach this event in the Events pane of the Properties window in Visual Studio.

Implementing Drag and Drop between Applications

The system intrinsically supports drag and drop operations between .NET Framework applications. You don't need to take any additional steps to enable drag and drop operations that take place between applications. The only conditions that must be satisfied to enable a drag and drop operation between applications are:

- The target control must allow one of the drag effects specified in the *DoDragDrop* method call.
- The target control must accept data in the format that was set in the *DoDragDrop* method call.

In this practice, you implement drag and drop functionality between two text boxes on a form. You implement functionality to drag the text from the first text box and copy it into the second text box when dropped. A completed solution to this practice can be found in the files installed from the companion CD.

EXERCISE 1 Implementing Drag and Drop

1. In Visual Studio, create a new Windows Forms application.

2. From the toolbox, drag two *Textbox* controls onto the new application.

3. Select *Textbox2* and, in the Properties window, set the *AllowDrop* property to *True*.

4. In the Properties window, click the Events icon to display events instead of properties. Select *Textbox1* and double-click the space next to the *MouseDown* event in the Properties window to create the default event handler for the *Textbox1.MouseDown* event.

5. Add the following code to the *Textbox1_MouseDown* event handler:

   Sample of Visual Basic Code

   ```
   TextBox1.DoDragDrop(TextBox1.Text, _
   DragDropEffects.Move Or DragDropEffects.Copy)
   ```

   Sample of C# Code

   ```
   textBox1.DoDragDrop(textBox1.Text,
   DragDropEffects.Move | DragDropEffects.Copy);
   ```

6. In the designer, select *TextBox2* and double-click the space next to the *DragEnter* event in the Properties window to create the default event handler for the *TextBox2.DragEnter* event.

7. Add the following code to the *Textbox2_DragEnter* event handler:

   Sample of Visual Basic Code

   ```
   If e.Data.GetDataPresent(DataFormats.Text) = True Then
       e.Effect = DragDropEffects.Copy
   End If
   ```

   Sample of C# Code

   ```
   if (e.Data.GetDataPresent(DataFormats.Text))
   {
       e.Effect = DragDropEffects.Copy;
   }
   ```

8. In the designer, select *TextBox2* and double-click the space next to the *DragDrop* event in the Properties window to create the default event handler for the *TextBox2.DragDrop* event.

9. Add the following code to the *Textbox2_DragDrop* event handler:

Sample of Visual Basic Code

```
TextBox2.Text = e.Data.GetData(DataFormats.Text)
```

Sample of C# Code

```
textBox2.Text = (string)e.Data.GetData(DataFormats.Text);
```

10. Press F5 to build and run the application. Type some text into the first text box. Using the mouse, drag from anywhere in the first text box to the second text box. The text from the first text box is copied to the second text box.

Lesson Summary

- The drag and drop operation is initiated by calling the *DoDragDrop* method on the source control. This is usually done in the *MouseDown* event handler for the source control. The *DoDragDrop* method takes two parameters: an *Object* parameter that contains the data to be dragged and dropped, and a *DragDropEffects* enumeration parameter that represents the effect or effects that are allowed for this operation.

- The *DragEnter* event on the target control is used to set the allowed effects for the target control. You can examine the data in the *e.Data* object present in the event parameters and determine whether the data is appropriate for the control. If the data is not appropriate for the control, you can cancel the *DragDrop* operation by setting the *e.Effect* property to *None*.

- The drag and drop operation is completed in the *DragDrop* event on the target control. You must write code to complete the appropriate operation in this event.

- Data can be dragged and dropped between controls in different applications. No additional steps need to be taken to enable drag and drop operations that take place between applications.

Lesson Review

The following questions are intended to reinforce key information presented in Lesson 3, "Implementing Drag and Drop." If you are unable to answer a question, review the lesson materials and try the question again.

> **NOTE ANSWERS**
>
> Answers to these questions and explanations of why each answer choice is correct or incorrect are located in the "Answers" section at the end of the book.

1. Which of the following events must be handled to execute a drag and drop operation?

   A. *MouseDown*

   B. *MouseUp*

   C. *DragLeave*

   D. *DragDrop*

2. Which of the following is necessary to implement a drag and drop operation between two applications? (Choose all that apply.)

   A. You must call the *DoDragDrop* method.

   B. The target control must allow one of the drag effects specified in the *DoDragDrop* method call.

   C. The target control must accept data in the format that was set in the *DoDragDrop* method call.

   D. The target control must have the *AllowDrop* property set to *True*.

Case Scenario

In the following case scenario, you apply what you've learned about the topics presented in this chapter. You can find answers to these questions in the "Answers" section at the end of this book.

Case Scenario: The Configurable Application

You are about to deploy an application to the entire company. This application must serve the needs of all the employees, including some who require high-contrast color schemes. In addition, you want to enable all employees to personalize this application by creating their own custom color schemes.

How can you implement this functionality with limited development time?

Suggested Practices

To help you successfully master the exam objectives presented in this chapter, complete the following tasks.

- **Practice 1** Create an application that stores a color scheme for each user and automatically loads the correct color scheme when the user opens the application.

- **Practice 2** Create an application that enables users to rearrange the nodes in a *TreeView* control but gives them the option of placing moved nodes before, after, or as a child of the target node.

Take a Practice Test

The practice tests on this book's companion CD offer many options. For example, you can test yourself on just the content covered in this chapter, or you can test yourself on all the 70-511 certification exam content. You can set up the test so that it closely simulates the experience of taking a certification exam, or you can set it up in study mode so that you can look at the correct answers and explanations after you answer each question.

> **MORE INFO** PRACTICE TESTS
>
> For details about all the practice test options available, see the "How to Use the Practice Tests" section in this book's Introduction.

CHAPTER 11

Testing and Debugging WPF Applications

Testing and debugging your application is a vital part of any development cycle. Because all but the very smallest of development projects is nearly certain to have mistakes in the first draft, finding and correcting those issues is important for the overall integrity of your work. In this chapter, you learn about techniques and technologies for debugging WPF applications. You learn how to use user interface (UI) automation to test the user interface and the WPF Tree Visualizer to explore the properties of the WPF visual tree. You learn how to use *PresentationTraceSources* to view trace information associated with WPF applications and to use Intellitrace to view highly selected trace data.

Exam objectives in this chapter:

- Implement a WPF test strategy.
- Debug XAML by using the WPF Visualizer.
- Debug WPF issues by using *PresentationTraceSources*.

Lessons in this chapter:

Before You Begin

To complete the lessons in this chapter, you must have:

- A computer that meets or exceeds the minimum hardware requirements listed in the "About This Book" section at the beginning of the book.
- Microsoft Visual Studio 2010 Professional installed on your computer. Microsoft Visual Studio 2010 Ultimate is required for Intellitrace.
- An understanding of Microsoft Visual Basic or C# syntax and familiarity with Microsoft .NET Framework 4.0.
- An understanding of Extensible Application Markup Language (XAML).

 REAL WORLD

Matthew Stoecker

Debugging WPF user interfaces is often an exercise in frustration. Because many failed WPF operations (such as failed bindings) do not raise errors, it can be difficult to pinpoint the source of these logical errors in code. However, using debugging tools such as Intellitrace, *PresentationTraceSources*, and the WPF Tree Visualizer provides greater insight into exactly what is going on in your application and greatly speeds locating and resolving these errors.

Lesson 1: Testing the User Interface

After you have created your application, you must test it for proper functionality. In WPF, creating tests for and getting information about the user interface can be challenging due to the tree-based nature of the WPF user interface. However, you can create tests for individual user interface elements by using UI Automation and the *AutomationPeer* classes, and the WPF Tree Visualizer helps you explore the user interface at debug time to learn debugging information. In this lesson, you learn how to use UI automation and the WPF Tree Visualizer.

> **After this lesson, you will be able to:**
> - Use UI Automation to automate the WPF user interface.
> - Use the WPF Tree Visualizer to inspect the WPF tree.
>
> **Estimated lesson time: 30 minutes**

Using Automation Peers to Automate the User Interface

UI Automation enables you to run a user interface programmatically as though you were actually running the application through keyboard and mouse inputs. For example, UI Automation enables you to programmatically click a button, scroll a scrollable container, toggle a check box, or perform any action that can be executed through the user interface programmatically.

The base class that enables all this functionality is the *System.Windows.Automation.Peers .AutomationPeer* class. An automation peer represents an automation representation of an actual user interface control and encapsulates all the base functionality required to interact with the automation system. Individual WPF control types all have their own corresponding *AutomationPeer* class, named *<control>AutomationPeer*, in which *<control>* represents the name of the control. For example, the corresponding class for a WPF *Button* control is *ButtonAutomationPeer*. These classes implement functionality specific to the automation of their corresponding controls.

Useful Methods of *AutomationPeer* Classes

All classes that inherit *AutomationPeer* share a core group of methods. Table 11-1 describes some important methods for automation.

TABLE 11-1 Some Important Methods of *AutomationPeer* Classes

METHOD	DESCRIPTION
GetChildren	Gets the collection of *GetChildren* elements that are represented in the UI Automation tree as immediate child elements of the automation peer. This method returns a list of *AutomationPeer* objects.
GetName	Gets text that describes the element associated with this automation peer.
GetParent	Gets the *AutomationPeer* class that is the parent of this *AutomationPeer* object.
GetPattern	When overridden in a derived class, gets the control pattern associated with the specified *PatternInterface* object.

The *GetName* method returns the name of the control associated with the current *AutomationPeer* class. The *GetParent* and *GetChildren* methods enable navigation through the control tree. The *GetPattern* method enables you to retrieve implementations of the various pattern interfaces that provide the actual automation functionality, as described in the section titled "Pattern Interfaces," which follows shortly.

Creating an *AutomationPeer* Class

You can create an *AutomationPeer* class from any WPF control that has a corresponding class that derives from *AutomationPeer*. The following example demonstrates how to create an instance of a *ButtonAutomationPeer* class based on an existing WPF *Button* control named *Button1*.

Sample of Visual Basic Code

```
Dim ButtonPeer As System.Automation.Peers.ButtonAutomationPeer
ButtonPeer = New System.Automation.Peers.ButtonAutomationPeer(Button1)
```

Sample of C# Code

```
System.Automation.Peers.ButtonAutomationPeer ButtonPeer;
ButtonPeer = new System.Automation.Peers.ButtonAutomationPeer(Button1);
```

Pattern Interfaces

Each non-abstract *AutomationPeer* class implements one or more pattern interfaces, which contain the required methods to invoke the functionality of their associated control. Table 11-2 summarizes these pattern interfaces.

TABLE 11-2 Pattern Interfaces

INTERFACE	DESCRIPTION
IDockProvider	Exposes methods and properties to support UI Automation client access to controls that expose their dock properties within a docking container.
IExpandCollapseProvider	Exposes methods and properties to support UI Automation client access to controls that visually expand to display content and collapse to hide content.
IGridItemProvider	Exposes methods and properties to support UI Automation client access to individual child controls of containers that implement *IGridProvider*.
IGridProvider	Exposes methods and properties to support UI Automation client access to controls that act as containers for a collection of child elements. The children of this element must implement *IGridItemProvider* and be organized in a two-dimensional logical coordinate system that can be traversed (that is, a UI Automation client can move to adjacent controls) by using the keyboard.
IInvokeProvider	Exposes methods and properties to support UI Automation client access to controls that initiate or perform a single, unambiguous action and do not maintain state when activated.
IItemContainerProvider	Exposes a method to enable applications to find an element in a container, such as a virtualized list.
IMultipleViewProvider	Exposes methods and properties to support UI Automation client access to controls that provide, and are able to switch among, multiple representations of the same set of information or child controls.
IRangeValueProvider	Exposes methods and properties to support UI Automation client access to controls that can be set to a value within a range.
IScrollItemProvider	Exposes methods and properties to support UI Automation client access to individual child controls of containers that implement *IScrollProvider*.
IScrollProvider	Exposes methods and properties to support UI Automation client access to a control that acts as a scrollable container for a collection of child objects. The children of this control must implement *IScrollItemProvider*.
ISelectionItemProvider	Exposes methods and properties to support UI Automation client access to individual, selectable child controls of containers that implement *ISelectionProvider*.

ISelectionProvider	Exposes methods and properties to support UI Automation client access to controls that act as containers for a collection of individual, selectable child items. The children of this control must implement *ISelectionItemProvider*.
ISynchronizedInputProvider	Exposes methods to facilitate UI Automation client access to controls that support synchronized input.
ITableItemProvider	Exposes methods and properties to support UI Automation client access to child controls of containers that implement *ITableProvider*.
ITableProvider	Exposes methods and properties to support UI Automation client access to controls that act as containers for a collection of child elements. The children of this element must implement *ITableItemProvider* and be organized in a two-dimensional logical coordinate system that can be traversed (that is, a UI Automation client can move to adjacent controls) by using the keyboard.
ITextProvider	Exposes methods and properties to support UI Automation client access to controls that contain text.
ITextRangeProvider	Exposes methods and properties to support UI Automation client access to a span of continuous text in a text container that implements *ITextProvider*.
IToggleProvider	Exposes methods and properties to support UI Automation client access to controls that can cycle through a set of states and maintain a state once set.
ITransformProvider	Exposes methods and properties to support UI Automation client access to controls that can be moved, resized, or rotated within a two-dimensional space.
IValueProvider	Exposes methods and properties to support UI Automation client access to controls having an intrinsic value that does not span a range and that can be represented as a string.
IVirtualizedItemProvider	Exposes a method to support the virtualized item control pattern.
IWindowProvider	Exposes methods and properties to support UI Automation client access to controls that provide fundamental window-based functionality within a traditional graphical user interface (GUI).

Refer to the documentation for each *AutomationPeer* control to determine which interfaces are implemented by which *AutomationPeer* controls.

Retrieving a Pattern Interface

You can use the *GetPattern* method to retrieve a default implementation of each pattern interface implemented by a particular automation peer. The following example demonstrates how to retrieve an implementation of *IInvokeProvider* from a *ButtonAutomationPeer* control named *Bap1*.

Sample of Visual Basic Code

```
Imports System.Windows.Automation.Peers
Imports System.Windows.Automation.Providers
' Omits class and method declarations
Dim InvProvider as IInvokeProvider
InvProvider = CType(Bap1.GetPattern(PatternInterface.Invoke), IInvokeProvider)
```

Sample of C# Code

```
using System.Windows.Automation.Peers;
using System.Windows.Automation.Providers;
// Omits class and method declarations
IInvokeProvider InvProvider;
InvProvider = (IInvokeProvider)Bap1.GetPattern(PatternInterface.Invoke);
```

After an instance of a pattern interface implementation is obtained, you can use it to automate the associated control. For example, to automate the button click of the associated button in the preceding example, you would call the *IInvokeProvider.Invoke* method, as shown here:

Sample of Visual Basic Code

```
InvProvider.Invoke
```

Sample of C# Code

```
InvokeProvider.Invoke();
```

Note that if you specify a pattern interface that is not implemented by *AutomationPeer*, a null value will be returned by the *GetPattern* method.

Using the WPF Tree Visualizer to Inspect the User Interface

The WPF Tree Visualizer enables you to examine the user interface while in debug mode. You can view visualizations of user interface elements, inspect the WPF dependency properties for objects in the tree, and navigate through the entire WPF visual tree.

The WPF Tree Visualizer is available in break mode when debugging an application. You can start it from the Watch window, the Locals window, the Autos window, and the data tips in break mode.

To open the WPF Tree Visualizer:

- In break mode, in the Watch window, the Locals window, the Autos window, or a data tip next to a WPF object name, click the arrow next to the magnifying glass icon to display a list of visualizers.

Click WPF Tree Visualizer to open the WPF Tree Visualizer, as shown in Figure 11-1:

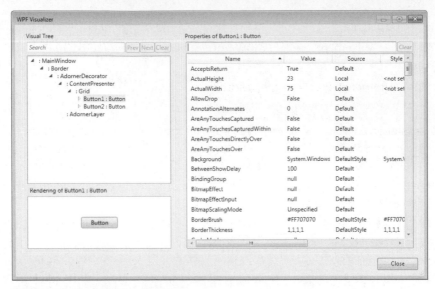

FIGURE 11-1 The WPF Tree Visualizer.

The WPF Tree Visualizer is divided into three sections. In the upper left pane is a representation of the WPF visual tree. Each object in the visual tree is represented in this pane and can be selected by the user. In the lower left pane is a rendering of the selected visual tree object, and in the right pane, all the properties of the selected object are displayed.

In complex WPF visual trees, you might want to search for an item in the visual tree.

To search in the WPF Tree Visualizer:

- In the Visual Tree pane, type the string you want to search for in the Search box. The objects that match the search string are displayed in the Visual Tree pane. You can go to the next object that matches the search string by clicking Next, go to the previous object that matches the search string by clicking Prev, or clear the search box by clicking Clear.

Similarly, you can search the Properties pane for items that match a search string. You can search for a property name, a value, or any other string that appears in any of the displayed properties.

To filter properties in the WPF Tree Visualizer:

- In the Properties pane, type the string you want to search for in the Filter box. The list now displays only those properties matching the string you have typed. Type more characters to find a more accurate match.

In this practice, you create an application that automates a preexisting application representing a pizza order form. You automate *RadioButton*, *CheckBox*, *ListView*, *ListViewItem*, and *Button* controls.

EXERCISE Automate a Preexisting Application

1. In Visual Studio, open the partial solution for this application.

   This solution contains a UI for a pizza-ordering application as well as an unimplemented form that you will use to automate the main window. Note that references to *UIAutomationProvider* and *UIAutomationTypes* have already been added, and the *System.Automation.Peers*, *System.Automation.Providers*, and *System.Automation* namespaces have been imported.

2. In the designer, open the designer view for AutomationWindow.xaml. You will see four buttons, each of which indicates functionality to be automated.

3. In the designer, double-click the button marked Automate Select Calzone to open the code window to the *Button1_Click* event handler. In this event handler, add the following code to automate selecting the second radio button:

   Sample of Visual Basic Code

   ```
   Dim RBAutomationPeer As New RadioButtonAutomationPeer(aWindow.RadioButton2)
   Dim SelectProvider As ISelectionItemProvider
   SelectProvider = RBAutomationPeer.GetPattern(PatternInterface.SelectionItem)
   SelectProvider.Select()
   ```

   Sample of C# Code

   ```
   RadioButtonAutomationPeer RBAutomationPeer = new RadioButtonAutomationPeer(aWindow
   .RadioButton2);
   ISelectionItemProvider SelectProvider;
   SelectProvider = (ISelectionItemProvider)
       RBAutomationPeer.GetPattern(PatternInterface.SelectionItem);
   SelectProvider.Select();
   ```

4. In the designer for AutomationWindow, double-click the button labeled Automate Select Pepperoni And Sausage to open the *Button2_Click* event handler. In this event handler, add the following code to automate selecting the first two *Checkbox* controls.

   Sample of Visual Basic Code

   ```
   Dim CBAutomationPeer1 As New CheckBoxAutomationPeer(aWindow.CheckBox1)
   Dim CBAutomationPeer2 As New CheckBoxAutomationPeer(aWindow.CheckBox2)
   Dim ToggProvider1 As IToggleProvider
   Dim ToggProvider2 As IToggleProvider
   ToggProvider1 = CBAutomationPeer1.GetPattern(PatternInterface.Toggle)
   ToggProvider2 = CBAutomationPeer2.GetPattern(PatternInterface.Toggle)
   ToggProvider1.Toggle()
   ToggProvider2.Toggle()
   ```

```
CheckBoxAutomationPeer CBAutomationPeer1 =
    new CheckBoxAutomationPeer(aWindow.CheckBox1);
CheckBoxAutomationPeer CBAutomationPeer2 =
    new CheckBoxAutomationPeer(aWindow.CheckBox2);
IToggleProvider ToggProvider1;
IToggleProvider ToggProvider2;
ToggProvider1 = (IToggleProvider)
    CBAutomationPeer1.GetPattern(PatternInterface.Toggle);
ToggProvider2 = (IToggleProvider)
    CBAutomationPeer2.GetPattern(PatternInterface.Toggle);
ToggProvider1.Toggle();
ToggProvider2.Toggle();
```

5. In the designer for AutomationWindow, double-click the button labeled Automate Select Bellevue Location to open the *Button3_Click* event handler. In this event handler, add the following code to automate scrolling of the *ListBox* control and selection of the last *ListBoxItem* object:

Sample of Visual Basic Code

```
Dim LBAutomationPeer As New ListBoxAutomationPeer(aWindow.ListBox1)
Dim ScrProvider As IScrollProvider
ScrProvider = LBAutomationPeer.GetPattern(PatternInterface.Scroll)
ScrProvider.Scroll(ScrollAmount.NoAmount, ScrollAmount.LargeIncrement)
ScrProvider.Scroll(ScrollAmount.NoAmount, ScrollAmount.LargeIncrement)
Dim LBIAutomationPeer As +
    New ListBoxItemAutomationPeer(aWindow.ListBox1.Items(3)LBAutomationPeer)
Dim SelItemProvider As ISelectionItemProvider
SelItemProvider = LBIAutomationPeer.GetPattern(PatternInterface.SelectionItem)
SelItemProvider.Select()
```

Sample of C# Code

```
ListBoxAutomationPeer LBAutomationPeer = new ListBoxAutomationPeer(aWindow
.ListBox1);
IScrollProvider ScrProvider;
ScrProvider = (IScrollProvider)LBAutomationPeer.GetPattern(PatternInterface
.Scroll);
ScrProvider.Scroll(System.Windows.Automation.ScrollAmount.NoAmount,
    System.Windows.Automation.ScrollAmount.LargeIncrement);
ScrProvider.Scroll(System.Windows.Automation.ScrollAmount.NoAmount,
    System.Windows.Automation.ScrollAmount.LargeIncrement);
ListBoxItemAutomationPeer LBIAutomationPeer =
    new ListBoxItemAutomationPeer(aWindow.ListBox1.Items[3],
        LBAutomationPeer);
ISelectionItemProvider SelItemProvider;
SelItemProvider =(ISelectionItemProvider)
    LBIAutomationPeer.GetPattern(PatternInterface.SelectionItem);
SelItemProvider.Select();
```

6. In the designer for AutomationWindow, double-click the button labeled Automate Click Order Button to open the *Button4_Click* event handler. In this event handler, add the following code to automate clicking the Place Order button.

Sample of Visual Basic Code

```
Dim BAutomationPeer As New Automation.Peers.ButtonAutomationPeer(aWindow.Button1)
Dim InvProvider As IInvokeProvider
InvProvider = BAutomationPeer.GetPattern(PatternInterface.Invoke)
InvProvider.Invoke()
```

Sample of C# Code

```
ButtonAutomationPeer BAutomationPeer = new ButtonAutomationPeer(aWindow.Button1);
IInvokeProvider InvProvider;
InvProvider = (IInvokeProvider)
    BAutomationPeer.GetPattern(PatternInterface.Invoke);
InvProvider.Invoke();
```

7. Press F5 to run your application. Two windows appear, MainWindow and AutomationWindow. In AutomationWindow, click each button in turn and notice that the controls in MainWindow are automated as expected.

Lesson Summary

- UI Automation enables you to control a user interface programmatically. The *System.Windows.Automation.Peers* namespace contains automation peers that correspond to existing WPF controls and can be used to automate those controls.

- Each implemented automation peer implements one or more pattern interfaces that provide the functionality required to automate WPF controls. You can retrieve a default implementation of these interfaces by calling the *GetPattern* method from the automation peer you are using.

- The WPF Tree Visualizer enables you to inspect the WPF visual tree at debug time. You can visualize the rendering of a selected WPF control and explore its dependency properties.

Lesson Review

You can use the following questions to test your knowledge of the information in Lesson 1, "Testing the User Interface." The questions are also available on the companion CD if you prefer to review them in electronic form.

> **NOTE ANSWERS**
>
> Answers to these questions and explanations of why each answer choice is correct or incorrect are located in the "Answers" section at the end of the book.

1. Which of the following is NOT required to automate a WPF control? (Choose all that apply.)

   A. Create an instance of *AutomationPeer* that corresponds to the control you want to automate.

   B. Cast your instance of automation peer as the required pattern interface for the functionality you want to invoke.

   C. Obtain a reference to an implementation of the pattern interface that encapsulates the functionality you want to automate.

   D. Call methods on an instance of the correct pattern interface to automate the desired functionality.

2. From which of the following are you able to open the WPF Tree Visualizer at debug time? (Choose all that apply.)

   A. The Watch window

   B. The Auto window

   C. The Locals window

   D. The Output window

Lesson 2: Debugging with Intellitrace and *PresentationTraceSources*

Trace was introduced in .NET Framework 1.0 and represents a technology that enables the user to emit information to the console window or other attached logs. Tracing technology has improved over the years, and in this lesson, two of the most recent innovations in Trace will be discussed: Intellitrace, which enables you to selectively examine and filter Trace messages emitted by your application, and *PresentationTraceSources*, which are specialized trace sources for debugging WPF applications.

After this lesson, you will be able to:

- Enable Intellitrace.
- Select and filter Intellitrace data.
- Configure *PresentationTraceSources* through the app.config file.
- Configure *PresentationTraceSources* in code.
- Emit trace messages with *PresentationTraceSources*.

Estimated lesson time: 30 minutes

Using Intellitrace

Intellitrace is a new tracing technology available only to users of Visual Studio 2010 Ultimate. With Intellitrace, messages about Intellitrace events are automatically emitted by Visual Studio in the background to an .iTrace file, where they can be retrieved and examined for debugging purposes. Intellitrace is highly configurable with regard to the type and amount of information you want to record and, with the default settings, has very little impact on application execution and performance.

Enabling Intellitrace

Intellitrace is enabled by default, and Intellitrace events are recorded automatically. These events represent application events, and recording this data has a very small, usually unnoticeable, impact on application performance. You can also configure Intellitrace to record events, function calls, and parameter information. Recording this information is more processor-intensive and can degrade application performance, but it can also provide valuable information for deep debugging.

To enable Intellitrace:

1. In Visual Studio 2010 Ultimate, from the Tools menu, select Options and then click Intellitrace and Enable Intellitrace to open the Enable Intellitrace pane.

2. To enable Intellitrace, ensure that Enable Intellitrace Checkbox is selected. To disable Intellitrace, clear this box.

3. To enable collection of call and parameter information, select the option button labeled Intellitrace Events And Call Information.

Setting the Location for Intellitrace Recordings

Intellitrace files are recorded to disk for later viewing. You can select a disk location for your Intellitrace files.

To set the location for Intellitrace recordings:

1. In Visual Studio 2010 Ultimate, from the Tools menu, select Options and then click Intellitrace and Advanced to open the Advanced pane.

2. Click the Browse button and browse to the directory location for Intellitrace files.

3. You can also set the maximum size for Intellitrace files by selecting the maximum amount of disk space to be used from the drop-down box in this pane.

   Note that if you enable collection of call and parameter information, you will likely need more disk space for your Intellitrace file and should adjust this amount accordingly.

Selecting Intellitrace Events to Record

The types of events you want Intellitrace to record are highly configurable. You can record all available events or limit Intellitrace recording to only the events in which you are interested.

To configure Intellitrace events to record:

1. In Visual Studio 2010 Ultimate, from the Tools menu, select Options and then click Intellitrace and Intellitrace Events to open the Intellitrace Events Pane.

2. In the Intellitrace Events pane, you will see a list of types of events to record. To select an event type, ensure that the check box next to the event type is selected. Note that you can also collect subsets of these events. By expanding the arrow to the left of the event type, you are presented with a list of event subtypes that can also be selected or cleared.

3. To restore the default settings, click the Restore button.

Viewing Intellitrace Events in Debug Mode

You can view Intellitrace events and calls that pertain to your application through the Intellitrace window. Although the Intellitrace window can be open at any point in Debug mode, you can view Intellitrace events only in Break mode.

To view Intellitrace events:

1. While the application is executing, from the Debug menu, choose Intellitrace and then Intellitrace Events. Note that if you are collecting call and parameter information, you can open this window by selecting Intellitrace Calls.

2. In the Intellitrace window, click Break All to break application execution. Intellitrace events are now displayed in the Intellitrace window. Clicking an Intellitrace event will cause the code window to highlight the code that is the source of this event.

Filtering Intellitrace Events

When viewing Intellitrace events, you can filter the event types you want to view.

To filter Intellitrace events:

1. In the Intellitrace window, filter by event type by selecting the appropriate type from the left drop-down list.

2. You can also filter by originating thread by selecting the appropriate thread from the right drop-down list.

3. To search for an event that matches a given string, simply type that string in the search box, and matching events will be displayed automatically.

Opening an Intellitrace File

In addition to viewing Intellitrace data while in Break mode, you can examine the Intellitrace information for past application runs by viewing the recorded Intellitrace file. To do so, navigate to the Intellitrace file location and double-click the .iTrace file. The Intellitrace information opens in the Intellitrace window. You can view and filter this information just as if the application were in Break mode.

Using *PresentationTraceSources*

PresentationTraceSources is a static class that exposes a set of preestablished trace sources which can emit information about an application's execution. Trace sources can be configured to emit information at various levels and can be turned on and off by associated trace switches. You can attach trace listeners to record trace information in a variety of formats. *PresentationTraceSources* can be configured either in code or in the app.config file.

WPF *PresentationTraceSources*

PresentationTraceSources incorporates eleven trace sources that each emits information about its area of functionality. For example, *AnimationTraceSource* emits information about animations being executed in your application. Table 11-3 summarizes the available *PresentationTraceSources* trace sources.

TABLE 11-3 *PresentationTraceSources*

TRACE SOURCE NAME	NAMESPACE	DESCRIPTION
AnimationSource	*System.Windows.Media.Animation*	Writes information about events pertaining to animations.
DataBindingSource	*System.Windows.Data*	Writes information about events pertaining to databinding.
DependencyPropertySource	*System.Windows .DependencyProperty*	Writes information about events pertaining to dependency properties.
DocumentsSource	*System.Windows.Documents*	Writes information about events pertaining to documents.
FreezableSource	*System.Windows.Freezable*	Writes information about events pertaining to freezable objects.
HwndHostSource	*System.Windows.Interop*	Writes information about events pertaining to Hwnd hosts.
MarkupSource	*System.Windows.Markup*	Writes information when XAML or BAML is loaded.
NameScopeSource	*System.Windows.NameScope*	Writes information when a name is registered.
ResourceDictionarySource	*System.Windows .ResourceDictionary*	Writes information about events pertaining to logical resources.
RoutedEventSource	*System.Windows.RoutedEvent*	Writes information about events pertaining to routed events.
ShellSource	*System.Windows.Shell*	Writes information about events pertaining to shell operations.

You use the name of the trace source when using it in code, and you use the namespace when configuring the trace source in the app.config file. Both of these scenarios are described in greater detail later in this chapter.

Enabling *PresentationTraceSources*

By default, *PresentationTraceSources* is disabled. To enable tracing with these sources, you can call the *PresentationTraceSources.Refresh* method as follows:

Sample of Visual Basic Code

```
PresentationTraceSources.Refresh
```

Sample of C# Code

```
PresentationTraceSources.Refresh();
```

Configuring *PresentationTraceSources* with the App.Config File

The most common way to configure *PresentationTraceSources* is through the app.config file, an XML file that contains a node called *<System.Diagnostics>*, which is where *PresentationTraceSources* trace sources are configured. The *<System.Diagnostics>* node has three important subnodes, *<sources>*, *<switches>*, and *<sharedListeners>*, where *PresentationTraceSources*, trace switches, and trace listeners are configured, respectively.

The first step in configuring *PresentationTraceSources* through the app.config file is actually to add an app.config file to your application.

To add an app.config file:

1. From the Project menu, choose Add New Item. The Add New Item window opens.

2. In the Add New Item window, select General in the left pane. In the center pane, choose the Application Configuration file and click Add. A new app.config file is added to your project.

You can configure *PresentationTraceSources* in the *<sources>* node of the app.config file. You can add a new source by adding a *<source>* node, which requires two attributes: the *Name* attribute, which specifies the namespace for the *PresentationTraceSources* trace source to be added (see Table 11-2 for a list of namespaces); and the *switchName* attribute, which specifies the name of the switch that controls this trace source. (See the following text for information on configuring a trace switch.) Each *<source>* node also contains a subnode called *<listeners>* where you can add trace listeners, which receive the output from the trace sources.

To activate a presentation trace source, create an entry in the *<sources>* node of the app.config file that specifies the *Name* and *switchName* attributes. The following example demonstrates how to add the *System.Windows.Media.Animation* trace source with a switch name of *mySwitch*.

```
<source name="System.Windows.Media.Animation" switchName="mySwitch" >
</source>
```

In the preceding example, a new trace source has been added to the configuration file, but you will not see any difference in tracing for your application at this point. You still need to add a switch to control the level of trace information you receive and one or more listeners to record the trace output.

To add a trace switch, create an entry in the *<switches>* node that specifies the switch name and the level, as shown here:

```
<switches>
  <add name="mySwitch" value="All" />
</switches>
```

By specifying a new switch with the name that matches the switch name specified in the *<source>* node, you automatically associate that trace switch with the source. Possible values for the *Value* attribute are *Off*, which disables trace activity; *Warning*, which emits only warnings and errors; *Activity*, which emits information about activity; *Verbose*, which emits verbose information; and *All*, which emits all trace information produced by this source.

Even when a trace source has been added to the app.config file and associated with an active trace switch, you still will not receive any output from this trace source until you create and associate a listener to receive and process the output. There are three kinds of trace listeners: console listeners that direct trace output to the Output window, text listeners that write trace output to a text file, and XML listeners that write trace output to an XML file.

You can add a trace listener by creating a new *<add>* node in the *sharedListeners* node of the app.config file. In this node, you must specify the *Name* attribute, which indicates the name of the listener; the *Type* attribute, which specifies the .NET Framework type to instantiate for the listener; and the *initializeData* attribute, which provides the initial file name for text and XML listeners and receives a value of *False* for console listeners.

After a new listener has been specified, you must associate that listener with one or more sources before it will receive any output. You can associate a listener with a trace source by creating an *<add>* node in the *<listeners>* node of the source node. The *<add>* node must specify the name of the listener in the *Name* attribute.

To add a trace listener:

1. Add a node specifying the new listener to the *<sharedListeners>* node. The following example demonstrates how to add a console listener, a text listener, and an XML listener:

```
<sharedListeners>
  <!-- This listener sends output to the console -->
  <add name="console"
      type="System.Diagnostics.ConsoleTraceListener"
      initializeData="false"/>
  <!-- This listener sends output to an Xml file named xmlTrace.xml -->
  <add name="xmlListener"
      type="System.Diagnostics.XmlWriterTraceListener"
      traceOutputOptions="None"
      initializeData="xmlTrace.xml" />
  <!-- This listener sends output to a file named textTrace.txt -->
  <add name="textListener"
      type="System.Diagnostics.TextWriterTraceListener"
      initializeData="textTrace.txt" />
</sharedListeners>
```

2. Set *AutoFlush* to *True* to flush the trace listener output automatically by adding a *<trace>* node to the *<system.diagnostics>* node that sets the *Autoflush* attribute to *True*, as shown here:

```
<trace autoflush="true" ></trace>
```

3. Add a *<listeners>* node that specifies the trace listener to the source node you want to associate with the listener. The following example demonstrates associating the *System. Windows.Media.Animation* trace source with the text listener defined in step 1:

```
<source name="System.Windows.Media.Animation" switchName="mySwitch" >
```

```
      <listeners>
        <add name="textListener" />
      </listeners>
    </source>
```

Configuring *PresentationTraceSources* Programmatically

If you prefer, you can configure *PresentationTraceSources* programmatically rather than through the app.config file. *PresentationTraceSources* classes are initialized with a trace switch, but you must still set the trace level on that switch and add a trace listener to receive output.

To set the trace level, set the *Level* property of the *Switch* property on the presentation trace source you want to configure, as shown in the following example.

Sample of Visual Basic Code

```
PresentationTraceSources.AnimationSource.Switch.Level = SourceLevels.All
```

Sample of C# Code

```
PresentationTraceSources.AnimationSource.Switch.Level = SourceLevels.All;
```

To add a trace listener:

1. Initialize the trace listener in code, as shown in the following example:

   Sample of Visual Basic Code

   ```
   Dim listener as TextWriterTraceListener
   Dim myFile As System.IO.Stream = System.IO.File.Create("trace.txt")
   listener = New TextWriterTraceListener(myFile)
   ```

   Sample of C# Code

   ```
   TextWriterTraceListener listener;
   System.IO.Stream myFile = System.IO.File.Create("trace.txt");
   listener = new TextWriterTraceListener(myFile);
   ```

2. Add the listener to the *Listeners* collection of the trace source, as shown here:

   Sample of Visual Basic Code

   ```
   PresentationTraceSources.AnimationSource.Listeners.Add(listener)
   ```

   Sample of C# Code

   ```
   PresentationTraceSources.AnimationSource.Listeners.Add(listener);
   ```

PRACTICE **Practice with *PresentationTraceSources***

In this practice, you work with *PresentationTraceSources* in code to set the trace level on a trace source, create a new text listener for it, associate the two, and, finally, examine the trace output.

EXERCISE Working with *PresentationTraceSources*

1. Open the partial solution for this lesson.

   This is, in fact, the completed solution from the previous lesson. You will trace the routed events in this application.

2. In Visual Studio, open the code window for AutomationWindow.

3. In the constructor for AutomationWindow (C#) or the *AutomationWindow_Loaded* event handler (Visual Basic), call the *PresentationTraceSources.Refresh* method as follows. For C#, this call should be added after the call to InitializeComponent().

   Sample of Visual Basic Code

   ```
   PresentationTraceSources.Refresh()
   ```

   Sample of C# Code

   ```
   PresentationTraceSources.Refresh();
   ```

4. Beneath the code you added in step 3, add the following code to create a new TextWriter trace listener:

   Sample of Visual Basic Code

   ```
   Dim listener As TextWriterTraceListener
   Dim myFile As System.IO.Stream = System.IO.File.Create("trace.txt")
   listener = New TextWriterTraceListener(myFile)
   ```

   Sample of C# Code

   ```
   TextWriterTraceListener listener;
   System.IO.Stream myFile = System.IO.File.Create("trace.txt");
   listener = new TextWriterTraceListener(myFile);
   ```

5. Beneath the code you added in step 4, add the following code to set the trace level to *All*, thus emitting output for all events associated with that trace source.

   Sample of Visual Basic Code

   ```
   PresentationTraceSources.RoutedEventSource.Switch.Level = SourceLevels.All
   ```

   Sample of C# Code

   ```
   PresentationTraceSources.RoutedEventSource.Switch.Level = SourceLevels.All;
   ```

6. Finally, beneath the line of code added in step 5, add the following line of code to add the text listener to the *Listeners* collection of *RoutedEventSource*:

   Sample of Visual Basic Code

   ```
   PresentationTraceSources.RoutedEventSource.Listeners.Add(listener)
   ```

   Sample of C# Code

   ```
   PresentationTraceSources.RoutedEventSource.Listeners.Add(listener);
   ```

7. Press F5 to build and run the application. Click each of the buttons in *AutomationWindow* and then close the application. Note that you will have to close both windows to end the application.

8. In Visual Studio, in Solution Explorer, click the icon for Show All Files. Expand the bin and then the Debug nodes and double-click trace.txt. Your new trace file opens. Note that every routed event that occurred in the short application run was recorded, including many you might not even have been aware of. By choosing different values for the *Switch.Level* property, you can filter the amount of information a trace source emits.

Lesson Summary

- Intellitrace enables you to view trace information that is automatically emitted by your application. Intellitrace data can be filtered to narrow down specific tracing events and can be stored in .iTrace files for future examination.

- *PresentationTraceSources* is a static class that exposes several preconfigured trace sources that emit information about WPF applications.

- You can view information emitted by *PresentationTraceSources* by associating one or more listeners with the trace source and by enabling its associated trace switch by setting the trace level to any value other than *Off*.

- You can configure *PresentationTraceSources* either in the app.config file or directly in code.

Lesson Review

You can use the following questions to test your knowledge of the information in Lesson 2, "Debugging with Intellitrace and *PresentationTraceSources*." The questions are also available on the companion CD if you prefer to review them in electronic form.

> **NOTE ANSWERS**
>
> Answers to these questions and explanations of why each answer choice is correct or incorrect are located in the "Answers" section at the end of the book.

1. Which of the following is required to view Intellitrace data?
   A. You must enable Intellitrace data collection through Visual Studio.
   B. You must set the file size and location.
   C. You must open the Intellitrace window.
   D. You must be running Visual Studio 2010 Ultimate.

2. Which two of the following XML samples, when added to the correct nodes of the app.config file, correctly configure *AnimationTraceSource* to write data to *TextWriterTraceListener*? Assume that any trace switches have been appropriately set. (Choose all that apply.)

A.

```xml
<source name="System.Windows.Media.Animation" switchName="mySwitch" >
  <listeners>
    <add name="myListener" />
  </listeners>
</source>
```

B.

```xml
<sharedListeners>
    <add name="myListener"
    type="System.Diagnostics.XmlWriterTraceListener"
    initializeData="myTrace.xml" />
</sharedListeners>
```

C.

```xml
<sharedListeners>
    <add name="myListener"
    type="System.Diagnostics.TextWriterTraceListener"
    initializeData="myTrace.txt" />
</sharedListeners>
```

D.

```xml
<source name="System.Windows.Media.Animation" switchName="mySwitch" >
  <listeners>
    <add name="textListener" />
  </listeners>
</source>
```

Case Scenario

In the following case scenario, you apply what you've learned about testing and debugging WPF applications. You can find answers to these questions in the "Answers" section at the end of this book.

Case Scenario: Debug Drama

Boy, we're in it now! Customer demand for your new WPF application has pushed the ship calendar up a couple of months and now you're dealing with a beta that is full of bugs. Most of the straightforward ones have been resolved, leaving a lot of tricky ones, including several that are hard to reproduce. In addition, many of your junior testers are Windows Forms users with little exposure to WPF, and they are finding debugging data binding to be particularly frustrating.

Answer these questions for your manager:

1. What general strategies can you use to speed up resolution of the remaining tricky bugs?

2. Are there any tools that can be used to help locate and resolve the data-binding errors?

Suggested Practices

To help you successfully master the exam objectives presented in this chapter, complete the following tasks.

- **Practice 1** Modify the solution to Lesson 2, "Debugging with Intellitrace and *PresentationTraceSources*," so that it receives trace output from several trace listeners but writes only warnings and errors. Then modify the application so that errors are produced and examine the trace output.

- **Practice 2** Test the user interface for solutions to previous chapters by creating an application that accesses all the controls in the completed solution through automation.

Take a Practice Test

The practice tests on this book's companion CD offer many options. For example, you can test yourself on just the content covered in this chapter, or you can test yourself on all the 70-511 certification exam content. You can set up the test so that it closely simulates the experience of taking a certification exam, or you can set it up in study mode so that you can look at the correct answers and explanations after you answer each question.

MORE INFO **PRACTICE TESTS**

For details about all the practice test options available, see the "How to Use the Practice Tests" section in this book's Introduction.

CHAPTER 12

Deployment

After you have developed your application, it must reach its intended audience. Microsoft Visual Studio provides several methods for deploying your application. ClickOnce technology enables you to deploy your application quickly and easily and provide for automatic updates. For more detailed deployments, Windows Installer technology provides a highly configurable deployment environment. In this chapter, you learn how to deploy your applications by using ClickOnce and Windows Installer technology.

Exam objectives in this chapter:

- Configure a ClickOnce deployment.
- Create and configure a Windows Installer project.
- Configure deployment security settings.

Lessons in this chapter:

Before You Begin

To complete the lessons in this chapter, you must have:

- A computer that meets or exceeds the minimum hardware requirements listed in the "About This Book" section at the beginning of the book.

- Microsoft Visual Studio 2010 Professional installed on your computer.

- An understanding of Microsoft Visual Basic or C# syntax and familiarity with Microsoft .NET Framework 4.0.

- An understanding of Extensible Application Markup Language (XAML).

 REAL WORLD

Matthew Stoecker

Deployment can pose some difficult challenges to the developer. I find it especially difficult to deploy applications that require frequent updates. ClickOnce addresses this problem and enables me to deploy applications that are updated regularly. And for complex deployments, I still like to use Windows Installer technology, which provides the greatest degree of control and customization.

Lesson 1: Creating a Windows Setup Project

Although ClickOnce provides simple and easy deployment for a variety of applications, you might need a more configurable environment for complex programs. *Setup projects* enable you to create highly configurable deployment plans. In this lesson, you learn how to create a setup project.

After this lesson, you will able to:

- Create a Windows Forms Application setup project.
- Set deployment project properties.
- Configure Setup to add icons during setup.
- Configure conditional installation based on operating system versions.
- Configure a setup project to deploy the .NET Framework.
- Add a custom action to a setup project.
- Add error-handling code for custom actions to a setup project.

Estimated lesson time: 45 minutes

Setup Projects

You can add a setup project to a solution to create a Windows Installer application for your solution. Setup projects are highly configurable and enable you to create directories on the target computer, copy files, modify the registry, and execute custom actions during installation. When compiled, a setup project produces an .msi file, which incorporates a setup wizard for the application. The .msi file can be distributed by disk, download, or file share. When it is clicked, the .msi file launches the application setup wizard and installs the application.

To add a setup project to your solution:

1. From the File menu, choose Add and then click New Project to open the Add New Project dialog box.

2. In the Project Types pane, expand Other Project Types and then click Setup And Deployment.

3. In the Templates pane, expand Visual Studio Installer, click Setup Project, and then click OK.

Setup Project Editors

Each setup project includes six editors with which to configure the contents and the behavior of the setup project. These editors are:

- **File System Editor** Enables you to configure the installation of your application to the file system of the target computer.

- **Registry Editor**   Enables you to write entries to the registry upon installation.
- **File Types Editor**   Enables you to set associations between applications and file types.
- **User Interface Editor**   Enables you to edit the user interface seen during installation for both regular installation and administrative installation.
- **Custom Actions Editor**   Enables you to define custom actions to be performed during installation.
- **Launch Conditions Editor**   Enables you to set conditions for launching the installation of your setup project.

You can open any of these editors by selecting the deployment project in Solution Explorer and then selecting the appropriate editor from the View menu.

Adding Files to a Setup Project with the File System Editor

The File System editor represents the file system on the target computer. You can add output files to various directories, create new directories on the target computer, or create and add shortcuts to the target computer. Figure 12-1 shows the File System editor.

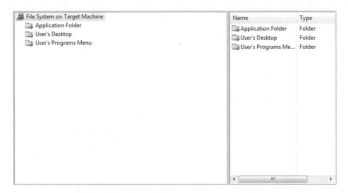

FIGURE 12-1 The File System editor.

The File System editor is split into two panes. The left pane represents the directory structure of the target computer. Each folder in the left pane represents a folder on the target computer that exists or will be created by the setup application. The right pane displays the contents of the directory selected in the left pane. Initially, the File System editor consists of three folders: Application Folder, User's Desktop, and User's Program Menu. You can change the folder for a particular file by selecting the file in the right pane and dragging it to the appropriate folder.

You can add folders to the File System editor by right-clicking the left pane and choosing Add Special Folder. Using this menu, you can add a special folder to the File System editor or create your own custom folder. If you choose to create a custom folder, this folder will be created in the target computer's file system upon installation.

To add output from a project to a deployment project:

1. Right-click Application Folder in the left pane of the File System editor, choose Add, and then choose Project Output. The Add Project Output Group dialog box (pictured in Figure 12-2) opens.

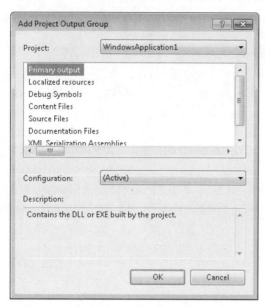

FIGURE 12-2 The Add Project Output Group dialog box.

2. Choose the project outputs you want to add to your setup project. All .exe and .dll files created by the project are contained in Primary Output. You can also add other project files to your setup project—such as localized resources, content files, or documentation files—or, less frequently, debug symbols, source files, or Extensible Markup Language (XML) serialization assemblies. After you have selected the output to be added to the folder, click OK.

To create a shortcut and add it to the target computer:

1. In the right pane of the File System editor, right-click the file for which you want to create a shortcut and choose Create Shortcut. A shortcut to the file is created and added to the pane.

2. Drag the shortcut from the right-side pane to the appropriate folder in the left-side pane.

Configuring the Setup Project to Add an Icon during Setup

You can use the File System editor to associate an icon with your application at installation. Shortcuts to your application will be displayed with the icon you specify.

To associate an icon with an application at setup:

1. In the File System editor, right-click a folder, choose Add, and then select File. The Add Files dialog box opens.

2. Browse to the .ico file you want to associate with a shortcut and click Add to add it to your setup project.

3. Create a shortcut to your application as previously described.

4. In the File System editor, select the shortcut.

5. In the Properties window, select the *Icon* property and then choose (Browse...) from the drop-down list. Browse to the icon you want to associate with your application.

6. Select the icon and click OK.

Configuring Conditional Installation Based on the Operating System Version

You can use the *VersionNT* system property to determine the operating system at installation time and to create installation conditions that allow the installation to continue or abort based on the operating system.

The *VersionNT* property is an integer that is calculated by the following formula: MajorVersion * 100 + MinorVersion. Thus, Microsoft Windows 2000 would report a *VersionNT* value of 500 or greater, depending on the minor version.

To configure conditional installation based on the operating system version:

1. In the File System editor, select the file that contains the primary output for the application.

2. In the Properties window, select the *Condition* property and type a condition that evaluates the operating system based on the formula previously described. For example, if you want to restrict installation to Windows 2000 or later, you would type the condition *VersionNT>=500*.

Setting Setup Project Properties

The setup project properties provide information about your project and set actions relating to versions of your project. You set setup project properties in the Properties window. Many setup project properties can provide descriptive information about your application. These properties include:

- **AddRemoveProgramsIcon**   Specifies an icon for the Add/Remove Programs dialog box on the client computer.
- **Author**   Contains information about the author of the program.
- **Description**   Contains a description of the application.
- **Keywords**   Contains keywords to be associated with the application.

- **Localization**   Provides the locale information for the application.

- **Manufacturer**   Contains information about the manufacturer of the application. It is commonly used to define the default install folder within the Program Files folder.

- **ManufacturerURL**   Contains the URL of the manufacturer's Web site.

- **ProductName**   Contains the name of the product.

- **Subject**   Contains information about the subject of the application.

- **SupportPhone**   Provides a phone number for support for the application.

- **SupportURL**   Contains a URL for support for the application.

- **TargetPlatform**   Specifies the target platform of the installer: x86, x64, or Itanium.

- **Title**   Contains the title of the application.

Other properties of the setup project determine the behavior of the setup project at installation time. These properties include:

- **DetectNewerInstalledVersion**   Looks for a more recent version of the application on the target computer and aborts the installation if one is found.

- **InstallAllUsers**   Specifies whether the package is installed for all users or only for the installing user.

- **PostBuildEvent**   Specifies a command line that is executed after the build ends.

- **PreBuildEvent**   Specifies a command line that is executed before the build begins.

- **RemovePreviousVersion**   Looks for earlier versions of the application and, if any are found, uninstalls them in favor of the new version.

- **RunPostBuildEvent**   Specifies the condition under which the post-build event runs. The value is either *On Successful Build* or *Always*.

- **SearchPath**   Specifies the path used to search for assemblies, files, or merge modules on the development computer.

- **Version**   Holds the information used by the previous two properties to determine versioning.

There are two additional properties: *ProductCode* and *UpgradeCode*. These are used by the setup program and should never be altered manually.

You can change these properties at design time by selecting the project in Solution Explorer and altering the appropriate property in the Properties window.

Configuring a Deployment Project to Deploy the .NET Framework

All applications created with Visual Studio 2008 require .NET Framework 3.5 to run. If you are uncertain of the deployment environment for your applications, you can configure your setup project to install prerequisites, such as the .NET Framework, as part of the installation. The .NET Framework is configured to be installed by default, but you can verify that this configuration is still valid by the following procedure.

To configure a deployment project to deploy the .NET Framework:

1. In Solution Explorer, select the setup project.

2. From the Project menu, click Properties. The *<project>* Property Pages dialog box opens.

3. In the *<project>* Properties dialog box, click Prerequisites to open the Prerequisites dialog box.

4. If it is not already selected, select the check box labeled Create Setup Program To Install Prerequisite Components.

5. In the Choose Which Prerequisites To Install list, select the check box labeled .NET Framework 3.5.

6. In the group labeled Specify The Install Location For Prerequisites, select the option button labeled Download Prerequisites From The Component Vendor's Web Site.

7. Click OK and then close the *<project>* Property Pages dialog box.

Custom Actions

Custom actions are an advanced installation technology. With the Custom Actions editor, you can configure code to be executed during installation. Custom action code must be contained in an *Installer* class. You can use custom actions to execute code upon four *Installer* events: *Install*, *Commit*, *Rollback*, or *Uninstall*. Install actions occur after the files have been installed but before the installation has been committed. Commit actions occur when an installation is committed on the target machine. Rollback actions are executed when an installation fails and is rolled back, and Uninstall actions are executed when an application is being uninstalled. You can use the Custom Actions editor, shown in Figure 12-3, to associate code with these *Installer* events.

FIGURE 12-3 The Custom Actions editor.

Any executable code can be executed as a custom action as long as it is contained in an *Installer* class. (Although technically it is possible to configure a custom action in code other than an *Installer* class, this text will limit discussion of custom actions to *Installer* classes.) You can add a new custom action in the Custom Action editor by right-clicking the event in which you want your custom action to run and choosing Add Custom Action from the context menu. This opens the Select Item In Project dialog box, from which you can select an item in your project to set as a custom action. A new custom action representing the item you selected is added to your setup project.

For the item you select to function as a custom action, it must contain an Installer class. *Installer* classes expose methods—such as *Install*, *Rollback*, *Uninstall*, and *Commit*—that the setup project uses to execute custom actions. These methods are present in the base *Installer* class and must be overridden in the *Installer* class you create in order to contain a custom action. For example, the following code example demonstrates how to override the *Install* method of an *Installer* class:

Sample of Visual Basic Code

```
Public Overrides Sub Install(ByVal stateSaver As System.Collections.IDictionary)
    MyBase.Install(stateSaver)
        ' Insert code for the custom action here
End Sub
```

Sample of C# Code

```
public override void Install(System.Collections.IDictionary stateSaver)
{
    base.Install(stateSaver);
    // Insert code for your custom action here
}
```

You can write code for any or all these methods, but code written in an *Installer* class will not be executed unless the project that contains it has been designated as a custom action. Note that the *Installer* class must be added to the project you want to deploy, not to the setup project.

To add an *Installer* class to your project:

1. In Solution Explorer, select the project to which you want to add the *Installer* class. Note that this should be the project you want to deploy, not the setup project.

2. From the Project menu, select Add New Item. Choose Installer Class in the Add New Item dialog box and click Add.

When you are in the Custom Actions editor, you can configure a custom action by selecting the custom action and then setting the properties in the Properties window. Custom action properties are shown in Table 12-1.

TABLE 12-1 Properties of Custom Actions

PROPERTY	DESCRIPTION
(Name)	This is the name of the selected custom action.
Arguments	Supplies any required command-line arguments to the application represented by the custom action. This property is applicable only when the custom action is implemented as an executable (.exe).

Condition	Provides a Boolean statement that will be evaluated before the custom action is executed. If the statement is *True*, the custom action will execute. If the statement is *False*, the action will not execute. You can use the *Condition* property to evaluate properties chosen in custom dialog boxes.
CustomActionData	Passes any additional required data to the custom action.
EntryPoint	Specifies the name of the method to execute for the custom action. If left blank, the custom action will attempt to execute a method with the same name as the event with which the custom action is associated (for example, *Install*). This property applies only to custom actions implemented in dynamic-link libraries (DLLs) and is ignored when the *InstallerClass* property is set to *True*.
InstallerClass	A Boolean value that represents whether your custom action is implemented in an *Installer* class. This property must be *True* if the custom action is implemented in an *Installer* and *False* if it is not.
SourcePath	Contains the actual path on the developer's computer to the file that implements the custom action. This property is read-only.

To create a custom action:

1. Write, test, and debug the code for the custom action you want to add to your setup project.

2. Add an *Installer* class to the solution you want to deploy.

3. Add the code written in step 1 to the appropriate overridden method (for example, Install, *Rollback*, *Commit*, or *Uninstall*) of the *Installer* class.

4. In Solution Explorer, select the setup project. From the View menu, choose Editors and then choose Custom Actions Editor.

5. Right-click the installation event you want to associate with your custom action and choose Add Custom Action. The Select Item In Project dialog box opens.

6. Browse to the file that implements your custom action, select it, and then click OK.

7. Select the new custom action in the Custom Actions window. In the Properties window, configure the properties of the custom action.

Handling Errors in Custom Actions

Although Windows Installer handles most errors in deployment, you must write error-handling code to trap errors in custom actions. Because custom actions are executed code, errors that occur and are not handled can cause unexpected results on installation. Use *Try/Catch* blocks to catch and correct any errors that can be corrected. If an error occurs that cannot be corrected, such as a missing file, throw a new *InstallException* exception. Throwing an *InstallException* exception causes the installation to be rolled back without leaving any lasting effect on the system. The following example demonstrates how to test for the existence of a file and throw a new *InstallException* exception if the file is not found:

Sample of Visual Basic Code

```
Dim myInfo As New System.IO.FileInfo("aFile.txt")
If Not myInfo.Exists Then
    Throw New System.Configuration.Install.InstallException("File not found")
End If
```

Sample of C# Code

```
System.IO.FileInfo myInfo = new System.IO.FileInfo("aFile.txt");
if(!(myInfo.Exists))
    throw new System.Configuration.Install.InstallException("File not found");
```

 Quick Check

1. How can you associate an icon with an application?

2. How can you roll back installation of a setup project in a custom action?

Quick Check Answers

1. You can associate an icon with your application by creating a shortcut in the File System editor and then setting the shortcut's *Icon* property to the icon you want to associate with your application. The icon is automatically added as the shortcut.

2. You can throw an *InstallException* exception. Custom actions that encounter unrecoverable errors should throw an *InstallException* exception to roll back the installation and prevent harm to the system.

PRACTICE **Create a Setup Project**

In this practice, you create a setup project for the same application that you installed in Lesson 1, "Creating a Windows Setup Project." You use the File System editor to install files to different directories and create a custom action that displays a message box at installation time.

EXERCISE Use the File System Editor and Create a Custom Action

1. From the samples installed from the companion CD, open the partial solution for this exercise.

2. From the File menu, choose Add and then choose New Project. The Add New Project dialog box opens.

3. Expand Other Project Types, select Setup And Deployment, and then expand Visual Studio Installer. Select the Setup Project template and click OK. The Setup Project opens to the File System editor.

4. In the File System editor, right-click Application Folder, choose Add, and then choose Project Output.

5. In the Add Project Output Group dialog box, select your project in the Project drop-down list and select Primary Output in the list of output categories. Click OK.

6. In the File System editor, right-click the left pane, choose Add Special Folder, and then choose Custom Folder to add a custom folder.

7. In the File System editor, select Custom Folder #1. In the Properties window, set the *DefaultLocation* property to **C:**.

8. In the File System editor, right-click Custom Folder #1, choose Add, and then choose File. Browse to the Lesson 1 subfolder in the folder that contains your partial solution and select myFile.txt. Click Open.

9. In Solution Explorer, select your application project (the Lesson 1 project).

10. From the Project menu, choose Add New Item. In the Add New Item dialog box, select General from the Installed Templates pane and then choose Installer Class. Click Add.

11. In Solution Explorer, right-click the Installer1 file and select View Code to open the code editor.

12. In the code editor, add the following code to override the *Install* method of the *Installer* class:

Sample of Visual Basic Code
```
Public Overrides Sub Install(ByVal stateSaver As System.Collections.IDictionary)
    MyBase.Install(stateSaver)
    MsgBox("Install custom action executed")
End Sub
```

Sample of C# Code
```
public override void Install(System.Collections.IDictionary stateSaver)
{
    base.Install(stateSaver);
    System.Windows.Forms.MessageBox.Show("Install custom action executed");
}
```

13. In Solution Explorer, right-click the Setup1 project, choose View, and then choose Custom Actions.

14. In the Custom Actions editor, right-click Install and choose Add Custom Action to open the Select Item In Project dialog box.

15. In the Select Item In Project dialog box, double-click Application Folder and select Primary Output From [*application*], where [*application*] is the project that contains your *Installer* class. Click OK.

16. From the Build menu, choose Configuration Manager. Make certain that check boxes for both projects are selected in the Build column, and click Close.

17. From the Build menu, choose Build Solution to build your solution.

18. Close Visual Studio. In Windows Explorer, navigate to your solution folder.

19. Open the Setup1\Debug folder and double-click Setup1.msi to install your application. Follow the instructions in the wizard and respond to any security prompts. Note that a message box appears when the custom action is executed. You might have to move the Setup1 progress dialog box to see the message box.

20. Navigate to the folder in which you installed your application and double-click your application. It opens and runs.

Lesson Summary

- Setup projects enable you to create Windows Installer applications you can use to install your solutions. Windows Installer projects are highly configurable and provide a great deal of control over the configuration of the installation process.

- Setup projects provide several editors by which you can edit aspects of the installation process. They are the File System editor, the Registry editor, the File Types editor, the User Interface editor, the Custom Actions editor, and the Launch Conditions editor.

- Use the File System editor to add output from your projects and other files to your setup project. The File System editor can create directories on the target system and install files to those directories. You can also use the File System editor to install shortcuts and associate icons with your application and install files conditionally, based on the operating system.

- The setup project has several properties that expose descriptive information about the application and affect the behavior of the setup project at installation time. You can change these properties by selecting the setup project and changing them in the Properties window.

- Custom actions are code executed at installation time or uninstallation time. You can create a custom action by writing custom code in an *Installer* class, adding the *Installer* class to the project for which you want to create a setup application, and, finally, designating the project that exposes the custom action in the Custom Actions editor.

- When errors that are unrecoverable occur in a custom action, you should throw an *InstallException* exception to roll back installation without damaging the target system.

Lesson Review

The following questions are intended to reinforce key information presented in Lesson 1, "Creating a Windows Setup Project." The questions are also available on the companion CD if you prefer to review them in electronic form.

> **NOTE ANSWERS**
>
> Answers to these questions and explanations of why each answer choice is correct or incorrect are located in the "Answers" section at the end of the book.

1. Which setup project editor is used to add project outputs to a setup project?

   A. File System editor

   B. File Types editor

   C. Custom Actions editor

   D. User Interface editor

2. Which of the following is an appropriate installation condition if you want to restrict installation to Windows 2000 or later?

   A. VersionNT=500

   B. VersionNT>=500

   C. VersionNT<=500

   D. VersionNT<>500

3. Which of the following are required to execute a custom action upon installation of your setup project? (Choose all that apply.)

   A. You must add an *Installer* class to your setup project.

   B. You must add an *Installer* class to the project you want to deploy as a custom action.

   C. You must write your custom action in the *Install* method of an *Installer* class.

   D. You must specify the project that contains the custom action in the Custom Actions editor.

Lesson 2: Deploying Applications with ClickOnce

Although not as complex as Windows Installer, ClickOnce provides you with a wide range of control over the installation of your application. You can configure applications for stand-alone deployment or require the user to run the application from a server. This lesson describes the various options presented by ClickOnce deployment.

After this lesson, you will be able to:

- Deploy a WPF application with ClickOnce for stand-alone access.
- Deploy an XBAP with ClickOnce.
- Configure a deployed application for a partial-trust environment.

Estimated lesson time: 30 minutes

Deploying with ClickOnce

ClickOnce is a deployment technology by which you can create self-updating applications that can be installed from a variety of media and that require minimal user interaction. Any WPF application can be published as a ClickOnce application, including Windows applications, Navigation applications, and XAML browser applications (XBAPs). You can use ClickOnce to create applications that are deployed from a Web site, a file share, or a CD-ROM. You can configure ClickOnce applications to be run only while the user is online or while the user is offline as well.

ClickOnce applications are isolated from the rest of the system. Because they are completely self-contained, they share no components with any other applications installed on the computer and run no risk of breaking other applications' installations. Windows and Navigation applications require full trust to be installed on a local computer via ClickOnce, but XBAPs and applications that run online execute in the Internet security zone by default (or in the local intranet security zone if they are run from a file share on the local intranet).

 EXAM TIP

Although WPF applications can be deployed with either Setup projects or ClickOnce, ClickOnce is usually considered the preferred technology for WPF deployment. Have a good general knowledge of Setup projects for the exam, but focus on learning the intricacies of ClickOnce.

Deploying an Application by Using ClickOnce

You can deploy an application directly in Visual Studio from the Publish tab of the project properties dialog box. To open the Publish tab, right-click the project in Solution Explorer, choose Properties, and then select the Publish tab. This displays the Publish properties page, as shown in Figure 12-4.

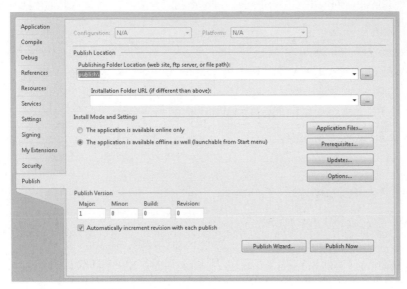

FIGURE 12-4 The Publish properties page.

You can publish your application, using ClickOnce, by setting the Publish properties in this page and then clicking Publish Now. The process of configuring Publish properties is described in the following sections. The information contained in these sections applies to both stand-alone applications and XBAPs, unless noted.

Selecting the Publishing Location

You can specify the publishing location in the Publishing Folder Location combo box in the Publish properties page. The publishing folder location can be a file path, a network share, a local Microsoft Internet Information Services (IIS) folder, a Hypertext Transfer Protocol (HTTP) address, or a File Transfer Protocol (FTP) address. This is generally the address to which users go to install the application.

Clicking the button to the right of the Publishing Folder Location combo box opens the Open Web Site dialog box, shown in Figure 12-5. The Open Web Site dialog box enables you to select the type of site to which to deploy your application (file address, HTTP address, FTP address, or local IIS installation) and to browse to and configure each location option.

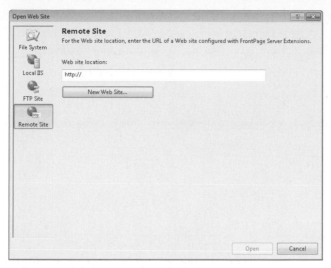

FIGURE 12-5 The Open Web Site dialog box.

Publishing to a Temporary Location

You can specify a separate location for publishing your application and the installation Uniform Resource Locator (URL). You might want to do this if you want to deploy your application to a staging server first and then have an administrator copy the files from the staging server to the final location from which users download the application. You can specify an installation URL that represents a temporary location or staging server in the Installation Folder URL combo box immediately beneath the Publishing Folder Location combo box. You can also click the button to the right of the Installation URL combo box to open the Open Web Site dialog box, which enables you to browse to and configure the final location. Note that if you designate an installation URL, you have to copy the files manually from the staging server to the final installation server to complete the deployment.

Online and Offline Deployment

You can configure a ClickOnce application to be available only when the user is online or when the user is online or offline. By selecting The Application Is Available Online Only in the Install Mode And Settings group of the Publish properties page, you require the application to be run directly from the location specified in the Publishing Folder Location combo box. This ensures that the user always runs the most recent available version of the application.

> **NOTE ONLINE ONLY MODE**
>
> When an application is available in Online Only mode, the application still runs on the client machine as opposed to the server. However, it is not installed to the client machine and must be retrieved from the server each time it is run.

You can select The Application Is Available Offline As Well to make the application available both online and offline. In this case, the application is copied to the local computer and added to the Start menu and the Add/Remove Programs box in Control Panel in Windows.

Specifying Application Information

You can specify information about the application by clicking the Options button in the Publish properties page. This opens the Publish Options dialog box, shown in Figure 12-6.

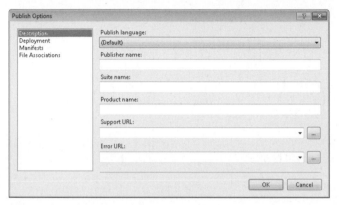

FIGURE 12-6 The Publish Options dialog box.

In the Publish Options dialog box, you can set Publisher Name, Product Name, Support URL, and the name for Deployment Web Page, which is generated when the application is published.

Of particular interest for stand-alone applications are the Publisher Name and the Product Name settings. When an application is installed for offline use, an entry is made in the All Programs folder in the Start menu. The entry appears under Product Name, which in turn appears under Publisher Name, so these values must be set in the Publish Options dialog box.

Configuring ClickOnce Update Options

ClickOnce enables you to configure applications to check for updates automatically. By clicking Updates in the Publish properties dialog box, you can open the Application Updates dialog box, shown in Figure 12-7.

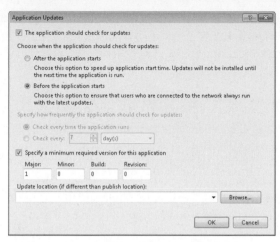

FIGURE 12-7 The Application Updates dialog box.

Configuring Update Settings with Visual Studio

To enable the application to check for updates, select the check box labeled The Application Should Check For Updates. Doing so enables the other options in the dialog box.

You can specify when the application checks for updates by selecting either After The Application Starts or Before The Application Starts. If you select Before The Application Starts, the application checks for new updates every time the application starts. This ensures that the user always runs the most recent version of the application, but it also slows the application's performance at startup.

If you select After The Application Starts, you can specify that the application should check for updates every time it is run, or at a designated time interval, by choosing the appropriate option under Specify How Frequently The Application Should Check For Updates. You also can specify a minimum required version for the application, and you can specify a different location for updates if your updates are hosted in a location other than the install location.

Loading Updates Programmatically

Rather than scheduling updates, you might want to give the user the option to check for updates. Although there is not a way to do this built into the Properties page, you can add functionality to your application to check for and install updates manually. For example, you might provide a menu option entitled Check For Updates.

You can check for updates in code by using the *ApplicationDeployment* class. This class represents a ClickOnce deployment. To use this class in code, you first must add a reference to *System.Deployment*. After this reference has been added, you can retrieve an instance that represents the current deployment from the static *CurrentDeployment* property, as shown here:

Sample of Visual Basic Code

```
Dim aDep As System.Deployment.Application.ApplicationDeployment
aDep = _
    System.Deployment.Application.ApplicationDeployment.CurrentDeployment
```

Sample of C# Code

```
System.Deployment.Application.ApplicationDeployment aDep;
aDep =
    System.Deployment.Application.ApplicationDeployment.CurrentDeployment;
```

After you have obtained a reference to the current deployment, you can check for updates by using the *CheckForUpdate* method, and, if updates are available, you can update the application by using the *Update* method, as seen here:

Sample of Visual Basic Code

```
If aDep.CheckForUpdate Then
    aDep.Update()
End If
```

Sample of C# Code

```
if (aDep.CheckForUpdate())
{
    aDep.Update();
}
```

The *CheckForUpdate* and *Update* methods also have asynchronous counterparts, called *CheckForUpdateAsync* and *UpdateAsync*, respectively, which can perform updates asynchronously. When *CheckForUpdateAsync* returns, it raises the *CheckForUpdateCompleted* event. By handling this event, you can query the *CheckForUpdateCompletedEventArgs* argument in the event handler to determine whether an update is available. If an update is available, you can call *UpdateAsync* to download and install the update asynchronously. If the application is running, updates are applied after the application ends, so the updates are not seen until the application is restarted.

These techniques are demonstrated in the following example:

Sample of Visual Basic Code

```
Dim aDep As System.Deployment.Application.ApplicationDeployment
Public Sub New()
    ' This call is required by the Windows Form Designer.
    InitializeComponent()
    ' Add any initialization after the InitializeComponent() call.
    aDep = _
        System.Deployment.Application.ApplicationDeployment.CurrentDeployment
    AddHandler aDep.CheckForUpdateCompleted, AddressOf UpdateCheckCompleted
End Sub
Public Sub UpdateApp()
    aDep.CheckForUpdateAsync()
End Sub
```

```
Private Sub UpdateCheckCompleted(ByVal sender As Object, ByVal e As _
    System.Deployment.Application.CheckForUpdateCompletedEventArgs)
    If e.UpdateAvailable Then
        aDep.UpdateAsync()
    End If
End Sub
```

Sample of C# Code

```
System.Deployment.Application.ApplicationDeployment aDep;
public myApplication
{
    InitializeComponent();
    aDep =
        System.Deployment.Application.ApplicationDeployment.CurrentDeployment;
    aDep.CheckForUpdateCompleted += UpdateCheckCompleted;
}
public void UpdateApp()
{
    aDep.CheckForUpdateAsync();
}
private void UpdateCheckCompleted(object sender, System.Deployment.Application.
CheckForUpdateCompletedEventArgs e)
{
    if (e.UpdateAvailable)
    {
        aDep.UpdateAsync();
    }
}
```

Migrating Settings and User Data

Application settings and default user settings are stored in the application's .config file. These are typically updated with each new application update. However, user settings that have been modified by the user are stored in a local file that is separate from the .config file. Thus, no additional effort is required to migrate user settings when an application is updated. Similarly, you should take steps to avoid overwriting any custom files that store user data.

Deploying an XBAP with ClickOnce

With ClickOnce, XBAPs can be deployed in much the same way as a Windows or Navigation application. All the ClickOnce publishing properties also apply to XBAPs, but there are a few XBAP-specific concerns as well.

XBAPs run in the browser and are typically run from a Web site. Thus, they are almost always run under partial trust. You must design your XBAP applications for execution in a partial-trust environment and test them in the same trust environment in which you plan for users to execute them.

Considerations for Deploying in Partial-Trust Environments

When designing an application for execution in a partial-trust environment, you should avoid coding features that require access to protected system resources. For example, you should not attempt to access the file system or registry in an XBAP.

Choosing a Local Persistence Mechanism

Because XBAPs generally do not have access to the local file system, you must use a different mechanism to save user information. User-specific data can be written to the isolated storage file store, a specialized technology that allows isolated access to the file system under partial-trust conditions.

Configuring the Application Manifest

Application Manifest is a file created by Visual Studio during ClickOnce deployment that describes the files and dependencies required by an application, the identity and trust information of an assembly, the entry point for the application, and any associations between file types and the application. All these aspects, except for file associations, are configurable through the Visual Studio user interface, as has been described earlier in this chapter. To create a file association, you must edit the Application Manifest file manually.

Adding a File Association

A file association is described in the Application Manifest by the *<fileAssociation>* element. The attributes of this element are listed in Table 12-2. All four attributes are required.

TABLE 12-2 Attributes of the *<fileAssociation>* Element

ATTRIBUTE	DESCRIPTION
extension	The file extension to be associated with the application.
description	A description of the file type for use by the shell.
progid	A name uniquely identifying the file type.
defaultIcon	Specifies the icon to use for files with this extension. The .icon file must be described in the application manifest and, thus, must have been added to the application with the Build Action property set to Content.

You can add a *<fileAssociation>* element to your application manifest by adding it to the App.Manifest file in Visual Studio. This file is added to your project when you select Enable ClickOnce Security Settings on the Security tab of your project's property pages. The content in the App.Manifest file is folded into the application manifest at publish time. The following procedure describes how to create a file association for an application.

To create a file association:

1. Select or create an icon for your file type.

2. From the Project menu, choose Add Existing Item. The Add Existing Item dialog box opens. Set the filter to All Files and navigate to your icon, select it, and click Add.

3. With the icon selected in Solution Explorer, in the Properties window, set the Build Action property to Content and the Copy To Output Directory property to Copy Always.

4. In Solution Explorer, right-click your project and select Properties. Select the Security tab.

5. In the Security properties window, select the Enable ClickOnce Security Settings check box. The App.manifest file is added to your solution.

6. In Visual Basic only, in Solution Explorer, select View All Files and expand My Project.

7. Double-click App.manifest to open the App.manifest file.

8. Just before the final closing tag, add a *<fileAssociation>* element that includes values for all four required attributes. An example is shown here:

```
<fileAssociation xmlns="urn:schemas-microsoft-com:clickonce.v1"
    extension=".fnord"
    description="Fnord file"
    progid="SecretsMWNMTK.fnord"
    defaultIcon="fnord.ico"
/>
```

Note that you can only create file associations for applications that are installed as stand-alone applications, and you can create no more than eight file associations per application.

Associating a Certificate with the Application

Certificates are digital signatures issued by certificate authorities (CAs) that guarantee the identity of the application's publisher. You can use Visual Studio to associate a certificate with your application.

To associate a certificate with your application, right-click your project in Solution Explorer, choose Properties, and then choose the Signing tab to open the Signing properties page, as shown in Figure 12-8.

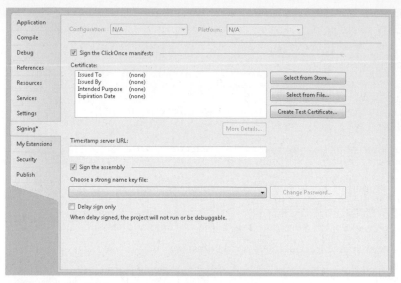

FIGURE 12-8 The Signing properties page.

To enable certificate signing for your application, select the Sign The ClickOnce Manifests check box. You can then choose a certificate, either from your local certificate store or from a particular file, by clicking the appropriate button and browsing to the correct store or file. You can also create a test certificate by clicking Create Test Certificate and providing a password for certificate creation. You can view the details of the certificate by clicking More Details.

PRACTICE **Publishing Your Application with ClickOnce**

In this practice, you publish your application by using ClickOnce.

EXERCISE Publishing Your Application

1. Open the partial solution for this exercise from the companion media.

2. In Solution Explorer, right-click your project and choose Properties.

3. On the Properties page, click the More Settings icon and then select the Publish tab.

4. In the Publishing Folder Location drop-down box, select a folder in which to publish your application. The completed solution on the CD-ROM that comes with this book uses the default entry (publish\), which is a subfolder in the project folder. If you have access to a Web or FTP server, you might want to try publishing to a server location instead.

5. Click Options to open the Publish Options dialog box. Add a suitable Publisher Name and Product Name and click OK.

6. Click Publish Now to publish the application to the selected location. If you are publishing to a file, Visual Studio opens the publish folder in Windows Explorer for you when the process is complete.

7. In Windows Explorer (for the file system) or Windows Internet Explorer (for HTTP or FTP sites), browse to the publish location for your application if the publish location is not already open. Double-click Lesson 2.application to launch the application installation. The Application Install dialog box opens.

8. In the Application Install dialog box, click Install. The installation process installs and starts the application. Close the application.

9. In Windows, click Start, select All Programs, and look for the Publisher Name you added. Then confirm that the Product Name is present in the Start menu hierarchy.

10. Open Control Panel and then click Uninstall A Program. If you are using Classic View, open Programs And Features instead. Right-click the name you designated for your product (Lesson 2 in the partial solution) and choose Uninstall/Change to open the Maintenance dialog box. Alternatively, you can select Lesson 2 and then click Uninstall/Change.

11. Select Remove The Application From This Computer and click OK to uninstall the application.

Lesson Summary

- ClickOnce is a versatile and flexible deployment technology. It enables you to publish an application to a disk location, a file share, an FTP site, or an HTTP address. ClickOnce application installations are segregated from the rest of the system and do not use shared components. Thus, installing a ClickOnce application runs no risk of breaking other application installations.

- You can install a ClickOnce application so that it is available online or offline. If an application is available online only, it runs from its server rather than from a location on the local machine. If an application is available online only, a shortcut to it is not added to the Start menu.

- ClickOnce applications can be configured to be self-updating. You can designate an application to check for updates every time it starts or on a set schedule, such as every week. You can also implement code to check for updates manually.

- Stand-alone ClickOnce applications must be installed to a local computer under full-trust conditions. Applications that are run online are executed in the Internet security zone (if run from a Web site) or the local intranet security zone (if run from a file server on the local intranet).

- XBAPs are designed to run in partial-trust conditions, and, as such, they should not attempt to access system resources that are not allowed by the default Internet security zone settings. Because they cannot use the file system, XBAPs should persist user data through isolated storage or user settings.

- You can create file associations for ClickOnce applications by editing the App.manifest file. Visual Studio also provides tools for adding certificates to your application.

Lesson Review

You can use the following questions to test your knowledge of the information in Lesson 2, "Deploying Applications with ClickOnce." The questions are also available on the companion CD if you prefer to review them in electronic form.

> **NOTE ANSWERS**
>
> Answers to these questions and explanations of why each answer choice is correct or incorrect are located in the "Answers" section at the end of the book.

1. For an XBAP that is installed with ClickOnce to run from an Internet Web page, what is the default security mode under which the XBAP executes?

   A. Full trust

   B. Intranet zone

   C. Internet zone

   D. Custom zone

2. You are converting a WPF application that formerly executed under full trust to execute under partial trust. This application previously stored user data in a small local file, but now it cannot because it lacks FileIO permissions. What is the appropriate way to store user data in a partial-trust environment? (Choose all that apply.)

   A. Use isolated storage to store user data.

   B. Create a Web service that saves data back to the deployment server.

   C. Save user data as user settings.

   D. Call *FileIOPermission*.Demand to gain temporary access to the file system.

3. Which of the following code samples manually checks for updates and installs updates if any are available? For examples C and D, assume that the *UpdateApp* method has been called after execution of the constructor. (Choose all that apply.)

   A.

   Sample of Visual Basic Code
   ```
   Dim aDep As System.Deployment.Application.ApplicationDeployment
   aDep = _
       System.Deployment.Application.ApplicationDeployment.CurrentDeployment
   If aDep.CheckForUpdate Then
       aDep.Update()
   End If
   ```

   Sample of C# Code
   ```
   System.Deployment.Application.ApplicationDeployment aDep;
   aDep =
       System.Deployment.Application.ApplicationDeployment.CurrentDeployment;
   if (aDep.CheckForUpdate())
   {
   ```

```
    aDep.Update();
}
```

B.

Sample of Visual Basic Code

```
Dim aDep As System.Deployment.Application.ApplicationDeployment
aDep = _
    System.Deployment.Application.ApplicationDeployment.CurrentDeployment
If aDep.CheckForUpdateAsync Then
    aDep.Update()
End If
```

Sample of C# Code

```
System.Deployment.Application.ApplicationDeployment aDep;
aDep =
    System.Deployment.Application.ApplicationDeployment.CurrentDeployment;
if (aDep.CheckForUpdateAsync())
{
    aDep.Update();
}
```

C.

Sample of Visual Basic Code

```
Dim aDep As System.Deployment.Application.ApplicationDeployment
Public Sub New()
    ' This call is required by the Windows Form Designer.
    InitializeComponent()
    ' Add any initialization after the InitializeComponent() call.
    aDep = _
        System.Deployment.Application.ApplicationDeployment.CurrentDeployment
    AddHandler aDep.CheckForUpdateCompleted, AddressOf UpdateCheckCompleted
End Sub
Public Sub UpdateApp()
    aDep.CheckForUpdate()
End Sub
Private Sub UpdateCheckCompleted(ByVal sender As Object, ByVal e As _
    System.Deployment.Application.CheckForUpdateCompletedEventArgs)
    If e.UpdateAvailable Then
        aDep.UpdateAsync()
    End If
End Sub
```

Sample of C# Code

```
System.Deployment.Application.ApplicationDeployment aDep;
public myApplication
{
    InitializeComponent();
    aDep =
        System.Deployment.Application.ApplicationDeployment.CurrentDeployment;
    aDep.CheckForUpdateCompleted += UpdateCheckCompleted;
}
public void UpdateApp()
{
```

```
        aDep.CheckForUpdate();
    }
    private void UpdateCheckCompleted(object sender,
        System.Deployment.Application.CheckForUpdateCompletedEventArgs e)
    {
        if (e.UpdateAvailable)
        {
            aDep.UpdateAsync();
        }
    }
}
```

D.

Sample of Visual Basic Code

```
Dim aDep As System.Deployment.Application.ApplicationDeployment
Public Sub New()
    ' This call is required by the Windows Form Designer.
    InitializeComponent()
    ' Add any initialization after the InitializeComponent() call.
    aDep = _
        System.Deployment.Application.ApplicationDeployment.CurrentDeployment
    AddHandler aDep.CheckForUpdateCompleted, AddressOf UpdateCheckCompleted
End Sub
Public Sub UpdateApp()
    aDep.CheckForUpdateAsync()
End Sub
Private Sub UpdateCheckCompleted(ByVal sender As Object, ByVal e As _
    System.Deployment.Application.CheckForUpdateCompletedEventArgs)
    If e.UpdateAvailable Then
        aDep.UpdateAsync()
    End If
End Sub
```

Sample of C# Code

```
System.Deployment.Application.ApplicationDeployment aDep;
public myApplication
{
    InitializeComponent();
    aDep =
        System.Deployment.Application.ApplicationDeployment.CurrentDeployment;
    aDep.CheckForUpdateCompleted += UpdateCheckCompleted;
}
public void UpdateApp()
{
    aDep.CheckForUpdateAsync();
}
private void UpdateCheckCompleted(object sender,
    System.Deployment.Application.CheckForUpdateCompletedEventArgs e)
{
    if (e.UpdateAvailable)
    {
        aDep.UpdateAsync();
    }
}
```

Case Scenarios

In the following case scenarios, you apply what you've learned about deployment. You can find answers to these questions in the "Answers" section at the end of this book.

Case Scenario 1: Distributing the Application a Little Early

Well, here it is! All your work for Fabrikam, Inc. on its big widget has come to fruition, and the application is ready to distribute to clients! The clients are very excited because this application is just what they've been waiting for. Unfortunately, the picture is not so rosy. The application is full of bugs, and Fabrikam's clients cannot wait any longer. You have to release the buggy version, even though you have a team working around the clock to fix these bugs. Your requirements are that:

- You must release the buggy version now.
- You must provide updates that incorporate bug fixes as quickly as possible.
- This application must be installable by the end user, who does not have administrative privileges.

What is a deployment strategy that will accomplish all the key requirements?

Case Scenario 2: Installing the Server Core

Fabrikam has decided to make its server application and core database available for sale to some of its high-end clients. You have been directed to determine a distribution strategy. You will need to install the server application, create a new directory structure and registry keys, and check for prerequisite files in the installation phase.

Which deployment strategy can accomplish all these goals?

Suggested Practices

To help you successfully master the exam objectives presented in this chapter, complete the following tasks.

- **Practice 1** Publish your favorite application to a Web site and a file share using ClickOnce. Experiment with expanded permission requirements and update schedules.
- **Practice 2** Expand on the practice in Lesson 1, "Creating a Windows Setup Project," to include an icon for your application and a custom action that tests for a condition and aborts if the condition is not found.

Take a Practice Test

The practice tests on this book's companion CD offer many options. For example, you can test yourself on just the content covered in this chapter, or you can test yourself on all the 70-511 certification exam content. You can set up the test so that it closely simulates the experience of taking a certification exam, or you can set it up in study mode so that you can look at the correct answers and explanations after you answer each question.

> **MORE INFO** **PRACTICE TESTS**
>
> For details about all the practice test options available, see the "How to Use the Practice Tests" section in this book's Introduction.

Answers

Chapter 1: Lesson Review Answers

Lesson 1

1. **Correct Answer: B**

    A. **Incorrect:** A content control can host a single nested control.

    B. **Correct:** A content control can host a single nested control.

    C. **Incorrect:** Although a content control can host a list control, which can host an unlimited number of nested members, the content control itself can host only a single control.

    D. **Incorrect:** All content controls can host only a single nested control.

2. **Correct Answer: B**

    A. **Incorrect:** You must use the *Grid.Column* and *Grid.Row* attached properties to designate the cell for controls.

    B. **Correct:** This example shows the correct use of the attached *Grid.Column* and *Grid.Row* properties.

    C. **Incorrect:** No *Grid.Column* or *Grid.Row* values are set for this button.

    D. **Incorrect:** You must use the *Grid.Column* and *Grid.Row* attached properties to designate the cell for controls.

3. **Correct Answer: D**

    A. **Incorrect:** Context menus cannot be part of a visual tree.

    B. **Incorrect:** This structure would require the context menu to be a visual child of a higher-level element, and context menus cannot be part of a visual tree.

    C. **Incorrect:** Context menus must be an instance of the *ContextMenu* class, not the *Menu* class.

    D. **Correct:** The context menu must be defined as a property of the control it is associated with.

4. **Correct Answer: C**

    A. **Incorrect:** Item controls can contain a list of items, the number of which has no defined limit.

    B. **Incorrect:** Item controls can contain a list of items, the number of which has no defined limit.

C. Correct: Item controls can contain a list of items, the number of which has no defined limit.

D. Incorrect: All item controls can contain a list of items, the number of which has no defined limit.

5. **Correct Answer: C**

   A. Incorrect: Although you can use a *Grid* control to create an evenly spaced control layout, *UniformGrid* requires much less work to implement this kind of layout.

   B. Incorrect: Although you can use a *Canvas* control to create an evenly spaced control layout, *UniformGrid* requires much less work to implement this kind of layout.

   C. Correct: The *UniformGrid* control automatically lays out controls in an equidistant manner irrespective of control *Margin* properties.

   D. Incorrect: *WrapPanel* lays out controls in a horizontal wrapping layout and does not guarantee equidistance.

6. **Correct Answer: A, C**

   A. Correct: With the *Canvas.Right* and *Canvas.Bottom* properties set to 0 and the *Margin* property set to 20, the *Button* control maintains 20 units between the button edges and the right and bottom canvas edges.

   B. Incorrect: Because the *Canvas.Right* and *Canvas.Bottom* properties are not set, the button location will default to the upper left corner.

   C. Correct: Using absolute positioning with the *Canvas.Top*, *Canvas.Left*, *Canvas.Right*, and *Canvas.Bottom* attached properties is the preferred way to handle control position when using the *Canvas* control.

   D. Incorrect: Because the margin is set to 20 and the *Canvas.Right* and *Canvas.Bottom* properties are also set to 20, the control edges actually are 40 units from the edges of the canvas.

Lesson 2

1. **Correct Answer: A**

   A. Correct: This is a correctly formatted pack URI.

   B. Incorrect: In this URI, component and MyFolder are transposed from their correct locations.

   C. Incorrect: The assembly name must come before the semicolon.

   D. Incorrect: In this URI, the folder name is not specified.

2. **Correct Answer: B**

   A. Incorrect: The *Embedded Resource* setting embeds the image by using a different resource-handling technology, making it more difficult to access.

   B. Correct: The *Resource* setting makes this image accessible to the *Image* control through pack URI syntax.

C. **Incorrect:** With the *None* setting, the file is neither embedded nor copied into the output directory.

D. **Incorrect:** The *Content* setting does not embed the file; rather, it copies it as a loose file.

3. **Correct Answer: D**

A. **Incorrect:** *MediaElement* cannot access resources of any kind.

B. **Incorrect:** *MediaElement* cannot access resources of any kind.

C. **Incorrect:** With the *None* setting, the file is neither embedded nor copied into the output directory.

D. **Correct:** The *Content* setting allows *MediaElement* to access the files. You also should set the *Copy To Output Directory* property to *Copy Always*.

4. **Correct Answer: D**

A. **Incorrect:** Because these *Brush* objects need to be used in many elements, defining them at the individual element level would require a great deal of redundancy.

B. **Incorrect:** Because these *Brush* objects need to be used in each window, defining them at the window level would be redundant.

C. **Incorrect:** Although defining these resources at the application level would enable use across the entire application, it would not facilitate reuse across multiple applications.

D. **Correct:** By defining your resources in a resource dictionary, you can share the file between applications as well as import the resources contained therein at the window or application level as needed.

5. **Correct Answer: D**

A. **Incorrect:** Because the foreground is bound to the resource as a dynamic resource, it detects when the resource changes and turns green. Also, because the background is bound as a static resource, and a property on the brush that paints the background is changed, the resource detects that change through change notification, and the background turns black.

B. **Incorrect:** Because the foreground is bound to the resource as a dynamic resource, it detects when the resource changes, and the foreground turns green in addition to the background turning black.

C. **Incorrect:** Because the background is bound as a static resource and a property on the brush that paints the background is changed, the resource detects that change through change notification, and the background turns black in addition to the foreground turning green.

D. **Correct:** Because the foreground is bound to the resource as a dynamic resource, it detects when the resource changes, and the foreground turns green. Also, because the background is bound as a static resource and a property on the brush that paints the background is changed, the resource detects that change through change notification, and the background turns black.

Lesson 3

1. **Correct Answer: D**

   A. **Incorrect:** *Button1* does not reference or explicitly set a style; thus, the background is not affected by the style defined in *Window.Resources*.

   B. **Incorrect:** *Button1* does not reference or explicitly set a style; thus, the background is not affected by the style defined in *Window.Resources*.

   C. **Incorrect:** *Button1* does not reference or explicitly set a style; thus, the background is not affected by the style defined in *Window.Resources*.

   D. **Correct:** *Button1* does not reference or explicitly set a style; thus, the background is not affected by the style defined in *Window.Resources*. Therefore, the background remains the default.

2. **Correct Answer: C**

   A. **Incorrect:** A multi-trigger requires all conditions to be met before activating its setters.

   B. **Incorrect:** A multi-trigger requires all conditions to be met before activating its setters.

   C. **Correct:** A multi-trigger is active when all conditions defined in it are met.

   D. **Incorrect:** A multi-trigger requires all conditions to be met before activating its setters.

   E. **Incorrect:** A multi-trigger is active only when all conditions are met.

3. **Correct Answer: C**

   A. **Incorrect:** An explicitly set property always takes precedence over a property set by setters or triggers. Because the *Content* property is set explicitly, it displays *Button*.

   B. **Incorrect:** An explicitly set property always takes precedence over a property set by setters or triggers. Because the *Content* property is set explicitly, it displays *Button*.

   C. **Correct:** An explicitly set property always takes precedence over a property set by setters or triggers. Because the *Content* property is set explicitly, it displays *Button*.

   D. **Incorrect:** An explicitly set property always takes precedence over a property set by setters or triggers. Because the *Content* property is set explicitly, it displays *Button*.

Chapter 1 Case Scenario Answers

Case Scenario 1: Streaming Stock Quotes

1. Because the *Stock Quote* control needs linear space but not two-dimensional space, a *StatusBar* control is a natural choice to display this information. Controls used to configure the application could be hosted in a *ToolBar* control.

2. A couple of layout controls could be used to create the layout. A grid is an obvious choice; by creating multiple grid rows, you can control where and how each control is positioned. A possibly better choice would be *DockPanel*. By setting *DockPanel.LastChildFill* to *True* and adding

the chart control last, you can dock the *ToolBar* and *StatusBar* controls to the edges, fill the remaining space with the chart, and even allow the application layout to be reconfigured to dock *ToolBar* to different edges at run time.

Case Scenario 2: Cup Fever

There are several possible approaches to this problem, but the one that seems to make the most sense is to create a style for the elements in your user interface that defines the appropriate color scheme. The style should incorporate setters to set the color scheme of the object, and the value of the *Setter* objects should be bound to the value of the drop-down list. Using a custom converter, you can return the appropriate *Brush* objects for the style based on the content in the drop-down list.

Chapter 2: Lesson Review Answers

Lesson 1

1. **Correct Answer: B**

   A. **Incorrect:** No *Button1_Click* method is defined as a handler for the *button1* click event in this example.

   B. **Correct:** *Click* is a bubbling event, so *stackPanel1_Click* will execute first.

   C. **Incorrect:** *Click* is a bubbling event, so *stackPanel1_Click* will execute first.

   D. **Incorrect:** *Click* is a bubbling event, so *stackPanel1_Click* will execute first.

2. **Correct Answer: B**

   A. **Incorrect:** *MouseDown* is a bubbling event and thus is raised after corresponding tunneling events, which are prepended with "Preview," are raised.

   B. **Correct:** *PreviewMouseDown* is a tunneling event and thus is raised by controls from the top down in the visual tree.

   C. **Incorrect:** Because the *StackPanel* is contained in *Grid, PreviewMouseDown* will be raised by the grid first.

   D. **Incorrect:** *Click* is a bubbling event and thus occurs after all preview events are raised.

3. **Correct Answer: A**

   A. **Correct:** Because the *Activated* event is raised the first time the window is shown and every other time it is activated, this is the correct event to handle.

   B. **Incorrect:** This event will execute code only when the application begins.

   C. **Incorrect:** Because the *Activated* event is raised the first time the window is shown and every other time it is activated, you do not need to handle the *Startup* event as well.

   D. **Incorrect:** This event would execute code when the application is started and every time the window loses focus.

Lesson 2

1. **Correct Answers: A, B, D, and F**

    A. **Correct:** You must create a new instance of *CommandBinding* for each command you register.

    B. **Correct:** The *CommandBinding.Command* property specifies which command is to be bound.

    C. **Incorrect:** A command does not required any input gestures to be registered.

    D. **Correct:** If the *CommandBinding.Executed* event is not handled, no code will be executed when the command is invoked.

    E. **Incorrect:** Although handling the *CanExecute* event enables you to determine when the command is unavailable, it is not required to register a command.

    F. **Correct:** You must add *CommandBinding* to one of the *CommandBindings* collections for it to be registered.

2. **Correct Answer: C**

    A. **Incorrect:** *CanExecute* is a method, not a property, and cannot be set to a value.

    B. **Incorrect:** The *Execute* method requires a target element where the run time begins looking for *CommandBinding*.

    C. **Correct:** You call the command's *Execute* method to execute the command, specifying the parameter and the owning control.

    D. **Incorrect:** There is no *CanExecute* method on the *Window* class.

Lesson 3

1. **Correct Answer: D**

    A. **Incorrect:** Because the *RepeatBehavior* property is set to a time span, it repeats for the duration of that time span. Because the span is 1 minute and the duration of the animation is 15 seconds, it repeats three additional times after the first iteration.

    B. **Incorrect:** Because the *RepeatBehavior* property is set to a time span, it repeats for the duration of that time span. Because the span is 1 minute and the duration of the animation is 15 seconds, it repeats three additional times after the first iteration.

    C. **Incorrect:** Because the *RepeatBehavior* property is set to a time span, it repeats for the duration of that time span. Because the span is 1 minute and the duration of the animation is 15 seconds, it repeats three additional times after the first iteration.

    D. **Correct:** Because the *RepeatBehavior* property is set to a time span, it repeats for the duration of that time span. Because the span is 1 minute and the duration of the animation is 15 seconds, it repeats three additional times after the first iteration.

2. **Correct Answer: D**

   A. **Incorrect:** Because the default value for *FillBehavior* is *HoldEnd,* the final value of the animation holds after this animation has completed. Because both the *To* property and the *By* property are set, the value of the *By* property is ignored.

   B. **Incorrect:** Because the default value for *FillBehavior* is *HoldEnd,* the final value of the animation holds after this animation has completed. Because both the *To* property and the *By* property are set, the value of the *By* property is ignored.

   C. **Incorrect:** Because the default value for *FillBehavior* is *HoldEnd,* the final value of the animation holds after this animation has completed. Because both the *To* property and the *By* property are set, the value of the *By* property is ignored.

   D. **Correct:** Because the default value for *FillBehavior* is *HoldEnd,* the final value of the animation holds after this animation has completed. Because both the *To* property and the *By* property are set, the value of the *By* property is ignored.

Chapter 2: Case Scenario Answers

Case Scenario 1: Validating User Input

The key to implementing these requirements is routed events. Because all the *TextBox* controls in this form will be contained in a *Grid* or other layout control, you can implement the validation rules by handling the *PreviewKeyDown* event. Because *PreviewKeyDown* is a tunneling event, it will be raised by the layout control before other events are raised by the *TextBox* controls, and you have an opportunity to cancel invalid keystrokes before they are entered into the user interface. The global validation rules can be applied directly and then individual validation rules can be applied based on the *e.Source* property, which will indicate in what control the event originates.

Case Scenario 2: Humongous Insurance User Interface

Commands enable you to implement much of this functionality. By using commands, you can assign a command to the *Command* property of each menu item. When that command is unavailable, as determined by the handler for its binding's *CanExecute* event, the corresponding menu item will be disabled. Shortcut keys and mouse gestures can be added to the *InputGestures* collection of the command, and these will be inactivated as well when the command is unavailable.

To implement auto-fill functionality in your *TextBox* controls, you can handle the *TextBox.KeyDown* event. In this event, you can test whether appropriate keystrokes have been entered and then complete the entry automatically as necessary.

Chapter 3: Lesson Review Answers

Lesson 1

1. **Correct Answer: B**

   A. Incorrect: To keep the coordinates of the rendered control the same, you must set the *RenderTransformOrigin* property to .5,.5.

   B. Correct: You must set the *ScaleY* property to –1 and the *RenderTransformOrigin* property to .5,.5 to achieve the specified effect.

   C. Incorrect: You must set the *ScaleY* property, not the *ScaleX* property, to –1. In addition, to keep the coordinates of the rendered control the same, you must set the *RenderTransformOrigin* property to .5,.5.

   D. Incorrect: You must set the *ScaleY* property, not the *ScaleX* property, to –1.

2. **Correct Answer: D**

   A. Incorrect: When the *StartPoint* and *EndPoint* properties are not set, they default to (0,0) and (1,1), respectively, which creates a diagonal gradient.

   B. Incorrect: This example creates a horizontal gradient.

   C. Incorrect: This example creates a horizontal gradient. In addition, it fades from yellow to red, not from red to yellow.

   D. Correct: With *StartPoint* of (1,0) and *EndPoint* of (1,1), the gradient is vertical.

Lesson 2

1. **Correct Answer: C**

   A. Incorrect: Because *MediaElement* elements do not throw exceptions, a *Try...Catch* block never detects them.

   B. Incorrect: Although *MediaElement* elements do not throw exceptions, ignoring a failure of media to load would create a confusing and frustrating user experience at best.

   C. Correct: Even though *MediaElement* does not throw exceptions, you can access the original exception that is thrown from the media failure through the event arguments. Then you can notify the user or take any other appropriate action.

   D. Incorrect: The *MediaOpened* event is raised only after media has been opened; thus it will be raised only when there is no problem.

2. **Correct Answer: D**

   A. Incorrect: *SoundPlayer* can be a good choice, but if your application needs to control volume or balance, these elements are inaccessible.

   B. Incorrect: *MediaPlayer* can be a good choice, but if you need to play sound as an action or want a lightweight sound element, *SoundPlayer* is a better option.

C. Incorrect: Although *MediaElement* plays sound files, either *MediaPlayer* or *SoundPlayer* is a better choice because neither has a visual representation.

D. Correct: Depending on application requirements, either *SoundPlayer* or *MediaPlayer* can be a good choice.

Chapter 3: Case Scenario Answers

Case Scenario: The Company with Questionable Taste

1. Obviously, the stark black and white of the background is not a problem; it is simply a matter of setting the correct properties. The tie-dyed user input is somewhat more challenging, but that should not be a problem either. To create this effect, you should develop a *RadialGradientBrush* object that achieves the right mix of colors and set the *Foreground* property of all user input controls to this brush.

2. You can produce the video in the shape of a dancing bear by adding a *MediaElement* element to the application and setting the *Clip* property to the *Path* object supplied by the art department. Because the client wants continuous footage, you should handle the *MediaElement* *.MediaEnded* event and supply code to restart the media file when the end is reached.

Chapter 4: Lesson Review Answers

Lesson 1

1. **Correct Answer: D**

    A. Incorrect: There is no *CreateForm* method on a *Form* class. You create a new instance by using the New keyword.

    B. Incorrect: You must create a new instance of *Form1* with the New keyword before calling methods on that instance.

    C. Incorrect: *myForm* is not declared, and you cannot assign an instance variable to a class, although in Microsoft Visual Basic, "Form1" would return the default instance of *Form1*.

    D. Correct: *myForm* is correctly declared and instantiated.

2. **Correct Answer: A**

    A. Correct: All properties are set to appropriate values.

    B. Incorrect: The *FormBorderStyle* property should be set to a member of the *FormBorderStyle* enumeration, not to a string.

    C. Incorrect: The *Opacity* property should be set to a value between *0* and *1*, not to a string value, and the form's *Size* property should be set to a new instance of the *Size* structure.

    D. Incorrect: The *Opacity* property should be set to a value between *0* and *1*, not to a string value.

3. **Correct Answer: C**

 A. **Incorrect:** The *Button* class does not expose a *SetFlowBreak* method.

 B. **Incorrect:** Flow breaks are set by *FlowLayoutPanel*, not by the hosted control.

 C. **Correct:** Use the *SetFlowBreak* method to set a flow break.

 D. **Incorrect:** You cannot access contained controls as members of a container control.

4. **Correct Answer: D**

 A. **Incorrect:** The *TableLayoutPanel* control is best for organizing controls in a tabular style. Although it might be a good choice for a single set of properties, it is not a good choice for separating groups.

 B. **Incorrect:** The *FlowLayoutPanel* control is best for organizing controls that reorient themselves in response to resizing of the control, but it is not a good choice for presenting multiple groups of controls.

 C. **Incorrect:** The *GroupBox* control is best used for presenting option buttons that provide the user with exclusive choices between two or more options.

 D. **Correct:** The *TabControl* control is best used for organizing related controls into individual related groups.

5. **Correct Answers: A, B, C, and D**

 A. **Correct:** Each of these methods is valid. You can select a control in the Toolbox and double-click the form.

 B. **Correct:** Each of these methods is valid. You can select a control in the Toolbox and draw on the form with the mouse.

 C. **Correct:** Each of these methods is valid. You can double-click the control in the Toolbox.

 D. **Correct:** Each of these methods is valid. You can select the control in the Toolbox and drag it to the form.

6. **Correct Answer: B**

 A. **Incorrect:** You cannot add a type to the controls collection. You must create an instance of the control first.

 B. **Correct:** You must first instantiate the control and then add it to the form's controls collection.

 C. **Incorrect:** The *Add* method is a member of the *Form.Controls* collection, not a member of *Form* itself.

 D. **Incorrect:** The *Add* method is a member of the *Form.Controls* collection, not a member of *Form* itself.

7. **Correct Answer: D**

 A. **Incorrect:** You cannot add panels to the *SplitContainer* control, so you cannot use the *Controls.Add* method to add a new panel.

 B. **Incorrect:** You cannot add panels to the *SplitContainer* control, so you cannot use the *Controls.Add* method to add a new *SplitterPanel*.

C. **Incorrect:** You cannot add panels to the *SplitContainer* control, so you cannot use the *Add* method to add a new *SplitterPanel*.

D. **Correct:** You cannot add additional panels to the *SplitContainer* control, although you can add new panels to the individual *SplitterPanel* controls.

Lesson 2

1. **Correct Answers: A and D**

   A. **Correct:** You can resize controls by grabbing and dragging the edges.

   B. **Incorrect:** You cannot alter individual controls from the View menu.

   C. **Incorrect:** Smart tags do not appear on all controls and, when they are present, generally do not allow you to resize controls.

   D. **Correct:** You can modify the *Size* property directly in the Properties window.

2. **Correct Answers: A, B, and C**

   A. **Correct:** You can set the *Location* property in the Properties window.

   B. **Correct:** Grabbing the control and repositioning it with the mouse is the most natural way to relocate a control.

   C. **Correct:** The Layout toolbar enables you to adjust the spacing and alignment of controls on your form.

   D. **Incorrect:** There is no Location window.

3. **Correct Answer: C**

   A. **Incorrect:** The control will maintain a constant distance from the top edge.

   B. **Incorrect:** The control will maintain a constant distance from the top and bottom edges.

   C. **Correct:** The control is not anchored to any edge and will float when the form is resized.

   D. **Incorrect:** The control will maintain a constant distance from the right and left edges.

4. **Correct Answer: B**

   A. **Incorrect:** This setting will dock the control to the top edge of the control.

   B. **Correct:** A value of *Fill* will cause the control to fill the form or container control.

   C. **Incorrect:** The *Dock* property can be set to only a single value. A value of *Top, Left, Right, Bottom* is invalid.

   D. **Incorrect:** The *Anchor* property does not allow you to fill a form or container control.

5. **Correct Answers: A and C**

   A. **Correct:** The *Click* event responds to the left click of the mouse, as well as to some keyboard events, if the button has the focus.

   B. **Incorrect:** The *LinkClicked* event exists in the *LinkLabel* control but not in the *Button* control.

   C. **Correct:** The *MouseDown* event can respond to any button a mouse has.

   D. **Incorrect:** The *MouseOver* event does not respond to clicks.

6. **Correct Answer: D**

   A. **Incorrect:** The *FlatAppearance.MouseOverBackColor* property controls the *BackColor* property of the button when the mouse pointer is on the button.

   B. **Incorrect:** The *FlatAppearance.MouseDownBackColor* property controls the *BackColor* property of the button when the mouse clicks the button.

   C. **Incorrect:** The *FlatAppearance.BorderSize* property controls the width of the border when *FlatStyle* is set to *Flat*.

   D. **Correct:** The appearance of the text does not change when the *FlatStyle* property is set to *Flat*.

7. **Correct Answers: A, B, and C**

   A. **Correct:** You must set the *TabOrder* property to an appropriate value.

   B. **Correct:** You must set the *UseMnemonic* property to *True*.

   C. **Correct:** You must set the *Text* property with an ampersand to indicate the access key.

   D. **Incorrect:** The *CausesValidation* property is not required to create an access key.

8. **Correct Answer: D**

   A. **Incorrect:** The *MultiLine* property enables you to enter and display multiple lines, but it has no effect on the actual length of text entry.

   B. **Incorrect:** The *WordWrap* property affects how text is displayed in a multiline text box, but it has no impact on the maximum length of the string.

   C. **Incorrect:** The *ScrollBars* property influences whether scroll bars are displayed, but it does not affect the maximum length of the text.

   D. **Correct:** The *MaxLength* property is the only property that affects the maximum length of the *Text* property.

9. **Correct Answer: C**

   A. **Incorrect:** The 9 character indicates an optional numeric character in *MaskedTextBox*. All entries for a social security number should be required.

   B. **Incorrect:** The 9 character indicates an optional numeric character in *MaskedTextBox*. All entries for a social security number should be required. Additionally, the slash (/) character represents a date separator and is inappropriate in this context.

   C. **Correct:** The zero (0) character indicates a required numeric character. Additionally, the hyphen (-) is a literal character that is traditionally used for formatting social security numbers.

   D. **Incorrect:** The slash (/) character represents a date separator and is inappropriate in this context. The hyphen (-) character literal is more appropriate.

10. **Correct Answer: B**

   A. **Incorrect:** If the *CutCopyMaskFormat* property is set to *ExcludePromptAndLiterals*, the hyphen (-) literal character will be excluded. If the *TextMaskFormat* property is set to *IncludeLiterals*, the hyphen (-) literal character will not be excluded from the *Text* property.

B. Correct: The *CutCopyMaskFormat* property should be set to *IncludeLiterals* to include the literal characters, and the *TextMaskFormat* property should be set to *ExcludePromptAndLiterals* to exclude all but the user input.

C. Incorrect: If the *CutCopyMaskFormat* property is set to *ExcludePromptAndLiterals*, the hyphen (-) literal character will be excluded. If the *TextMaskFormat* property is set to *IncludePrompt*, the hyphen (-) literal character will be excluded from the *Text* property, but any prompt characters that remain in *MaskedTextBox* will be incorporated into the *Text* property as well.

D. Incorrect: If the *TextMaskFormat* property is set to *IncludeLiterals*, the hyphen (-) literal character will not be excluded from the *Text* property.

Lesson 3

1. **Correct Answers: B and C**

   A. Incorrect: The *IndexOf* method returns the index of an object to which you have a reference, but it does not detect selected objects.

   B. Correct: The *SelectedIndex* property will return the selected index. Note that if more than one item is selected, this property might return any of them.

   C. Correct: The *SelectedIndices* property will return all selected indexes.

   D. Incorrect: The *Select* method will select an object programmatically in *ListBox*, but it does not detect which index is selected.

2. **Correct Answer: D**

   A. Incorrect: The *Items.Add* method adds a specified item to the *Items* collection.

   B. Incorrect: The *Items.Insert* method adds a specified item to the *Items* collection at a specified index.

   C. Incorrect: The *Items.AddRange* method can be used to add an array of objects to the *Items* collection.

   D. Correct: The *Items.Contains* method determines whether a collection contains a specified item, not whether to add items to a collection.

3. **Correct Answer: C**

   A. Incorrect: Setting the *View* property to *LargeIcon* displays the *ListView* items with their associated large icons.

   B. Incorrect: Setting the *View* property to *Details* will display the *ListView* items with their associated *SubItems*.

   C. Correct: The *ListView* property cannot be used for displaying hierarchical data. For items with a tree structure, use the *TreeView* control.

   D. Incorrect: Setting the *View* property to *SmallIcon* displays the *ListView* items with their associated small icons.

4. **Correct Answers: B and E**

   A. Incorrect: The *Checked* property is a Boolean value and can be only *True* or *False*. The *CheckState* property can be set to *Checked*, however.

   B. Correct: The *Checked* property is a Boolean value and can be only *True* or *False*.

   C. Incorrect: The *Checked* property is a Boolean value and can be only *True* or *False*. The *CheckState* property can be set to *Indeterminate*, however.

   D. Incorrect: The *Checked* property is a Boolean value and can be only *True* or *False*. The *CheckState* property can be set to *Unchecked*, however.

   E. Correct: The *Checked* property is a Boolean value and can be set only to *True* or *False*.

   F. Incorrect: The *Checked* property is a Boolean value and can be only *True* or *False*. No property of the *CheckBox* control can be set to *NotChecked*.

5. **Correct Answers: A, C, and D**

   A. Correct: The *MaxSelectionCount* property determines the number of days that can be chosen in the *SelectionRange* property.

   B. Incorrect: The *SelectionRange* property is set to a new value when the user chooses dates, so setting it at design time will not facilitate this scenario.

   C. Correct: The *MaxDate* property determines the latest date that can be chosen, so setting it to the last day of the month in question will prevent the user from choosing any date after this day.

   D. Correct: The *MinDate* property determines the earliest date that can be chosen, so setting it to the first day of the month in question will prevent the user from choosing any date before this day.

6. **Correct Answers: C and D**

   A. Incorrect: The *Image* property directly sets an image for the control and cannot be set to an *ImageList* component.

   B. Incorrect: The *ImageKey* property takes a string and indicates the key for the image in the associated *ImageList* component. You cannot set the *ImageKey* property to a value of *Image*.

   C. Correct: You can set the *ImageList* property of the control to the *ImageList* component in question and set the *ImageIndex* property to the index of the image in the *ImageList. Items* collection.

   D. Correct: You can set the *ImageList* property of the control to the *ImageList* component in question and set the *ImageKey* property to the key of the image in the *ImageList.Items* collection.

Lesson 4

1. **Correct Answer: C**

   A. Incorrect: *ToolStripMenuItem* controls have no *UseMnemonic* property, and create access keys automatically when a letter is preceded by an ampersand.

B. **Incorrect:** *ToolStripMenuItem* controls have no *AccessKeys* property, and create access keys automatically when a letter is preceded by an ampersand.

C. **Correct:** *ToolStripMenuItem* controls create access keys automatically when a letter is preceded by an ampersand.

D. **Incorrect:** The *ShortcutKeys* property creates shortcut keys, which provide direct access to the command. Access keys are defined by preceding a letter in the *Text* property with an ampersand.

2. **Correct Answer: D**

A. **Incorrect:** *ToolStripManager* does not contain a *Menus* collection.

B. **Incorrect:** The *ToolStripManager.Merge* method is used for merging two tool strips or menus, not for adding a menu to a form.

C. **Incorrect:** *ToolStripManager* does not contain a *Controls* collection.

D. **Correct:** To add a menu to a form at run time, you add it through the form's *Controls* collection.

3. **Correct Answer: A**

A. **Correct:** All that is required to enable a context menu for a control is to set that control's *ContextMenuStrip* property.

B. **Incorrect:** Controls do not have a *ShowPopUp* property.

C. **Incorrect:** *ContextMenuStrip* controls do not have a *ShowPopUp* method.

D. **Incorrect:** *ContextMenuStrip* controls do not have a *Control* property.

4. **Correct Answer: B**

A. **Incorrect:** The *ToolStrip* class does not have a *Merge* method. You must use the *ToolStrip-Manager* class.

B. **Correct:** Use the static *ToolStripManager* class to merge tool strips.

C. **Incorrect:** The *ToolStripManager* class is static, so it cannot be instantiated.

D. **Incorrect:** The *ToolStrip* class does not have a *Merge* method. You must use the *ToolStrip-Manager* class.

5. **Correct Answer: A**

A. **Correct:** Use the *Add* method of the *Items* collection to add a new item at run time.

B. **Incorrect:** The *ToolStripManager* class is used to manage the tool strips themselves, not the items they contain.

C. **Incorrect:** The *ToolStrip* class contains a single collection, *Items*, for all the tool strip items. It does not contain a separate collection for each type of tool strip item.

D. **Incorrect:** Use the *Items.Add* method to add a new item. There is no *Items.NewItem* method.

Chapter 4: Case Scenario Answers

Case Scenario 1: Designing a Simple User Interface

1. You can use *TextBox* controls to receive input for the interest rate and time span parameters and a *MaskedTextBox* control that uses the currency symbol for the current investment value parameter. You should use labels to clearly identify each input control.

2. You can set the *TabOrder* property for each control to provide an ordered means of navigating with the Tab key. In addition, you can use the *Label* controls to create access keys for the *TextBox* and *MaskedTextBox* controls in your UI.

Case Scenario 2: Designing a User Interface

1. For the name and address fields, *TextBox* controls are most appropriate. For fields that have a defined format, such as postal code and credit card number, use *MaskedTextBox* controls. A multiline text box will make general comments easier to enter and read. You should use labels to clearly name each control.

2. By setting the *PasswordChar* property of *MaskedTextBox*, you can keep the credit card information from displaying inappropriately. Although this might make it more difficult to ensure that the correct data was entered, you can overcome the problem by requiring this data to be entered twice and for both entries to match.

Chapter 5: Lesson Review Answers

Lesson 1

1. **Correct Answers: A and B**

   A. Correct: Composite controls consist of preexisting Windows Forms controls bound together by common functionality.

   B. Correct: You can add new properties, methods, and events to a composite control.

   C. Incorrect: Composite controls provide their own rendering code.

   D. Incorrect: Properties of constituent controls are not generally available to the developer. You can wrap the properties of constituent controls in new properties to make them available to the developer, but this is not available by default.

2. **Correct Answers: A and D**

   A. Correct: A Toolbox bitmap must be a 16-by-16 pixel bitmap.

   B. Incorrect: Size is important because a Toolbox bitmap must be a 16-by-16 pixel bitmap.

   C. Incorrect: The *Image* property determines what image is displayed in the control at run time, not what image is displayed next to the control in the Toolbox.

D. Correct: The *ToolboxBitmap* attribute enables you to specify a path, a type, or a type and a resource name to specify the Toolbox bitmap.

3. **Correct Answer: C**

A. Incorrect: Although you must override the *OnPaint* method to provide a new appearance for an extended control, you are not required to provide a new appearance.

B. Incorrect: If a Toolbox bitmap is not provided, the control will use the same bitmap that is used by the inherited control.

C. Correct: All that is required to create an extended control is to inherit a base control. All other steps are optional.

D. Incorrect: The extended control will expose all of the same properties and methods as the control it inherits.

Lesson 2

1. **Correct Answers: C and D**

A. Incorrect: You must use either *TemplateBinding* or *Binding* to bind a property.

B. Incorrect: When using *Binding,* you must set the *Path* property to the appropriate property name and somehow specify the source object.

C. Correct: *TemplateBinding* enables you to bind directly to a property on the templated parent.

D. Correct: You can specify the templated parent as *RelativeSource* and set the *Path* property to the appropriate value.

2. **Correct Answer: A**

A. Correct: The *Style* element sets the target type to *Label* and includes a setter that sets the *Template* property to the referenced template. The *Style* element is defined after *Template* in XAML so it can be parsed.

B. Incorrect: A *Style* element that sets the *Template* property, but which has that *Template* element defined either inline or before *Style*, is defined in the XAML code.

C. Incorrect: The *Style* element contains no *Setter* to set the template property.

D. Incorrect: Templates are not applied automatically to elements without the aid of a *Style* element.

Lesson 3

1. **Correct Answer: C**

A. Incorrect: No preexisting Windows Forms controls have this functionality.

B. Incorrect: Because no current WPF elements incorporate this functionality, a new template would not achieve the desired effect.

C. Correct: Because the visual interface can be achieved with existing WPF elements, the best choice is to create a user control that binds the preexisting WPF elements with custom functionality.

D. Incorrect: Although you could achieve your goals with a custom control, creating a completely new template is unnecessary; thus, creating a user control is a better choice.

2. **Correct Answer: D**

A. Incorrect: No preexisting Windows Forms controls have this functionality.

B. Incorrect: Because no current WPF controls incorporate this functionality, a new template would not achieve the desired effect.

C. Incorrect: Because the visual interface cannot be achieved with existing WPF elements, a user control is not the best choice.

D. Correct: Because this element requires both custom visual effects and custom functionality, you should create a custom control.

3. **Correct Answers: A, C, and D**

A. Correct: Each theme needs to have a separate template in an appropriately named file.

B. Incorrect: All templates should exist in the Themes folder or in the appropriate external folder.

C. Correct: *ThemeInfoAttribute* must be set to point to the correct folders.

D. Correct: You always must have a fallback template that is used if the chosen theme is not supported.

Chapter 5: Case Scenario Answers

Case Scenario 1: Full Support for Styles

The most common approach in this situation would be to use the Windows Forms *MaskedTextBox* control hosted in *WindowsFormsHost*. Unfortunately, because of the specific requirement for all elements to be visually extensible, this is not an option because Windows Forms controls cannot have *Style* or *Template* applied to them. The only other possible solution is to spend the developer hours implementing a WPF-based *MaskedTextBox* control by creating a custom control that inherits *TextBox*. We have already implemented the presentation logic, and we can focus on developing the mask engine and incorporating it into the new control.

Case Scenario 2: The Pizza Progress Bar

1. Because the control the client is requesting is essentially a *ProgressBar* control with an alternative appearance, the best approach is to build a new control template.

2. You can create the disappearing-pizza effect by starting with an image of a pizza in the background and then, as the *Value* property goes from the minimum to the maximum, gradually overlaying a partially filled ellipse. You can implement this functionality by creating a custom converter that converts the current value of the progress bar to a fraction of 360 degrees and by painting the appropriate filled arc over the pizza image, making it seem to disappear.

Chapter 6: Lesson Review Answers

Lesson 1

1. **Correct Answers: A and D**

   A. Correct: The *ElementName* property establishes the source object, and the *Path* property establishes the source property for that object.

   B. Incorrect: Although setting the *DataContext* property establishes the source object, you still must define the path to the source property for that object by setting the *Path* property (or by other means, as discussed in Lesson 2, "Converting Data," of this chapter).

   C. Incorrect: Although setting the *Source* property establishes the source object, you still must define the path to the source property for that object by setting the *Path* property (or by other means, as discussed in Lesson 2 of this chapter).

   D. Correct: The *RelativeSource* property identifies the source object, and the *Path* property indicates the path to the source property.

2. **Correct Answer: B**

   A. Incorrect: A binding mode of *OneTime* does not update the user interface with any changes made to the database while the application is running.

   B. Correct: This mode enables the user to view the data but not to change it.

   C. Incorrect: This mode enables the user to update the data source.

   D. Incorrect: When the need is explicit, it is best to declare the binding mode explicitly rather than relying on defaults.

3. **Correct Answer: D**

   A. Incorrect: Because this application requires a specialized update procedure, using the default setting is not the best practice.

   B. Incorrect: This setting would update the source whenever it changed, rendering it unacceptable for the scenario described.

   C. Incorrect: This setting updates the data source whenever the control loses focus, which is unacceptable for the scenario described.

   D. Correct: This setting updates the source only when explicitly called.

Lesson 2

1. **Correct Answer: A**
   - **A. Correct:** The *Content* property is bound to the *Date* path, and the *Background* property also is bound to the *Date* path, while setting the *Converter* property of that binding to the *myConverter* predefined static resource.
   - **B. Incorrect:** Although the properties are bound correctly, you must designate the converter that returns a *Brush* object for the *Background* property.
   - **C. Incorrect:** Although it is possible to define a resource in an element's resource collection, you still must designate the converter that returns a *Brush* object for the *Background* property. In addition, the question assumes that the converter has already been defined as a resource in the *Windows.Resources* collection.
   - **D. Incorrect:** Because the converter is a resource, you must refer to it using the *{StaticResource}* syntax.

2. **Correct Answer: C**
   - **A. Incorrect:** To bind to a multi-value converter, you must use a *MultiBinding* object. This example shows a source called *ShapeName* and a path called *ShapeSize* that would result in binding to a single field rather than binding to both of them.
   - **B. Incorrect:** To bind to a multi-value converter, you must use a *MultiBinding* object. This example shows a path called *ShapeName/ShapeSize* that would result in binding to a single field rather than binding to both of them.
   - **C. Correct:** This example correctly uses a *MultiBinding* object, and the arguments are bound in the correct order.
   - **D. Incorrect:** Although this example correctly uses a *MultiBinding* object, the arguments are bound in the incorrect order. Thus, the first member of the object array will be an integer instead of a string, as the converter expects.

Lesson 3

1. **Correct Answers: A and D**
   - **A. Correct:** Exceptions are never surfaced to the user in data binding.
   - **B. Incorrect:** The *Validation.HasError* property is set to *True*.
   - **C. Incorrect:** A new *ValidationError* object is added to the *Validation.Errors* collection.
   - **D. Correct:** Because the *Binding.NotifyOnValidationError* property is not set to *True*, the *Validation.Error* event is not raised.

2. **Correct Answer: C**
   - **A. Incorrect:** The *PropertyChanged* event must be raised to implement data change notification.
   - **B. Incorrect:** The *PropertyChanged* event is raised before the property actually changes, which can lead to unpredictable results.

C. Correct: The *PropertyChanged* event should be raised after the property is changed.

D. Incorrect: Because the property does not change in the getter, it is incorrect to raise the *PropertyChanged* event there.

3. **Correct Answer: B**

A. Incorrect: Although it is possible to implement a data object by inheriting from an *ObservableCollection* collection of *Object* types, this would require a lot of casting code and would make coding the application more prone to error. It is better to use an *ObservableCollection* collection of *Employee* objects.

B. Correct: Using an *ObservableCollection* collection of *Employee* objects is the best choice.

C. Incorrect: Although it is possible to implement a data object by declaring an observable collection of objects, this would require creating wrappers to access the collection's members. The better choice is to inherit *ObservableCollection*.

D. Incorrect: Although it is possible to implement a data object by declaring a member collection, this would require creating wrappers to access the collection's members. The better choice is to inherit *ObservableCollection*.

Chapter 6: Case Scenario Answers

Case Scenario 1: The Currency Trading Review Console

1. You can provide the currency conversion data by using a value converter. By creating an instance of the Web service in your value converter, you can access up-to-date exchange rates and convert the transaction from dollars to yen, pounds, euros, won, bhat, or any other currency desired. Because you are not changing the culture of the thread, however, you are unable to use built-in string formatting to get culture-specific currency formatting. Thus, you have to implement your own currency formatting code.

2. You can alert the users to trades that exceed the individual trader's limits by creating a multi-value converter, which would evaluate the trader's trade limit and the total value of the trade. If the value exceeded the limit, you could return a *SolidColorBrush* element of an alert color, such as red, and bind the background of your display control to that color, thus easily alerting the manager to the issue.

Case Scenario 2: Currency Trading Console

You can implement this requirement through a validation rule that would evaluate the identity of the individual trader logged on to the console and the total value of the attempted trade. If the value of the trade exceeded the trader's limit, a validation error would be raised, and the trade would not be submitted to the database.

Chapter 7: Lesson Review Answers

Lesson 1

1. **Correct Answer: C**

   A. Incorrect: The *DataContext* property is set, incorrectly, to the data set, not to the data table.

   B. Incorrect: The *Path* property does not recognize the data set named *mySet*.

   C. Correct: The *DataContext* is set correctly to the *Customers* table, and the *Display MemberPath* property is set to the correct property.

   D. Incorrect: The *DisplayMemberPath* property is set incorrectly.

2. **Correct Answer: C**

   A. Incorrect: The *Path* property must be set to the CustomersOrders/OrdersDetails relation. In this answer choice, it is not set.

   B. Incorrect: The *Path* property must be set to the CustomersOrders/OrdersDetails relation. In this answer choice. it is incorrectly set to just OrdersDetails.

   C. Correct: The *Path* is set correctly to the CustomersOrders/OrdersDetails relation.

   D. Incorrect: The *Path* property incorrectly includes the Customers table. Because *DataContext* is set to the Customers table already, the *Path* property incorrectly looks for a Customers table within the Customers table.

Lesson 2

1. **Correct Answer: D**

   A. Incorrect: The *<DataTemplate>* tags must be enclosed in *<ListBox.ItemTemplate>* tags to set the data template to the *ItemTemplate* property.

   B. Incorrect: The data template must be set to the *ItemTemplate* property, not to the *ItemsSource* property.

   C. Incorrect: The data template must be enclosed in *<DataTemplate>* tags.

   D. Correct: The data template is correctly set.

2. **Correct Answer: A**

   A. Correct: You set the *Filter* object to a *Predicate<object>* parameter that specifies a filtering method that returns a Boolean value.

   B. Incorrect: The specified method must return a Boolean value.

   C. Incorrect: You must set the *Filter* property, not the *CustomFilter* property.

   D. Incorrect: You must set the *Filter* property, not the *CustomFilter* property. In addition, the specified method must return a Boolean value.

Chapter 7: Case Scenario Answers

Case Scenario 1: Getting Information from the Field

Because the application needs to read XML flies in a queue, harnessing the power of *XmlDataProvider* seems like a logical choice. By specifying the file name, you can bind your controls to the XML files and view the data that way. Because the original XML files cannot be altered, you should use a binding mode of *OneWay* to keep any changes from being propagated back to the XML file. When the data has been edited, it can be added to the central database manually by using ADO.NET data access.

Case Scenario 2: Viewing Customer Data

The first step is to separate the records that meet the criteria from the records that do not. To achieve this, you should create a complex filtering subroutine that examines each record and determines whether it is a member of any of the groups you are looking for. You should then create a custom grouping by implementing *IValueConverter* and group the records based on criterion group.

Chapter 8: Lesson Review Answers

Lesson 1

1. **Correct Answer: B**

    A. **Incorrect:** Using the column and row index of the selected cell is not the best way to determine the currently selected cell because it requires more coding than using the *DataGridView.CurrentCell* property.

    B. **Correct:** Using the *DataGridView.CurrentCell* property is the best way to determine the currently selected cell.

    C. **Incorrect:** Using the cursor position's *x* and *y* coordinates is not the best way to determine the currently selected cell because it would require complicated coding to determine this information.

    D. **Incorrect:** Using the currently selected column and row in the bound *DataTable* control to determine the clicked cell is incorrect because it requires more coding than using the *DataGridView.CurrentCell* property.

2. **Correct Answer: C**

    A. **Incorrect:** Adding validation code to the *CellPainting* event handler is not the preferred method of validating data in *DataGridView*.

    B. **Incorrect:** Adding validation code to the *DataGridView.CellClick* event handler is not the preferred method of validating data in *DataGridView*.

C. **Correct:** Adding your validation code to the *DataGridView.CellValidating* event handler is the correct way to validate value changes in cells in *DataGridView*.

D. **Incorrect:** Adding code to the *DataGridView* partial class file is not the preferred method of validating data in *DataGridView*.

3. **Correct Answer: B**

A. **Incorrect:** Configuring *DataGridViewTextBoxColumn* to display *True* or *False* is one way to display a Boolean value, but it is not the preferred way.

B. **Correct:** Configuring *DataGridViewCheckBoxColumn* to display a check box that is selected or cleared is the preferred way to display Boolean values in *DataGridView*.

C. **Incorrect:** Configuring a *DataGridViewButtonColumn* class to display a button that indicates pressed or not pressed is not correct.

D. **Incorrect:** Configuring a custom column to display *Yes* or *No* is also one way to present a Boolean value, but it is not the preferred method.

Lesson 2

1. **Correct Answer: B**

A. **Incorrect:** The *Error* property is not used directly by WPF and is frequently not implemented in implementations of *IDataErrorInfo*.

B. **Correct:** This information is passed automatically to the *ErrorContent* string.

C. **Incorrect:** The *Validation.Errors* collection is read-only and cannot be set directly. Also, the *Error* property is not used directly by WPF and will never be called in this scenario.

D. **Incorrect:** The *Validation.Errors* collection is read-only and cannot be set directly.

2. **Correct Answer: C**

A. **Incorrect:** The *Leave* event is raised before the *Validating* event is raised.

B. **Incorrect:** The *Leave* event is raised before the *Validating* event is raised, and the *LostFocus* event is the last focus event raised.

C. **Correct:** This is the correct order in which focus events are raised.

D. **Incorrect:** The *Validating* and *Validated* events are raised after the *Leave* event, which follows the *GotFocus* event, and are then followed by the *LostFocus* event.

Chapter 8: Case Scenario Answers

Case Scenario: The Writer Completeness Chart

The best way to address this issue is to use a data grid, which will display information for all the writers in one easily browsable control. For the percentage of the project done, you can develop a custom WPF control that displays this information, and then display it in the data grid by creating a *DataGridTemplateColumn* property that binds this control to the ratio of the two relevant fields by using a custom data converter class.

Chapter 9: Lesson Review Answers

Lesson 1

1. **Correct Answers: A and B**
   - **A. Correct:** *RunWorkerAsync* raises the *DoWork* event, which must be handled to run code on the background thread.
   - **B. Correct:** The *DoWork* event handler contains the code that will be run on the background thread.
   - **C. Incorrect:** Handling the *ProgressChanged* event is not required.
   - **D. Incorrect:** Setting *WorkerSupportsCancellation* to *True* is not required.

2. **Correct Answers: A and C**
   - **A. Correct:** The *Dispatcher.BeginInvoke* method will execute a method asynchronously and safely on the main thread.
   - **B. Incorrect:** Invoking a delegate in this manner attempts direct access of the user interface from a background thread, which is not allowed.
   - **C. Correct:** Using the built-in mechanism of *BackgroundWorker* for reporting is the preferred way to report progress that can be expressed numerically.
   - **D. Incorrect:** Calling a method that directly accesses the user interface from a background thread is not allowed.

Lesson 2

1. **Correct Answer: C**
   - **A. Incorrect:** The *CurrentUICulture* determines the localized version of the form that is loaded, but it does not control data formatting.
   - **B. Incorrect:** Culture is set by the thread, not by the form. In this example, you attempt to set *CurrentUICulture* with the form.

C. **Correct:** The *CurrentCulture* setting determines the formatting methods used for application data.

D. **Incorrect:** Culture is set by the thread, not by the form. In this example, you attempt to set *CurrentCulture* with the form.

2. **Correct Answers: C and D**

A. **Incorrect:** Because the default value for the *RightToLeft* property is *Inherit*, you need to set only the *Form.RightToLeft* property to *True* for the control text to be displayed right to left. Thus, you do not need to set the Label.RightToLeft property.

B. **Incorrect:** Because the default value for the *RightToLeft* property is *Inherit*, you need to set only the *Form.RightToLeft* property to *True* for the control text to be displayed right to left. Thus, you do not need to set the Button.RightToLeft property.

C. **Correct:** Setting the *Form.RightToLeft* property to *True* will cause all controls with a *RightToLeft* property value of *Inherit* to display text right to left.

D. **Correct:** Setting the *Form.RightToLeftLayout* property and the *Form.RightToLeft* property to *True* will cause the entire form to display in a right-to-left manner.

Lesson 3

1. **Correct Answers: B and D**

A. **Incorrect:** The background of *WindowsFormsHost* is never visible, and setting this property has no effect on the user interface.

B. **Correct:** You can set properties for a hosted control in XAML just as you would for a WPF element.

C. **Incorrect:** Even though it is named in XAML, the child of *WindowsFormsHost* cannot be accessed directly in code.

D. **Correct:** The correct way to gain a reference to a child of *WindowsFormsHost* is to cast *Child* to the appropriate type.

Chapter 9: Case Scenario Answers

Case Scenario 1: The Publishing Application

The central issue in this application design is the list of documents for download. Both the UI thread and the background downloading thread must access this list. You should protect access to this list by using *SyncLock* or *lock* blocks where appropriate to allow access to the list by only one thread at a time. A background thread should be used to download the documents. When download of a particular document is complete, the UI should be updated through the thread-safe *Control.Invoke* method.

Case Scenario 2: Creating a Simple Game

The *BackgroundWorker* component enables you to implement separate process threads with relative ease. In the preceding example, you can create a single *BackgroundWorker* component that takes the path to the file to play as a parameter and then plays the sound on a background thread. When it is finished, the *BackgroundWorker* component can be used again without reinitializing.

Chapter 10: Lesson Review Answers

Lesson 1

1. **Correct Answers: A and B**

   A. Correct: Selecting (Custom) enables you to edit the app.manifest.xml file.

   B. Correct: The *applicationRequestMinimum* node governs requested code acess security permissions.

   C. Incorrect: The *requestedPrivileges* node governs requested user account control permissions.

   D. Incorrect: Software restriction policies function independently of code access security.

2. **Correct Answers: B and D**

   A. Incorrect: File IO is considered an unsafe operation in most partial-trust environments and will usually be denied in these environments.

   B. Correct: Isolated Storage is a safe way for applications to have limited File IO access in a limited-trust environment.

   C. Incorrect: Most security policies will restrict untrusted applications from modifying the registry because this can cause serious damage to the integrity of the system installation.

   D. Correct: Although specific bitmap effects can be considered unsafe, simply loading an image into a content control is a safe operation for partial-trust environments.

Lesson 2

1. **Correct Answer: C**

   A. Incorrect: Individual settings are exposed as properties on the *Settings* object, not as members of a collection.

   B. Incorrect: Individual settings are exposed as properties on the *Settings* object, not as members of a collection. In addition, you must call the *Settings.Save* method to persist changes to the settings.

   C. Correct: You first set the named setting and then call the *Save* method.

   D. Incorrect: You must call the *Settings.Save* method to persist changes to the settings.

2. **Correct Answer: D**

   A. Incorrect: Settings are strongly typed and therefore do not need to be cast.

   B. Incorrect: Settings are strongly typed and therefore have no conversion methods.

   C. Incorrect: Assigning a strongly typed setting to an object will require the object to be cast as a *System.Window.Media.Color* type.

   D. Correct: Because settings are strongly typed, you can assign a setting directly to a variable of the correct type.

Lesson 3

1. **Correct Answer: D**

   A. Incorrect: Although most drag and drop operations begin in the *MouseDown* event on the source control, they are not required to begin there.

   B. Incorrect: Although it is recommended that the *DragEnter* event handler be used to examine the data object and set the *Effect* property as appropriate, it is not required.

   C. Incorrect: The *DragLeave* event is used to execute code when data is dragged out of a control, but it is not necessary for the drag and drop operation.

   D. Correct: The *DragDrop* event is the only event that must be handled to complete a drag and drop operation.

2. **Correct Answers: A, B, C, and D**

   A. Correct: The *DoDragDrop* method begins the drag and drop operation.

   B. Correct: If the target control does not allow one of the specified effects, the operation will not be completed.

   C. Correct: If the data format is not correct, the operation cannot be completed.

   D. Correct: If *AllowDrop* is set to *False*, no drag and drop operation can occur.

Chapter 10: Case Scenario Answers

Case Scenario: The Configurable Application

You can implement this functionality through user settings. By storing these preferences in settings, you can provide a storage mechanism that is configurable by the user without having to implement any additional infrastructure.

Chapter 11: Lesson Review Answers

Lesson 1

1. **Correct Answers: A, C, and D**

   A. **Correct:** You must create an instance of the appropriate automation peer to automate your control.

   B. **Incorrect:** Although you must obtain a reference to an implementation of the appropriate pattern interface, the preferred way to do so is to call the *GetPattern* method.

   C. **Correct:** You must obtain a reference to an implementation of the pattern interface that encapsulates the functionality you want to automate.

   D. **Correct:** After a reference to an implemented pattern interface is obtained, you can call the methods that pattern interface exposes to automate your control.

2. **Correct Answers: A, B, and C**

   A. **Correct:** You can open the WPF Tree Visualizer from the Watch window. Additionally, you can select it from the drop-down list next to the magnifying glass in a tool tip.

   B. **Correct:** You can open the WPF Tree Visualizer from the Auto window. Additionally, you can select it from the drop-down list next to the magnifying glass in a tool tip.

   C. **Correct:** You can open the WPF Tree Visualizer from the Locals window. Additionally, you can select it from the drop-down list next to the magnifying glass in a tool tip.

   D. **Incorrect:** The Output window displays console output from the application and cannot open the WPF Tree Visualizer.

Lesson 2

1. **Correct Answers: C, D**

   A. **Incorrect:** Intellitrace data collection is enabled by default.

   B. **Incorrect:** The file size and location can be modified, but they function with default values and do not need to be set.

   C. **Correct:** You view Intellitrace data in the Intellitrace window.

   D. **Correct:** Intellitrace is enabled in only Visual Studio 2010 Ultimate.

2. **Correct Answers: A, C**

   A. **Correct:** This sample correctly initializes the trace source and adds a listener named *myListener*.

   B. **Incorrect:** This sample initializes *XmlWriterTraceListener*, not *TextWriterTraceListener*.

   C. **Correct:** This sample correctly initializes *TextWriterTraceListener*.

   D. **Incorrect:** No listener named *textListener* is defined in any of the other samples.

Chapter 11: Case Scenario Answers

Case Scenario: Debug Drama

1. For the difficult bugs, Intellitrace can be a valuable tool. By configuring Intellitrace to collect only the data in which you are interested, you can collect target information that will assist in the resolution of these bugs.

2. Since data-binding errors in the WPF user interface do not raise exceptions, it can be difficult to locate the exact cause of the error, making these errors frustrating to debug. By enabling the data-binding *PresentationTraceSource* class, you can examine data binding in minute detail. By setting the trace level to *Warning*, you can filter out all but the most important messages.

Chapter 12: Lesson Review Answers

Lesson 1

1. **Correct Answer: A**

    A. **Correct:** The File System editor is used to determine which files will be distributed by a setup project.

    B. **Incorrect:** The File Types editor is used to set associations between file types and applications.

    C. **Incorrect:** The Custom Actions editor is used to add custom actions to your application.

    D. **Incorrect:** The User Interface editor is used to edit the user interface of the setup wizard.

2. **Correct Answer: B**

    A. **Incorrect:** This specifies a particular value for the operating system version that might not exist. You should use >= to specify that the operating system should be greater than a specified version.

    B. **Correct:** You should use >= to specify that the operating system should be greater than a specified version.

    C. **Incorrect:** This requires the operating system to be less than Windows 2000. You should use >= to specify that the operating system should be greater than a specified version.

    D. **Incorrect:** This enables installation for any operating system except a particular version of Windows 2000. You should use >= to specify that the operating system should be greater than a specified version.

3. **Correct Answers: B, C, and D**

   A. **Incorrect:** The *Installer* class should be added to the project you want to deploy, not to the setup project itself.

   B. **Correct:** You must add an *Installer* class to the project you want to deploy as a custom action.

   C. **Correct:** You must write your custom action in the *Install* method of an *Installer* class.

   D. **Correct:** You must specify the project that contains the custom action in the Custom Actions editor.

Lesson 2

1. **Correct Answer: C**

   A. **Incorrect:** Applications and XBAPs that run from a Web page execute under the Internet security zone by default and not under full trust.

   B. **Incorrect:** Applications and XBAPs that run from a Web page execute under the Internet security zone by default and not under the intranet zone.

   C. **Correct:** Applications and XBAPs that run from a Web page execute under the Internet security zone by default.

   D. **Incorrect:** Applications and XBAPs that run from a Web page execute under the Internet security zone by default and not under the custom zone.

2. **Correct Answers: A and C**

   A. **Correct:** Isolated storage provides a safe way to persist data to the file system in a partial-trust environment.

   B. **Incorrect:** Web service access is typically curtailed in a partial-trust environment, so this strategy cannot be relied on to give acceptable results.

   C. **Correct:** Because user settings are persisted safely in a partial-trust environment, this strategy can be used if the data to be persisted is of an appropriate size and format for settings.

   D. **Incorrect:** A permission demand is used to check for permission, not to temporarily gain permission.

3. **Correct Answers: A and D**

   A. **Correct:** This example demonstrates correct usage of the synchronous methods *CheckForUpdate* and *Update*.

   B. **Incorrect:** *CheckForUpdateAsync* does not return a value; rather, it uses a callback. Thus, in this example, the call to *aDep.CheckForUpdateAsync* produces an error because it cannot be evaluated as a value.

   C. **Incorrect:** In this example, *CheckForUpdate* is called and returned, but the expression is never evaluated and no subsequent code path leads to the installation of updates.

   D. **Correct:** This example correctly demonstrates the use of the asynchronous methods *CheckForUpdateAsync* and *Update Async*.

Chapter 12: Case Scenario Answers

Case Scenario 1: Distributing the Application a Little Early

Using ClickOnce technology, you can provide the version that is available now through a Web site that is accessible by your clients. By setting the application to check for updates every time the application is run, you can ensure that your clients receive the most up-to-date version every time they run the application. Additionally, with a ClickOnce application, your clients do not have to be administrative users to install the application.

Case Scenario 2: Installing the Server Core

By creating a setup project to install the document core, you can create a setup environment that accomplishes all these goals. You can define directory structures in the File System editor, and you can create registry keys by means of the Registry editor. You can check for prerequisites in a custom action and, if they are not found, use the custom action to either install the prerequisites, if possible, or throw an *InstallException* exception to abort installation if it is not possible to install them.

Index

Symbols and Numbers

A

M

N

S

X

About the Author

MATTHEW A. STOECKER started programming in BASIC on a TRS-80 at the age of nine. In 2001, he joined Microsoft Corporation as a writer and programmer writing about Microsoft Visual Basic .NET. He has authored numerous technical articles about Visual Basic .NET and Microsoft Visual C# and has written or contributed to multiple books about these languages. He holds a PhD in microbiology (which he hopes he will never have to use again) and lives in Bellevue, Washington.

Resources for Microsoft Exchange Server and Forefront

**Microsoft®
Exchange Server 2010
Best Practices**

Siegfried Jagott and Joel Stidley
with the Microsoft Exchange
Server Team

ISBN 9780735627192

Apply real-world best practices, field-tested
solutions, and candid advice for administering
Exchange Server 2010 and SP1—and optimize
your operational efficiency and results.

**Microsoft Forefront®
Threat Management
Gateway (TMG)
Administrator's Companion**

Jim Harrison, Yuri Diogenes,
and Mohit Saxena from the
Microsoft Forefront TMG Team
with Dr. Tom Shinder

ISBN 9780735626386

Help protect your business from Web-based
threats with this essential administrator's reference
to planning, deploying, and managing Forefront
TMG—successor to Microsoft ISA Server.

**Microsoft
Exchange Server 2010
Inside Out**

Tony Redmond

ISBN 9780735640610

Pre-order now
This supremely organized reference packs all
the details you need to deploy and manage
your Exchange Server 2010–based system—
from the inside out. Covers SP1.

**Microsoft
Exchange Server 2010
Administrator's
Pocket Consultant**

William R. Stanek

ISBN 9780735627123

Portable and precise, this pocket-sized guide
delivers ready answers for the day-to-day
administration of Exchange Server 2010.

microsoft.com/mspress

Windows Server 2008 Resource Kit—
Your Definitive Resource!

**Windows Server® 2008
Resource Kit**

Microsoft® MVPs with
Microsoft Windows Server Team

ISBN 9780735623613

Your definitive reference for deployment and operations—from the experts who
know the technology best. Get in-depth technical information on Active Directory®,
Windows PowerShell® scripting, advanced administration, networking and network
accessprotection, security administration, IIS, and other critical topics—plus an
essential toolkit of resources on CD.

ALSO AVAILABLE AS SINGLE VOLUMES

**Windows Server 2008
Security Resource Kit**

Jesper M. Johansson et al. with
Microsoft Security Team

ISBN 9780735625044

**Windows Server 2008
Networking and Network
Access Protection (NAP)**

Joseph Davies, Tony Northrup,
Microsoft Networking Team

ISBN 9780735624221

**Windows Server 2008
Active Directory Resource Kit**

Stan Reimer et al. with
Microsoft Active Directory Team

ISBN 9780735625150

**Windows® Administration
Resource Kit: Productivity
Solutions for IT Professionals**

Dan Holme

ISBN 9780735624313

**Windows Powershell
Scripting Guide**

Ed Wilson

ISBN 9780735622791

**Internet Information
Services (IIS) 7.0
Resource Kit**

Mike Volodarsky et al
with Microsoft IIS Team

ISBN 9780735624412

Get Certified—Windows® 7

Desktop support technicians and administrators—demonstrate your expertise with Windows 7 by earning a Microsoft® Certification focusing on core technical (MCTS) or professional (MCITP) skills. With our 2-in-1 *Self-Paced Training Kits*, you get a comprehensive, cost-effective way to prepare for the certification exams. Combining official exam-prep guides + practice tests, these kits are designed to maximize the impact of your study time.

EXAM 70-680
MCTS Self-Paced Training Kit: Configuring Windows 7
Ian McLean and Orin Thomas
ISBN 9780735627086

EXAM 70-685
MCITP Self-Paced Training Kit: Windows 7 Enterprise Desktop Support Technician
Tony Northrup and J.C. Mackin
ISBN 9780735627093

EXAM 70-686
MCITP Self-Paced Training Kit: Windows 7, Enterprise Desktop Administrator
Craig Zacker and Orin Thomas
ISBN 9780735627178

GREAT FOR ON THE JOB

Windows 7 Resource Kit
Mitch Tulloch, Tony Northrup, Jerry Honeycutt, Ed Wilson, and the Windows 7 Team at Microsoft
ISBN 9780735627000

Windows 7 Inside Out
Ed Bott, Carl Siechert, Craig Stinson
ISBN 9780735626652

Windows 7 Administrator's Pocket Consultant
William R. Stanek
ISBN 9780735626997

Microsoft® Press

microsoft.com/mspress

Get Certified—Windows Server 2008

Ace your preparation for the skills measured by the Microsoft® certification exams—and on the job. With 2-in-1 *Self-Paced Training Kits*, you get an official exam-prep guide + practice tests. Work at your own pace through lessons and real-world case scenarios that cover the exam objectives. Then, assess your skills using practice tests with multiple testing modes—and get a customized learning plan based on your results.

EXAMS 70-640, 70-642, 70-646

MCITP Self-Paced Training Kit: Windows Server® 2008 Server Administrator Core Requirements

ISBN 9780735625082

EXAMS 70-640, 70-642, 70-643, 70-647

MCITP Self-Paced Training Kit: Windows Server 2008 Enterprise Administrator Core Requirements

ISBN 9780735625723

EXAM 70-640

MCTS Self-Paced Training Kit: Configuring Windows Server® 2008 Active Directory®

Dan Holme, Nelson Ruest, and Danielle Ruest

ISBN 9780735625136

EXAM 70-647

MCITP Self-Paced Training Kit: Windows® Enterprise Administration

Orin Thomas, et al.

ISBN 9780735625099

EXAM 70-642

MCTS Self-Paced Training Kit: Configuring Windows Server 2008 Network Infrastructure

Tony Northrup, J.C. Mackin

ISBN 9780735625129

ALSO SEE

Windows Server 2008, Administrator's Pocket Consultant, Second Edition

William R. Stanek

ISBN 9780735627116

EXAM 70-643

MCTS Self-Paced Training Kit: Configuring Windows Server 2008 Applications Infrastructure

J.C. Mackin, Anil Desai

ISBN 9780735625112

Windows Server 2008 Administrator's Companion

Charlie Russel, Sharon Crawford

ISBN 9780735625051

EXAM 70-646

MCITP Self-Paced Training Kit: Windows Server Administration

Ian McLean, Orin Thomas

ISBN 9780735625105

Windows Server 2008 Resource Kit

Microsoft MVPs with Windows Server Team

ISBN 9780735623613

Windows Server 2008—Resources for Administrators

Windows Server® 2008 Administrator's Companion

Charlie Russel and Sharon Crawford

ISBN 9780735625051

Your comprehensive, one-volume guide to deployment, administration, and support. Delve into core system capabilities and administration topics, including Active Directory®, security issues, disaster planning/recovery, interoperability, IIS 7.0, virtualization, clustering, and performance tuning.

Windows Server 2008 Administrator's Pocket Consultant, Second Edition

William R. Stanek

ISBN 9780735627116

Portable and precise—with the focused information you need for administering server roles, Active Directory, user/group accounts, rights and permissions, file-system management, TCP/IP, DHCP, DNS, printers, network performance, backup, and restoration.

Windows Server 2008 Resource Kit

Microsoft MVPs with Microsoft Windows Server Team

ISBN 9780735623613

Six volumes! Your definitive resource for deployment and operations—from the experts who know the technology best. Get in-depth technical information on Active Directory, Windows PowerShell® scripting, advanced administration, networking and network access protection, security administration, IIS, and more—plus an essential toolkit of resources on CD.

Internet Information Services (IIS) 7.0 Administrator's Pocket Consultant

William R. Stanek

ISBN 9780735623644

This pocket-sized guide delivers immediate answers for administering IIS 7.0. Topics include customizing installation; configuration and XML schema; application management; user access and security; Web sites, directories, and content; and performance, backup, and recovery.

Windows PowerShell 2.0 Administrator's Pocket Consultant

William R. Stanek

ISBN 9780735625952

The practical, portable guide to using *cmdlets* and scripts to automate everyday system administration—including configuring server roles, services, features, and security settings; managing TCP/IP networking; monitoring and tuning performance; and other essential tasks.

ALSO SEE

Windows PowerShell 2.0 Best Practices
ISBN 9780735626461

Windows® Administration Resource Kit: Productivity Solutions for IT Professionals
ISBN 9780735624313

Windows Server 2008 Hyper-V™ Resource Kit
ISBN 9780735625174

Windows Server 2008 Security Resource Kit
ISBN 9780735625044

microsoft.com/mspress

Systems Requirements

Hardware Requirements

You should use a computer that is not your primary workstation to do the practice exercises in this book because you will make changes to the operating system and application configuration.

To use the companion CD, you need a computer running Microsoft Windows XP with Service Pack 3 (SP3), Windows Vista with SP2, Windows 7, Windows Server 2003 with SP2, Windows Server 2003 R2, Windows Server 2008 with SP2, or Windows Server 2008 R2. The computer must meet the following minimum requirements:

- Personal computer with at least a 1-GHz 32-bit (x86) or 64-bit (x64) processor
- At least 1 GB of RAM (x86 systems) or 2 GB of RAM (x64 systems)
- At least a 40-GB hard disk
- DVD-ROM drive
- Super VGA (800 x 600) or higher-resolution video adapter and monitor
- Keyboard and Microsoft mouse or compatible pointing device

Software Requirements

The computer used with the companion CD-ROM should also have the following software:

- A web browser such as Windows Internet Explorer
- An application that can display PDF files such as Adobe Acrobat Reader, which can be downloaded at *www.adobe.com/reader*
- Microsoft Visual Studio 2010 Professional, a trial version of which can be downloaded at *http://www.microsoft.com/visualstudio/en-us/products/2010-editions/professional*

These requirements will support use of the companion CD-ROM.

What do you think of this book?

We want to hear from you!

To participate in a brief online survey, please visit:

microsoft.com/learning/booksurvey

Tell us how well this book meets your needs—what works effectively, and what we can do better. Your feedback will help us continually improve our books and learning resources for you.

Thank you in advance for your input!

Stay in touch!

To subscribe to the *Microsoft Press® Book Connection Newsletter*—for news on upcoming books, events, and special offers—please visit:

microsoft.com/learning/books/newsletter